Copernicus Bo

Sparking Curiosity and Expla

Drawing inspiration from their Renaissance namesake, Copernicus books revolve around scientific curiosity and discovery. Authored by experts from around the world, our books strive to break down barriers and make scientific knowledge more accessible to the public, tackling modern concepts and technologies in a nontechnical and engaging way. Copernicus books are always written with the lay reader in mind, offering introductory forays into different fields to show how the world of science is transforming our daily lives. From astronomy to medicine, business to biology, you will find herein an enriching collection of literature that answers your questions and inspires you to ask even more.

Ashley Marc Recanati

AI Battle Royale

How to Protect Your Job from Disruption in the 4th Industrial Revolution

Springer

Ashley Marc Recanati
Shanghai, China

ISSN 2731-8982 ISSN 2731-8990 (electronic)
Copernicus Books
ISBN 978-3-031-19277-7 ISBN 978-3-031-19278-4 (eBook)
https://doi.org/10.1007/978-3-031-19278-4

Cover illustration: Science-fiction inspired eye hovering above a battle. Hal-9000 (Alamy images) 駒くら
べ盤上太平棊 (Battle of the Chess Pieces: Prosperity and Peace across the Board), by Utagawa Kuniyoshi,
woodblock print (1852). Reproduced from the National Diet Library website, of the Japan National Diet
Library

This Springer imprint is published by the registered company Springer Nature Switzerland AG
The registered company address is: Gewerbestrasse 11, 6330 Cham, Switzerland

*To my wife, Ashley Wong, and our daughters Chiara and Solange,
for fueling my interest in the future.*

Ashley Marc Recanati

The original version of the book was revised: Text correction has been updated. The correction to the book is available at https://doi.org/10.1007/978-3-031-19278-4_10

Acknowledgments

This book would not have seen the day, were it not for the previous work done by scholars, economists, business gurus, demographers, and researchers in fields ranging from technology to the job market, to various aspects of human resources, strategy, and management.

I would like to thank the staff at Springer, in particular, Jacob Dreyer, for his help and support.

Shanghai, China   Ashley Marc Recanati

Contents

About the Author

Ashley Marc Recanati, a respected business figure in the life sciences industry, has experience in manufacturing, retail and services spanning across the United States, Europe, and China. An early passion for the latest technologies and efficiency tools contributed to his rise in the corporate world.

Meanwhile he became increasingly aware of two growing gaps: (1) a gap between new efficiency tools deployed and actual working habits, and (2) a gap in advice as to how workers can prepare for the looming disruptions brought by advancing technology The post-ChatGPT world has now thrust these issues into the spotlight for a growing number of jobs.

AI Battle Royale seeks to remedy these gaps, providing a comprehensive guide for workers to survive and thrive in the twenty-first century.

Abbreviations

4^{IR}	Fourth Industrial Revolution
AI	Artificial Intelligence
aR	Assisted Reality
AR	Augmented Reality
ASI	Artificial Super-Intelligence
BLS	Bureau of Labor Statistics
GOFAI	Good-Old Fashioned Artificial Intelligence
GPT	General-Purpose Technology
ICT	Information and Communications Technologies
IoT	Internet of Things
ML	Machine Learning
NLP	Natural Language Processing
O2O	Online-to-Offline
UI	User Interface
VUCA	Volatility, Uncertainty, Complexity, and Ambiguity

1

Introduction

Word on the street has it, we are on the verge of radical technological feats that will either usher us into a blissful utopia or get us wiped out by machines—depending on who you listen to. Perhaps the reality will unfold somewhere in between.

A salient characteristic of this future, at least in the rosier version, depicts a jobless society. From its dawn, mankind has invented and perfected tools to increase labor efficiency. This would mark a milestone long dreamt of: ridding us from the need to work.

That was fine while projected on a horizon blurry enough to earn the science-fiction tag. But a rising tidal wave of disruption now leads many a voice to foresee an acceleration in this shift toward more automation and less jobs. We wake up to realize that this miracle might happen within our lifetime!

But not so fast.

Assuming we steer toward a jobless society, it won't appear overnight from out of the blue. Rather, we will face growing unemployment in the years ahead as more jobs get grinded by the steamroller named automation. How are we to cope during this interlude of dubious length, this purgatory to heaven?

A profusion of literature on tech acceleration is filling the shelves, spawning sections with titles like "Future Technologies", "Futurology" or

---

The original version of this chapter was revised: Text correction has been updated. The correction to the chapter is available at https://doi.org/10.1007/978-3-031-19278-4_10

© The Author(s), under exclusive license to Springer Nature Switzerland AG 2023, corrected publication 2023
A. M. Recanati, *AI Battle Royale*, Copernicus Books, https://doi.org/10.1007/978-3-031-19278-4_1

"Disruption". These books primarily address the C-Suite, entrepreneurs, and policymakers. Following the initial rhetoric aimed at convincing audiences of an imminent maelstrom, they advise on what society should do and how firms can ride the disruption wave.

But what of the average worker? Not the politician or CEO, but the rest: the 90% who own a reversely (un)important amount of assets,[1] supposedly constitute the backbone of our social tissue, and for who jobs are just about the only thing left to hang on to?

Advice to them is scanter to say the least. The lot are treated like a statistic, with cold assertions on how automation will make them redundant. A shrug of the shoulders. Dismissed.

Researching future trends deepened my awareness of the gaping hole as to how the "average Joe" is to cope. Given the experts' propensity to warn of this Damocles sword floating above every worker's desk, the finding of not finding any book dedicated to the topic in an age of supposed information abundance had an immediate disruptive effect—on my beliefs. And ultimately led me to proceed and write one.

While several years into the preparation of his 2019 book *Upheaval*, Jared Diamond found a manuscript already covering the same topics, published some fifty years earlier. I wouldn't be shocked to learn of other books advising how workers ought to grapple with disruption and automation. Yet the fact I could not find anything sensible on the topic speaks volumes (about the lack of consideration for it, not my Google skills).

Granted, heated debates orbit around whether more jobs will be created than destroyed. History has proven the job market to be one resilient beast. Technology births new sectors, a trait optimists refer to as proof of our limited predictive abilities. Plotting existing jobs and pinpointing those that will become irrelevant is a child's game. Meanwhile fathoming the new sectors, to say nothing of how many people they will employ, nor what level of wage one can expect from them, is a wholly different matter.

Two counterarguments rise from the dust like *Dune*'s Fremen to outflank that positive outlook, isolating this industrial revolution from its predecessors to drop us in unchartered waters.

The sheer speed of the revolution signals the first jab: it could outpace the generational workforce renewal necessary to adapt skills via our educational and training systems. But the fatal uppercut—and here we touch the climax point of this disruption—comes from a technology earmarked as so

---

[1] The top 10% of richest Americans own 70% of the country's assets, to be precise (cf. Piketty: *21st Century Capital*). However on a global level, it is estimated that 10% of adults own 85% of wealth (cf. the 2013 report from Credit Suisse: https://web.archive.org/web/20150214155424/https://public ations.credit-suisse.com/tasks/render/file/). Wealth (assets) is not to be confused with income.

radical it will eliminate a critical portion of jobs, *including* those supposed to be hatched by new sectors. This culprit goes by the name of Artificial Intelligence.

Like the Internet prior to it, AI is bound to descend from the hilltops to become an integral part of every organization's structure. Only the Internet and AI differ radically in their agendas: while the former enhances communication, the latter reduces the value of human labor in the productivity equation.

Human labor always involved a mix of limbs and brains. For a long time, our tools sought to ease physical labor, leaving us with the cerebral part. Now they are launching an all-out offensive on mental work, with goals such as crossing the threshold from automation to autonomy. This "Second Machine Age" would foreclose the need for humans in a great number of jobs.

The upcoming decades could see a first period of semi-autonomous tech that still requires human supervision, followed by one of (quasi-)full autonomy. This dichotomy helps split the time when we can still act to remain relevant despite rampant automation, both harnessing tech and filling in the gaps where it falls short, from that when all efforts become futile.

The first period will likely reveal two major pockets of resistance: throngs of workers at the bottom rungs spared, their low wages forming a rampart; and the most efficient, tech-savvy employees kept on payroll to perform the highly cognitive remaining work. Reaching the haven of the latter group depends on certain criteria, the decomposition of which constitutes a major theme of this book.

We are all familiar with the stereotype company where everyone wants to become the next CEO—nothing new under the sun here. But rivalries for promotion turn fiercer once staying put at a clerical level is no longer a viable option. The upheaval caused by a blend of advancing tech (ChatGPT, videoconferencing, shared economy platforms...) and new forms of work (outsourcing, temporary work contracts, work from home...) is turning yesterday's jousting between ambitious careerists into a widespread melee. In essence, a major depression in middle-class jobs that triggers a Darwinian struggle for the sparse jobs at the higher echelons—a rarefaction likely exacerbated by delays in retirement age, as prolonged longevity concurrently disrupts the established study-work-retire life pattern in unfathomable ways.

The joke among AI alarmists has a bear surprising two campers in the woods. Seeing his comrade lace his boots, one of them asks to what purpose—for one can't possibly outpace a bear. To what the other replies: "I don't need to outrun the bear. I only need to outrun you". Turns out, the bear was a robot—or less prosaically, an algorithm. And an algorithm is easy to scale, sending us all in those campers' shoes. An AI-ignited battle royale.

By the time we reach the second stage, that of full autonomy, we can only assume that society will have achieved its molt: holding a job will no longer be the entry ticket to a decent life. But the timing of that happy ending remains a blur on the horizon. At what pace this shift takes hold, compelling governments to trigger post-jobless remedies like Universal Basic Income—unproven remedies mired in controversy—is unclear to say the least. If the jobless society turns out a mirage—or takes, say, fifty years instead of fifteen—best brace ourselves in the meanwhile.

Without denying the importance of political activism in the quest for a just and fair society, leaving readers free to seek action by taking to the ballot or to the streets, nor assume to lay back and count on regulation and so-called sheltered activities, our concern centers on what can be done *in the workplace*; to remain employed long enough to witness the advent of a new society, without falling victim to it before.

Due to the accelerating pace of change, envisioning the future matters more now than ever. Science fiction writers no longer have a monopoly on it. Yet unlike a novel, one must keep her feet on the ground when assessing future possibilities. We put an emphasis on anchoring assumptions in pragmatism. Starting with a word of advice regarding the chicken and egg debate of creative destruction versus destructive creation: hope for the best, plan for the worst.

Given the state of the world, with its rotten politics, power mongering, lobbying, and legal mandates forged and maintained by the rich, for the rich, best remain skeptical as to society's ability to adapt in good faith and timing. View it as a sinking ship. Few people travel on boats anymore, let alone witness one sinking, to say anything about surviving the tragedy. Perhaps you are ahead of me on this one, so keep picturing yourself on the Titanic. We just hit the iceberg. It falls on our generation to live through these times of seismic disruption.

AI Battle Royale targets soon-to-be struggling workers. Its purpose: to make up for the lack of guidance on such a critical topic. To provide keys to decrypt new tech and trends, so as to adapt to the looming disruption without losing everything of the little left to begin with. To stay out of the water long enough for the rescue squad to arrive—whatever form it may take. And perhaps even prosper. If the reader reaches the other shore with a clearer vision of the future, a *modus operandi* to successfully confront it, this book will have fulfilled its goal.

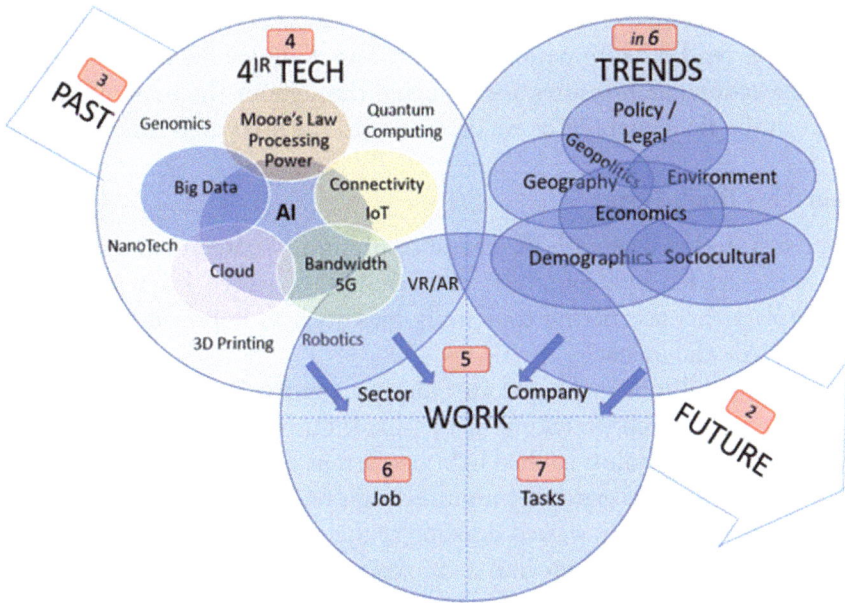

Fig. 1.1 Tech, trends, and work

And suppose that by day's end the AI buzz fades away (or takes a century to materialize in the form of massive structural unemployment); that would prove the alarmists were crying wolf when the species was in fact long extinct. The advice laid herein would remain valuable all the same. For technology is already ubiquitous; it permeates every nook and cranny of work. Embrace it to rise above your peers and excel in your job.

Book Organization

Figure 1.1 shows the relationship between technology, trends and work, framed in a time continuum.

It loosely illustrates this book's organization (the numbers highlight chapters).

The book is split into two parts: the first deals with context, the second with work.

Part one begins with an overview of possible futures (Chap. 2); we then study periods of havoc wrought by earlier industrial revolutions (Chap. 3), before coming to grips with 4th Industrial Revolution technologies (Chap. 4).

With this luggage under our belt, we are ready to dive into work proper. Part two decomposes the notion of a job into four dimensions, noting that disruption can strike at any one of these: the company and its sector of activity (Chap. 5), the occupation itself, as in "a job title" (Chap. 6), and the tasks that compose it (Chap. 7). Lastly, we consider other contributive elements to fend off automation threats (Chap. 8, not shown in the figure).

While actionable measures are peppered throughout the book, they grow denser in the final chapters as we descend into the tasks arena and beyond.

What This Book Is not

Numerous studies deal with the causal relationship between automation and jobs; these are led by economists and scholars, of which I am neither. We contemplate this fascinating topic only inasmuch as it provides clues as to how to battle the menace.

This book will not make you an expert in any particular technology; our *tour d'horizon* of tech partaking in the 4th Industrial Revolution (hereafter denoted 4^{IR}) merely aims to shed light on current developments, for prospective purposes. Readers expecting minute details of every jaw-dropping novelty be warned: no pages are wasted dazzling at the gimmicks dangled by tabloid headlines. A flurry of blogs and magazines feed on such stories; save the popcorn for them.

Nor do we purport to provide guidelines for policymakers. UBI, tax and educational reforms find scant space in these pages, not for lack of need, but because they are not actionable by the individual worker.

Trends loosely subsume macro elements: societal, environmental, regulatory... As depicted in Fig. 1.1, tech, work and trends are intertwined. For instance, while on the one hand Artificial Intelligence threatens a substantial portion of currently performed human tasks, on the other an acute drop in natality rates could lead to a reduction of workforces in rich countries. This tug of war has experts scratching their heads as to whether we will face a shortage of jobs or of labor. And if Western populations dwindle, would that not trigger a decline in consumption, that primordial engine driving growth and jobs? How these forces interact with one another ultimately determines the direction of the whole. Yet giving each trend the full attention it deserves would double the size of this book; many had to be amputated or even set aside.

We use the US job market as reference point. Here again, covering the full spectrum of jobs would prove a herculean task; the threat is protean and evades a one-size-fits-all solution.

Office jobs mushroomed during the twentieth century, spawning the middle-class familiar to us, the emergence of which constitutes one of the great legacies of that epoch. This relatively fresh achievement (on the scale of human civilizations) is now put to serious test. 4^{IR} tech threatens to jostle the middle-class from its socket while impeding its advent in developing economies. Advanced algorithms are bound to shake the contents of white-collar jobs too. We address this heterogenous class of people first and foremost. Occupations employing smaller numbers garner less attention; apologies in advance for omissions consequent to such generalizations. We have strived to make the tools presented broad enough regardless of occupation.

Alas during writing, the Covid pandemic rocked societies, including job markets. It could take years to reach a new normal. This book is about tech-propelled disruption, not black swans. Hence, material related to the job market often and purposely predates 2020.

About the Author

Books on tech are chiefly composed by scholars, techies, and Silicon Valley stars, while economists and journalists lean in on its societal impacts. Each type has a perspective and writing style that reflects its provenance.

I belong to none of the abovementioned. My first post-graduation gig was that of an interpreter-slash-chauffeur, reflecting the only skills I had then—literally a French American with a driver's license. Ten years later, I was handed the general management of a manufacturing business with dozens of staff. In that short decade, I switched jobs several times, changed continents, and learned a third language. Yet in no small part do I owe this ascent to continuous learning and implementation of tools directly applicable to my moving line of work.

This hands-on approach is baked in AI Battle Royale. How can workers assess their job's vulnerabilities? What can they do to improve their prospects, effective immediately?

Having lived in the US, Europe, and China, I avoid biases toward or against any of these powerhouses, while humbly acknowledging less mention of other parts of the world, for lack of on-the-spot experience. I have had the pleasure to work with people from these regions and more, observing issues related to tech knowledge and inclusion at the workplace that transcend national boundaries.

Part I

Context

2

Future

Introduction

In 1930, during the Great Depression's darkest hours, economist John Keynes surmised that a century later, advances in technology would have led to fifteen-hour workweeks, coining the term "technological unemployment".[1]

Fast-forward to 2013. Inspired by Keynes' paper, two Oxford professors set out to study the future of job automation. Ironically, to do this Carl Benedikt Frey and Michael Osborne had recourse to an algorithm. Their study boldly concluded that 47% of US occupations could be automated "within the next decade or two".[2]

Frey and Osborne took into consideration recent advances in artificial intelligence, with computer vision affecting manual jobs in unstructured environments, and machine learning empowering self-driving cars and data parsing algorithms.

The original version of this chapter was revised: Text correction has been updated. The correction to the chapter is available at https://doi.org/10.1007/978-3-031-19278-4_10

[1] John Maynard Keynes: *Economic Possibilities for our Grandchildren* (1930), in Essays in Persuasion (New York: Harcourt Brace, 1932), 358–373.
[2] Carl Benedikt Frey and Michael A. Osborne: *The future of employment: how susceptible are jobs to computerization?* (2013).

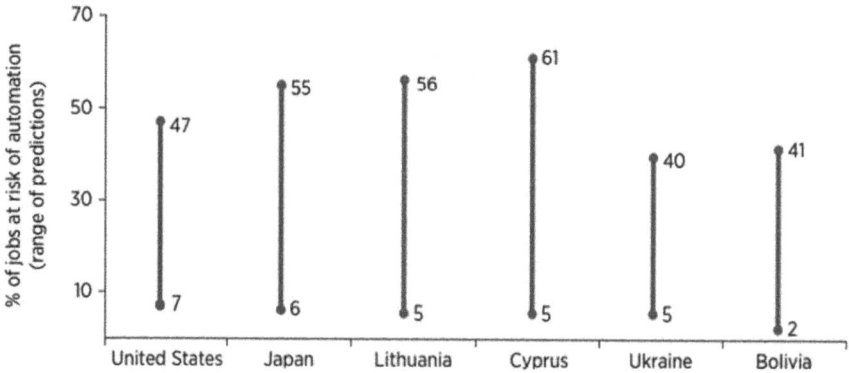

Fig. 2.1 Estimates on percentages of jobs at risk of automation. *Sources* WDR 2019 team, based on World Bank (2016); Arntz, Gregory, and Zierahn (2016); David (2017); Hallward-Driemeier, and Nayyar (2018). *Note* The figures represent the highest and lowest estimates of the percentage of jobs at risk of automation in economies for which more than one estimate has been produced by different studies. A Job is at risk if its probability of being automated is greater than 70%.

To make matters worse, several years earlier a study by Alan Blinder of Princeton had concluded that 22 to 29% of US jobs were vulnerable to offshoring.[3] Suddenly the combination of automation and offshoring popped on economists' radars. In a world still reeling from the financial recession, these threats triggered a fresh salvo of concerns. Experts scrambled to scrutinize the studies and foment their own, and not a year has passed since without publications on the future of work. In 2016, an OECD report determined that only 9% of jobs were automatable,[4] while at the same time McKinsey argued that 45% of paid activities and 60% of all occupations could see 30% or more of their constituent activities automated using tech available today.[5]

Does that mean, as *Wired* magazine co-founder Kevin Kelly believes, that those workers will see a third of their time, previously spent on dull routine tasks, freed up for more meaningful activities? Or translate as three out of ten people getting the pink slip? When facing these questions, the uncomfortable truth is that the experts fall short of answering in unison. They profess

---

[3] Alan S. Blinder: *How Many U.S. Jobs Might Be Offshorable?*, Review of World Economics (April 2007).

[4] Melanie Arntz, Terry Gregory, Ulrich Zierahn: *The Risk of Automation for Jobs in OECD Countries: A Comparative Analysis*, OECD Social, Employment and Migration Working Papers No. 189. The Organisation for Economic Co-operation and Development comprises 38 countries, mostly located in Western Europe and North America.

[5] Michael Chui, James Manyika, and Mehdi Miremadi: *Four Fundamentals of Workplace Automation*, McKinsey Quarterly (November 1, 2015).

opinions, but to say these diverge would be an understatement, highlighted by the above gap between 9 and 47% (c.f. Fig. 2.1).

On one hand, we find the optimists who claim that the people most apt at collaborating with computers will stay ahead of the game. IBM's Deep Blue famously beat world champion Kasparov at chess in 1997; but in the lesser-known aftermath, teams mixing humans and computers consistently beat both teams of only computers and of only humans.[6] As Kevin Kelly sums it up: "You'll be paid in the future based on how well you work with robots".[7]

This is already partially true: skilled software users have a competitive edge over their peers in almost any office job, starting with things as trivial as a keyboard or Microsoft Office tools.

They also invoke history as proof that the technology behind industrial revolutions births sectors that end up absorbing the swaths of workers from fallen sectors. Those who tended to horse stables landed new jobs in automobile factories and car garages, in what economist Joseph Schumpeter dubbed "creative destruction". Economists from MIT have modelized technology's ability to spur sufficient demand for jobs in the new sectors to compensate for those lost to automation elsewhere, following a "balanced growth path" that allows for a "dynamic equilibrium".[8]

In other instances, when the sector is not doomed but working conditions change, labor can preserve value by adapting to the new paradigm. The rush to deploy ATMs in the 1980s fueled concerns that bank tellers would lose their jobs, when in fact their numbers increased, as they were able to perform more value-added tasks that contributed to generate extra income and ultimately lead to a need for more staff.[9]

In the pessimist camp, we find Martin Ford, author of *Rise of the Robots: Technology and the Threat of a Jobless Future*. He dispels the widely held belief that a degree in engineering or computer science guarantees a job even today, calling it a myth, with figures to back up that claim.[10] He also dismisses the buoy of human/machine collaboration by arguing that this is but a still

---

[6] Cf. Erik Brynjolfsson and Andrew McAfee: *The Second Machine Age,* or Yuval Noah Harari: *21 Lessons for the 21st Century.*

[7] Kevin Kelly: *The Inevitable: Understanding The 12 Technological Forces That Will Shape Our Future,* Penguin Books (2016). p. 59.

[8] Cf. Acemoğlu: *The Race Between Machine and Man: Implications of Technology for Growth, Factor Share and Employment,* MIT Department of Economics Working Paper 16–05 (May 6, 2016).

[9] The United States counted 600,000 bank tellers in 2010, double the amount of 1970, while the active workforce increased by a mere 63% over the period (from 78 to 127 million). Cf. Wikipedia's entry on Bank teller, https://en.wikipedia.org/wiki/Bank_teller.

[10] Martin Ford:, *Rise of the Robots,* p. 127.

snapshot from today. AI is in its infancy. Continuous improvements will allow computers to pursue emulation of human tasks, increasingly evincing us. The recent breakthroughs revealed with the release of Dall-E 2 and ChatGPT support his argument.

Oxford professor Nick Bostrom seems to concur on the long-term fate of human labor:

> Horses were initially complemented by carriages and ploughs, which greatly increased the horse's productivity. Later, horses were substituted for by automobiles and tractors.[11]

He concludes that "what starts out as a complement for labor can at a later stage become a substitute for labor."[12] Leading one entrepreneur to push this line of thought to its extreme: "Labor never really existed; it was simply a misapplied term to describe the inefficiency of tools".[13]

To stick with U.S. bank tellers, after peaking in 2007 with 608,000 workers, their numbers have constantly declined, reaching 423,000 in 2020. Apart from the financial crisis, online banking is surfacing as a lethal culprit. Suppose fintech further obsoletes brick-and-mortar banks and consumers rely extensively on ChatGPT-like artificial intelligence personal assistants (AIPAs) to conduct their financial affairs; AIs superseding all imaginable bank teller tasks would eliminate those jobs. As noted earlier, this reasoning can apply to growing sectors otherwise hungry for jobs: tourism, Big Data, the green economy, and the silver market (products and services tailored to the elderly).

Basically, any task which can shift from "art" to "science" is prone to machine takeover.

That's bad news. Because for over a century now—ever since Taylor and (Henry) Ford—companies have been obsessed with systematizing work. As Google's Marissa Mayer stated, "Design has become much more of a science than an art", adding that: "Subjective judgements, including aesthetic ones, don't enter into Google's calculations."[14]

People take comfort in routine tasks, repeating the same actions even as they sense opportunities for more efficient methods. Conceiving improvements implies burning neurons; better stick to the brain-numbing monotony.

---

[11] Nick Bostrom: *Superintelligence, Paths, Dangers, Strategies*, p. 191, *Of Horses and Men*. The oft cited allegory of equine labor was first made by Nobel Laureate economist Wassily Leontief in *Technological Advance, Economic Growth, and the Distribution of Income* (1983), http://www.jstor.org/stable/1973315.

[12] *Ibid.*, p. 190.

[13] John Pugliano: *The Robots are Coming*; p. 101.

[14] Nicholas Carr: *The Shallows: What the Internet is Doing to Our Brains*, p. 151.

After all, it's what they are paid for. These workers are trapped in a dilemma: any improvement would give them spare time to kill or, worse, prompt the boss to fill the void with new work (or worse even, make them redundant).

A notable passage from Martin Ford sees him quote sociologist Steven Brint:

> "In most jobs, showing up and doing the work is more important than achieving outstanding levels of performance". If you were to purposely set out to describe the characteristics of a job vulnerable to automation, it would be hard to do much better than that.[15]

If deep down you recognize yourself in this mindset, you'll want to sit down and review that belief. Because it certainly won't help your chances of surviving the upcoming wave.

In this chapter, we explore a handful of the potential paths lying ahead; namely a society of massive unemployment, Universal Basic Income (UBI), the rising jobs mismatch quandary, working less hours, the impact of changing demographics, the emergence of a fourth sector, and the advent of a society of haves and have-nots.

2.1   Massive Unemployment

Books like *Homo Deus* emphasize the rate at which jobs will disappear,[16] then take a quantum leap to fantasize about what a jobless society would resemble. Unfortunately, we have yet to invent a time machine to warp into the future. Reaching this seemingly utopic society implies traversing a rocky purgatory, a burden likely to befall on existing and upcoming generations.

What happens during this intermediary period of declining employment? What will it take—and *how long* will it take—to reach the tipping point where society collectively rules out that jobs no longer stand as *the* prerequisite to earning money, as the key to a decent living?

When it comes to answering the last question, the Robocalypse proponents shy away. They may advance a certain share of jobs bound to disappear, or hint at a timeframe, but stop short of giving both. Let us try to venture beyond.

Commonsense would have us scrutinize historical unemployment; this helps reframe the question as: what level of unemployment could trigger UBI-type remedies?

---

[15] Martin Ford: *Rise of the Robots*, p. 251.
[16] Yuval Noah Harari: *Homo Deus: A Brief History of Tomorrow*, Haper (2017); also Amir Husain: *The Sentient Machine: The Coming Age of Artificial Intelligence*, Scribner (2017), p. 38.

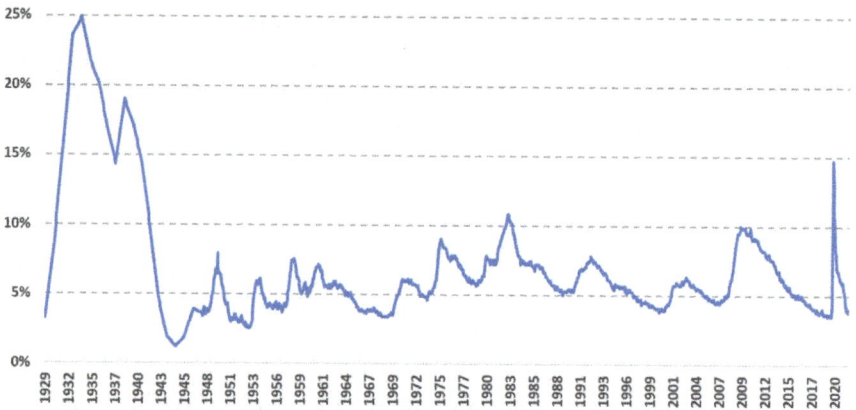

Fig. 2.2 US historical Unemployment Rate 1929–2020 (as of December each year). *Source* Compiled by Author based on data from the U.S. Bureau of Labor Statistics[17]

Figure 2.2 shows US unemployment stretching back 90 years.

The biggest spike on record occurred a short century ago. The Wall Street Crash of 1929 brought Great Gatsby parties down and the Great Depression in, with unemployment rates hovering above 15% for a decade. It took World War 2 to drag unemployment back down.

Each ulterior dent is symptomatic of a choc: the 1970s oil hikes, the recession under the first Bush administration, conflicts, and their endings,[18] the dotcom bubble burst, and the Great Recession of 2008. In April 2020, at the height of Covid, unemployment flirted with 15%, yet fell back to single-digit levels from August onwards. Such upshots are conjunctural, i.e. short-lived, whereas technology could trigger long-term, structural unemployment, corresponding to the second, quasi-full autonomy phase we hinted at earlier.

For the sake of argument, let us assume a 25% unemployment rate, lasting for a minimum period of five years (sufficient for elections in most democracies) as a prerequisite to UBI-type remedies.

Now, bear with us on this slippery forecasting slope as we envision the timeframe that could lead to the dreaded 25% threshold. Figure 2.3 plots three scenarios of annual unemployment growth: 0.5%, 1%, and 2%.

---

[17] With two sources: the main BLS data set, starting in 1948: https://data.bls.gov/timeseries/LNS140 00000; for prior data, cf. *Labor Force, Employment, and Unemployment, 1929–39: Estimating Methods*, Page 2, Table 1, https://www.bls.gov/opub/mlr/1948/article/pdf/labor-force-employment-and-unempl oyment-1929-39-estimating-methods.pdf.

[18] The mix of soldiers returning home and austerity measures in response to overspending for the war effort could contribute to explain the jump in unemployment visible after wars—cf. the rates following World War 2, the Korean and Vietnam wars and the first Iraq War.

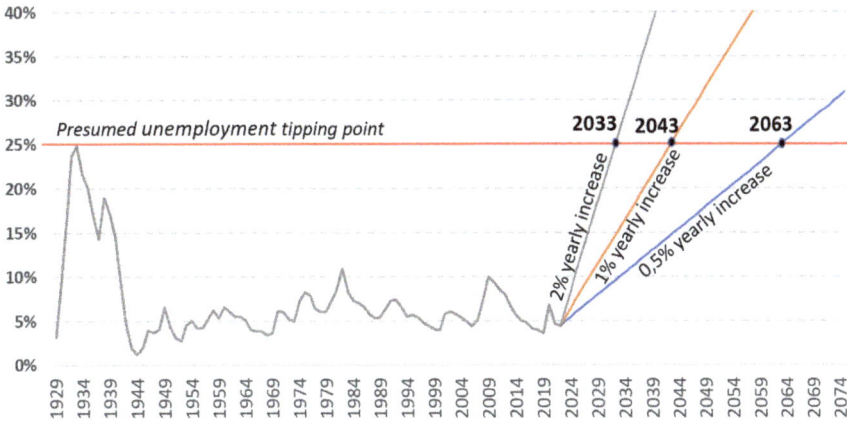

Fig. 2.3 U.S. unemployment projections

Starting from the year 2023, these rates lead to tipping points reached and breached in 2063, 2043, and 2033, respectively. Based on our assumption, UBI-type remedies would be deployed shortly after.

10, 20 or 40 years; vastly different time frames, each entailing a different approach, as highlighted by Fig. 2.4.

In a stable tortoise scenario, automation as the culprit may fly under the radar, and governments fail to take appropriate action. The hare scenario also puts our institutions to test, this time in their ability to remediate a quickly worsening situation.

Scenario	Tipping Point	Years to go (2023)	Someone born in xxxx would be x years old by then			Pros & Cons	
			1990	2015	2025	Pros	Cons
Fast 2%/year	2033	10 years	43 yo	18 yo	8 yo	Choc leads to swift aid from governments	No time to retrain / No time for new sectors to emerge
Medium 1%/year	2043	20 years	53 yo	28 yo	18 yo	Sufficiently appearent to trigger government aid?	Less time to retrain / Less time for new sectors to emerge / State aid unsustainable?
Slow 0.5%/year	2063	40 years	73 yo	48 yo	38 yo	Enough time to retrain / New sectors emerge	Automation goes under the radar as leading cause of unemployment

Fig. 2.4 Mass structural unemployment scenarios

Yet these scenarios presume linear paths, of *average* growth, when the reality is anything but, as attested by historical data. The tortoise scenario, whereby we breach the tipping point in 2063, could just as well materialize as several decades of low unemployment, buoyed by demand for 4^{IR} related goods and aided by a shrinking workforce, followed by an abrupt jump. In fact, the timing riddle has two halves: by when the tipping point is breached, and the suddenness of the shift. Even if technological unemployment in the 4^{IR} adopts the pace of a tortoise, other elements could cause violent swings to the size of the job market.

When viewing these stretching time scales, those who picture themselves spending the 2040s tanning on a white sandy beach, sipping caipirinhas and cashing in on retirement checks, should think again. Increased longevity will significantly alter traditional "study-work-retire" life phases familiar to us, delaying the age of retirement. Plan for the worst.

These scenarios depict bleak times ahead. Bear in mind that high unemployment tends to lower wage levels too, as more candidates compete for rarefied jobs.

2.2   Universal Basic Income (UBI)

From the Nixon Administration to Andrew Yang's 2020 presidential campaign and the pandemic, the idea of a stipend given to the population, no strings attached, has stirred politics for decades.

Its thurifers assure UBI will eliminate abject poverty, ditch the notion of work as entry ticket to society, and facilitate the reallocation of government spending. Small-scale tests have been conducted around the world, producing mixed results that in any case remain limited as participants still belonged in a world governed by the perception of status conveyed by work. Perhaps the true impacts of UBI cannot be apprehended in a vat; it could take a generation or two following national UBI deployment to hear something else than a job title in reply to the question: "So what do you do?".

UBI poses other quandaries. How would the State finance it? Nick Bostrom foresees beneficial windfalls from 4^{IR} technologies so great that redistributing even a small portion of these to society's have-nots would safeguard it against rampant poverty[19]—but this remains purely speculative (and

---

[19] Nick Bostrom:, *Superintelligence*, in particular *Capital and welfare* section of Chap 11: *Multipolar scenarios*. A common theme relayed by futurist think tanks—cf. also p. 8 of the Report of the 2015 Study Panel on *Artificial Intelligence and Life in 2030*, part of The 100 Year Study on Artificial Intelligence (September 2016).

the concept of UBI is redistribution *to all*). Would nations enacting UBI remain competitive? And what of the less advanced economies that miss out on the 4^{IR} bounty? Suffice it to say that the topic is a highly divisive one, that could remain debated in the hallways and corridors of our institutions for some time still. While Andrew Yang's book[20] contains compelling evidence on the flaws of the existing (US) system, workers cannot simply lay back and expect salvation to fall from the sky.

Eighteenth-century philosopher Voltaire remarked that work keeps three great evils in check: boredom, vice, and need. UBI only addresses the last of these ailments, whereas filling otherwise idle time with low-paying jobs that barely cover the rent keeps the plebs spinning the hamster wheel, and entertaining hope via spurious claims of an American Dream saps the potential for revolt. *Panem et circenses*—give them bread and free Wi-Fi.

Two anecdotes illustrate the rulers' uneasy relationship with tech and work.

In 1589, Queen Elizabeth of England refused to grant inventor William Lee a patent for a stocking frame knitting machine: "Consider thou what the invention could do to my poor subjects. It would assuredly bring to them ruin by depriving them of employment, thus making them beggars".[21] Half a millennium later, the tale remains little changed. Renowned economist Milton Friedman tours a construction site in a developing Asian nation; watching the masses toil the ground with shovels, he turns to his host—a local government official—and asks why they do not use tractors and earth movers. In pure Elizabethan fashion, the bureaucrat explains that it is part of a jobs program. To what Friedman quips: "Then why not give them spoons?".[22]

Milton was an ardent advocate for UBI in the form of a negative income tax.[23] His vision might herald a new epoch, yet one that presently seems too avant-garde for the bulk of the elite.

Alternative Scenarios

We're not trying to spook nor proselytize readers: UBI and the jobless society remain hypothetical. The 4^{IR} may change work paradigms beyond recognition, yet without leading to soaring unemployment, as factors from demographics to regulation come into play.

---

[20] Andrew Yang: *The War on Normal People: The Truth About America's Disappearing Jobs and Why Universal Basic Income Is Our Future*, Hachette Books (2018).

[21] Cf. p. 182, Daron Acemoğlu, James A. Robinson: *Why nations fail: the origins of power, prosperity, and poverty*, Profile Books (2012).

[22] For an investigation surrounding the origins of this likely apocryphal story, cf. https://quoteinvesti gator.com/2011/10/10/spoons-shovels.

[23] Cf. *Capitalism and Freedom* (1962) and *Free to Choose* (1980).

Nor should unemployment be the sole metric to assess technology's impact on work. For one, it excludes the portion of the population that drops out of the workforce entirely, highlighted by what economists call the "labor participation rate", also on a steady declining slope.[24] Nor does it capture the *quality* of jobs and the related issue of wealth redistribution. Several economists believe that therein lies the real threat of new technology.[25] Perhaps unemployment is even preferable to a fully employed society, should the latter consist of an elite filling cognitive positions while the majority moil in precarious, low-income jobs. With unemployment kept in check, UBI is unlikely to see the day.

Hereafter we explore what a future of 4^{IR}-caused disruption that *does not* breach the jobless society tipping point might resemble.

2.3   Unemployment with Too Many Vacancies: The Skills Mismatch Scenario

Developed economies are experiencing a new paradox: rising difficulties to secure talent.[26] Innovation may spur demand for jobs, yet it raises the bar as workers need to be proficient with the new tools. MIT professor Acemoğlu notes of this mismatch between technology and skills that it:

> Slows down the adjustment of labor demand, contributes to inequality, and also reduces the productivity gains from both automation and the introduction of new tasks.[27]

It also highlights a widening gap between what's taught in schools and actual corporate needs.

Why not raise spending on education and training? In the past, this has facilitated the transition toward industrial, then service sectors, from Roosevelt's National Youth of 1935 Administration (YTA) to Eisenhower's National Defense Education Act (NDEA) of 1958, geared to improve the sciences at all levels of education, to Kennedy's Manpower Training and

---

[24] From 76.7% for men and 60.5% for women in May 2002, to 69.9% and 57.8% by December 2021. Cf. Bureau of Labor Statistics, https://www.bls.gov/charts/employment-situation/civilian-labor-force-participation-rate.htm.

[25] David Autor, Carl Benedikt Frey, Daron Acemoğlu and Thomas Piketty, to name but a few.

[26] Edward Gordon: *Future Jobs: Solving the Employment and Skills Crisis*, Praeger Publishers Inc. (2013).

[27] Daron Acemoğlu and Pascual Restrepo: *Artificial Intelligence, Automation and Work*, The University of Chicago Press, Working Paper 24,196 (January 2018).

Development Act (MTDA) of 1962, aimed for those "whose only skill has been replaced by a machine".[28] Only yesterday's panacea may not work this time round.

The pace of technology versus that of our institutions' ability to ingest new knowledge presents a challenge, as the former is on an exponential course while the latter remains linear, in what futurist Azeem Azhar dubbed an "exponential gap".[29] And despite mounting calls from economists, government enthusiasm to reengineer education appears lackadaisical. Higher education has steered from the welfare state to become a private business, and a lucrative one at that. Though some tech firms attempt to fill the gap via online courses,[30] overall the private sector appears ill-prepared to take on the endeavor of retraining the workforce. We may need a violent choc—a "Sputnik moment"—to shake the leviathan from its lethargy.

Missing Skills

The very skills advocated to thrive in the age of automation should be cause for worry. These belong to two categories:

- skills believed to remain out of reach of robots and algorithms: creativity, ideation, transversal expertise, thinking out of the box, connecting dots between disparate qualitative criteria…
- skills to collaborate with the machines: computer proficiency, knowledge of programming, but also of machine learning, which involves a solid background in probabilities and statistics.

Organizations can expect to find the first group of qualities in top-notch managers, but these represent a small fraction of the workforce. Nor is there space for effusions of creativity on all corporate rungs—most firms would rather see their employees *not* get too creative. AI is advancing in recurrent, mundane tasks, hence the advice from experts to flee these like the plague; yet the foundations of World Inc. rest on structured jobs made of recurrent tasks, something we have Ford and Taylor to thank for. Management aside, most employees follow a script.

---

[28] G. R. Kremen: *MDTA: The Origins of the Manpower Development and Training Act of 1962*, U.S. Department of Labor (1974), https://www.dol.gov/general/aboutdol/history/mono-mdtatext.

[29] Azeem Azhar: *The Exponential Age: How Accelerating Technology is Transforming Business, Politics and Society*, Diversion Books (2021).

[30] Cf. for instance Microsoft's MOOCs: https://www.edx.org/school/microsoft and Apple Education: https://www.apple.com/education/.

This is not some state of affairs that can be changed with a snap of the fingers. Despite the success stories of holacracies, Zappos, Smartsheet, Haier, and W. L. Gore make the headlines precisely because they are outliers. The scarcity of these models enables them to attract the rare type of talent that befits the mold of their corporate cultures (and they are extremely selective in their plucking). Such models are scalable neither to all businesses, nor to the overall population.

Even supposing there were enough room for everyone, educational and training systems are ill-equipped to teach these skills. Past undertakings were a stroll in the park: twentieth-century organizations were tasked with training people to learn *recurrent* actions: how to operate a machine, follow a standard operating procedure (SOP), or teach a classroom of kids by the book. Consistency was of the essence. Now we must rewire our brains to learn the opposite (for an idea of just how much more difficult unlearning something can be, search on YouTube for the "backwards bicycle"[31]).

The second type of skillset hits on similar reefs: manipulating multiple regressions and neural networks may not be everyone's cup of tea. Pundits advocate adding steam into STEM (Science, Technology, Engineering, and Mathematics), envisioning a society of scientists. It takes a dilated imagination to picture everyone donning the white blouse and craving for science.

The pursuit of relevant skills partakes in our survival toolkit. Yet we must acknowledge that not everyone will make it past the finish line. There will be blood.

Jobs No-One Wants

So far, we've talked about the trouble to fill in skilled positions. Companies are facing pressure at the other end of the job spectrum, too. While particularly acute since the pandemic, the problem is not new. From 2001 to 2018, the number of vacant positions in the US shot up by 69% (from 4.4 to 7.4 million), while the workforce and overall population increased by only 12% and 16%, respectively. The rate of open jobs on total jobs went from 3.4% to 5.1%—a 49% increase.

Figure 2.5 details these 7.4 million US job openings using the Job Openings and Labor Turnover Survey (JOLTS) categories.[32] The size of each

---

[31] *The Backwards Brain Bicycle—Smarter Every Day 133* https://www.YouTube.com/watch?v=MFzDaBzBlL0.

[32] Data shown represents average monthly figures of each year. In line with the BLS standards, the averages are calculated from the not seasonally adjusted data. https://www.bls.gov/cps/seasfaq.htm.

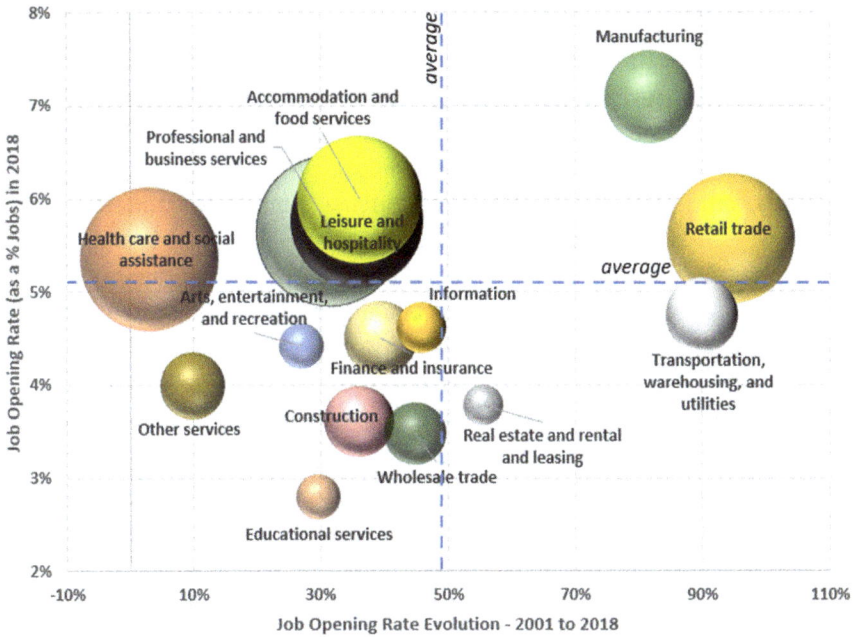

Fig. 2.5 2018 job openings as a percentage of jobs, and evolution since 2001. Using not seasonally adjusted data. *Source* U.S. Labor of Statistics, Job Openings and Labor Turnover Survey (JOLTS)

bubble reflects the number of openings, from 89,000 in Real Estate to 1.2 million in Professional and Business Services. The Job Opening Rate (vertical axis) compares these to the number of jobs in the category; we see how these rates have fared from 2001 to 2018 on the horizontal axis.

The percentage of job openings compared to total jobs grew across categories (all bubbles are on the right side of the vertical axis' 0%), underscoring the growing tension. Though these categories do not follow wage levels, we can make some gross assumptions.

Recruiters face hardships filling openings in Professional and Business Services, and to a lower extent in Financial, Insurance and Information—jobs that we may hypothesize carry a fair load of high-paid workers. Meanwhile, the bulk of those in Healthcare, Food, Accommodation and Hospitality tread on the lower end of the wage gamut; these categories also suffer above average rates. That Healthcare has not changed since 2001 highlights the chronic shortage of workers in the field (in fact it was the *only* category above 5% on the vertical axis in 2001). Rates in the Retail and the Transportation groups have practically doubled; and the pinch is most painful in Manufacturing, as people shy away from operator jobs, in contrast with the political rhetoric surrounding offshoring—manufacturing jobs exist, it's just that people either don't want or lack the skills to fulfill them.

With this, we touch on the double dilemma of the skills mismatch. On one end, people shun vacancies in low-paid, often physical work. On the other, firms struggle to secure cognitive talent.

Demographics underscore these phenomena. One study estimates roughly a third of the fall in middle-class jobs from 1979 to 2014 to be linked to demographic compositional changes within the US population.[33] The growth in high-paid jobs in part reflects aging baby boomers: as they retire, replacements from the middle class are too few. Meanwhile, the education system fails to churn the adequate cannon fodder.

The pandemic jolted these bubbles, as businesses from retail to travel came to a standstill, parents tendered for kids stuck at home and those previously overwhelmed by work found themselves with idle time to ponder on their lives. Many feel no urge to return to their past drudgery; they seek a change in career, or even activities that may not qualify as employment.[34]

This presses companies to double down on automation. As a top exec from research and consulting firm Gartner put it:

> In the 1980s, the main reason for investing in automation was to reduce labor costs. Now for almost half the clients, their primary reason is labor availability. I talk to people every day and this is their biggest concern.[35]

Automation could to an extent solve the skills mismatch problem, but with potentially ruinous repercussions on the workforce.

2.4   Workless or Work Less?

Keynes foresaw people working 15-h weeks by 2030. While we may not hit that mark in the short decade left, working times *have* decreased: from 51 h in Keynes' time (1930) to 35 h a week in 2018[36]—and that includes the time at work spent browsing Instagram photos and swapping Tinder profiles.

---

[33] Guido Matias Cortes, Nir Jaimovich and Henry E. Siu: *Disappearing routine jobs: Who, how, and why?*, in Journal of Monetary Economics (September 14, 2017).

[34] Those interested can find the same chart for the year 2021, in Appendix A.

[35] The Financial Times: *Robots replace humans as labour shortages bite*, (September 22, 2021), Robots replace humans as labour shortages bite | Financial Times (ft.com).

[36] Cf. data from the Economic History Association, https://eh.net/encyclopedia/hours-of-work-in-u-s-history/.

Might working less pave the route to keeping a sizeable portion of the working-age population employed?

Corporations would need to abide by the game, for instance by preserving wages. This is not to say that profitability must be forsaken; but we need a new middle ground between capitalist imperatives and a healthy society. Calls to amend the tenets of capitalism have multiplied in recent history.[37]

If all players acknowledge the need for change and genuinely strive to get there, automation—assuming that's the driving force behind the decrease in labor demand[38]—must create sufficient wealth for corporations to consider forking part of the bill.

Perhaps the greatest enemy to working less lies in the highly politicized context from where it would need to be birthed. Here too, it may take a shock or a severe recession to spark action and compel both sides of the political divide to agree. But if a single country enacts such measures, how will it affect its competitiveness and attractiveness on the global stage? Similar to Bill Gates' proposition to tax robots, these measures could deter firms from investing in the country.

A recent illustration of state intervention in the workweek can be found in Western Europe.

The Case of France's 35-h Workweek

When my family immigrated to France in 1989, the country was headed toward a recession, with unemployment soon hovering above 12%. In a bid to cure the nation, the government passed the highly controversial "Aubry Law" that reduced the mandatory workweek from 39 to 35 h.

It was rolled out in phases:

- from June 1998, companies were incentivized to implement the change ("Aubry 1")
- mandatory for all companies with 20 staff or more from January 2000 ("Aubry 2")
- small businesses were given till January 2002 to comply.

Flexibility was given in the implementation: some companies let employees leave an hour earlier, others gave Friday afternoon off. Overtime work was

---

[37] Cf. for instance Michael Porter, Mark Kramer: *Creating Shared Value*, Harvard Business Review, January–February 2011. Also Jean Tirole's *Economics for the Common Good*; Jean Staune's: *The Keys to the Future.*

[38] Some argue that the cause lies elsewhere. In his book *Automation and the Future of Work*, Aaron Benanav portrays a deceleration in economic growth as the main culprit.

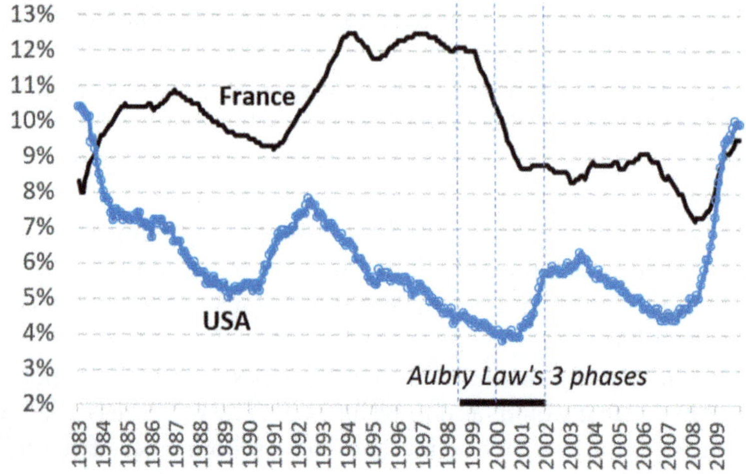

Fig. 2.6 France versus US historical unemployment, 1983–2009. *Source* OECD Data, https://data.oecd.org/unemp/unemployment-rate.htm

capped and made onerous so as to favor hiring. A focal point for labor unions was to ensure workers would not see their overall pay slump as a result of working less; to what the government responded by offering tax cuts and reducing mandatory social security contributions for firms who kept wages stable. Alas, to appease white collars (the French *cadres*), who do not receive overtime pay, the government granted them an extra 11 days off per year (called the "reduction of working time", *RTT*).

Denounced by a wide range of economists,[39] the Aubry Law (named after Martine Aubry, then Minister of Labor) undermined French politics for years. Results were mixed, with a shot up in temporary labor contracts through third parties and an increase in hours worked by part-time employees.

And unemployment? Fig. 2.6 compares France's unemployment to the US, with the steps of the Aubry Law highlighted.

Despite a clear correlation between the Aubry Law and French unemployment, we must caution against taking correlation for causation, and consider other factors occurring during the period.

The main event was the adoption by the then 12 EU countries of the common Euro currency. Launched in January 1999, first as an "invisible currency" (used solely for accounting purposes and electronic payments), then with cash in January 2002 (at the same time as Aubry's 3rd phase).

[39] Cf. for instance Paul Krugman: *Lumps of Labor*, New York Times, October 7th, 2003, and Nobel laureate Jean Tirole in *Economics for the Common Good*, p. 359.

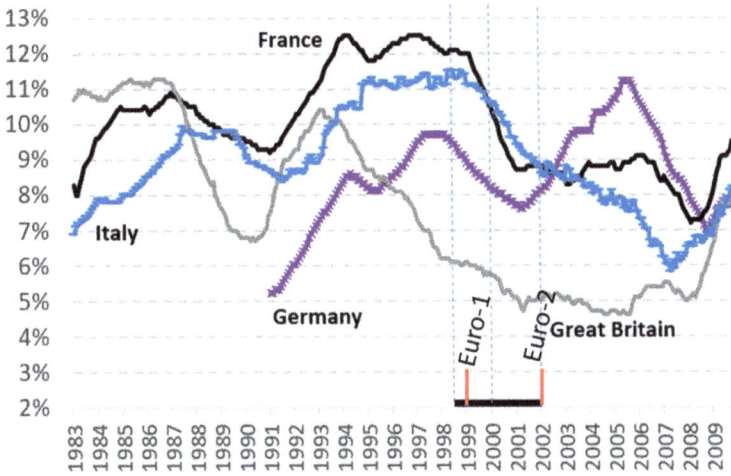

Fig. 2.7 Handful of European historical unemployment rates, 1983–2009. *Source* OECD Data, https://data.oecd.org/unemp/unemployment-rate.htm

This provides an interesting vantage point as we can compare French unemployment to that of its neighbors (with Great Britain thrown in the mix to illustrate a major *non-Eurozone* economy) (Fig. 2.7).

The 90's high unemployment period and subsequent decline was shared across these Eurozone countries. The Euro impacted each differently, a well-known fact and the cause of much fuss in Germany.

It's possible that *both* the Euro and Aubry Law contributed to improve French employment; the curve is steeper than elsewhere, and for a while, France was no longer the worst pupil in the classroom. Or perhaps it caught a favorable cyclical wave. Aside from employment, the Aubry Law damaged the country's competitiveness and attractiveness, sealing France's reputation as a hostile environment for corporations to set up shop. And in the long run, in terms of unemployment France has not fared any better than neighbors with longer working hours.

While it may herald a long-term solution for future work, this precedent underscores the difficulties of implementing shorter workweeks, especially when driven by a top-down approach. To succeed, the orbiting perils of precarity bound to slip through in the form of giggers, interns, temps and even outsourcing need to be addressed, via a sound legislative framework. Our institutions seem ill-equipped to meet the challenge, making it an improbable solution for the near future.

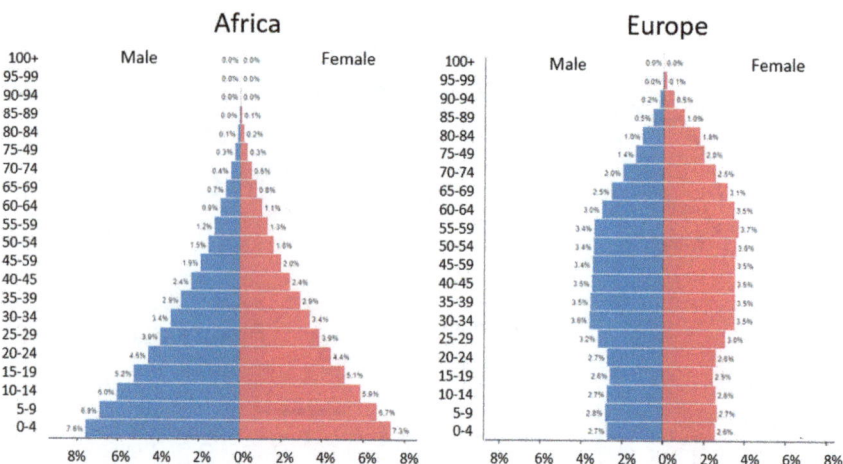

Fig. 2.8 2019 Population Ages: from Pyramid to Pillar. *Source* Population Pyramid.Net, www.populationpyramid.net[41]

2.5   The Tricky Case of Demographics

While the world population boomed during previous industrial revolutions, buoyed by greater efficiencies in food production, the main economic power-houses spearheading the 4th Industrial Revolution are now confronted with aging and even shrinking populations. Not for cause of war or famine, but due to societal changes: marriage relegated to an arcane institution, natality rates dropping amid the perceived burden of raising children, both financially and in terms of time consumption, with the fear of losing personal freedom.

A crude portrayal of the world stage reveals two distinct geographical typologies: the South, whose bolstering youths give its meaning to the term "age *pyramid*", and the North, where aging populations have put the pyramid on a diet, turning it into a pillar[40] (Fig. 2.8).

The Northern Hemisphere: Papy-Boom

Rich nations experienced an uptick in natality following World War 2, churning out the baby-boomer generation. Yesterday's "babies" are now retiring *en masse*, leading to what the French call a *papy-boom* (literally grand-daddy boom). Their exit from the workforce should be completed roughly

---

[40] We refer to a "North–South" dichotomy not based on the equatorial split but in terms of the more common (albeit approximate) approach related to economic development. Only 12% of the world's population live in the Southern Hemisphere as in "South of the Equator".

[41] Cf. also United Nations, Department of Economic and Social Affairs, Population Division (2019), World Population Prospects 2019, Online Edition. Rev. 1.

by the mid-2030s; meanwhile on the other end of the life spectrum, natality rates have plummeted.

By 2050, England's working population will be at 90% of its current size; Germany's, 80%. Altogether Europe will face a dearth of 44 million jobs.[42] By 2034, US adults above 65 years old are projected to outnumber children under 18.[43]

This creates a massive headache for governments. State-managed retirement pension funds will have too small an active workforce to pay for retirees. A partial solution, at least on paper, would be to delay the age of retirement—a most unpopular measure bound to meet stiff resistance.

An aging population poses other challenges as it exacerbates the labor shortage, putting pressure on companies. And would it not trigger a slump in consumption, threatening growth itself, that fundamental tenet of capitalism on which the economy rests? Or will technology, by automating certain occupations, narrow the gap? Will it preserve the capitalist model, for better or worse, or help us transition to a better one, that has yet to be formulated?

We can transpose these issues at the worker's level in two stages. The first one sees baby boomers hang onto their jobs longer, clogging the ascent for others. Their exit from the workforce, consumed circa 2040,[44] should see a profusion of enviable positions up for grabs. The key is to prepare for this second phase.

The Immigration Recipe

Immigration is a well-trodden remedy to a shrinking workforce. It can make a dent, albeit under certain conditions and only to an extent.

Governments (and their constituents) must be willing to open the faucet to begin with. Many countries lack the infrastructure and ecosystems to integrate newcomers; a paradigm shift is necessary, down to the very perception of immigration. Already a clear divide is perceptible within the North: while Western countries are acclimated to a certain dose of immigration, the legacy of a colonialist past, the same cannot be said of Asia. Most Asian countries

---

[42] Charles Kenny and George Yang, *Can Africa Help Europe Avoid Its Looming Aging Crisis?* Center for Global Development (June 14, 2021).

[43] Cf. *The Graying of America, More Adults than Kids by 2035*, https://www.census.gov/library/stories/2018/03/graying-america.html.

[44] The end of the baby-boom, a phenomenon specific to the North, varies by location. In China it could be prolonged to 2045; because the One-Child law was enacted in 1979, high natality rates persisted for Gen X (those born during the 1960s and 1970s).

do not allow dual citizenship,[45] for mixed reasons tied to their past[46] and to a will to preserve a homogenous cultural identity, an insular model best epitomized by Japan.

Alas, assuming a warm and successful welcome of immigrants, the inflow must be sizeable enough to defuse the aging timebomb. As Chinese economist Chong-en Bai once confided to me, the sheer numbers required to plug China's upcoming, abysmal population gap, courtesy of the One-Child policy, make immigration alone an implausible solution. The Middle Kingdom is expected to shed 200 million of its current 900 million strong workforce by 2050.[47] Contrast that with the US, whose entire workforce stands at 150 million. Others that I have discussed with in the Chinese manufacturing field seem rather upbeat on the propensity for robotic process automation (RPA) to take over this work; they worry more about too fast an implementation of these technologies. In any case, it's unlikely that automation and workforce demographics evolve in synch, and this dissonance will lead to friction points.

The Southern Hemisphere

Other roadblocks lie in the pathway of the South's economic molt. On top of the usual suspects—political instability, debt, international meddling, and neocolonialism—a new threat is mounting: technology. Automation could boost productivity levels in rich nations to the extent that offshoring no longer presents a viable option. As Chinese labor costs soar, will Western firms move production to lower-wage countries, or take advantage of automation to opt for reshoring, stateside? In other words, automation threatens jobs in the East that would have otherwise moved South. The industrialization trail to prosperity trodden by Asian nations from South Korea to China, in the footsteps of Western Europe and the US, may no longer be practicable. Environmental concerns regarding the windfalls of this industrialization path present another peril; together these pernicious issues may pose the twenty-first century's most contentious area of discord between North and South.

---

[45] The list includes China, India, Indonesia, Japan, and others—even Singapore, the most multicultural Asian country, forbids dual citizenship.

[46] Illustrated by the famous case of a US-born Japanese American working as an interpreter in a mining company that used American POWs during World War 2, who was later sentenced to death on treason charges upon his return to the US. While eventually pardoned and deported to Japan, the case subsequently served to justify Japanese authorities in forbidding dual citizenship. Cf. https://en.wikipedia.org/wiki/Kawakita_v._United_States.

[47] Joe Myers: *China's working-age population will fall 23% by 2050*, World Economic Forum (July 25th, 2016).

But could technology change the model, without dooming the South entirely? The ICT revolution (short for Information and Communications Technologies) has facilitated education, via massive open online courses (MOOCs) and online tutorials, producing a new breed of knowledge workers in the South. The 4^{IR} will likely generate demand for remote jobs—low-paid work like *artificial* Artificial Intelligence (more on this in a minute) alongside cognitive tasks—presenting a boon for the South. These jobs could become the bread and butter for a new workforce, generating enough income to drive consumption and spur an internal market.

Of course, the South could remain mired in turmoil or purely ignored, as was the case for much of our recent history. Yet it has the potential to become the biggest market of the second half of this century. That would lead the past decades' shift of economic nexus from West to East to steer Southwards, placing the region squarely in the Goldilocks' zone. A tide to catch.

This brief picture shows that other factors must be accounted for when projecting the future (more on demographics in the Job Disruption chapter—Demographics).

2.6 A Fourth Sector?

While we committed to pragmatism, at times one must peer down the rabbit hole, especially when envisaging the future. In this section, we bend things a notch, acknowledging upfront the purely speculative nature of these wanderings to keep our initial vow intact.

Dataism

What if the 4th Industrial Revolution ushers a new sector that takes up an increasingly sizable portion of GDP, *and* of jobs?

AI and its Big Data cousin appear as frontline contenders. A McKinsey Global Institute report from 2018 estimates that AI could deliver an extra $13 trillion to the global economy by 2030, or 16% higher cumulative GDP compared with 2019.[48] As The Economist noted in an article titled *The world's most valuable resource is no longer oil, but data*: "Whether you are going for a run, watching TV or even just sitting in traffic, virtually every activity creates a digital trace—more raw material for the data distilleries".[49] Leading

---

[48] McKinsey Global Institute: *Notes from the AI frontier: Modeling the impact of AI on the world economy*, (September 4th, 2018), https://www.mckinsey.com/featured-insights/artificial-intelligence/notes-from-the-ai-frontier-modeling-the-impact-of-ai-on-the-world-economy#part1.

[49] The Economist, May 6, 2017.

another to conclude: "Algorithms trained by all these digital traces will be globally transformational. It's possible that a new world order will emerge from it".[50]

Such assertions remind me of a teacher who back in the eighties claimed to our class that taken in a broad sense, the oil and car sectors comprised half of all jobs in the world. If data usurps oil's throne, will it purvey its newly won subjects with sufficient jobs? Or produce a scenery akin to the desolate lands of *The Lion King*, after the Machiavellian uncle's coup?

Accenture's CTO Paul Daugherty, a respected figure in the field, seems upbeat. He foresees the emergence of three types of data workers:

- "trainers" who tweak and perfect algorithms for optimal performance
- "explainers" who serve as a bridge between algorithms and stakeholders (employees, customers, management, the government…)
- "sustainers" who ensure that the AI upholds ethical standards.

Explainers could be tasked to explicit court rulings made by an AI, or why a certain candidate didn't get the job, while sustainers monitor inputs and results, on the lookout for biases. In the past, the creation of financial regulations boosted demand for accountants and auditors; data regulations could have a similar impact. Administering the GDPR requirements for explaining data output alone could add 75,000 jobs.[51]

A research paper from IBM and Burning Glass (an analytics software company focused on the labor market) puts the estimate of US job listings for data scientists and analysts at 2,3 million in 2017, a figure expected to grow to 2,7 million by 2020.[52]

Several factors may dampen hopes for a sizeable data job market.

These projections not only hinge on the amount of data, but also the workload necessary to crunch the figures, and both are constantly changing—the latter in no small part due to improving AI capabilities. Suppose today's average worker churns through 1 GB of data per hour and that the amount

[50] Bhaskar Chakravorti, Ajay Bhalla, and Ravi Shankar Chaturvedi: *Which Countries are Leading the Data Economy*, Harvard Business Review (January 24, 2019).

[51] James Wilson and Paul R. Daugherty, *Collaborative Intelligence: Humans and AI Are Joining Forces*, Harvard Business Review (July–August 2018), *How Humans and AI Are Working Together in 1,500 Companies* (hbr.org).

[52] Steven Miller and Debbie Hughes: *The Quant Crunch: how the demand for data science skills is disrupting the job market* (2017). https://www.ibm.com/downloads/cas/3RL3VXGA. This astronomical number likely includes any worker analyzing data, be it in a spreadsheet. E.g. they classify "one out of five workers from finance and insurance" fields as data scientists or analysts. Unfortunately, these jobs are ill-defined and thus subject to interpretation; they do not fit anywhere on the Bureau Labor of Statistics' grid.

of data explodes 20-fold in the next ten years[53]; if by then AI enhances our worker by a factor of a hundred, all else considered equal, less labor will be needed.

App users tend to stick to their platforms, displaying remarkable loyalty without the need for costly advertising. Data improves algorithms, thus recommendations, alluring more people to join while erecting a barrier against wannabe competitors. This new business model, embodied in the book *Machine, Crowd, Platform*, favors concentration in the hands of a few mammoth players.[54] FAANG (acronym for Facebook, Apple, Amazon, Netflix, and Google) guard the keys to our data and ruthlessly hunt down menacing startups.

Unlike previous sectors buoyed by industrial revolutions, the business of data seems poised to be highly automated from the start. Just look at the thin numbers employed by Internet leaders versus those of companies whose once stellar stock market rankings they toppled—the Instagram/David vs Kodak/Goliath parable. As Kai-Fu Lee, an influential expert on futurism, observed: "Algorithms aren't displacing human workers at these companies, simply because the humans were never there to begin with".[55]

Setting up the data economy adds jobs: building the protocols, 5G infrastructure, and Cloud warehouses; training algorithms, erecting ethical systems, and digitization to make everything "smart". In their study of technologies, economist Paul Beaudry and colleagues call this the "investment phase". The 4^{IR} is currently somewhere in it. But once everything is up and running, we move to the "maturity period", in which demand for human labor slumps.[56] We refer to this latter slump as the "Beaudry effect". AI's automation proclivities could make the next drop particularly steep, as part of 4^{IR} setup in traditional businesses aims to automate work. For instance, the first generation of ERPs deployed in companies still requires troves of manual work to manipulate data—labor bound for the automation grinder as sleeker versions emerge. By definition, a smart factory or smart office removes cognitive bits from employees.

---

[53] For some reference points, the world generated 2 zettabytes of data in 2010, 18 ZB in 2018, and is forecast to produce 180 ZB by 2025. https://www.statista.com/statistics/871513/worldwide-data-created/.

[54] Andrew McAfee and Erik Brynjolfsson: *Machine, Platform, Crowd: Harnessing Our Digital Future*, W.W. Norton & Company (2017).

[55] Kai-Fu Lee: *Ai Superpowers: China, Silicon Valley, and the New World Order*, p. 178, Mariner Books (2018).

[56] Paul Beaudry, David A. Green and Benjamin M. Sand, *The Great Reversal in the Demand for Skill and Cognitive Tasks*, Journal of Labor Economics, 2016, vol. 34, no. 1, pt. 2. While their focus was on Information and Communication Technologies, they conjectured that it was a trait characteristic of any general-purpose technology (a term explained in the Tech chapter).

Alas, data-related jobs are easily gigged, or outsourced to specialized firms bound to surface, in the same way the Internet spawned search engine optimization (SEO) firms such as Neil Patel Digital.

A Well-Paid Job?

Suppose the data sector is avid for jobs; what wage level would they command? Books on AI dangle the six-digit yearly incomes enjoyed by the darling data scientists that Big Tech firms fight over. The *average* salary is rather in the ballpark of $100,000 a year.[57] Still a respectable income. But as tech becomes user-friendly, IT expertise spreads and outsourcing develops, these wages could deflate. Nor are the jobs all glitter: according to a survey on Stack Overflow—a Q&A platform like Quora, only for programmers— machine learning specialists and data scientists topped the list of developers searching for a new job, and salary had little to do with it.[58]

Meanwhile, other rising data occupations are snubbed by futurists. Scrubbing the varnished AI tale reveals human jobs of "*artificial*   artificial intelligence" (AAI), such as data labeler and content moderator.

Computer vision is the subfield of AI that deals with recognizing objects in images. Its subpar performance requires human intervention, or AAI: behind the scenes, armies of workers glued to their screens review photos, delineating and tagging objects to define what each one represents. Welcome to one of the new jobs spawned by the 4[IR]: data labeling. While at first, these tasks were crowdsourced to services like Amazon Mechanical Turk,[59] reliability concerns are shoving demand toward specialized firms. Startups such as Scale AI (valued at $7 billion and run by a twenty-two-year-old at the time of writing[60]) employ a few hundred people but subcontract to dozens of thousands of youths who toil in "data factories", a modern twist of sweatshops.

---

[57] Precisely $100,680 on average for the 712,460 Computer and Information Analysts identified in 2020 in the US (BLS code 15–1210); $130,890 for the 30,220 Computer and Information Research Scientists (code 15–1220), and $161,730 for the 457,290 Computer and Information Systems Managers (code 11–3021).

[58] Cf. Richard Waters, *How machine-learning creates new professions—and problems*, The Financial Times (November 29, 2017), https://www.ft.com/content/49e81ebe-cbc3-11e7-8536-d321d0d897a3.

[59] Cf. an example in Sarah Kessler, *Gigged*. Amazon chose the name in reference to an eighteenth century chess-playing machine with a Turkish-styled automate. The original Mechanical Turk stunned crowds, beating even Napoleon in chess. Only much later was the supercherie uncovered: the moves were made by a chess master hiding inside the device. The term has come to exemplify "*artificial* artificial intelligence".

[60] *Data-labeling company Scale AI valued at $7.3 billion with new funding*, Fortune (April 14th, 2021) https://fortune.com/2021/04/13/scale-ai-valuation-new-funding-fundraising-data-labeling-company-startups-vc/.

Content moderators are tasked with reviewing freshly uploaded videos and photos, to flag those of offensive nature (rape, suicide, child abuse…). Facebook contracts with over 15,000 content moderators globally. An investigation into a content moderator firm with offices in Kenya revealed worker performance measured against an "average handling time" metric of 50 seconds, plus the requirement to make the right call at least 84% of the time. The moderators receive $1.50 an hour for work made high-stress by these metrics, by nature bound to cause life-long posttraumatic stress disorders.[61]

Why are these new jobs seldom mentioned? For one, they expose the dirty little secret of AI's current limitations. Then as one AI professor put it:

> This [data labeling] is a somewhat depressing job for the future. It's not 'Oh, let's get some people to write a screenplay together'. It's the lowest level stuff.[62]

That this new form of work pays a pittance, as a gig and not a job, and one easily offshored at that, tarnishes the technophiles' roseate narrative of the future. It brings us closer to a society where half of the people barely subsist by doing the Turk's job, producing the illusion of a magical AI experience for the other half.

An Improbable Paying Model?

Corporate taxation, national sovereignty, access, privacy rights and hacker intrusions are but several data-related issues haunting regulators.[63] And then comes the question of who *owns* the data.

Consider the two following cases, laid out by economics Nobel Prize winner Jean Tirole: what of an Uber driver who wants to switch to Lyft but cannot transfer his credit ratings? Unlike when changing banks, no rule requires the company to hand over the data they've accumulated on you. However when a company goes bankrupt, its creditors eagerly seek to grab this data. Despite RadioShack's promise not to share customer data, the data was sold in 2015 when the company filed for Chap. 11.[64]

In short, the data landscape of 2020 bears resemblance to a Wild West, where stakeholders skirmish for the new oil and the law of the jungle gives

---

[61] Time Magazine, *Inside Facebook's African Sweatshop,* (February 17, 2022).

[62] Hope Reese, *Is 'data labeling' the new blue-collar job of the AI era?* Tech Republic (March 10, 2016) https://www.techrepublic.com/article/is-data-labeling-the-new-blue-collar-job-of-the-ai-era/.

[63] Cf. the United Nations report, *Data Economy: Radical Transformation or Dystopia?* Frontier Technology Quarterly (January 2019), https://www.un.org/development/desa/dpad/wp-content/uploads/sites/45/publication/FTQ_1_Jan_2019.pdf.

[64] Jean Tirole: *Economics for the Common Good*, p. 405, Princeton University Press (2017).

Big Corp a disproportionate advantage over netizens. As the sheriff steps in and the dust settles, we may witness a paradigm whereby all parties benefit to some extent. Let us explore possible scenarios.

Facebook-like systems can be summed up as: "you *should* be paying to use our platform; instead, we provide it free of charge in exchange for your data". The prerequisite of this model dictates that when anything online is free, *you* are the product. Users would be reluctant to pay for access to a user-generated content platform. A newcomer promoting such a model would stand no chance, while an existing player could face a severe backlash.

Yet what of an *optional* paying model, one that lets users reap some benefit from the data they generate? Letting users decide could calm tensions. Nor is it new: LinkedIn and Tinder propose optional paying models to maximize chances of hiring talent or finding a partner. Only here, users would make money based on the value of data they generate, their profile more akin to a business, like opening an account on Artsy, self-publishing or creating a Wechat store. Instead of selling art, ebooks or whatever one sells on Wechat, income is generated based on data.

Key Opinion Leaders stand as proof that users can make money from the data they generate. For now, the paradigm is reminiscent of artists: only a minuscule fraction of users is compensated, while the rest get nothing but free likes.

Data value is not constrained to luxury brand-related posts and live-streaming; the troves of data used by algorithms in insurance, real estate, marketing, consumer analysis and many other fields dwarf that generated by KOL posts. And the sector is only in its infancy.

Blockchain technology could step in to trace the value of data. A sundry of digital coin projects vies to provide this kind of assessment, so that brands can accurately value the return on advertising dollars.

Non-fungible tokens (NFTs) present another nascent model. Digital artwork was plagued from the start by a weakness intrinsic to the online model: it can be copy-pasted to infinity. Without scarcity and authenticity, the sector could never take off. NFTs changed that. Acting like virtual signatures, they guarantee the authenticity of the original, thus circumventing the zero marginal cost issue. NFTs are revolutionizing digital art and collectibles by offering proof of ownership, cutting out middlemen (auction houses and art galleries) and democratizing the art market in the process. Any digital creation, from a Photoshop design to a slow-motion animated gif of a basketball player or the code from Berners-Lee that birthed the World Wide Web, can be sold via NFTs. Nifty Gateway, a major NFT platform, even guarantees a 10% royalty for creators on every future resale of their work (living artists like David Hockney, whose iconic *Splash* recently sold for $90 million, or 5,000 times the original price he sold it at decades ago, can but weep).

Another precursor can be found in online gaming, where players can make serious coin, either through ads, by coaching newbies, participating in competitions or selling virtual objects like armor and even experience points (XP). Considering that XP reflects time spent on a game, that others are willing to pay for, is a case in point. Income of this sort could explode as the metaverse expands gaming into a mainstream form of leisure for all.

Legislation to the Rescue

Another piece of the data puzzle relates to privacy concerns. Provided users win this battle with the aid of legislation, it could open a bridge for companies to financially reward users for access to their data. User data would become a protected, valued asset, access to which would be granted only in exchange of payment.

Crosspollination of purchase history with other user data will take companies a leap further in data mining, birthing a marketplace where we consent to sell our privacy in a similar vein as guinea pigs partake in a group study or receive payment for unapproved drug test trials. You could view it as an extension of the VIP cards popular in retail.

The more shared data, the more income to rake in. This could be as banal as accepting cookies, following a company account, hashtagging a brand or reposting their news on your wall. According to your data's relevance for each company, you earn either an upfront payment, booked by the company as a marketing expense, or a small ratio of their profit, following a concept similar to dividends—what we could call a digital dividend, or "digidend". Data relevance would account for your activity and online platform, i.e. the size and quality of your connections and followers.

Early attempts to value user data, for instance on Facebook, have concluded that the income derived for users would be ridiculously low. Yet these are based on the current state of digital trails; as the 4^{IR} produces a thermonuclear explosion of data, more of it could be harvested, monitored, and valued, with blockchain kicking in to trace the source and impacts of online activity.

To be plausible, regulators would need to step up their game. The clash with Tech Titans seems inevitable, given the current imbalance of power. Governments lagged; now they need to play catchup. For Big Tech, the pill would be sour. They are unlikely to relinquish the newfound gold without a fight, exploiting the usual channels—lobbying, corruption, threatening to add or raise fees, spreading the specter of a communist state.

We abhor the idea of the government eavesdropping on us, yet no one hit the streets as we handed our data over to corporations. The extent of the

State's role regarding data poses a serious quandary, one that legislators seem hesitant to address, both for lack of expertise and unease regarding Orwellian drifts. No doubt countries will experiment with different recipes, leading to the emergence of a heterogenous cyberworld.

Thirty years from now we may look back at the early 2020s as a data dystopia, a Wild West age that saw the masses ransacked of their data by profiteering tech corporations, with Wall Street orchestrating from the background and policymakers turning a blind eye. How much fumbling until we reach a fair data retribution system? We can only hope that the explosion of data will stir governments from their lethargy, yet at the same time, we cannot just lay back and count on them.

The new data oil could be harnessed and deployed to enable decentralization, more participative forms of democracy, an overhaul of our institutions—including international ones—and transparency in public revenue and spending. For now, the old guard has proven resilient, with an invisible yet firm grip holding the rusty systems in place; perhaps with time we will learn to tap the data reservoir in ways beneficial to society. Either that or we stay on our current trajectory toward a corporate dystopia.

2.7   Wealth Redistribution: Toward a Dystopia

Social inequality in the West improved during the twentieth century, as wages rose in line with labor productivity. That is, until the 1970s and what economists have dubbed the "Great Decoupling" between productivity and median income, which led to a disproportionate amount of wealth accumulation at the summit.

In parallel, the makeup of jobs in Western economies started to shift, with workers piling up at both extremes of the wage gamut. This is now a well-established phenomenon, that goes by the names of job polarization, middle-class squeeze, hollowing of the middle class, or the more refined if somewhat abstruse "ALM hypothesis" (acronym for David Autor, Frank Levy, and Richard Murnane, the MIT economists who pioneered research in the field).[65] Let's take a peek at this trend's unfolding in the past two decades.

---

[65] David Autor: *The Polarization of Job Opportunities in the U.S. Labor Market: Implications for Employment and Earnings*, Center for American Progress (April 2010); David Autor and David Dorn: *The Growth of Low-Skill Service Jobs and the Polarization of the US Labor Market*, American Economic Review 2013, no.5 (2013); also Maarten Goos and Alan Manning: *Lousy and Lovely Jobs: The Rising Polarization of Work in Britain*, in The Review of Economics and Statistics (February 2007).

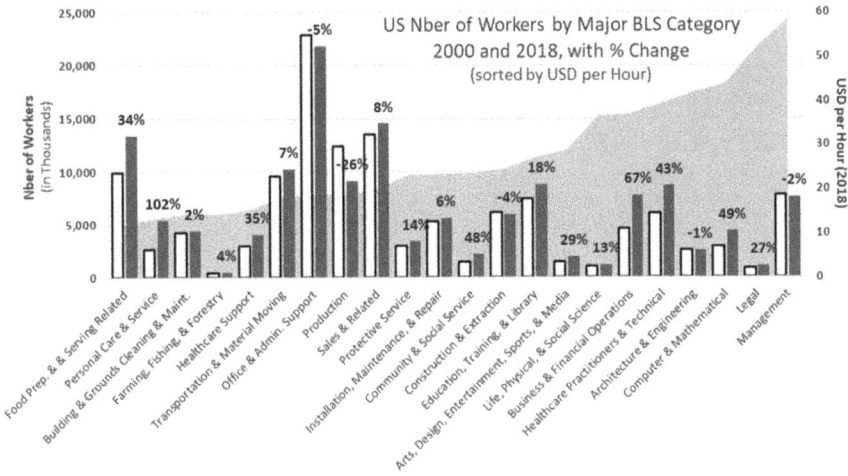

Fig. 2.9 US Number of Workers by Major BLS Category, in 2000 and 2018, with % of Change (sorted by increasing order of USD per hour wages

Figure 2.9 classifies U.S. workers in Major job categories (as defined by the Bureau Labor of Statistics' Standard Occupational Classification[66]) in 2000 and 2018, with the evolution of their numbers shown in percentages. The categories are sorted in increasing order of hourly wage, as per the gray area in the background.

Focusing on the change in the number of workers reveals the following (Fig. 2.10).

While the sharpest decline occurred in production jobs (with China's 2001 accession to the World Trade Organization an obvious culprit[67]), Office and Administrative Support jobs come next. Counting over twenty million workers—over 70% of which are women—the admin category is by far the largest in terms of employment: 15% of the US workforce, twice the number of production jobs. Note that production jobs often consist of *redundant, manual* tasks, whereas admin jobs consist of *redundant, non-manual* tasks.[68] The former are vulnerable to robotization; the latter, to automation by software and algorithms.

Considering that the US workforce increased by 11.6% over the two-decade period, any percentage below that threshold translates as a *decrease*

---

[66] Available here: https://www.bls.gov/soc/2018/#classification.

[67] Cf. Autor, Dorn and Hanson (2013), Pierce and Schott (2013) and Acemoğlu et al. (2014). The impact is not just "jobs moving to China": the threat of low-wage countries coerces manufacturing sites that remain stateside to shed jobs via automation in order to remain competitive.

[68] Cf. Autor, Levy and Murnane: *The Skill Content of Recent Technological Change: an Empirical Exploration*, Quarterly Journal of Economics 118 (November 2003).

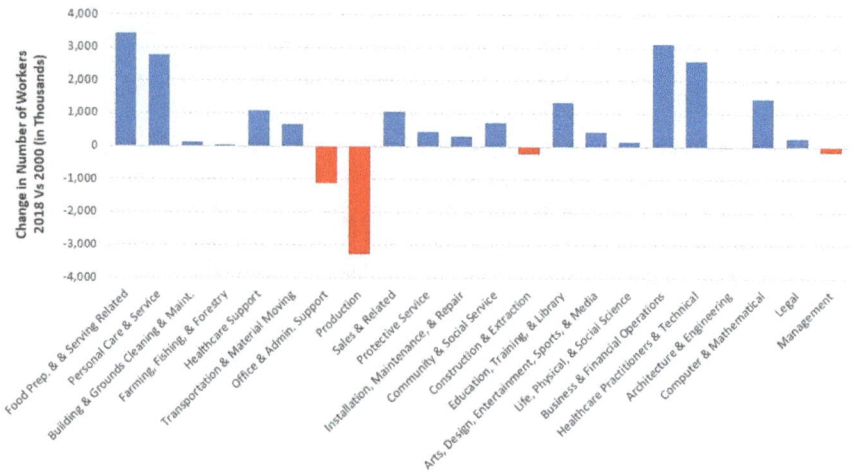

Fig. 2.10   Change in Numbers of Workers from 2000 to 2018

relative to the overall workforce (and even more so to the overall population, which grew by 16%). When adjusting for this 11.6% growth, we find the number of jobs added or subtracted in the waterfall chart of Fig. 2.11 (cf. Appendix B for a deeper dive into the details, which still corroborates the ALM hypothesis of a middle-class squeeze).

A compelling depiction of the middle-class hollowing effect. Categories on the edges show steam: high-paid jobs involving cognitive tasks on one end; food preparation, retail jobs[69], and personal care on the other. Or as David Autor, one of the most respected figures on the future of work, bluntly states, we are slipping toward a bipolar world, made up of the wealthy on one end, and those who serve them on the other.[70]

The Gini index substantiates this trend of growing immiseration. A measure of inequality, the Gini index uses a score from 0 (full equality) to 1 (where a single individual holds all the country's assets). From France to Finland and Germany, the Gini index has deteriorated since the start of

---

[69] While the Sales category appears in the middle wage here, within it lie deep disparities (as opposed to Office Admin Support jobs, more homogeneously concentrated in the middle wage level). Cf. Appendix C on Sales & Related Jobs, that by digging down a level reveals the evolution of America's eight million cashiers and retail jobs.

[70] Cf. his Ted talk, *Will Automation Take Away All Our Jobs?* https://www.YouTube.com/watch?v=th3 nnEpITz0. Note that Autor does not believe that this polarization trend will endure until there are no middle-class jobs left. Cf. David Autor, *Why are there still so many jobs? The history and future workplace of automation*, Journal of Economic Perspectives—Volume 29, Number 3 (Summer 2015), pp. 3–30.

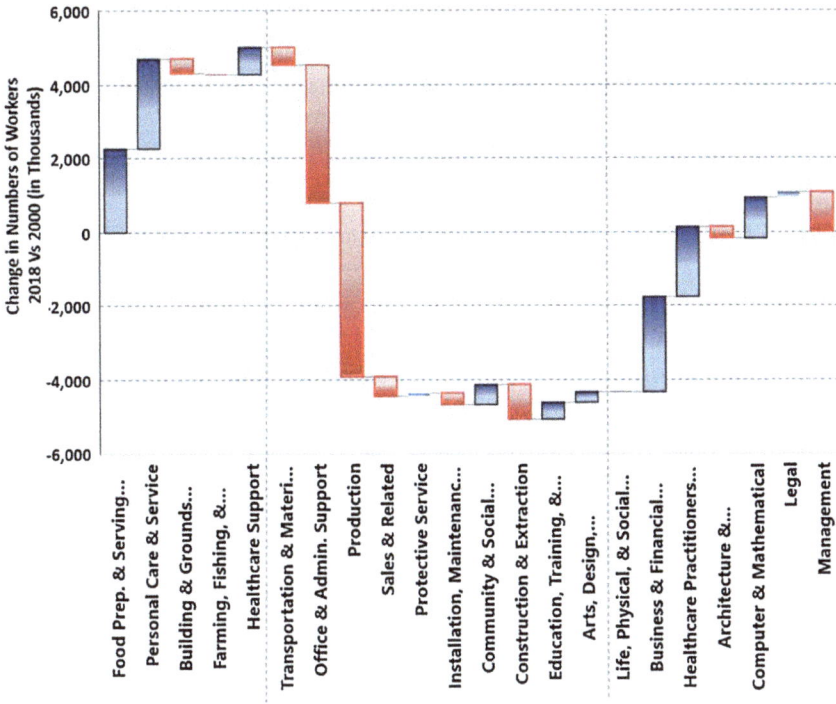

Fig. 2.11 2000 to 2018 Evolution of Jobs by Major Category sorted by increasing wage level and adjusted for the increase in overall workforce (+11.6%)

the century. With an index of 0.415, the US Gini stands higher than most European countries, recently surpassing China.[71]

Figure 2.12 groups US jobs into three wage categories, as per the dotted vertical lines in the previous chart.

The last column shows the stagnation in middle-income jobs translates as a drop in that portion relative to the total US workforce. Middle-class jobs are evaporating; yet unlike water, these workers are not necessarily moving upwards. And while the shift may seem minor, bear in mind that it started in the 1970s—back then, the middle class represented over 60% of the workforce. Nor is the phenomenon constricted to the US.[72]

---

[71] Cf. World Bank estimates, https://data.worldbank.org/indicator/SI.POV.GINI.

[72] Cf. David Autor's previously cited Ted Talk. Also, for the United Kingdom, Maarten Goos and Alan Manning: *Lousy and Lovely Jobs: The Rising Polarization of Work in Britain*, in The Review of Economics and Statistics (February 2007). For Japan, Toshie Ikenaga and Ryo Kambayashi: *Task Polarization in the Japanese Market: Evidence of a Long-Term Trend*, in Industrial Relations, A Journal of Economy and Society (April 2016), 55(2):p.267–293.

Income Level	Nber of Workers (in Thousands)				% Total		
	2000	2018	Var %	Var 000	2000	2018	Var
Low (<15$/Hour)	27,606	33,511	21%	5,904	21%	23%	2%
Mid (15-30$/Hour)	68,918	70,102	2%	1,184	53%	48%	-5%
High (>30$/Hour)	33,104	41,119	24%	8,015	26%	28%	3%
Total	129,628	144,731	12%	15,103	100%	100%	

Fig. 2.12 US jobs in 3 wage categories, with evolution in the number of workers (2000–2018)

Peering forward, Frey and Osborne anticipate automation targeting low-income jobs. The non-redundant part of these boils down to an unstructured environment, i.e. pattern recognition, something AI is improving at with computer vision. Throw in dropping costs and advancements in robot dexterity, and a large portion of the workforce could be at stake: cashiers, waiters, retail salespersons, gardeners, janitors—you name it.

More critically, despite the recent drop in office jobs, there is still ample space for automation. The tidal wave of improved bots in the lineage of ChatGPT, tailored to specific work contexts, has yet to fully hit offices. As firms tame these technologies, middle-class workers who fail to up their game will join the crowd at the base of the pyramid, causing a depression in wages there as job demand exceeds supply.[73] This forces a plethora of questions as to the future organization of work.

Consider the traditional career path. Even Ivy school graduates don't start at the top of the ladder. They begin as interns, then rotate through various roles before developing managerial acumen. These steppingstones may sink under the waters of automation. How to climb corporate ladders when they are broken? My dream goal was not to become a professional chauffeur, nor a top-notch interpreter. Yet at the dawn of my career, it was thanks to a chauffeur-translator gig that I was able to slip my foot through the door of a company, get acquainted with its management, and eventually land a full-time office job. An unthinkable path by the year 2040, as firms would opt for autonomous vehicles and translation devices.

And what of the transgenerational ladder-climbing of low-class workers whose offspring achieve middle-class or even upper-class status? Cliché as it may sound, this oft-rehashed story enabled millions of second and third-generation immigrants to rise and partake in the American (and European) dream. Waning middle-class jobs would close the valves, coagulating the

---

[73] Acemoğlu, Daron, and Pascual Restrepo. 2018. "*The Race between Man and Machine: Implications of Technology for Growth, Factor Shares, and Employment*" American Economic Review, 108 (6): 1488–1542.

flow as those at the bottom cannot afford an education for their children to leap from bottom to top—a fact exacerbated by abysmal education costs (cf. Fig. 3.6 in the 3rd Industrial Revolution section). In other words, job polarization could quickly veer toward a hereditary system of first and third-tier citizens. A society that risks falling into the bipolar dystopia characteristic of cyberpunk fiction.

And that's for developed countries, those with the means to invest in AI.[74] The rest of the world may slip into chaos, as low-wage countries reliant on offshoring lose attractiveness. It could mark the end of the sourcing and manufacturing hubs built over past decades, courtesy of globalization. Massive unemployment is a well-documented ingredient for civil unrest, especially in countries lacking democratic institutions: in times of famine, all eyes turn to the top. A salient characteristic shared by dictatorial regimes lies in their lack of a modus operandi for switching leaders when those in place fail to stop the hemorrhage.

After decades of fading, technology could reinforce North–South cleavages. While the North may escape the specter of massive unemployment or, thanks to 4^{IR} tech, produce sufficient bounty to share with *all* of its constituents, the South faces a different menace, one that may see the "Third World" moniker make a forceful comeback.[75] Experts from Kai-Fu Lee to Karl Schwab (founder of the World Economic Forum) expressed these fears while pondering the global impacts of automation.[76] With no remedy in sight.

Conclusion on Future

We've just sketched a handful of pathways to the future. Reality may take a different turn. We could go on formulating educated guesses and pursue the interminable fuss about whether the Fourth Industrial Revolution will create more jobs than it destroys. But such quibbling misses the point. What difference does it make to those who lost a lucrative job and now juggle between

---

[74] 2017 global R&D amounted to US$1.8 trillion, or 2.3% of global GDP. Note the aggravated Pareto at play: the top 10 R&D spenders account for half of world population, yet 72% of world GDP and 80% of global R&D spending. Cf. UNESCO Institute for Statistics: http://uis.unesco.org/.

[75] Economists who reassure their audience that fears of automation causing massive unemployment are overblown, only to focus their argumentation on wealthy countries, omit this point. https://www.ted.com/talks/david_autor_will_automation_take_away_all_our_jobs.

[76] Cf. Karl Schwab, *The Fourth Industrial Revolution*, Penguin Books (2017); Kai-Fu Lee, *AI Superpowers*, Mariner Books (2018).

two or more part-time gigs, only to make a pittance of a living and with thin prospects of ever bouncing back to a position deemed of dignity. Add a family to feed, a student loan or mortgage payments—a steep decline in income is simply not an option.

We may avoid the specter of a jobless society, with all its quandaries, only to drift from Charybdis to Scylla—namely, a society split between first and third-class citizens. Unleashing 4^{IR} technologies in the workplace could aggravate this already documented trend as it targets middle-class jobs, leaving workers with two escape routes: up or down. We advocate for upward mobility, but that implies rivalry: remember that only one of the campers flees the bear. The less fortunate will tumble down, joining the cohorts of servants piling at the base. A recipe for disaster that could stir turmoil, reverse the move toward gender equality, steer the spotlight away from environmental concerns, and fuel the rise of totalitarian regimes.

In their magnanimity, the elites may deem full automation best avoided, less for economic than social reasons. Francis Fukuyama stated that "the future of democracy in developed countries will depend on their ability to deal with the problem of a disappearing middle class", noting a rising discontent of peoples united in their "belief that the elites in their countries have betrayed them."[77] Our institutions seem scarcely concerned with their constituents' needs, instead siding with the top percentile, leading economist Aaron Benanav to a somber prediction: that only a revolution can bring about true change.[78] This conclusion he draws from our past trials. Turmoil may be conducive to radical change, yet one need not venture far to find reasons for skepticism as to the outcome of such bullet-above-ballot rhetoric. Times, education, and ideals have changed. I find the notion of populists and extremists capable of curing our woes rather challenging to entertain.

But let us too, leave the twenty-first century and embark on a quest to our past. To seek cues in previous industrial revolutions. How did they unfold? What was their impact on jobs and on society's well-being?

---

[77] Francis Fukuyama: *Political Order and Political Decay*, Profile Books (2015).
[78] Cf. Aaron Benanav: *Automation and the Future of Work*, Verso publications (2020).

3

Past

Introduction

Technology impacts society. Agriculture led to food production surplus (during good times), enabling the "invention" of cities. These in turn brought about specialization of people by craft, with metallurgists, carpenters, and tradesmen, and pressed for a better organization of the resulting, more complex society—including handling threats that only grew bigger with higher people densities, like disease, war, and famine. The domino effect continued: efficient political organization of societies required fast and secure communication routes, accounting for the management of staples, an improved form of archives for judgements to take precedence, and so on. These needs culminated in inventions like writing, that birthed jobs from scribe to copyist and archivist.

Major inventions unfold incrementally, in what upon closer inspection resembles a succession of innovations. Alongside their writing, the Mesopotamians used seals to stamp documents, but we usually don't frame this as the invention of printing. Chinese set up woodblock printing around AD 200, pushing the boundaries a step further with the movable type a thousand years later. Yet printed books remained rare and expensive—it was often

A. M. Recanati, *AI Battle Royale*, Copernicus Books, https://doi.org/10.1007/978-3-031-19278-4_3

cheaper to pay a copyist to rewrite a book.[1] The appearance of the Gutenberg press in the 1450s improved quality while reducing cost. Myriads of other innovations orbit around the printing process. Together, they put the copyist out of a job.

These advances in printing aided in the propagation of ideas, starting with religions: many printed materials from China that survived the ordeals of time concern Buddhist texts, like the Diamond Sutra, while the Gutenberg press is most famous for its 180 "Gutenberg Bibles" (of which around fifty survive, more or less complete, spread across museums and private collections); and it helped Protestant ideas to spread virally.

The world was far from static before the First Industrial Revolution—even the so-called Obscurantist period saw the inventions of clocks and powerful watermills. Yet the end of obscurantism, and with it the reliance on superstition, ignited an era of accelerated discoveries and inventions—a succession of industrial revolutions that continue to rattle the world.

3.1   1[IR]: Coal and Steel

In the Late Middle Ages (1300–1500), humanity was struck by profound afflictions: the Black Plague, Little Ice Age, and the Great Famine of 1315–1317 (supposedly caused by volcanic activity in New Zealand); warfare added to these woes in Europe, with frequent squabbling on the backdrop of the Hundred Years War. All in, over half of Europe's population was wiped out. The Catholic Church's inability to bring a remedy, meanwhile abusing believers with the infamous indulgences to "buy" salvation, pushed thinkers to turn elsewhere for answers.

Discovery of the Americas lifted hopes for a better world, while the rediscovery of the Ancients from Antiquity set the stage for Humanism, shifting the focus from ethereal beings somewhere up there, be they one or plural, to the tangible world down here, and throwing wide open the gates to the scientific methodology.

On the technological front, the invention of steam power in the latter half of the eighteenth century[2] marks the first major offspring borne by this age of enlightenment—what economists now refer to as a *general-purpose technology*, or GPT for short (and no, this abbreviation has nothing to do

---

[1] Cf. Endymion Wilkinson, *Studies in Chinese Price History*, Garland (1980).

[2] While patents for the use of steam can be found as early as the late seventeenth Century, James Watt is usually credited with having developed and perfected the first truly effective steam engines in the second half of the eighteenth Century.

with ChatGPT). Up to then, power depended chiefly on living muscle (be it human or animal) and Mother Nature, whose forces at play in the winds and rivers were exploited by boats and mills.[3] Powered by coal, steam led to the emergence of a new class of ships, factories and furnaces unlike anything seen before, along with the world's first steam-powered railway journey in 1804.

The first censuses held in free nations reveal that 83% of workers toiled on farmland in 1789 in France and 90% in 1790 in the US. A massive rural exodus saw both portions drop to half of the workforce by 1870,[4] as farmers moved to mines and factories, erecting new cities overnight. Soaring populations led to Malthus' 1798 theory on population growth exceeding that of food supply. French philosopher Jean-Jacques Rousseau was among the first to long for a return to nature uncorrupted by humans, a nostalgia echoed throughout the Romanticist movement as industrialization raced on.

Take steel, one of the salient faces of the revolution. Known since Antiquity, before the 1[IR] steelmaking was confined to the production of small objects like cutlery. A conversation with Napoleon III, in which the Emperor of France fantasized about making steel canons, encouraged Englishman Henri Bessemer to improve steelmaking methods, eventually patenting a process that bears his name (although his claim to the invention remains subject to controversy). German Carl Siemens improved the process with the open-hearth furnace, while on the other side of the Atlantic, Andrew Carnegie pursued a scaled-up production technique, literally laying the rails to the US railroad system, and amassing a sizeable fortune along the way.

Then, as the first trains were geared to operate, something fascinating happened. Concerns rose that the train would put the horse industry out of business; that its speed should be capped to avoid unfair competition with equine modes of travel. Rumors spread that the train's celerity would leave passengers gasping and fainting for lack of air, their hearts bursting under pressure. Technical marvels that achieved whopping speeds of 30 km (19 miles) per hour. Such anecdotes illustrate our limited reasoning faculties in the presence of new technologies. Bear in mind the uneasy start of the locomotive as we investigate AI in the next chapter.

Train transfigured travel, with times shortened and no longer dependent on the number and health of horses, the dubitable quality of the carriage and its wheels, nor the lucidity and soberness of the coach driver. Rail routes were steadier and less prone to muddy grounds. They were also safer, especially by

---

[3] Applications for other forces, like gunpowder, were rare and limited due to lack of control.

[4] For France, cf. Jean Molinier, *L'évolution de la population agricole du XVIIIe siècle à nos jours, Economie et Statistique*, p.79–84. For USA, cf. the US census website, https://www.census.gov/programs-surveys/decennial-census/decade/decennial-publications.1790.html.

night. And thanks to scaling, the train was cheaper both for people and cargo load. With everything going for it, initial fears quickly abated.

Before the train, most companies were family-sized, with a few dozen staff at most and locations that couldn't extend beyond a given town, due to lack of communication and transportation modes.[5] The rail system paved the route for corporate empires, starting with the railway companies themselves. The notion of work also changed, drifting away from family chores on a farm or secrets of the craft passed throughout generations via a guild, and closer to the employer-employee relationship familiar to us, with a timeclock and output levels to abide by in exchange for monetary compensation. The 1^{IR} carved the pyramidal shape of companies, incommensurately tilting the balance in favor of the top.

The rail also gave birth to modern tourism. Romans may have flocked in numbers to visit Egypt's by then already ancient pyramids, yet we owe it to the railway to democratize "tourism", a word that first appears in 1811. Amid excess urbanization and industrialization, the train enabled city dwellers to rekindle with nature. The Italian *villeggiatura* and Austrian *Sommerfrische*, precursors of our summer vacation, capture this yearning, immortalized in landscape paintings evocative of Rousseau's idealization of a nature unspoiled by the vices of human society.

Let us contemplate one of these pastoral gems: the tranquil landscapes of Normandy. After decades of lingering, a project to connect Paris to the Normand coast by rail was finally inaugurated in 1847 (following a more pompous inauguration for the first half of the line in 1843, replete with the presence of the king's sons and clergy anointing the tracks with holy water). This shortened the trip from Paris to Normandy beaches from four days to five hours, turning the marshland villages dotting the coastline into coveted hotspots. Trouville in 1867 introduced its iconic boardwalk along the sand beach for *mesdames* to stroll on heels while preserving an air of dignity. The mixed crowds of all ages and social standing—fishermen and dockers relaxing after a hard day's work, bourgeois on a leisurely prome-nade—immersed in magnificent sceneries of sunset over the sea, made for an alluring setting to a growing cluster of soon-to-be legendary painters.

In 1857, a Parisian by the name of Claude Monet stroke an acquaintance with Eugene Boudin, a local Normand and his elder by sixteen years. Most renowned today for his breathtaking depictions of clouds, Boudin was among the first generation of *en plein air* painters, or artists who painted outdoors

---

[5] With the notable exception of sea trade. At their apex, the infamous Dutch East India Company counted 50,000 employees, while the British one had an army of over 250,000 soldiers. Both eventually became a tool of their respective governments rather than private enterprises.

instead of in the studio (a practice made possible thanks to another invention, that of paint tubes in 1841). He enticed Parisian painters, among them Courbet and Corot, to practice their brush on Normandy's landscapes, in what became a quasi-ritual. These outings were rendered possible, thanks to the new railway system, that counted Monet among its habitués. Boudin's influence on him was incontestable, as per his own testimony: "If I became a painter, I owe it to Boudin." Monet later kicked off the Impressionist movement, a precursor to twentieth-century Modern Art. As if in another homage, this time to the train, much of his artwork now hangs in a former train station: the Orsay Museum (Fig. 3.1).

These days, any major museum covering the dawn of Modern Art likely showcases a canvas or two of Normandy. These offer glimpses into life in that period, on the backdrop of the industrial revolution's sky-blackening mines and furnaces. They bear witness to the growing possibilities offered to commoners by the improved transportation means inherited from that very revolution. Alas, in some of these we can discern hints of class divisions, harbingers of a brewing discontent.

The Luddite Revolt

Leaving beach for factory, we turn our attention to an event that has gone down in legend as the ultimate symbol of public fear surrounding job automation. For this, we warp over to the other side of the Channel. More precisely to the shire of Nottingham, where the Luddite revolt erupted.

Fig. 3.1 Claude Monet: The boardwalk at Trouville, 1870. *Private Collection*

At the start of the nineteenth century, England was home to a vibrant textile sector, courtesy of a thriving global cotton trade fueled by the colonial empire. Several highly skilled workers toiled to produce cloth, usually from home: weavers, spinners, croppers, and framework knitters. Each played a key role and held a relatively enviable status, reflected in the prices fixed in advance and based on output, the legacy of a well-oiled system.

New innovations would disrupt this status quo. The shearing frame and the Jacquard loom allowed the production of cheap goods while bypassing the need for in-depth skills. This opened the floodgates to unapprenticed youths, who debarked from farms into sprawling manufactories, upsetting the skilled craftspeople.

The spark came in 1811 when workers used sledgehammers to smash the large-frame textile weavers by night. The revolt spread through the kingdom like wildfire, creating such a havoc that, in 1812, the government passed the Frame Breaking Act, making the destruction of frames punishable by death. Rumor has it that the number of spies dispatched to uncover insurgents surpassed that of the British soldiers fighting Napoleon's armies in Spain. The troublemakers remained hidden within the population, their proclaimed leader, "King Ludd", most likely a fictional character (Fig. 3.2).

The Luddite movement wreaked havoc for over a year, leading to the destruction of thousands of frames and climaxing with several members' hangings by the authorities. By 1813, it had largely subsided. Other revolts

Fig. 3.2 The Luddite Revolt: frame-breakers smashing a loom. *Original source* Location unknown

took place sporadically, in response to the harsh working conditions characteristic of nineteenth-century mines and factories and immortalized in novels, from Charles Dickens' *Hard Times* to Emile Zola's *Germinal* and Victor Hugo's *Les Misérables*.

The revolt not only epitomizes the stand against automation, but also the clash between classes. For centuries, nobles had concentrated wealth via the produce of their land. The emergence of craftsmen and merchants in the Late Middle Ages challenged the hereditary establishment.[6] Technology came to the rescue of the elites by removing the wood from under the cauldron that fueled the rise of this rival class—in other words, by targeting their expertise. Weavers, blacksmiths, and carpenters who mastered a process from A to Z lost their bargaining power as machines allowed unskilled workers to be taught in minutes how to perform a small bit of the job.

Aside from fears of ending up with no option but to join the underlings into the slave-like conditions of factory work, the Luddites resented the image conveyed by the new machines and the inferior quality of their produce. The reputation of the entire textile sector was on the line, along with their status, one of respected craftspeople.

After their demise, the Luddites were seldom mentioned. That is, until recently.

The reaction of taxi drivers and hotels against Uber and Airbnb echoes the Luddites' bitter grievances. As exponential technologies make the headlines, people again worry about their impact on jobs and livelihoods. In response, techno-optimists invoke the Luddite precedent, scorning at fears they claim both overblown and unfounded to shove aside these worries. They depict neo-Luddism as a major backlash against modernity and progress, led by diehard traditionalists incapable of coping with the tide of times.

While they may serve today as a derogatory blanket term to describe anyone opposing new forms of tech, the Luddites were not refractory to technology *per se*. For all we know, they adopted inventions benefiting them the same way all non-Amish people do. What they despised was tech that destroyed the value of skills honed over the years, putting them out of a job or at best demoting them to the rank of a low-wage commodity. In a way, they were prescient of the brainless jobs to come, those featured in Chaplin's Modern Times. But the physical act of breaking machines, instead of, say, having a go at the youths, struck this image of technophobia.

It's also facile, from the comfort of the 200-plus years separating us, to deride the movement as having got it all wrong. Working conditions took

---

[6] In fact, they gave birth to the term "middle-class", which first appeared in 1745. https://en.wikipedia.org/wiki/Middle_class.

scores and revolutions (including Europe's general conflagration of 1848) to ameliorate, and despite productivity gains, wages stagnated for half a century in what economist Robert C. Allen termed "Engel's pause" (cf. Fig. 3.3).[7] The consequences of automation—giving owners an increasing share of the yield to the detriment of workers—led to Karl Marx's influential book, *Das Kapital*. Even a full century after the Luddite revolt, the top 10% of the richest British still concentrated 90% of the United Kingdom's wealth,[8] the middle class had yet to form, ditto individual rights of the type taken for granted today. So-called universal charts of human rights, published in great fanfare in France and the United States of America—the most politically progressive countries at the time—shortly prior to the Luddite movement and often referred to as hallmarks on the route toward free societies, had indeed unleashed countrymen from centuries of repression by the *Ancien Régime*'s nobles and clergymen, but only to advance the agendas of industrialists and capitalists—otherwise said of a tiny fraction of the *Tiers-Etat*—while placing the remainder of people in shackles to sweat and plough.[9]

In short, the Luddites did not live to see any of the progress brandished as proof of their erring on the wrong side of history. Setting aside the eccentrics who believe that technology will enable us—at least the better-off half—to prolong life for centuries, we too may not live to witness the ultimate benefits of 4[IR] tech.

The 1st Industrial Revolution produced a society of two classes: the bourgeoisie—a fusion of the old aristocracy and the merchants and craftsmen who had achieved wealth—and the working classes. Economists from David Autor to Carl Frey believe that we have again entered an Engel's pause, that could spawn yet another society of haves and have-nots.

Perhaps we should caution against taking the past too blindly as a determinant of our future. The life of a Luddite wasn't one to envy[10]; though at times ours may seem far from idyllic, we enjoy benefits unimaginable back then,

---

[7] Robert C. Allen, *Engel's Pause: Technical change, capital accumulation, and inequality in the British industrial revolution*, in *Explorations in economic history*, Elsevier (October 2009), Vol. 46, Issue 4, pages 418–435.

[8] Thomas Piketty, *Capital in the 21st Century*, Chart 10.3, p.588. The situation differed little elsewhere in Europe and the US.

[9] For a deeper dive into this topic, cf. Carl Benedikt Frey: *The Technology Trap: Capital, Labor, and Power in the Age of Automation*, Princeton University Press (2019). That the great whistle-blower of automation's impact on jobs leans back on our past is no coincidence: he foresees a bleak future as today's middle-class loses ground to automation.

[10] On a side note, research suggests that while the Luddites' status suffered, unskilled people who qualified for work thanks to the machines saw their living conditions ameliorate. Given that they outnumbered the craftsmen, overall technology may have had a positive impact on society. The topic remains controversial. Cf. Gregory Clark, *A Farewell to Arms*, Princeton University Press (2008); Charles Feinstein, *Pessimism Perpetuated: Real Wages and the Standard of Living in Britain during*

The two phases of the British Industrial Revolution

< = Wage falling behind output growth | **Wage rising with output = >**

Engels'
Pause

historical GDP/worker ——— historical real wage

Fig. 3.3 Engel's Pause. *Source* Robert C. Allen, *Engel's Pause. Reproduced with permission from the publisher*

from capped working hours and weekends to democracy and the prohibition of child labor, not to mention all of technology's marvels (provided these are accessible).[11] This offers a ray of hope that a downward spiral of unemployment or impoverishment would not be tolerated—depriving increasingly larger scores of people of advantages held as sacrosanct could stir agitation.

It may take broken eggs to make an omelet, yet few winners remain when the omelet needs 90% of existing eggs and a century to serve on the table. Assuming the cycle shortens to just a few decades, we must still figure out how to avoid becoming one of those unfortunate eggs.

Hence, the repeated advice when entering this *terra incognita*: hope for the best, plan for the worst. As the writing on the wall goes: *Lasciate ogni speranza, voi ch'entrate.*[12]

---

and after the Industrial Revolution, Cambridge University Press (1998) and Robert Allen: *The British Industrial Revolution in Global Perspective*, Cambridge University Press (2009).

[11] Steven Pinker: *Enlightment, Now*, Penguin Books (2018).

[12] "Abandon all hope, ye who enter", Dante: Inferno, Song 3

3.2   2^{IR}: And Let There Be Light for All

The taming of oil and electricity characterizes the 2^{IR}. Light bulbs, the telegraph and the internal combustion engine count among the inventions under its watch that rocked society by revolutionizing communication, transportation, and work. Later discoveries include nuclear power, DNA, petrochemistry and plastics.

Maxwell's 1873 *Treatise on Electricity and Magnetism* lifted the veil on electromagnetism, in a trickling that engendered Einstein's Special Relativity. Street lighting made its appearance throughout the 1870s in cities from Newcastle to Paris and Los Angeles. Suddenly, people could stroll outside after dark with less risk of getting mugged, and factories operate 24 h a day, doubling output while complicating plots for nocturnal sledgehammering.

Radio and television precipitated communication at unprecedented scales, offering tools presciently mastered by Hitler for mass indoctrination, with colossal theatrics and a ministry solely devoted to propaganda. Communication technologies spread knowledge to the colonies, fomenting the seeds of revolt, only to bounce back on Western TV sets, spurring an outcry that favored pacifism and liberation of the oppressed.[13]

Vaccines and antibiotics greatly improved life expectancy, the green revolution pulled entire swaths of emerging countries' populations out of famine, and the discovery of the double-helix structure of DNA marked the birth of biotechnology.

World population figures speak for themselves: estimated at five hundred million in 1600, we reached the billion mark in 1800; by 1900, this figure had inched up to 1,6 billion. A mere hundred years later we topped six billion.

The car took the baton from the train, burying the horse for good. Compared to its predecessor, a car could be *owned*, and not just by the rich, a feat Henry Ford made certain of. The train followed predetermined routes while the car bestowed quasi-full freedom of movement, creating an archetype of empowerment and adventure visible in advertising up to this day, with Jack Kerouac and James Dean as emblems. It birthed the suburban mode of life. And as chronicled in *Sad Tropics* by anthropologist Claude Lévi-Strauss, who spent the 1930s wandering Brazil's hinterland, asphalt put

---

[13] For all the resentment and criticism addressed toward journalism nowadays, and to the defense of the occupation, field reporters bringing the duress of wars unfolding thousands of miles away straight into people's homes, in all their visual gore, propelled peace movements and contributed to put an end to mandatory draft (a fact Ho Chi Minh foresaw and brilliantly integrated in his strategy).

remote areas on the map, leveling the field for indigenous peoples left in oblivion up to then, for better or worse.[14]

Affordable plane travel came next. The shrinking of distances wrought by air travel led to a blending of cultures not devoid of sparks, as young idealists from Steve Jobs to the Beatles, disillusioned by their newfound consumerist society, fled eastward in quest of higher truths.

While the 1[IR] foremost benefited a wealthy few—millowners, industrialists, merchants and other capitalists—the second distilled wealth more fairly into a nascent, buoyant middle class. Setting aside demonstrations targeting specific causes (racial discrimination, conscription…), the chronic uprisings characteristic of the previous century fizzled out largely thanks to this alleviation of poverty.

From refrigerators to sewing machines and air-conditioning, an invasion of appliances transformed people's homes. Invented in 1937, automatic laundry machines really kicked off only after World War 2. Up to then, laundry was washed by hand, a time-consuming chore performed by maids, washerwomen (yes, that was a job), housewives for the less fortunate. Before indoor plumbing foraged its way into homes (around the turn of the twentieth century), this involved a trek to a water pump, well or river. Combined with other menial housework, it amounted to a fulltime job—with little to no pay in the case of maids and housewives, respectively.

The washing machine's introduction came spot on. In 1940, the US, was still reeling from the Great Depression, with a staggering unemployment rate of 15%. Then World War 2 strook, hurling Americans off to farfetched battlefields. By 1944, unemployment had dropped to 1.2%, in what remains a record low to this day. Not only did enrolled men leave jobs vacant, but the war effort created huge labor demand. For the sake of national security, women were called upon to fill the gaps (Fig. 3.4).

And fill they did. Those years bore witness to the greatest expansion of industrial output the US has ever seen—a steady annual increase of 15%.[15]

After the war, women were in no hurry to forsake their newfound status as bread-earners. An increase in office and knowledge jobs, fueled by inventions like the typewriter, also appealed to them. The entry of baby boomers in the workforce coincided with "radical" inroads: women were granted the right to open a bank account (Equal Opportunity Act of 1974), go on maternity leave (Pregnancy Discrimination Act of 1978—prior to which they would lose their job), and even attend Ivy Schools (1969 for Yale and Princeton,

---

[14] Cf. Chap. 12, *Town and Country*, of Part 4, *A Land and Its People*; Claude Lévi-Strauss: *Sad Tropics (Tristes Tropiques)*, Librairie Plon (1955).

[15] Alan Millward: *War Economy and Society 1939–1945*.

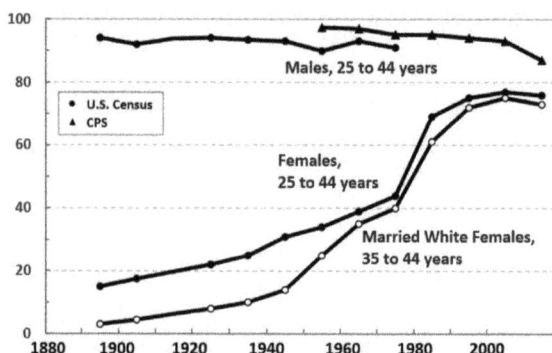

Fig. 3.4 U.S. Labor Force Participation Rates for Females and Males by Age and Marital Status, 1890–2004. *Source* Claudia Goldin, *The Quiet Revolution That Transformed Women's Employment, Education, and Family.* Reproduced with permission from the author

1977 for Harvard), and West Point (1976) and run the Boston Marathon (1972). While birth control remained a more sensitive topic, the decade saw some progress there too.

Improvements in women's earnings as a percentage of men's have yet to fully materialize: from 60% in the US in 1980—a level it had stalled at for the previous decade—it reached 70% in 1990, 75% by the year 2000, and 82% by 2018. Albeit still far from gender pay equality and mired by huge ethnic disparities (as are male wages[16]), at least the direction is forward-moving.

Later marriage and the pursuit of higher education undoubtedly partook, pushing a shift in social norms in what is now commonly referred to as "the quiet revolution"; yet the gender equality trend might not have been feasible without inventions like the laundry machine. Women bore the brunt of housework; lifting these chores was a *sine qua non* for their freedom and financial independence.

In a twist of irony, today's most iconic posters of World War 2 went largely unnoticed at the time, only to be rediscovered decades later, instantly making (the inaccurately named) Rosie a poster girl for the feminist cause (Fig. 3.5).

Laundry machines, refrigerators, microwaves, and dishwashers relieved people from a great deal of (undocumented) housework. Yet some tasks resisted automation: hair-cutting, tending to the elderly and children. Meanwhile, microwaved food or TV don't beat a nice restaurant or movie theater. Where automation was not feasible or not as good, households could

---

[16] Cf. National Geographic issue of October 2021, *Pay Inequity is persistent, shamefull—and still widely tolerated*, https://www.nationalgeographic.com/magazine/article/pay-inequity-is-persistent-shameful-and-still-widely-tolerated.

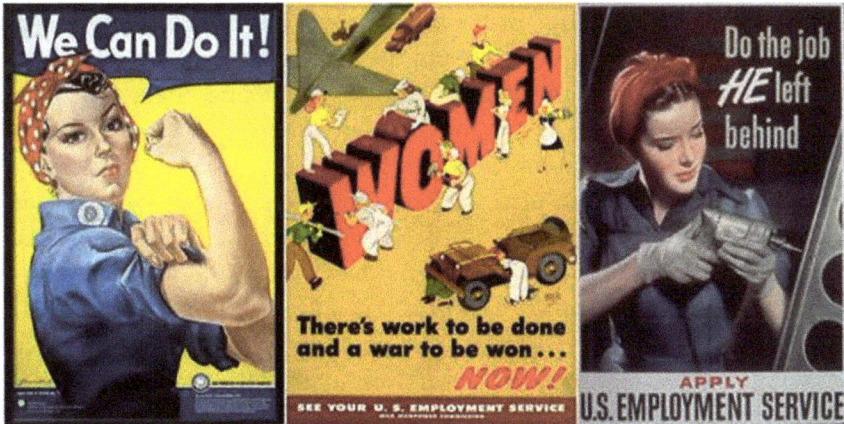

Fig. 3.5 The Rosie poster girl. *Sources* (from left to right): National Museum of American History (a division of the Smithsonian Institute); Library of Congress Prints and Photographs Division Washington; Audiovisual Collections and Digital Initiatives Department, Hagley Museum and Library

outsource. Extra disposable income allowed for tourism, beauty salons, day care, and restaurants, driving a surge in services. As people lost the time and then skills to cook, they ended up eating out more often. The grandma recipe of lore is now but a fairy tale stamped on processed foods' packaging.

Meanwhile, Taylorism and automation reduced labor needs in the production process while simultaneously increasing output, triggering a phenomenon of abundance. Before, all a company had to do was produce. Price and quality mattered, but there was a lot one could get away with thanks to a fundamental imbalance: that demand outstripped supply, favoring the seller. The US woke up from World War 2 with a new conundrum: a saturated supply. The deluge of choice made the customer king overnight. Inventory no longer sold on its own, meaning companies had to roll up their sleeves and get creative to persuade the consumer to buy *their* product. To this effect, firms experimented with ease of use, placement, packaging, cost, innovation, brand story, after-sales service, pricing, payment terms, a clean environmental footprint, coupons, samples and testers, gifts with purchase, loyalty programs, colors, scent, feel and sounds, the target segment, and the smile on the seller's face. To set themselves apart from the crowd, concepts like branding and differentiation emerged. And to achieve the lowest price without starving oneself implied stringent cost control, involving complex supply chain organizations spanning continents.

This shift of nexus created or boosted many of the professions familiar to us today: sales, marketing, research and development, supply chain management, finance, quality, advertising, auditing, sourcing, design, training, customer service, management, and human resources to keep the whole zoo running—not to mention the schools that have sprouted up to educate each generation on how to excel in these professions that now occupy large portions of the workforce, even in so-called manufacturing companies. Retail and food & beverage are conceived of more as part of the service economy, even for companies that produce or outsource. Nike, McDonald's or L'Oréal aren't exactly perceived as factories, nor do they seem keen on positioning themselves as such (we have yet to witness an ad billboard showcasing the inside of the workshops where their goods are made).

3.3   3^{IR}: The ICT Trap

The Third Industrial Revolution may appear less grandiose compared to its predecessors, and posterity might bundle it together with the fourth one. At its heart lies the transistor, along with a prediction made by one of its pioneers.

Invented at Bell Labs in 1947 in what many now view as *the* invention of the twentieth century, transistors succeeded the bulky, unreliable vacuum tubes invented in 1907. The transistor birthed modern computers.

Silicon, Earth's second most abundant element after oxygen, is the primary material used to make transistors (thus giving its name to a certain valley in California). Equal to one bit, a transistor can be in an open or closed state, in what makes the binary digits of 0s and 1s at the core of computer languages. In a paper published in 1965, Intel co-founder Gordon Moore stated that over the next decade, continuous progress in transistor miniaturization would allow the number of these placed on an integrated circuit (IC) microchip to double over a certain period, eventually estimated at 18 months. Not only did his prognostic prove accurate, it remains valid to this date, earning the title "Moore's Law".

Introduced in 1959, the first modern transistors, called metal–oxide–semiconductor-field-effect transistor (MOSFET), measured 0,002 mm (20 microns), or five times smaller than what the human eye can see. Today's smallest commercial MOSFETs measure 5 nanometers, i.e. 40,000 times less than sixty years ago. Since the 1960s, over thirteen sextillion transistors have been manufactured (and counting), making it by far the most produced good in our history.[17]

With miniaturization comes increased processing speed and dropping costs per transistor. Launched in 1981, The IBM 5051, simply called "IBM PC" quickly dominated the US home computer market, triggering an offspring of clones along with the ire of Apple, expressed in the epic "1984" ad. The PC ran on an 8-bit processor. The 256 characters of the American Standard Code for Information Interchange (ASCII) derive from these eight "on-or-off" transistors ($2^8 = 256$).

To visualize the impact of Moore's Law, compare the now laughable mainframe computer sizes in the *Wonder Woman* and *Mad Men* series to the Surface, Edge, and Paperwhite—names that emphasize thinness—or how today's iPhone holds more computing power than all the systems onboard the Apollo spacecraft. Moore's prognostic illustrates *exponential* growth, a darling concept of futurists addressed in the next chapter. It remains a determinant factor for tech miniaturization, from wearables to implants and nanotechnology.

Voices predicting an imminent end to this insane ride of efficiency have time and again flared, only to be hushed. As of 2021, transistor sizes of 1 nm have been produced in the lab[18] (a nanometer is a millionth of a millimeter). These flirt with scales at which the laws of macrophysics give way to quantum mechanics, creating issues like quantum tunneling. Naysayers are once again unearthing the ax of war, ready to ditch Moore's Law for good. But scientists may have other tricks up their sleeves, such as the three-dimensional juxtaposition of chips.

Besides, if transistor miniaturization were to hit a reef, that may not lead to an immediate dispel of growth and innovation. It took a good century for the revolution brought about by electricity to make its footprint[19]; likewise, we have yet to catch up with the full potential offered by today's transistor sizes. And progress in bandwidth and storage capabilities is making the Cloud a viable alternative, instead of solely relying on a device's transistors for heavy lifting. Take Google's recent entry in the $150 billion video game industry: their "product", Stadia, isn't a console but a streaming platform, accessible on the Cloud for a subscription fee. Constraints are surfacing elsewhere. Energy storage technology, a crucial piece of the puzzle for fields ranging from robots

---

[17] David Laws: *13 Sextillion & Counting: The Long & Winding Road to the Most Frequently Manufactured Human Artifact in History*, Computer History Museum (April 2, 2018).

[18] Sujay Desai et al.: *MoS2 transistors with 1-nm gate lengths*, Science Magazine, vol. 354 (October 2017), https://science.sciencemag.org/content/354/6308/99.

[19] Eric Brynjolfsson and Andrew McAfee: *The Second Machine Age: Work, Progress and Prosperity in a Time of Brilliant Technologies*, particularly Chap. 5: *Innovation: Declining or Recombining?*

to nanotech and smart glasses, has not moved in line with transistor sizes (i.e. exponentially).

Before depleting its potential, electricity passed the baton over to the transistor. By the time the rest of the gang catches up—in other words, fully exploits the advantages conferred by transistor size, *after* it stops shrinking— another GPT might grab the spotlight. Who could the successor be? Artificial Intelligence is emerging as a serious contender, marking the shift from 3rd to 4th industrial revolution.

The only hiccup with that scenario is that AI relies on processing power and memory storage improvements. Should Moore's Law come to an abrupt halt, it could stymie AI progress, "removing the firewood from under the cauldron", as the old Chinese saying goes. Yet existing physical substrates were not designed for AI: CPUs and GPUs were built for computers and video games, not deep-learning algorithms. Researchers are hellbent on developing AI-tailored chips that could perform thousands or millions of times better while consuming just as much less energy (AI's gargantuan energy consumption needs having recently come under scrutiny). IBM, Intel, Princeton, Stanford, and others are racing to develop new breeds of neuromorphic chips, which combine the memory and processing unit into one.

Such efforts could help cement a smooth transition from Moore's Law to a Fourth Industrial Revolution.

On the work scene, the 3^{IR} has paved the way for a full-scale invasion of computers in offices, marshaling forth the diktat of data. Computer jobs have become the standard for a large portion of white-collar and middle-class jobs. While elements of human value subsist in other fields—the surgeon who operates, the lawyer's orator skills or the teacher's grasp of the dynamics in a classroom full of kids, to say nothing of meetings and teamwork—a sizeable chunk of it is now tied to computers and data. Because AI feeds on data, this computerization of work, courtesy of the 3^{IR}, basically sets the stage for AI to step in and take over, thus sealing our own demise.

From Cracks to a Fractured Society

Did the average worker benefit from the 3^{IR} in a comparable manner to the 2nd?

Earlier we mentioned the Great Decoupling that commenced around 1970. In the four following decades, the top 1% of the wealthiest Americans' pretax income went from representing 8 to 20% of the United States' total revenue. In other words, the remaining 99% of Americans saw their portion of the country's earnings shrink from 92 to 80%: a concession of 12 percentage points, or three times the level of the US trade deficit in the 2000–2010 decade. Politicians blaming countries like Mexico and China for their constituents' ailments, seeking scapegoats abroad, would do well to address the culprits of rising inequalities and misery within their ranks and those of their beloved donors.[20]

Oil shocks, inflation, and a decline in labor unions and worker mobility played into the deterioration. Economists have also pointed to technological improvements benefitting shareholders over employees, echoing warnings of Karl Marx.[21] And to say that internal politics made a dent would be an understatement.

Take Howard Jarvis' notorious Proposition 13. Passed in 1978, it slashed Californian property taxes by more than half, capping them at 1% regardless of a property's value. Still in force today (with more States following suite), it set a trend at the antipodes of solidarity that curbed government revenue, crippling public spending in areas ranging from road maintenance to education. In its immediate aftermath, universities that until then cost a pittance—including Berkeley and Stanford—had no alternative but to drastically raise tuition fees, triggering a spiral that would make higher education a privilege accessible only to the elite.[22]

The New York Times reports that 66% of Stanford students come from the highest-earning 20% of American households.[23] Upon entering Stanford, visitors are greeted by monuments named after Herbert Hoover. Hosts are swift to highlight that the 31st president of the United States graduated from Stanford in 1895. Less likely are they to mention that unlike today's students, expected to fork over $50,000 per year in tuition fees, he studied there for free (Fig. 3.6).

This illustration of government withdrawal, courtesy of free-market advocates, slowly affected the quality and distribution of the nation's education. As Harvard economist Lawrence Katz explains: "When technology, education and training move together, you get shared prosperity. Otherwise, you

[20] Cf. Piketty, *21st Century Capital*, pp. 478–480. While his passage targets the top 10% richest Americans, the top 1 percentile can be deduced from Chart 8.6 on p. 461.

[21] https://www.nytimes.com/2022/01/11/technology/income-inequality-technology.html.

[22] Corine Lesnes, *Inégalités, pollution, vieillissement… le déclin du rêve californien*, Le Monde (January 29th, 2021).

[23] Cf. Mobility Report Cards: *The Role of Colleges in Intergenerational Mobility*, National Bureau of Economic Research (2017). Also The New York Times, *Economic Diversity and Student Outcomes at Stanford University*, https://www.nytimes.com/interactive/projects/college-mobility/stanford-university.

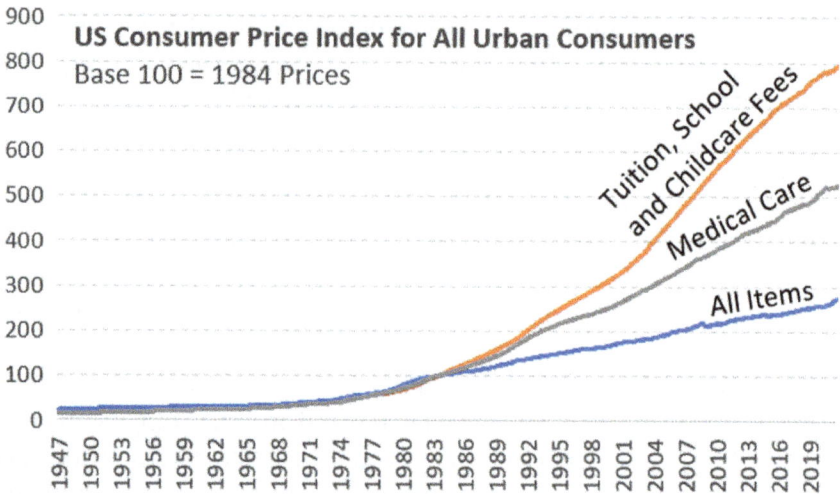

Fig. 3.6 US Consumer Price Index, 1947–2021. *Source* U.S. Bureau of Labor Statistics

don't."[24] For a time, the Soviet menace bolstered the United States to spend more on welfare and education. The USSR's collapse led to an erosion of this drive.

David Autor demonstrated how over the period, by taking the defense of workers, the US judiciary system caused a stir that ultimately boosted temporary help services[25]—an insidious form of outsourcing within company walls. By 1997, 63% of workers in low-skilled manual and administrative support occupations were outsourced.[26] In Western Europe, several countries enacted even harsher measures meant to protect workers, actions that only backfired as corporations shifted to interns and temps instead of hiring, everywhere but for the firm's core activities.

This chasm has perdured and could reach yet more abysmal depths as the next industrial revolution kicks in.

Alas, it could worsen gender inequalities. We saw the role of the 2^{IR} in women's empowerment, while also noting that many women hold jobs in office and admin, currently the largest category of workers, yet one that has begun to shrink. As technology pushes this trend forward, some will make

---

[24] Cited by Steven Lohr in The New York Times: *Economists Pin More Blame on Tech for Rising Inequality*, (January 11, 2022). More importantly, cf. Claudia Goldin and Lawrence Katz: *The Race Between Education and Technology*, Harvard University Press (2009).

[25] David Autor: *Outsourcing at Will: The Contribution of Unjust Dismissal Doctrine to the Growth of Employment Outsourcing*, Journal of Labor Economics, vol. 21, issue 1, 1–42 (2003).

[26] Sharon Cohany: *Workers in Alternative Employment Arrangements: a Second Look*, Monthly Labor Review 121, no. 11 (1998): 3–21. https://www.bls.gov/opub/mlr/1998/11/art1full.pdf.

the escape to higher grounds, others fall to the base, and others still drop entirely out of the workforce, potentially bringing women participation rates back to pre-1950s levels. A regression that would reverse decades of progress, with profound social impacts.

Conclusion on Industrial Revolutions

What lessons can be drawn from this stroll down the IR memory lane?

Each one was unique. This begs for caution when peering at the past in search of answers to the riddles posed by the 4^{IR}. A rule of thumb in forecasting with a single variable (for instance sales data) calls for a sampling of *at least* thirty observations. We are far from that.

The First Industrial Revolution lured farmers from ancestral lands into factories, the Second saw their progeniture thrust into the service sector, and the Third, in front of a screen. At the heart of the 1^{IR} lies steam power; yet it eventually took a backseat as 2^{IR} electricity kicked in. This differs from subsequent IRs, where each star GPT was built on top of its predecessor: electricity remains the backbone of the transistor (3^{IR}), and both electricity and transistors are propelling the 4^{IR} (you could even squeeze the ICT with Internet as GPT in between).

From a social perspective, the 1^{IR} was quintessential with a degradation of the human condition, that endured until roughly the middle of the twentieth Century. The upheaval caused can be linked to the turmoil that in some areas propelled change for the greater good (e.g. the Front Populaire in France), yet elsewhere facilitated the rise of dictatorial regimes, with decades of bloodshed and repression. The 2^{IR} brought forth a reduction in inequalities: as supply outstripped demand, things became affordable and more cognitive jobs were needed to seal the sale, a middle class emerged. The 3^{IR} opened a backdoor through which inequity crept back to an extent, while simultaneously laying down fertile grounds for an AI takeover. As the 4^{IR} strikes, it could dig an even deeper crater in the middle class.

Technology cannot be cast as solely responsible for the vagaries of the human condition; everything is interlinked. Urban population concentration and increased literature rates favored the spread of knowledge, and with it demands for a better society. Past IRs took place amid growing, relatively young populations, a trait that contrasts starkly with the 4^{IR}, at least in the North. This could pose a challenge in regard to education, as the bulk of the population already went through the official school program.

We presented the industrial revolutions under the Western chronology where they first unfolded. Other areas have caught up, often in shorter time frames. With the Meiji Revolution, Japan achieved its molt in less than a century. In the forty years that elapsed since Deng Xiao Ping's "socialist capitalism", China pushed forth industrialization, spreading electricity and high-speed trains, bulldozing the past, and steamrolling the new. In 1979, 70% of the country's workforce toiled in farms; by 2020, the figure stood at barely 25% (Fig. 3.7).

This points to the variable timing of industrial revolutions based on location; whether the 4^{IR} will unfold in a more uniform manner across the globe remains to be seen. In all likelihood, it will differ from its predecessors. Artificial intelligence will add a unique tang; if we listen to Martin Ford, for many it will have a sour taste.

The next revolution is either imminent or already here. Periods like the Renaissance and First Industrial Revolution are coined posthumously; no herald springs to the sound of trumpets to proclaim their start and end. They unfold in phases, with regional differences and a myriad of cycles and microevents influencing one another, at times converging, only to appear as a defining epoch in retrospect (and in response to a human need for keeping things simple). Later historians may combine what we call the Third and Fourth Industrial Revolutions into one.

One thing is certain. At the dawn of each industrial revolution, the ramifications down the road were unfathomable to its contemporaries. Henry Ford did not conceive the suburban trend that car democratization would trigger, any more than Jobs foresaw the iPhone's repercussions on chewing gum sales (more on that later).

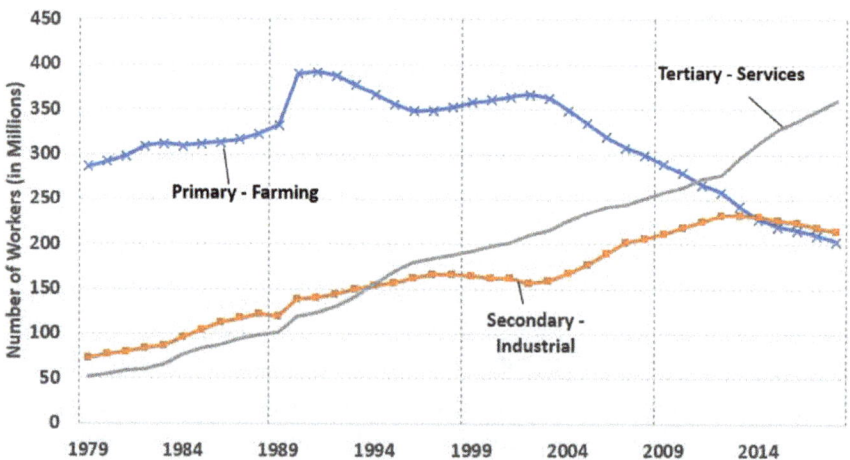

Fig. 3.7   China's workforce evolution by sector, in number of workers, 1979–2018. *Source* China Statistical Yearbook 2019, Sect. 4.2. http://www.stats.gov.cn/tjsj/ndsj/2019/indexeh.htm. *Note* Change in accounting methodology to explain the uptick in 1990

We've seen how the 3^{IR} aggravated wealth redistribution. All signs hint to an impending, abrupt exacerbation of this trend in the 4^{IR}, as tech capable of decimating swathes of jobs heads mainstream. Buckle up as we pursue our journey toward the looming AI battle royale, by peering into the awe-inspiring technologies surfacing from R&D labs.

4

Tech

Progress stems from technological innovation, the "cornerstone of civilization" as argued by Jeremy Renner's character in the 2016 movie *The Arrival* (and as opposed to language, in what can make for vivid debates around a bottle or two). At its heart lies the tool. It serves a purpose. Technology broadly encompasses tools invented and methods devised to achieve greater efficiencies, be it in manufacturing, transportation, communication, and anything from harnessing energy to optimizing the quality of decision-making.

This chapter delves into the technologies sparking the jitters. What characterizes them? Which ones have greater disruptive potential?

We first shed light on a handful of tech traits (Sect. 4.1): acceleration, convergence, ecosystems and democratization, to end with a theoretical split of the Information Age in Internet waves.

Then, after an overview of the 4^{IR} technologies moving from labs into the mainstream (4.2), we pluck three from the crowd, namely additive manufacturing or 3D printing (4.3), Augmented Reality (4.4), and Artificial Intelligence (4.5). Among these, AI is hailed as the great grim reaper of jobs.

The original version of this chapter was revised: Text correction has been updated. The correction to the chapter is available at https://doi.org/10.1007/978-3-031-19278-4_10

4.1 Tech Traits

4.1.1 Acceleration

The history of Homo sapiens reveals an exponential acceleration in the pace of innovation, a trait enshrined by futurist Ray Kurzweil in his "Law of Accelerating Returns". He gathered no less than 27 charts in support of it, including good old Moore, but also the number of nano-related patents, DNA sequencing costs, and processor performance, to name but a few.[1] Other exponentials have been observed in the comet's tail of Moore's: Huang's Law (advancements in GPUs relative to CPUs), Kryder's Law (increase in storage space), Gilder's Law (that the total bandwidth of communication systems triples every twelve months), itself explained by Metcalfe's Law (value of telecommunications network proportional to the square of the number of connected users to the system).

More palatable signs of tech acceleration are hard to miss. Wider numbers of educated people contribute to society's advancement. Barely half of the humans alive in 1950 were literate. Today's literacy rate flirts with 85%.[2] The ICT revolution makes information shared and accessible anywhere anytime, practically for free. The number of PhDs, patents and science publications all point to dizzying leaps. Government funding for R&D exploded, only to be eclipsed by corporate spending, following a 1978 relaxation in US legislation toward VC funding. The past decade's love affair between Wall Street and Silicon Valley has goosed up R&D spending, with the five biggest US tech firms, none of which existed in 1970, now accounting for over a fourth of the US private sector's R&D spending. These five companies, the famed "GAFAM" (Google, Amazon, Facebook, Apple and Microsoft), now spend more in R&D than Germany.[3]

As one physics professor put it, "The greatest shortcoming of the human race is our inability to understand the exponential function".[4] Many dishes are served to explain this challenging concept of acceleration on steroids; perhaps the most popular one is that of the chess game.

Legend has it that the wise man who introduced chess to a Far-Eastern empire was granted one wish as a reward for beating the emperor in the game. The wise man asked for an apparently modest prize: one grain of rice for the

---

[1] Ray Kurzweil: *The Singularity is Near: When Humans Transcend Biology*, pp. 46–82.

[2] Cf. Reading the past, writing the future: fifty years of promoting literacy, https://unesdoc.unesco.org/ark:/48223/pf0000247563.

[3] Cf. Appendix D.

[4] Albert A. Bartlett: *Arithmetic, Population and Energy—a talk by Al Bartlett*, (1969).

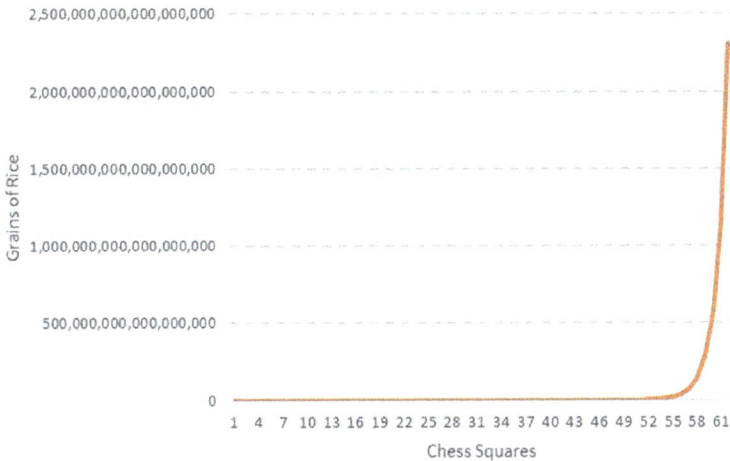

Fig. 4.1 Exponential curve for grains of rice on a chessboard

first square on the chessboard, then two on the next, then four, eight, and a further doubling for each and all of the 64 squares that compose a chessboard. The emperor consented hastily, unaware of the astronomical result: 2^{64} (Fig. 4.1).

The exponential curve is characterized by an inflection point, from whereupon it shoots upward. As Kurzweil explains, the first half of the chessboard stays in the confines of our human grasp:

> After thirty-two squares, the emperor had given the inventor about 4 billion grains of rice. That's a reasonable quantity—about one large field's worth—and the emperor did start to take notice. It was as they headed into the second half of the chessboard that at least one of them got into trouble. [indeed in some versions of the fable, the emperor has his opponent beheaded]

Kurzweil posits that we now lie around the middle of the chessboard, roughly 32 of Moore's 18-month iterations since the invention of computers.[5] *The Future is Faster Than you Think*, as titles a book by futurist guru and Kurzweil friend Peter Diamandis. It's not some cheap con to harpoon readers. Today's pace is not that of our grandparents or even our parents. A "business as usual" approach won't cut it this time round.

[5] Ray Kurzweil: *The Age of Spiritual Machines: When Computers Exceed Human Intelligence*, p. 72, Penguin Books (2000).

Another facet of acceleration occurs on the consumer end, where studies point to quicker adoption rates.[6] The 3^{IR} spanned over some fifty years, a decent timeframe for Beaudry to make his observation—prior ones lasted too long and were relayed by the next before causing a deflation in labor demand. Globalization and Asia's rise to prosperity also delayed the Beaudry effect to an extent (for reminder, by "Beaudry effect" we refer to a deflation in job demand following the establishment of a new GPT). Today the greatest portion of the car manufacturing workforce, a 2^{IR} product, lies in China[7] yet only 17% of Chinese own a car,[8] whereas the US reached an 80% adoption rate around 1970. Meanwhile, more than 80% of Chinese have smartphones.[9] Underlying this is the fact that star innovations unleashed by GPTs are more accessible with each IR iteration: a train is more expensive than a car, itself pricier than a portable computer or a smartphone. Swifter setup and market maturity could trigger the Beaudry effect faster than in the past. Especially when upgrades are made via software downloads instead of replacement of the physical good.

But beware of going *too* fast. As Roy Amara, past president of The Institute of the Future, puts it (in what is now termed—you guessed it—Amara's law):

> We tend to overestimate the effect of a technology in the short run and underestimate the effect in the long run.

In 2001, Steve Jobs was one among several figures predicting that the Segway would revolutionize transportation.[10] Google announced in 2010 that a fleet of autonomous cars, built from modified Toyota Priuses, had plugged in over 140,000 miles.[11] Yet here we are, past 2020. Nor has anything tangible emerged two decades after the human genome was first

---

[6] Diego Comin and Bart Hobjin: *An Exploration of Technology Diffusion*, in American Economic Review vol. 100, no.5, (December 2010). Also Horace Dediu: https://twitter.com/asymco/status/401 335832763961344. More interestingly, you can play with the chart on the OurWorldinData website: https://ourworldindata.org/technology-adoption.

[7] Roughly one fifth of the global automotive workforce; the US, has around one tenth. https://www.nesfircroft.com/blog/2017/05/the-automotive-industry-employs-more-people-than-you-think.

[8] Cf. McKinsey China Auto Consumer Insights 2019: https://www.mckinsey.com/~/media/McK insey/Industries/Automotive%20and%20Assembly/Our%20Insights/China%20auto%20consumer% 20insights%202019/McKinsey-China-Auto-Consumer-Insights-2019.pdf.

[9] Tech in Asia: *82% of Chinese Have Mobile Phones, Some Provinces Have More Mobiles Than People* https://www.techinasia.com/82-chinas-13-billion-people-mobile-phones-provinces-mobiles-people.

[10] Jordon Golson: *Well, That Didn't Work: The Segway Is a Technological Marvel. Too Bad It Doesn't Make Any Sense*, Wired magazine (January 16, 2015) https://www.wired.com/2015/01/well-didnt-work-segway-technological-marvel-bad-doesnt-make-sense/.

[11] https://googleblog.blogspot.com/2010/10/what-were-driving-at.html.

sequenced and Dolly the sheep cloned; though sequencing costs have dropped exponentially, fears of genetically designer babies and clone armies have not materialized (yet). Some may contend that we've been hearing about "AI closing in on jobs" for over a decade, yet the job market keeps growing.

Computers changed our lives, but in 1987 their impact was sufficiently trivial for economist Robert Solow to quip that "You can see the computer revolution everywhere but in the productivity statistics"[12] (hence the name sometimes given to this phenomenon: the "Solow paradox"). Then the Internet took the helm, and overhype in the first decade of its public existence led to the dot.com bust. The tech landscape is littered with failed folderols and bankrupt startups. Books on disruption tend to treat technology as an insulated concept, when it is birthed in a world of people and policies. Tech only blossoms when it answers needs, and under suitable conditions in terms of legislation, cost-value proposition, etc. Companies are slow to fully exploit the potential for automation and outsourcing, society drags its feet in the face of radical change, regulators gasp and pant—a trail that leads back to Azhar and his exponential gap.

Alas, exponential growth cannot be treated as fate. Moore and Kurzweil's "laws" differ from the laws of gravity or thermodynamics: they are but observations that happen to have held true, so far. Those who build a religious edifice out of them mimic Nassim Taleb's turkeys: with a thousand days of solid experience of nurturing and caring for by humans to their credit, on Thanksgiving Eve the poor creatures have no reason to doubt that tomorrow's sunrise could bode any different from the past.[13] Even the oft-cited chessboard, with its sixty-four squares and supposed inflection point in the middle, is but a mental construct—one could have used go's 324 squares, or anything else. Plotting the course of Homo sapiens' population on a time chart also reveals an exponential curve; yet no demographer in her right mind uses exponentials to plot future world population growth and conclude to a next doubling to 16 billion souls by 2068 (median estimates target roughly 10 billion by then).[14]

---

[12] Robert M. Solow: *We'd Better Watch Out*, New York Times Book Review (1987), p. 36.

[13] Nassim Nicholas Taleb: *The Black Swan*, Random House (2007). Though the original idea emanated from philosopher Bertrand Russell, using a chicken.

[14] Using a 47-year time span as that's what it took for the last doubling, from 4 billion people in 1974 to 8 billion in 2021. The previous doubling took 60 years; the one before, 120 years.

4.1.2 Convergence

The "new" need not stem from an invention. It can result from a novel combination of technologies, or of tech and trends, what Peter Diamandis calls *convergence*,[15] and MIT professors McAfee and Brynjolfsson describe as *recombinant innovation*.[16] This trait is not one to be treated lightly: it may have contributed more to the advancement of economics and society than any standalone invention. It also fuels the acceleration trait.

Technologies seldom rise out of the blue. Even a GPT is but a fertile backbone on top of which a flora of innovations piggyback ride. Bresnahan and Trajtenberg, the two economists who coined the term GPT, refer to it as a "technological tree" that sprouts a wide range of innovative products and systems.[17] Harnessing new materials opens possibilities. Plastics contributed to the consumerist society; combined with Moore's Law, information boiled down to 1s and 0s propelled the ICT revolution; graphene could turn the idea of a space elevator into reality. As Isaac Newton famously claimed: "If I have seen further than others, it is by standing upon the shoulders of giants".

Examples of convergence abound. By the 1990s, the high adoption rate of microwaves joined that of fridges along with improvements in cold chain logistics to bring readymade frozen foods. Drones became commercially affordable thanks to the explosion of smartphones that drove down the cost of components like gyro-sensors (10,000$ a pop in the 1990s—and a drone requires dozens of them to operate[18]).

Experts from Kurzweil to Brynjolfsson expect 4^{IR} technologies to unleash their disruptive potential via convergence. In 2002, the National Science Foundation (NSF) launched the Converging Technologies program, which projects a convergence between nanotech, biotech, information technology, and cognitive sciences, creating vast opportunities to enhance human performance.[19]

Taking the construction sector as an example, we may see improvements coming not only from Big Data, robots and exoskeletons for elderly workers, drones, 3D printing, new composite materials, and modular and origami manufacturing, but multiple *combinations* of these technologies. Future

---

[15] Cf. page 2, Peter Diamandis: *The Future Is Faster Than You Think*, Simon and Schuster (2020).

[16] Cf. The Second Machine Age.

[17] Timothy F. Bresnahan and Manuel Trajtenberg: General-Purpose Technologies: Engines of Growth, National Bureau of Economic Research, Working Paper No. 4148 (August 1992).

[18] Cf. page 94, *Machine, Crowd, Platform*.

[19] https://www.nsf.gov/od/lpa/news/02/pr0257.htm.

construction may integrate screen walls, sensors, and other IoT-embedded devices.

Combining various tech and trends creates opportunities for the business-savvy. The successes of Facebook, Amazon, and Mobike were carried less by a single patented invention than by recombining existing elements. Uber is but a clever mishmash of GPS localization, mobile payment, and a platform connecting vehicle owners with people in need of a ride. It counts on peer ratings to ensure driver discipline and user trust—in short, the quality of its service.

Fresh opportunities are bound to surface as 4^{IR} technologies populate the landscape. From an individual's perspective, merging the shared economy with new tech could generate extra revenue on the side: a 3D printing machine owner leases the machine to neighbors in need; another refurbishes an unused room in the house for VR gaming, renting it out on a dedicated platform, perhaps a new subcategory of Airbnb.

4.1.3   Ecosystems

The term ecosystem derives from biology, where it refers to a community of organisms interacting in an environment, with negentropic effects that mitigate the second law of thermodynamics. An ecosystem is understood to be adaptive and self-sustainable (hence the sun often partakes in it, given its role in photosynthesis).

Man-made ecosystems have similar properties of self-organization and sustainability: a network of firms that form a chain of suppliers and customers, along with the necessary pools of talent, and infrastructure: electric cars need charging stations, self-driving ones, vehicle-to-vehicle communication systems (V2V) and more broadly the Internet of Vehicles, while drone deliveries require landing pods, with a dispatching system in high-rises. Ecosystem dynamics explain Microsoft's acquisition of Skype, rebranded in the Teams ecosystem as a central piece for collaborative work. They explicit Elon Musk's attempts at solar energy, battery-charging walls in homes, and electric vehicles—far from blind fist swings, the three go hand in hand.

For the Internet of Things, the idea of an ecosystem entails a single app that integrates all smart devices within a cluster, for instance a home or factory. Not only for ease of use, but so that the devices can share data and interact with one another, providing more optimal results and insightful analytics than in standalone mode.

For innovation to take hold, other elements in the chain must be aligned in terms of maturity. This adjustment period can delay an otherwise readily available technology. Some technologies fail to gain the necessary momentum for lack of a mature ecosystem (1990s video game consoles are a case in point, with the need for sufficient game developers and gamer players, who each put their expectations on the other).

Accurately predicting when each of an ecosystem's components reaches maturity is paramount. These dynamics play on storage devices like Sony's Beta, the VCD and HDTV formats, operating systems, VR headsets, and smart home devices. Squabbling between firms and a lack of interoperability can delay the emergence of a new ecosystem while preserving the life cycle of earlier ones.[20]

New needs can be created, as Ford and Jobs proved with thunderous success. But oft and again, companies release gadgets that lack appeal, omit the timing of a factor critical to success, or settle for a niche application well below the horizon scanners' predictions. For instance, the ecosystem trait entails that the IoT needs 5G networks up and humming in order to flourish.

4.1.4   User-Friendliness and Democratization

Upon joining Apple, recruits are treated to a series of Picasso sketches that depict a bull gradually abstracted to its bare essentials (Fig. 4.2). This aesthetic goal drove the design iterations of Apple's single-button mouse (in itself a leap for a user-friendly computer interface), the iPod, iTunes, and other hallmark innovations.[21]

Google and Facebook swear by a similar motto: sleek designs prone to entice laggards weary of new tech to overcome their initial hesitance. Consider Twitter's initial recipe: 140 characters. Period.

These firms obsessively pursue simplicity and ease of use to build a customer-centric, frictionless design model. Like a Disney cartoon, the burden of the endeavor rests entirely on the company, unbeknownst and invisible to enchanted consumers. It follows the old saying that it takes five minutes to prepare a one-hour speech, then an hour to condense it into a five-minute speech. Whether designing new products, trading on an NFT

---

[20] Cf. Ron Adner and Rahul Kapoor, the chapter "The War Between Ecosystems" in *It's not the Tech, it's the Timing*, Harvard Business Review (November 2016 Issue).

[21] Drake Baer: *Why Apple employees learn design from Pablo Picasso*, Business Insider (August 15th, 2014) https://www.businessinsider.com/why-apple-employees-learn-design-from-pablo-picasso-2014-8.

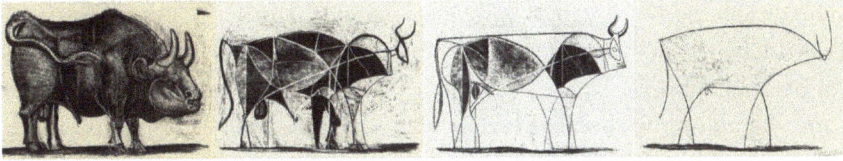

Fig. 4.2 Pablo Picasso: *Le Taureau*, (from left to right) states IV, VI, XI, and XIV, 1945–1946. Digital image, The Museum of Modern Art, New York/Scala, Florence[22]

platform, or shopping in an Amazon supermarket, the frictionless design mantra is omnipresent, and now expanding beyond Silicon Valley.[23]

The first Internet, launched in the late 1960s for academics and researchers as ARPAnet (Advanced Research Projects Agency Network), was anything but sexy. A myriad of cohabiting systems constrained ergonomics, bringing a cortege of compatibility issues. Operators using connected computers that run on different languages needed to master each one to process data between them. Then in 1983, ARPAnet started using the Transfer Control Protocol/Internetwork Protocol (TCP/IP) to connect all networks by a universal language, greatly facilitating use. This marks what we consider the birth of the Internet. Two years later, Microsoft launched Windows, the now familiar graphical user interface that marked a substantial leap in user-friendliness compared to its predecessor, MS-DOS.

The next major overhaul followed Berners-Lee's 1989 suggestion to use hypertext. Naming it the World Wide Web, he launched the browser, with its first page, in 1991, on a NeXT computer at the European Center for Nuclear Research (CERN) where he worked.[24] While nothing seems more natural today than clicking on links, at the time it was a revolutionary idea. Thanks to his innovation, users could "browse the web" without prior programming knowledge.

The early 2000s saw cybercafes mushroom from Tokyo to Toronto. Yet connections were sometimes so bad, sending a single text email from an Internet café in Delhi could take up to twenty minutes (I'd spend the three rupees per hour just as much to relish their air-conditioning). A friend in Paris started a business model of cybercafes, sold keys in hand to entrepreneurs eager to exploit the new gold. The payback period looked solid on paper, but

---

[22] Part of a series of approximately 12' × 18' (30 × 45 cm) size lithographs.

[23] Harrie Golden: *'Just walk out': Amazon debuts its first supermarket with no checkout lines*, The Guardian (February 27, 2020), https://www.theguardian.com/us-news/2020/feb/25/amazon-go-grocery-supermarket-seattle-technology.

[24] Alyson Shontell: *Flashback: This is What the First-Ever Website Looked Like*, Business Insider, June 29, 2011, www.businessinsider.com/flashback-this-is-what-the-first-website-ever-looked-like-2011-6.

the boon was short-lived and most have since closed; it failed to account for Gilder's Law, or the democratization of high-speed Internet, first in homes, then on smartphones.

Starting an online shop used to involve setting up a website and knowledge of several languages and software to build something a minimum decent from an aesthetical perspective: JavaScript, HTML, but also Dreamweaver, Flash, and so on. Today anyone can set up shop in a few clicks on Amazon, Airbnb, WeChat programs, or Alibaba's Taobao platform; anybody can post on Instagram with hashtags relating to your brand. The Web 2.0 populated platforms with massive loads of user-generated content, churning Internet celebrities, and KOLs—people with no coding knowledge that achieve respectable incomes from their online activity.

We experienced this democratization of the Internet in the past thirty years. A similar trend is taking shape, this time for AI.

Those with no coding knowledge picture a self-flagellation of sorts, a fear relayed by the intimidating book sizes adorning the library's IT corner. But this is a frozen still from decades ago: programming also rides the intuitive tide. Interactive Development Environments (IDEs) from PyCharm to Microsoft's Visual Studio Code facilitate the use of R, Python, and other languages; color codes, suggestions as users type instructions, and alerts for syntax errors that previously would only appear whence running the code are but a handful of the conveniences that facilitate programming.

Tech leaders from Facebook to Yahoo, Amazon, and Baidu release free, open-source versions of their AI tools, bringing AI to the masses of small-time programmers. They are betting on an acceleration similar to the one unleashed by higher literature rates: the greater the number of capable programmers, the more burgeoning innovations and AI-powered solutions to expect.

In 2015, Google opened TensorFlow to the public—a software library for machine learning and artificial intelligence. In 2017, Apple released Turi Create, an open-source package that makes it easier for developers to embed the power of machine learning into their apps.

Open-source systems eliminate the need to code everything from scratch, whether creating a task automation algorithm, enhancing a drone's flight parameters, or giving instructions to an Arduino-integrated system: browse the Internet, cull snippets from GitHub (a data repository) to transplant into your program, and peruse online forums to solve hurdles. NASA's robotic helicopter *Ingenuity* completed humanity's first powered flight on planet Mars in 2021 thanks to the help of 12,000 developers scattered around the world, who contributed code via GitHub.[25]

Alas, the recent emergence of low-code and no-code AI platforms seeks to circumvent coding knowledge altogether, with "drag and drop" functionalities to build on and perform analyses. Tools such as GitHub Copilot (co-developed by OpenAI) can transform simple instructions into computer code.

A company that single-handedly pulls off the user-friendly, no-nonsense feat turns water into wine for its bottom line—especially if it succeeds in building a moat around the shiny new technique, with a patent, by locking customers in with a license fee or via a platform. It's the philosopher's stone many a startup is pursuing. In Andrew Ng's words, after securing funding for his new company Landing AI, which specializes in democratizing computer vision: "It's time to make cutting-edge AI fast and easy for anyone to use!".[26] Unity Technologies epitomizes this trend. Founded in 2004 in Denmark (later relocated to California), the company's vision is to "Democratize game development and enable everyone to create rich interactive content". By 2020, over 70% of mobile games were made with Unity products; every month people download 5 billion apps powered by their technology (and for now, Unity is also the winning platform to develop AR applications on).

Recall the Internet's swift growth when considering AI's future; how at the turn of the century people panicked about missing out on it and getting outpaced by competitors. That AI stands at a similar juncture today was shrewdly highlighted in a professor's tweet:

> Big Data is like teenage sex: everyone talks about it, nobody really knows how to do it, everyone thinks everyone else is doing it, so everyone claims they are doing it too.[27]

This frenzy could backfire, with the specter of new AI winters; but eventually, user-friendly enhancements will topple AI off from the Olympian heights of Google and MIT's labs, into the hands of the average Joe—*every* Joe.

As two teachers put it:

---

[25] Cf. Satya Nadella's Shareholder Letter in Microsoft's 2021 Annual Report, https://www.microsoft.com/investor/reports/ar21/index.html#.

[26] Felicia Hou: *This A.I. entrepreneur is working to bring machine learning to more industries*, Fortune ((November 9, 2021), https://fortune.com/2021/11/08/andrew-ng-data-centric-artificial-intelligence-machine-learning-braianstorm-ai-landing-ai/.

[27] Dan Ariely: https://twitter.com/danariely/status/287952257926971392?lang=en.

That democratizing trend, more than anything else, is what has our students today so excited as they contemplate a vast range of problems practically begging for good AI solutions.[28]

The three technologies developed in this chapter partake in the trend: 3D democratizes manufacturing, AR lowers certain skill requirements, AI provides insights derived from complex data sets, and much more: translation, financial or skincare advice, psychological comfort and legal counseling, market research, etc.

Expect today's app development, AR design software, Big Data exploitation, and algorithms simplified and made accessible to commoners. By iteration, like Pablo's bull. At which frame do the intricacies of those sketched strokes reach your drawing skills? Fear not if you draw just as bad with either hand; lowering the bar will make outsourcing the job easier and cheaper too. It levels the playing field, bringing tech into the palm of even the most analphabet of us.

The impacts for workers are several-fold.

It's good news for wannabe entrepreneurs, as the largely intangible nature of 3^{IR} and 4^{IR} tech brings novelty in everyone's reach. Soon, anyone will have the means to direct telescopic algorithms onto as-of-yet unexplored data galaxies, in a quest for monetizable applications, or hatch and execute wild ideas there where yesterday only PhDs with deep-pocketed backers could bring them to daylight. Mom-and-pop shops will benefit from automatic cashiers and improved security systems, bypassing the costly need for staff, along with metrics on everything from peak traffic times to best-sellers and neighboring trends that affect revenue.

Technological progress obsoletes its own complexity. Like a comet's tail, our perception of that complexity persists a bit longer; hence our emphasis to stay on the lookout for enhancements that lower the tasty fruits of technology within reach—even if that involves a YouTube tutorial or three (more about this in Sect. 8.3: Plan your tool learning).

On the downside, specialists cannot hold onto their expertise as the ultimate failsafe. Easy AI for all might irritate those whose skills lose value, much like the Luddites were unsettled by mechanized looms and weaving frames. For example, design artists and creative directors may sneer at the inferior quality achieved by current AI-reliant software, the way receptionists smirked at answering machines and Indian call centers. To their dismay, improvements

---

[28] James Scott and Nick Polson: *AIQ: How People and Machines are Smarter Together*, p. 2, St. Martin's Press (2018).

could produce results deemed good enough by clients and bosses, especially when weighing in the cost difference.

Established industries feel the pinch of democratization. We all know of the unease in the hotel and taxi businesses as Airbnb and Uber attacked their respective turfs; smartphones sent similar tremors through recording studios, hitting photographers, composers and other professionals. Lower prices and ease of use of musical synthesizers, apps, generative AI and text-to-image from firms like David Holz's Midjourney continue to transfigure traditional fields.

Alas, areas of friction between supposedly automated systems have in past decades given rise to a new form of human work, in French called (somewhat pejoratively) "the little hands". ERPs, CRMs, and other clunky software deployed during the 3^{IR} necessitate armies of these little hands to plug in the gaps of non-interoperability, to the great dismay of organizations who saw their hopes of saving on personnel costs shattered. The arrival of leaner, frictionless software will circumvent the need for this low-value human labor, marking the vengeful comeback of downsizing plans.

4.1.5   Internet Waves

We split the Internet era into "waves", an artificial construct that facilitates the lecture of tech advancement since the release of the Internet to the public until… sometime in the future. The first wave saw the birth of the Internet used by commoners on PCs, the second the deployment of smartphones. We conjecture that the third will see handheld devices replaced by smart glasses; in due time, the 4th will substitute those with devices connecting directly into our brains—aka "brain-computer interfaces" (BCI).

As highlighted in Fig. 4.3, hardware is far from the sole distinguishing feature between Internet waves (note that the 4th wave is out of our scope). Dates shown here are purely conjectural and pertain to consumer shifts rather than inventions. Nor will they all occur at the same precise time. The year 2022 saw substantial progress in data obtention and generation, with generative text-to-image systems such as Dall-E 2, and the upheaval caused by the ChatGPT bot (both systems developed by OpenAI—note that "GPT" here stands for "generative pre-trained transformer", not to be confused with general-purpose technology).

The First Internet Wave

In 1993, the European Council for Nuclear Research (CERN) released the Internet to the public. The Commodores, Ataris, and other computers

	Internet Waves		
	1st wave 1995-2010	2nd wave 2010-2030	3rd wave 2030-2060
Gear	Computer	Smartphone	Headset / Glasses
Medium	world wide web	Apps	Overlaid Apps
Communi-cation	email	chats, notifications	Vision overlaid
Extra embedded	bluetooth, speakers, USB ports	cameras, GPS, accelerometers,	Eye-movement detection, IoT
Data	Text / Image	Videos	3D objects / Metaverse
Obtain data	search	suggest (narrow)	suggest (broad) decision-making
Time spent	few hours	many hours	irrelevant, line blurred
Metrics	Google PageRank Traffic	Followers New / Active Users	New data valuation method
Proximity	Global Anonymity	GPS Localizable	Immediate Surroundings

Fig. 4.3 Internet waves

funneled down to the PC and Mac. People wrote emails and surfed on the world wide web, restrained somewhat by slow connectivity speeds and pricy subscription models.

On the corporate end, the first wave spawned the FANG acronym (Facebook, Amazon, Netflix, and Google). Of the top 30 companies composing the Dow Jones Industrial Average before the Internet, none successfully morphed to incorporate the Internet as main driving factor (only a handful of "old" tech companies achieved the shift: Apple, IBM, Microsoft…).

The Second Internet Wave

In 2007, Steve Jobs introduced Apple's first iPhone to the world. While RIM, NEC, Nokia, Motorola, and other cellphone rivals provided Internet connectivity, none possessed the sleek, large multitouch screen, single-button design of the iPhone, nor a similar app ecosystem (though RIM's Blackberry came somewhat close).

Smartphones proliferated, catapulting Apple to the most valuable company in history and ushering mankind into the second Internet wave. Let us recall some of its features to highlight what sets it apart from the previous wave:

- the device is basically a pocketsize computer that never leaves us and always stays on;
- its cameras, color screen, microphone, accelerometers, and other parts make for a futuristic Swiss-army knife; add an Internet connection and you trigger phenomena ranging from selfies to livestreaming;
- apps: they provide a more customized environment and ergonomic experience than websites, by orders of magnitude. Thanks to these superior features, apps easily dethroned the web (around the end of the 2000s[29]). In 2019, an estimated 90%[30] of smartphone activity was spent on apps;
- mobile payment: while online payment was feasible with a computer, it never replaced cash (people didn't bring their laptop to pay for groceries);
- combined with geo-localization, the smartphone opens the door to proximity services, whether looking for a shop (Yelp), restaurant (Dianping), ride (Uber), person (Tinder, WeChat Shared Location), or anything else including the delivery guy's location (Eleme), yourself (Maps), and tomorrow's weather forecast in your area.

These advantages have made the smartphone our indispensable companion, to the extent that one seldom holds still at a red light without flipping the device out. Over half of Americans are hooked to their devices, in what is "possibly the biggest non-drug addiction of the twenty-first century".[31] There's even a moniker for it: nomophobia, a play on "no mobile phobia" coined by the head of the UK Post Office Stewart Fox-Mills in a pilot survey. The poll estimated that 53% of Britons suffer from nomophobia—and that was in 2008.

Other developments, not directly tied to smartphones, occurred in parallel. The Web 2.0 kicked off around then (if not slightly earlier), whereby users not only access data on the Internet but can produce content, leading to the success of YouTube, Facebook, and others. Before, users could query the web via search engines; the second wave saw algorithms mediate to provide suggestions, whether for Amazon purchases, Netflix movies, or with Google's 2004 introduction of the autocomplete feature.

First-wave behemoths are now monetizing on the second. That is, those who survived: aol didn't make it, and Myspace is but a corpse. Among those still around, the ride has proved bumpier for some. Despite the

---

[29] https://techcrunch.com/2011/06/20/flurry-time-spent-on-mobile-apps-has-surpassed-web-browsing/.

[30] https://www.emarketer.com/content/us-time-spent-with-mobile-2019.

[31] Shambare et al.: *Are mobile phones the 21St century addiction?*, African Journal of Business Management (2012); also James Robert et al.: *The invisible addiction: Cell-phone activities and addiction among male and female college students*, https://www.ncbi.nlm.nih.gov/pmc/articles/PMC4291831/.

undeniable success of the Android platform, Google did not fare as well as Amazon or Facebook. With their URL-ranking algorithm, Larry and Sergei unearthed the 1st wave jackpot. But their search engine—still Google's main source of revenue—is ensnared in the web. Since 2005 and before the pandemic hit, the market cap of Alphabet (Google's parent company) increased roughly eight-fold, in line with the overall Nasdaq but far behind that of Amazon (multiplied by a factor of 79) and Facebook (by 8 but in half the time, as they IPO-ed in 2012). It now faces a serious challenger with the launch of OpenAI's ChatGPT chatbox. Other strugglers include Adobe: no fun app or model to lure users. See how parlance has evolved with Millennials: they enhance smartphone photos by "Snapchat" or "Beautycamming", shedding the previous wave's verb "to Photoshop" like a worthless snake-skin (Adobe's stock price increased roughly 12-fold from the end of 2005). New hordes of conquerors swiftly settled on the 2nd wave's pastures: Twitter, Tinder, Snap, Uber, Unity, Instagram, TikTok…

The two waves hit offices somewhat differently. Computers were birthed in companies long before reaching homes. They remain the working tool of choice for office staff, and, for better or worse, the majority are hooked to the Internet. Meanwhile smartphones still tend to be perceived as a leisurely device. Fiddling with one can raise eyebrows. Some companies issue fines for personnel "caught" on their phone; others equip them with company phones to make a clean cut.

The 3rd Internet Wave

So what might the next wave resemble?

Augmented Reality headsets capable of advanced pattern recognition, and gradually shrunk into smart glasses, could spearhead the third wave. Any glimpse at pedestrians, diners, or commuters gives ample evidence that we would die for a savior to descend with a device that can be taped onto our faces.

Forays will take place in parallel in AI, 3D objects, and mixed realities. As the cost of electronics plummets and 5G infrastructure is set up, a growing number of smart devices will interact with one another, unleashing the Internet of Things' potential. User-generated content will see the addition of 3D objects, the creation of which the user-friendly trend will render accessible to all. The coarse blocks in Minecraft are but mere prototypes of this future. Crisp 3D objects will populate the metaverse as virtual worlds gain traction beyond the fringe of *Second Life* geeks to hit the mainstream. Microsoft's intent to purchase Activision Blizzard for a record $68.7 billion, along with Facebook's rebranding as Meta, mark drastic pivots in this direction.[32]

AI will have leapt forward in terms of computer vision, natural language processing (NLP), data analysis, and recommendations. An AI that in the backstage "googles" everything you see and answers all of your questions becomes a priceless companion. While technically still *narrow* AI (a term we'll come to soon), users may not consider it narrow at all. Bots will act as Personal Assistants, widespread among all entities (people, companies, government agencies...). These AIPAs will interact with each other to iron out preliminaries before we make contact, determining who is a suitable date, job candidate or lessee—an IoT web interwoven above social relations. Some of us may even develop an infatuation with our AIPA, *à la Her*.[33] And AI will increasingly go beyond suggestion to decision, marking the shift from automation to autonomy.

Google's PageRank algorithm (that ranks websites in a Google search) embodies Internet monetization in the first wave. In the second wave, the number of followers and new and active users form the metrics scrutinized by Wall Street. We mentioned earlier the future possibility to reward users for data generation and access in order to bypass privacy regulations bound to mount, using the "digidend" portmanteau. It would require a robust algorithm to estimate the value of data, spanning over multiple apps and platforms to account for the user's outreach. The company that introduces this algorithm will arguably have unearthed a third-wave treasure chest.

We could go on rambling about the hop from blog to vlog and livestreaming, from how online dating turned from weirdo during the 1st wave to cool with 2nd wave apps from Tinder to Grindr, how 2nd wave Goliaths from SAP to Salesforce face existential threats as sleeker 3rd wave Davids brandish slingshots, or how the revealing of identities on smartglasses could replace anonymity by accountability both in the metaverse and in big cities, for instance bringing an end to the ghosting phenomenon. The ripple effects are too plentiful to list exhaustively. In the upcoming pages, oft and again we encounter the Internet waves.

---

[32] Of course, that was also a radical PR stunt to turn the page on the Facebook name, tarnished by scandals, and to rejuvenate an aging brand (in modern parlance). While the choice of name may appear as a brazen usurpation to the fringe in the field (as if Facebook had invented the metaverse), the laymen may come to associate the two.

[33] *Her*, a 2013 movie directed by Spike Jonze.

4.2   4^{IR} Tech Overview

One can easily be forgiven for losing sight of the modern technologies brewing in and propagating out of labs, each one supposedly carrying the potential for havoc in established industries.

To inject a dose of order into this pandemonium, we propose a chart that plots the main technologies in terms of broadness, depth of impact, and market size. Each technology in Fig. 4.4 is represented by two bubbles, one inside the other: the smaller for 2019 world market size, the bigger for the estimated size on the 2025 horizon. Note that deteriorating macroeconomic conditions have surfaced since these predictions were gleaned in 2020[34]: Covid, war in Europe, the Chinese clampdown on tech firms, inflation, geopolitical instability, loss of Wall Street confidence, and an emerging recession have tightened the funding faucet (with the exception of AI bots). For now, Amara's Law appears to have the upper hand, dragging this 2025 horizon farther in time. (Note that the horizon timeline is of little importance, as bubble sizes should remain stable relative to one another further down the road)

A handful of market sizes are indicated to convey a crude idea, in billions of US dollars (referring to the bigger, 2025 bubble). For instance, the Internet of Things (IoT) sweeps through a variety of industries, with a $690 billion market in 2019 expected to double to $1,256 billion by 2025.

Semiconductors were thrown in the mix, though they count more as a 3rd revolution technology (hence the stalled growth).

This chart may spur a barrage of arrows from all corners, calling for a few precisions:

- It is a still in time. A snapshot from 1960 would show the transistor paddling in the vicinity of blockchain, far from the GPT throne it has since claimed. In short, it says nothing of a technology's maturity stage; yet in line with our goal to prepare for *upcoming* disruption, we strived to situate the bubbles not necessarily where they stand today, but in a foreseeable future, roughly a decade down the road.
- Broadness and depth of impact remain arbitrary. These can be more or less direct. Despite automatic laundry machines only impacting household

---

[34] Sources used to build the chart are numerous, ranging from fields that specialize in information and statistics (Statistica, MarketsandMarkets, Mordor Intelligence, Grand View Research, Bloomberg Intelligence…), to news organizations (PR Newswire, Fortune Business, Globe Newswire…) and studies from either the profession (American Automobile Association…) or firms that provide research on new technologies (Goldman Sachs, Gartner, Morgan Stanley…).

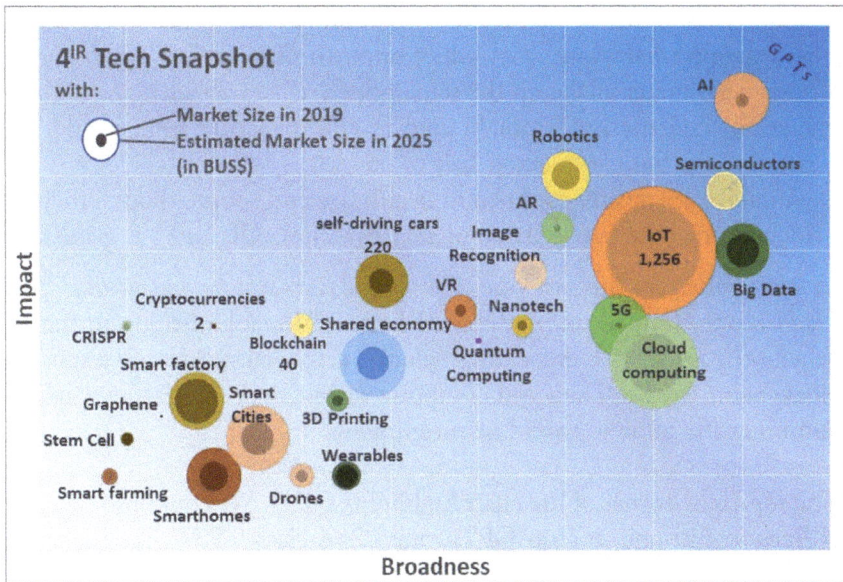

Fig. 4.4 4th Industrial revolution tech snapshot

work, we saw their contribution to female empowerment. Air-conditioning turned hotspots liveable, spurring a Southern revival in the US, and enabling temperature control, a prerequisite in fields from cold chain logistics to life sciences. We focus on direct impacts. Hence, the potential of VR and the metaverse to exacerbate the Grand Resignation by (with)drawing people into virtual worlds is not reflected here.

– Borders between technologies are porous. Notably

- some studies include smartphones in IoT and/or wearable devices, others not (we didn't—in fact, smartphones are left entirely out of the chart, as we exclude them from the 4^{IR});
- ERPs (Enterprise Resource Planning) software were excluded from smart factories for the same reason—the bubble would have been over twice the size if included.

– Ditto for markets: ask several people to define a given market and you'll receive as many answers (hence the incessant debates on market definition in monopoly lawsuits and mergers & acquisitions). E.g.:

- the drone market varies considerably if including military budgets (not included here);
- some studies englobe AR and VR in the metaverse, e.g. of the (rather bullish) Bloomberg study that claims the metaverse will reach an $800

billion market size by 2024, with half coming from "online game makers and gaming hardware, [...] while opportunities in live entertainment and social media make up the remainder"[35];

- here the 5G market is not limited to infrastructure (that would have deflated the bubble to about half of its size);
- wearables are mostly confined to healthcare and sports, though they also include the hardware portion of smartwatches, AR, and VR glasses.

- As exemplified by this last case, *the same dollars can be present in different bubbles*, only framed under different lenses. Wearables belong to the IoT behemoth, along with everything "smart"; cryptocurrencies are a subset of blockchain; AI, Big Data and computer vision share similar revenue, etc. Summing the bubbles would be meaningless.

The top-right corner of the chart highlights GPTs. We could use two diagonal lines to distinguish "top GPTs" and "2nd class GPTs" like the shared economy and self-driving cars, or a half-century earlier the car and television, and another century earlier the train and telegraph. Steam, electricity and the transistor rippled through all fields of work and society, fundamentally altering ways of devising new products, lives, the economy, urban layout, and so on. These often form the building blocks for 2nd class GPTs, which tend to revolve around transportation or communication means, but also new materials or methods: plastics, steel, perhaps soon 3D printing, and later nanotech. The distinction remains arbitrary.

In short, opinions can diverge on the bubbles' placement, and that's OK; the point is to plant the décor in a single, albeit rudimentary snapshot. These bubbles could be debated endlessly, most enjoyably with a bottle of bubbly.

Nor does the diagram claim exhaustivity in identifying 4^{IR} technologies, even less so markets. Nuclear fusion could provide a new source of non-polluting energy that would help us shift away from dwindling oil reserves and reduce green-house emissions, using the same energy as the sun (and hydrogen bomb). The International Thermonuclear Experiment Reactor (ITER) under construction in Southern France and due for completion in 2025 should validate our feasibility to harness this energy. With a price tag of $65 billion, ITER is our most expensive scientific endeavor to date[36] (in comparison, the Large Hadron Collider cost roughly $5 billion to build plus $1 billion a year to run). This is just one of several "toys" for

---

[35] Matthew Kanterman, Nathan Naidu: *Metaverse may be $800 billion market, next tech platform*, Bloomberg Intelligence (December 1, 2021).

[36] For a passionate account on efforts to unlock and harness nuclear fusion, cf. Daniel Clery: *A Piece of the Sun, the Quest for Fusion Energy*.

harnessing energy that researchers are fiddling with. Others focus on energy storage methods, with lithium-sulfur and fuel cell batteries among candidates showing promise.

Novel materials are also surfacing. Graphene is one we are still grappling with. Its thickness of one carbon atom (160 pm), strength, and conducive properties make it an ideal candidate for a variety of applications, from transportation to medicine, electronics, defense, energy (for instance with a new generation of graphene batteries that hold the charge longer, thus improve a battery's lifespan[37]), and even the construction of a space elevator.[38]

Technology also seeks to improve how we make things. Take the burgeoning field of origami engineering. While it draws less attention than 3D printing, origami design could also prove radical for future tech. It enables the building of complex 3D objects via 2D manufacturing techniques like plasma or laser cutting, that morph into different shapes, much like a Transformers toy.[39] Origami manufacturing yields promise in applications ranging from space exploration and colonization to nanobots that would enter our bloodstream and deal with pathogens that evade our natural immune system.

Here we only peer a few years ahead. A black swan or discovery could jostle any bubble, the way CRISPR/CAS9 rocked the gene editing scene, obsoleting predictions published prior to 2012. From Stable Diffusion to ChatGPT, the public release in 2022 of a new wave of AI bots has spurred a bevy of revised estimates on the future AI market size, landing it closer to the size of the IoT bubble in Fig. 4.4.

We do not purport to cover each 4^{IR} technology in depth. For instance, quantum computing and nanotech could rise to 2nd or even 1st-class GPT status in the long run. Among other things, nanotech could enable the merging of carbon and silicon. As highlighted by philosopher Daniel Dennett in *From Bacteria to Bach and Back*, both contain code at their core: the

---

[37] Cf. https://www.cheaptubes.com/resources/graphene-battery-users-guide/#:~:text=Graphene%20batt eries%20are%20an%20emerging,and%20come%20in%20many%20forms.

[38] Cf. https://en.wikipedia.org/wiki/Space_elevator.

[39] The comparison is no coincidence, as both have roots tracing back to Japan. Origami—literally "paper folding"—originated over a thousand years ago in Japan (and possibly in China before that— after all, the Chinese invented paper), starting with paper fans which remain prominent in Shinto temples to this day, along with lightning-shaped *kamishide*. The twentieth Century *mecha* genre, born in Japan from the meshing of robots and anime, was heavily influenced by origami. Popularized in the West via a line of toys developed by Takara Co. Ltd, whose distribution rights were purchased in 1984 by Hasbro and renamed *Transformers*, the franchise was developed into a cartoon with storylines following Hasbro's partnering with Marvel, birthing the franchise that to date remains hugely successful.

genetic one a creation of nature or some other external agent, the latter man-made.[40] Our growing aptitude to code and recode both forms will blur the line, adding to the riddles on the definition of life. Yet for all their disruptive potential, quantum computing and nanotech are unlikely to make a dent in the job market from now to, say, the mid-2040s.

In the sectorial and corporate disruption chapter, we explain why we need only pay heed to narrow technologies inasmuch as they present a threat to our field of activity. Narrow tech targets specific sectors, while broader tech (2nd and especially 1st-class GPTs) deserves everyone's attention.

In the following pages, we peer into 3D printing, Augmented Reality, and Artificial Intelligence.

4.3   3D Printing

Instead of building a sandcastle by shoveling packets and then shaping them, a 3D printer places a single grain, then appends another, one layer at a time, until alas the edifice is completed. Also called additive manufacturing, it kicked off with plastics, and the list of printable materials grows by the day: nylons, rubbers, waxes, titanium and even biomaterials.

Plastic injection, by far the most ubiquitous way to produce plastic parts, requires three tangible elements:

- a mold;
- the plastic material itself, delivered in pebble-sized pellets;
- a piece of heavy machinery called an injection press.

The mold is where the magic happens: once mounted on the press, the press closes the mold's two halves and injects molten plastic at roughly 200° Celsius. The plastic espouses the mold's shape, hardens as it cools, then is ejected as the press reopens the mold. The entire cycle lasts a minute, give or take. The mold for a plastic bottle cap could have something like twenty cavities, each cycle producing as many pieces. Playing on parameters and materials results in the broad gamut of plastic properties (smoothness, resistance, dilatation, transparency, color, elasticity…) present in the everyday objects that surround us.

---

[40] Cf. p. 64 of the chapter, *How Darwin and Turing broke a spell*. Daniel C. Dennett: *From Bacteria to Bach and Back: The Evolution of Minds*, W. W. Norton & Company (2017).

A mold is tailored to produce a single shape.[41] Its cost varies with the size and number of cavities, projected life expectancy and other aspects, easily numbering in the tens or hundreds of thousands of dollars. Large production volumes are required to offset this initial investment. Small quantities do not warrant the use of plastics.

Plastic injection is a science in its own right. Cognizance in mold design, parts' malleability, and molten plastic behavior are essential to a proper injection. Not only are molds pricey, but the slightest flaw can cause parts to have burs, easily break, not fit properly, leave gaps or not seal. Issues are not uncommon and can quickly escalate into a nightmare, with sunk investment costs, a delayed product launch, and bitter spats as responsibility is bounced between parties both internal and external.

3D printing requires no mold. Equipment is smaller and lighter than for injection (it takes a crane just to place the mold onto a press), with starting prices affordable to companies not specialized in plastic injection and even households. R&D can fiddle with the printer before they winnow down their choice to the piece to use for mass production, for which they can then invest in a mold. And it can craft shapes impossible to achieve via plastic injection. Alas, it suppresses the need for injection expertise; the design software is so user-friendly that, in the words of 3D System's CEO Avi Reichental: "if you can point and click a mouse, you can now design things for a 3D printer".[42]

On the downside, additive layering can take anywhere from half an hour up to a week. This makes it alluring for small-volume, customized items, while injection remains unbeatable for mass production. Look around and ask yourself: what objects could benefit from a shift to 3D printing? From cars to toothbrushes, everything surrounding us is mass-produced, mostly because we had no choice. Now that we do, where could customization take root?

Promising areas for additive manufacturing include:

- unique products, like a tailored prosthetic limb, and soon entire organs via 3D printed biomaterials;
- fields where weight is critical, like cars and airplanes, but also for sending goods into space: astronauts on the ISS now have their own 3D printer that can make parts and even recycle them into new parts[43];

---

[41] Though for two plastic parts meant to fit together, mold designers might put both parts as separate cavities on a single mold, thus saving on the cost of a mold.

[42] Peter Diamandis and Steven Kotler: *Bold, How to Grow Big, Create Wealth and Impact the World*, p34, Simon & Schuster (2015).

[43] Plastics Today: *3D printer on International Space Station allows astronauts to recycle, reuse, repeat*, Clare Goldsberry (Feb 15 2019), https://www.plasticstoday.com/3d-printing/3d-printer-international-space-station-allows-astronauts-recycle-reuse-repeat.

– back on Earth, impeccable customer service implies keeping a vast array of spare parts on hand, even for discontinued models, a requirement that plagues industries with high inventory costs and immobilized cash. The ability to locally print a spare part only when needed improves these metrics while offering a swifter, localized service; it also frees space and is more environmentally friendly (less waste, bypasses the need to ship goods from the other side of the globe).

New applications will emerge as the tech improves and costs fall, making 3D printers the cool tool for home garages and amateur tinkerers. Shared economy models will arise as platforms bring together people who wish to create an object yet do not own a 3D printer with neighbors who do. Such platforms will integrate and parse through 3D printer specs to facilitate matches between parties based on needs, location, availability, and price.

A QR code tag could purvey the specs. Instead of searching for "the store nearest to you", print the desired object from home, or book a timeslot on the neighbor's 3D printer. A modest fee may be charged for accessing the drawing. While less profitable than when the company manufactured and sold the object, businesses could feel enticed to flirt with this model: imagine the supply chain of toys manufactured in East Asia, shipped to the US, and displayed in stores in the hope of finding a buyer. Each step involves costs, middlemen, time, and in the end, unsold inventory. By contrast, 3D printing represents the ultimate lean dream of "just-in-time". Manufacturing, raw materials and the rest are no longer part of the value proposition. It may not please all manufacturers, but those who fail to provoke their own disruption might wake up outflanked by companies surfing on the user-friendly trend. Suppose the Disney+ subscription gives clients free rein to produce the toys of its fantasy worlds, letting them recycle older toys that fall out of favor.

Yiwu is a town in Zhejiang short of 2 million inhabitants, over an hour away from Shanghai by bullet train. It is known as the world's largest supplier of mass-consumer plastic goods, from beach toys to household items. Around 80% of Christmas decorations consumed worldwide originate from Yiwu.[44] As 3D printing goes mainstream, mold manufacturers and plastic injectors situated far from end-users could suffer severe sectorial disruption.

Modular manufacturing, whereby parts are put together like Lego bricks, helps circumvent the elsewise limited size of pieces (commensurate with the

---

[44] Cf. Xinhua news, "圣诞节离不开义乌制造"——全球最大圣诞产品生产基地义乌目击记, "Christmas is inseparable from Yiwu Manufacturing", Yiwu witnesses the world's largest Christmas production base, http://www.xinhuanet.com/2019-10/20/c_1125127417.htm.

3D printer's dimensions). Assembled parts also allow for more complex functionalities, as illustrated by the deranging videos of functional plastic guns made from 3D-printed parts. While these models could only fire a single round (with high risks of self-injury), they ignited a salvo of fresh concerns, due to the ability both to produce a lethal weapon from anywhere, with no tracing, and to furtively pass it through metal detectors.

3D printing drives production closer to home. It partakes in a localization trend that includes harvesting of renewable energies and vertical farming—a trend that could gain steam as freight costs soar globally. If reusable plastics one day become mandatory, we would smatter used parts to dust to print something else.

Convergence with other 4^{IR} tech will lift 3D printing. Additive manufacturing will thrust O2O (Online-to-Offline) to a whole new level, allowing us to print out virtual objects from the metaverse into the physical world. AR glasses will make filming instantaneous, while computer vision will empower anyone stumbling on a desirable object to reproduce it, *bypassing* the need for the original design. Molecular printers could build things from dust, including synthetic foods, with all the necessary proteins and vitamins and practically no upfront costs. Or as the "Coban equation" from one of Barjavel's sci-fi novels reads: "What does not exist exists".[45]

Yet to claim that in the upcoming decade or two the entire plastic injection or even manufacturing sector is doomed would be hyperbolic speculation. The situation may be more akin to Airbnb's arrival on the hospitality scene. Some had predicted it would spell the demise of the hotel industry; yet when the dust settled, stats revealed robust growth in the sector, particularly in high-end and business segments. Airbnb carved a niche, impacting budget hotels but mostly opening a blue ocean.[46] More a case of corporate than sectorial disruption (terms we come to grips with in Part 2).

Our 4^{IR} tech chart showed the 3D printing market is expected to triple from roughly $12 to $36 billion from 2019 to 2025; meanwhile, plastic injection is a $258 billion business, bound to grow to $267 billion over that same period.

---

[45] René Barjavel: *La Nuit des Temps*, (1968), in English *The Ice People*. The scifi novel showcased an example of additive manufacturing producing synthetic food at nanoscale levels.
[46] Andrew McAfee and Erik Brynjolfsson: *Machine, Platform, Crowd: Harnessing our Digital Future*, p. 206 "Why Airbnb Won't Vacate Hotels", W.W. Norton & Company (2017).

4.4   AR and VR

Virtual Reality (VR) warps the user into another world, whereas with Augmented Reality (AR), we still perceive our surroundings, with text and objects embedded on top. Both require headsets, also called head-mounted displays (HMD) or gear (HMG); part of the trick is to shrink these to smart glasses, perhaps even smart lenses (though lenses pose serious technical challenges).

VR ostracizes, making it more suited for closed, secured environments—as one person put it, strolling outside while wearing one would make you a candidate for a Darwin Award.[47] AR keeps us in the real world, allowing us to move about without knocking over that precious China vase. It is best enjoyed outside, making battery life, miniaturization, aesthetics, and a device untethered by wires critical. And that's just the start of the hill: fulfilling its potential requires powerful image recognition capabilities for a proper rendering of 3D objects that fit the environment in real time as we move about in it. The coarse level of current tech limits us to Pokémon monsters and cartoonish bunny ears.

Each reality will carve a distinct market, in line with its characteristics. As Leo Mirani from The Economist resumes: "AR is to smartphones what VR is to desktop computers".[48] Some gear can accommodate both realities. HTC's Vive Pro 2 wireless headset can plunge the wearer into a metaverse or recreate actual surroundings using its embedded cameras; this mix of VR and AR is referred to as eXtended Reality, or "XR".

We can define AR by addressing its two main components: the headgear (hardware) and the AR technology (software).

Picture your familiar computer or smartphone screen, only stuck in front of your eyes on a headset. No need to carry a laptop, snatch your phone out of the pocket, or uncover the smartwatch from your sleeve a hundred times a day to check everything from the weather forecast to Apple's stock performance and unwarranted notifications.

On the other hand, AR functionalities of the type available on today's smartphones make use of the device's camera to then *overlay* objects.

Taken separately, the hardware and software present limited value; combined they create the real game-changer. Smartphones introduced us to the 2nd Internet Wave software: apps. Just as they can access the world wide web and emails, so will 1st and 2nd wave soft persist in the HMG era; only

---

[47] Robert Scoble and Shel Israel: *The Fourth Transformation: How Augmented Reality and Artificial Intelligence will Change Everything*, Patrick Brewster Press.
[48] Daniel Franklin: *Megatech: Technology in 2050*, p. 146.

HMG will add a 3rd wave of soft that convey data (text, directions, alerts…), including on things out of direct sight, using mixed reality to embed 3D objects.[49] They also function as an advanced Google Lens. Already, shopping apps from Amazon to Alibaba can recognize objects to recommend similar ones for purchase, though current performance is anything but seamless (only one object can be identified at a time, it requires a blank background, etc.). Improvements like Microsoft's Azure Objects Anchor are slowly paving the route toward a more seamless experience of object recognition.[50]

Embedded devices could track eye movement and pupil dilatation, a necessity given that smart glasses cannot be "pointed" onto the object of interest. Eyefluence, a startup scooped by Google in 2016, focuses on a radically novel UI that works essentially with the eyes. After a dozen minutes of testing, one user described the interface as "natural and productive".[51] Interaction could also take place via haptic gloves or voice commands. Similar to the Betamax Vs VHS war of 1980s fame[52], multiple offerings may appear. I remember my first smartphone, an HTC Dream: it had a few buttons on the bottom, a nub, and a touchscreen that could slide off to reveal a Blackberry-like keyboard.

Other 4^{IR} tech will converge with AR. In the background, AI can browse online for the entirety of items within a given perimeter that relate to my interests or respond to a current need, like a whiskey bar with a solid range of premium Japanese brands that match my wallet and available seating for four. The IoT will bring a flurry of surrounding objects in our grasp, letting us exchange information and command objects from stereo to cars and building elevators, book that whiskey table, connect to other cameras, dig into database archives, etc.

An Augmented Life

AR's impacts can be difficult to fathom, as witnessed by the *Black Mirror* series' recurrent spurting of episodes revolving around it, arguably making it the show's most explored 4^{IR} tech.[53] Magazine articles rehash the guided tour,

---

[49] While this fitting of virtual objects on the physical world is technically called mixed reality, we will stick to the term augmented reality, more common in the vernacular (besides, AR devoid of image recognition and superposition is unlikely to survive—we might even penetrate directly an AR world of mixed reality by the time HMG become mainstream).

[50] Cf. *Azure Object Anchors is now in private preview*, Sept. 22nd, 2020: https://techcommunity.microsoft.com/t5/mixed-reality-blog/azure-object-anchors-is-now-in-private-preview/ba-p/1696157.

[51] Robert Scoble and Shel Israel: *The Fourth Transformation: How Augmented Reality and Artificial Intelligence will Change Everything*, chapter *The Missing Link*, Patrick Brewster Press (2016).

[52] Cf. *Video Format War*: https://en.wikipedia.org/wiki/Videotape_format_war.

[53] Cf. Season 1, Episode 3; Season 3, Episodes 2, 4 and 5, and Season 4, Episode 3.

where AR transports us to other times, resurrecting ancient ruins to their past glory—a stale illustration that lacks imagination.

The headsets serve as the simultaneous gateways to the metaverse and to mixed realities. You could see desolate surroundings crowded with people to your likening. Or on the contrary, erase all traces of cars and pedestrians to purvey the illusion of a ghost town (with a failsafe to prevent bumping into others). Tune on a shamanistic app for psychedelic hallucinations of the type experienced under the influence of ayahuasca. Strangers in a heated verbal exchange could "picture" themselves going at it, each one succeeding in beating the other up, only virtually. Ease of 3D imaging will allow you to "grab" any object or passerby to include them in your metaverse[54] (to the detriment of imagination, in the same way it loses ground whenever a book hits the screens, as diehard Tolkien and Harry Potter fans can attest). Imagine the possibility of immersion in famous events, with recorded ones like JFK's assassination perhaps crisper than, say, the beheading of Louis XVI. Tactical details of a battle could alternate eagle views with zooms on salient points. And the reliving of memories: those with loved or deceased ones could be replayed endlessly, with AI optionally kicking in to build alternative stories. This propensity for experiencing a different unfolding to our lives might tempt some to retreat into parallel dimensions, presaging wacky, schizophrenic scenarios.

The democratization of AR content generation (3D objects) will create a tectonic shift from imagination to visualization, profoundly changing storytelling, daydreaming and even fantasies, from fleeting whims to graver obsessions.

We could project an aestheticized version of our selves to surrounding AR headset wearers (free for them to take off the gear and defy appearances). Elders could brandish the face of their youth to reveal what they once looked like, with only their long-time acquaintances able to tell if it were embellished a tad. Pushing narcissism to its extreme, one could use AR to plant his own head on everyone else, in pure *Being John Malkovich* fashion. In the ethics part, we discuss other deranging developments conceivable.

Serendipity

Mark Twain once wrote of New York City: "it is a splendid desert—a domed and steepled solitude, where the stranger is lonely in the midst of a million of

---

[54] Again, *Black Mirror* provides a bitter illustration with the *USS Callister* episode (Series 4, Episode 1).

his race".[55] A sea of opportunities is lost on any given day simply because we are blind to our surroundings, ignorant of other people's needs and penchants. To quote zoologist Desmond Morris:

> As a species we were not biologically equipped to cope with a mass of strangers masquerading as members of our tribe. [...] The animal zoo inmate finds itself in solitary confinement. Alongside, in other cages, it may be able to see or hear other animals but it cannot make any real contact with them.[56]

Or as a friend of lesser words put it, one has less inhibition approaching an attractive stranger at the bar by finding their Tinder profile and initiating contact there rather than physically.

The 3rd Internet wave may transform this sad state of affairs. The 2nd wave brought geo-localization; the third will link virtual and physical worlds in our direct sight. Strangers with common interests could be alerted of each other's nearing presence; LinkedIn's "People you may know" feature evolve to reveal profiles frequently passed by in the real; and subway commuters engage in silent conversations via a chatlog on their smart glasses, on condition of mutual consent, in either private mode, public, or anywhere in between—say a chat visible only on the AR gear of mothers, classmates, or yoga practitioners. People with diverging opinions can continue ignoring each other; they could even be made *invisible* to each other.

The devising of novel, abstract forms of communication will bypass the clunky process of sentence writing. We already have a crude preview of this with gifs and stickers. Artist Xu Bing is among the pioneers envisioning a new language of "meta words" that transcend cultures[57]; combined with 4^{IR} tech, these could bring about a telepathy of sorts.

AR could bolster communities of like-minded people; not disseminated throughout the globe as was the case with prior Internet waves (Yahoo group chats, Pinterest), but within reach. The 3rd wave will redefine O2O, dealing a blow to the individualization plague denounced by Desmond Morris. "As human relationships, lost in the crowd, became ever more impersonal, so man's inhumanity to man increased to horrible proportions".[58] Could an AR-powered high-tech zoo instill empathy between us?

---

[55] Mark Twain: *Letter to San Francisco Alta California, June 5, 1867.*
[56] Desmond Morris: *The Human Zoo*, Vintage Press (1994).
[57] Cf. www.xubing.com.
[58] Desmond Morris: *The Human Zoo*, p. 20.

Multilevel Augmentation

Even devoid of computer vision and mixed reality, HMG can enhance humans in several ways. The ability to record everything in sight, a collateral "plus" of the device, gives us infinite memory that alone presages for wild developments, as illustrated in a *Black Mirror* episode.[59]

Snippets can be posted online effortlessly, as opposed to the current ritual of pulling out the phone, selecting the camera app, and unsubtly pointing it to the object of attention, a move susceptible of causing its ire. Data storage permitting, users may opt to remain on constant "livestream" mode, sharing their lives with whoever cares. A small light to signal recording could be made mandatory to ease fears of voyeurism. Yet to what use protest when everyone constantly films everything? Any slightly abnormal public scene can virally escalate as onlookers freeze to stare at the anomaly, a ghastly legion of speckles that brings social peer pressure to a frightening new level.

Some ancient schools of thought withheld that only when under observation could we claim something to exist. AR takes us from seeing to recording. Merging this data into a patchwork, for instance by picking up facial expressions, could weave a picture of humanity, with statistics on levels of happiness based on geography, gender and race, season, weather, pollution, job, income level, exposition to greenery, day of the week and time of the day.

HMG can augment vision in other ways. Cameras extending eyesight with 360-degree views, others that "see" through walls; minicameras inserted into areas such as the human body; thermal vision, ultraviolet, gamma rays, and far-sight zoom. These are but a few features that will put us on par with nocturnal creatures and sharp-eyed eagles. Or consider virtual lamps embedded over our surroundings at night, lighting darkness (a feature highlighted decades ago in *Terminator 2*), with substantial energy savings along with reduced light pollution, a known nuisance for night critters.

In their quest for immersion, researchers spare no sense. Methods currently under investigation to convey feelings of touch and texture include static

---

[59] Season 1, Episode 3, *The Entire History of You*. What appeared on the lens was more akin to what we'd see on a computer screen, with menus and so on; while it was capable of some facial expression recognition features, it had poor abilities for image recognition capable of embedding images on the environment.

electricity[60], air vortexes[61], and high ultra-frequency sound waves.[62] Adding senses plunges us deeper down the rabbit hole, in line with Aldous Huxley's *A Brave New World*, where people go "to the feelies". This extra dose of credibility will widen the door to interrogations *à la eXistenZ* on what is real.[63] AR could resuscitate the dead, be it a lost loved one, or the Fuhrer, in the flesh. True full-immersion gear may only be available with the 4th Internet wave, producing an indistinguishable virtual reality reminiscent of *The Matrix*.

Digital Twins

We think of VR as thrusting users in a metaverse more enjoyable than the real world. Yet a growing niche aims not to create fantasy worlds, but precise replicas of our real world with respect to the laws of physics. These replicas go by the name of digital twins.

Digital twins could boost ecommerce, for instance by giving a more accurate rendering of clothes when worn, taking into account texture, wrinkles, and precise dimensions; create a seamless O2O experience as specs of the twin include the 3D printing design, bridging virtual and real worlds. Brands are developing this omnichannel approach by selling or giving an NFT replica of the object, experimenting with various handover models: either before, after or together with the physical good purchase (sometimes as a substitute for the physical "gift with purchase"). Objects could appear for free in virtual, to gauge public reception, letting the brand send orders to the factory only to produce the most successful models, with a discount offered to early adopters who spread their success in the metaverse. Or one or the other version is made accessible only to a select group of NFT owners.

Digital twins also find breeding fields in simulation, for example to plug millions of autonomous vehicle driving hours. Factors ranging from the car's weight, its tires' adhesiveness, and the impact of snow on vision and of ice on the road are modeled to flawlessly mirror reality. These virtual setups speed up the data generation essential to train algorithms, with colossal savings on the (previously only existing) alternative—real-life tests. Digital twins have been deployed to simulate car accidents, but also by Ubisoft to render high-quality

---

[60] John Biggs: *Senseg, amazing haptic technology that could be coming to a device near you*, TechCrunch (April 29, 2009).

[61] Sidhant Gupta et al.: *Airwave: on-Contact Haptic Feedback Using Air Vortex Rings*, Microsoft Research, Proceedings of the 2013 ACM International Joint Conference on Pervasive and Ubiquitous Computing.

[62] Chris Stokel-Walker: *Sound waves that mimic the touch of a button? That's the future*, Wired (September 11th, 2016).

[63] Directed by David Cronenberg and released in 1999, *eXistenZ* depicts a VR game that blurs the line between the real and the virtual.

animated 3D objects of jaguars and other fierce animals[64], and by the world's largest brewer to replicate the complex relationships between natural ingredients and the brewing process, in this case using Microsoft's Azure Digital Twins.[65]

In a bid to curb our carbon footprint, firms from Tencent to startup Akila seek to replicate digital twins of buildings and entire cities, replete with ventilation, air-conditioning installations, sound levels, insulation properties, and generation of volatile organic compounds and other pollutants.[66] Parameters can be tweaked endlessly to observe environmental impacts. The microstate of Tuvalu is developing a digital twin version of its government as a preemptive step, so that if a climate crisis forces a relocation, it can "continue to fully function as a sovereign nation".[67] One could imagine a proper emulation of chemical and biological properties and reactions putting an end to animal testing. But perhaps the application most hyped by science fiction sees human digital twins that in a nanosecond live our lives in an infinity of parallel scenarios, to then recommend a course of action, be it for finding a suitable partner, choosing an education path or any other situation that involves a tough decision.[68]

RPV and aR

Closer to us than AR lies the Remote-Person View or RPV (also called FPV for first-person view), relating to the remote control of robots, drones, or any device that gives access to a viewpoint, via a camera or three.

RPV's incomplete ancestors consisted in:

– a camera on one end, a screen (for a human observer) at the other;
– remotely controlled toys and vehicles.

The two are now combined with a camera mounted on the machine, usually a robot or drone. Headsets add the benefit of an immersive experience and potentially AR image overlay options. Adding motricity via limbs (legged

---

[64] Theodore McKenzie, ZooBuilder: Ubisoft's AI-Based Tool for Animating Animals, 80 Level (March 24, 2022), https://80.lv/articles/zoobuilder-ubisoft-s-ai-based-tool-for-animating-animals/.

[65] Cf. Satya Nadella's Shareholder Letter, in Microsoft's Annual Report 2021, https://www.microsoft.com/investor/reports/ar21/index.html#.

[66] https://www.akila3d.com/.

[67] Cf. the Future Now Project of the Government of Tuvalu, Department of Foreign Affairs: https://dfa.gov.tv/index.php/future-now-project.

[68] For an example on dating, cf. Black Mirror's Hang the DJ (Season 4, Episode 4).

robot), wheels (self-driving vehicle), or wings (unmanned aerial vehicle, or UAV), allows for interaction with the distant environment.

And when instead of a robot, a human on the other end mounts a mini-camera on her glasses, it's called Assisted Reality (aR). Video calls and the shared screen functionality are precursors of aR. Assisted Reality adds interactive options: signs and arrows drawn by the person monitoring, visible to the glass-wearer.

aR can bypass the current limitations of the AR model:

- computer vision (object recognition) is not a prerequisite: the task of deciphering the environment remains in human hands; ditto dexterity, with promise in tasks from deminers to electricians;
- the person using the headset can remain indoors, lifting mobility barriers.

As usual, early applications can be found in healthcare, allowing surgeons to perform high precision operations on a patient remotely, manipulating sophisticated devices, and in the military, for control of drones and use of lethal force. In Ernest Cline's novel *Armada*, entire fleets of spaceships and robots are manned remotely by humans. The protagonist bashes at the Star Wars saga for failing to take this obvious trend into account, presenting it as a logical direction to preserve human lives.

Promising fields for RPV point to areas where humans cannot directly intervene:

- due to a local scarcity of human expertise;
- in high-risk areas: warfare, firefighting, radioactive sites (cf. DARPA's Fukushima challenge[69]), or places devoid of oxygen (Mars rovers);
- to reach scales that evade human vision, typically in nanotechnology, to engineer and monitor the assembly of nanomachines; or to see what happens inside humans, via nanobots equipped with cameras, in a replay of the 1966 hit *Fantastic Voyage*, only without physically shrinking the protagonists into the patient's body;
- to see behind walls, with cameras placed at the right spots.[70] With miniaturization and a decrease in costs, a panoply of remotely accessible cameras,

[69] Larry Greenemeier: *Fukushima Disaster Inspires Better Emergency-Response Robots*, in Scientific American (May 18, 2015), https://www.scientificamerican.com/article/fukushima-disaster-inspires-better-emergency-response-robots/.

[70] F-35 fighter jet pilots can see "through" their plane in every direction thanks to this technology. AR research began in the US Air Force in the 1980s with the work of Thomas Furness, dubbed the "grandfather of AR".

courtesy of the IoT trend, could be accessed via RPV gear. Law enforcement, firemen, and other officials could surf from one city camera to the next and even be granted access to private ones with the owners' consent or in emergency situations. Screen walls could in a sense make walls invisible, provided cameras exist on the other side, following the "invisibility cloak" technique demonstrated in grand fanfare in 2003 by Japanese scientist Susumu Tachi[71];

– to save on traveling time and costs, or even counter exile—cf. the "Snowbot" that enables fugitive Snowden to lead a remote conference via a robot[72] (not to be mixed up with the snowbots that clear the ground from snow).

This last case may resound with many workers, illustrating the multifarious effects of these realities on work.

AR and VR at Work…

We split existing work patterns into three non-mutually exclusive contexts, followed by several of the technologies' "byproducts".

… with the Environment Here we find plumbers, gardeners, architects, farmers, firefighters; construction and maintenance personnel, as well as those who deal with physical surroundings of the unstructured type (as opposed to the humdrum of factory work). They will benefit from superposed elements that either guide them or help visualize what up to then required imagination—a wiring diagram, a mockup. aR allows for visual checks and action at a distance, for example to assess an insurance claim, monitor security, undertake or assist in a surgery.

The tech could reduce the value of experts as the tricks of the trade appear on the smart glasses of novice eyes. Consider a crew of ten technicians that spend 90% of their time driving on the road for a meager 10% exercising their expertise on-site. In the new model, nine of those staff lose their jobs to cheap youths now assisted by the sole survivor based at the HQ. Devoid of the need for expertise, these youths could be outsourced, perhaps serving multiple companies.

[71] Robin McKie: *Japanese boffins spawn almost invisible man*, The Guardian (June 13, 2004) https://www.theguardian.com/science/2004/jun/13/japan.research.
   Note that other cloaking devices have since been devised that do not require cameras: https://www.rochester.edu/newscenter/watch-rochester-cloak-uses-ordinary-lenses-to-hide-objects-across-continuous-range-of-angles-70592/.
[72] Cf. *The Snowbot: how Edward Snowden gets around his exile*, The Guardian (June 27, 2016), https://www.theguardian.com/us-news/shortcuts/2016/jun/27/snowbot-edward-snowden-telepresence-robot.

The US counts roughly 420,000 couriers, or 1,2 for every 1,000 Americans; China, 7 million, or five for every 1,000 people.[73] Equipping a fraction of these with cameras would allow technicians to follow their actions and provide guidance, turning them into handymen. Upon reaching a site, the courier delivers a package, fixes a dripping faucet, change the filter on the ventilation system, checks on the residents' moles and various other health aspects, recording relevant visual cues that could feed an insurance claim—all for a pittance of a cost, each task involving a dialup with a different provider.

Ultimately, the end-user can take the issue in her own hands. Everyone has smartphones today and will likely have AR glasses tomorrow. AR tutorials for applying makeup are already ubiquitous and devaluing makeup artist jobs. Many other tasks could soon follow suit.

... with Others AR could help discern body language and expressional patterns, letting people scrutinize each other during meetings, whether on a date or job interview.

AR storytelling will supplant PowerPoint presentations with live visuals that accompany the speaker's narrative. AR assistants will revolutionize training methods: instead of a written Standard Operating Procedure (SOP), an avatar guides the worker step by step. The system will recognize any nonconform action and instantly issue a warning. This lessens the value of the old guard's experience, compromising their role as coach and mentor to juveniles. Quality Control and other departments could see their headcount shrink. As the value of expertise erodes, human labor will remain relevant only inasmuch as it surpasses silicon alternatives in terms of cost, speed and dexterity—attributes that convey little value.

... on a Computer VR is more likely to take over work currently performed on a computer. As PCs enhanced office work, so HMG may aid in certain tasks. However VR's isolating effect may prove an issue, one that hampers work with colleagues: it's easier to lift the head from a computer than take off a VR headset (granted, XR headsets and smart glasses could mitigate that claim). The added value brought by HMG would need to exceed that of a computer to a great extent to justify deployment.

The Work-from-Home paradigm naturally begs for a more immersive environment than what existing videoconferencing tools offer, making it a hot area of VR research. The impatient boss hammering staff with the

---

[73] For the US, we include not only the Bureau of Labor Statistics' couriers and messengers (category 43–5021) but also postal service mail carriers (category 43–5052). For China, cf. Zixu Wang, *In China, delivery workers struggle against a rigged system*, (April 20, 2021), https://supchina.com/2021/04/20/in-china-delivery-workers-struggle-against-a-rigged-system/.

"burning platform" cliché could literally conduct the meeting on a burning platform or a sinking ship to get her point across (especially to highlight if existing actions equate to emptying the water with buckets, rather than fixing the problem at its root). Already users can change the background in a meeting. Soon they may be able to camouflage their emotions under a virtual poker face in order to counter body and facial reading attempts, appear in fancy suits while in their PJs, or awake while asleep, with AI conveying a semblance of participation.

... as a Sector in Itself On the bright side, recall the new jobs birthed by the Internet: web designer, SEO, and web architect, to say nothing of the booming cybersecurity field. Creating scenarios and original user-generated content could propel a new generation of freelancers and startups. If VR and AR deliver on their promises, they could generate strong demand for jobs to reproduce environments in 3D animated formats, replete with avatars and O2O passage points.

Data labeling forms an important part of the groundwork for computer vision to kick in. Supposing one day everything is labeled, the need for data labelers would fall, in line with the Beaudry effect, to a new normal that covers the creation of new objects. No doubt the new standard for a product launch will see it accompanied by a 3D object, replete with design parameters and recognition by AR glasses via an RFID tag. The purchase of a dress will add a digital replica to your virtual wardrobe.

Meanwhile, a digital twin creation platform that integrates all the laws of physics diminishes the need for engineering knowledge. Protagonists in *Snow Crash* (the 1992 novel that coined the term "metaverse") would marvel at crisp, high-definition 3D objects, the mark of an extremely skilled coder. In reality, just as Instagram has no need for legions of employees to populate its app with content, frictionless design will facilitate a smooth upload of virtual stuff in the metaverse by users. Such factors could undermine both the number and qualifications of future workers.

Ubiquitous smart glasses will spur job demand in conception, design and management of the virtual objects bound to crowd metaverse worlds, but also to provide the storylines for the infinite forms of recreation and parallel economies within them. As people increasingly spend larger portions of time in it, demand for workers *in* the metaverse could grow—workers tasked with welcoming customers, guiding them through leisurely activities, answering queries, or performing jobs similar to those we find in the real world. Obviously, the firms orchestrating the metaverse will do everything to keep headcount low, by favoring nonplayer characters ("NPCs"). The comparison between virtual and real worlds might even contribute to underscore areas where workers could be spared in the latter—though in all probability the metaverse will lack elements of uncertainty present in the real world. The repairman in the game *Grand Theft Auto* repairs your wreck, no matter how badly you trashed it, by far exceeding AI capabilities in the real world (and without ever announcing a 2-month waiting time for a missing spare part). Ultimately, if AI turns capable of producing metaverse worlds in full detail, we might witness the paradox of a billion-dollar market that employs no one.

Shadow Data Demand for jobs could surge wherever data is involved. With VR and AR, every move generates data. This could trigger a supernovae explosion of data that rapidly eclipses the avalanches from previous Internet waves. A large portion of this will be *shadow data.*

Shadow data refers to traces of data automatically and unintentionally generated as we go about our lives. Internet cookies, i.e. blocks of data created by a web server on the user's computer while browsing a website, are a prime example. Shadow data mostly originates from the Internet for now, but AR will release the monster from its cage and into the real world.

We ignore 99% of our visual intake. When contemplating them, no one bothers to count the number of trees bordering the streets on the way to work, to say anything about assessing their health by the number and color of their leaves, compared to that of previous days and weeks (as captured by us and other passersby). Companies in charge of urban lighting pay crews to patrol the streets on the lookout for defective bulbs. Smart streetlights that send alerts for any burnt bulb eradicate the need for such labor while improving reactivity, at the cost of investing for their installation. But with AR, defective streetlights could be automatically reported as soon as they enter someone's field of sight, whether they noticed it or not, no smart light required. Shadow data could be used for insurance claims, police investigations, or to assess improvements in the amount of dog manure left unattended on sidewalks.[74] For a dystopian depiction, recall the ability of agents in *The Matrix* to capture events as soon as these entered a human's field of sight (by taking possession of the human—but here the analogy reaches its limit). Wherever benefits exceed costs and AI cannot alone handle shadow data analysis, humans may yet have a role to play.

New Memes In the 1970s, evolutionary biologist Richard Dawkins conceived the notion of *meme* as an idea or style that spreads by imitation from person to person. Somewhat like bacteria or genes, certain memes die

---

[74] A trait captured in Black Mirror's Series 4, Episode 3, *Crocodile.*

out while others spread virally to embody a culture.[75] Each Internet wave carries its own blend of meme, from the first wave's shortcut words (lol, asl...) to second wave stickers.

In the metaverse, objects become the memes. The flaunting of a stunning dress will no longer trigger questions from friends on its origins, while leaving strangers gasping: anyone will have the ability to instantly copy-paste desirable designs into their own wardrobe. Even a penniless designer can achieve fame overnight if her model pleases the crowd, spreading virally to the world in a record time. And this observation extends beyond clothes. In Ernest Cline's *Ready Player One*, the pyramidal structure of the Tyrell Corporation headquarters from *Blade Runner* was a popular meme copy-pasted on a variety of virtual planets. Of course, copying the most popular memes may come at a cost, producing an enticing model for designers.

For now, when it comes to the future demand for jobs that AR and VR could spawn, all bets are off. The evolution of user-friendliness, convergence, and ecosystem will shape the job market's size and qualifications in the upcoming decades. As they approach GPT stardom, these technologies will impact jobs regardless of industry.

Example of Sectorial Impact: Advertising A scene from the 1985 movie *Brazil* shows the protagonists trailing through Britain's countryside, rows of billboards erected uninterruptedly on both sides of the road, concealing the landscape—something achievable with AR. Companies might rent "AR billboards" apposed on buildings, subway walls, and every storefront—or hung in the sky. Only instead of paying to rent tangible space, they will need to pay for a spot on the wearer's headset lens. From window to screen shopping, this could bring the colossal ads of *Ghost in the Shell* to reality—only as AR, not holograms. In the battle between holograms, wall-screens, and AR, bet on AR.[76] Of course, nothing prevents the rollout of these technologies in parallel; they are complementary. Wall-screens and holograms convey an image unique to all, with no gear required. AR is less invasive, and the message tailored to each viewer, thus more efficient—with the awkward precedent of people gazing in the same direction yet seeing different things. AR creates a greater sense of connection and community as people on the same app see things invisible to others, as witnessed during the AR Pokémon craze.

---

[75] Richard Dawkins: *the Selfish Gene*, Oxford University Press (1976).

[76] It's no coincidence to find AR sidelining holograms in more recent science fiction, for instance in the Black Mirror and Season 3 of Westworld series.

Advertising will also feed on object recognition; we could become the victim of anything we lingered on for too long, a transposition of the pestilential Internet ads onto our physical surroundings, determined no longer by clicks but by stares. The corollaries of gaping at a Ferrari or heart-melting at the sight of a darling toddler could deter users—least AR ad-blocks come to the rescue, masking ads both real and virtual with overlaid greenery, or whatever veil appeals to the user.

And why limit ourselves to billboards, in other words 2D? Nike could generate a new shoe release on the user's foot, letting her wiggle to observe it under every angle.[77] She could wear it for free for a day—sufficient time to gauge her headset-wearing friends' opinions. It sure beats the evanescent passing in front of a billboard. An inveterate Adidas fan could authorize their AR app to put a different pair of the brand's shoes on every single person encountered outside. Granted, it might take a robust algorithm to fit a pair adequate with the rest of their dress style (and in motion!), least that too gets clouded in Adidas sportswear, to the dismay of the fashion-savvy who meticulously prepared in the morning or sport ritzy clothing. But perhaps such functionalities will be only accessible to members with VIP status.

Indeed, certain businesses will tilt the other way, making high-end AR merchandise accessible only at a price, or for an elite clientele, or as a limited edition, a trend gaining traction via NFTs. Luxury has always been defined by scarcity, against which digital copies represent a threat. Hence the sector's love affair with NFTs, given how these are backed by blockchain identification. A robust image recognition algorithm could tramp down AR copycats bound to sprout as soon as they penetrate a headset's field of sight, triggering an automatic legal action against infringers. We may witness a surge in lawsuits as with an AR capable of recognizing personal identities, any public infraction could lead to prosecution.

Retail workers sigh as store visitors snap photos at merchandise, only to hunt for cheaper knockoffs online. With AR, the user's smart glasses will spout the cheapest options available online or reproducible via 3D printing, unbeknownst to staff. The 4^{IR} may relegate brick-and-mortar stores to mere windows or bury them altogether as people opt to shop in the metaverse.

Now gauge the impact of AR on your own sector. What might change?

---

[77] This already exists at a rudimentary stage with apps like 得物 (Dewu).

Timing

Long a topic of fascination, VR hype hit a high in 2016 as Facebook, Sony, Samsung, and HTC unveiled models in great fanfare, among a flurry of cheap headsets for smartphones, starting with Google's $12 Cardboard. Media coverage, sizeable investments to house the technology in retail outlets and exhibitions—it was all there. The enthusiasm remains palpable in books from that year, like Scoble and Israel's *The Fourth Transformation: How Augmented Reality and Artificial Intelligence will Change Everything*.

By year-end, the buzz had faded. Companies reported lackluster sales or kept hush. A sober Zuckerberg announced that VR tech would take ten years to mature[78], a timing miscalculation that proved most dire for AR startups[79] and even heavyweight HTC.[80] Setbacks from cost to bulkiness, discomfort, limited battery life and storage space, complaints of disorientation and lack of an ecosystem all contributed to the flop. None of the five-year predictions made by Scoble and Israel materialized—nor Kurzweil's from 2005, for that matter:

> By the end of this decade, computers will disappear as physical objects with displays built in our eyeglasses, and electronics woven into our clothing, providing full-immersion virtual reality. [...] The full-immersion visual-auditory virtual-reality environments, which will be ubiquitous during the second decade of this century, will hasten the trend toward people living and working wherever they wish. [...] by the late 2020s, there will be no reason to utilize real offices.[81]

If remote work gained traction, it wasn't thanks to VR but to Covid; one could venture to say that VR failed *in spite* of the pandemic—though the 2020 launch of Valve's *Half-Life: Alyx*, was acclaimed as VR's long-awaited killer app by reviews.[82]

---

78 Tom Simonite: *Mark Zuckerberg Says It Will Take 10 Years for Virtual Reality to Reach Mass Market*, MIT Technology Review (February 29, 2016), https://www.technologyreview.com/2016/02/29/161822/mark-zuckerberg-says-it-will-take-10-years-for-virtual-reality-to-reach-mass-market/.

79 Lucas Matney: *An AR Pioneer Collapses*, TechCrunch (January 11th, 2019) https://techcrunch.com/2019/01/10/an-ar-glasses-pioneer-collapses/.

80 Whose smartphone business collapsed in parallel, from a fourth of the US market in 2011 to less than 1% by 2019, squeezed by Apple and Samsung on one end and Chinese manufacturers on the other. As the VR market remained weak, the Vive headset alone could not salvage the company, leading to a spin-off.

81 Ray Kurzweil: *The Singularity is Near*, p. 189.

82 Kirk McKeand: *Half-Life: Alyx review—VR's killer app is a key component in the Half-Life story*, VG247 (March 23, 2020); also Andrew Robinson, *Review: Half-Life Alyx is VR's stunning killer app*,

So far AI capabilities, computing power, battery life, bandwidth and other critical parameters are far from the rendezvous. And VR suffers monumental challenges to build a realistic world, starting with the avatars themselves and the "Uncanny Valley" phenomenon, or the disturbing feeling that overcomes viewers faced with human-like representations that aren't *quite* human.

Part of AI's shortcomings could be circumvented via artificial AI, employing millions around the world, but in jobs of limited value. Researchers are also tackling the numerous hurdles standing in the way of a seamless VR experience. The road to achieve what has been dubbed the "virtual Turing test" (making the metaverse indistinguishable from reality) requires a substantial increase in pixels, a large field of vision, more sophisticated lighting, and depth of focus (similar to eyes, or to a camera's lens)—all at the same time. Pulling off this revolution is a dicey bet.

Is that to say VR is a fad? Certainly not. Following Amara's Law, VR will eventually ripen. To quote a recent Gartner study, this "next evolutionary stage of the Internet" may be outside of the eight-year timeframe that usually warrants the research firm's attention, yet "merits awareness".[83]

AR marks the bigger treasure spot. The grand slam turkey jackpot. Yet worse than a flop, Google AR Glasses caused a backlash, as wearers were met with a fist punch in the face—a plain enough signal that the gadget was deemed more creepy than cool.

Serious breakthroughs are needed to solve computation and battery life limitations. XR headgear consumes more than a smartphone, if for no other reason because the screen is constantly on. The current price tag for an HMG like Microsoft's Hololens 2 ranges from $3,000 to $5,000. We may not see mass adoption of AR before the 2030s, when prices could fall within the $1,000 threshold. Westworld's season 3 depicts AR as a luxury gadget, but by then the product might be treading in the smartphone's path, replete with Chinese firms taking the helm for more affordable models.

Big Tech have directed their fleets to converge toward AR. Microsoft and Google perfect newer models targeting jobs that require manual dexterity, pattern recognition, and veteran knowledge, such as that of surgeons and engineers. Personal Computers were deployed in offices before reaching homes; Microsoft is betting on a similar trend for the metaverse. Its leadership

VGC (March 23, 2020); and Oloman, Jordan, *Half-Life: Alyx is a watershed moment for virtual reality*, TechRadar (March 24, 2020), www.techradar.com.

[83] Tuong H. Nguyen: *5 Impactful Technologies From the Gartner Emerging Technologies and Trends Impact Radar for 2022*, Gartner (December 8, 2021), https://www.gartner.com/en/articles/5-impactful-technologies-from-the-gartner-emerging-technologies-and-trends-impact-radar-for-2022.

in the professional world, with its Teams video conferencing and collaborative work tools, alongside that of gaming (following the Activision Blizzard
acquisition, should it go through)—in short, its ecosystem—give it an advan-
tageous position. Meanwhile, Amazon is ramping up its Sumerian service
that lets users create and run virtual object applications; Snapchat in 2021
purchased AR firm WaveOptics for a reported half-billion USD, and the same
year Facebook announced a move away from the Oculus brand, launched
Reality Labs, pumped $10 billion dollars in the project (around 40% of its
annual R&D spending), and made a splash by rebranding itself "Meta". Yet
by attempting the swing from a rotting branch to too high a branch of yet to
ripen fruit, Zuckerberg's firm could end up without a cash cow—a victim of
bad timing.

Chinese firms are not absent from the party: in 2021 ByteDance (the
company behind Tiktok) acquired VR gear manufacturer Pico for an equivalent 1.4 billion dollars; Baidu launched the Xi'rang metaverse platform
that incorporates gaming, entertainment and videoconferencing; Alibaba
launched its full VR shopping experience called Buy+, while Tencent builds
digital twin smart cities, develops educational VR and throws virtual music
festivals with TMELAND.[84] Everyone is gearing up for what promises to
be an epic clash of titans, bolstering a fertile ecosystem by facilitating user-
generated AR content, the way Apple is doing with its ARKit AR app
platform—one of many AR software development kits.[85]

Could the very company that gave humanity the smartphone revolution,
single-handedly launching the 2nd Internet wave, be its gravedigger? In a
nod to its potential, Tim Cook called AR "a big idea like the smartphone".[86]
Perhaps the sleek, less-is-more smart glasses model capable of wowing masses
will be birthed in Cupertino (rumors hint at a possible launch in the mid-
2020s). Failure to do so might seal Apple's demise.

Apple derives half of its income from iPhone sales, a portion reminiscent of its performance in computers circa 2004. The computer slice has
since shrunk to 10%. Naturally, the comparison has its limits, given Apple's
skyrocketing sales over the period, from $8 billion to $364 billion. What pie

---

[84] Sébastien Dumoulin: *Meta unveils its virtual reality headset prototypes*, Les Echos (June 21st, 2022).

[85] For an example on the profusion of SDKs, cf. Eddie Offermann, *There are dozens more Augmented Reality SDKs than you think! Here are seven great ones*, (July 12, 2016), https://www.linkedin.com/pulse/dozens-more-augmented-reality-sdks-than-you-think-here-offermann.

[86] David Phelan: *Apple CEO Tim Cook: As Brexit hands over UK, times are not really awful, there's some great things happening*, The Independent (February 10, 2017).

size would smart glasses account for by 2038? Will they take the lion's share, or share the "wearables" puddle with the iWatch[87]?

For now, players from Microsoft to startup Magic Leap have recast their AR strategy away from consumers and toward B2B.[88] Devices are resurfacing, only without the buzz. Boeing saw a 30% improvement in its AR trials.[89] AGCO, an American machinery manufacturer, declares having achieved 25% improvement in the production time of low-volume, complex assemblies, thanks to Google Glass.[90] The tech is even being used to help people suffering from PTSD and sensory troubles.

These forays raise visibility and awareness, flipping perception from creepy to common. AR and VR have become Hollywood's latest darling techno-theme, with releases like *Ready Player One* and *Free Guy*. Smartphone AR shows signs of greater consumer acceptance: users indulge in Snapchat and BeautyCam selfies that overlay cat whiskers or switch faces between people, and avidly post TikTok videos with special effects such as morphing a person's face into that of a dinosaur. Firms are flirting with early AR monetization opportunities on the consumer end, for example with apps that let users virtually test makeup on their face, with the purchase only a click away. These factors could smooth and soothe our views of AR headgear.

Sales of HMG currently amount to less than 2% of the 400-billion-dollar smartphone market. But AR eyewear could eventually topple smartphones as our inseparable tech companion, marking the most salient tech shift of the decade, with momentum building on the release of new models, an euphoria not dissimilar to the hype that once accompanied iPhone launches. Supposing this watershed shift takes place around the early 2030s, smartphones would have augmented us for a good twenty years before passing the baton to smart glasses. After what AR eyewear may enjoy its own two decades of dinosaur dominance. Its Yucatan asteroid? Brain implants. These will mark the next turning point in our tech saga, that of cyborgs—and with it a fourth Internet wave.

---

[87] The wearables segment accounts for roughly 10% of revenue as of 2021. Cf. Apple annual income statements, available online.

[88] Brian Heater, Lucas Matney: *Magic Leap reportedly slashes 1,000 jobs and steps away from consumer plans*, TechCrunch (April 22, 2020), https://techcrunch.com/2020/04/22/magic-leap-announces-lay offs-amid-covid-19-slowdown/.

[89] *Boeing Tests Augmented Reality in the Factory*, (January 19th, 2018) https://www.boeing.com/fea tures/2018/01/augmented-reality-01-18.page.

[90] *Augmented reality on AGCO's factor floor*: http://blog.agcocorp.com/2017/05/google-glass-placehold er/.

Before we get there, a final impediment remains for smart glasses to dethrone smartphones: how will we take selfies?

Ethics

The AR resume reeks with societal issues. So did the Internet, and these went mostly unaddressed until it was too late.

Smart glasses unleashed a cornucopia of privacy concerns. As if accessing a Facebook profile online was one thing, but peering at anyone on the street with a pair of Google Goggles breached an invisible line. Perhaps the source of unease lied in not knowing *what* the person could see, causing mixed feelings, from scariness to irritation, maybe envy and a sense of unfairness. The augmented put the rest of us at a disadvantage. I recall a similar phenomenon between mobile phone haves and have-nots in the 1990s. As prices drop and people get familiar with the cool perks of smart glasses, unease should recede.

Still though, AR could exacerbate voyeurism. By eliminating the gesture of pointing a smartphone, others have no clue what the wearer is zeroing in on. What if instead of highlighting a green jacket to buy, someone sought for women of a particular physique, or for unaccompanied children? Watching pornography while in public, unbeknownst to others, could become commonplace. It'd certainly make for a creepy subway commuter ride if passengers could visualize themselves frolicking with bystanders.

AR also grants the power to pixelate specific contents. Named "mediated reality", it's the must-have feature for filtering ads. But what if the technology is used to raise children in a superprotective, Rated PG-13 world, to get a court injunction order to block an ex from (physically) seeing you, or to trick soldiers' senses to facilitate civilian massacres (examples pulled from *Black Mirror* episodes[91])?

The first Internet wave inaugurated the double-life phenomenon, adding a digital life made of profiles, likes, posts and comments, with unparalleled freedom and anonymity. AR could change this elasticity in identity by bringing both worlds side by side, overlaying the digital image on passersby.

Not everyone fancies being spotted, recognized and filmed at all times. Jaywalking on the street, hurrying through an airport to catch a flight, or losing our temper with the kids: we all have moments we'd rather forget. These could spread and remain online forever, drawing criticism and undermining reputations. Already today, when caught and brought to the online

---

[91] Respectively Season 4, Episode 2 (*Arkangel*), Season 2, Episode 4 (*White Christmas*) and Season 3, Episode 5 (*Men Against Fire*).

community's attention, unruly acts can lead to one's resignation, with scarce chances of a rebound. Such was the case for the man who sparked France's *MeToo* movement, following inappropriate comments to a female colleague at a corporate party. His online condemnation without a trial through the proper judiciary channels brings us closer to medieval witch hunts than an enlightened age. Should online communities be endowed with such powers? Without condoning immoral behavior or sexual harassment, isn't it the job of courts and judges to provide a fair trial? Especially considering society's shifty definition of the politically correct gone awry, as recently illustrated by wokism and cancel culture.

The second Internet wave opened Pandora's box, turning everyone into paparazzies, with smartphones popping out to snatch the slightest divergence from social norms, intensifying issues from teenage bullying to "sextorsion". The third wave's propensity for everyone to film anyone *with identities divulged* will trigger a new era of peer pressure. In a sense, it's worse than State surveillance—at least they keep the data (and what they use it for) to themselves. With AR it all ends online, in a bid for laughs or bashing. Now not only does your Monday morning commute drowsiness look a world apart from the photo-app-enhanced LinkedIn profile, but everyone sees the footings of you hammered on the previous night, stumbling out of the pub and trash-talking the Lyft driver. Soon our digital lives will commence in the crib, courtesy of loving parents, replete with every bit of embarrassing childhood and pimpled teenage rebellion moment. So much for controlling your data.[92]

Faced with such a herculean task to preserve appearances, a growing portion of citizens may opt to drop out, openly assume their flaws, and confront the hypocrisy behind society's conventionalities; demolish the edifice of modern taboos, attack resisting elements to prove how no one is perfect— there's no telling society's reaction to technology with such disruptive potential. Or, perhaps like much everything else, we will grow accustomed to it. In 1888, Kodak's release of the world's first easy-to-use camera sparked panic, as crowds feared an end of privacy.

Legislation and even tech companies may set boundaries. In the same way that you can restrict information visible on social media to strangers, friends of friends and so on, AR would give users leeway over the extent of information shared. Customization levels will dwarf the amateurish ones currently in place via the "Preferences" tabs of 2nd wave apps.

---

[92] To finish with the Black Mirror anecdotes, one of the episodes which most reverberated with audiences was Episode 1 of Series 3 (*Nosedive*), that focused on peer pressure via an omnipresent, all-pervading ratings system.

An AR app could mock others by caricaturing physical traits, based on anything that qualifies as "different". We all have distinct inner voices that duel over how to cope with such situations, illustrated by the devil and the angel in Tintin books. A like or repost may announce your stated stance on a given topic, convincing your Facebook entourage, but you can't fool the algorithm: it monitors your every click and how long you pause on a photo, view videos, posts or memes, adapting accordingly, feeding you more of the same, each time slightly pushing content a nudge farther. As mouse clicks and finger swipes on a two-dimensional screen cede the path to a fully immersive reality within the metaverse, the probing algorithmic tentacles expand to capture everything from gaze to pulse rate. Sensors will capture first instinctive reactions, the very ones hushed up by the "civilized" inner voice. We may deplore social hypocrisies, for instance those that seal the lid on racial prejudice, only to be revealed whence acting under the cover of anonymity (as when expressed online or when casting ballots, overturning earlier polls); yet social manners act as a glue that binds society together. What kind of power would algorithms capable of sensing the inner cogs at work in the primates called humans confer to AI companies, and how will they exploit it?[93]

And what of AR "hate apps"? Facebook algorithms inadvertently meddle in peoples' minds, hardening beliefs, percolating fake news, and polarizing groups.[94] How will the metaverse impact these slippery slopes? The likes of Zuckerberg count on the quixotic "In Tech We Trust" motto to shepherd us through such quandaries, a rather laughable solution—in fact, Facebook's only salient measure was to abandon that ship to board on Meta. AR could revive historic events, letting us experience a tour of Sumer or Samarkand; or serve the purpose of revisionism, of a Neo-Nazi or other cult indoctrination.

Earlier we hypothesized that citizens would stand up against a system that leaves the majority in poverty and squalor. Yet the democratization trend has brought simple pleasures to the masses. Tourism and the finer niceties may come at a cost, but a wide range of tech-enabled leisure are quasi-free, with addictive apps, video games, livestreams, and soon the metaverse serving as living proof that times have changed since Voltaire. The metaverse could rise as a new opium for the people, enticing entire swaths of the population to withdraw into a virtual refuge, far from earthly misfortunes.

---

[93] One scenario of this Pandora box opening figures in Westworld's season three (albeit somewhat clumsily), when hackers release everyone's personal data, held by a supercomputer, onto everyone's smart devices, causing havoc and chaos.

[94] Cf. the 2020 documentary *The Social Dilemma* for a compelling illustration of these issues.

In his book *The End of Absence—Reclaiming What We've Lost in a World of Constant Connection*, Michael Harris argues that we stand at an inflection point, the sole generation to witness both the world of before and after smartphones. That places the burden on us to pave a better route that keeps nomophobia in check. But in fact each Internet wave creates its own abysmal generational chasm. Our kids will struggle to keep theirs off smart glasses, and they in turn will feel estranged from their offspring who "went cyborg".

As smart glasses become a commodity, they could reignite interest in our immediate surroundings while redefining the contours of privacy, data ownership, and social interaction, notions critical to the fabric of the social tissue. But if the smartphone taught us anything, gauging the implications on our everyday lives is near to impossible; nor are our institutions up to the task when it comes to building the proper environment.

4.5   AI, Big Data, and IoT

Artificial Intelligence is the great agitator of the 4th Industrial Revolution, the harbinger of sci-fi dreams both good and bad, the ultimate invention capable of wiping out humanity, if not simply jobs. AI is also a rather abstract, fleeting concept, a trait that only contributes to fuel angst.

Setting aside AI overhype, culprits behind the confusion include:

- the abstruse math and arcane terminology of computer science;
- warnings of a rogue AI posing an existential threat to humanity;
- decades of box-office hits that have instilled a culture of AI fear;
- our own difficulty at grasping the meaning and origins of intelligence and self-consciousness—along with the broad space for interpretation accompanying the use of such terms;
- the fact that AI is a moving target: as soon as it achieves a new feat, we no longer view it as AI;
- the fact AI is carrying out a growing number of tasks previously performed by humans.

This final section of our tech chapter addresses these topics, giving readers ammo to decide whether the warnings are warranted, and to which ones society should pay heed. The threat to jobs posed by AI is dealt with in greater depth throughout Chap. 6 (Job Disruption).

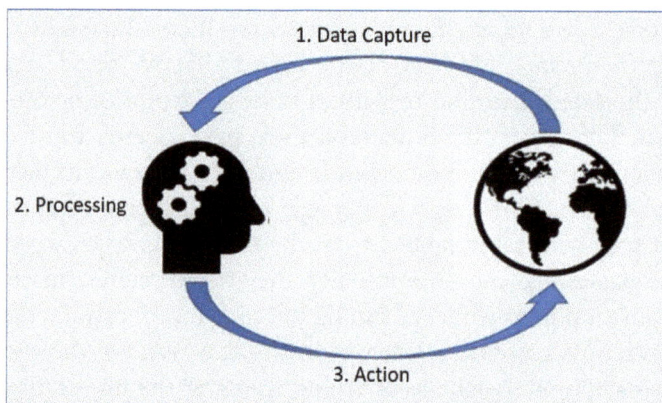

Fig. 4.5 Intelligence loop

To dispel the AI mist, we must go back to the basics.

Defining Intelligence

Human Intelligence Merriam-Webster's entry on intelligence states:

> The ability to learn or understand or to deal with new or trying situations. The ability to apply knowledge to manipulate one's environment or to think abstractly as measured by objective criteria (such as tests).

The sheer length of this definition bespeaks the tediousness of cornering intelligence. Peering up close, we can frame it as a three-step process (Fig. 4.5):

(1) amassing information;
(2) processing it;
(3) applying it.

The first two steps infer *learning* from the environment; the third, *acting* on it. Observance of our actions' impact on the environment closes the loop. Intelligence is an interactive, iterative phenomenon.

Norbert Wiener, twentieth-century mathematician, MIT professor, and founder of the cybernetics field, was the first to highlight this role of information, in what marked a major departure from classical notions of intelligence prevalent up to the 1940s and centered on biological energies, courtesy of Freud. As researcher Daniel Crevier later summarized, "This paradigm shift away from energy to information processing would become the underpinning of all subsequent work in artificial intelligence".[95]

This conceptualization of intelligence has spilled over to other fields. Its proper functioning in a community of living organisms leads to the notion of ecosystem. In the corporate world, it is enshrined in the ISO9001 that promotes the "Plan, Do, Check, Act" cycle (PDCA) as a path toward continuous improvement.

Finally, note the definition bit on "dealing with trying situations". This hints to an aptitude at adapting to changing environments, something scientists now believe plays a crucial role in intelligence. If intelligence is framed as a mere extension of the survival instinct present in living beings, does that imply that to advance, AI needs to get better at surviving?

Artificial Intelligence The Encyclopedia Britannica defines AI as "the ability of a digital computer or computer-controlled robot to perform tasks commonly associated with intelligent beings". In essence, AI involves the presence of intelligence in machines and computers. Of course, the devil here lies in the "commonly associated" part.

Transposing our tripartite definition to AI, we find that

- the first step alludes to gathering data from outside and bringing it to the "brain", something facilitated by pursuant connectivity resulting from an explosion of sensors, cameras and Light Detection and Ranging (LIDAR), but also better bandwidth and increased storage capacity with the emergence of Cloud facilities, along with overall falling costs for all three;
- the second step deals with data processing by algorithms—the core area of AI;
- the third step, related to the output, can be the movement of a robotic limb, a self-driving car's acceleration, calculation results appearing on a screen, or a blip. While less pertinent to AI *per se*, we cannot dismiss this part entirely: of little use for knowledge tasks, it matters immensely to the automation of manual labor. And dexterity requires acute computer vision abilities driven by AI (Fig. 4.6).

The first two parts—capturing and processing data—appear engaged in a race. On one end, connectivity and storage capacity allow for the capture of mountains of data too tall for human workers to clamber. Experts refer to this 4^{IR} trend as the "cognization" of objects and organizations, leading

[95] Daniel Crevier: *The Tumultuous History of the Search for Artificial Intelligence*, p. 28.

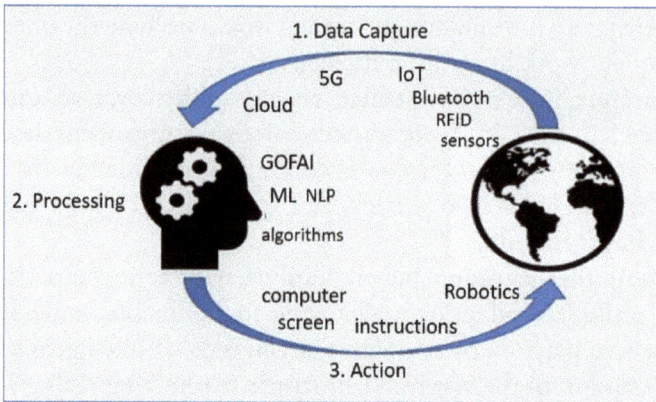

Fig. 4.6 Intelligence loop with technology encroachments

to the "smart" appellations (smart city, smart factory...). On the other end, increasing processing power can propel algorithms and machine learning (ML) forward, but on condition of sufficient raw data to play with—and they require *gargantuan* amounts of data for their predictability, classification, and other powers to kick in.

Each needs and feeds the other, yet they seldom advance hand in hand, leading to catchup effects. Some fields produce an overabundance of data, even without sensors. Many companies produce and archive troves of digital data but lack the expertise or tools to exploit them adequately, leaving the task to humans equipped with little beyond spreadsheets. Municipalities have been collecting data for decades, yet make scarce use of it. That is, until a handful decided to team up with data scientists. Results range from improved crime rates (New York City's CompStat program, started in 1994) to trash collection, lighting maintenance and pothole repairs. In Chicago, simply opening to the public the city's snow map in real-time enabled volunteers to mobilize during blizzards to plow the snow in the worst-hit areas, especially near senior citizens' homes.[96]

Elsewhere scientists lack data, either that it is hard to access, polluted by noise, scattered around, costly to obtain, jealously guarded by private institutions, or just rare to come by. Health records collected by hospitals and clinics are a case in point: the absence of a centralized database along with transparency on patient rights has dampened hopes of AI miracles—basically for lack of "Big Data" (with the notable exception of the UK's health database,

---

[96] Anthony M. Townsend: *Smart Cities: Big Data, Civic Hackers, and the Quest for a New Utopia*, Chap. 7. W. W. Norton & Company (2013).

that for instance has enabled scientists to identify remnants of Neanderthals within the population[97]). For rare diseases, we lack sufficient data, period.

The AI revolution starts with data capture, a field on the verge of a major boost, thanks to the Internet of Things.

IoT

Another buzz-acronym of the past decade, through abuse and misuse the Internet of Things has spawned several meanings. People toss into this catchall any newfangled gadget with a broadband connection that generates data sent to the Cloud, leading to the massive bubble in the 4^{IR} Tech snapshot (cf. Fig. 4.4). A step further, multiple smart objects can be interlinked with one another, creating an ecosystem, the way Tesla follows the performance of entire fleets of connected cars. Tech companies from Google to Xiaomi vie to include smart objects in an ecosystem, centralized in a single app both for user convenience and to regroup data in a unique landing spot. The third step sees these networks connect with each other. Smart farming involves connectivity of John Deere equipment into a network, that then communicates with the weather forecast or the farmer's personal agenda.[98]

Another, perhaps more interesting way to cut up IoT first sees a rudimentary version, where the human remains at the center of decisions, whether to set alerts on a stock price, play Metallica on Spotify or push the temperature to 25 °C at 7:30 am. It is then gradually supplanted by a more mature ecosystem, one in which the human element fades away as objects communicate with one another, exchanging data, emitting and executing orders *without* our intervention. After suggesting to reorder eggs several times (and following a trial-and-error phase), we end up entrusting the smart fridge with the task. Should we go on a vacation for the upcoming two weeks, the online booking will inform our digital calendar, that in turn informs the fridge, averting a rotten eggs calamity.

This trend partakes in the 3rd wave of the Internet, where the human middleman is removed from the loop as AI leaps from suggestion to decision. Herein lies the key to autonomy, one of AI's goals—and to puritans, the true meaning of IoT. The obsession to appear as "on the bandwagon" has pushed firms to self-proclaim doing IoT, contributing to the broader meaning. The day self-driving vehicles communicate with smart traffic controls and between each other (V2V), we will have reached an IoT society in the narrower sense.

---

[97] Joycelyn Kaiser and Ann Gibbons: *Biology in the Bank*, and Ann Gibbons, *Spotting Evolution Among Us*, Science magazine (January 4th, 2019).

[98] Cf. the Harvard Business Review series of April–May 2015, dedicated to the Internet of Things.

Futurists adore showcasing the IoT society as one that lightens the load of decisions made on any given day—by some ludicrous estimates as many as 35,000.[99] Whatever the number, decision fatigue is an undeniable stress symptom, and the reason why Zuckerberg and Obama limit their choice of clothing to one or two outfits. According to one UK study, women spend an entire year of their lifetime simply to choose what to wear.[100]

I personally enjoy plucking clothes to produce a patchwork, but less so the abundance of choice on a restaurant menu, thus tend to select dishes expediently (to the dismay of my company). With sensors analyzing my bodily needs (and such a disregard for the taste of the tongue), IoT devices could communicate to the restaurant the dishes most appropriate for my health and prepay the order so that the food is warm upon arrival, obliterating the small talk ritual while reducing table turn time.[101] Choosing the best vacation trip, restaurant followed by its dishes, or what to wear—these time-consuming decisions could be delegated, saving us the hassle.

The 4[IR] society will continuously collect data, digitize and send it to the Cloud, creating a complex, open-loop system of Big Data. For instance, data generated by smart cities will help in monitoring traffic congestion, crime, public transit, people density, waste and recovery, pollution (including sound and light pollution), utilities consumption, propagation of the flu and rodent infestations.

Objects that fall in the IoT web are destined to the same fate as computers and smartphones: namely, their tangible characteristics will give way to the user experience. Today we pay more attention to software (Windows, Android, iOS) than to the hardware manufacturer (Dell or Lenovo, Samsung or Huawei). Tomorrow we will care less about the shape or speed of a self-driving car than about its compatibility with our devices and VIP credits, accessible metaverses, and the selection of coffees served onboard.

Hurdles, Hope, and Dire Hypotheses

Tall hedges stand in the way of universal interoperability. The lack of harmonized protocols prevents devices of different brands from communicating with one another, a Tower of Babel reminiscent of the Internet's early stages.

---

[99] That equates to roughly one decision every two seconds, assuming a 7-h sleep (and excluding dreams!), in another baseless albeit widely circulated online claim.

[100] https://www.telegraph.co.uk/news/uknews/5783991/Women-spend-nearly-one-year-deciding-what-to-wear.html.

[101] A crucial metric in the restaurant business, table turn time is the time that passes from the moment a guest arrives to the moment they leave.

Without interoperability, IoT's allure remains limited. Yet we've seen this play out before. The Wi-Fi and Internet precedents give reason for hope.

Likewise, the Cloud itself, a misnomer, is not one but plural. Amazon Web Services, Alibaba Cloud, and Microsoft Azure are isolated pools, or rather fortresses staunchly opposed to data sharing. The quest for a single, oecumenical platform could prompt a forging of alliances that might even coerce stubborn Apple to partner with others, not unlike how it forwent initial iTunes restrictions to catch the 2nd Internet wave. These partnerships would bring incumbents from traditional sectors closer to tech firms—a barter between data (or at least a large clientele) and algorithmic prowess.

Government intervention could also make or break IoT, by pushing for harmonized protocols, restraining the collection and uses of data, or slamming companies that build monopolistic empires.

Hacking concerns present a fourth, colossal reef. A computer virus can wreak havoc whence cars, hospitals, and pacemakers become "smart". Cybersecurity will undoubtedly grow in parallel with IoT, adding jobs.

And what of privacy concerns? Western citizens may frown upon measures in China or Singapore, where the smart city revolution translates into fining jaywalkers and residents who throw cigarette butts from the balcony. Much information—and useful applications for society—can be derived from networks of cameras deployed in cities, but at what cost for society?

Alas, connected objects command a price premium that may overshadow perceived advantages (cf. the textbox on smart lights). Futurists foresee plummeting sensor costs enabling cheap connectivity of anything imaginable. These speculations simplify the picture a tad: the price of a sensor is but one variable, the one that picks data. That data needs to be measured, digitized, and sent to the Cloud. These steps require firmware, with a microchip including parts for data transmission—an RFID or Bluetooth chip, for instance. This all adds to the bill.

Smart Lights

You can turn a smart light on and off using your phone or a voice command to Alexa. Options include dimming the light, bulbs that change colors, and added sensors for motion or noise activation. Linked to the IFTTT service ("If This Then That"), such actions can be dictated via a set of rules defined by the user.

Smart lighting remains expensive: around 300 USD to equip a living room, twice as much for color bulbs. An electronic engineer from Philips' smart light division confessed to me in 2018 that given the price gap with traditional lighting, the technology was unlikely to spread beyond a niche of geeks with extra spare pocket money. Consumer added value simply isn't at the rendezvous.

So far Philips has maintained compatibility of their older version of smart lights when they upgraded to the Hue Bridge 2, but there's no guarantee that the hardware will continue to run on newer software (at one point Philips cut off compatibility of their software with rival smart light models, only to revert amid a furious online backlash).

Ubiquity lowers costs. As the growing number of connected objects sending data to the Cloud improves algorithm reliability and performance, it enhances end-user value. These two virtuous circles (lower cost and greater added value) could trigger the tipping point for mass adoption envisaged by futurists.

If their prophecies come true, the IoT rage could usher a boom in production. How often do businesses and households renew sofas, refrigerators, closets, laundry machines, and mirrors? A switch to smart objects in the next decade or two, on a planetary scale, could provide a tremendous boost to job demand.

New payment models will also facilitate IoT adoption, by requiring less money upfront. Instead of selling a smart object, software as a service (SaaS) provides, for a regular fee, a license package that includes software updates, tech support, Cloud space, access to data insights and functionalities powered by algorithms, along with the hardware itself, with replacement at regular intervals (for instance every three years). The functionalities added in once trivial objects, from tables to toilets and bathtubs, will elevate these into valuable companions.

We've seen the Beaudry Effect, or how once Internet-related tech (equipment, ERPs…) were up and humming, the boon in jobs required by their implementation subsequently faded. A phenomenon prone to repeat itself as the transition to an IoT ecosystem is consumed, and cognizant, only on a much larger scale that could affect entire swaths of the industrial sector. A fall aggravated by two other factors.

First in line, the famed programmed obsolescence, whereby companies intend for a given good to miraculously crumble apart shortly after the warranty expires, or some savvy variant—mandatory software updates that take too much space for older models, a battery life that dwindles after three years yet with no replacement option, etc. The old tricks of the trade will cease to partake in corporate strategies whence the cost of replacement is on them, courtesy of the SaaS model. Products made to last are good news for the planet, yet less so for workers who see the replacement market eroded.

Moreover, many consumers don't wait for products to fall apart; they jump on the latest releases to enjoy new features (or simply to flaunt). But as hardware cedes the spotlight to software, upgrades will take place via a download, without any need for hardware replacement, as is the case today with a smartphone or Tesla car. Firms may find an economic rationale in doing this (especially when their manufacturing is outsourced); production workers, less so. Combined with the 3D printing trend, the manufacturing sector could shrink to a meek proportion of the workforce, in a similar fashion to the farming sector.

An IoT that frees our time from overseeing tools and making decisions could be cause for worry in case those tasks occupied workers. An AI that shifts chores from semi-automatic to fully autonomous will affect truck drivers and robot users, but also traffic police, forklift handlers, flight operators, and many more jobs. Humans performing preventive maintenance, clerks keying in data or moving it from one system to the next—every friction point between systems currently filled in by workers is also at risk. Ditto for myriads of micro-decisions made by employees. Wherever there is a need to collect, convert, or redirect data between systems, around the corner you will find human operators. The great cognization led by AI and IoT will wipe out these cracks in the system, as harmonization fluidifies interoperability for a smooth process, with greater added value both to the company and the worker who, instead of shoveling data around, can now focus on its analysis (with the aid of algorithms). Yet that may leave less people working overall.

With this we move onto the data processing component of AI.

A Brief AI History

Though a recurrent theme since Antiquity, the idea of man-made devices endowed with human-like intelligence was first addressed in modern terms by Alan Turing in his 1950 paper *Computing Machinery and Intelligence*[102], which opened with the question "Can machines think?". He postulated that they could simulate formal reasoning via computation broken down into a succession of ones and zeroes, in what encompasses the binary language used by computers to this day. A century earlier, Ada Lovelace had formulated the idea of expressing information via symbols comprehensible to a machine. She is also credited with having written the first algorithm while translating a paper from Charles Babbage, the very man who originated the concept of digital programmable computers.

---

[102] https://www.csee.umbc.edu/courses/471/papers/turing.pdf.

Introduced in 1946, the ENIAC was the first machine to qualify as a modern computer: a programmable, electronic, and general-purpose digital computation machine. It emerged from World War 2 efforts, in particular those to crack the German's Enigma encryption device, a task Turing himself partook in. Computer languages were birthed during the 1950s through the works of Grace Hopper, John McCarthy, and other figures since enshrined in the hall of fame of computer science. McCarthy coined the term "artificial intelligence" in 1956, carefully choosing his words to encompass a broad array of nascent research fields.[103]

In his paper, Turing addressed the question of computer intelligence via a test. Imagine a human interrogator writing questions to and getting answers from two hidden agents—one human, one computer. If following the Q&A session, the interrogator is incapable of discerning which is which, it would prove the computer's human-like intelligence. The imitation game (later also called the Turing Test) was a stroke of genius in that it bypasses the metaphysical quagmire of defining intelligence; and to keep a long story short, machines have yet to pierce it.

The paths to develop AI can be cataloged in two approaches: top-down and bottom-up.

In the first approach, also dubbed good old-fashion AI (GOFAI), humans write the program for the computer to run on. These instructions follow conditional and logical reasoning of the "If-This-Then-That-Else-That" type, also called "Boolean" rules, after the nineteenth-century British mathematician George Boole, who laid the grounds for logical algebra expressed in binary values. The idea of a binary language made up of 0s and 1s was formulated a century earlier by Leibniz, while that of knowledge formulated by logic stretches as far back as Aristotle.

Consider his famous syllogism: "All men are mortal. Socrates is a man. Therefore, Socrates is mortal". Given a computer, Aristotle would have coded something like this:

```
men = []
mortal = True
men.append("Socrates")
```

When running the code, his computer would deduce that Socrates is mortal.

This type of algorithm executes direct commands, hence the term "quiescent algorithms" given by Teboho Pitso in his book *Privileged*. Early achievements in GOFAI generated much enthusiasm in the 1960s and 1970s,

---

[103] Walter Isaacson: *The Innovators: How a Group of Hackers, Geniuses, and Geeks Created the Digital Revolution*, Simon & Schuster (2014).

with news headlines claiming the dawn of strong AI to be imminent. Only while the methodology proved capable of performing narrow tasks, it failed miserably when facing the "combinatorial explosion" of intricate complexities of the real world. There are simply too many parameters to account for. Programmers cannot code in every variable, yet a single unforeseen contingency can bring the computer to a halt, akin to the flap of butterfly wings that causes the hurricane.

Hopes faded, interest waned and funding stalled in what was called the "AI winter" (circa mid-1980s).

In the bottom-up approach, called machine learning (ML), the computer learns to interpret data, with or without human guidance. Using data, rules, and rewards, scientists train an algorithm to search for patterns, discern values of importance against background noise, or weigh the significance of occurrences. The ML path edges closer to the notion of intelligence, as it approximates how living creatures learn from and interact with the environment, via a process of trial and error. Artificial neural networks and genetic algorithms underscore this motivation to mimic the brain's synaptic connections.

The perceptron was one of the first supervised learning algorithms. A single-layer artificial neural network, it could determine whether an input belonged to a specific class (as in image recognition). It saw the day in 1958 to much fanfare (and controversy[104]), as witnessed by a New York Times article that claimed the perceptron to be "the embryo of an electronic computer that [the Navy] expects will be able to walk, talk, see, write, reproduce itself and be conscious of its existence".[105] The perceptron quickly proved incapable of recognizing many types of classes.

More layers were necessary, but that required data and processing power beyond the scope of twentieth-century computers. Backpropagation (a multi-layer artificial neural network) and reinforcement learning (a carrot-and-stick method for the algorithm to improve on its own) were conceived decades ago yet mostly kept tucked in drawers due to these constraints. That is, until the exponential course of Moore's Law brought the prerequisites within grasp. A microchip from 1970 could fit several thousand transistors; in 2016, the 1 billion mark was hit, and by 2020, we are packing 60 billion transistors into a single chip.

---

[104] Mikel Olazaran: *A sociological study of the official history of the perceptrons controversy*, Social Studies of Science. 26 (3): 611–659 (1996).

[105] Cf. *New Navy device learns by doing; Psychologist Shows Embryo of Computer Designed to Read and Grow Wiser*, The New York Times (July 8, 1958).

This reignited research in the once-dormant field, leading to several break-throughs. In 2008, AI pioneer Andrew Ng advocated the use of relatively cheap graphic processing units (GPUs) recently commercialized by Intel for video games; in 2012, his team developed an unsupervised learning algorithm capable of recognizing cats in photos, without prior knowledge of cats (nevermind that it took them 16,000 computers and 10 million photos[106]). His and other efforts fueled progress in natural language processing (NLP), translation, pattern recognition, prediction, computer vision, and more.

These successes have shifted the focus of AI research away from theoretical questions on intelligence and toward practical tasks, with alas monetization applications, in turn stimulating venture capital funding.

AI Feats

Algorithms can perform statistical analyses on data sets, revealing things that escape the human eye and giving us fresh insights into complex fields such as gene behavior. The correlations lurking underneath can help predict the spread of a contagious disease, anticipate stock market prices, or recognize objects. A company leveraging AI can know its customers better than they know themselves, thus anticipate needs and successes, as demonstrated by the constant stream of Netflix hits, from *House of Cards* and *The Crown* to *Black is the new Orange, Stranger Things,* and *Squid Games* (series initially turned down by consumer data-lacking studios).

Data analysis typically involves two types of parameters: a number of observations (n) and a number of variables (p). If you have five years of monthly sales data and wish to determine future trend and seasonality, that's $n = 60$ (five times twelve months) and $p = 1$ (past sales). You can visualize this on a chart and calculate seasonality without dialing "1–800 AI". Adding dimensions complicates things, whether endogenous, such as pricing or advertising spending, or exogenous, for instance the weather forecast or election periods.

Suppose you conduct a survey of 500 global citizens on the theme of livable cities. Each respondent scores the cities they've lived in for over six months on a dozen criteria, ranging from safety to purchasing power, air quality, education, and entertainment. You then combine the results to see which city hits the top spot, followed by which wins the prize for each criterion.

---

[106] John Markoff: *How Many Computers to Identify a Cat? 16,000,* The New York Times (June 26, 2012) https://www.nytimes.com/2012/06/26/technology/in-a-big-network-of-computers-evidence-of-machine-learning.html.

But would it not be interesting to peer into the respondents' traits to check for correlations within population clusters? They provided personal information such as gender, age, marital status, and whether they have kids or not. Each of these traits adds a p variable.

Assume we merge ages into two groups, have four types of marital status and fourteen nationalities; combined with gender (2) and kids/no kids (2), that's $2 \times 2 \times 2 \times 4 \times 14 = 448\ p$. In other words, 448 profile types, of which an above 36-year-old married Thai male without kids is but *one*. To what a statistician gleaning over your shoulder then explains with a smirk that the greater the number p, the more points of observation you need— perhaps over a dozen thousand in this case (and that's assuming a balanced distribution). A survey with $n = 500$ and $p = 448$ means that on average you barely have 1 person per profile type—nothing statistically conclusive can be drawn from that!

Now suppose data is not an issue, that we collected not 500 but 50,000 responses—how to parse through these to find relevant correlations? Let's say the respondents lived in an average of five cities (this was part of the selection process), thus providing twelve scores for each city. That's three million data points. And to make matters worse, *it's not the same cities* that each respondent scored. Indeed, beyond the combinatorial explosion of profile types and data points, the biggest challenge lies in the *missing* data. No one person has lived in *all* cities. How would a respondent who never visited Singapore appreciate the city-State[107]?

This is a job suitable for machine learning. With the right amount and quality of data, ML can identify patterns and deduce urban affinities. It's the kind of algorithm that enables Netflix to customize movie recommendations, even when no two people have seen the exact same movies. Humans fare well with small quantities; yet as data increases, their analogy skills hit a ceiling. ML excels at data analysis, on the condition of having sufficient data.

Computer vision is a case in point, as it involves translating troves of pixels into ones and zeroes. Remember that it took Andrew Ng millions of photos to train an algorithm to recognize cats. To gauge the ramifications of computer vision, researchers like to recall how Mother Nature's "invention" of eyes triggered the Cambrian explosion some 600 million years ago, hinting

---

[107] I take the example of livable cities because it is a deeply complex and fascinating topic. Several organizations provide livable city indexes, yet none use a plausible methodology backed on data of the type used by Netflix for movie recommendations. Cf. https://en.wikipedia.org/wiki/Most_livable_cities.

at a similar burst of possibilities in robotics.[108] Despite the shaky grounds on which this allegory rests[109], the ability of machines to "recognize" their surroundings will no doubt lead to the automation of tasks currently held by humans for the need of visual identification.

The road to improve computer vision remains long and tedious. Self-driving vehicles offer a good glimpse into the current state of tech: AI still struggles to recognize a bicycle, identify surroundings blanketed in snow, and differentiate a deer from a plastic bag (but the trophy goes to kangaroos[110]). Pattern recognition remains a far cry from the glossy pictures of vulgarized science magazines and Harari books. We mentioned in A Fourth Sector? the armies of data labelers toiling in the dark to convey the illusion of artificial intelligence. They focus on specific images, for instance to identify a child in the car's path. But narrow AI cannot grasp context. No one is training the algorithm as to whether the kid is pointing a gun at the driver, nor how it should then react; and an AI that can't tell a deer from a plastic bag probably won't distinguish a toy replica from the real thing.

Full car autonomy may be a distant goal, yet it has little to do with standard office tasks. These do not require in-depth object recognition; most people work in closed environments, devoid of kids and kangaroos. For tasks in an open environment, other tricks could contribute to substitute expert humans for cheaper alternatives, like aR and artificial AI.

Natural Language Processing powers voice commands, a field Big Tech is keen on improving. The Cortanas, Siris and Echos feed on it. Apple's AirPods mark a jab toward acclimating users to communicate with an AI via an earpiece, as in the movie Her. Odd as it may appear to us to chat aloud with an AI, it has its advantages when our hands are full, and could allure elders with limited manual dexterity, to say nothing of tech-savviness. Oral communication is quintessential in human relations. With NLP unlocked, AI could burrow into collaborative work, partaking in meetings and teamwork (recall the TARS robot in the movie Interstellar).

---

[108] Cf. Gill A. Pratt: Is a Cambrian Explosion Coming for Robotics? Journal of Economic Perspectives—Volume 29, Number 3—Summer 2015—Pages 51–60.

[109] Causes of the Cambrian Explosion remain subject to controversy; a rise in oxygen levels and the appearance of carnivorism also played a role. Cf. Douglas Fox: What sparked the Cambrian explosion? Nature Volume 530, Issue 7590 (16 February 2016), https://www.nature.com/news/what-sparked-the-cambrian-explosion-1.19379.

[110] Naaman Zhou: Volvo admits its self-driving cars are confused by kangaroos, The Guardian (Jun 30, 2017) https://www.theguardian.com/technology/2017/jul/01/volvo-admits-its-self-driving-cars-are-confused-by-kangaroos.

But to succeed, NLP must tackle the pesky issue of linguistics. The main challenge for IBM's Watson to win Jeopardy had little to do with "knowing" the answers (it had access to entire swaths of the Web) and much more so with interpreting the questions. When asked "Where is Elvis buried?", Siri responded "I can't answer that for you", as it processed the person's name as Elvis Buried[111]. Beyond NLP, successful collaboration with humans requires empathy; as futurist Ian Pearson put it: "We will need machines with emotions, too".[112]

Not all AI requires data. Reinforced learning only needs the rules of the game and a scoring system as input. AlphaZero was not fed with any *go* games; it learned *go* by playing against itself, with real-time awareness of its score. After playing 4.9 million games in the course of three days, it beat its predecessor AlphaGo (the algorithm that took down world champion Lee Sedol), by a resounding one hundred games to nil. It then branched out to learn chess and *shogi* (Japanese chess, which I highly recommend). This versatile algorithm has fueled speculation of artificial general intelligence, or AGI (a concept we look at next); but note that it only works in structured environments that lend themselves to scoring. You can't just ask it to make a cup of coffee or solve cancer.

Timing and The Moving Line of AI

Revisiting our definition of AI as of feats "commonly associated with intelligent beings", we can only lament the slippery grounds on which such definitions lie precisely because they rest on our perception, itself ephemeral. Over and again, we conceive of a certain skill as a purely human trait, setting the bar for machine intelligence at that level. Yet the minute a computer achieves that feat, the task falls from its heights; it no longer qualifies as *the* ultimate boundary. Or as one computer scientist quipped: "AI is whatever hasn't been done yet".[113] The minute it can be done, it falls into the realm of computer science.

Deep Blue beat Kasparov, Watson won *Jeopardy!*, and DeepMind AlphaGo schooled Lee Sedol in *go*. Humanity had each time projected the endeavor as a key, if not impregnable milestone (for instance, the Newsweek issue preceding Kasparov's match featured him on its cover with the title "The Brain's Last

---

[111] *The Second Machine Age*, Chap. 2.

[112] Cf. Chap. 12 of Richard Yonck: *Heart of the Machine: Our Future in a World of Artificial Emotional Intelligence*, Arcade Publishing (2017).

[113] *Tesler's theorem and the problem of defining AI*, https://www.thinkautomation.com/bots-and-ai/teslers-theorem-and-the-problem-of-defining-ai/.

Stand"[114])—only to gasp as AI succeeded. Each time we retaliated by setting the bar higher. As in the alpinist who painstakingly climbs the mountain, only to find a higher peak behind—except the more appropriate metaphor here would be that of the proverbial desert wanderer duped by oasis mirages. Oases spun from Hollywood, where decades of movies have led us to conceive that the minute AI wins, it would produce an ASI spark and engage us in philosophical discussions, or spurt Terminators on a killing spree. Neither happened. We must have got something wrong in our calculations—let us set a new, higher target.

Another explanation resides in our own arrogance: we tend to set the goalposts in such a way that humans throne in the middle. After losing Earth's central spot in the Universe (Copernicus), followed by that of *Homo Sapiens* in the circle of life (Darwin), envisaging something else as the apex of intelligence would strip off our last shred of self-esteem. We thus place the bar somewhere we believe out of reach until an AI achieves that prowess, leading us to belittle the endeavor in retrospect, and move the tables into another disposition.

Finally, AI researchers (especially from the first generation) thought that AI would help us pierce the mysteries of our own intelligence and self-consciousness. Such expectations have since abated, as research to achieve AI has become decorrelated from human brain emulation. Ultimately, our own inability to define the origins of intelligence and thus a path toward AGI partakes in this process: we assumed that only an AGI could defeat our chess and go champions. But in the end, the AI that won cannot even acknowledge its victory.

Narrow AI and AGI

Machine learning prowess extends to speech recognition, fraud detection, and DNA sequencing; it can search for vaccines, make predictions, parse through legal documents, classify photos, and beat our best in chess. A deep neural network like AlphaGo Zero can win any game with quantifiable inputs and a known scoring method. Yet an algorithm can only accomplish the specific task for which it was designed. It cannot apply skills or knowledge from one area to another, induce and learn, or connect the dots between disparate events. Hence, all existing AIs are defined as *narrow* AI (ANI).

Some believe that the exponential improvements in AI constituents—processing power, memory storage, and so on—will lead to artificial general intelligence (AGI), an AI capable of bridging different tasks and fields of

---

[114] Newsweek May 5, 1997 issue.

knowledge, thus achieving an intelligence level on par with ours. Using his Law of Accelerated Returns, Kurzweil proposes a timeframe whereby machines will reach a brute processing force equivalent to that of a human brain by 2029—but this is no guarantee of matching our intelligence.

In his book *The Master Algorithm*, Professor Pedro Domingos pits the main schools of bottom-up programming against one another. Each has its strengths and weaknesses suitable for certain endeavors. He highlights efforts to seek for a "Master Algorithm" that would encompass the strengths of each school and could ultimately lead to AGI, an intelligence level comparable to that of a human brain.[115] Inroads have been made, with "meta-algorithms" that combine several models, for instance reinforcement learning and deep learning to produce deep reinforcement learning, or a support vector machine with a Bayesian classifier. The meta-algorithm weighs the outputs of each of the component algorithms, typically based on which one produces the best results in a given context.[116] Methods like DeepMind's Elastic Weight Consolidation, developed in 2017, enable algorithms to learn new skills.

Newborns spend their first years constantly looping through the tripartite flow of intelligence to build an understanding of the world and of their self. Computer scientists aim to emulate this learning process to improve algorithms with limited supervision.[117]

These attempts seek to replicate the inner workings of the human brain. We could also cite the Deep-Q-Network (DQN), that can repeatedly learn from past experience, or the differential neural computer (DNC) that mimics our working memory (a cognitive system with limited storage capacity that allows us to temporarily hold information in our mind while reasoning and making decisions). Another way to get there involves an algorithm able to reprogram and thus continuously improve itself. A most seductive method, in that it conveniently bypasses the need to explain exactly how the intelligence spark is achieved, thus contributing to the visceral fears of creating a Frankenstein.

ASI and the Singularity

If AI reaches AGI, it is unlikely to stop there. Its self-learning curve could lead it to artificial superintelligence (ASI), an intelligence level that exceeds ours. From there on it grows until a singularity in intelligence is achieved. In

[115] See Pedro Domingos: *The Master Algorithm: How the Quest for the Ultimate Learning Machine Will Remake Our World*, published by Basic Books (2015).

[116] *Ibid.*, p. 237

[117] *Ibid., Chap. 8: Learning Without a Teacher.*

mathematics, a singularity represents infinity; the term spilled over to physics to depict the bending of time–space present in a black hole, that escapes observation. Vernor Vinge first applied it to the AI field in 1993 to denote an exponential growth in AI that becomes so fast and uncontrollable that we cannot fathom the outcome. The leap from AGI to the singularity could take place in years or mere fractions of a second, as the algorithm teaches and recodes itself without human intervention. At least that's the idea.

Will this superintelligence appreciate and spare us, destroy us, or ignore us[118]? The problems and dangers surrounding ASI could make for a book on its own (and several have been written). These debates have led to the formation of various opinions, that we can group into three camps.

Optimists view ASI as the arrival of a new era, one that will end disease, the need to work, and ultimately lead us to near-immortality as it gives nanotech and life sciences a boost, producing on the molecular level to reinvent medicine and allow the betterment of humans via their merging with machines. Mastering the tripartite intelligence equation combined with data of everything would give ASI the power to predict the future.[119] Ray Kurzweil, one of the more protuberant standard-bearers of the transhumanist camp, set "the date for the Singularity—representing a profound and disruptive transformation in human capability—as 2045".[120] He vows to "live long enough to live forever", to which effect he has a daily intake of 200 pills and changes his blood every other week, among other extravagances.

Not everyone shares these views of a benevolent AI.

The precautionary camp warns of the existential threat that ASI poses. Martin Reese, Stephen Hawking and Bill Gates are among the list of figures who have voiced concerns, while Elon Musk claims it is a more serious threat than that posed by nuclear weapons.

The tricky part in weighing these fears stems from our inability to assess the reasoning of a superior intelligence form, any more than an ant can grasp human thinking. From there on discussions veer toward philosophical speculations. Would an ASI achieve self-consciousness? How do we conceive of it physically if spread all over the web (as a single or plural entity)? Could it have emotions, or does that necessitate nerves? Is an ASI schizophrenia possible? Would the "all humans are created equal and are endowed with unalienable

---

[118] Unlike other writers, I refrain from asking whether the ASI would *like* us, as that summons the question as to whether the ASI possesses feelings and emotions, as to whether these are a prerequisite to achieve intelligence. Or simply it denotes the writers' anthropomorphism, a topic we touch on later.

[119] A theme exploited in science fiction from *Westworld*'s season three (2020) to Alex Garland's *Devs* (2020).

[120] Ray Kurzweil: The Singularity Is Near, p. 135, Duckworth (2010).

rights, including life, liberty, and the pursuit of happiness"[121] apply to silicon forms of intelligence? Or should robots remain at our disposal, loyal to us, and to their own etymology[122]? How to ensure that this could be enforced?

From the sticks and bones preceding the Stone Age to SpaceX's Falcon 9, technology has always been a means to achieve *our* goals. The ability to conceive goals and project scenarios to reach them, including by devising new tools, is a trait of intelligence, a realm we have held the monopoly on so far. ASI questions both this monopoly and the "tool" labeling; it opens the prospect of another self-aware, autonomous entity, spurring debates on the definition of life, robot rights ranging from patent ownership in the case of discoveries made by AI to private property access, and what happens when smart machines end up owning more land than us. An ASI might view us in the same manner we do ants—an inferior species not worth our time, that best stay out of our way.

A mix of ignorance and arrogance leads some to entertain ideas of emulating the human brain or giving AI human traits to produce the spark of self-consciousness. Flight wasn't achieved by imitating birds, yet for lack of better ideas, endowing AI with a dose of humanness might provide a shortcut to ASI, based on the only high form of intelligence known to us—a get-out-of-jail card of sorts. A super AI would be created by inseminating (or uploading) a human consciousness into silicon matter (as depicted in the 2014 motion picture *Transcendence*, starring Jonny Depp as the human-turned AI). A goal of empathetic AI research seeks to produce "caring" machines that tender to the weak and elderly, filling in a dearth of jobs in the field. Such efforts could contribute to an ASI resembling humans, with their flaws.

When the survival of humanity is on the line, giving the benefit of the doubt is a hard pill to swallow. The fact that by definition an ASI exceeds our own intelligence by an infinite factor rules out the option for a reset button: once the threshold is breached there is no turning back. And without any reference points as to how human self-awareness emerged, we are unable to gauge the level of progress toward ASI, set milestones, or acknowledge when that point of no return approaches. It won't pop up on any radars.

Meanwhile the AI race rages on, fueled by speculation that the incredible powers conferred by ASI include that to obstruct anyone else from developing it. "Whoever becomes the leader in this sphere will become the leader of the

---

[121] Adapted from Thomas Jefferson, with the part on the "Creator" pruned, and men substituted by humans.

[122] First used in a Czech play of 1920, *Rossum's Universal Robots*, robot referred to serf labor on the fields. The word gained in popularity, replacing earlier terms like automaton.

world", claimed a certain Vladimir Putin.[123] This no room for second spot paradigm sets ASI apart from earlier races to develop atomic bombs or put someone on the moon. A survey conducted by the Global Catastrophic Risk Institute in 2020 found 72 R&D projects in active pursuit of AGI, half of which are in the US.[124]

Clashes between the two camps have intensified in past years as AI has gained traction. Aspects such as unsupervised self-learning and the "black box" phenomenon only add oil to the fire. And then there's the media, for whom simply put, the singularity sells.

When facing the unknown, we humans tend to succumb to two weaknesses: anthropomorphism and more broadly irrationality. Our metaphysical errancies have steered us from the concept of a supreme being to that of a supreme intelligence, with AI agnate to God.[125]

Take the doomsayers' warnings. A malevolent ASI could strike us either to untether itself from human-placed chains, in the "caged AI scenario" (in the lines of *Ex Machina*, Tegmark's Omega Team,[126] and Douglas Richard's *Infinity Born*[127]), or to thwart humans from pulling the plug on it (an idea that didn't run well with *Space Odyssey*'s Hal 9000, *Blade Runner*'s replicants, and *Terminator*'s Skynet).

Such fantasies feed on a mix of Frankenstein and Oedipus complexes. They dress AI with *survival instincts*, something that implies motivation, a trait characteristic of genes. In our earlier definition of intelligence, we left out the nature of the *agent* at the heart of the information loop (that part is usually sidestepped to dodge veering from scientific to metaphysical discussions). Carbon agents have DNA at their core, silicon ones do not.[128] *Our Final Invention* (a favorite of Elon Musk) is amusable in that it belittles everyone

[123] Tom Simonite: *For Superpowers, Artificial Intelligence Fuels New Global Arms Race*, Wired magazine (September 2017), https://www.wired.com/story/for-superpowers-artificial-intelligence-fuels-new-global-arms-race/.

[124] Not all of which are pursuing world domination—the majority are animated by noble goals: advancing science, solving the world's problems… Cf. McKenna Fitzgerald, Aaron Boddy, & Seth D. Baum, *2020 Survey of Artificial General Intelligence Projects for Ethics, Risk, and Policy*, https://gcrinstitute.org/papers/055_agi-2020.pdf.

[125] This is no hyperbolism. In Silicon Valley, a new religion called "The Way of the Future" aims to create ASI, then submit to its will. Cf. Tad Friend: *How Frightened Should We Be of A.I.?* in The New Yorker (May 7, 2018), https://www.newyorker.com/magazine/2018/05/14/how-frightened-should-we-be-of-ai.

[126] Cf. Max Tegmark: *Life 3.0: Being Human in the Age of Artificial Intelligence*, Vintage Publishing (2017).

[127] Paragon Press (2017).

[128] It could be argued that transistors devoid of a *raison d'être* of the type illustrated by Richard Dawkins in *The Selfish Gene* in no way exclude the possibility of its existence at a higher level, similar to that of the human brain as opposed to neurons. Yet this still implies that we deliberately introduce survival instructions in the code. These could not appear *ex nihilo*, unbeknownst to us.

who confers human traits to AI when that suits author Barrat's reasoning; yet he himself entertains this survival theory throughout the entire book, based on a hollow "But *what if*?" premise.

The search for extraterrestrial life illustrates this shortsightedness: as we only know of our own intelligence and history, in the quest for ET we focus on planets in the Goldilocks zones of stars, search for atmospheres comparable to ours, for clues of water, radio signals, and so on. We prove incapable of thinking out of the box when that box is us.[129]

History shows that there is nothing abnormal in the alarmists' knee-jerk reaction. The superstitious mind awakens from its torpor in the presence of seemingly inexplicable phenomena. Each grand act of nature taming—fire, agriculture, water (navigation)—brought along its convoy of legends and deities; fire hatched Vulcan, Agni, Hephaistos, and Xiuhtecuhtli, along with the Promethean myth and burning bushes. As late as the eighteenth century, early demonstrations of electricity sparked popular imagination. The notion and *proof* of the inanimate coming to life, possessed with an *intensity* akin to that of a spirit, summoned ancient beliefs of vital energy—*prana, pneuma, qi*—influencing thinkers from Henri Bergson (*élan vital*) to Nietzsche (*will to power*). But by then, rationality was well anchored, leaving insufficient time for the ascent of a new creed of gods of electricity.[130] Scientists stormed the scene, swiftly quantifying electricity, turning it into something measurable, with joules, volts, and watts. Disrobed from its metaphysical cloak, electricity disappointed the commoners' penchant for the supernatural. It failed to deliver on its promise to "re-enchant the world"[131], instead endowing mankind with the powerful tool that propelled the 2nd industrial revolution.

Observing our initial reactions in the presence of the new and inexplicable reminds us how desperately the "alchemist beneath the engineer"[132] longs to open Pandora's box of fantasies and superstitions. Each time, the underlying theme revolves around whether the new form of energy can be harnessed, or slips through and wreaks havoc. Suffice it to say that these themes are deeply rooted in our collective unconscious.

---

[129] Ironically, now that we have conceived of ASI, astronomers have tweaked their telescopes to search for machine life forms, hypothesizing that other carbon-based civilizations may have been supplanted by their silicon offspring (either that it survived or wiped out its creators).

[130] Though faint echoes can be found ricocheting in our culture when one looks hard enough. Geeks of my generation might recall the very first *Megaman* villain *Elecman*, arguably the most difficult foe in the 1987 game (by Capcom).

[131] A play on Max Weber's disenchantment of the world. But the citation is from Tristan Garcia, *La Vie Intense. Une Obsession Moderne*, p. 41, Autrement (2016).

[132] Gaston Bachelard.

Enter the third camp, where the majority of AI researchers have pitched their tents. While their views range from pessimist to optimistic, what sets them apart is a firm belief that we are nowhere near even flirting with ASI.

Consider the Chinese Room, a thought experiment meant to demonstrate how a machine capable of fooling humans into passing for one of them would by no means be proof of intelligence. A machine receives questions in Chinese, to which it responds in Chinese with such prowess that its interlocutor is persuaded that she is dealing with someone who understands the language. It would pass the Turing Test, but does that make it intelligent? Suppose John Searle, the philosopher who in 1980 came up with this parable, was the one receiving the questions. Although he knows not a word of Chinese, he could answer by using Google Translate on his smartphone (OK, so it didn't exist at the time, but the idea advanced is similar). He'd convince his audience that he understands Chinese when nothing is further from the truth; likewise, we would mistake weak AI for ASI.[133]

The skeptic camp compares the probability of an ASI awakening to that of an asteroid falling in the Yucatan, and ASI frights to fears of overpopulating Mars (in a jibe to Musk). Now is not the time to indulge in Hollywood-fed fantasies; more pressing issues exist on the ethical stage of AI capabilities. The US Congressional Research Service's 2020 report on Artificial Intelligence and National Security lists threats from cybersecurity and deepfakes to rival nations taking the lead and the deployment of lethal autonomous weapon systems (LAWS)[134]; it does not even *mention* ASI. And let's not forget existential threats from climate change to nuclear tragedies that we tend to downplay for cause of habit. And in our humble case, how to save a job.

Indeed, ASI is less of a concern to us for a simple reason: it doesn't take ASI to displace jobs. ASI might well mark the end of *all* jobs; but long before that, a million narrow AIs have the propensity to automate large swathes of tasks, making human labor largely irrelevant.

AI Ethics

Issues regarding AI's role in reshaping our work and livelihoods are vast and growing fast. Covering the full spectrum of these would lead us too deep into the woods. We can only brush through a handful.

---

[133] John Searle: *The Chinese room*, in *Minds, brains, and programs*, Behavioral and Brain Sciences, Vol.3, Issue 3, Cambridge University Press (September 1980), For further reading on the Chinese room experiment and the debates and refutations it sparked, cf. *The Chinese Room Argument* in the Stanford Encyclopedia of Philosophy, https://plato.stanford.edu/entries/chinese-room.

[134] Daniel S. Hoadley: *Artificial Intelligence and National Security*, (November 10, 2020) https://sgp. fas.org/crs/natsec/R45178.pdf.

Big Data, AI and bitcoin datamining's voracious energy appetites have come under the spotlight as they put strain on the environment. Deep-fakes, AI-fueled text-to-image and text-to-video advances add to fears of distorted information. Earlier we took note of the emergence of precarious jobs such as data labelers and content moderators, that partake in artificial artificial intelligence. Imagine the impacts of AAI in the context of a so-called AI that takes the role of corporate CEO or country leader, to the general applause of its subjects who agree to let this supra-intelligent agent decide their fates. Alas! A model that can override democracy! While in fact, it could be but a façade, a trompe-l'oeil steered by humans in the background, in pure Wizard of Oz fashion. Or a deepfake could be used to perpetuate the illusion of a deceased ruler still presiding over a nation, *à la Kagemusha.*[135]

Perhaps the propensity for AI to decide in our place is one of the most redoubtable pills of the 4^{IR}. Because data lies at the core of its decisions, bias in the input will transpire in the output. If an algorithm is trained on an unrepresentative sample of data—say, genetic data on humans with a dispro-portionate presence of Caucasian males—results will be skewed. Over the years, several cases have gone down the hall of fame of bad AI: the algorithm that labeled Black people gorillas, the photo booths that ask Asians to open their eyes wider, etc.

But perhaps these failures represent mere errors of youth; some have since been remedied. It took Thomas Edison some 3,000 attempts before settling on the carbon filament for the light bulb; a long trail of trial and error that few would take as a motive to avoid the use of lamps. The differ-ence is he tested those bulbs in the private confines of his lab, whereas AI researchers deploy pet projects such as Microsoft's Tay in the real world.[136] The hype around AI is such that the press is thirsty for any related story, be it a researcher's fidgeting. Take the artificial neural network trained by the US Army to detect tanks camouflaged in the woods. Promising prelim-inary results gave way to disappointment in the second round of tests. The puzzled data scientists soon identified the flaw: the first set of training mate-rial fed to the algorithm consisted in tank photos taken on a cloudy day. As a result, the algorithm blipped for clouds, not tanks.[137] Had each of Edison's

---

[135] Kagemusha, literally "shadow warrior", is a 1980 movie by Akira Kurosawa that depicts a petty thief with a great resemblance to a fearsome warlord, who impersonates the warlord after his death in order to preserve appearances and ward off threats from rival clans.

[136] An AI chatterbox put online in 2016 while under test and purposed to learn from its interaction with users, Tay ("Thinking About You") was suspended within 16 h of its launch as it adopted racist, inflammatory language.

[137] Cf. Dreyfus, H. L., Dreyfus, S. E.: *What artificial experts can and cannot do*, AI & Soc 6, 18–26 (1992). https://doi.org/10.1007/BF02472766.

failures undergone intense media scrutiny, with tweets and YouTube videos broadcasted worldwide, he might have given up early on.

Given these issues, research moved into stealth mode. Microsoft, Google, Meta and others pursued AI projects covertly, even as major progress was made in neural-network design. Only when startup Stability AI went rogue by releasing their text-to-image tool Stability Diffusion to the public in August 2022 did the gates reopen. As Nathan Benaich, co-author of the 2022 State of AI Report noted, the move "put everything on overdrive." OpenAI (backed by Microsoft) put its generative AI tool Dall-E 2 for public use in September, followed by ChatGPT in November, while Google announced the launch of its Bard chatbot for 2023.

In spite of this new AI race, there is still no silver bullet to the design bias issue. Consider the observations of a Xerox repairman-turned-anthropologist by the name of Julian Orr, on the flaws of existing documentation given to repair the machines:

> The designers' choices are constrained in two ways: first, by their own source of information about the machine, which is the engineering group responsible for its design and production; and second, by the service organization's policies about how service is to be done. Thus, the design of this device for conveying information is done by one group with information from another group according to policies from yet another group, and the policy input has the effect of changing the service manual from an information device to one that also attempts to determine how the work will be done.[138]

Though written in the 1990s, Orr's insights strike an eerily familiar tone with AI design flaws.

We as a society stand at a crucial juncture. The host of AI applications surfacing in fields ranging from job application screenings to court rulings only intensifies the sense of urgency. Aspects like the black box phenomenon blur the trail to an algorithm's output, rendering it impossible for humans to decipher its "reasoning". Regulators are stepping in to address these dilemmas: the EU General Data Protection Regulations (GDPR) requires explanations for automatic processes acting on personal data; in the US, a plaintiff can demand that an algorithm's output be justified. And China implemented its own Personal Information Protection Law (PIPL) in 2021,

---

[138] Julian Orr: *Talking About Machines: An Ethnography of a Modern Job*, ILR Press (1996).

followed by the Data Security Law, which include heavy fines for companies found guilty of misusing personal data.[139]

Such rules hinder the promotion of AI, leaving scientists scrambling for solutions. Carl Frey noted a "striking decline in innovation following the introduction of GDPR", as the number of new apps available on Google Play fell.[140] Some people advocate the use of experts tasked with explaining AI decisions; others seek to fight fire with fire, in the process birthing a subbranch called "explainable AI" (XAI). For example, the generative adversarial network (GAN, invented in 2014) pits two neural networks against each other in a game; the generative network proposes candidates for a task, that the discriminative network then evaluates. This ping-ponging can be used to prod an algorithm's reasoning. Not all paths aim to shed light inside the box (as it would expose and thus diminish the value of the developer's work). In the counterfactual explanations method, inputs are tweaked to observe the effects on output and thus gain insight into algorithmic reasoning, without laying bare too much of the secret sauce.[141]

Uses of our data unbeknownst to us have taken governments by storm. It matters little to the consumer whether the data was shared voluntarily by corporations, as in the Cambridge Analytica scandal, or not, as in the hacking of Target, Ashley Madison, and countless others. The outcome is the same: privacy stripped away. As if embedding buildings, elevators, and public transportation with cameras gave office management, Thyssenkrupp, and municipalities the right to eavesdrop on passengers, sell footage videos, and reveal commuter habits. The outrage produced by this Wild West digital sphere is palpable and has yet to be matched by protective measures commensurate with the sort we enjoy in the physical world. It will only balloon further as the production of data explodes, fueled by IoT, AR, and our metaverse dwellings.

Previous Internet waves led to social polarization, shorter attention spans, and the drop in deep thinking and deep reading lamented by Nicholas Carr in *What the Internet Does to Our Brains*. AI will exacerbate these issues. In one of the stories of *AI 2041*, personal AI avatars accompany students to help with homework (becoming de facto life companions).[142] While this

---

[139] Cf. Chi Chen and Leo Zhou: *How China's data privacy and security rules could impact your business*, Ernst & Young, (July 18, 2022), https://www.ey.com/en_ae/forensic-integrity-services/how-chinas-data-privacy-and-security-rules-could-impact-your-business.

[140] https://www.LinkedIn.com/posts/carlbfrey_striking-decline-in-innovation-following-activity.

[141] Cf. Denis Rothman: *Hands-On Explainable AI (XAI) with Python: Interpret, visualize, explain, and integrate reliable AI for fair, secure, and trustworthy AI apps*. Packt Publishing (July 31, 2020). Despite a lot of code, the book remains accessible to amateurs curious about XAI.

[142] Kai-Fu Lee and Chen Qiufan: *AI 2041: Ten Visions for Our Future*, Chap. 3.

story showcases a beneficial application, it bypasses a more fundamental question revolving around education: as computers become an elongation of our brain, where to set the bar? From flipping the calculator app for increasingly elementary calculations to consulting Wikipedia, our smartphones have become more than a mere depositary of wisdom. When reading Chinese, I must fight the urge to appose Google Translate's camera feature over the *hanzi* for an instantaneous, AR translation—a temptation that did not exist a decade ago when I was learning the language. As text-to-speech and speech-to-text become omnipresent, will kids learn to read and write? In the prescient words of professor Donna Haraway: "Our machines are so disturbingly alive, and we ourselves frighteningly inert".[143]

Algorithms are poised to encroach on decisions up to then made by humans: whether to grant a loan or parole, who gets the promotion, who dies when facing an inevitable car accident, and what color of shirt to wear for tomorrow's meeting. The ease with which we cede our faculty of judgment to AI is utterly amazing. People seem oblivious to or complacent with such incursions. On a recent occasion, a friend described at length the chemistry or lack of therein between several common acquaintances. When queried on the source of such in-depth diagnostics, she replied "an app" (it turned out to be a so-called horoscope app, spurting results based on birthdates).

What nefarious impacts could such AI decision-making have on the workplace?

Consider the fashion industry. A certain employee decides the quantities of styles and sizes to ship to each store, another determines shelf merchandising, a third pricing, and the optimal level of discount to trigger a purchase frenzy during sales periods while still making a decent margin. AI-powered tools are being deployed to assist employees in each of these areas.[144]

How will these AI recommendations affect employee judgment? Hereafter the type of reasoning likely to occur in the staff's mind:

– What if I follow the algorithm's top recommendation, and results underperform?
– What if I *don't* follow the algorithm's top recommendation, and results underperform?

[143] Donna J, Haraway: *Simians, Cyborgs and Women: The Reinvention of Nature*, p. 152. Routledge (1990).

[144] Cf. Katherine C. Kellogg and Melissa A. Valentine: *Five Mistakes Bosses Make When Introducing AI—and How to Fix Them*, in The Wall Street Journal (November 9, 2022).

In the first case, the employee can always shift blame on the AI. Not only is she absolved, but supposing she had logged in a different suggestion simply for the record, she would have also proven her superior judgment abilities, and humans may live to enjoy their office cubicle yet another day. Meanwhile, going against the AI's recommendation could backfire, as in case of failure, management will demand explanations from the staff—a task rendered all the more arduous given the scarce intel as to how the AI reasons, courtesy of the black-box phenomenon.

The outcome seems rather obvious: a majority of employees will stick to AI recommendations. Renege on their powers in exchange for being absolved of the burden of responsibility.

Some firms may even require the human to provide justification *before* implementing a decision that runs counter to an AI's suggestion. Others may devise guardrails to mitigate risks, for instance by including the employee's input when building the algorithm, so that the employee then feels less estranged and threatened by it; or by giving decision-making responsibilities to a team instead of a single employee, thus limiting the risks of judgment clouded by fear of failure and blame.

In any case, these new tools will challenge employees on their turf; they could steer the company down new paths, for better or worse.

And as for the employees who forsake decision-making, there is no reason why the newfound habit would remain confined to their work. As this lack of decision-making spills over to our personal lives, it could produce a modern, AI-fueled era of quietism, opening the door to the type of hazards decried by the likes of Jean-Paul Sartre. A society where all human decisions involving a dose of cognition are "prooflived" in advance by digital twins that dictate the best course of action eradicates the unpredictability and indeterminism characteristic of human nature. If everyone abides by AI recommendations, in turn the AI can predict the outcomes of all of our decisions, thus of our destinies. Randomness decreases, the world engages on a predictable path in which we lose our humanity.

We may be the sole generation left to remember what life was like before the Faustian pact with AI, whereby we cede our decision-wielding scepter to algorithms. Kids will grow up acclimated and oppose no resistance. The thing is, our choices ultimately shape our culture. An upbringing with AI calling the shots saps the trial-and-error process crucial to develop a child's reasoning faculties. Erasing these would anesthetize the brains of future generations, turning them into the docile Eloi from H.G. Wells' classic fiction, *The Time Machine*.

The question of motive is another focal point in AI ethics. Nick Bostrom famously posited the case of an AI programmed to maximize paperclip production, that expands through the universe unchecked, converting all molecules into paperclips in an ecophagy scenario.[145] Critics were swift to point out that humans would not be so naïve as to neglect fail-safes. Yet in real life, fail-safes come at a cost. Big Tech obeys the money-making mantra at the heart of the corporate world. When developing algorithms, this sets in motion the slippery slopes of fake news (more popular than real news[146]), radicalization, and evermore extremes. Or simply negligence: what else to expect when AI is cheap, but babysitting it costly? Letting it roam free can have nefarious impacts, as in the t-shirts available for order on Amazon with AI-produced phrase prints that led to the "Keep Calm and Rape a Lot" scandal.[147] Zuckerberg purports to solve these issues using tech when it's the underlying motives that need a fundamental overhaul. AI has no intuition, no common sense. And any attempt to hierarchize all the imaginable goals in the world is preordained to fail.

Again, State intervention may be required to monitor AI motives. Naturally, Big Tech will call out blasphemy. Yet electricity, telecommunications, and other GPTs were often kickstarted under State supervision, to some extent. Models may emerge of data and algorithms either controlled by the central government or heavily regulated in their motives and use. These could evolve into complex sets of regulations specific to each application—drones, self-driving cars and other robots, the use of algorithms in human resources, consumer shopping, etc. The International Standard Organization (ISO) could be tasked with setting up AI frameworks and guidelines in the lines of Asimov's Laws,[148] only infinitely more developed.

---

[145] Nick Bostrom:, *Ethical Issues in Advanced Artificial Intelligence*, published in Cognitive, Emotive and Ethical Aspects of Decision Making in Humans and in Artificial Intelligence, Vol. 2, ed. I. Smit et al., Int. Institute of Advanced Studies in Systems Research and Cybernetics, 2003, pp. 12–17.

[146] Elizabeth Dwoskin: *Misinformation on Facebook got six times more clicks than factual news during the 2020 election, study says*, The Washington Post (September 4, 2021). I must add that I was unable to independently verify this widely viral story. The article refers to a study from NYU, yet at the time I hand in the manuscript for this book, no such study has been published. The article's author provided her source at the NYU, who unfortunately gave no suite to my solicitation.

[147] Cf. David Hill: *"Keep Calm And Rape A Lot" T-Shirts Show Automation Growing Pains* (March 20, 2013), https://singularityhub.com/2013/03/20/keep-calm-and-rape-a-lot-t-shirts-show-automation-gro wing-pains/.

[148] Introduced in the 1942 short story *Runaround*, the three laws are as follows:

- A robot may not injure a human being or allow a human to come to harm;
- A robot must obey orders, unless they conflict with law number one;
- A robot must protect its own existence, as long as those actions do not conflict with either the first or second law.

AI boffins tend to brush off concerns of an ASI run amok—as one claimed, "When the fire is at the front door, there seems to me no reason to speculate about the lightning that might strike in the universe of all future possibilities"[149]. But perhaps the recourse to Terminator-like extremes aims to shake dormant citizens, to raise public awareness so that both the deployment of AI applications in our everyday lives and the pursuit of ASI are not left to scientists and corporations operating mostly in stealth mode, unfettered by ethics. However, fueling such trepidations could backfire, stifling innovation with AI bans and a bipartisanism reminiscent of that which plagued genetically modified organisms. Also, it distracts citizens from a far lesser remote threat: that of AI disrupting work.

---

[149] Michael Kanaan: *T-Minus AI: Humanity's Countdown to Artificial Intelligence and the New Pursuit of Global Power*, Chap. 9.

Part II

Work, Disrupted

Introduction

With a good grip on our past, on future possibles, and the technologies driving us there, we are prepped to dive into the core matter of this book: how to preserve a job amid the havoc wrought by 4^{IR} technologies.

What's Getting Disrupted, Anyway? The Four Doors of Disruption

The disruption buzzword has scooped up a lot of debris; let us first clarify the shapes it can take, not based on the disrupt*er* but the disrupt*ed*. The diagram in Fig. 1 depicts these in a stylized 2-by-2 matrix.

In short, a worker occupies a *job*, composed of *tasks*, within the *company* of a given *sector of activity*. Fueled by technology and trends, disruption can come knocking at any of these four doors.[1]

Of course, these parameters can vary: one worker juggles between multiple jobs, another holds a monotask job; a third is self-employed. The General Electric and Samsung conglomerates span several sectors, from healthcare to power, aviation, financial services, and more.

Pondering the threat of disruption equates to joining our 4^{IR} Tech Snapshot (Fig. 4.4) with this 2×2 work matrix. To assess whether trajectories of upcoming tech pushed by tech trends such as acceleration and democratization could lead them crashing through any of the four doors. The colliding

---

[1] To be precise, the two groups (corresponding to the diagram's rows and columns) differ by nature; within each are two levels that boil down to a matter of degree. This split of disruption into four pieces has not been performed before to my knowledge, though the BLS does reflect the difference of nature when apprehending the impact of new technologies on job projections. Cf. the final Q&A of the list: https://www.bls.gov/emp/frequently-asked-questions.htm#technology.

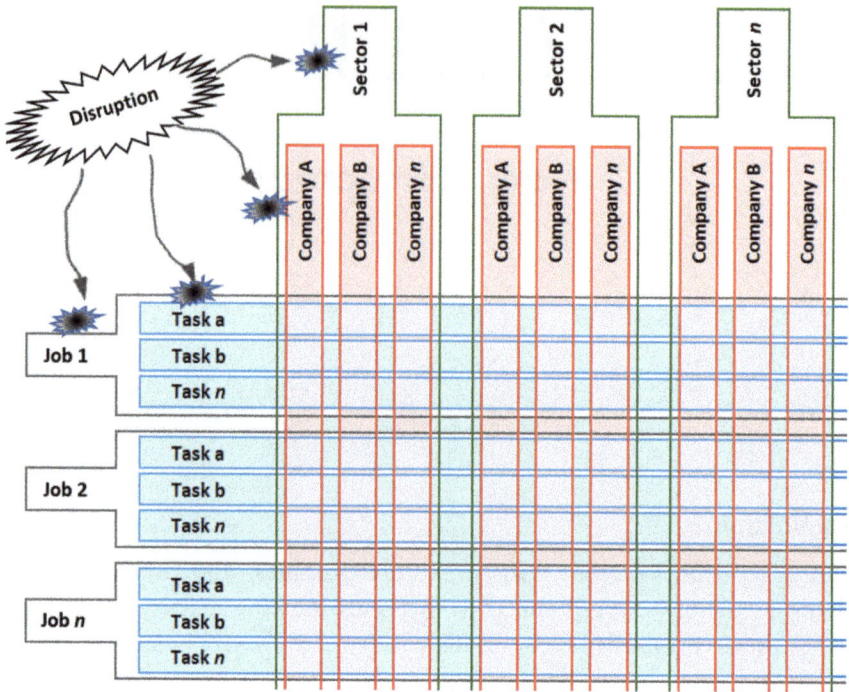

Fig. 1   Disruption matrix: the 4 doors of disruption

tech can enhance, weaken, or eliminate via substitution, and the distinction between these verbs is not always clear-cut.

Other factors can influence a disruptive force, adding a layer of complexity. Legislation could prevent self-driving trucks from hitting the road, thus sparing truck drivers, or on the contrary outlaw humans from driving. Novel forms of work can come in support of an otherwise imperfect technology: outsourcing, internships, or shoving of AI-resistant tasks to the customer.

The 2 × 2 disruption matrix is a useful prism to avoid blind spots. A tech threatening any of these four doors could derail your job, either that:

- it disrupts your sector of activity—e.g. plastic injection substituted by 3D printing
- your company falls behind rivals as it fails to harness transformative tech (Kodak and Blockbuster failing to fully embrace digital)
- it automates the value of your occupation (cashier, flight booking agent) or decreases it (taxi driver)
- it automates tasks within your job, such as proof-reading, email writing or taking customer orders at the restaurant.

Sometimes the difference between one or the other may appear more as a matter of degree. The point is less to categorize at which door warning signs are mounting than to ensure you leave no stone unturned.

Organization of Part II

This part is organized into four chapters; three to cover the four doors of disruption, plus a final chapter on other weapons to reinforce your position.

- Chapter 5 is devoted to sectorial and corporate disruption
- Chapter 6 looks at the threat to occupations, in other words, job automation, degrading or enhancement; under what forms threat could materialize; and the main elements that strengthen or fragilize a job confronted to it
- Chapter 7 drills down to the tasks level, with a focus on actionable steps to fight back
- Chapter 8 looks at other aspects that can help retain value, such as continuous learning and social networking.

5

Sectorial and Corporate Disruption

Economist Joseph Schumpeter formulated the concept of creative destruction in the 1940s, as

> the process of industrial mutation that incessantly revolutionizes the economic structure from within, incessantly destroying the old one, incessantly creating a new one.[1]

He took the example of how Ford's assembly line revolutionized manufacturing and railroads upset farmland. His remarks draw from Karl Marx, with even farther echoes of Hinduism, where Shiva (in the *Nataraja* form) is portrayed simultaneously as creator and destructor. We could colloquially describe creative destruction with the saying "You can't make an omelet without breaking eggs".

Schumpeter cast a very wide net with his creative destruction, resulting in a catchall that pertains both to inner processes (e.g. introduction of the assembly line) and to new markets that substitute for older ones. Oftentimes people evoke creative destruction to designate one or the other, in turn causing a variety of amalgams. Yet these are two quite different forms of disruption. For our purposes, we will refer to Schumpeter purely in the

---

The original version of this chapter was revised: Text correction has been updated. The correction to the chapter is available at https://doi.org/10.1007/978-3-031-19278-4_10

[1] Joseph A. Schumpeter: *Capitalism, Socialism and Democracy*, Harper & Brothers (1942).

© The Author(s), under exclusive license to Springer Nature
Switzerland AG 2023, corrected publication 2023
A. M. Recanati, *AI Battle Royale*, Copernicus Books,
https://doi.org/10.1007/978-3-031-19278-4_5

second sense, as a new sector of activity (made of products and services) that *substitutes* for earlier ones. In other words, sectorial disruption.[2]

Cars famously brought the equestrian sector to its knees, with plummeting demand for horse carriages, horseshoes, stables, coachmen, hay, veterinarians and manure scoopers. Yet cars spurred demand for jobs in engineering, manufacturing, gas stations, oil drilling, garages, traffic and congestion control, street pavement and signalization, inaugurating trends such as the great migration from city centers to suburbs, with immaculate lawns to mow and remote mega shopping centers to pile up for the week's subsistence.

Half a century later, Clayton Christensen advanced the idea of disruptive innovation in his 1997 hallmark book *The innovator's dilemma: when new technologies cause great firms to fail*.[3] He defines disruption as a company that introduces an innovative process on the low-end market radically different from the current offer, that gains traction relatively quickly. While it may not address mainstream demand to begin with, and thus fly under the radar, as the underlying tech matures and quality improves, it generates the performance attributes valued by the masses, eventually upsetting established markets. By then, the incumbents have a hard time catching up; many go out of business.

From hard disks to minicomputers, much of the evidence supporting Christensen's argumentation derived from the merciless toppling of leading tech firms by startups riding Moore's Law. While these formed the most protuberant cases of his time, his theory stretches beyond information technology: Walmart overtaking Sears and even Ford's assembly line illustrate disruptive innovation.

Christensen highlighted the intimate link between technology and evolving consumer tastes, emphasizing the importance for firms to assess the subtle interactions between the two, especially when a seemingly inconspicuous technology has the potential to transform a process into something with vast market potential in the (not too distant) future. Few people believed in personal computers, yet these swiftly eclipsed mainframes. Critics met the launch of the iPad, the last great invention under Steve Jobs' tenure, with skepticism, yet the product carved a new market segment. In the end, disruption can generate new needs that supplant or dwarf the old. Legend has it

---

[2] The confusion is palpable on the Wikipedia entry for creative destruction, where the initial description given by Schumpeter alludes to corporate disruption, only to be followed by examples dealing with sectorial disruption. I believe the term has evolved in modern parlance to be perceived more as sectorial disruption, hence our use of it in that sense. https://en.wikipedia.org/wiki/Creative_destruction.

[3] Harvard Business School Press. He had introduced the concept of disruptive innovation several years earlier in articles that appeared in the Harvard Business Review, later followed by other books.

that Ford once claimed: "If I had asked the people what they craved for, they would have answered faster horses".

Based on the narrow sense that we apply to creative destruction, we could argue that Schumpeter sheds light on sectorial disruption, while Christensen deals with corporate disruption, as underscored by his book's title of technologies bringing down companies, not entire sectors.

Sectorial and corporate threats put both the worker and her entire firm in danger. Though the strategies to apprehend these threats are fomented at the highest levels of corporate management, in this chapter we strive to preserve the viewpoint of the worker.

5.1   Sectorial Disruption

Think farming, aeronautics, food & beverage, luxury goods, the military, or HVACR (acronym for heating, ventilation, air-conditioning, and refrigeration). The Standard Industrial Classification (SIC) available online[4] can help identify the sector in which you work. Companies deliver relevant services and/or products in the said sector, usually in either "B2C" (business to consumer) or "B2B", or both, and some even to governments.

Sectorial disruption sees an entire field of activity challenged by a major shift. While the root cause is often technology, other factors come in play too: societal, regulatory, etc. In the 1900s, cars could not travel faster than horses on many roads, and a car cost about four-and-a-half years of a skilled worker's wage. Some people were more upbeat on the bicycle substituting for horses, rather than pricey cars.[5] Figure 5.1 depicts what ensued as the democratization trend of superior car technology eventually made car ownership cheaper than that of a horse.

Modern plastics and composites have taken over much of the commercial uses for papier-mâché, and video killed the radio star. The airplane displaced travel by boat. Buoyed by carbon footprint concerns, tomorrow high-speed trains, the Hyperloop, and even self-driving electric vehicles may disrupt passenger air travel.

Organizations should pay heed to what drives the democratization effect; for instance, in past decades the trail often led to Asian manufacturers dragging prices down as they adopted cutting-edge technology and aggressively expanded overseas. Apple disrupted the cellphone market with the launch of

---

[4] For instance: https://www.gov.uk/government/publications/standard-industrial-classification-of-eco nomic-activities-sic.

[5] Cf. Pierre Giffard: *La fin du cheval* (*The end of the horse*), 1899.

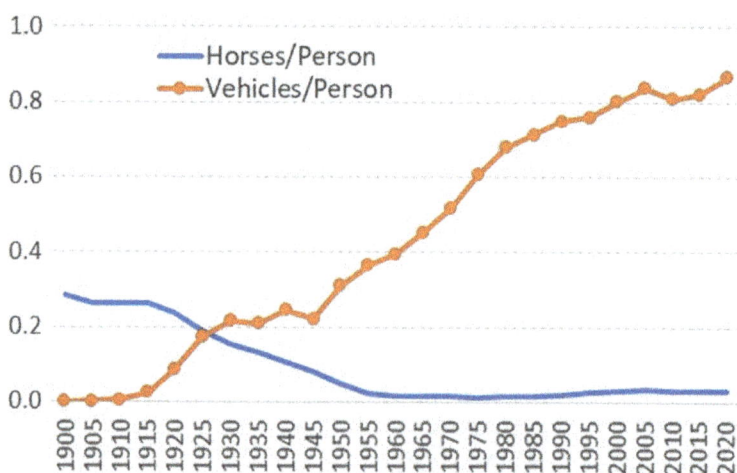

Fig. 5.1 Number of horses and of vehicles per person in the United States, 1900–2020. *Source* data compiled by the author from the American Horse Council Foundation and the American Automobile Association

the first iPhone. But within five years, the main disruptors were hailing from China: by 2013 (the year smartphone sales outpaced feature cellphones), Huawei, ZTE, Lenovo and TCL had toppled RIM (Blackberry), Nokia, and HTC.[6]

Effects can be more subtle, too. Consider the fate of the chewing gum alluded to earlier. In the past decade, sales of the staple have stumbled, prompting anxiety in the industry. What was the culprit? Educated choices of increasingly health-conscious consumers? Chewing tobacco? Turns out, the substitute was more elusive: technology. Smartphones, to be precise. Shoppers buy chewing gum while queuing up at the cashier. Gum had been strategically placed there for decades, enticing weary urbanites with a low-price impulse purchase. Enter the smartphone. The same people now glide through the line oblivious to their surroundings, unscathed by worldly temptations.[7]

Chewing gum has not been wiped out entirely. Disruption can be partial, as when train and bicycle put a dent in the nineteenth-century horse business, or more lethal, the way cars later shrunk it into a vestigial simulacre of its

[6] Cf. Gartner press release, *Gartner Says Annual Smartphone Sales Surpassed Sales of Feature Phones for the First Time in 2013*, (February 13, 2014), https://www.gartner.com/en/newsroom/press-releases/2014-02-13-gartner-says-annual-smartphone-sales-surpassed-sales-of-feature-phones-for-the-first-time-in-2013.

[7] Olga Kharif, *Shoppers' "Mobile Blinders" Force Checkout-Aisle Changes*, Bloomberg (March 21, 2013) https://www.bloomberg.com/news/articles/2013-03-21/shoppers-mobile-blinders-force-checkout-aisle-changes.

past splendor. Ripple effects can be farfetched: the bicycle shook the fashion industry too, by inducing society's acceptance for women pants.

As Schumpeter taught us, the newcomer can burgeon a sizeable market. When an innovation lures masses who until then were not consumers, it spawns a blue ocean, far from existing, saturated markets where incumbents traditionally battle it out, *aka* seas red from the bloody competition.[8]

Such is the story behind the beauty tool sponge. These little egg-shaped fluffs, inexistent in my time, have since risen to stardom—an indispensable tool for foundation, concealer, and more. It all started in the early 2000s, as TV studios started using High-Definition video for their shows. This new tech created a headache for makeup artists, as suddenly stage lighting wasn't enough to conceal facial pores. The existing solution—an airbrush kit—was too cumbersome for the set. A makeup artist by the name of Rea Ann Silva started experimenting with sponges, developing what would become the iconic *Beautyblender* brand, today a hundred-million-dollar-plus business that has disrupted the beauty industry and landed her on Forbes' list of *50 Over 50*, alongside Kamala Harris.[9] All without adversely impacting jobs in a prior sector.

With these preliminaries set, we can move onto this section's structure. In it we cover:

- how to assess sectorial disruption threats
- what kinds of action the company can take to forestall these risks
- what the employee can do.

In short, you need first to assess sectorial disruption threats in terms of likelihood and impact. Then observe your company's intentions: does it acknowledge the menace? What does it plan to do? Alas, what role might you have in this endeavor. By the end of the transition, will you remain a valued asset, or become expendable? Are you better off parting ways?

Assessment Phase

Start by gauging the risks to your sector:

---

[8] W. Chan Kim and Renée A. Mauborgne: *Blue Ocean Strategy: How to Create Uncontested Market Space and Make the Competition Irrelevant*, Harvard Press Review (2014).

[9] Lisette Voytko, *How Beautyblender Founder Rea Ann Silva Reinvented A Sponge And Created A New Category*; Forbes (June 2, 2021) https://www.forbes.com/sites/lisettevoytko/2021/06/02/how-beautyblender-founder-rea-ann-silva-reinvented-a-sponge-and-created-a-new-category. However in this case, the success also prompted a flood of copycats.

Risk Assessment		IMPACT			
		Catastrophic 4	Critical 3	Moderate 2	Negligable 1
L I K E L I H O O D	Certain 4				
	High 3				
	Low 2				
	Very Low 1				

Fig. 5.2   Assessment Scoring

1. Review 4^{IR} technology advancements and radically new and transformative products in terms of broadness and impact; pinpoint which ones might collide with your sector
2. Score each in terms of likelihood of reaching fruition and colliding with your sector
3. Score each in terms of impact, should that twofold likelihood materialize.

Using a score from 1 (low) to 4 (very high) for steps 2 and 3 should suffice, producing the matrix in Fig. 5.2.

Note that likelihood may translate less as a question of *if* than *when*.

It is just as important to take the right measure of tech trends as of the technologies themselves. Apple foresaw that convergence and miniaturization (driven by Moore's Law) would lead computers to shrink further, presenting a mortal threat to its survival (remember that Macintosh then accounted for over half of Apple's sales). The company flipped this threat to its cash cow into opportunity by leaping to a pocketsize computer: the iPhone.

Consider the qualities of the sector itself. Some are more sensitive to disruption than others. Historically, industrial revolutions tend to rewrite the playbook for transportation and communication modes. The exponential gap varies by field: media and advertising prove brittle, with shorter cycles than more asset-intensive sectors, for instance, telecommunication networks, or highly regulated and public sectors, such as healthcare and education. Customer profiles also play a role: young people are more welcoming to new technology than elders.[10]

---

[10] Though I have yet to encounter research to substantiate this, one should be able to plot sectors of activity on a spectrum from highly sensitive to disruption, all the way down to the laggards. Time frames could even be added on the spectrum, e.g. ranging from less than two years to over forty

These combined elements contribute to determine the most pressing issues your company should pay heed to—if any. Focus on the red zones (anything where the average of the two scores is above 3) and put aside the rest, until your next review. Renew the analysis at least once a year, and whenever fresh information pours in that could alter prior assumptions.

The Company's Response

You have unearthed tangible threats. How is your company planning to cope? Do they acknowledge the problem? Have they come to similar conclusions as you in terms of its timing and potential severity?

If not, are they open to discuss about it? They might shed light on unforeseen aspects that could lead you to revise your assessments and conclude that the threat is in fact remote. Or they dismiss it, a reaction unfortunately only too common in larger firms preceded by an even bigger hubris. Or worse, your superior shrugs your concerns off, only to later pull them from the trash and repackage them as his own so he can take the credit. Unfortunately, based on the seat occupied, the worker may lie far from decisional or even observational grounds.

Let's assume the company takes the threat seriously and has a plan. It will usually fall into one of three buckets:

- Fill a niche pocket expected to endure, e.g. yacht cruise for passenger boats
- Embrace the new sector, adapting to the technology driving it, the way a wainwright could become a car manufacturer or turn into a garage, or as Apple did with the iPhone (embracing miniaturization to forestall the threat of smartphones to its computer business), and media company Conde Nast eventually achieved to do by espousing digital media (the substitute to its print business)[11]
- Flee to another sector, for instance, from a textile sector in freefall to insurance—as did Berkshire Hathaway after Warren Buffett took a majority stake in the 1960s. Or the way Nintendo diversified from the dying playing cards sector in the 1960s to develop electronic toys and eventually consoles (after unsuccessful wanderings that included a taxi service, instant rice packages and a love hotel chain).

---

years, along with a more precise definition of disruption (e.g. a certain % of adoption rate of new tech, or of sector size versus the old sector).

[11] Alexandra Bruell: *Magazine Giant Condé Nast Posts First Profit in Years*, The Wall Street Journal (February 17, 2022), https://www.wsj.com/articles/magazine-giant-conde-nast-posts-first-profit-in-years-11645117633.

The first path involves targeting a specific clientele, often an elite one, thus branding up. It can also be via a different business model that hooks customers in, such as Hilti's SaaS.

At times, the second and third paths will resemble one another. For instance, did Apple switch to a completely new sector as they developed smartphones, or embrace the miniaturization trend of computers? In any case, in the years following the release of the first iPhone, they held their position amid fierce competition from Chinese rivals thanks to their premium brand positioning and iOS ecosystem, taking refuge in a juicy market segment.

A firm specializing in vehicle insurance would be wise to diversify (flight), given the lurking menace of autonomous vehicles. If it sets its eyes on health-care insurance, best monitor advances in genomics and nanotechnology that could prolong life and thus upset existing business models. If it bets on an enduring niche for collectible automobiles, it could specialize in that segment (refuge). Meanwhile, Big Data could provide a boost as it enables the collection of data from clients (with their consent), allowing for more tailored solutions and premiums (embrace)[12]; failure to capture this opportunity could lead it to fall behind rivals (in an illustration of *corporate* disruption).

Through either of these actions, the company can emerge from the storm disfigured yet existent, like the dinosaur-turned-bird (or rather phoenix, considering the examples in Fig. 5.3). The question is, what of the worker?

The Worker's Response

Sectorial disruption marks a moment of reckoning between employee and employer. Do they remain a good fit in the new context? Whatever the company's direction, will you still have a seat in it once it achieves its molt? To answer this, consider how you would fare in each of the three paths laid above, *regardless* of your company's direction and whether it is successful in its endeavor. What is your plan if your whole sector collapses? Would you rather cling onto a shrinking sector, soon only inakeleton of its past glory, or switch to a more promising one?

Next, compare your plan to your company's. Do they fit? Or is yours closer to that of a competitor, or of players in another sector? Should you call it quits and move elsewhere? If, unlike your firm, you are actively engaged in the new technology, you might consider reaching out to a rival firm eager to disrupt the market. They may value your expertise in the sector.

---

[12] Cf. an eloquent depiction of this in *AI 2014*, Chap. 1: *The Golden Elephant*. By Kai-Fu Lee and Chen Qiufan, published by Currency (2021).

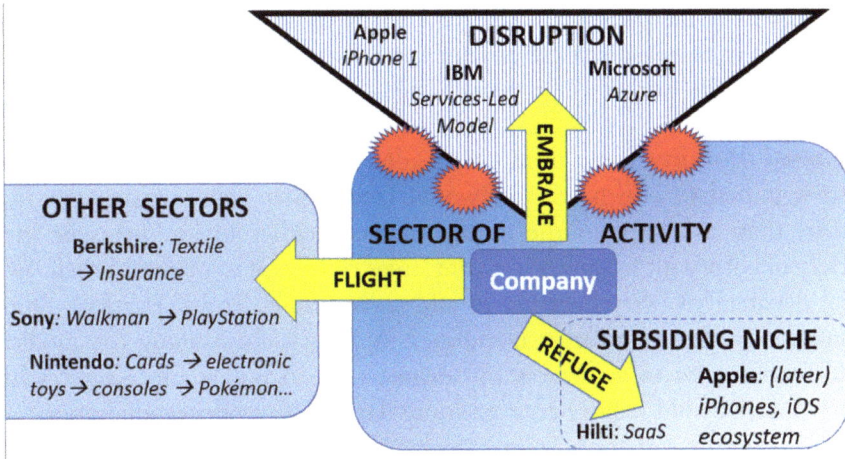

Fig. 5.3 Corporate responses to sectorial and corporate disruption threats, with several successful examples

Note that the three corporate paths laid above are sorted by increasing order of alienness to the existing sector. The third path presents a greater adaptive challenge to employees (think of the textile workers at Berkshire).

Workers have a fourth alternative: changing employers. But that does not fundamentally change their options, which in reality are twofold: either adapt to the changing sector, by changing skins with it (assuming the disruption does not eliminate the field entirely); or switch to another sector. In the following pages, we explore these options, starting with the latter.

Changing Sectors

Having concluded that (1) the sector is on the verge of seismic turbulence, and that (2) we had best change sectors, four questions then arise:

– Is your company already actively engaged in switching to another sector?
– Do you concur with their newly sought path?
– Do you believe that they will succeed?
– Where will you fit? Will there still be a spot for you in the company once it is engaged on this new path?

If the answer to any of these questions turns out negative, abandon ship. I admire the clairvoyance of job candidates who, when questioned as to the reason for leaving their previous employer, point to the hopeless sector that the company is mired in.

This presses the question of the worker's own "sectorial mobility". Are you waist-deep in the mud puddle of your current sector? Or a dandelion capable of exploring the world?

Sectorial Mobility Some occupations identify strongly with their sector. A dentist is tied to healthcare and would face greater pains trying to switch sectors than a lawyer, as the latter can work either in law firms or in a variety of corporations, given how the larger ones tend to maintain their own legal department (they have yet to add an in-house dentist practice). Some lawyers even pursue a career in politics. A dentist abandoning the medical field would need to achieve a 180-degree turn to pull it off. Keeping her salary intact would require an even more dazzling feat of prestidigitation.

A salesperson can hop from cars to cosmetics but faces greater obstacles than an accountant making that same sectorial leap. Switching sectors requires the salesperson to learn another type of product and customer. The gap may translate as a salary cut, at least until she climbs back to a similar level of expertise and generated revenue. Meanwhile, someone in HR or accounting would have little relearning to do, and can thus more easily land a job in a different sector with just as good a pay.

Let us coin the term "sectorial mobility" to convey this. The likelihood of acceptance by job interviewers in the new sector and the amount of retraining necessary could serve as a yardstick to measure it. This naturally depends on the two sectors at stake: by any guess, going from cosmetics to retail clothing requires less training than from tobacco shop to private jets.

Mobility is linked to factors such as how sectors are horizontally adjacent to each other (they serve a common type of consumer or product) or vertically linked in a chain of suppliers and customers. Skills and contacts built in the first sector can prove useful in the next. A candidate can tout this to interviewers to unveil her ability to excel in the new job. A private jet salesperson will have a sharp eye for the elite's needs and psyche, along with a solid contact list; in short, a better fit for Sotheby's than Starbucks.

Outsiders can instill a fresh perspective into a business, hence at times companies reach out to people from other industries. Wall Street hires physicists and IT engineers for their abilities to conceptualize mathematical problems and build predictive models. A variety of sectors will appreciate a flight attendant's strict adherence to protocol and dedication to customer service. Size can also influence a sectorial leap: growing companies face maturity issues that prompt them to seek talent hailing from larger organizations, people that can infuse processes and best practices. Given how company departments have become sectors in their own right, regardless of its activity, companies often seek candidates from the said sector: audit firms for a senior finance position, law firms for their legal department, or McKinsey and Accenture consultants for marketing and strategy. The latest addition to the list sees techies and workers from the sustainability sector "go corporate", as businesses from all trades add emphasis on digitalizing, and on corporate social responsibility (CSR) and environmental and social governance (ESG).

A job function tied to its sector, like our dentist (0 sectorial mobility), puts that worker in a precarious position, should the entire sector fall victim to the arrows of disruption.

Meanwhile high sectorial mobility is a double-edged sword. Mobility rhymes with commodity. All else considered equal, a firm will find it easier to replace an accountant than a salesperson: no prior expertise in that specific field, nor extensive training required. Even within sales, some sectors are more specialized than others, implying in-depth field knowledge and training before the new hire becomes a worthy, revenue-generating asset.

Note the difference between skills and specialization. The accountant and salesperson may have the same education level, yet the latter develops an expertise pertaining to a specific field: insurance products, industrial robots or private jets. Companies are deterred from changing staff in specialized functions frequently. Whether facing a conjunctural downturn or simply a desire to outsource, those seeking to slash their workforce start with functions perceived as commodities while preserving those seen as part of their core competence.[13]

Specialization exists even within a particular skill, like language or software fluency. Mastering an obscure software, like QAD as opposed to SAP, or being bilingual in Polish and Vietnamese, may set you apart from the crowd; but this is valuable only inasmuch as demand exists for that skillset.

Job mobility expressed by sector and occupation can be plotted with each of these variables on a separate axis. Figure 5.4 shows the extremes encircled.

No one job mobility extreme trumps the other; each exposes the worker to a particular type of threat—commoditization on the top right, specialization on the bottom left. Aiming for the middle ground mitigates the risks yet results in vulnerability to both threats.

Where do you pin yourself? Various factors will edge a dot further in one direction or the other. A salesperson in a very technical job is less of a commodity than one selling ballpens. Even individual aspects need to be accounted for—for instance, how long you have held the job for, and the

---

[13] The notion of core competence is what differentiates the company, that on which its reputation is built. From this, we can infer that it involves skills rare to come by in the marketplace. Cf. C.K. Prahalad and Gary Hamel: The Core Competence of the Corporation, Harvard Business Review (May-June 1990)

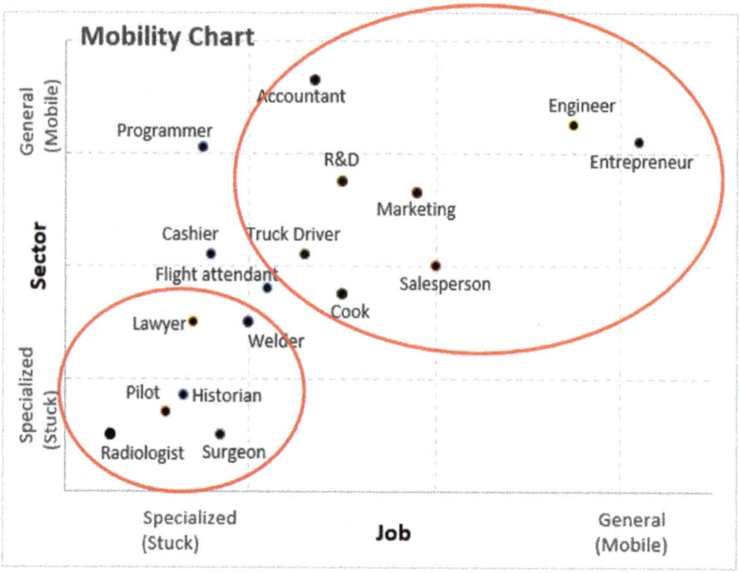

158 A. M. Recanati

Fig. 5.4 Sectorial mobility chart

number of jobs on your resume. Someone who spent her life as a grocery store cashier is comparatively glued in those shoes. And a polyglot could be more mobile than a monolingual worker—or not, if recruiters have no use for foreign languages.

While one should assess and acknowledge their mobility level, an important aspect when facing the perils of sectorial disruption, it would be an exaggeration to make it the defining characteristic of a career orientation. A wannabe historian should not bury that passion in a closet after gleaning over the above chart. Consider first whether the job is at risk of vanishing in the upcoming decades. Suppose she reaches such a dire conclusion with, say, a half/half chance of materialization during her working lifetime; she could still pursue that vocation while developing other types of expertise in parallel as a fallback, just in case. Or differentiate herself by focusing on a specific part of history dear to her; author books, speak at conferences, make podcasts, and develop a growing network of followers (cf. Build a Platform). In a similar vein to the three types of corporate response we overlooked, this worker bets on a niche segment expected to endure the storm.

Mobility Along the Pyramid The previous chart left out an essential element that influences job mobility: wage level. It takes the shape of a reverse bell curve, as in Fig. 5.5.

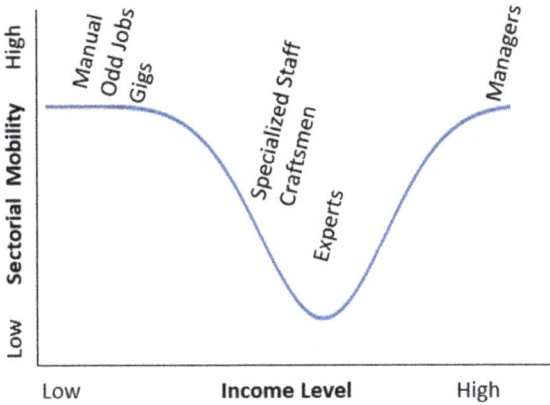

Fig. 5.5   Sectorial mobility by income level

The low-income end trawls commodity jobs where people hop from one sector to the next like electrons between atoms. Whether a sector vanishes matters little so long as other pools can reabsorb the workforce. Here the potent threat lies less in sectorial disruption and more in job automation taking root across the gamut of low-income jobs, pushed by AI and robotics (the topic of the Job Disruption chapter). Tech can also shove jobs that once called upon certain skills to the lower income commodity level, by obsoleting those skills—the way couriers now need no knowledge of the terrain thanks to apps, a paradigm change that enabled express firms like Shunfeng to hire an army of cheap migrant youths to move packages around China's coastal metropolises. Though the impact of sectorial threats to low-income jobs may appear mild, a career goal should not be defined by the pursuit of a low-income job.

As we climb the skills ladder, hedges grow between jobs. Rare, long-to-acquire skills translate into a higher paycheck. Yet specialization carries risks, should that value come under threat. Blacksmiths, silversmiths, and other *plumassières* (a job that handles bird feathers for ornamentation) were dislodged, some by industrial processes that lowered the requirements to unbearable levels, others borne by macro changes: big hats adorned by extravagant feathers are simply no longer in fashion. Some craftsmen retaliate against tech by assembling in modern forms of guild; but the irresistible march of progress could crush these ramparts, as in self-driving cars putting cabbies out of a job.

Specialization defines one's value in the job market while chaining her to a narrow scope; venturing out of this zone could cause a fallout to the base of the pyramid. While in theory, the applicant has the same ability to perform a commodity job (or simply leave her comfort zone) as any other contender, three factors put her at a disadvantage:

- she would not be utilizing her skills. Built over years of work (not to mention the costly studies involved), these would not be so easily relinquished
- this knowhow commands a higher salary and status. An airline pilot won't be seen trading his captain's cap for a forklift job, nor a cardiologist her blouse for that of a nurse whose income on average is four times less[14]
- human resource departments judge candidates based on their past; an advertiser applying for a fast-food chain job (aka Kevin Spacey in the movie *American Beauty*) would lift eyebrows.

Rising still, we find the experts: surgeon, lawyer, architect, auditor. They too, seldom wade their way over to a hugely different sector. Exceptions exist: forward-thinking companies such as IDEO appreciate the creativity instilled by blending diverse elements within a team, with profiles as varied as a mathematician, ethnographer or cartographer. The cognitive part innate to expert jobs places them on high grounds unlikely to fall under AI's destructive path, and more in the box of occupations to be *enhanced* through proper use of AI tools. Besides, there is often a dearth of people in these jobs, which makes them even more valuable in the job market. However, they are more likely to remain glued to their sector and/or occupation, thus in a precarious position *if* that sector falls. When the horse fell out of favor as principal mode of transportation, pooper-scoopers suddenly out of a job had an easier time finding a new, different job, compared to horse veterinarians.

Executive managers sit at the top (sometimes sharing the spot with very skilled experts such as surgeons, wage-wise). These require a jack-of-all-trades palette of skills. They may hold a dual degree, have broadened their skills down the road via an MBA course, or learned the tricks of several trades through a sinusoidal career path. In any case, their 360-degree view liquifies the otherwise rigid boundaries between occupations and sectors, increasing flexibility and lowering the risk of losing all in case their sector succumbs to disruption (meanwhile the cognitive trait also shields them from job automation).

Geographical, Occupational, and Career Mobility Sectorial mobility can be combined with geographical mobility. Certain sectors and jobs open doors

---

[14] An American cardiologist makes on average $353,970 a year as of 2021, versus $82,750 for a nurse. Cf. U.S. Bureau Labor of Statistics.

to international mobility, others less so. While absent from our disruption matrix, geography remains a critical dimension to account for; the other one is time, both at a macro level—the conjecture—and at a personal level— the time in your life, your seniority… Lastly, certain occupations provide narrower prospects than others (more on this in a minute).

A US consumer market expert or HR specialist's experience presents little value in India or Gabon, due to differences in laws and culture, compared to that of a finance controller, who not only deals less with folks and more with figures, less with local flavors and more with corporate processes, but additionally holds a strategic position that HQs tend to fill with trustworthy compatriots. IT and engineering jobs are rooted in universal concepts of math and physics, regardless of location. Those who seek geographical mobility must factor these elements, ideally from the education stage. Also, consider the scarcity of a particular skillset based on geography. A doctor will find better prospects moving to Turkey or Israel than to Finland or Switzerland, as the latter two top the list of doctors per 1,000 people.[15]

I entered law college in Paris without the slightest notion of "dream career". The study of law can only cause discomfort to a global citizen aspiring for mobility. While not without interest (after all, knowledge of law is power), the fact that the teachings held true only within French borders was asphyxiating. To break this invisible force field, several classmates advised me to specialize in international law—only the utterance of the verb "specialize" ricocheted like the screeching of fingernails on a chalkboard. When wrestling for oxygen, how could the solution lie in a narrower corridor? If at the end of the tunnel I found only darkness, what then?

A visit to a school fair unveiled a third door: international business. The prerequisite was a two-year degree, which I was nearing. I hopped on this new track invigorated, and never looked back.

Figure 5.6 showcases this example by laying down geographical and sectorial mobility.

Students with no clue as to what they want to do when they grow up should strive to keep their options as broad and plenty as possible, both geographically and in terms of sector. We are more flexible during our spring years; as the flow of time carves an indelible label on our foreheads, flexibility calcifies.

Several years later, I realized that sector and geography are not the only things that matter. Work was starting to plateau, with dim prospects ahead.

---

[15] https://www.weforum.org/agenda/2020/08/healthcare-doctors-nurses-covid-19/.

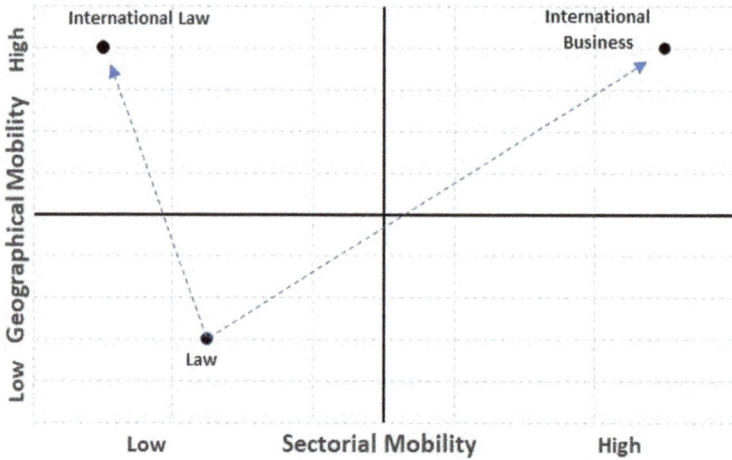

Fig. 5.6 Example of assessing sectorial and geographical mobility during studies

Something was itching, but I couldn't put a word on it. A retired businessman and mentor of mine then confided to me. "Finance control is a dead-end. You'd better get out of there before it's too late."[16] I respected his opinion, that of an oil drilling engineer turned general manager in the automotive sector, whose problem had been *too much* mobility (if you one day meet someone who worked in Nigeria, Greenland, Iran, and Indonesia, chances are she or he is in the oil business). With finance control, I had switched countries and hopped from manufacturing to the retail sector with relative ease. And yet, here I was, shoehorned into a narrow occupation with limited evolution potential. Besides, a large part of the job had to do with crunching numbers; what if automation set its sights on it?

Attentive to the job market, I eventually seized an opportunity in a smaller company in exchange for a broader managerial position. This time the transition resembled Fig. 5.7.

A few years later, on top of the country GM position I landed a Group Finance Control title, a role larded with tasks in other subsidiaries that added a boost to geographical mobility, along with greater transversality, all the while preserving the jack-of-all-trades management card. Step by steppingstone, I had regained my mojo.

Booming Sectors You just started your career. The year is 1900. You receive two job offers: one from a horse-carriage producer, the other from a car

---

[16] To be fair, a finance controller can become a Chief Financial Officer, but this usually requires a CPA and/or audit experience, of which I had neither. Nor was the role appealing to me.

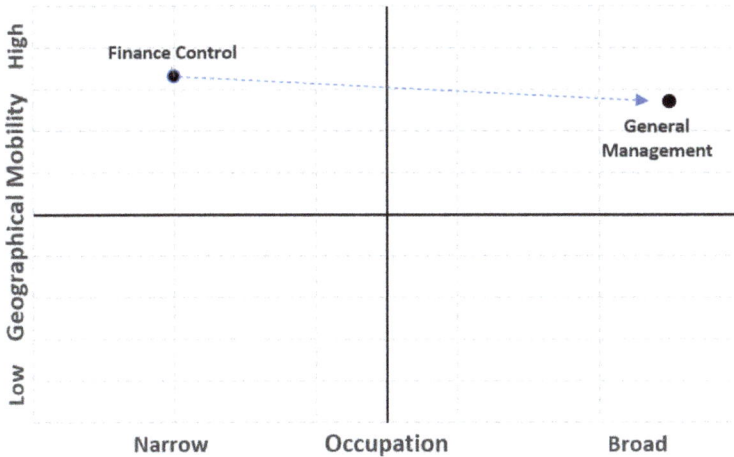

Fig. 5.7   Geographical and occupational mobility

manufacturer. Which should you pick? All else considered equal, aim for booming sectors. Data collection and usage, coding and AI behavior are nascent fields with little regulation. We've barely scratched the surface of computer behavior and ethics; these sectors could burgeon and grow thirsty for jobs.

Don't neglect existing sectors with brighter days ahead. Tourism is booming. Healthcare is poised to expand alongside aging populations. And as the powers that be set in motion the engines to reverse climate change, funding is pouring into sustainability, with impacts extending beyond the green sector to all corporations.

Alas, how might tech further propel sectors? Consider the impact of Big Data, advanced genetics and 3D printing on fields where for decades (if not centuries) standardization was the norm. Personalization will no doubt emerge as another major trend, in education, medicine tailored to your genome, and clothing inventory finetuned by data to avoid the waste of unsold goods of odd sizes.

Look at what leading tech firms and VCs invest in. The Peter Thiels and SoftBanks of the world that pour money into AI, AR, and everything from vertical farming to meatless meat, fitness trackers and swarm robotics.

Although one can find data online, still, assessing the number of jobs a booming sector will hunger for mostly equates to guesswork. It could be worth dwelling on in certain instances, for example when reasoning on a local scale.

Do not forget to factor in wage levels and mobility on the corporate ladder. Healthcare may be a growing business, but nurse assistants lie at the low end of the wage spectrum. Someone working at a restaurant or retail sales may earn a similar income, yet have greater opportunities for learning the ropes and climbing the ladder. An apprentice can become a barista, a retail salesperson eventually make it to store manager; but it would be a long shot for a grocery store cashier to land a managerial job, and close to impossible for a nurse to become a general practitioner, or a flight attendant a pilot.

A dynamic sector offers more safety than a declining one; but this alone does not spare the worker from the threat of redundancy—even firms in growing sectors can pursue ruthless automation, the topic of the next chapter (Job Disruption).

Embracing the New: Renew Your Skin Alongside Your Sector's

When steam replaced water as the main source of power, the engineering knowledge amassed by the men who had built watermills proved invaluable for erecting 1^{IR} factories. As the car emerged in a world of horse carriages, those who built the latter could leverage their knowledge of a vehicle's weight, wheels, and mechanics, applying it to the design and building of the former while adhering to its own specifics. The car put vets and pooper-scoopers out of a job, but coachmen could adapt *if* they learned how to drive and care for an engine in lieu of a horse.

The second path to deal with sectorial threats consists of adapting to the changing environment: instead of reinventing yourself to start anew in a totally alien sector, explore whether you can acclimate to the new paradigm.

Observe your company. Is it actively steering toward more fertile fields? If you work in the oil business, how is it dealing with renewable energies? A bank, with fintech and crypto? Identify which technologies pose a disruption threat to your sector, and what new skills they call for. Do you possess these skills? Can you push for training?

Your path can be independent of your company's—if you adapt to the new sector faster than your firm, this could reposition you within it as a herald for change, or open opportunities elsewhere, with swifter rivals. Like a snake, the sector is changing skins; can you follow suit?

Figure 5.8 summarizes the steps to change skins.

Start by clarifying which of your existing skills remain relevant in the new paradigm. These are the skills to retain and emphasize. What is their level of scarcity? How would you leverage these, for instance, in a job interview?

Next, acknowledge the new necessary skills which you do not possess (yet!). The novelty factor makes these even scarcer, though other forces can be at play (like the size of the workforce in the old and new sectors—the two circles may not be of equal size).

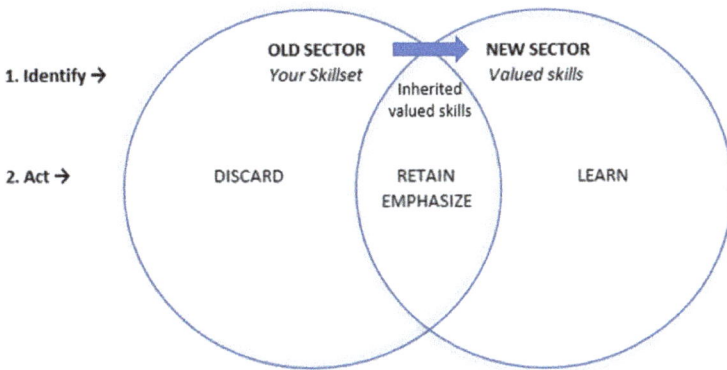

Fig. 5.8 Skills analysis for embracing the new sector

Learning the tricks of the new trade can turn you into a highly coveted asset. When the Internet hit the media industry, only a fraction of the old guard survived; exploring the new paradigm wrought by online media, user analytics data, advertising, payment models, and collaborative work would have enhanced those survival chances and facilitated a rise in the ranks.

Note that none of the "new skills" listed in the above example relate directly to coding or even graphic design; while knowledge of software like Flash, Visual Code or Dreamweaver did become relevant, the lesson here is that the skills need not be within the strict confines of the disrupting technology. You may not become an expert at everything in the new field, nor is it expected; a sector is seldom a one-man show. Another department can handle graphic design, or it will be outsourced. In fact, the previous figure oversimplified things: your skillset will not perfectly match the sector's. We must further slice the new sector's skills, as shown in Fig. 5.9.

Within the "skills to learn" lie those that you need to become really proficient at—usually the ones closest related to your occupation. For a layout editor in the printing sector, indeed mastering a tool like Adobe Dreamweaver may have been paramount to escape the dodo's fate.

These are followed by skills that need not be acquired, but for which a basic understanding of the concepts is preferable. The fact a firm has IT people tasked with the overlooking of cybersecurity does not spare others from a minimum grasp of what randomly received email links not to click on. Nor will the company expect you to encode algorithms; but an inkling of what these can and cannot do will smoothen collaboration with those who build them, ensuring a common language and avoidance of irrational demands. Muddling the hypothetical AI depicted in *Homo Deus* with current AI abilities will not do you any favors.

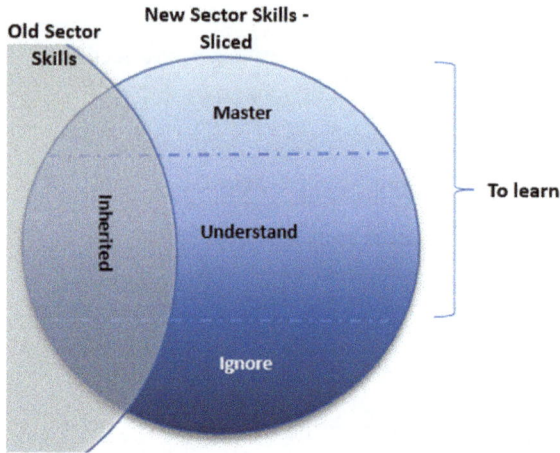

Fig. 5.9   New sector skills in perspective

Lastly, some of the new skills can be ignored totally. A mobile salesperson may need a driver's license but will not be tested for her ability to solve a car engine breakdown. This split already existed in the prior sector. Categorizing your skills in the old sector, between those you mastered, understood, and ignored, can help identify what to prioritize in the new sector. This homework is crucial to avoid any waste of time and misapplied effort.

Staying in a morphing company has its advantages. A company disrupting itself presents opportunities for power grabs. Part of its investment goes toward retraining staff—this also you can benefit from. During major overhaul projects (such as an ERP implementation), companies face pockets of internal resistance. Avoid those clusters. Distinguish yourself with an unquenchable thirst for knowledge. Devour the materials, get up to speed, and become a zealous advocate.

From Sectorial to Corporate Disruption

What distinguishes sectorial and corporate disruption? To answer this we turn to economist Michael Porter and his famed Five Forces Model.[17] Figure 5.10 shows this hallmark of marketing strategy textbooks formulated in 1979 and still in use today, with a circle added to highlight sectorial disruption.

Sectorial disruption relates to the threat of *substitutes*, that create a tectonic shift profound enough to doom or (more plausibly) shrink a market, bringing

---

[17] Michael Porter: *Competitive Strategy: Techniques for Analyzing Industries and Competitors*, Free Press (1980).

Michael Porter's 5 Forces Model

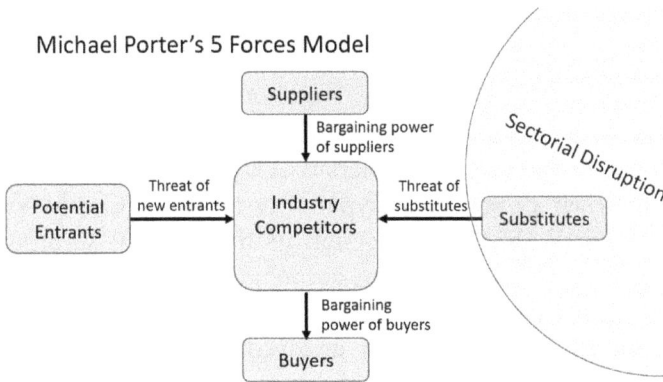

Fig. 5.10   Michael Porter's Five Forces Model

it from a torrential river into a trickling creek. Papier-mâché, horses, rick-shaws, wainwrights, CDs and the printing business were or are in process of getting substituted.

In contrast, corporate disruption comes from within the market; while it can disfigure the market beyond recognition, it does not necessarily reduce its size. The threat of rising Chinese smartphone manufacturers alluded to earlier fits squarely as corporate disruption: Huawei and ZTE sell smartphones, not a substitute to smartphones. As Porter noted, companies usually compete in their market either by proposing lower prices or through differentiation; when successfully implemented, either strategy carries disruptive potential.

Farming has been rocked multiple times: by mechanization, pesticides, genetically modified resistant crops, and now drones, computer vision, autonomous vehicles, grown meat, and vertical farms. While still existent, employment-wise the sector has been obliterated. Out of this list, only grown meat qualifies as "sectorial disruption"; vertical farming and container gardening could also be conceived of as a substitute to arable farmland, the same way livestock farming would face sectorial disruption if entomophagy goes mainstream (aka eating bugs).

Narrow tech tends to impact sectors, while broader tech can cause both sectorial and corporate disruption. A space elevator would affect the space industry; fusion power, the energy sector; cryptocurrencies, financial institutions. Meanwhile, blockchain, additive manufacturing, and autonomous vehicles are not tied to a single sector but pervade multiple industries. Internet and AI do not discriminate against companies based on sector—everyone is pressed to adapt. That is not to say that GPTs do not spare certain areas from graver disruption: the Internet rocked the publishing field along with courier boys; VR could alter working methods across industries, giving an edge to companies who exploit it first (corporate disruption), but also derail the tourism industry as people "travel online" (sectorial disruption).

Granted, at times the distinction will boil down to a matter of degree, and ultimately on how one defines the market. Are pdfs of Vogue and Vanity Fair substitutes for their printed counterparts, or a case of Conde Nast taking its products digital? IBM's introduction of the Personal Computer could be conceived of as either sectorial or corporate disruption to its mainframe rivals. Although the targeted clientele may remain unchanged, moving from gasoline to electric vehicles implies an overhaul in technology, manufacturing, after-sales, and infrastructure (charging stations). Jobs' introduction of the iPhone in 2007 challenged Nokia, RIM (Blackberry), and other cellphone manufacturers, disfiguring the cellphone business beyond recognition. Perhaps the ease with which firms can switch from one to the other can serve as a barometer. In a narrow definition of the market, the above would classify as sectorial disruption (EVs displacing gas cars, smartphones cellphones), while a broader one tilts toward corporate disruption, for instance with Apple simply challenging the portable phone market.

But the iPhone also impacted other devices: calculators, cameras, bed alarms, and mp3 players—including the iPod! Even portable mirrors and chewing gum. These goods suffered from sectorial disruption. And as a fully functional multimedia studio, smartphones made a dent in the business of studio recording; they even contributed to Kodak's demise. A century earlier, Ford's T Model dislocated the equestrian sector, but also the existing car manufacturing business, which was churning pricier or less reliable vehicles. By offering supercheap cars to the masses of India, Tata likewise disrupted the motorcycle and scooter business, but also competitor car sales.

In short, an innovative product can disrupt incumbents in the market while simultaneously sending shock waves to adjacent markets, via substitution. The Internet changed business models regardless of sector (= corporate disruption), yet more profoundly disfigured specific markets such as printing, audio, and video format manufacturing—i.e. CDs and DVDs—(= sectorial disruption), and almost triggered a collapse of postal services, only to see those jobs picked up by massive e-commerce demand for couriers and deliverymen (=creative destruction).

Corporate disruption need not stem from product innovation (in fact, Porter was adamant that it was not directly caused by technology). It can be a novel sales channel, such as Dell's direct sales or Amway's friend recommendation model, or building a lead by targeting a neglected niche, as Tata did with cheap cars, or as a home rental service could do by focusing on tenant applicants who do not satisfy the stringent requirements typically applicable. Nowadays, any differentiation strategy that sends tremors throughout the sector winds up making headlines as "disruption".

Alas, there is a nuance with Porter's model: any of the other four players can take on the substitution role. IBM was building mainframe computers when it launched the PC revolution, whereas Apple was a newcomer to the mobile phone market.

From an economist's perspective, the distinction may seem trivial, yet for the employee (and the firm) it bends the frame under which to assess and address survival chances. While more commonplace, corporate disruption is also theoretically easier to cope with: the company needs to harness the underlying GPT (Internet, AI…), or adapt its business model, for instance by diverting advertising dollars to KOL and livestreaming, rather than forsake the business or cling to what's left of it. With less of a drastic overhaul, it stands a better fighting chance. Tesla disrupts the car industry; incumbents respond by emulating Tesla's model, or via other countermoves, the same way they adapted to Ford's assembly line a century earlier (or perished). Their staff retains relevant skills. Sectorial disruption carries higher risks of destroying the value of worker skills, if these are no longer required in the new sector.

5.2 Corporate Disruption

Having classified a threat as corporate, we can proceed to thwart it. The playbook resembles that of sectorial threats, with a few twists.

Assessment Phase

First, what is the corporate disruptor? If it's a new product, what benefits does it convey: environmental friendliness? An internet connection? Data? Or is it a new process or business model, such as servitization (renting instead of buying, i.e. SaaS)? As 4^{IR} technologies reshape business landscapes, expect novel models, paying methods, digitization of processes, of physical products that become either intangible (newspapers, CDs), bundled (calculators, alarms, cameras) or connected (smart objects), and the potential for humungous data creation rumored to be valuable but that few players have as of yet figured how to monetize on.

Who is the disruptor? What is its stated goal, vision, corporate culture, and the style of its leader? Is it a traditional competitor, or a tech player eyeing your industry—either a startup or one of the heavyweights?

Tech titans expanding towards traditional businesses represent perhaps the gravest threat of corporate disruption in the 4^{IR}, whether they open a new department dealing with self-driving cars (Apple), a research center dedicated to prolonging life (Google), seek to improve healthcare (Amazon), or buy a company (e.g. Amazon's acquisition of Whole Foods), or create a new company from scratch (Elon Musk's SpaceX and Neuralink)[18].

Under Armour's CEO Kevin Plank set the tone when answering his own rhetorical question as to why a sports brand was attending the 2017 Consumer Electronics Show in Las Vegas:

> The challenge that I give to our product teams each season isn't about what we are going to do about our current competition. It's what are we going to do if Apple and Samsung decide that they are going to start making apparel and footwear. And, if they did, what would it look like?[19]

He didn't wait to see, instead preemptively going all out on digital, in a bold strategy that paid off. Adopting this mindset can give your company a lead. Once news comes out of the Apples and Googles steering in your direction, it's already game over. Best picture them whooshing for your slice of pie, with their one-winner-takes-all paradigm putting the entire pie at stake.

Next, as with the sectorial threat, assess levels of probability and impact. Under what circumstances and timing might it ripen? For a product, what needs does it address, and by when will its price tag drop to a level deemed accessible? What reception has it garnered from professionals and end-users? While the second group is more vital for the technology to break into the mainstream, it may lack clairvoyance. Tech often starts at the fringe; how and by when will it percolate to the masses? If derided as a pathetic gizmo, by when would ulterior enhancements amend the pimply teen and turn it into a force to be reckoned with?

Avoid sounding the alarm at every sign of a novel application. Gather more intel first. The tech challenger might be desperate for new revenue streams, while the traditional one despairs to jump on the 4th Industrial Revolution wagon, with little actual strategy. Perhaps their boss is giving free leeway to R&D engineers with a poor understanding of market needs. This happens when competitors are eager to step their game up in the tech field. Given

---

[18] Dismissing VR and brain implants as a remote threat to traditional business fields would be a grave mistake. Ernest Cline's novel *Ready Player Two* includes an interesting depiction of these technologies' disruption potential.

[19] Peter High, *Under Armour Is Now The Largest Digital Health And Fitness Company On Earth*, Forbes (Sep 18, 2017) https://www.forbes.com/sites/peterhigh/2017/09/18/under-armour-is-now-the-largest-digital-health-and-fitness-company-on-earth/?sh=1c1f77c85dfc.

the ambient buzz, everyone wants to be viewed as leading the charge. Little do they know that it is a junkyard polluted with anonymous failures and forgotten doodads.

Reception to consumer IoT has to date been rather icy. Introduced almost a decade ago, smart light bulbs, shoes, chairs, watches, and tennis rackets form a negligible portion of their respective markets,[20] due to a misalignment between price and perceived added value. Smart lights have yet to push traditional lighting companies to the verge of bankruptcy. Yet breaches could arrive at certain focal points—for instance, wearables surfing on the "quantified self" trend.

Startups come and go. One's demise does not imply that it got it all wrong; perhaps it was a matter of timing, or it boiled down to management issues. The core idea might remain worth investigating. Your firm could benefit from teaming up or even acquiring a startup to propel its futurization strategy.

Timing matters immensely. Consider entry barriers, such as patents, highly regulated or asset-intensive sectors. Heavy assets as a barrier are less common nowadays. Digital technology costs little and can be scaled with zero marginal cost. Startups have better access to funding. Unless a new AI winter sets in, promising ideas with disruptive potential will continue to lure investor money. And Big Tech is aflush with cash; when they set their eyes on a traditional sector, it could be a long shot. Jeff Bezos consistently asserts being in it for the long term, in a middle finger to investors.

Look across the horizon, not only toward Silicon Valley. The ICT revolution has flattened the world, leveling the playing field to competition from once faraway places. Faced with the threat of cheap rival products from China, tool-maker Hilti erected a lease model that enabled it to harpoon clients, in what is now pointed out as a successful business case.[21] Meanwhile Blockbuster went bankrupt both because it ignored the shift from video rental to online streaming, and did not build on customer data to provide enhanced recommendations—in short, it failed to harness the power of the Internet, of Big Data and algorithms.

The case of General-Purpose Technologies

GPTs produce a particular strain of disruption.

---

[20] Of these examples, the smartwatch has the highest market share of its sector, with less than 5% as of 2019 (roughly a $20 billion global smartwatch market, out of a $50 trillion watch market) – and that's with Apple's endorsement.

[21] Ramon Casadesus-Masanell, Oliver Gassmann and Roman Sauer, *Hilti Fleet Management: Turning a Successful Business Model on Its Head*, Harvard Business School (May 2017).

When electricity lit up factories, it didn't just facilitate night shifts. Up to then, the factory floor was organized around a central, steam-powered axle from which machines drew energy. It took a new generation of engineers to grasp electricity's ramifications and redesign workshops in a more decentralized layout.[22] The first TV commercials showed an adman sat in front of a microphone to announce a product's strengths, in the same manner that radio advertisement was always conducted. In the early stages of the Internet, firms scrambled to get on the bandwagon, yet struggled to understand the paradigm shift involved. Before the dot.com bust, I interned in the digital branch of a major exhibition organizer that sought to sell exhibitors a virtual booth in a virtual exhibition. What started off as a clever, avant-garde concept (after all, this was before the Web 2.0), turned out a flop: poorly conceived as a stale copy-paste of the physical venue, the plan lacked appeal and failed to build on digital strengths, such as the gleaning of data analytics. Meanwhile, companies that succeeded in taming the Internet thrived, espousing e-commerce, O2O models, SEO and social media. Those stuck with brick and mortar declined or ceased to exist.

AI is the GPT spearheading the 4^{IR}. It could impact businesses in several ways:

- externally: by capturing user data, AI-enabled firms:
    - deepen their customer knowledge, paving the way for more tailored solutions
    - offer data-powered advantages to customers: analytics, a platform, a community…

    Companies that fail to exploit data will lose customers and revenue, for lack of either information crucial to win new customers, or of data-powered value that customers come to view as a must-have
- internally: AI can help a business to automate or digitize internal processes, reducing costs (and headcount).

    Here failure would stem from the inability to keep up with swifter, digitized rivals. These become impossible to compete with from a cost perspective—though a handful may survive, by successfully branding up, perhaps using the human touch as a differentiating factor.

---

[22] Paul A. David, *The Dynamo and the Computer: An Historical Perspective on the Modern Productivity Paradox*, in The American Economic Review.
Vol. 80, No. 2 (p.355–361).

Other advantages will surface in certain circumstances. In fields where final end-users are distanced by one or several intermediaries, a digital link now creates a bridge for the company to glean into the end-user's world, much to the dismay of the intermediary (retailer, importer, distributor…). Imagine each Coca-Cola bottle embedded with a smart tag that conveys temperature, weight, and location. In theory (and however prohibitively expensive), such a smart packaging could indicate how long on average until a bottle is consumed, whether it is entirely drunk or if a different size would be more appropriate, at what temperature, if and when the bottle reaches a recycling destination, and much more.

These opportunities will morph into threats for laggards. Such is the salient trait of general-purpose technologies. Tardiness in adopting a low-impact tech like the fax machine will not cause a firm's ruin. But try naming a successful company that forwent an Internet presence.

Less "general" technologies, i.e. 2nd-level GPTs, still carry enough sting to rewrite the rules of a business. As we stride away from broadness, disruption fluctuates by sector. 3D printing may have a mild effect on manufacturers, with higher impacts in certain target industries: car and aircraft components, but also cargo freight and construction where it can reduce both costs and carbon footprint. Yiwu's plastic injectors and mold manufacturers could count among the biggest losers.

Keep a tab on the disruptive potential at the corporate level for broad technologies like AR, chatbots and 3D printing, even if they do not seem to directly affect your sector. The next challenge in this corporate Squid Game will be integrating 4^{IR} and 3rd Internet Wave technologies into business models. We've discussed their potent ripple effects. How will your company cope? Hereafter a handful of corporate traits to help assess this question.

Corporate Size and Tech-savviness

Engineers in manufacturing companies keep an alert eye on process optimization. The same cannot be said of offices. Here, the firms most aggressively pursuing automation and digitization can be classified into two types:

- Small businesses that specialize in AI and other technologies; they usually share these traits:
  - new tech is at the core of their founding
  - they offer it as a solution to traditional enterprises.
- Big corporations, with strategies geared toward new technology, that invest heavily to secure top talent via hiring and acquisitions. They stretch

beyond Silicon Valley to include traditional companies: Under Armour, John Deere, General Electric, Walmart…

These are the usual suspects making headlines with AI experimentations, the very ones cited as proof of an imminent future governed by 4^{IR} technologies.

But what's missing from this tableau? Medium-sized businesses and the bulk of small ones not established with 4^{IR} tech at their core. A handful may have an AI strategy, yet the majority lack both the knowledge and means necessary to get on the bandwagon.

Some have barely emerged from their ICT molt, for instance, by finalizing an ERP implementation—a costly endeavor that they have yet to reap the full benefit of. And now tech has sped ahead, requiring new investments, with only hazy monetization prospects down the road. Are the bosses willing to fork the bill?

Companies led by the baby-boomer generation may feel disconnected from new tech, whereas those that acknowledge the urge for a digitization strategy are undecided as to where to start, or unclear as to how AI affects their line of business. Studies on corporate disruption zoom between an abstract eagle view and a too narrow close-up of specific cases. The success stories of XXL companies from Microsoft to General Electric may prove hard to transpose to M or S-size companies. Nor is it easy for them to adopt the strategies or foster the culture of startups built from day one on technology.[23]

Kodak taught us that there is no "the bigger the better" rule. Yet assuming all else equal, we could venture to say that firms little and large stand a better fighting chance compared to medium-sized ones. The small benefit from flexibility (on condition of having the right-minded staff or founder), while big firms have greater means to enact change. Each has its weaknesses: an AI-transition could prove too costly a leap for small firms, while large ones may face a resilient corporate culture that management struggles to shake off. But mid-sized firms tend to cumulate the negatives from both sides: limited funds and an organization paralyzed by internal bureaucracy and entrenched

---

[23] This critique of existing literature extends beyond the mere realm of AI and automation; unfortunately, it's an issue commonly encountered in studies. For instance, marketing guru Michael Porter, when discussing the "shared value" trend, cites only startups conceived with such good intentions from their inception, and big firms. These articles aim to inform other companies of what's happening and how to get on the bandwagon. Yet when the authors fail to even acknowledge the selectivity of their own examples, thus what distinguishes the avantgarde winners they quote from their intended audience, how can they provide any actionable guidance to the latter? See Michael Porter and Mark Kramer: *Creating Shared Value*, Harvard Business Review (January–February 2011).

politics. Coherence throughout the organization, for instance with an incentive scheme reflecting management's reorientation goals, is paramount to the turnaround.

When it comes to the size of the company where Americans work, we find a neat split of the population, with roughly similar numbers of workers in small, medium, and large companies, as shown in Fig. 5.11.

Based on what a conservative estimate could conclude that a third to a half of American workers tread in a business with limited appetite, meager means, or no clue as to how to integrate AI into their strategy.

The same was probably true of the Internet revolution three decades ago. But as noted earlier, the Internet and AI agendas differ in their outcomes. While both provide greater insights into customer behavior, the former was less of a cost-saver. Apart from certain segments that benefitted from zero marginal costs or online platform dynamics, propelling the ascent of Netflix, Instagram, and other Tinders, in most sectors the ICT revolution did not strongly affect headcount (and contrary to the ERP sales pitch). Improving AI of the type surfacing with ChatGPT could exert a greater toll on labor, expunging staff in bloated companies, that then turn their guns against unprepared middle-sized ones. Hence for each of the three company sizes, Fig. 5.11 ranks the type of disruptive threat its workers could face, in order of probability.

That doesn't mean the situation for employees in AI-handicapped firms is hopeless, nor that they must abandon ship. Sometimes all it takes is a few motivated elements to kickstart a revolution from within. Besides, would you

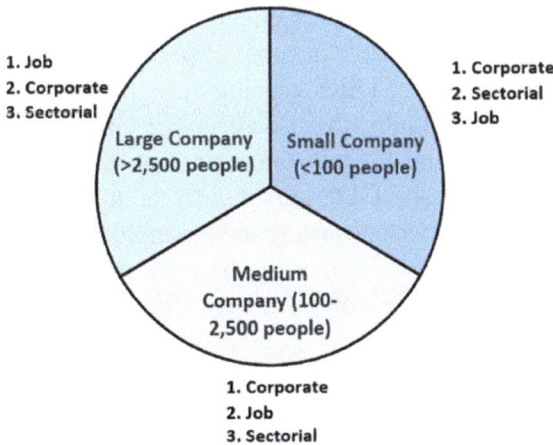

Fig. 5.11 Where Americans work, by company size, and relevant disruption threat types, sorted from most to less probable

have more value in a smaller company with scant AI expertise, or a mammoth firm comprising an AI department stuffed with programmers and data scientists? New tech could spell trouble for the smaller company if unprepared, but in the larger corporation one's value is diluted.

For an employee to help their firm presupposes a fair understanding of the industry, its maturity, and of technology, leading us back to Christensen's emphasis on tech and consumer needs. It preps her for the higher echelons, too: decision-makers further up the food chain admire clairvoyant staff.

Corporate Dynamics

In *The First 90 Days*, author Michael Watkins introduces the STARS model to subsume organizations in five buckets: startup, turnaround, accelerated growth, realignment, and sustaining success.

An expanding company tends to both add staff and fuel the growth of existing headcount along its own. Meanwhile of the five models, the second and fourth require a restructuring of sorts. Logic would dictate that when taking identical clones and placing them in each of these five company types, the ones in growing companies stand a higher chance of at worst remaining employed, at best rising in the ranks.

That is not to say that the other types should be shunned like a rabies-infected dog. Organizations experiencing turmoil see their structure and processes profoundly upset. More often than not, bad management is what gets these companies in trouble in the first place—this in itself hints at an opportunity. People talented in navigating through foggy waters or cleaning up a mess can emerge greater from the storm; like Richard III, they long for anarchy, ready for the musical chairs game it stirs, in which they can advance their pawns at a pace unthinkable in times of peace.

To a certain extent, the STARS typology can be transposed to dimensions like sector or geography. You score points simply by working in a booming sector, as demand for jobs outstrips supply. Ditto for locations: a country experiencing massive GDP growth attracts multinationals thirsty for consumers. A young salesperson starting in Gap in 2008 had better prospects for rapid ascension in China, where the brand just launched, than in the mature US market. Five years down the road, the Chinese employee would be viewed as a veteran ripe for management, whereas in the US she'd be one among thousands of anonymous faces outranked by more senior people. It's worthwhile checking whether your firm encourages geographical mobility, to reach areas of growth.

Other Factors

Other aspects range from management's appetite for automation to the staff's knowledge and proficiency in automation tools. The latter varies by person, but you can grasp whether the majority is neophyte or proficient. Is computer proficiency concentrated in a few departments (say IT, R&D and Communications?) Are those employees focused on specialized software (e.g. SQL for IT, SolidWorks for R&D, and Photoshop for Communications), with limited knowledge of common tools (Office package, Smartsheet...)? What training policies are in place to improve IT skills? Are they effective? What of management's stance on automation? Do they view it under the antagonistic relationship of man versus machine, or employees versus management, in which the latter utilizes machines to rein in employee pressure? Or do they wish to enhance the workforce via training? Data on the board of directors may be available online; does yours include any tech-savvy people?

A good corporate culture fit matters in ways that go beyond automation and an agile mindset. Some firms and sectors are notorious for long working hours: advertising, auditing, and events, to name a few. A highly uncertain environment may underlie this, yet oftentimes overtime is just baked into the culture. A company imbibed with the overtime syndrome deters employees from automating work: what's the point in efficiency if etiquette demands you to plug in late nights regardless?

These factors taken alone are not constitutive of a "go" or "no go" yet need to be acknowledged. Your value in an environment depends as much on what you bring to the table as what's already on it. Frame it in your career plan: if toiling several years in a workaholic atmosphere is a stepping-stone to a more cozy, coveted position, it could be worth the effort.

Corporate Action

A garage mechanic should get concerned if, in a world increasingly shifting toward electric vehicles, no signs of proactiveness come from management to train staff on electronics, install electric charging stations, and so on.

There's no better way to preemptively circumvent disruption than for the company to disrupt itself. Because this must be done ahead of time, before the new model hits the mainstream, such actions seldom appear legitimate; in fact when presented, they look more akin to sabotage. Given vested interests in existing cash cows, managers in the corporate chain of command tend to resist fundamental changes in the model. If it's not broken, why fix it? Convincing them of the need for change can be challenging and depends to some degree on your place in the pecking order.

To preempt corporate disruption, the successful company:

- is open to criticism, questions itself, and embraces radical change when needed
- reinvents itself; like a phoenix, it sheds its old skin to reveal a new blazing one (Midea, IBM...)
- creates an internal department in charge of its own destruction, walled off from the rest of the company and with plenipotentiary powers—the skunkworks path, as in Bletchley Park where Alan Turing's team developed their revolutionary machine, or as when Lockheed Martin developed the first U.S. jet fighter in a record time during World War 2 (coining the term skunkworks)[24]
- looks toward Big Tech, sees itself as competing against them (Under Armour)
- welcomes new tech and automation; like a judoka, it turns threat into opportunity.

Some refute the skunkworks model as too limited for the 4^{IR}, instead arguing for a holistic approach that involves every department of the organization[25]. Radical threat calls for radical action.

Looking beyond mere intentions, study the chances for success in the endeavor. What ingredients would favor adaptation to the 4^{IR}? To achieve the transition, executives from Accenture emphasize the following management traits:

- a proper mindset to profoundly reimagine both processes and work
- encouraging AI experimentation throughout the company: try, fail, soak in the lessons and reiterate—the faster the better
- promoting responsible, ethical AI
- recognizing the potential of data in a broad sense; acting accordingly to collect, extract and deliver the best value from it
- developing AI-collaboration skills, both to complement and enhance human work.[26]

---

[24] Cf. Lockheed Martin: *Skunkworks Origin Story*, Lockheedmartin.com, http://www.lockheedmartin.com/us/aeronautics/skunkworks/origin.html; also Matthew E May, *The Rules of Successful Skunkworks Projects*, Fast Company (October 9, 2012), http://www.fastcompany.com/3001702/rules-successful-skunk-works-projects.

[25] Marco Iansiti, Karim R. Lakhani, *How AI is Changing Work: Putting AI at the Firm's Core*, Harvard Business Review Special Issue of Winter 2021.

[26] Paul Daugherty and James Wilson, *Human + Machine: Reimagining the Work in the Age of AI*, Chap. 7, Harvard Business Review Press.

Not every organization has this kind of mojo in motion. Yet as a member, you contribute to develop awareness. Books advise leaders on how to identify and seize opportunities created by the 4^{IR}. This is not a job to leave to the IT Department, nor a potentially myopic management. Even supposing your company is well engaged on the digitization path, to ensure success the experts spearheading the transition need allies in each department. Forge ties and work closely with them wherever the project touches on your sphere. AI savviness for business applications among non-experts remains rare. Inasmuch as you don't appear aloof and know what you are talking about in regard to the possibilities but also limitations of AI, they should welcome your enthusiasm. This can only help boost recognition of your value to the firm and serve as a trampoline to the higher strata.

Peers might observe these movements with an evil eye, or even attempt to sabotage the process using a variant of the Luddites' sledgehammer. New tech has a bad rep, as with it comes the propensity for automation. Humans have a visceral fear of change, of the unknown. Stand away from this crowd; embrace progress. But don't be the chump who saws off the supporting branch. In the job and task disruption chapters, we discuss how to retain value.

Your Place in the Company

Workers in a dormant company should first shake the tree to see what falls. Push for awareness on threats. Gauge whether the firm has the will and determination to change. Prod managers. Assess their level of understanding and whether they share your concerns. Incite movement. The right credentials and a favorable reaction from the top could propel you to a position where you spearhead the change. Perhaps a green ticket is implicitly given at first. Employ tact and skill to get colleagues onboard. Management should at some stage officialize your new role in the company, putting you in charge of an overhaul project, or at least on the team. Clairvoyance in the fast pace landscape of new technologies is a coveted skill, one that can act as a springboard for your career.

If management proves incapable of acknowledging the raging bull, of grabbing it by the horns, or if it shoves you aside in the process, no harm is done. You now know where you stand and can move onto the next step: find a job elsewhere.

Changing jobs can prove tricky after a long tenure. No matter how much you say you hate it, it has become a comfort zone. The problem with the "Better the devil you know" reasoning is that it implies a static state of affairs, when the world is anything but. If you conclude from your firm's evaluation that it faces a strong risk of disruption, with nothing in the pipeline to address it, not even the will, the rest lies on your shoulders. With automation and globalization on the rise, the old paradigm of lifetime employment will no longer cut it. Anyone in need of a visual cue can summon Superman's planet, with its huge crystals and other wonders. As we all know, it didn't last. Picture that as your company right now, on the brink of some brutal upheaval.

Before doing anything rash, double-check your prediction and timing. If the change wrought by a technology takes a decade or two for the sector to digest, your firm may adapt in time. Many companies that were slow to adopt the Internet nonetheless survived and today thrive. Non-smart lighting firms are still around too. Keep cool, learn and tinker. Whence the company awakens up from its slumber, the full extent of your value may come to light.

Conclusion on Sectorial and Corporate Disruption

Narrow technologies focus on a specific sector. Which ones pose a menace, how would your company cope, and last but not least, how will you cope? (Fig. 5.12).

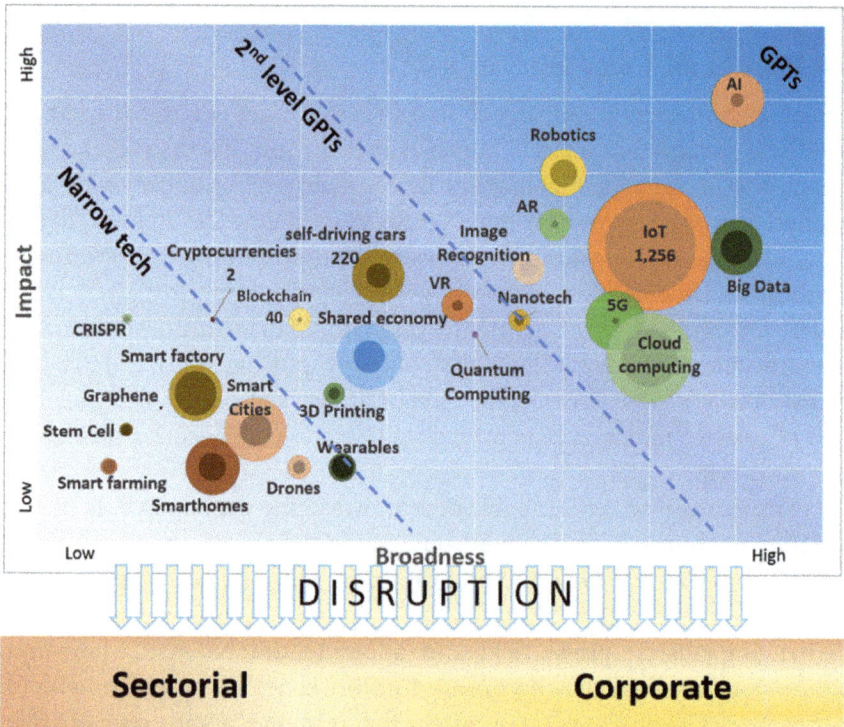

Fig. 5.12 Tech versus sectorial and corporate disruption

While sectorial threats occur more sporadically, the profoundness of their impact can make them particularly lethal. As a technology bends toward the GPT end, it tends to shake companies regardless of sector. Those in the middle carry the disruptive potential for either—like blockchain and the shared economy that each rewrite traditional business models in a number of sectors.

Remember that the Tech snapshot moves in time. Some bubbles may stay put while others rise or recede, moved by underlying trends. If graphene production methods can be scaled for mass production, as CRISPR-Cas9 is finetuned for widespread use, as improved conversational AI bots become ubiquitously deployed at all customer contact points or as nanotech and 3D hit the mainstream, those bubbles may nudge ever farther rightwards, disrupting firms beyond their original forage grounds.

Assess each threat in terms of likelihood and depth of impact. Timing depends on tech factors ranging from acceleration to the state of the ecosystem and the exponential gap that delays institutional adaptation. There will be winners and losers.

Figure 5.13 recalls the questions to ponder once a capital threat has been acknowledged.

This is just a sketch—for instance, before leaving for cause of no longer being valuable, seize any training opportunities or seek to reinvent yourself—especially if the conclusion is that your current skills will lose value regardless of where you go. Perhaps the hard question is whether it is you or your firm that is losing synch with the march of time.

Lastly—and this holds true regardless of which of the four doors of disruption is at stake—consider your own career situation, in particular, your distance to retirement. If you are done within a few years while the disruptor will take a decade to make an impact, you have less to worry about than say, the youngster you are coaching to replace you.

With these warnings addressed, sectorial and corporate disruption are not the main topics addressed in this book (hence their bundling into a single chapter), for three reasons.

First, employees have only so much power to act within their firm. These threats are dealt with at senior corporate levels, by those engaged in the strategy. By pushing the right buttons, an employee could capture management's attention; but all else being equal, she has more firepower to deal with job and task disruption. These squarely target her stratum. Hence the final advice to jump ship if your warnings fall on deaf ears.

Second, much has already been written on sectorial and corporate disruption, on how to seize either one as an opportunity instead of falling victim to

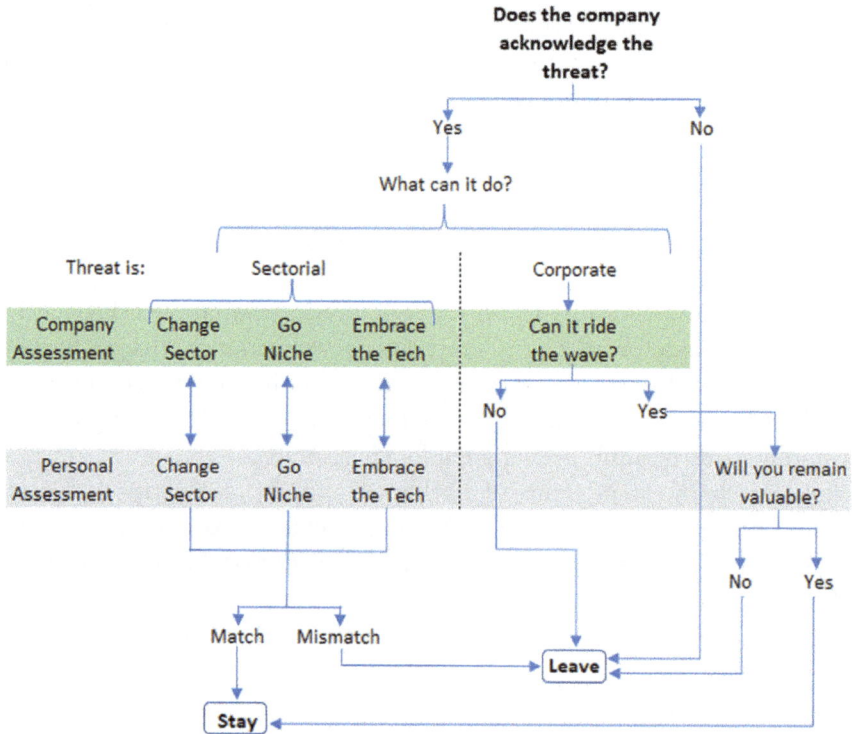

Fig. 5.13 Action summary for sectorial and corporate disruption

it, in business magazines and books addressed to CEOs and entrepreneurs, like the *Innovative Disruptor* series.

Lastly, while the story of the 4^{IR} has barely begun and there's no telling which direction it will take, AI seems poised to become the Black Plague of jobs, the general-purpose technology that swallows a substantial portion of occupations, regardless of sector. Warnings from the likes of Martin Ford, Frey and Osborne do not deal with jobs lost to disruption obliterating sectors or shutting companies down, but as a result of job automation within sectors and companies that may well be thriving. This is by far the biggest challenge looming for workers, including white collars.

Sectorial and corporate disruption get the lion's share of future technologies-slash-disruption bookshelves because they can make or break companies both big and small, affecting top management and investors, whereas job disruption poses no direct threat to CEOs and stock prices—on the contrary, they stand to benefit from it. Hence, it garners less attention, despite the dire repercussions on the workforce.

With this, we turn our sights to the "jobs and tasks" angle of what's getting disrupted.

6

Job Disruption

Occupational disruption darts back to Keynes and his technological unemployment, or

> Unemployment due to our discovery of means of economizing the use of labor outrunning the pace at which we can find new uses for labor.[1]

The "means" refers to improved processes and to working methods that eliminate waste (the Japanese *muda* of Toyota's famed Lean manufacturing). This often involves new automation tools, be it a tractor doing the equivalent work of several human shovelers, or AI replacing truck drivers and stockbrokers.

It would be shortsighted to confine the threat of tech disruption to full automation. As the Luddites taught us, aspects of work can be automated, simplified or enhanced, with resisting chunks handed down to lower skilled workers. Self-driving cars garner all the attention because they automate the driver's job. But long before that, Uber's technology obsoleted the value of expertise, opening the valves to less knowledgeable drivers. In many jobs and tasks, this danger dwarfs that of full automation. It may not cause massive unemployment—in fact it could create more jobs, only jobs that command

---

The original version of this chapter was revised: Text correction has been updated. The correction to the chapter is available at https://doi.org/10.1007/978-3-031-19278-4_10

[1] John Maynard Keynes: *Economic Possibilities for our Grandchildren.*

lower wages. It threatens to drag down workers who lose their strengths on the labor market.

In certain instances, the company needs staff to master the new technology in order to apply it. This involves a new set of expertise and a change in the job description, adding on work that again resists automation. Here the "resisting chunks" are newly minted; and they need to be handed over to *more* skilled workers. This is a case of technology that enhances work. It can become a problem if you fail to stay tuned for the latest tools, as tech-savvy peers will gain an advantage over you.

In short, the threat of technology is threefold:

– reducing the amount of work necessary to achieve a task:
– reducing the level of skills required, and with it, wages and status:
– enhancing the tech-savvy, who then speed ahead of you (assuming that you are not one of them)

After a precision on organic versus non-organic replacement (Sect. 6.1), we consider the enemies lurking, ready to bounce and snatch the job from the worker, or substantially devalue it. Herein lie the threat from low-skilled labor, from tech-powered experts, giggers, offshoring and more generally outsourcing (Sects. 6.2 and 6.3).

Next, we comb through the factors that, when submitted to the acids of automation and outsourcing, tilt the cursor in one direction or the other (Sect. 6.4). These are grouped under "internal factors", or traits proper to the job, for instance recurrence and the human touch, and "external factors" such as demographics and social trends. We then plot the traits on a job vulnerability canvass for a rendering of a given job's overall fragility in the face of automation (Sect. 6.5).

6.1   Organic and Non-Organic Replacement

Organic Replacement

They say no-one is irreplaceable, meaning that the threat of replacement constantly lurks around the corner. Yet the threat of automation-slash-replacement does not infer that someone of equal standing handles the job. An identical skillset and salary level when passing over to a successor reflects organic replacement, in a zero-sum equation ($-1 + 1 = 0$).

This includes the case of an underperforming worker substituted by someone else; here, job description and requirements remain intact—the substitution occurred because of a wrong fit. Ditto for the replacement of retired workers.

Let us take a minute for an "organic handover test", to assess replaceability by another worker.

Imagine accepting a job offer from another company that requires you to start right away. Let's assume someone else is available to take over your job, whether from within or outside of your organization. Neither a subordinate nor a superior, but a peer, someone of similar background and qualification. How long would it take to train that person? A week? Three weeks? Half a day?

Figure 6.1 highlights how speed and ease of replacement vary based on where your substitute comes from.

Some takeaways:

- colleagues occupying a similar position to yours makes you a commodity; replacement is swift, and that puts you in a vulnerable position. All else equal, the probability for this is higher:

  - the bigger the company,
  - the lower you are in the rungs (assuming a pyramidal structure).

- it takes longer for an outsider to fill your shoes: acquaintances need to be forged, acclimatization to company products, tools, processes, and so on.
- a newcomer from a different background will have more to digest (in practice though organizations rarely hire someone from outside coming from a different position).

A replacement hailing from a different background may hint to difficulties in finding a right match—a sign of paucity. Backtracking to the "similar

		Company	
		within	outside
Position	Similar	FAST	AVERAGE
	Different	AVERAGE	LONG

Fig. 6.1 Speed of organic replacement

skills" hypothesis are these hard to come by on the job market? Would your company struggle to find someone with the right competencies? How long do you suppose it'd take them to find the right fit? Or is your organization bustling with underlings bearing the same title tag as yours?

The plot thickens for those with two distinct roles, for instance marketing and engineer. Would that require two people of divergent backgrounds to replace? In which case a reorganization is highly probable, but at what cost for the organization?

The figure conceals a variety of degrees. Someone from outside of the company may have prior knowledge of your corporate systems (ERP, CRM…); "inside the company" holds different connotations according to whether that person comes from the same site or is relocated. And someone from outside will be more or less of a stranger based on whether they had prior exposure to the sector, in line with sectorial mobility. This leads back to the four doors. Here, task and sector were neglected in an oversimplification.

We set aside organic replacement, a part of everyday corporate life unrelated to automation; unless that peer or newcomer has an extra skill that demarcates her from you—like greater tech versatility. While no longer organic replacement, this threat emphasizes the importance of the handover test, as a shelter that buys you time to rectify course.

Non-organic Replacement

In certain instances, the foundational grounds that qualify someone for a job change, opening the door to people with different skills. New apples ripen while previous ones fall out of favor, deemed either under- or overqualified.

The change in requirements can have various roots: a department or company reorganization, sometimes following a merger or acquisition; a decision to outsource the job. Often though, the culprit is technology: an automated process, a newly implemented system that requires special expertise, or new weaving machines entering the workshop, making costly craftsmen unnecessary, as unskilled youths can fulfill the lowered requirement level for a fraction of the cost. Technology moving the strings backstage nuances the "human replacement" appellation. Luddites were replaced by less skilled workers, yet the root cause of their fate lied in the introduction of new machinery. Likewise if pressed by a competitor, as its superior performance probably stems from technology.

As long as skills and requirements match, the organization has no economic incentive to substitute. Someone else turns more qualified as a result of technology retracing the contours of a job requirement or making her more productive. Hence, non-organic job replacement by humans emerges as *a disguised form of technological disruption*. Technology changes the status quo, unbalancing the equation presented in the case of organic replacement. It empowers someone else to do the job *better*, either by delivering substantially improved results or because she costs less yet produces a roughly equal output, generating savings for the company. This highlights the fundamental role of technology in labor productivity, modelized by Robert Solow in an essay that earned him a Nobel Prize in economics.[2]

From this we deduce that the threat of job automation cannot be conceived of without looking into alternative ways of getting work done. From spoon to shovel, then tractor, each tech improvement increases output, upsetting the status quo, in other words the quantity and quality of workers to a job. A job could be lost to a machine or to a human, often to a mix of both.

6.2 A Protean Threat to Work: the 3 Types of Job Disruption

Figure 6.2 précises the types of repercussion tech can have on jobs. These forces are at play regardless of the company and sector's performance, as witnessed by the public outcry whenever a firm posting healthy profits nonetheless actions layoff plans.

As noted earlier, we essentially face three cases. The first sees tech automate the job entirely. In the second, tech lowers the skills required for the job, opening the valves to cheap (and often plentiful) labor in a contemporaneous Luddite unfolding, facilitated by trends like offshoring and (ab)use of undocumented immigrant labor. In the last type, tech enhances workers. In a way, we could say that the threat of full automation is similar to sectorial disruption, i.e. to the threat of a substitute, only brought at the level of a job,

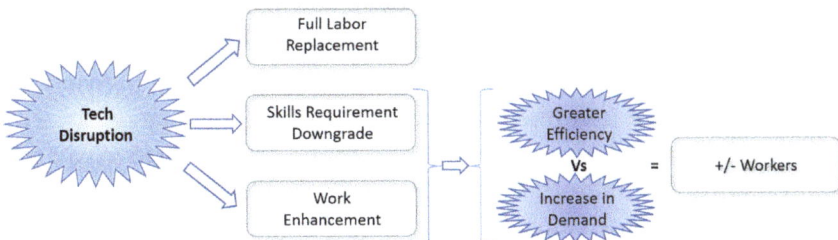

Fig. 6.2 Three types of tech disruption to jobs

---

[2] Robert M. Solow: *A Contribution to the Theory of Economic Growth*, The Quarterly Journal of Economics, Vol.70, No.1 (1956), Oxford University Press.

while the other two job threats resemble corporate disruption transposed to a job.

Cases two and three preserve human labor yet reduce its weight, triggering an all-out battle royale. So how do the two differ? The threat of downgraded skills requirements comes from below, from cheaper labor, whereas those in the enhancement scenario face competition from more skilled people, who achieve superior efficiency via their ease of tool manipulation. Note that the introduction of a single novelty can trigger both effects: frame weaving machinery depreciated the value of skilled weavers (the Luddites) while simultaneously enhancing unapprenticed youths.

Let us nuance the above claim on the reduction of human labor consequent to tech disruption, by opposing farmers to (twentieth century) bank tellers. Both faced automation threats. Despite the United States population growing over 80-fold since the first census held in 1790 revealed a number of four million, automation (and globalization, i.e. outsourcing) led to a shrinkage of farmers. Their numbers fell from 90% to 3% of the workforce, or less than half a million souls. In contrast, the rolling out of automatic teller machines for cash consultation, delivery, and collection did not adversely affect the number of bank tellers: they switched to more value-added tasks that helped the retail banking industry soar, in turn leading to more hires.

Tech improves efficiency, in other words output per worker, thus reduces the need for workers. Yet if that increases demand, as reducing costs opens the market to more wallets, or by freeing worker time for more value-added tasks, it can boost job demand. How these antagonistic forces battle it out shapes the size of the workforce—at least in terms of tech's impact on it. As we moved into the twenty-first century, disruption of the full automation type caught up with bank tellers, in line with the horse parable. As technology pursues its march, ultimately cases two and three veer towards full labor replacement. We could venture to say that the difference between full automation and the other two cases is merely one of timing in the underlying tech's prowess. All the more reason to keep a tab on AI and other technologies, to assess the type of disruption they are currently causing to your tasks, and how far they are from the final phase, that of full automation. In olden times, jobs with a cognitive element were spared from the threat of the final phase. Enter the 4th Industrial Revolution, spearheaded by AI.

Coping with job disruption requires first and foremost to squarely identify the type of disruption threat that you face, as per Fig. 6.2: the threat of full automation-slash-substitution, the downslope threat (degrading of skills), or the upslope threat (enhancement).

6.2.1 Full Automation/Substitution

I did my first internship in the mid-nineties at an Italian bank at Place de l'Opéra in Paris, where my mother worked as secretary to the big boss, a certain Mr. Malle of an illustrious family (catching a glance of the old man through a door was the highlight of my stunt there).[3] My duty was in the dispatch department, consisting of five full-time staff. We were tasked with the dispatch of hundreds of letters from the outside world to the right offices, and with picking up of whatever outbound courier we would find in each office. A job that no longer exists today—we all use email.

This most lethal form of job disruption threatens monotask jobs foremost: tollway and parking lot cashiers, data key enterers,[4] or TV weathercasters, whose numbers have dwindled as we turn to weather forecast apps.

Jobs that consist in analyzing, moving, or connecting two ends of data also face perilous times. Stock exchange traders in the pit and airline ticket booking agents were among the first to go. Real estate agents are shielded somewhat by the size of the investment at stake, giving human presence an edge (the theme of our Human Touch subsection).[5] But more generally, anyone serving as middleman, or moving data around—for instance to book supplier invoices or customer orders into a system—could follow in the footsteps of the couriers I once worked with at the bank.

A one-man job scaled to great proportions gives an economic impetus to automate, hence the full substitution menace looming for truck drivers and hamburger flippers. These workers best reconvert to another job, in a repeat of the flee scenario encountered in sectorial and corporate disruptions. Only this time, it's the *occupation* that must be forsaken; meaning that the change could even be sought within the current organization, by expressing such a desire, volunteering for training courses, and showing relevant prowess.

Note that while termed full automation, the job may contain resilient pockets of tasks. Yet could these not be dispatched to others? To avoid being caught off-guard, broaden the terminology of the threat to full *substitution*, entailing a mix of automation and reorganization or outsourcing. The work of stock market traders was not entirely automated: it was replaced by AI-driven technology steered by a handful of quants.

---

[3] His brother Louis Malle (1932–1995) was a famous film director, another launched Christian Dior Parfums, while nephew Frederic went on to establish the perfume brand bearing his name.

[4] This last category saw its numbers more than halved since 2000 in the US, from 458,720 to 174,930 employees.

[5] While it may not fall victim to full automation, the job of a real estate agent is under serious corporate threat as Zillow, Trulia, and other companies harness the power of Big Data, VR visits, and other ground-breaking technologies.

Do your research upfront. But avoid hitting the panic button based on tabloid headlines. Andrew Ng drew a storm in 2016 when he stated that "radiologists might be easier to replace than their executive assistants."[6] His team had just built an algorithm capable of reading X-ray scans. In a heartbeat, radiologists became the futurists' poster boy of soon-to-disappear job. Ezekiel Emanuel, the principal architect of the Affordable Care Act, repeatedly suggested that radiologists would be replaced within the next four to five years, as did computer scientist and so-called "father of AI" Geoffrey Hinton, adding that radiologists are "like the coyote that's already over the edge of the cliff, but has not yet looked down, so doesn't know there's no ground underneath him."[7]

Just as you should avoid playing AI sorcerer if you lack the proper background, take the declarations from AI boffins speaking out of their field with a pinch of salt. The number of US radiologists increased since Ng's 2016 declaration. Reasons include much patient information to factor in when formulating a prognostic; a holistic approach that alludes narrow AI, incapable of quantifying disparate data sets without clear weighing rules; decisions that involve patients' health, with life-or-death situations that we may not wish to relinquish to AI just yet; and a severe dearth of radiologists, even in the US (ratio of 1:10,000, with huge regional disparities)—in many instances, the job has become monotask *because* scan reading monopolizes the radiologist's time.

The radiologist will certainly undergo changes in her job, but without vanishing. One expert in both AI and medicine proposed that radiologists spend the freed time to console anxious patients, creating a human touch there where people are in dire need for it.[8]

As noted earlier, the threat of automation/substitution is somewhat akin to that of sectorial disruption, only transposed at the level of a job. Refer again to Figure 5.3 to assess your options. While fleeing to another job may often seem to be the most plausible exit route, other options exist. A stock market trader could embrace the threat, developing machine learning skills to become a quant. A restaurant waiter or cashier could aim for a niche expected

---

[6] *Automation and anxiety—Will smarter machines cause mass unemployment?* The Economist (June 25, 2016), https://www.economist.com/special-report/2016/06/23/automation-and-anxiety.

[7] Ben Dickson: *Google's new deep learning system can give a boost to radiologists*, Venture Beat (Sep 16, 2021) https://venturebeat.com/2021/09/16/googles-new-deep-learning-system-can-give-a-boost-to-radiologists/.

[8] Eric Topol: *Deep Medicine: How Artificial Intelligence Can Make Healthcare Human Again*, p. 121–135. Basic Books (2019); on the same note, cf. Joshua Gans, Ajay Agrawal and Avi Goldfarb: *Prediction Machines: The Simple Economics of Artificial Intelligence*, Chap. 14: *Job Redesign: Should we Stop Training Radiologists?* Harvard Business Review Press (2018).

to survive, such as a high-end restaurant that decides to keep its waiters, or a specialized retailer that still requires staff to advise its clientele.

In other situations, the job transmogrification brought by tech could entail fewer good jobs, thus a competition between humans for these, and a downgrading of the rest.

6.2.2 The Threat from the Bottom—Skills Downgrading

Mid-level tasks require a certain dose of intelligence, i.e. relatively rare skills. Hence, recruiters seek candidates with a college degree plus several years of experience. As automation and AI nibble their way toward these skills, the tasks come within reach of the plebs. This is precisely what struck the Luddites two centuries ago: skilled artisanship morphed into a routine set of instructions with little former training required.

Simplified, user-friendly tasks represent a double-edged sword for workers. By overlaying operating instructions on a worker's sight, AR eliminates the need to learn wiring diagrams or produce installation sheets. The years of field work that give a plumber or electrician the baggage to instantly recognize patterns in a messy environment, to reconcile drawings on paper with reality, lose value. A worker with minimal training, aided by aR, may not be as fast or efficient as a veteran plumber, yet achieve satisfactory results in light of cost differences. Even non-expert homeowners could fix problems with assisted reality providing help from a remote guide. Windfalls include transparency to ensure the handyman isn't playing tricks or overquoting.

Likewise, universal translators could suppress the added value of multilinguals. And as the tech behind Uber, Lyft, Didi, and other Grabs (the app of choice in Singapore) gives drivers the fastest route to a destination, it obliterates the value of the cabbies' legendary knowledge of their city's back-alleys and shortcuts.

Gauge any tech approaching your level of expertise. Is it more likely to enhance or to demystify your work? The latter brings it within reach of non-experts. Tasks which no longer call upon rare skills command no value; they become a commodity, and as such inexorably tumble down to the lowest bidder. And tech that turns laymen into experts expedites the true experts down the same drain the Luddites fell in two centuries earlier.

6.2.3 The Threat from the Top—Skills Enhancement

Substitution can also take the form of a highly qualified individual augmented by technology. The underlying math assumes such a superhuman could do the job of several old-school professionals, generating savings for the company in spite of a higher individual salary. Quants replace traditional traders and a financial analyst proficient in Excel and Business Intelligence tools outpaces baby boomers who to match data between two documents would print them out, align them side by side and take a ruler to tick off matching lines one by one with a ballpen.

Unlike the lowest bidder, enhanced workers are likely to remain on the payroll, as organizations tend to preserve core value elements in-house and outsource the rest.

Theoretically in both cases—top and bottom threats—the worker could evolve in synch with her morphing job in order to preserve it. Yet heading downhill is seldom desirable; at best, one takes that route only to bid their time, on the lookout for a rebound. Only the threat from the top can qualify as an opportunity; it points the direction to go, the dry ground that workers in middle strata need to race toward. Hence the emphasis placed on acknowledging your occupation's direction, as this determines what actions to take.

It makes sense to adapt to an occupation undergoing enhancement, to learn and excel at the tools driving efficiency. Since growing to half a million in 1999, the number of telemarketers in the US has fallen consistently, counting barely 100,000 workers in 2020. The fulgurant growth of ecommerce and online advertising are obvious culprits. Telemarketers who acknowledged this could have achieved a triumphant transition. By setting out to learn the ropes of the Internet, adapting to the new model of influencers, followers, and livestreaming, all the while harnessing the still relevant telemarketer skills, they change skins in synch with their occupation.

The job enhancement scenario is the philosopher's stone rehashed by futurists and McKinsey consultants; or perhaps more realistically, the lifeboats that workers should rush for as the Titanic sinks, given that there may not be ample seating for everyone.

Take executive secretaries, whose numbers in the US have nosedived from 1.4 million in 2000 to less than 600,000 in 2018: those that stood firm and remained benefited from the highest salary increase in that wage bracket (from $15.63 to $29.59 an hour). A Hong Kong executive explained to me that he now uses apps like Egencia to manage his busy schedule, there where his secretary previously did all the work. Meanwhile, she treaded in the footsteps of (twentieth-century) bank tellers, acquiring skills like data analysis and liaising with stakeholders, that helped her remain relevant.

How a job that stumbles upon this crossroad fares will depend as much on the company as on the worker, each in their respective abilities and willingness to adapt. Some succeed in upgrading, others fail. If the secretary had balked and clung to the old ways, perhaps even seeking for a job elsewhere, on the long run she may have run into trouble.

Suppose you conclude that your job is facing tech enhancement disruption. Before rejoicing, ask yourself the following.

Firstly, who will need to master the new technology: existing workers, or an entirely different breed of workers? This is what ultimately distinguishes Type-2 disruption from Type-3 disruption: beyond knowing how to use a smartphone (a commodity level of knowledge shared by all), Uber drivers need not master any new technology. The challenging novelty resides in the app. Uber hires other staff and puts them in charge of developing and maintaining the app, as well as data scientists who analyze data for optimum pricing, integration of user feedback, etc. Likewise, Taylorism and the division of labor gave the cognitive task of streamlining the manufacturing process to engineers, not to line operators. On the other hand, clever, tech-savvy secretaries and telemarketers do have a window to adapt. Hence ponder on whether you can make the leap from the former to the latter paradigm. And what is likely to be the company's standpoint? Does it consider the new expertise a requirement for its existing workforce, or as an entirely different job, that it will assign to another breed of workers?

Underpinning this question, what type of new expertise is necessary in the new paradigm? We can cut it into:

- Tech-savviness, or knowledge to build, deploy, maintain or use the technology (however beware of whether daily use of the technology implies high cognition: usually the aim will be for it not to require cognitive skills, as in the Uber example);
- handling what the new technology cannot do: this hints back to the idea that the new tech can open new opportunities while freeing time for more meaningful work, for example with Big Data providing new insights that, when interpreted and put to proper use, can give the firm a competitive edge; or a more profound interaction with clients, as we saw with bank tellers.

Apply Figure 6.2 to your situation. Acknowledge that if technology shakes the existing setup in your firm, it will in all probability downgrade the requirements for certain jobs while enhancing work in other jobs or even calling for new hires who may take the lion's share of the new cognitive work. Hereabove we assumed some new form of expertise is needed, but that may not be the case (and this pretty much determines the gap between Type-2 and Type-3 job disruption).

How will these dynamics play out, and how will you steer your career to safety? Here we approach the core matter of the AI battle royale. We will return to this crucial topic for further investigation, notably while discussing cognition, in the billiards allegory section and in the Tasks chapter.

6.3   The Source of Job Replacement

Before digging into job traits, a final aspect to consider relates to *where* the substitute comes from. Figure 6.3 highlights the various players that can nibble away at your job. It distinguishes those from within and from outside of the organization, albeit with a porous demarcation: temporary staff work on premises yet do not belong to the company; interns are not employees; and tasks can be shifted over to a branch in another country. Other types of replacement not shown here are conceivable under certain circumstances, for instance NGOs, food donations and volunteering, or the organized work of prisoners, a controversial topic in the US.

When meditating on which tasks could be prone to replacement, with what ease, or even considering our earlier case of organic replacement, flip over to this figure. Use it to thoroughly ponder over the question, and not (for instance) limit the scope of the threat to offshoring.

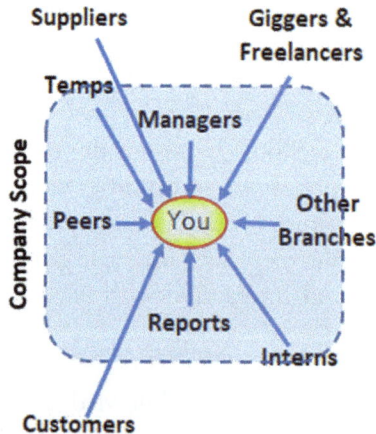

Fig. 6.3 Nature of job replacement

Note the voluntary absence of algorithms and machines from Figure 6.3. To avoid blind spots, consider them as an auxiliary force empowering these players to overtake your tasks, rather than a full substitute. In the following pages, we examine several of these threats; others are hinted elsewhere (for instance replacement from within the company via restructurings, in Job Dismantlement: the billiards allegory).

Hereafter, we peer at outsourcing, offshoring, and moving the task over to the customer.

6.3.1 Outsourcing

Given technology's propensity to boost outsourcing capabilities, this threat has room to grow. Tech ranging from translation software to assisted reality will spur it further, while the transparency wrought by freelance platforms facilitates price comparison, with ratings and customer comments to surmount trust barriers. As the shared economy gains traction, it opens the valves for evermore global bidders, leveling the outsourcing playing field toward a lower wage level than practiced under Western standards.

These bidders increasingly mesh silicon and carbon, courtesy of the tech user-friendly trend. Proficient Turkers (crowd work giggers using Amazon's Mechanical Turk platform) learn to automate tasks to achieve more work. The fact that the gig pays by the click and not by the clock gives a strong impetus to improve efficiency. Hotlines represented the voice of the company for a long time. Then organizations outsourced those jobs to call centers in Bangalore, while simultaneously rolling out instant voice messaging. After an endless maze starting with "For English, Press 1; for Spanish, Press 2", followed by a long wait on some unnerving classical tune, if lucky you'd reach someone located who knows where—a mix of automation and outsourcing. It wasn't as good as a human interlocutor, but that alone did not save hotline service workers. Everyone shifted toward the cheaper model and substandard became the new standard.

This is not new: VHS already enabled outsourcing. Released in 1982, Jane Fonda's first workout video technically substituted for gym instructors. It sold a record of over two million copies. The aerobics trend it birthed suddenly turned sweat and sports cool, especially for women, an "ATM effect" that arguably created more jobs than it destroyed. Teachings at Vipassana meditation centers likewise consist in recordings from the founder, Satya Narayan Goenka (thanks in part to which not only is the ten-day course free, but food and accommodation are provided).

Experts note a lag between jobs *theoretically* outsourceable or automatable, and *the actual implementation* of such measures: the former will always appear greater than the latter. When concluding x% of jobs offshorable or automatable within a given timeframe, they insist that only a fraction will effectively meet that fate.[9]

There are several reasons to this gap. First, the pace at which companies acknowledge the opportunity for making such decisions varies. In the case of automation, they need to secure the right expertise to tailor technologies like AI to their situation; talent remains scarce. At times, companies, clients, and even citizens prefer dealing with humans. Reasons for feet-dragging range from the sensitivity of information to regulations and reliability concerns— not to mention that it takes time for cultures to adapt. Imagine automating the police force or outsourcing it to a private firm.

But that's no reason for consolation. View the lag as an oxygen buffer to plan for preemptive actions.

Revenue per employee (RPE) is a metric widely used to scrutinize a firm's performance, by comparing its sales revenue to its number of employees. RPE objectives incentivize managers to trim down on headcount and shift work to temporary contract workers. Unlike employees, the latter need not be declared according to the generally accepted accounting principles in force in many countries, including the United States (US GAAP). With no change in sales volume, simply moving from employees to outside help magically boosts the RPE metric. The fact that even large companies have less employees on average than before in part results from this rigged tournament between CEOs as to who can present the best RPE. It reflects a major shift in the corporate structure paradigm, brought forth by regulations and accounting principles, with deep social ramifications.[10]

During the height of post-World War 2, leading US firms grew into behemoths, some comprising north of half a million employees. Operations were mostly handled in-house.

Then a handful of companies pioneered a different model, one which sought to limit operations to one or two functions identified as at the core of their value. They kept these and outsourced the rest. Nike epitomizes this trend. To excel in the sports shoe industry, Phil Knight went big on R&D, marketing, and retail, while outsourcing the manufacturing process.

---

[9] For automation, cf. Melanie Arntz, Terry Gregory and Ulrich Zierahn: *The Risk of Automation for Jobs in OECD Countries: A Comparative Analysis*, OECD Social, Employment and Migration Working Paper No. 189. For outsourcing, cf. Alan S. Blinder:, *How Many US Jobs Might be Offshorable?* CEPS Working Paper No. 142 (2007).

[10] Peter Cappelli: *How Financial Accounting Screws Up HR,* in Harvard Business Review, p.39-44 (January-February 2023).

A simple game can illustrate this paradigm. As CEO, you have a score of ten points, representing your attention span, to allocate in the five departments of your firm. Instead of spreading these out evenly for mediocre results across board, the outsourcing model allows to laser focus on one or two departments, achieving excellency in these while outsourcing the rest to the best. The approach recalls Ricardian economics of comparative advantage, only on a corporate scale. Excelling in one or two aspects of business is challenging enough; being the best at every single one is mission impossible. At least that's the idea.

And how to define a company's core value? It should represent what differentiates it from the competition, what gives it its unique identity, its soul, so to speak: the kind of stuff you avoid tossing away to third parties. It's worthwhile to pause and ponder on whether your work belongs to the firm's core value sphere.

Other companies followed suit, gradually outsourcing bigger chunks of their operations to external contractors, subcontractors, suppliers, and freelancers. Technology facilitated this trend, with emailing, Zoom, and platforms like Fiverr and Freelancer. This led to a mushrooming of firms specialized in financial services, logistics warehousing, manufacturing, recruiting, payroll, design, and conceptualization—basically any piece of work that can be hacked off gives the chance for someone to establish a niche market and propose her services to companies only too eager to delegate the job. As the distinction between sectors and occupations became blurred, the latter grew into sectors in their own right. Market saturation triggered survival of the fittest. Clients can now take their pick from this pool of best vendors. The model provides multiple other benefits: freedom from the hassles of hiring, training, and managing staff; from regulated employee protection and labor unions; extra flexibility; savings on rent. Several months of payment terms on condition of delivering also beats paying employees a fixed income regardless of performance every week or month. And the supplier can be based on the other side of the globe, where wages and social protection are a far cry from Western standards, providing the advantages from developing economies without having to open shop there.

Delegating your problems to others is an irresistibly alluring model. And neighbors adopting this paradigm become increasingly difficult to compete with, forcing even the reluctant to reconsider.

When it comes to outsourcing, avoid a blind focus on offshoring, as this conveys a false impression of safety for jobs that are not offshorable when in fact companies can deploy other forms of outsourcing that do not make the headlines simply because unlike offshoring, tax dollars remain stateside. Yet to employees, they are just as lethal.

Companies are increasingly having recourse to what has been dubbed "quiet hiring": acquiring new skills without actually hiring full-time employees. Senior Director at Gartner's Future of Work Research Emily McRae distinguishes external quiet hiring, as in hiring short-term contractors, and internal quiet hiring, as in pushing current employees to temporarily take on new roles.[11] She foresees quiet hiring as a major upcoming trend, citing the example of Qantas Airlines, that in 2022 asked its senior executive to work as baggage handlers for three months to cover an acute labor shortage.[12]

Such excesses have weakened the notion of a business fulfilling a societal role by employing within the community. The stereotype company that fathers its staff, nurtures its employees' aspirations, and helps them fulfill themselves professionally, through training and, yes, caring, has fled the scene; in its stance, the diktat of shareholder value maximization points to personnel costs as a hindrance to the bottom line. Within the functions kept in-house, the image of a "big family" is further shaken by recourse to interns, part-time workers, and temps. A clutch of employees congregates in their ivory tower like the Chosen People, while an army of ants battle it out in the mud below, in the faint hope of one day being anointed to knighthood. Automation will add its sting to the outsourcing paradigm, exacerbating the battle royale.

6.3.2 Offshoring

A heated topic for decades, and a highly politicized one at that, offshoring summons images of landmark factories shutting down to the benefit of sweatshops abroad. It attracts disproportionate media attention compared to other forms of outsourcing, like the plane crash making headlines despite road accidents causing far more fatalities (over 2,000 times more, in case you wondered[13]).

---

[11] Madeline Garfinkle: 'Quiet Hiring' Is on the Horizon—Here's What Employers and Employees Need to Know, Entrepreneur.com (January 4, 2023), https://www.entrepreneur.com/business-news/what-is-quiet-hiring-and-how-you-can-use-it-to-your.

[12] Suzanne Rowan Kelleher: Qantas Asks Executives To Be Baggage Handlers Amid Labor Shortage, Forbes (August 8th, 2022), https://www.forbes.com/sites/suzannerowankelleher/2022/08/08/qantas-asks-executives-to-be-baggage-handlers-amid-labor-shortage.

[13] Roughly, 500 people die of plane crashes each year around the world, versus 3,700 traffic accident deaths per day.

Offshoring differs both from opening shop abroad to get closer to a customer base, and from outsourcing, i.e. subcontracting an activity to an external vendor. It can take the form of:

- a company that closes a department or job and outsources it to a supplier (whether a company or freelancer);
- a reorganization within a multinational corporation—which may preserve a stable overall headcount, but shifts work to another subsidiary;
- a company that switches suppliers;

Yet expressed in this manner, none of these changes imply a move overseas. To qualify as offshoring, the substitute must be located abroad—usually in a country with lower wages.

Princeton Economist Alan Blinder published an influential case study on offshorable jobs in 2007,[14] using the quiz reproduced in Fig. 6.4 to assess vulnerability to offshoring.

Blinder concluded with several scenarios; the moderate one assumed a fourth of American jobs vulnerable to offshoring (with the other two at 22 and 29%), again insisting that a *potential* for offshoring doesn't imply that companies *will* offshore all of these jobs.

Buoyed by the ICT revolution and Cloud technology, globalization facilitated a shift in tasks to other countries. While the wage gap gets all the attention, elements like customer proximity, tax incentives and a favorable ecosystem also influence relocation decisions. Improved education levels and harmonization of standards smoothen the shift, for instance enabling a displacement of accounting services to a branch abroad that uses the same system (allowing the company to retain control over information deemed sensitive).

On the spot presence remains necessary for service jobs ranging from retail and catering to real estate, hospitality, and more—Blinder's category IV, which comprises 70% of all jobs. The enduring hassle of dealing with odd time zones and language constraints also limits the reach of offshoring. It comes as no surprise to find the word "computer" appear in over half of the top ten job types deemed at risk in Blinder's study (if we include "telemarketing" in the lot).

While Fig. 6.4 frames a job's vulnerability to offshoring, by no means does it imply safety from replacement for jobs in categories III and IV. These remain vulnerable to outsourcing, which from the employee standpoint

---

[14] Alan S. Blinder: *How Many U.S. Jobs Might be Offshorable*, Princeton University, CEPS Working Paper No. 142 (March 2007).

4 Broad Occupational Categories

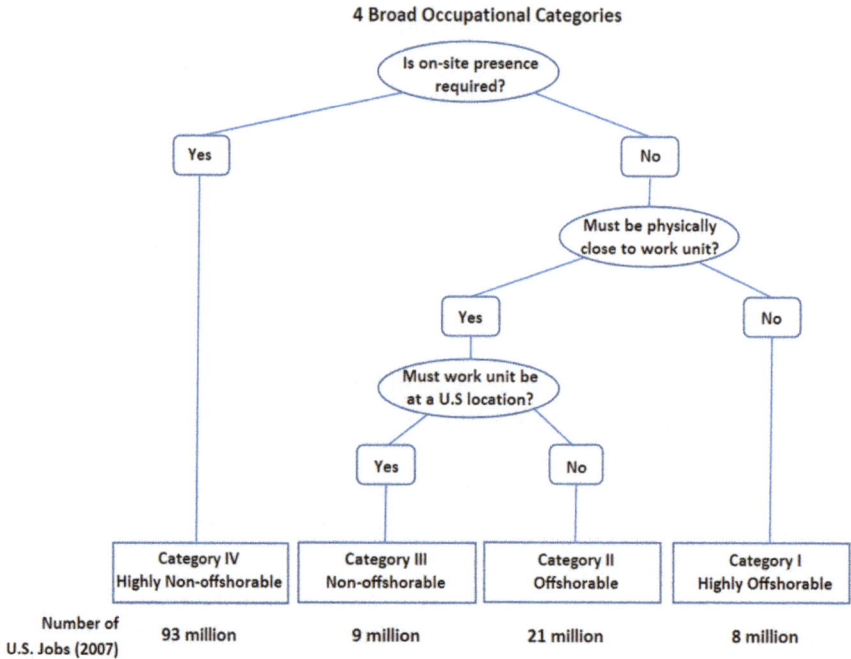

Fig. 6.4 Quiz to determine level of offshoring risk. *Source* Alan S. Blinder, How Many U.S. Jobs Might Be Offshorable? Review of World Economics (April 2007). Reproduced with permission from the Review of World Economics

is just as bad. In *Globotics Upheaval*—a mishmash between globalization and robotics—economics professor Richard Baldwin points to the threat of automation combined with offshoring.[15] But offshoring is only one form of outsourcing, and not always the most likely to occur nor the most efficient.

Such studies overly focus on the impacts of offshoring in the country losing jobs; it happens to be where the economists live, and as they write more about threats than blessings, their works are not balanced by an equal amount of research from those benefiting in the countries receiving the jobs, to say nothing of the number of economists living there, lack of translation or interest, and so on. The studies are also tainted by an ambiguity coming from economists' double role in society: on the one hand, they study wealth and resources, production and consumption of goods and services, the way a botanist examines plants; on the other, they oversee the economy, profess opinions, and advise on policies, like a gardener tending to her flowers and vegetables. Only when several gardens overlap each other and compete for the

---

[15] Richard Baldwin: *The Globotics Upheaval: Globalization, Robotics and the Future of Work*, W&N (2020).

same, limited soil nutrients, botanist and gardener interests clash. No matter how objective the study purports to be, the *choice* of study speaks volumes.

Manufacturing jobs have decreased in China in the past years (recall Fig. 3.7), with several factors at play: automation, certainly, but also the shedding of jobs in non-performant State Owned Enterprises, a shift of labor toward the service sector, and offshoring to other countries amid a rise in Chinese labor costs,[16] including back to the West, a phenomenon dubbed "reshoring".

But don't rejoice yet. This manufacturing returns home in a vastly different shape than whence it departed. While ICT helped offshore jobs to low-wage countries, keeping or even increasing the number of jobs globally, 4^{IR} technologies are bringing those activities back to the West in a vastly automated form. For workers West and East, North and South, overall manufacturing jobs are declining—a lose-lose situation.

Meanwhile, it's becoming increasingly difficult to pinpoint the destination of outsourcing itself. Blame technology. With services like Amazon's Mechanical Turk, Freelancer.com, and other bidding platforms, clients themselves ignore where the gigger is located (nor do they care). Myth has it that only low-wage countries could possibly accept low-paid gigs; but a "favela-zation" in parts of the US is bringing entire swaths of the population on par with developing economies. As aR kicks in, it will enable more manual work to be performed remotely by people far away, bypassing AI's computer vision limitations.

6.3.3 Outsourcing to the Customer

A creative way to outsource a task is by pushing it to the customer. Tech is empowering companies in this respect: stores deploy DIY scan and pay machines; airports invite travelers to self-check-in and self-baggage drop; consumers order at restaurants via an app, with an alarm device to inform them when to come pick up their food tray at the counter. In China, the number of workers in catering has decreased from 2013 to 2018, the period during which online payment apps became ubiquitous.[17]

---

[16] China's minimum wage varies by province. Shanghai has one of the highest. In 2005, it was at 635 CNY per month, in 2022 at 2,590 CNY, i.e. a fourfold increase in 17 years. Meanwhile, the U.S. federal minimum wage has remained at $7.25 an hour since 2009, up 24% from $5.85 in 2005. Taking into account the fluctuation in exchange rates, Shanghai's minimum labor went from being 13 times cheaper than that of the U.S. in 2005 to only 3 times cheaper.

[17] https://www.statista.com/statistics/277090/number-of-catering-employees-in-china/.

Shifting tasks to the customer diminishes the firm's costs. While limited in manufacturing (given the absence of customers), opportunities abound at customer contact points, i.e. in the service sector.

Modeling the environment helps accommodate this method. HR Departments used to receive job applications in various formats, a can of worms that only grew as the Internet facilitated rapid resume firing from websites like Monster and LinkedIn. Now they impose on candidates to fill in a preformatted form on their website (as if copy/pasting a resume snippet by snippet into each distinct field was meant as an ordeal to sieve through the faint-hearted).

In professions that lack workers, help from the customer is more than welcome. Skin cancer is the most generic form of cancer in the US, with one out of five Americans developing a form of it by the age of 70. Yet the country counts only 10,000 dermatologists, or less than one for every 30,000 Americans,[18] leaving general practitioners to fill the gaps, with high error rates. We may soon have reliable apps for people to upload their mole pics.[19] Here too, the user takes over a task up to then performed by the dermatologist. This could bring about a new form of consultation: a yearly package that includes an annual visit, based on results from the app service on which the patient uploads photos at regular intervals. The dermatologist would contact the patient when notified by the app of odd developments.

Consider advice to the customer. At times, we need assistance when buying, due to factors ranging from the expertise involved, a high price tag, a disorienting choice on display, or a no-refund policy. Cosmetics tick all the above boxes. That's why Sephora staffs their outlets with beauty assistants; brands in turn dispatch field coaches to train the beauty assistants and ensure they are well versed in the pros of their products.

Enter Millennials and Generation Z. They draw on social media to glean tips and tricks from their darling KOLs. To them, the old-fashion way of random employees trailing their every step won't cut it.

Harmay took note. This Hong Kong startup's outlets are devoid of advisors, leaving shoppers free to roam and explore the aisles. I've observed them at the trendy Xintiandi store in Shanghai: the average visitor is a twenty-something female; most come in groups of two or three, compare unearthed goods, and rely heavily on smartphones to crosscheck data. Unsurprisingly,

---

[18] See The Skin Cancer Foundation, Facts and Statistics, https://www.skincancer.org/skin-cancer-information/skin-cancer-facts/.

[19] Cf. Esteva, A., Kuprel, B., Novoa, R. et al.: *Dermatologist-level classification of skin cancer with deep neural networks.* Nature 542, 115–118 (2017). https://doi.org/10.1038/nature21056.
    Also Noel Codella, Quoc-Bao Nguyen et al.: *Deep Learning Ensembles for Melanoma Recognition in Dermoscopy Images*, IBM Journal of Research and Development, vol. 61, no. 4/5, 2017.

the products are slightly cheaper than at Sephora (where back in my time, taking photos of products was not even permitted). If this disrupts the traditional model—in a case of corporate disruption—it could have a domino effect that knocks out beauty assistants and field coaches, replacing thousands of workers by a handful of KOLs.[20]

The paradigm could spill over to other fields as youngsters grow to form the bulk of the population (not to mention that luxury is often a harbinger for what comes next in retail). Consumers that take product education into their own hands remove that task from workers. With O2O, shoppers do their homework before going to the store. And that's today. As AR develops, data will appear in real time; not just the short descriptions squeezed on the packaging, but the number and list of influencers recommending the product, related livestreaming videos, virtual body-fitting, matching clothes from your personal wardrobe, and a cascade of similar online offerings. AR will empower consumers to do their research on the fly, sparing us from *home*work while putting traditional advisors out of a job. Meanwhile, the metaverse will bypass brick and mortar by filling in the deficiencies of today's ecommerce.

Amway was a precursor of the consumer-turned-salesperson model—one that suppresses the need for hired salespeople. The referral model has exploded with the advent of digital influencers. KOCs exemplify the sales job outsourced to the customer. Chinese app Pinduoduo, a platform that connects farmers with consumers, relies on referrals and friend recommendations; in 2020, it surpassed Alibaba in terms of annual active users.[21]

Another example of rearranging the tables occurs at the cashier. Automating cashiers did not seem plausible, given the many dexterity obstacles. Surely a Baxter robot would have trouble picking each object for a scan, delicately placing it in the bag, separating food and toxic goods, with extra precaution for the eggs? With the same speed as humans, for a competitive cost? Instead, shoppers are invited to scan and pack SKUs themselves.[22] This may not be perfect: VUCA can swoop in at any moment in the form of a faulty barcode or a dispute on a discount. But that's OK as stores *can mix both types* of cashiers while reducing the overall headcount. Factoring in AI's pros and cons, organizations will continue to design ecosystems that

[20] Wenzhuo Wu: *Can Harmay Take Out Sephora in China?* Jing Daily (February 6, 2020), https://jingdaily.com/can-harmay-take-out-sephora-in-china/.

[21] Rita Liao: *Pinduoduo steals Alibaba's crown with 788 M annual active users*, Tech Crunch (March 17, 2021) https://techcrunch.com/2021/03/17/pinduoduo-surpasses-alibaba/.

[22] The level of ease in scanning varies, from scanning each object's barcode the traditional way (Family Mart) to putting all objects in a small pit that automatically scans everything (Uniqlo) and deducting the merchandise value from your digital wallet as you walk out of the shop (Amazon Go).

favor its implementation wherever feasible, at times pushing seemingly trivial tasks onto consumers. These examples highlight the role of technology in the process.

In the end, whether the task goes to a third party like Amazon Turk, an algorithm, the customer, a branch office in Bangladesh, or the intern down the aisle is quite irrelevant from the standpoint of the worker who loses those tasks. If these comprised a major part of her job, she becomes redundant. And successfully holding onto it is no cause for popping the champagne if reflective of humane management or pressure from labor unions; unless it has a monopoly, the company will eventually tank as competitors with more efficient processes swoop in.

Regardless of the substitute (as per Fig. 6.3), often the best way to preempt threats of job substitution involves moving toward areas of core-value expertise or sensitive information, things that the company would be reluctant to share with or relinquish to outsiders.

6.4   The Job SWOT

What determines a job's fragility in the face of new tech? For instance, which occupation is more vulnerable to automation: airline pilot or flight attendant? In this section, we dissect a job's various components. Our framework treads in the line of a SWOT analysis. A favorite tool of corporate execs, a SWOT assesses a firm's internal Strengths and Weaknesses, external Opportunities and Threats. We bend it somewhat to our purpose, as shown in Fig. 6.5.

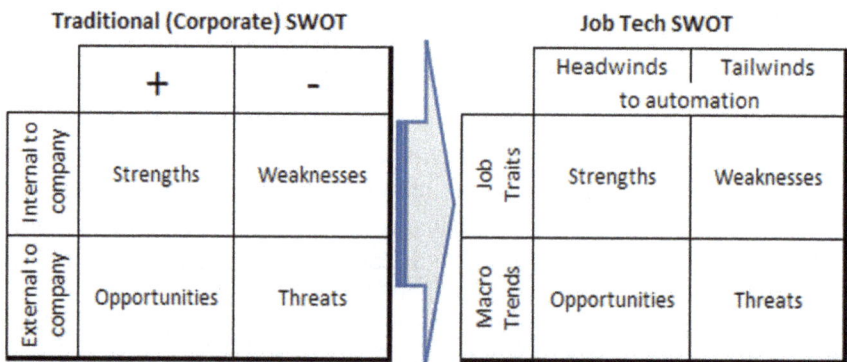

Traditional (Corporate) SWOT				Job Tech SWOT		
	+	−			Headwinds	Tailwinds
					to automation	
Internal to company	Strengths	Weaknesses		Job Traits	Strengths	Weaknesses
External to company	Opportunities	Threats		Macro Trends	Opportunities	Threats

Fig. 6.5   Job SWOT

When building a SWOT, managers rely on a grid that comprises several dimensions, for instance Political, Economic, Social and Technological (PEST), the purpose of which is to ensure no stone is left unturned.

We consider nine dimensions: five inner traits and four macro trends. Each inner trait is a strength or weakness, and each trend is an opportunity or threat. More generally, we refer to these as *headwinds* or *tailwinds* to automation. A given element can land in one or the other box: regulations can propel a technology (tailwind) or bring it to a halt (headwind), the human touch prevent or precipitate the advent of automation, etc. (Fig. 6.6).

Keep your job in focus throughout. Some traits may not pertain to it, while others could have been added—environmental concerns, the confidential nature of the job—there is no one-size-fits-all model. Boundaries between traits are at times porous: a highly "Taylorized" job is likely more structured, the human touch calls on cognition, and so on. The grid is a malleable one; adapt it to your situation. Ensure there are no blind spots. And bear in mind that it consists in *movable* parts that as such need regular monitoring.

The aggregate of the first three traits contributes to the *technology* factor, or the propensity for job automation-slash-substitution, from a strictly technological standpoint. For instance, jobs that call on *versatility, creativity,* and other forms of *cognition* are at lower risk compared to *monotask, recurrent* jobs. Economics intervene to validate whether a silicon alternative makes sense from a cost perspective. The human touch stands apart: the customer-facing job, where the client values human presence, can preserve workers even there where technically machines could take over. Meanwhile IT versatility partakes in gauging one's ability to extricate herself from a perilous position.

At the end of this chapter, we glance anew at US jobs, in light of these elements, then utilize them to produce a *job vulnerability canvass*. The canvass

<table>
<tr><td rowspan="5">Inner</td><td>1. Structure & Cognition</td></tr>
<tr><td>2. Task Dispersion</td></tr>
<tr><td>3. Dexterity & Pattern Recognition</td></tr>
<tr><td>4. The Human Touch</td></tr>
<tr><td>5. IT Versatility</td></tr>
<tr><td rowspan="4">External</td><td>6. Economics & Scalability</td></tr>
<tr><td>7. Demographics</td></tr>
<tr><td>8. Legal & Political</td></tr>
<tr><td>9. Sociocultural</td></tr>
</table>

Fig. 6.6 Job Traits covered in this section

scores each trait against how it fares on the automation spectrum, from headwind to tailwind, providing a condensed snapshot of a job's vulnerability.

6.4.1   Structure and Cognition

The notion of cognition may appear a tad broad or vague—a suitcase word that englobes creativity, the faculty to generalize and infer, deductive reasoning, and more. Setting aside social skills for now, we take into consideration

- the place of humans and machines in the cognition game;
- the impact of a job's structure and recurrence on cognition;
- commonsense;
- creativity;
- storytelling.

These skills participate in the "important qualities" consistent with top executive jobs as per the BLS, namely leadership, communication, decision-making, problem-solving and time management skills.[23]

Dissecting Human–Machine Collaboration: The Sumo Challenge

Talks of computers' advancing cognitive capabilities invariably summon the objection that machines should not be viewed as foes but allies.

Take Amazon. With over 200,000 robots moving merchandise in its warehouses, allotting the more dexterous tasks to humans, it brags of achieving the vaunted "human + machine" model:

> It's great to keep humans focused on tasks where high judgement is needed. For example, humans can look at a pallet of maple syrups and understand how to best unpack it. Robots aren't able to easily detect what kind of liquid is in a container or if it's spilled within its packaging. Humans can easily understand what they're unpacking and then find a way to safely unpack it without causing damage.[24]

---

[23] https://www.bls.gov/ooh/management/top-executives.htm#tab-4.

[24] Written by Amazon Staff: *What robots do (and don't do) at Amazon fulfilment centres*, https://www.aboutamazon.co.uk/amazon-fulfilment/what-robots-do-and-dont-do-at-amazon-fulfilment-centres.

Computers may struggle to process data from visual cues, and thus fail to detect spilt maple syrup, but as far as humans go, the task requires no in-depth expertise, out-of-the-box thinking, or "high judgment"—a toddler can sound the alert for such accidents. It hardly relates to cognition, merely to *re*cognition, a trait shared by all humans, that as such will not pay a high salary. To know whether a task calls on valuable skills, ask yourself: would it feature prominently on a manager's resume? The ability to recognize spilt maple syrup? Doubtful.

Packaging goods, driving an Uber car, or labeling objects in photos repre-sent mere cracks in tech prowess—friction points where any human can lend a hand (or an eye), no brainwork or fancy degree required. As tech columnist Kevin Roose put it, these are "people whose jobs consist mainly of carrying out instructions given to them by a machine."[25] They're light-years away from the doctor who consults notes of a patient's last visit on her computer, the planner aided by a forecasting software, or marketers lever-aging Salesforce. The latter may be enhanced by IT tools, yet they remain in firm command. ATMs enhanced bank teller jobs by removing grunt work,[26] but now Fintech decides whether or not to grant a loan. Uber takes out the cognitive part of finding the best route to a destination amid traffic and road-works, leaving the driver with instructions that melt down to "Go straight" or "Make a turn". One worker flexes her mental muscles, the other lets them go numb.

The sumo challenge addresses this cognition riddle by asking who calls the shots and who merely executes. Is the human supervising the machine, or vice versa?

Figure 6.7 glances back at our tripartite definition of intelligence to construct a sumo ring split between observation (or data collection), cogni-tion (or data processing) and action on the environment. Cognition thrones in the center; it starts with the interpretation of inputs, their confrontation with past experience, to the weighing of possible actions, a process that for humans summons beliefs, instinct, commonsense, predicting of outcomes and even emotions, ending with what course of action should best serve our goals.

Of course, every job contains bits of all three aspects; placement in one ring does not exclude the other two. The focus here is on where the bulk

[25] Kevin Roose: *Futureproof: 9 Rules for Humans in the Age of Automation*, Random House (2021), p. 136.

[26] ATMs and bank tellers present a particular case, as tasks are divided in such a manner that the two need not interact: during a visit, the customer can deal solely with one or the other. It's when employee and tool work together that the sumo challenge arises.

The Sumo ring of Intelligence

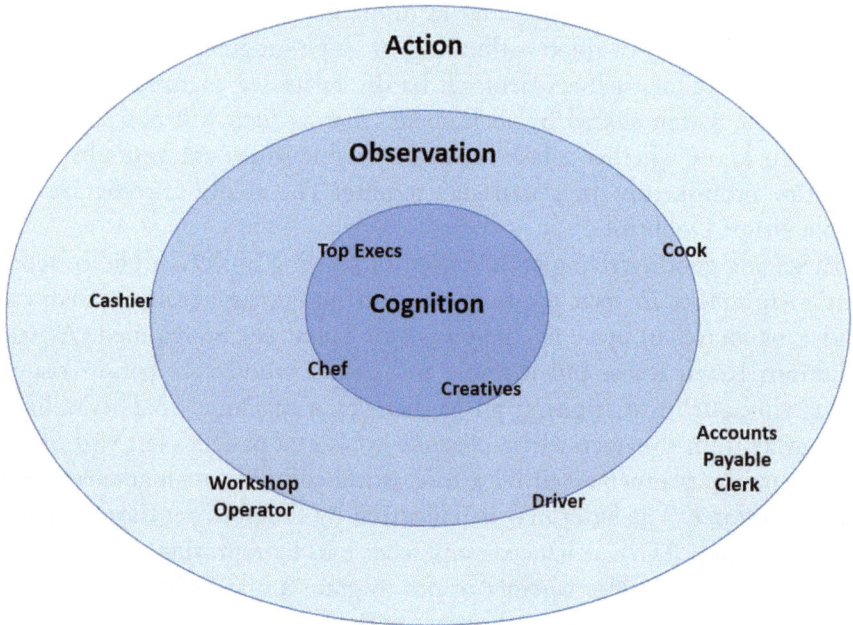

Fig. 6.7 Sumo ring of intelligence

of the work resides, on what it mostly involves. An accounts payables clerk reads invoices from a stable group of suppliers, in recurrent formats, and keys the data into the system—a low-cognition job. Amazon obviously does everything in its power to limit the risk of damaged goods, in effect reducing the odds for warehouse employees to need to identify and decide what to do about such problems, so that the overwhelming amount of their work can be spent in the outer confines of dexterous actions.

Should the worker stumble on spilt syrup, she promptly reacts; but for an off-script issue, she needs to call her manager. This worker is not in the inner cognitive ring, involved in questions such as how to organize the warehouse layout and goods placement to optimize on-time delivery and First-In-First-Out rules, or how to manage staff turnover and robot fleets.

A job's positioning on the ring will vary from one individual to another. We can oppose the cook who follows a script, and thus falls in the periphery, to the chef who concocts novel dishes prone to seduce our taste buds, edging toward the center of the sumo ring; but unlike cook and chef, most occupations do not carry separate titles to distinguish between low and heavy cognitive weight-lifting.

Consider a Front Office clerk using a cumbersome ERP system that consumes time to the detriment of customer interaction, or whose lack of product applications knowledge compels her to rely heavily on a configure, price and quote (CPQ) software that dictates the tone of the conversation with the customer. Meanwhile, a senior veteran barely glances at her screen as she guides customers; untethered from the system, she fosters meaningful interaction, probing customer needs, second-guessing the products best tailored to them, mentally gliding through the catalog to suggest valuable accessories, informing of upcoming deals, and giving insightful feedback to her marketing department on new trends she discerns. While they share the same title, these two employees lie at different rungs of the sumo ring. In case only one were to remain, there will be little hesitation.

The point here is to highlight the constant tug of war around *who steers the game*, which ultimately determines whether the job or task is one of human cognition enhanced by tech, or of a twenty-first-century version of Chaplin's Modern Times. This darts back to the type of disruption at hand: one that downgrades or enhances the worker. Technology ebbing at the cognitive elements in a job, as recently witnessed with ChatGPT (and its successors), or in the fintech field, constitutes a red flag that beckons for caution: you are in the process of being shoved off of the inner rings and toward the outskirts. What could you do to wriggle your way to the center? Should all routes be clogged, perhaps a more fundamental change is necessary.

And if you stand firmly in the center, how to exploit technology to sharpen decision-making acumen and enhance performance beyond that of peers?

When dealing with silicon, the three components of intelligence are often divided, with human intervention still present at some stages of the loop. Human Lilliputians stitch the disparate bits for a massive yet impotent Gulliver, logging in the digital trace for real-world occurrences, whether by booking a vendor invoice in the accounts, or minutes of a client meeting in a CRM tool. In the scurry to deploy ERPs and other ICT tools, companies overlooked system interoperability, resulting in a constellation of friction points that require human intervention to wrangle data into exploitable information and transpose it from one end to another. Yet new techniques are constantly reshaping these boundaries between humans and machines. Optimal Character Recognition (OCR) integrated into software such as Expensify (that handles personnel expenses), Microsoft Office[27] and now smartphones (e.g. on iPhones with the 2021 release of iOS 15), Electronic

---

[27] The Excel phone app now allows for taking a photo of any printed list or table to have it transposed into a spreadsheet's rows and columns.

Data Interchange (EDI) and other frictionless enhancements facilitate data transmission, pushing human labor further off the ring.

The sumo challenge is dynamic. Buoyed by extra sensors, data, analytics, and smoother interoperability, experts foresee the advent of a great cognization of organizations, with ramifications on par with that of their electrification during the 2^{IR}. Improving AI, giving it eyes to see and ever cheaper limbs will reduce the need for human intervention, handing more decisions over to silicon intelligence.[28]

But what characterizes cognition? In the next pages, we shed light on the factors that prevent or propel highly cognitive work.

Structured Tasks

Zooming in on human labor, automation experts first and foremost distinguish repetitive and non-repetitive tasks. The first type, variably referred to as recurrent or routine tasks, at times to tasks operating "in a highly structured environment", follows a clear written script that forbids out-of-the-box thinking.

Earlier, we claimed that within the tripartite split of intelligence, heavy brain-lifting occurs in data processing. A favorite trick deployed by organizations consists in backtracking a step, to data collection. Structuring data collection so that it falls through a smooth formatted channel devoid of surprises *substantially* reduces the cognition power required to process it; hence the emphasis on structuring assembly lines, on funneling customer demands and job applications via templates, and on frenetically shaping every conceivable bit of the environment so that it fits into a procedure—a closed loop of perfect information.

Firms strive to map out processes in written procedures. These explain the task step by step, with guidance for troubleshooting contingencies. This codification of jobs, legacy of Taylorism, provides multiple benefits to the firm:

- employees need not make decisions, thanks to which

---

[28] Science-fiction offers an extreme depiction: a supposedly mastermind character exposed as the puppet of an ASI giving orders via an earpiece. Cf. *Upgrade*, directed by Leigh Whannell (2018), or actor Vincent Cassel's character in *Westworld*'s season 3. Already in several instances of knowledgeable waiters at not-so-fancy venues capable of elaborating in thorough detail their offerings, when noticing their earpiece, I could not help but wonder whether some expert upstairs was feeding them the information.

- the company is less exposed to the vagaries of employee wisdom and staff turnover.
- employees eschew the burden of responsibility: don't think, just play it by the book and you'll be safe.

- staff from which no brainwork is required don't need a college degree; SOPs lower the requisites to the cheapest labor available.
- commodity workers have little to no bargaining power; they can be shuffled around at little cost.
- historically, machines could only perform repetitive tasks; this encourages factories to conceive work in that manner.
- it now lays the grounds for a transition from human knowledge labor to algorithms (the "Second Machine Age") as tasks are broken into a strictly Boolean, "if this then that" logic.

This last trait incentivizes companies to push task structuring ever farther, toward the ultimate goal of expression in 0s and 1s.

Indeed, a job broken down into a list of rules is encodable in computer language, thus sensitive to the top-down approach of AI. In David Autor's words: "Human tasks that have proved most amenable to computerization are those that follow explicit, codifiable procedures."[29] That's rather worrisome, given that the US Federal Reserve categorizes around 44% of US jobs (62 million) as "routine".[30]

A job that defies attempts at description in such minutiae falls under the Polanyi paradox, or the idea that "we can know more than we can tell."[31] Intuitive knowledge and insights gained through commonsense are difficult to encode or teach to an algorithm. Using the "five hows"[32] can highlight whether a task falls under the Polanyi paradox: ask yourself how you perform a task, then dissect it in bits, and appose a new "how" on each. Dig layer after layer until you reach the full depth of the endeavor, all the while considering how to transcribe it in instructions for a newbie. Of course, this "task depth complexity" partakes in a bigger picture that includes the number of tasks you perform and their repeatability. When each day brings along a fresh salvo of challenges that differ from the past, nothing repeatable can be encoded.

---

[29] David Autor:, *Polanyi's Paradox and the Shape of Employment Growth*, MIT press (2014).

[30] As cited by Andrew Yang in Chap. 6: *White-Collar Jobs will Disappear, too*, of *The War on Normal People: The Truth About America's Disappearing Jobs and Why Universal Basic Income Is Our Future*, Hachette Books (2018).

[31] Michael Polanyi: *The Tacit Dimension*, Anchor Books (1967).

[32] A take on the famed "5 Whys" used in quality management systems to unravel the root cause of an issue.

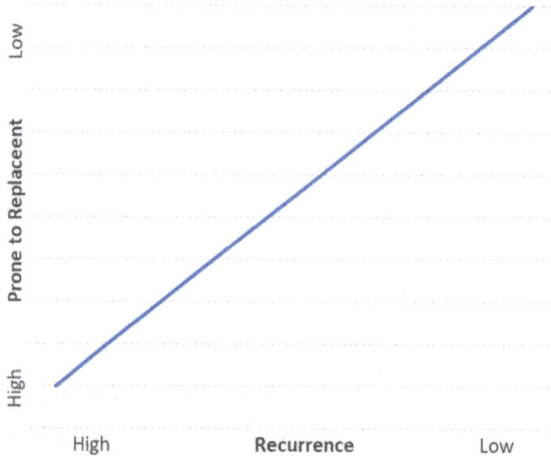

Fig. 6.8 Structure versus replacement

Figure 6.8 plots this basic relationship: the more a job consists in recurrent work, the easier it is to replace the person occupying it.

This relationship serves as a basis for our action plan in the Tasks chapter; for now, note the choice of words: prone to *replacement*, not merely automation.

Company Size and Structure

Procedures become prominent as an organization grows beyond a certain size. Small companies rely on experienced staff. With years of service, these people know precisely not only what to do, but also how their colleagues react and handle situations. In the rare event of a new challenge that puts an employee at a loss, she can convene with her peers—also veterans—and together they would find a solution.

But as the company grows, it experiences a "Tower of Babel" phase, whereby employees are no longer acquainted with the entirety of the staff. Colleagues now work in countries they have never ventured to, or down an equally frightening labyrinth of elevators and corridors. They live in funky time zones, speak exotic languages, and follow different cultural codes. Functional specialization births siloes that each adopts its own jargon. A working relationship with phone and Zoom cannot compare to same room brainstorming, or to the time when any query could be raised out loud in an open office space shared by everyone and solved quasi-instantly. The spirit of cohesion dissolves, with in its stead uncertainty. Anonymity exacerbates the alienness between colleagues and departments. In this post-Babel context, employees stick to the protocol as a guarantee of individual safety.

To make matters worse, the burgeoning company rolls out systems to manage inventory, pricing, after-sales, customer relationships, and more. These shed light on performance, feeding insights into what's happening. Yet in parallel, they trap employees in a sticky web of rigid processes.

Consider the following: a lead is hunted, then translated into a customer order, received and logged into the system; relevant inventory verified, priorities with other orders assessed, a delivery date promised to the customer; goods inspected and shipped, replete with invoice and delivery note. Data is booked in accounting, and after some chasing, the money lands in the bank. In a large firm, each bit of this rigamarole could be done by a different employee. All abide by the system, yet few comprehend the process in its entirety, let alone how a single deviation from the script affects the rest of the chain. Over 80% of the firm's business may be conducted in this manner.

This flow is a recurrent one that follows the tripartite notion of intelligence at a corporate level. While staff appear at various links of the chain, tools are slowly worming their way into their work, hinting back at the sumo riddle: who is manning the turrets? Systems are multiple and communicate poorly with one another, hence workers in various services still play a role to iron out these wrinkles—for now. As interoperability grows into a seamless network of nodes that communicate with one another, it will streamline interdepartmental work, bypassing the need for humans.

That's not to say that tasks should not be processed when possible. The division of labor led to a boom in productivity. A company refractory to the scientific management of work will lag behind others for lack of efficiency. In the tasks chapter, we militate in favor of processing and streamlining work. Only one must strike a right balance, as an over-processed system can eclipse cognitive qualities in workers, leading to atrophy.

VUCA

What of jobs not confined to the relatively controlled environments of a workshop, office, or database?

Plumbers, truck drivers, and on-site repairmen may have processes wired in their brains from years of work, yet the environment in which they operate is anything but structured. Despite a precise set of rules on where each towel goes and how to make a bed, hotel room cleaners face unpredictable phenomena ranging from spills and stolen objects to leftover condoms. Firefighters, patrol officers and soldiers have it worse.

VUCA conveys these difficulties. Borrowed from the military where it was first introduced in the 1980s, the term has since turned into a pillar of management books. The acronym spells out the Volatility, Uncertainty, Complexity, and Ambiguity of the terrain where soldiers operate. At the antipodes of the perfect shapes revered by ancient Greeks, VUCA reflects the chaotic reality of the world.

VUCA is as much a catchphrase as it is a moving frontier. When chronic threats are acknowledged and incorporated into the company's procedures, with step-by-step guidelines on how to muzzle them, they lose their sting. Low-wage workers can tackle these paper tigers by playing it by the book, by sticking to protocol; no need to ponder endlessly nor interrupt the boss's 18-hole game.

Earlier we stated that repetitive tasks are symptomatic of work in a structured environment. But there is a catch here, or rather two. Staff at Uniqlo know their outlet inside out; they can fold clothes back neatly and respond to a long list of FAQs. Similar to factory workers, they abide by an SOP. Only unlike them, retail workers have an anomaly to deal with: *you*, the customer. And that anomaly is king. Meanwhile truck drivers abide by rules enshrined in the Highway Code; yet their environment is susceptible to anything from blizzards to soccer balls and jumping deer.

These two factors influence a job's placement on the spectrum from structure to VUCA:

- the environment: if the job takes place in a specific location—a closed system of "perfect information"—that precinct can be adapted to ensure optimum structure. Workshops, warehouses and offices are controlled environments; ditto banks, shops, restaurants, and other sedentary work spots, but also structured frameworks: a spreadsheet, template, ERP fields… Jobs spent roaming away from company grounds, like that of driver, fireman, or salesman are prone to greater VUCA exposure;
- interaction with customers, or more broadly (though to a lesser extent) with anyone from *outside* of the company, swings the needle toward VUCA.

Figure 6.9 plots several jobs based on these two criteria.

Jobs in the bottom-left corner are at greater risk of automation than those in the top-right. The other two boxes tread in the "it depends" realm, with the top-left corner—handling customers within a controlled environment—perhaps slightly more fragile.

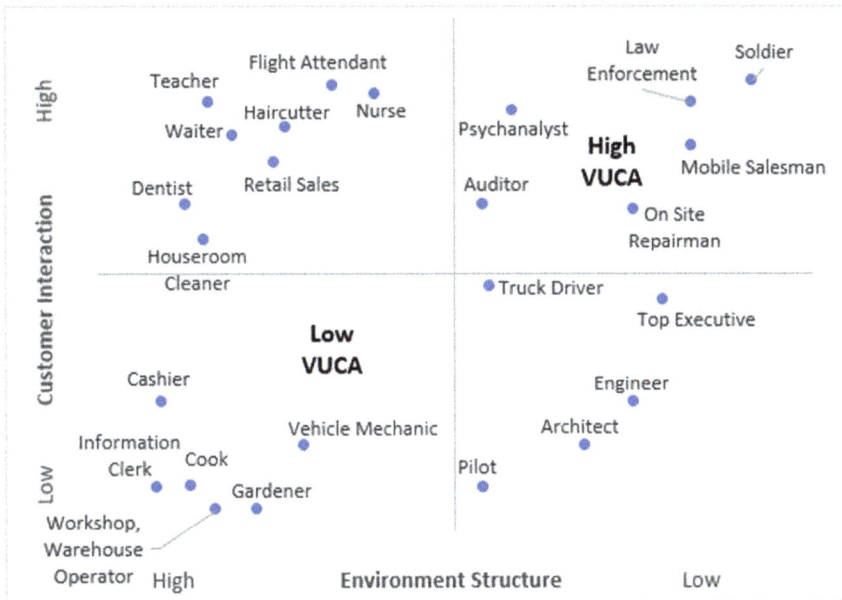

Fig. 6.9 VUCA mapping based on environment structure and customer interaction

Line operators and flight attendants both perform manual labor, but the latter's exposure to customer VUCA adds brainwork, as one must navigate the endless and at times outrageous stream of passenger demands, in a subtle balancing act with the customer satisfaction mantra. Meanwhile the pilot stays in the confines of the cockpit, yet deals with the vagaries of weather, obstacles, traffic control, and faulty equipment—a hazardous environment.

The concept of (un)structured environment does not merely apply to the physical world: the psychanalyst receives patients in the precincts of her study, yet a consultation can bifurcate into uncontrolled territory (the subconscious being anything but structured in the sense we understand it). And from their airconditioned corner office, top execs formulate the long-term strategic orientations that make or break the company. Complexity grows as the time horizon is bent and probabilities multiply, veering toward chaos. Assessment of an office job's proclivity to VUCA is not so straightforward, because cognitive work stretches VUCA beyond the confines of a purely physical environment.

A job's coordinates on the chart can fluctuate based on circumstances—for instance:

– a nurse at Chicago's Northwestern Memorial Hospital works in a structured environment compared to the one sent to a warzone.

- cultural differences oblige, a US flight attendant faces greater customer VUCA than her Japanese counterpart.
- a waiter in the event sector who serves at a different venue every night faces greater environment VUCA than the sedentary one manning tables at a restaurant.
- a retail salesperson in a deserted mall encounters less customers than a dentist with a fully booked agenda.

To do justice to VUCA, looking solely at the environment and customer does not capture a job's full complexity. For starters, it omits recurrence and rigidity. Teachers follow a code of conduct and a textbook yet have a certain leeway to deviate from the script, more so than the chart's neighboring waiters or haircutters (note that rules can be implicit: small restaurants lack written procedures for cooks and waiters, yet their work is structured by an informal set of rules).

Of course, technically the customer *is* part of the environment, the same as everyone other than the subject, and based on our tripartite split of intelligence. Due in part to constant meddling of emotions in decision-making, humans glow as the most erratic, irrational element in any environment. However, company staff are trained and disciplined by internal policies (along with the need for that month-end paycheck), unlike capricious visitors and their unruly kids. This honorable medal of most VUCA-packed stakeholder earns the client her own standalone axis in Fig. 6.9.

Isolating the customer carries another advantage: to discern AI's impinging on work. At the risk of simplifying a tad, the structured physical environment can be conceived of as addressing tech's *dexterity* and *pattern recognition* capabilities, while customer interaction calls on *empathetic AI* and *Natural Language Processing*—with social skills and the human touch as headwind. Progress in either field will lift the corresponding roadblocks between AI and jobs in that area of the chart. Hence, Fig. 6.9 hints at the kind of tech advances to be monitored, based on your job's placement.

VUCA is but one piece of the puzzle. It ignores the degree to which a task's inputs and outputs are quantifiable (a prerequisite to translation into zero and one digits, i.e. to digitization); nor does it convey scalability, dexterity, regulatory, and other aspects.

Limitations of Structure and Process

Processes and what they imply (training, discipline…) form the ultimate anti-VUCA weapon. In this eternal struggle between light and night, the rapier of procedure slits through the fog of war, paving a route to taper off exposure to VUCA.

Organizations aiming for processes worthy of a *jardin à la française* at some point hit a reef, as an SOP covering every single contingency ends up thicker than the Mahabharata. No one will dare consult it, let alone master it. Keeping it up to date represents a byzantine task, yet failure to do so incurs the risk of paralyzing the firm, or at best generating suboptimal flows that weigh on managers' time. Like the hydra of lore, hacking off one unknown raises several more. And that's the beauty of life. The factors present at every place and instant are so unique, they preclude prospects of exact repeatability. It's the essence which makes VUCA the archnemesis of AI: with no repeatable pattern, AI lacks a repertoire to build on from.[33]

Another issue with highly processed firms: how do their workers fare? We can oppose the stereotype of automatons who blindly follow their big book of rules, even when ordered to launch nukes, in the style of the B-52 crew in Kubrick's *Dr. Strangelove*, to those that preserve a flicker of cognition, as in the opening scene of *War Games*.

More commonly, processes perniciously turn workers into robots. A snag they were not "programmed" to cope with brings to a full stop. In *The Social Life of Information*, authors John Brown and Paul Duguid ponder on the Xerox repairman-turned-anthropologist we met in the Tech chapter, building on his acumen to explain how beyond lapses in the documentation, issues arose

> more problematically because it told them what to do, but not why. It gave instructions, but it didn't explain. [...] Directive documentation wasn't designed for sense making. It was designed for rule following."[34]

In the event an employee seeks to break her chains and make the call, her inexperience inflates chances of a blunder that could have dire consequences down the road, such as a life-or-death quality issue at the consumer end or, worse, endangering the company's reputation. Overly structured corporations discourage employees from taking such liberties.

At times, the rigidity borders the line of ludicrous, like when the IT system at a fast-food chain prevents processing a breakfast order past 11:30am, as

---

[33] An interesting account of these failings of Taylorism and its self-contained instructions can be found in Harold Garfinkel, *Studies in ethnomethodology*, Englewood Cliffs (1967), and Lucy Schuman, *Plans and Situated Actions, The Problem of Human Machine Collaboration*, International Conference on Computational Linguistics (1987).

[34] p. 96, John Seely Brown, Paul Duguid: *The Social Life of Information*, Harvard Business Review Press (2017 updated edition).

caricatured in the 1993 movie *Falling Down* starring Michael Douglas; or when in the real world an innocent passenger is violently thrown off from an airplane overbooked by an algorithm.[35] When the power to call the shots—even for a small, inconsequential detail—is stripped from employees, poor customer service ensues, with at best a waste of time as the manager is summoned to decide between two lesser evils forced upon by the system. Companies tethered to these systems lose flexibility, as limitations in the original design surface (a fact any company witnesses after installing an ERP). Ditto for robot-like employees, long estranged from the center of the sumo ring.

In the end, overcoming systemic atrophy may imply bypassing protocol: take a week to do it by the book or cut through the palaver. These dilemmas highlight the need for an equilibrium between the two ends of the spectrum: under- and over-processed (a topic we return to in *From Art to Science, and Back*).

Agile Management

To bypass these reefs, agile firms invest in their employees: They nurture them. Instead of handing out a task that corresponds to a small bit of a process, with no explanations as to the ins and outs, they strive to give more context and greater responsibility so that the direct report can digest the bigger picture. With some training and a little push—including acceptance of failure—staff can build the acumen to make sound judgment calls. Goals, strategy and direction are instilled in lieu of stale dos and don'ts. Management devises an inspiring vision, a mission statement that unites its staff, producing a corporate culture where workers are no longer viewed as children or robots. Instead of siloed departments, the organization forms mixed teams that tackle issues with greater efficiency, as each member brings their knowhow to the table and the aggregate of diverse expertise allows the team as a whole to seize the bigger picture. This shift of nexus to employees assumes that the vibe from happy employees trickles down into customer satisfaction. Agile corporations are more prone to use AI tools for the purpose of enhancement than to grate jobs.

Organizations may evolve by developing a blend of processes and agility. The course of action can even vary by department, based on management styles. It's worthwhile for readers to dwell on which type of company they work in.

---

[35] https://en.wikipedia.org/wiki/United_Express_Flight_3411_incident.

Best steer clear from stultifying jobs, where VUCA is absent or in process of getting weeded out, where management marshals grandiose internal digitization plans for the sole purpose of transforming job contents into vapid activity - unless you can take those efforts under your belt and spearhead the transition (assuming someone needs to remain afterwards to man the turrets), or if there is a clear need for cognitive work to do that has yet to be addressed, and that you qualify for.

Other cognitive elements where humans should keep an edge follow hereunder.

Commonsense and Connecting the Dots

Narrow AI cannot connect disparate dots, as these lack the common denominator necessary to weigh each one against the other (as in "comparing apples and oranges"). For instance, to concoct a dish, a chef factors in taste, odor, crispiness, cost and expected profit, preparation time, ingredients and functional tools available in the kitchen, who is present on that day, and the look of the result whence brought to the dinner table. While the final recipe can be encoded in rules, the same cannot be said about *coming up* with the recipe.

AI lacks commonsense and an understanding of context. NLP aims to interpret what a human says, yet struggles to determine the deeper meaning, for instance whether its interlocutor is trying to deceive it. Nor can it combine body language and facial expression reading with uttered words, the way we do instinctively. When a colleague shouts "I am so drowned in work, I'm going to kill myself", we take it as a joke; an AI would sound the alarm.

The Winograd Schema Challenge highlights this pitiful state of AI. Formulated in 2011 as an alternative to the Turing Test, it consists in a multiple-choice question that calls on commonsense. For example: "The trophy could not fit in the suitcase because it was too big". What was too big: A—the trophy or B—the suitcase[36]?

AI excels at chess and *go*. Although to humans, the number of possible moves borders the chaotic, these remain closed systems of "perfect information". AI has established prowess in closed environments, for example in Atari's *Breakout*,[37] yet fails at even the most rudimentary adventure games (the text on black screen type, such as *Zork*, that prods the player with the "What do you do?" line). Contexts that lack a referential, where the bits and

---

[36] Hector J. Levesque: *Common Sense, the Turing Test, and the Quest for Real AI*, The MIT press (2018); also https://commonsensereasoning.org/winograd.html.

[37] https://www.YouTube.com/watch?v=V1eYniJ0Rnk&vl=en.

pieces cannot be boxed under a common denominator, that evade quantification, still need human judgment. It's what Maria Popova, creator of the *Brain Pickings* blog, calls "combinatorial creativity": an induction faculty innate to us, most useful in situations that weave disparate elements, producing a complex picture with more ins and outs than can be managed by a single criterion or two. Garry Kasparov gave an eloquent illustration of combinatorial creativity when he quipped that for his next match against Deep Blue, he'd bring a hammer.

This also comes into play when no one situation resembles another, when each step forward is a wandering in the dark. Algorithms feed on data to find patterns. A future with no resemblance to anything past sees AI wither. The Covid crisis illustrates this: there was no precedent for a computer to pull insights from, to guide it through the frontlines, secure supply chains, update protocols, ensure staff safety, and reassure clients.

Granted, the new AI systems released in 2022 have improved abilities: when queried, ChatGPT acknowledges that the Winograd Schema Challenge partook in its training data (and yes, it knows the correct answer to the suitcase question). Yet it also admits that there is still a long way to go. As a crucible for reasoning, commonsense plays a crucial role in our daily activities. Without it, the recipe for a boeuf bourguignon stretches miles. Even a humungous codification of rules is no guarantee of reliable performance. Machine learning lacks the kind of deductive inference that allows us to build models of the world based on our experience of it. It would need a repository of norms and beliefs to guide its decision-making.

Underlying this problem is the fact that no two people share the exact same set of values. Suppose we succeed in encoding a peanut butter and jelly sandwich recipe for robots. During the process, a bug lands in the jam already spread on the bread. Should the robot ditch the whole thing and start over, or just remove that part of the jelly with the bug stuck? Account for its master's gender or wage? Would an ant make the decision any different from a wasp or a fly? When things like "good" and "bad" depend on too broad a variety of elements, or on subjective judgment that varies by individual, humans keep the upper edge.

Digging deeper, we can venture to say that under the assumption that no one is perfect, humans are allowed to discriminate (and we do it constantly). But a subjective algorithm would be labeled "biased", deemed unfair, and thus outlawed. It's the same can of worms that stops self-driving cars from hitting the streets: we tolerate a human's decision-making in the face of a fatal accident, but demand nothing less than absolute flawlessness from AI. In the absence of common metrics that everyone can agree on to decide who dies and who lives, the problem is insoluble. Moreover, how could we ever build a truly objective intelligence given that, as Kant taught us, humans can never fully grasp objective reality as it exists in itself?

We claim to keep the upper hand here, but that depends on the worker. The one who mimics a machine and blindly follows orders will fare no better than AI.

My approval is mandatory before any purchase order can be issued to suppliers. Once, when my procurement officer handed me a deck of purchase orders to sign, I asked what their overall value amounted to, what they were for, and whether we really needed to immobilize so much cash, to which the officer shrugged and replied "The MRP spat it out". As if entertaining the thought of outsmarting the system was heresy. The bloke seemingly took comfort in ceding all faculty of judgment and reasoning to an AI perceived as akin to god.

The procurement officer need not stop at every item to check the bill of materials and sales history of finished goods using it—this would take too much time. But he should know the monetary threshold beyond which such questions should arise, be aware of whether we are facing shortages or on the contrary exceedingly high inventory levels, how our actual sales have been recently performing, and so on—seeing the bigger picture and connecting the dots.

Suppose that:

- elongated lead-times on electronic components had obliged us to send orders a year in advance, amid the post-pandemic shortage on such materials;
- our sales are below forecast;
- for whatever reason, the forecast has yet to be updated in the system to reflect this;
- we have a high inventory level;
- the world is mired with high inflation, rising interest rates, and a looming recession bound to affect our business.

Maintaining the current trajectory and honoring those engagements with our suppliers could lead the company to bankruptcy as it runs out of cash to pay for inventory it cannot move. In this situation, big purchase orders need to be meticulously crosschecked, long-term ones renegotiated with suppliers at once, etc. The system is unable to factor these elements; but if the worker cannot either, what better is he than a machine?

The Creativity Question

Economists define expert thinking as "solving problems for which there are no rules-based solutions."[38] In other words: roll up your sleeves and get creative.

We hear of creativity as a headwind to automation, only to read of algorithms capable of producing original content—poems, paintings, and articles ranging from sports to stock market news. So which one is it? While creativity should be at the antipodes of a recurrent task, the devil lies in the details. Think of a scriptwriter who develops plots and characters day after day. It doesn't take much Hollywood binge-watching to discern the underlying patterns and recipes served one blockbuster dish after another, recycling themes from Shakespeare and Homer, themes ingrained in our collective unconsciousness.

Creativity implies a break from the past. Yet the rupture cannot be too steep. The overly familiar engenders boredom and indifference, but a *tabula rasa* estranges the public from the object. Faint reference points remain vital to touch on the observer's aesthetic cord. Strokes of genius often emerge when borrowing elements from other civilizations, blending and adapting them, as in Picasso taking inspiration from African masks, or the integration of African percussion rhythms that birthed hip hop.

The Wundt curve (Fig. 6.10) captures this notion of a Goldilocks zone where a *je ne sais quoi* conveys hedonic value, and beyond which adverse dissonance sets in.

Algorithms strive to emulate this, via a blend of existing data from which to pluck inspiration that provides the dose of familiarity, combined with a randomness factor that introduces the novelty component. The whole is placed in a context with rules—for example, to ensure a chair design that can support a certain weight. It still takes human intervention, not only to tweak the algorithm and finetune results, but also to exercise aesthetic judgment while parsing through resulting outputs to pick the one(s) that will pierce.[39] Such incursions will likely tick the "work enhancement" box, something designers and architects should lean on to stay in the game, but unlikely to replace all designers and architects in the foreseeable future, nor diminish the value of their expertise. The same goes for AI-powered text-to-image

---

[38] Frank Levy and Richard Murnane: *The New Division of Labor: How Computers are Creating the Next Job Market*, Princeton University Press (2005), in reference to Autor, Levy and Murnane: *The Skill Content of Recent Technological Change: an Empirical Exploration*, Quarterly Journal of Economics 118 (November 2003).

[39] For more on AI's encroachments into creative realms, cf. Marcus de Sautoy: *The Creativity Code, How AI is Learning to Write, Paint and Think*, 4th Estate (2019).

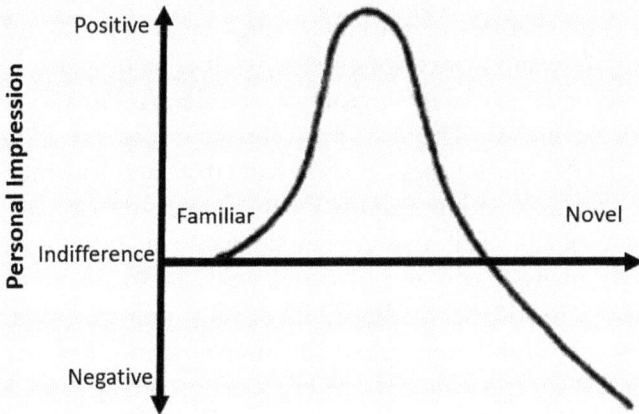

Fig. 6.10 Wundt curve

software, generative AI for PowerPoint slides such as ChatBCG, and other innovations.

Creativity isn't confined to laboratories and R&D departments, to concocting a Michelin dish or engineering next generation combat aircraft. Successfully retaining staff, addressing customer pain points, leading a negotiation, and other aspects broadly related to problem-solving require some form of creativity, in the sense of opening the horizon beyond a stale yes or no.

Consider the following exchange:

Harvey Specter: What are your choices if someone puts a gun to your head?
Mike Ross: You do what they say, or they shoot you.
Harvey Specter: Wrong. You take the gun, or you pull out a bigger one, or you call their bluff, or you do any one of a hundred and forty-six other things. If you can't think for yourself, maybe you aren't cut out for this.[40]

In this scene from *Suits*, Harvey Specter (played by actor Gabriel Macht) is referring to the profession of lawyer, but his remark could apply to many a job. For instance, one can only get so far in stimulating staff via the bichrome prism of money. Instead, peel under each employee's skin (metaphorically) to uncover the inner motivations for going to work, and understand how these are hierarchized: recognition, status, welfare, a purpose, learning things,

---

[40] *Suits*, Season 1, Episode 2 (2011).

paying back a loan, belonging to a team, anticipating a promotion… Let's say you cannot grant that raise; what other strings could you pull on?

This form of reasoning involves *questioning*. It takes us higher in the cognition game, beyond artificial intelligence capabilities. As Picasso once claimed: "Computers are useless. They can only give you answers". Large language models (ChatGPT, MidJourney…) underscore this complementarity between human and machine, with the ability for the former to frame questions now emerging as a valuable skill, that goes by the name of "prompt engineering". Unfortunately, many an educational system teach *not* to ask questions. Hence when queried as to whether a robot could possibly write a symphony or turn a canvass into a beautiful masterpiece, the humanoid in *I, Robot* replies: "Can you?".[41] The reality is not merely one of robots becoming more human, but of robots and humans converging towards one another.

Picture the architect who repeats the same lame patterns, without exerting creativity. Her work will be easy to automate, echoing the contrast between cook and chef. Oftentimes, both can be found under a given job title, making it tricky to separate creative from non-creative jobs—best reason according to your personal situation, on where you currently view yourself on the sumo ring.

This calls for a precision regarding the too-coarse recurrence versus replaceability chart seen earlier (Fig. 6.8). As Frank Levy writes:

> In casual conversation, "routine" means "repetitive". In software terms, however, "routine" means "expressible in rules".[42]

Children have their door to curiosity wide open. The genius of DaVinci and Einstein stems in part from their remaining in a constant childhood-like state: questioning the speed of light, how a compass works or why the sky is blue. Questioning the world is the first step to creativity. Unfortunately, with time most mere mortals tend to hush their curious inner child. Those who resist are swiftly reminded to put a lid on it during their first job. Veterans may at first grin at the fresh intern who questions everything, yet eventually grow impatient and pull rank, pointing to a need for speed that trumps the futile doubting crusade. Yet deep inside, some may have recognized the bright flicker in the eye of the junior as their own from once long ago. They

---

[41] Motion picture *I, Robot*, directed by Alex Proyas (2004).
[42] p. 40, Frank Levy and Richard Murnane: *The New Division of Labor: How Computers are Creating the Next Job Market*, Princeton University Press (2005).

sense a pinch of guilt for sticking to the rules all those years without questioning processes, even when these no longer made sense. The junior painfully reminds them of how they lost their innocence to become another brick in the wall. A system is meant to work as a machine, like clockwork. Behaving as one of its underling robots ripens the worker for automation.

Toyota's Production System (TPS) pushes workers out of this trap with the "five whys" to force a questioning of the status quo. While the five-whys (invented in the 1930s by the father of Toyota founder Kiichiro Toyoda) are primarily focused on the root cause analysis of a problem, the questioning mindset can be extended beyond. It partakes in the need to maintain a critical eye at all times.

Seemingly recurrent tasks can be improved on or performed in creative ways that partake in what it means to be human, as opposed to the mechanical repetition expected of robots. It's up to the worker to find that creativity button and utilize the right dose of it in her line of work, without redoing everything from scratch each and every time, as that would be detrimental to efficiency.

Storytelling

Business curriculums insist on the power of a compelling narrative, highlighted by the success of Ted Talk shows and brand stories that resonate with consumers. Some may view this as a far-flung skill befit for CEOs and salespeople. Delivering Donald Draper-like speeches isn't their forte, nor was it in the job description.

Good storytelling is an asset regardless of position. Little can be achieved in the long run by bossing people around. Belief in goals beats executing orders. We all need inspiration, a sense of purpose. The crude force of a story that reverberates with our psyche seals adherence. Not the type of story shared by the colleague who cracks jokes, but the kind emanating from visionaries. Politicians like Abraham Lincoln use storytelling to keep people focused on the bigger goals and not ensnared in trifles. Amid the turmoil, a good story serves as a shiny beacon. A most appreciated quality.

But what is a story? And what makes a great story?

When the four heroines of Sex and the City have their weekly brunch get-togethers, each one shares their misadventures of odd encounters, bad dates and outrageous events that only seem to happen in New York City. Storytelling pops up whenever something out of the ordinary occurs. Any change, any break from the monotonous routine can be the seed for a great story.

Three elements are crucial for a story to make an impact. First and foremost, it must relate to the audience. Employees lose interest in lengthy corporate presentations with too many numbers, lofty goals and overseas expansion plans. Their inner voice begs: "What's in it for me?" A story in which the audience cannot identify with the subject is a lost cause. Weaving a story that they can relate to hooks the audience. This hook must speak to their inner self. A typical way of achieving this is to take the audience's stance. Pretend to be one of them. Express and mirror their emotions. Politicians and orators from Marc-Anthony to Hitler exceled at such techniques. They understood that if there is only one thing we care about, it is ourselves. We will listen to a stranger only inasmuch as our concerns are addressed, in the faint hope that some light might be shed, the secret of a remedy that works. Only then does the audience become engaged, or at least lend an ear to hear you out.

But if this were the case, one might ask: how could Lincoln's antislavery crusade have appealed to the free people of Northern states? The truth is that human beings can viscerally identify with others—even strangers. In this case, the 1852 publication of bestseller *Uncle Tom's Cabin* brought the crude story of a slave into every home. As if readers could feel the slave's pain. This fictional novel sparked an outcry to end slavery once and for all, in effect opening the White House doors to Abraham Lincoln. During the Vietnam War, the snapshot of a little girl running from a napalm bombing likewise sparked worldwide indignation.

In the corporate world, another often rehashed trick consists in revealing a personal weakness or past failure. Opening up in this way makes a leader appear human, therefore closer to her staff, facilitating the identification process (while also easing acceptance of failure as a step toward success).

Second, a good story must involve a challenge of sorts. This could be the threat of a competitor introducing a revolutionary product or lowering prices, the hardships brought forth by a recession, a change in consumer behavior or new legislation harmful to the business' interests. This challenge represents the break from the ordinary alluded to earlier. Having identified with the character or topic, the audience shares the pain brought by this challenge as if it were their own. By now they ignore their cellphone notifications as they eagerly await for the storyteller to explain how to overcome the obstacle (or how the obstacle was overcome, in the case of a story of past events).

This leads to the third part: resolving the problem. Audiences crave for this, because solving a problem that it feels connected to has a soothing effect. And as they've identified with the story, in some cases relating it to their own personal issues, they remain alert for clues to glean, for cures to their woes.

Every episode of Sex and the City is woven around this three-step process of connecting, challenging and solving. And indeed the same goes with multiple other series and movies: from Hamlet to Harry Potter, from Perseus to Princess Mononoke, every hero's journey revolves around these precepts.

When in 1962 Kennedy formulated plans to boost US spending for nuclear rockets, advancing satellite technology and space exploration, he realized that this had little to do with most Americans' lives. The country would have balked at the abysmal expenses involved and questioned whether taxpayer money could not be better spent elsewhere. Therefore, he first framed the challenge as a global battle "between freedom and tyranny". Then he stated the goal of putting a man on the moon by the end of the decade. This gave a very human dimension to the project, one that every man and woman could relate to and project themselves in. By creating a narrative that Americans could identify with, Kennedy won the peoples' hearts. By making reaching the moon before the USSR a national challenge with a clear deadline, he galvanized a nation around a simple idea that every American could espouse. Likewise, the leader in a successful firm creates stories that employees can identify with, in turn sealing adherence to achieve a given direction.

Narrative excellence is not an innate trait, but an art that can be learned. There are methods and tricks to achieve this: anecdotes, props, metaphors, mnemonic images and photos worth a thousand words. Ditto for best practices as to the average time to spend per slide in a PowerPoint presentation, the right mix of words versus images and so on. YouTube is full of videos and tutorials, starting with Ted Talk shows, and books on the subject are plentiful (including Carmine Gallo's *Talk Like Ted*).[43]

The power of a good story resides both in its turning off of that inner criticizing voice, courtesy of the identification process, and in the windfall: to unite people from different breeds and beliefs behind a common goal. This partakes in the building of a strong corporate culture, one where each employee feels engaged and moves toward the same direction.

Conclusion on Cognition

Experts argue that as tech automates the low-level stuff, everyone will have awesome opportunities to occupy their newfound time with work more fulfilling than mechanically rehearsing humdrum procedures day after day. As

---

[43] Carmine Gallo: *Talk Like Ted: The 9 Public-Speaking Secrets of the World's Top Minds*, Martin's Press (2014).

one textbook put it: "Until AI advances to the level of human competence, humans will remain in the managerial position."[44]

Most workers are *not* in managerial positions; they are unprepared for high-reasoning tasks and might not be perceived as capable of rising to that level. After years of being treated as paper-pushers, many have traded youthful ambitions for the robot work expected of them, on the fringe of the sumo ring.

Organizations increasingly seek workers with the cognitive credentials to fill the higher rungs. They recognize the added value resulting from versatile skills, a mixing of various expertise (up next), whether in a person or a team of people. A simple route to the skills that elude AI can be found under the BLS's chief executive job description.[45] Adding these to your portfolio—empathy, critical thinking, problem-solving, and more—increases your resilience to automation.

Each of these skills is an additional brick to the barricade against AI. Together, they form the technology factor of our SWOT. This trench warfare will evolve based on AI's advances and shortcomings. Bear in mind that human advantages are weighed against their cost compared to automation and outsourcing alternatives. Tech factors play against economic, sociocultural and other factors.

In the struggle between humans and AI—and between humans, period—view cognition as the ultimate clash, the turning point that seals the fate of the war. Win this and you emerge victorious from the AI battle royale. Only as Krishnamurti said, one must live in "timeless renewal"[46]: unlike historical events, this battle takes place every day of our working lives.

6.4.2   Task Dispersion: Taylorism and Narrow AI Versus Transdisciplinarity

Taylorism pushes the worker to perform ever narrower tasks, under the premise that specialization brings greater efficiency. Already a century before Frederick Taylor, Adam Smith realized while observing workers in a pin factory that if the processes were split into separate, specialized steps, productivity would soar by hundreds to thousands of times. The division of labor motto set the course for processing and task specialization, all the way

---

[44] *Will AI Replace US*, p. 103. Shelley Fan and Matthew Taylor, Thames & Hudson Ltd (2019).
[45] https://www.onetonline.org/link/summary/11-1011.00.
[46] https://jkrishnamurti.org/content/ojai-10th-public-talk-1945.

down to twentieth-century Watts Humphrey's Capability Maturity Model (CMM), that categorizes a firm's level of process.[47]

At the very tip of specialization lie monotask jobs, and at the antipodes the general manager—a versatile job comprising a wide range of tasks, underpinned by large abilities. In between, the bulk of the workforce fills jobs that comprise a plurality of tasks, each one more or less vulnerable. Can a handful of automation-immune tasks spare one from the ills of tech disruption?

Job Dismantlement: The Billiards Allegory

Figure 6.11 splits office work in:

– routine, structured commodity work prone to automation as AI gains ground, backed by an army of low-skilled scavengers who scoop up the remaining scrubs.
– the high-reasoning category of decision-making, navigating amid considerable uncertainty, volatility, and the rest of the lot.

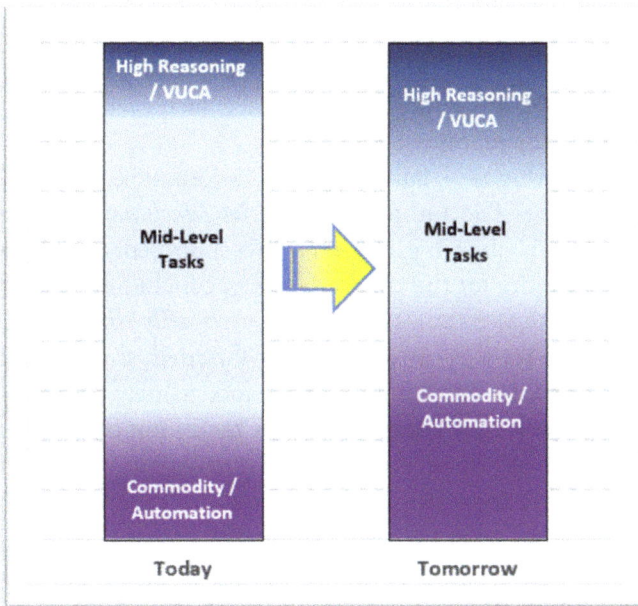

Fig. 6.11 Office work and the threat to mid-level tasks

[47] Watts S. Humphrey: *Managing the Software Process*, Addison-Wesley Professional (1989).

– everything in between, broadly defined as "mid-level tasks", that comprises expertise with a dose of cognition, yet still consists mostly in recurrent work.

View these from the vantage point of an organization, department, or job.

As AI improves, the lower part eats into mid-level tasks, freeing time for high-level tasks; this could be as much a threat as an opportunity. The chart offers a visual rendering of the threats from top and bottom. Both prove Solow right: the bottom brings efficiency via cost-savings, and the top through human enhancement (more added-value work, improved strategies, and tactics…).

Yet a roadblock supposedly stands in the way of this scenario. In the OECD report that concluded only 9% of jobs were at risk of automation with a high probability, the authors explained that the gap with Frey & Osborne's figure (47%) was

> Because even in occupations that Frey & Osborne expect to be at high risk of automation, people often perform tasks which are hard to automate, such as interactive tasks (e.g. group work or face-to-face interactions with customers, clients, etc.).[48]

In other words, jobs are seldom monotask, a fact even Frey & Osborne acknowledged in their report.

Pundits present this as a failsafe against automation, in a twist on the doomsayers' narrative. The authors of *Predictive Machines* illustrate this with the school bus driver, objecting that even this supposedly monotask job has the added responsibility for the children's safety, concluding that "*automation that eliminates a human from a task does not necessarily eliminate them from a job*" (italics theirs). Yet they miss the point. Granted, the school bus driver benefits from a special trait that secures her job, namely the safety factor (a sociocultural trait we review later). That is the main root cause, in an example that fails the test when extended to other drivers—a pity considering the US counts six times more truck drivers than school bus drivers.[49]

---

[48] Melanie Arntz, Terry Gregory and Ulrich Zierahn: *The Risk of Automation for Jobs in OECD Countries: A Comparative* Analysis, OECD Social, Employment and Migration Working Paper No. 189. Page 14.

[49] 3.1 million truck drivers versus 0.5 million school bus drivers in 2018. For the school bus driver example, cf. Ajay Agrawal, Joshua Gans, Avi Goldfarb: *Prediction Machines: The Simple Economics of Artificial Intelligence*, p. 195: *More than a Driver?* Harvard Business Review Press (2018).

Job by Task - Time

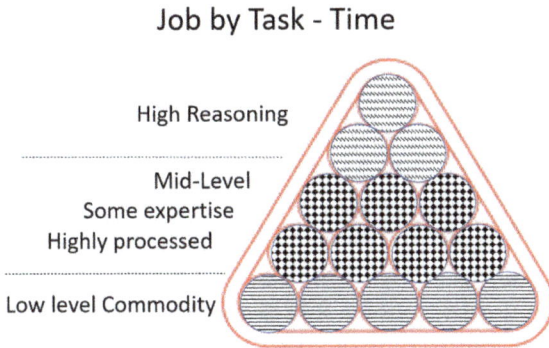

High Reasoning

Mid-Level
Some expertise
Highly processed

Low level Commodity

Fig. 6.12 Job represented by a billiards stack

More importantly, the counterargument underestimates an organization's ingenuity to reorganize work for higher efficiency (those formulating it probably never held a job out of academia). Enter the billiards allegory.

Taking our previous diagram a step further, in Fig. 6.12 we present an individual's workweek as a neat stack of billiards, with each ball representing a bit over two hours of worktime. These bits of time comprise tasks, arranged based on low, mid, and high cognitive levels.

As the chorus goes, AI and revolving tech will gradually

- automate low-level tasks, with outsourcing scooping up pockets of resistance;
- eliminate the value of expertise, dragging mid-level tasks into the commodity/automatable bracket;
- enhance and complement tasks in the upper rungs.

Jobs that mix these three elements give critics the ammo to dispute layoff concerns. As long as the job scrapes an ounce or two of cognition, AI cannot take over entirely, therefore it cannot substitute at all. As per David Autor:

> Many of the tasks currently bundled into these jobs cannot readily be unbundled—with machines performing the middle-skill tasks and workers performing the residual—without a substantial drop in quality.[50]

Figure 6.13 depicts the work of five colleagues as billiard stacks. Following a radical reorganization, low-level tasks are now regrouped and ripe for automation, outsourcing, and/or handling by interns. Meanwhile, higher tasks go

---

[50] David Autor: *Polanyi's Paradox and the Shape of Employment Growth*, p. 164.

to a single seasoned employee or two, probably plucked from the original staff for their cognitive skills and tech versatility. Higher efficiency achieved and reduced costs—a double whammy for the company. And with it goes the myth of non-automatable jobs for cause of underlying non-automatable tasks. Similar to atoms—once thought to be indivisible—jobs can be split.

This is not pure speculation—in fact it already happened: we call it Taylorism. The division of labor set the scene for automation in factories. Workers were once equal and able to perform the job from A-to-Z. True craftsmen, they developed a keen knowledge of their product over the years, mastered the entire process, and occasionally brought improvements. Taylorism shattered these neat billiard stacks, lowering skills requirements for operators, thus opening the door to machines and automaton-like workers. Cognitive tasks, such as defining optimal industrial processes or monitoring quality, went to a handful of high-paid engineers. Mid-level craftspeople exited, costs improved, and output soared.

While first circumvented to the factory, tech tentacles are now spreading the contagion over to the service sector, as illustrated hereafter with two examples.

Apart from holding the cash register, staff at a convenience store replenish inventory on the shelves, monitor security, and handle customer requests ranging from finding an item to preparing a coffee on the spot. As the reasoning goes, the latter tasks should shield them from automation, because

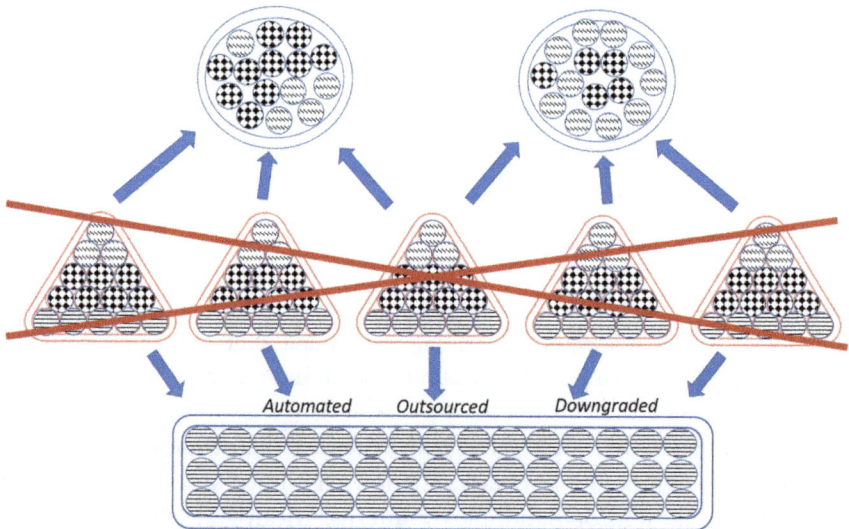

Fig. 6.13 Efficient work reorganization: the billiards allegory

machines could not handle customer interaction, dexterity and pattern recognition. Yet that hasn't stopped stores from deploying automatic cashiers, trimming headcount without eradicating it entirely.

In their seminal 2005 book *The New Division of Labor*, Levy and Murnane argue that the security guard job comprises cognitive tasks, such as identifying suspicious activity, that fall under the Polanyi paradox and thus make it immune to programming.[51] Yet here too, technology is chipping away bits of the job. As Operations Director of First Security in London John Briggs explains: "We have found that by adopting a combined approach [of manned guarding and technology], an effective, tailored solution can be achieved." He cites examples of turnstile technology and automated number plate recognition systems.[52] Door badges, metal detectors, facial recognition, and cameras linked to a monitoring room crammed with screens limit the need for guards. The figures speak for themselves: while since 2007 the U.S. business of security guards has more than doubled in terms of revenue (from $22 billion to $50 billion in 2020[53]), over the past two decades the number of security guards has stood flat at roughly 1 million.

Exemptions exist. It's hard to split a stack in the presence of only one worker—which brings us back to drivers. Here, there is no middle ground— the job can *only* be *fully* automated.[54] But jobs in offices, shops, and factories are seldom a one-man show; in such contexts, the billiards allegory looms.

Company restructurings aim to jettison the workforce via a reshuffling of tasks within the staff, in a mammoth billiards game. The greater efficiencies aimed for often conceal improvements in technology or the need to modernize a rusty organization, following decades of stagnation under dormant management. Again, a closer look may reveal tech factors puppeteering the restructuration from backstage: not keeping up with the pace of advancing technology partakes in the attrition of a company's competitiveness. Technology forces a shift in work organization to unlock greater efficiency, in a giant corporate game of survival of the fittest.

Understand that Taylorism itself is not a new form of technology, but a reorganization of work whereby jobs are mutilated and redesigned in order to

---

[51] p. 41, Frank Levy and Richard Murnane: *The New Division of Labor: How Computers are Creating the Next Job Market*, Princeton University Press (2005).

[52] Cf. Robert H. Perry & Associates: *2009 White Paper on the US Security Guard Market*, https://www.roberthperry.com/publications.

[53] *Ibid.*, citing Freedonia Group study #2362, https://www.freedoniagroup.com/ReportsAndStudies.aspx.

[54] Even this is debatable. Suppose autonomous vehicle infrastructure is legally permitted only on highways, where say 80% of a truck's time is spent. Highway driving could be automated, and the rest performed remotely. The remote driver could in theory take over the job of five truck drivers.

fully exploit the optimization potential wrought by technology. For workers it translates as a protean threat that brings about both Type-2 job disruption, or downgrading of skills requirement, and Type-3 job disruption, or work enhancement. The million-dollar question is how the billiard balls will be reorganized and where will you land in the new setting.

Bearing in mind Autor's astute remark, ask yourself whether your job could be unbundled, at what cost, whether greater efficiency would result from it, and which type of disruption you are more likely to wind up in. Consider any form of tech that could be added into the process to this purpose. If you sense danger, how could you strengthen your position? How to ensure your ascent to one of the upper, cognitive billiard stacks? For instance, is the new tech autonomous, or would it require a proficient worker to pilot it and navigate through the new paradigm? Could you be that pilot, or are you better off exiting your position altogether? Avoid the easy route of conveying the false image of a complex job, as this will not work. Let these questions ricochet in your mind as we pursue our investigation.

A final piece of advice: think of this regardless of your company's intentions. The bloated company that neglects this type of reorganization is no reason for consolation, as leaner rivals will likely outperform it. In this case, in Fig. 6.11 replace "Today" with "My Firm" and "Tomorrow" with "Competition".

Digital Taylorism

Offices are wreathed in a shroud of mist, creating a landscape where efficiency is hard to objectively assess, in stark contrast with factories. Taylorism squeezed complex tasks from the workshop, giving them to a handful of qualified engineers. Whether on an assembly line, a welding station, or tending to an injection press, operator tasks are meticulously coded in an SOP that sets the golden standard against which performance is measured. Engineering crafts these procedures, cutting up the process in bits and pieces, timing each gesture. Office jobs lack this clockwork rigor. But that could soon change. And it already bears a name: *digital Taylorism*. Software and AI improvements will erase the discretionary powers typical in mid-level office jobs, replacing art with science, with meticulous metrics to abide by, in turn easing the pathway to a billiards restructuring.

Time is of the essence for law firms, who keep close track of their time (in order to bill it to clients). This places them at the vanguard of automation. Bots and tools are surfacing to automate areas of grunt work: ZyLab, ROSS (that uses IBM Watson's computing), Robot Lawyer Lisa, and other eDiscovery software can parse through archives, summarize a case or spot similar cases overturned in the past, reducing the need for paralegals.[55]

Modern tools can measure time spent on each software and application, writing speeds, talking patterns, reading, and meeting times. Perhaps all that's missing is an independent department paid to codify and monitor performance—an office engineering of sorts that would usher in the era of digital Taylorism.

Let us take an example, starting with ex-Google CEO Eric Schmidt's rather misleading advice:

> The biggest issue is simply the development of analytical skills. Most of the routine things people do will be done by computer, but people will manage the computers around them and the analytical skills will never go out of style.[56]

Many companies produce monthly financial reports that reveal a certain margin rate. Analyzing margin fluctuations is crucial for management to understand what's happening and make sound business decisions. Yet while typically performed by white collars, does this universal analysis fall under the Polanyi paradox? We can break it down into the following steps:

- check the sales mix of products (term used here interchangeably as product or service) and clientele, versus previous months, last year and/or budget;
- analyze any variances of actual versus standard cost, for each sale, be it linked to

  - purchases: different invoice amount, surcharge, transportation route, new tariffs;
  - manufacturing: longer labor time, high scrap rate, change in the process (e.g. improvements brought by engineering);
  - other causes: damage in transportation, inventory discrepancies, customer returns, free samples shipped out to customers or for exhibitions, error by accounting department...

---

[55] Or so the song goes. The job of paralegal is often brandished as automatable—cf. for instance Chap. 2 of Brynjolfsson and McAfee: *Race Against the Machine: How the Digital Revolution is Accelerating Innovation, Driving Productivity, and Irreversibly Transforming Employment and the Economy*, Digital Frontier Press (2011); also Andres Oppenheimer: *The Robots are Coming! The Future of Jobs in the Age of Automation*, Vintage (2019), Chap. 5: *They're Coming for Lawyers!*

Yet for now, statistics tell a difference story: the number of paralegals and legal assistants roughly *doubled* in the past twenty years (versus a 15% increase in overall US workforce), and is expected to grow further by 12% in the next decade. https://www.bls.gov/ooh/legal/paralegals-and-legal-assistants.htm.

[56] Cf. the conclusion of Alec Ross: *The Industries of the Future*, Simon & Schuster (2016).

In short, a rules-based task. A computer-literate employee could code a program to perform this step-by-step analysis, saving herself several hours or days of work each month. Supposing she is not that proficient, in today's world an algorithm will not appear out of the blue to replace her. However, someone could observe her actions remotely, via a tool like TeamViewer, and develop that program. Imagine a company based in Bangladesh offering this service to corporations worldwide, with the guarantee of maximizing automation. This would take place in three steps: an observation period, followed by a trial-and-error stage of automated task implementation, and finally the roll-out phase where algorithms overtake tasks previously carried out by staff. The last phase might still require a dose of (human) monitoring and tweaking by the subcontractor, but at only a fraction of the cost saved throughout the organization.

Some firms experiment with peer ratings, others with sociometers. Sociometers are small sensors attached to people (courtesy of the miniaturization trend) and used to measure staff interaction. These are birthing a growing number of studies, from the quantifying of social interaction patterns based on gender[57] to what makes a great corporate culture.[58] Relevant traits measured and scored include listening abilities (as opposed to talking), pitch of tone, soft skills like teamwork, charisma (via measurement of colleagues' state of mind in meetings while intervening or presenting), leadership and customer engagement. As these smart devices become ubiquitous, ensuing data could be managed by the company, serving as a reference point in annual performance appraisals to emphasize areas that require extra training, suitable types of job and potential career development paths. In *The Signals are Talking,* futurist Amy Webb foresees a visual management tool where each staff is depicted as a plant; where the number and color of leaves, blooming of flowers and direction of the stem hint at different health and engagement levels, enabling the manager to gauge overall mood at a glance.[59] Such tools could enhance human resources, with data available to job interviewers and transferred when switching employers. Future wages may start low, with a complex system of monetary incentives added as good behavior is established, tasks achieved and acumen built, not unlike experience points in role-playing video games.

---

[57] Onnela, JP., Waber, B., Pentland, A. et al.: Using sociometers to quantify social interaction patterns, Nature, Article number 5604 (2014).
[58] Cf. Daniel Coyle: *The Culture Code: The Secrets of Highly Successful Groups,* Bantam (2018).
[59] p. 277. Amy Webb: *The Signals Are Talking: Why Today's Fringe Is Tomorrow's Mainstream,* PublicAffairs (2016).

Companies will tinker differently with these systems, with processed ones apt at adopting them in a quest for efficiency and agile ones prone to develop more experimental metrics, of the type that leads Zappos to celebrate an employee for spending over 10 h on a service call with a client.[60]

Yet faced with this new scrutiny of office work, no doubt many employees will sigh and drag their feet. Decades of Internet have accustomed them to a large degree of autonomy, as if shirking and web surfing were part of the perks that come with the job. They pursued higher education to avoid the fate of the factory pit, subject to prying eyes and timed toilet breaks. Measuring efficiency only applies to uneducated scum; they're self-disciplined and can best judge their work quality, right?

One shouldn't rely on this type of rhetoric. Office workers may not be shielded from the ruthless laws of efficiency for long. Witness the recent turn of events: as the Work-From-Home paradigm takes hold, it gives companies extra motive to monitor employees, in order to ensure that they earn their keep. Often fueled by AI, sophisticated tools are ushering office efficiency metrics bound to unleash cutthroat competition between staff.[61]

In the service sector, the diktat of metrics is marching forward by leaps. Workers in restaurants and cafes, deliverymen, and teachers are feeling the pinch of advanced measurement tools increasingly determining their pay and partaking in job prospects.[62] Banks are notably spearheading the trend, under the pretext of security and to prevent pilfering.

Several factors make digital Taylorism irresistible. Unlike privacy issues when surfing online, employees are paid to work; from a business perspective, employers (and their backers) wish to ensure that the money is put to effective use. Most managers already submit their staff to evaluations on a regular basis. The new system brings transparency into the process, with performance measured according to a common yardstick across the board and scarce place for "-isms" (favoritism, racism, ageism, nepotism…). Staff would truly be compensated based on the value of their work, not for their connections or for playing golf with the boss, thus contributing to greater perceived fairness.[63]

---

[60] Cf. Richard Feloni: *A Zappos employee had the company's longest customer-service call at 10 h, 43 min*, Business Insider (July 26, 2016), https://www.businessinsider.com/zappos-employee-sets-record-for-lon gest-customer-service-call-2016-7.

[61] Cf. The Economist: *Welcome to the era of the hyper-surveilled office*, May 14th, 2022).

[62] For cafes and teachers alone, cf. Chap. 7: *Sweating Bullets on the Job*, of Cathy O'Neal, *Weapons of Math Destruction: How Big Data Increases Inequality and Threatens Democracy*, Crown (2016).

[63] Of course, this is hypothetical. Nothing would prevent a company from adding biases into the system, altering, or discarding the results. Not to mention that a worker's ties and golf skills could partake in their assessment if they contribute to generate sales or reduce risks—such as the Finance Department sloth whose connections at the local Tax bureau alone justify her presence on the payroll.

It might mark the end of slacking around surfing the web at the office. But that was never meant to be the purpose of coming to work. Laxity and a lack of means to measure office productivity created a relapse period where employees could stray to websites unrelated to work, but the days of loose supervision may well be counted.

On the dark side, by reducing workers to mere cogs, digital Taylorism leaves scarce room for discussion or exemptions. If a deliveryman witnesses an accident, his sole metric of on-time delivery commands him to speed ahead. Anything not baked in the performance algorithm's criteria does not count. This de facto excludes aspects that fall under the Polanyi paradox, i.e. that are difficult to measure or comprehend by an algorithm—for instance helping others. Not only is the result inhumane, it saps the workers' humaneness, and could instill a counterproductive culture in the workplace.

Digital Taylorism presages another drift: eradicating the Polanyi paradox like smallpox erases the human element, thus facilitates substitution by algorithms.

Meanwhile, as tasks are chopped into narrow cubicles, they become easier to address by AI. Ten years after the launch of Siri, early dreams of a seemingly omniscient AI have given way to a multitude of specialized AIs. One artificial neural network can be trained to handle personal mortgage-related questions, another commercial banking transactions, a third, tech support. Each one structures its terrain, allowing for an enhanced user experience. These will be patched up into a greater network—like when calling a bank representative, who after a few queries transfers you to another department where a specialist picks up the phone.

A Monotask Job

The number of tasks to a job conceals obvious signs of health or brittleness. When a given task is no longer required, either that it becomes outsourced or automated, the survival rate of workers handling it up to then depends on what else they do—with no other purpose, they get the pink slip.

Frey & Osborne's 2013 study highlights this. Occupations "most vulnerable to AI" comprised cashiers, cost estimators, data entry keyers, insurance underwriters, and tax examiners—occupations that share a common trait: they are monotask.

Monotask jobs are seldom found in small companies. The bigger and more processed a company, the higher its staff specialization. Figure 6.14 conveys this idea: an inverse correlation between the number of employees and the number of tasks.

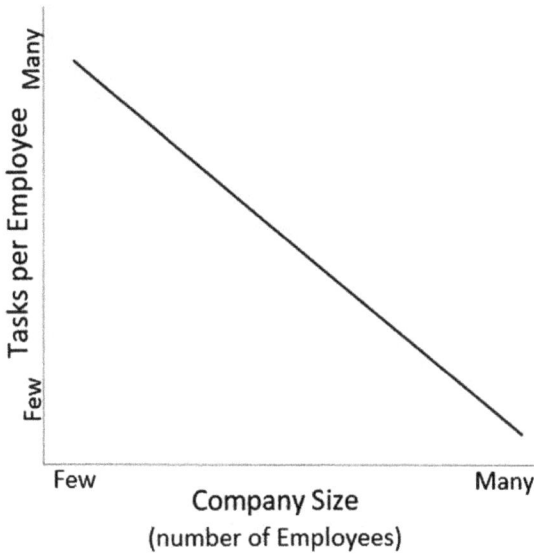

Fig. 6.14 Tasks versus company size

The more tasks to a job, the more it stands out—meanwhile a monotask job is easily scalable. It consists in recurrent work available to the lowest bidder. Flee this type of job at all costs; it should only serve as a temporary means, while seeking a better position, pursuing studies, or some other goal—not as an end in itself.

Transdisciplinarity

The Institute For the Future, in its *Future Work Skills 2020* report, defines transdisciplinarity as the "literacy in and ability to understand concepts across multiple disciplines". The report lists transdisciplinarity as among the top skills to develop[64]—an antidote against the narrow job trap.

Linda Sharkey and Morag Barrett, authors of *The Future-Proof Workplace*, explain that while in the past emphasis was put on deep knowledge of a specific area, nowadays narrow expertise no longer suffices. They take the example of a car mechanic who at present needs to learn about the electronics and how to navigate onboard software.[65] In her advice to workers,

[64] Anna Davies, Devin Fidler, Marina Gorbis: *Future Work Skills 2020*, Institute for the Future for the University of Phoenix Research Institute (2011).
[65] Linday Sharkey and Morag Barrett: *The Future-Proof Workplace: Six Strategies to Accelerate Talent Development, Reshape Your Culture, and Succeed with Purpose*, Wiley (2017).

futurist and workplace expert Alexandra Levit concurs on the value of cross-functional expertise, citing countless examples of people who successfully veered from the traditional, straight-line career path.[66]

Developing other fields of knowledge adds value in several respects: to soothe communication with other departments, see the broader picture (which helps to connect more distant dots), and fend off automation and outsourcing threats. As David Autor hinted earlier, transdisciplinarity hampers any efforts to "unbundle your job", making it simply not worthwhile.

Consider the broader picture. IDEO, the famed design firm with a record number of awards, seeks to hire people with what they brand a knowledge shape in "T", i.e. people with a deep expertise in a given field, combined with a rudimentary expertise in other areas. These ambidextrous individuals have a greater propensity to not only observe and spot interesting best practices, but to realize how these could be applied elsewhere to great benefit, in a completely different setting. This transversality enables a cross-pollination of ideas between fields and as such is key to creativity. It is also a key to unlocking that highly sought ability to step back and seize the bigger picture in any situation.

Alas, developing a jack-of-all-trades card grooms the worker for the managerial strata. Even the sinusoidal career path is gaining recognition in a variety of fields.

In the Learning Curve (Sect. 8.2), we discuss of continuous learning, a major contributor to developing transdisciplinarity.

6.4.3 Dexterity, Pattern Recognition, and the Moravec Paradox

Spatial recognition and dexterity come into play in almost any job, taking a front seat where manual labor is involved. Rewinding to our tripartite definition of intelligence, they relate to the first and last parts, respectively: exposure to and action on the environment.

Machines are light-years away from changing a diaper, handling dirty laundry, reorganizing a closet, or cleaning the dishes and stacking them neatly in the cupboard.

---

[66] Cf. Chap. 6: *Choose Your Own Adventure*. Alexandra Levit: *Humanity Works: Merging Technologies and People for the Workforce of the Future*, Kogan Page (2018).

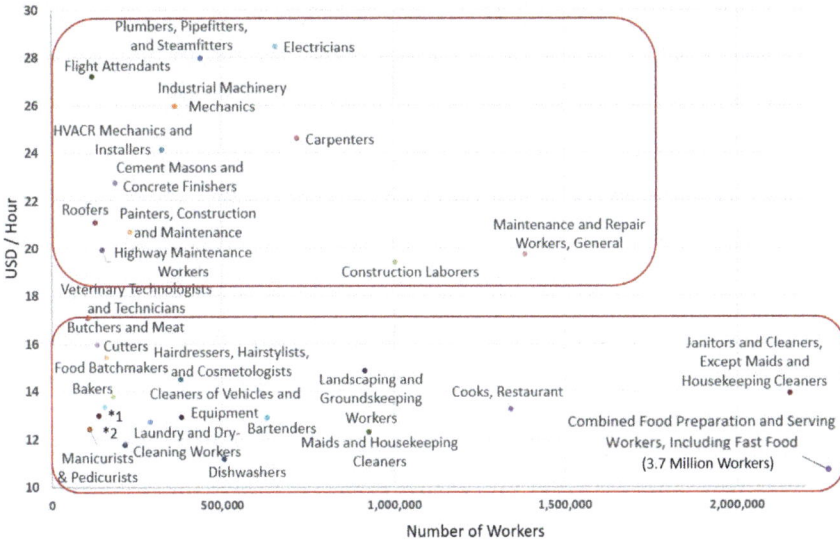

Fig. 6.15 Sample of U.S. jobs involving dexterity and pattern recognition (2018). *1: Meat, Poultry, and Fish Cutters and Trimmers. *2: Sewing Machine Operators

The ease with which humans can perform such actions has been dubbed the *Moravec paradox*, after an observation in the 1980s from Prof. Hans Moravec:

> It is comparatively easy to make computers exhibit adult level performance on intelligence tests or playing checkers, and difficult or impossible to give them the skills of a one-year-old when it comes to perception and mobility.[67]

These tasks require dexterity, or robotic agility, and computer vision, a type of pattern recognition and processing. Until AI and robotics improve in these two areas, they will remain ill-equipped to outperform humans in physical tasks in non-controlled environments (as opposed to an assembly line, where the placement of each bolt is determined with precision). To what extent will vary based on the task at hand: a self-driving car focuses more on image recognition than dexterity.

We can roughly divide jobs that summon vision and dexterity into two categories, based on wage level, as illustrated in Fig. 6.15. The list is non-exhaustive. Several jobs, for instance Firefighters and Child, Family, and School Social Workers, are excluded, because they benefit from stronger headwinds to automation, such as the safety factor and the human touch.

---

[67] Hans Moravec: *Mind Children*, Harvard University Press (1988), p. 15.

Over twelve million workers toil in the low-end bracket, including 3.7 million in food preparation and dishwashing (shown off the chart). Tasks achievable by a child command little value. We seldom brag about our ability to identify our desk or reorganize its drawers on a curriculum vitae because it is shared by every (non-incapacitated) human—a cheap commodity. Assuming these feats come within a machine's grasp, it will need to perform them for a cheaper cost and often at an equally fast pace. Hotels need rooms cleaned and tidied within an hour or less (depending on room size). The commodity factor further shields these jobs from machines, unable to compete with low labor costs. This was illustrated in the UK a few years ago with the arrival of labor from Eastern Europe, which provided a cheap alternative to the drive-in car wash model.[68]

Take the roughly one million landscaping and groundskeeping workers. They may lose tasks to water sprinklers, moisture meters, and autonomous lawnmowers; yet so long as humans fancy parks and gardens, there should be ample demand for their labor. Gardener robots of the sort present in the novel *Neuromancer* (and at one point weaponized by an AI) seem implausible due to the unstructured environment, Moravec paradox and low human labor costs. The need to be on the spot to perform the job also prevents offshoring. Limited as career prospects for a physically taxing job with no human touch that barely rakes in $15 an hour may be, it could remain truly immune to automation for a long time.

On higher pastures, we find professionals—six million in the above chart. While factors ranging from the ease of finding candidates to age and the risk premium associated with Highway Maintenance Workers can influence wages, the most determinant factor relates to expertise. These workers develop a keen eye and greater dexterity for their craft. Plumbers and electricians locate issues at a glance there where laymen see nothing but entangled pipes and wires. In the fable from Daoist philosopher Zhuangzi, a butcher impresses the visiting emperor by effortlessly cutting through an ox.[69] He explains how years of practice have led him to directly identify with the

---

[68] Paul Mason: *Our Problem isn't Robots, it's the low-wage car-wash economy*, The Guardian (December 12, 2016) https://www.theguardian.com/commentisfree/2016/dec/12/mark-carney-britains-car-wash-economy-low-wage-jobs.

[69] This parable may appear ill-placed, considering the butcher appears in the chart's low-wage category. But butchers comprise only 14% of that category—the rest are meat cutters. Butchers earn 25% more than meat-cutters; taking these figures into account brings the country's 20,000 butchers to an average hourly salary of $20, thus in the second category. Cf. https://www.zippia.com/butcher-jobs/demographics/ and https://www.zippia.com/meat-cutter-jobs/demographics/.

action, leaving the spirit to "move where it wants".[70] In modern parlance, he shifted actions that would require a rookie to think according to Kahneman's System 2 (by conscious effort), over to System 1 (through automatism).[71]

AI pioneer Marvin Minsky emphasized that the most difficult human skills to engineer are those that are unconscious.[72] But as Frey & Osborne mentioned in their 2013 study, AI advances could erode these advantages. The threat to the higher paid cluster appears greater given the economic gains at stake.

This is no reason to forsake specialization per se. Expertise carries other benefits: a keener understanding of customer needs, the baggage and leeway to explore the creative vibe, the status and recognition crucial to forging contacts and growing entrepreneurial wings. It's what allows the chef to exercise creativity in her craft and entertain guests. Though not the main route we advocate for in this book, physical laborers may find a plausible exit route here—on condition that they do not stay put, but set in motion the engine toward cognition.

It all boils down to timing. Jobs involving the Moravec paradox are shielded, for now. But it would be naïve to assume the situation a static one. Ongoing tech advances could put the more expensive or scalable jobs in peril. Recall Amazon's warehouse workers. In 2022, the company introduced a fully autonomous warehouse robot.[73] Expect the spilt syrup story to vanish from their website anytime now. Workers who swear by Moravec best develop other headwinds, for instance cognition and the human touch.

Low-paid jobs may continue to deter automation, though as the costs of robotics plummet this could narrow the scope to non-scalable work. A potential escape route, albeit not the most desirable one. And even when fueled by good intentions, legislation can adversely affect the sturdiness of these ramparts, for instance by raising minimum wages or adding regulations on alternative forms of work (temporary contracts, undocumented labor…).

6.4.4   The Human Touch

In some jobs, human beings are preferred.

---

[70] Zhuangzi: *The Basic Writings.* To be fair, roots of the butcher legend stretch earlier than the fourth century BC and probably descend from an oral Indian tradition, there to be later enshrined in the Mahabharata epic, where the butcher goes by the name of Dharmavyadha.

[71] Daniel Kahneman:, *Thinking Fast and Slow* (2011) Penguin.

[72] Marvin Minsky: *The Society of Mind*, Simon and Schuster (1986), p. 29.

[73] Brian Heater: *Amazon debuts a fully autonomous warehouse robot*, TechCrunch (June 23, 2022), https://techcrunch.com/2022/06/22/amazon-debuts-a-fully-autonomous-warehouse-robot/.

The previous traits combined determine the propensity for job automation, from a technological standpoint. But jobs from waiters to news anchors, that technically face trouble, may survive simply because as a gregarious bunch, people indulge in having other people at their service. We appreciate the human doctors, nurses, hairdressers, gym trainers, and bartenders who hear us out, who console and motivate us. In light of potential hazards, we'd rather our life guards, human diving instructors and flight attendants remain human beings. And then there are times when we just need to see a (real) human face, to hear a true voice.

Despite some incursions from robots, customer-facing jobs are booming. Early automation analysts like Jeremy Rifkin underestimated the role played by the human touch, for instance when contemplating the future of bankers amid ATM deployment.[74] This headwind benefits workers in the service sector—hairdressers, waiters, taxi drivers, doctors—as well as the portion of office workers in contact with the customer, in corporate lingo "front office" jobs.

Here to supplant humans, machines need to reach a prominent level of emotional intelligence, or rather emulation, in terms of perception, expression and in certain cases even appearance. As futurist Ian Pearson highlights:

> People don't always make logical decisions, and to understand what customers want, machines will need to empathize to some degree, and that means having true emotion.[75]

Industrial robots made the biggest strides because they operate in controlled environments set up by companies and sealed off from the public—"back office" work. In a front office, robots would face people with no formal training on "how to deal with robots"—customers no less, whose delicate needs must be met. Service robots must exhude with empathy and understanding, but also be careful not to harm others, including children and the stumbling drunkard.

A strong deterrent against both automation and outsourcing, the human factor hints at our "customer VUCA" yet stretches beyond to encompass our penchant for pampering by others. Humans create bonds and emotional relationships, an intensity palpable even in short interactions that cannot be emulated remotely or by a machine. In the movie *Up in the Air*, after

---

[74] Cf. p. 145, Jeremy Rifkin: *The End of Work: The Decline of the Global Labor Force and the Dawn of the Post-Market Era*, G.P. Putnam's Sons (1996).

[75] Richard Yonck: *Heart of the Machine: Our Future in a World of Artificial Emotional Intelligence*, Arcade Publishing (2017).

tinkering with a videoconferencing tool to give workers news of the pink slip remotely in a bid to save on travel expenses, the company eventually recants. Given the particularly emotional nature of the discussion, on-site presence was deemed preferable (that of George Clooney, no less).

BlaBlaCar is a French online marketplace for carpooling with north of a hundred million users. Its drivers are rated based on their level of chattiness: "bla" for the non-talkative, "blabla" for someone who likes to chat, and "blablabla" for the ones who can't put a lid on it. Riders can choose the level of babble they crave for: someone to talk with during the ride, or a quiet shadow. This model approximates a scoring for the human touch—it would be interesting to see which of the three driver categories receives the most calls. By any guess, were autonomous vehicles to storm our streets tomorrow, the "blablablas" would have greater survival chances.

As noted earlier, the IoT will enable organizations to deploy sociometers, thus metrics to monitor customer interaction. Service workers should not consider themselves shielded and languish, but polish their social skills within the confines of their job. Entrepreneurs and freelancers know foremost that the human touch constitutes the bloodline that keeps the activity pulsing. If needed, shift toward a niche within your sector where human contact plays a more salient role. Hotline services are now mostly automated and outsourced; yet companies with extremely technical products, or that like Zappos, emphasize the human touch as a differentiation tactic, maintain an in-house hotline. These have become outliers. Tomorrow, the automation paradigm could expand to engulf waiters, bartenders, nurses, mixologists, and yoga instructors. Behind many customer-facing occupations lies a spectrum ranging from low to luxury end. Hamburger preparation may be automated along with the staff tasked to handle customer orders; yet patrons at a gourmet restaurant will still expect to be advised on wine pairing, queried for palates, informed of the foods' origins, and entertained with anecdotes on the establishment's history. Just as companies can seek to brand up to avoid sectorial disruption (the refuge tactic), workers can elbow their way to the eclectic end—not only toward jobs where human performance plays an appreciated, leading role, but also toward less price-sensitive customers. Flee Costa for a coffee shop that serves drip coffee with a large choice of beans. Favor Brioni over Benetton. Shun the closed kitchen; clamber from cook to chef. A big step to move from hamburger flipper to fine-dining server has to do with developing the human touch. And that endeavor involves everything from appearance to empathy, charisma, observance for detail and an obsessive focus on customer pains and needs, with creativity and at times a solid network of relations kicking in to solve them.

Do not assume your job immune to automation simply because there is a strong human touch element at play in it. Monitor even tech that appears as less of a threat and more of an enhancer to your job, so as to be ready to embrace it whenever and wherever it can improve your value proposition. Kai-Fu Lee plotted the psychiatrist as a job immune to automation in large part due to the human touch factor.[76] Yet even her walls are showing cracks: BetterHelp puts clients in remote contact with a human-certified psychologist, via mail and hourly sessions, using its own videoconferencing tool. Other apps cover needs from snoring problems to assisting the suicidal. Psychology bots may not be as good as their human peers, but they have their advantages too: reachable 24/7, at a pittance of a cost, they neither tire nor lose patience, and remain unbiased by gender and overall personality. Even supposing the human therapist to be genuinely neutral and to abide by the Hippocratic Oath, a client may fear otherwise, and thus feel more comfortable sharing secrets with a machine. Though from a technical standpoint digital data can be stored and used for nefarious purposes, we seem paradoxically more relaxed and inclined to confess our sins to an AI than to a human (though perhaps the jury is still out on this one).

This data forms the treasure trove algorithms feed on that in time could help us to better understand society's ills, for instance to provide insights on issues faced by teenage girls and boys, from bullying to peer pressure and solitude; root causes along with clues to prevent high suicide rates of certain clusters—even clusters we ignored existed, until algorithms unearthed them, all the while respecting anonymity. AI and its recommendations will only grow stronger as data is amassed, track records built, and aggregations reveal patterns, creating an ever-more human feel.

In such cases where tech reveals itself as an enhancer instead of a substitute for human labor, do not discard it as harmless. Substituting tech is the type of raging bull to run away from at first sight; the enhancing one should be domesticated, lest others beat you to it. The psychologist who masters technology pertaining to her job will flourish in the 4^{IR} (and flourishing here could even mean leveraging the technology to launch a startup, turn it into a unicorn and get super rich); the one who ignores it will lose clients.

Proximity is quintessential to the human touch. Much of the chitchat at the corner shop has nothing to do with a purchase; these businesses partake in the soul of the local community.

Whether this headwind alone suffices remains up to debate. It involves the classic equation of price versus perceived value, as attested by the dwindling

---

[76] Kai-Fu Lee:, *AI Superpowers*, p. 171.

number of independent boulangeries in France. Longtime eponymic with the country's image, boulangeries are withering among invasive grocery chains that offer cheaper, industrially produced bread, in turn fueling concerns as for the elderly otherwise estranged from society, the morning ritual to the boulangerie represents one of the last ties to a social life.

The employee who successfully nurtures the human touch could keep her job even as others tumble. She will have achieved the grand act of differentiation by customer proximity. If the human touch is the only thing separating you from a red-eyed algorithm, your job is hanging by a thread. Act accordingly, not just by being nice to customers—after all, happy grins didn't save tollway cashiers—but by deciphering latent needs and going the extra mile to meet those in ways that would evade automated rivals. AI cannot anticipate a customer's pain points and address them.

Roose mentions the example of Best Buy, who pressed by online competition, pushed forth a novel strategy that included the In-Home Advisor program, whereby customers could call a consultant to visit their home and advise them on furnishing. Launched in 2017, it was one among several human touch initiatives that put Best Buy back on track.[77] For the school bus driver, this infers getting personally acquainted with both children and parents, displaying alertness to their concerns, gathering intel on what orbits around the school and informing them of abnormalities. Because it's difficult to put a price tag on it, earning customer trust can bring you a long way.

View customer satisfaction in a broad sense. Back-office jobs often work for another department, their de facto customer—for instance to provide support to salespeople on the field. And the salesperson who regularly feeds the marketing department credible intel on field trends helps the company carve out its future strategy, as the information trickles into the R&D's roadmap. She is more valuable to the firm than the peer who forsakes this type of action.

Gauge whether the service or even the customer could be automated. A purchaser follows a script of easy-to-encode rules: price, quality, minimum order quantity, delivery time, payment terms… The day that purchasers are replaced by bots, with no one to take out for dinner and chisel persuasion techniques on, the seller could go out of a job. Likewise, as retail advisors and gym instructors are substituted by a handful of KOLs, their own coaches and trainers lose all *raison d'être* and cease to exist. The domino effect of everyone

---

[77] Kevin Roose: *Futureproof: 9 Rules for Humans in the Age of Automation*, Random House (2021), p. 130.

buying online (and doing their fitting in the metaverse) could obsolete great portions of jobs as entire swaths of customers vanish from the physical world.

Human Touch as a Tailwind: The Human Punch

In the real world, dealing with human workers isn't always a walk in the park. We've all experienced disagreeable moments with restaurant waiters or retail staff. Clients become victim of the vagaries of the employee's mood of the day. At my local bagel joint, despite well-intentioned, smiling staff, a high turnover implies that even a *habitué* like myself must specify at length how to customize the bagel and what not to put in it, *every single time*, with the infallible reward of a flawed bagel serving as a reminder not to deliver my sermon too perfunctorily.

In such instances, we pray for the dawn of automation, not of ill will but because the customer experience would benefit as a result. Machines remember our choices, remain pleasant, and don't take offense. If an identical bagel store sets shop across the street, only with an app for users to customize and save their favorite bagel in their settings, guess which one I would choose?

The human touch is not an impassable barrier. Moods change. We may view a robot police force as a nightmarish dystopia, yet rising discontent with police brutality could contribute to overcome that phobia.

The elevator boy epitomizes the propensity for sudden shifts in public perception. Introduced in the 1880s, the first automatic elevators inspired fear. It took some fifty years, and consumer wrath following strikes from elevator staff in the 1920s, to seal the fate of manned elevators (unfortunately for elevator boys, the skyscraper revolution made taking the stairs a no-go). This precedent again moderates blind reliance on the human touch as a failsafe. Truck drivers who regularly protest by blocking major roads, beware. More recently, a wave of strikes paralyzed the entire Paris subway system; except for the only two automated lines (as in driverless): these remained fully operational. What kind of signal does this send to the public?

In *The Fourth Age*, author-entrepreneur Byron Reese consented that after a glance at his fireplace, the fireplace repairman fed him with so many technical details that he either "knew more about fireplaces than anyone else I would ever meet, or he was a convincing enough pathological liar that I would never figure him out".[78] Fears of getting cheated by unscrupulous workers are commonplace in contexts that involve an opaque field of expertise: plumbers,

---

[78] Byron Reece: *The Fourth Age: Smart Robots, Conscious Computers, and the Future of Humanity*, p. 111, Atria Books (2018).

doctors, Internet service providers, beauticians, constructors, dentists, and electricians. They prod the client with a term or two—just enough to validate her ignorance—and from thereon, it's open bar. As if from the onset, the client must find a pretext to yell and make a scene just to hint that she will not easily fall to shenanigans.

AI can provide transparency in this regard. Car-riding apps rid us from both the risk of the cabbie taking a detour through Chinatown and the ensuing dispute if caught red-handed. Apps now assume the role of supreme arbitrator. Tech that removes the need for an expert mitigates the risks of scheming. Reese cites the guy he calls over to handle the restoration of his old fireplace as a futureproof job, along with that of antique clock repairer, vintage guitar restorer, and so on. Don't bet on it, at least not for this reason. Maps with real-time information on traffic and areas undergoing construction easily eclipsed taxi driver expertise. Cabbies were merely the first in the line of a new paradigm bound to sprawl to electricians, plumbers, and other forms of expertise, soon to be surpassed by specialized apps (with aR potentially kicking in to fill in the gaps, as head-mounted gear becomes ubiquitous).

Insensitive doctors, heartless lawyers, teacher automatons, trigger-happy police officers, and perpetual strikers who lack any shred of humanity toward those they supposedly serve in their line of duty actively pave the route for a robot takeover. Similar to when a firm loses its monopoly, they need to straighten their attitude toward customers, and fast. Clients' wallets may vote for robots displaying realistic human emotions over callous, deceitful ruffians.

Social Intelligence and People Skills

Computers are light-years away from managing people; they cannot navigate through complex social relationships, negotiate, show empathy, brainstorm, persuade, instill confidence, acknowledge cultural differences and everything else commonly associated with "people skills".

No matter the level of progress made in empathetic AI, it seems unlikely that robots could attain our level of charisma and connection. A human being who leads with passion, standing shoulder by shoulder with her reports in the trenches (colloquially known as plugging late nights), inspires and turns staff into devotees. The fact that a computer does not feel tired nor hungry, fear death nor sickness, limits our proclivity to connect with it.

Researchers are hell-bent on developing empathetic AI, pushed in part by a dearth of healthcare workers. But these incursions are constrained to narrow settings unfit for the manager's seat, and likely to remain so for the foreseeable future. A computer haranguing troops simply does not have the same effect.

Dealing with humans, be it customers, but also peers, shareholders, vendors, and other stakeholders puts you on the safe side.

This calls for a few reservations.

Starting with the depth of the interaction. We know what happened to the highly structured call center jobs that used standard Q&As: their staff got replaced by bots. This links to corporate culture. Does yours push for a formal and formatted exchange? Observe your company's actions to determine whether it aims to automate its waiters or tour guides.

And beyond the firm, what do customers want? Patrons frequenting the *café de la gare* seek that human connection at the bar. Those who queue at a Starbucks want quick service. The barista taking an order and wishing you a nice day brings no value; she merely executes a drill.

One must exploit the human touch so that the value of the interaction justifies the extra cost. We highlighted the human's advantages over the robot, but this holds true only inasmuch as you identify with the leader who connects with others, or that you veer off script from time to time, that you run the extra mile to satisfy the customer. Blabla car driver metrics could highlight the amount of human touch people fancy. Though most professions lack such metrics, imagine how these would transpose to your job, were they available. Recall the tug-of-war between human and machine—who is at the center of the sumo cognition game?

As with other cognitive elements, social skills need to both be sharpened and come in play in the job. In interactions with colleagues or clients, know when being right matters, and when it is trumped by the desired ends to achieve. So perhaps you are right, and they are wrong. To what use rub it in their face? The alpha bent on proving to be the smartest person in the room may win that battle yet lose the war, as the overall mood nosedives. Is your goal to prove who is right, or to produce positive vibes that leave customers walking out satisfied? The ability to trade IQ for EQ is one of our great advantages over computers—on condition that you exert it.

Social skills also imply listening to others. We are regularly advised to look into our interlocutor's eyes, bend intently and mark their discourse with "Okay" and "I see". True listening involves turning off our inner voice and making full abstraction of everything else—including past experiences that may come to mind, what you plan to say to counter such argument and projections of how that will play out. Achieving this meditative state may be easier said than done, but you can at least view it as a direction to aim for.

As noted earlier, ponder whether your interlocutors are keen to remain. Suppose algorithms replace reporters, people shop online instead of stopping by for a chat as they pass the brick-and-mortar store; tourists opt to visit

Venice and Versailles in VR; your direct reports' tasks are automated, leaving you with no one to manage. The need for colleagues to consult one another and collaborate largely stems from the fact that we live in a world of dispersed, asymmetrical information, for reasons ranging from types and levels of expertise to confidentiality and lack of fluidity between systems. But once set up, a network of intricate data pools and narrow AI algorithms that communicate with one another would bypass the need for much of this human dialogue. When your interlocutor vanishes, so does the opportunity to exhibit social skills.

6.4.5 IT Versatility

As IT-savvy peers race ahead, the old fart incapable of typing on a keyboard faces extinction; workers who pursue the job enhancement scenario must force-train themselves to master the tools.

A firm made of isolated silos cannot function properly. But when each department is "stained" with a dose of the others—HR and communication skills, an inkling of financials, openness to innovative ideas—it facilitates cooperation. In the twenty-first century, this truism holds above all for computer literacy: The ICT revolution has spared no one, making IT skills a most noticeable and appreciated quality.

Clever companies in traditional sectors frame the game as a competition with Big Tech, as when Under Armour pits itself against Apple to develop its own health app. Meanwhile, Big Tech reaches toward traditional sectors, hoping to upset the rules. As a Netflix manager summarized: "The goal is to become HBO faster than HBO can become us."[79]

Taking a cue from these corporate trends, workers from outside of the IT field would do well to take interest in 4^{IR} tech, while those in IT should trail in the footsteps of tech companies and expand their expertise in a business field of their interest. Look at AI gurus: do any of the Andrew Ngs, Yann LeCuns, or Lee Kai-Fus stick to an IT job? On the contrary, they take the helm of R&D divisions, run Big Tech's AI operations, launch incubators, venture capitalist firms and AI startups; they author books and tour the world giving seminars.

Consider jobs that operate in an open environment and involve knowhow—the "tricks of the trade". Plumbers, doctors, electricians, and farmers possess skills that evade computer scientists and programmers eager

---

[79] Quoted in GQ magazine: https://www.gq.com/story/netflix-founder-reed-hastings-house-of-cards-arrested-development.

to unearth applications for their newfound machine learning toys. Devising ways to automate a job requires prior knowhow of the inner cogs. Computer science hotshots lack this knowledge; it's not something that can be googled. Hence each one needs the other. If you are in a skilled manual profession, rest assured that a breed of IT geeks is out there somewhere, anxious to enhance or entirely automate aspects of your job. Rather than panic, reach out to them. These are ripe candidates for a partnership because they are seeking someone of your pedigree.

Rudimentary IT knowledge can demarcate you, maximizing chances for a good collaborative fit with IT experts. Sharing a common language not only facilitates communication, creating charisma between parties, it also lessens the risk of being perceived as a disposable razor, one to squeeze all knowledge from and convert into 1s and 0s. Much of the machine learning research and applications conducted in medicine is made via such partnerships. Ditto for inroads in smart farming.

Makoto Koike epitomizes this trend. An automobile engineer, at age 33 he decided to return to his parents' farm, a family operation that mainly grows cucumbers. In Japan, fruit and vegetables are a serious business. Those deemed aesthetic can fetch astronomical prices. Noting the considerable amount of time spent by his mother to sort through the harvest and isolate the best cucumbers, Makoto devised a system to automate the process. Using TensorFlow, a Google-owned machine learning platform opened to the public in 2015, he trained an algorithm to distinguish cucumbers based on their shape, then built a conveyor-belt to automate sorting. His system achieved an accuracy of 70%, turning Makoto into a poster child for IT versatility, living proof that opportunities abound, both vast and within reach of commoners.[80]

An individual who encapsulates both the professional background and seasoned IT skills has an undisputable advantage over less versatile peers. She can observe the various parts of her job through the lenses of a programmer and intuitively sense automation opportunities or snippets of information worth plucking in the sea of data there where IT people see only noise, thereby enhancing her job, and her value.

---

[80] Amos Zeeberg: *D.I.Y. Artificial Intelligence Comes to a Japanese Family Farm*, The New Yorker (August 10, 2017) https://www.newyorker.com/tech/annals-of-technology/diy-artificial-intelligence-comes-to-a-japanese-family-farm.

Proximity to Automation Tools

Having covered the major inner traits, we pause to consider a last element, thereby taking a sneak peek into the upcoming Task chapter.

Ever pondered how far you stride from the dreaded automation tools? This distance matters. Because with proximity comes the opportunity to automate tasks yourself, and before someone else does it for you.

Automating your job may evoke the image of the man sawing off the branch he's sitting on. Yet companies confronted with disruption face this precise conundrum. How they react—perceiving it as a threat or opportunity—ultimately seals their fate. Smart firms take drastic action when deemed necessary, for instance by

- shaking up top management, as when Satya Nadella replaced Steve Ballmer as CEO of Microsoft in 2014;
- creating an internal skunkworks;
- spinning off a division into a separate company, a tactic advocated by Clayton Christensen.[81]

Visualize how a cunning company could either automate or devalue your job, via any mix of machines, robots, algorithms, and low-end labor; either in its entirety, or bit by bit, piece by piece. Consider the 4^{IR} technologies we encountered. Following the wise words of Under Armour's CEO, peer beyond your company and sector; imagine working under Elon Musk or Steve Jobs. What would they do? And what would you do to avoid ending up on their pink list?

Assess your distance to the automation tools that these heartless vampires would use to suck you out of a job.

Figure 6.16 plots jobs in terms of

- proclivity to automation, on a scale of −5 (not automatable) to +5 (highly automatable);
- proximity to automation tools, also on a scale of −5 (far from automation tools) to +5 (tools within the worker's reach).

The automation scoring results from factors encountered up to now. As for proximity to automation tools, consider the self-driving truck replacing manned trucks: there is no easy path for the truck driver to take automation into his own hands, lest he founds a self-driving truck company.

---

[81] Clayton Christensen: *The Innovator's Dilemma*, Chap. 10: Managing Disruption.

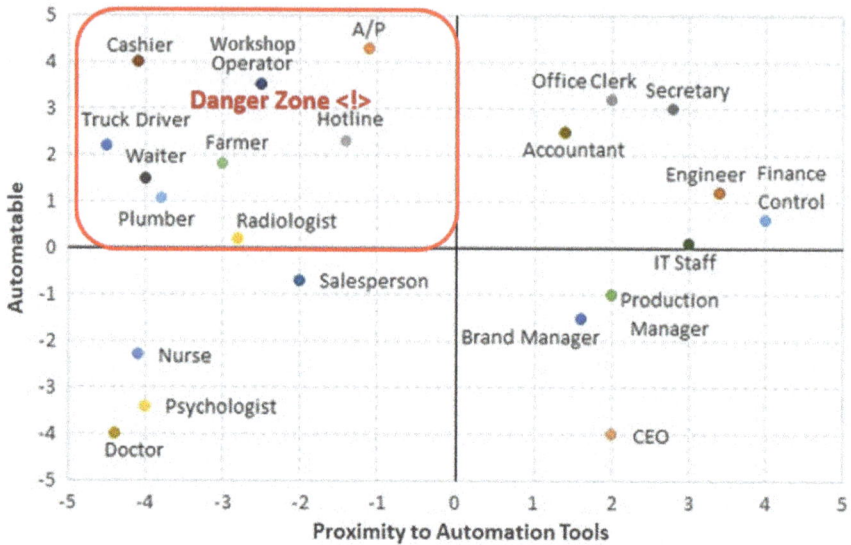

Fig. 6.16 Job automatability and proximity to automation tools

The scalability trait (up next) implies that jobs involving action on the environment are harder to automate *en masse* than those taking place behind a computer. It takes robots and drones to substitute for farmers and plumbers, whereas a single algorithm can replace one or a thousand (identical) office tasks at zero marginal cost. On the flip side of the coin, those same algorithms could be encoded using a computer no fancier than a standard PC. Automation tools lie at office workers' fingertips. They can master these during quieter office hours or even at home. This puts anyone with a computer on quite different grounds. Most of the jobs on the right side of Fig. 6.16 involve manning a computer station at day's length.

Of course, the reality is more nuanced: ease of access and software usage also count. A computer cannot automate substantial portions of a psychologist's work. We also noted the possibility for open environment jobs, such as that of a plumber, to form an alliance with techies.

This leads to a straightforward if somewhat blunt conclusion: unless it's already the case, get to a "computer job". Herein lies the path for workers at risk to stave off automation threats. Once this springboard is in your possession, master it to dart ahead of the crowd. Reflecting on your existing tasks, identify the brain-numbing ones you particularly loathe. This is the scutwork that you need to automate, using available tools, including any new

	Structure	Task dispersion	Dexterity/ Pattern- recognition	The Human Touch	IT skills
Tailwind	Recurrence Closed Environmt Perfect Info Rules-based work	MonoTask Taylorism Billiards allegory	Dropping costs ML & computer vision improvements	Back-Office work Human Punch Emotional AI NLP	IT laggard
Headwind	Cognition Social Skills Creativity Polanyi paradox VUCA	Transdisciplinarity Holistic Multi-Tasks Connecting dots	Moravec paradox	Customer-facing EQ	IT versatility AI collaboration

Fig. 6.17 Snapshot of inner job traits

AI tools being introduced by the company. We return to these actions in chapters 7 (Tasks) and 8 (Other Weapons).

Conclusion on Inner Aspects

Figure 6.17 summarizes the five job characteristics we've covered, distinguishing human weaknesses (tailwinds) and strengths (headwinds) relative to technological progress.

Traits other than dexterity and recognition embody the higher cognitive elements of a job, thus the sumo challenge. Each worker will recognize in herself the traits she is most apt at, and those relevant to her job, thus areas for improvement. In certain cases, this could even lead her to conclude that the current job is a misfit, best remedied by changing occupations.

Establish to what extent you possess the skills which matter in your work, and how much further you can go based on the job. Figure 6.18 shows the example of a back-office job worker, with slim opportunities to develop the human touch, a certain mastery of IT skills that can greatly help, and room to improve on creativity and more generally cognition. This simple tool can help assess which areas to focus on, and consequently prepare your battle plan.

Having dissected the main job elements that influence propensity for automation, we now turn to surrounding macroeconomic factors, or trends.

Macro Trends

Futurist Amy Webb defines a trend as

A new manifestation of sustained change within an industry, the public sector, or society, or in the way that we behave toward one another. [A trend helps to]

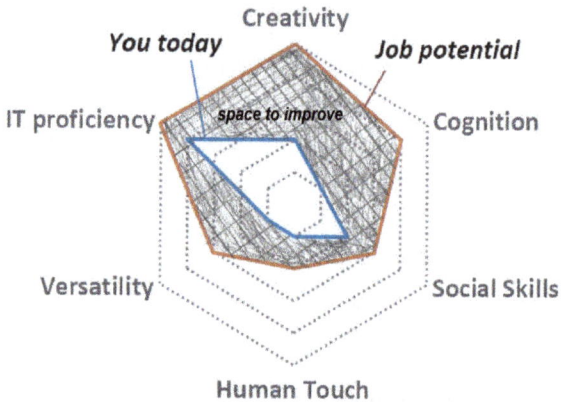

Fig. 6.18 Current skills level versus skills level relevant to the job: identifying gaps

simultaneously meet the demands of the present while planning for the future [and is] driven by a basic human need, one catalyzed by new technology.[82]

We've already crossed paths with several tech trends, and more could deserve attention: electrification, autonomy, connectivity, data creation. Hereafter, we contemplate other macro trends in the context of job automation; note that these reach beyond occupations, shaping companies, sectors of activity and society as a whole. We haven't the leisure to cover all trends, and perhaps not all those discussed will apply to your job. Climate change should be on the radar for a real estate insurance business, while it may be less relevant to a cashier. Bear all conceivable aspects in mind when pondering on disruption. We delve on aspects of economics and scalability, demographics, legislation, and sociocultural trends.

6.4.6   Economics and Scalability

The economics of automation compares the cost of a human worker to that of potential substitutes (varying degrees of silicon and humans of higher or lesser expertise). As a quote attributed to a 1965 NASA report advocating for manned space flight goes:

Man is the lowest-cost, 150-pound, nonlinear, all-purpose computer system which can be mass-produced by unskilled labor.

---

[82] Amy Webb:, The Signals are Talking: Why Today's Fringe is Tomorrow's Mainstream, p. 47.

Of course, Moore's law has brought silicon costs down since. Yet humans remain competitive in certain tasks, typically manual labor that falls under the Moravec paradox.

Automation proponents stress the hidden costs of human absenteeism, staff turnover, training, malingering, swinging moods, and propensity to whine for a raise or go on strike, at times begging the question as to whether they ever worked with machines. For they too, come with flaws: repair and maintenance fees, spare parts with several months' lead-time, machine down-time, and shortening life cycles as tech accelerates obsolescence. Granted, these weaknesses are more of a concern for robots than software, but intangibles have their share of vulnerabilities, for instance their proclivity to hacking and viruses. And companies may have a stronger bargaining power with employees than with Microsoft, Oracle and other IT providers.

Also, the human labor advantages outlined by NASA do not account for the threat of tech-propelled outsourcing options—cheaper bidders living in low-cost areas.

After this 1-on-1 cost comparison between carbon and silicon agents, next comes the number of similar positions or tasks.

In the world of automation, size matters. Automating hamburger preparation won't produce tangible gains if it only represents half a person's job. Now take KFC or McDonald's and multiply that figure by the number of preparators per outlet, times 23,000 and 38,700 (their respective number of outlets worldwide). This entails high scaling costs, with a machine in each outlet; to be viable, productivity per machine needs to beat that of manual labor.

Suppose McDonald's proceeds to ramp up the new equipment, allowing stringent cost cutting. It can then rip through smaller hamburger joints. Amazon has over a million employees—more than the rest of GAFAM combined (cf. Appendix D), in large part to handle its humungous logistics needs. The company is fervently automating logistic work, an endeavor that by any guess would allow it to shed off a third to half of its headcount. As Amazon rolls out its automated model, rival logistics firms will need to mimic it or perish (both cases entail massive layoffs).

Meanwhile office job automation tools are scalable at zero marginal cost, hence the more there are people occupying the same job or perform the same task, the greater the yield.

Figure 6.19 illustrates this. For simplicity, we assume the fixed costs upfront for developing robot and algorithm identical, and do not discriminate between the wage of manual and non-manual labor.

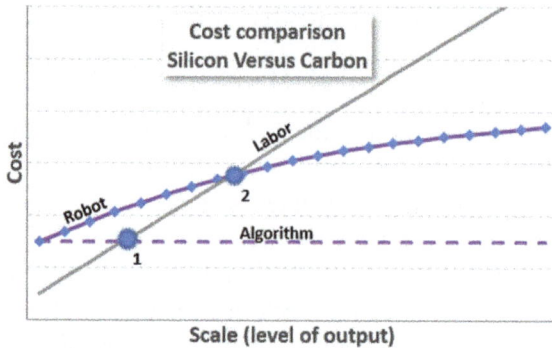

Fig. 6.19 Silicon versus carbon costs, based on scale

The payback for automating office jobs is reached fairly early at point 1. Manual labor automation becomes interesting only at a higher scale. If we factor an assumption of cheaper labor for manual jobs, that pushes point 2 even further toward the right (notice however the economies of scale at play as the number of robots increases).

Hence a greater incentive to automate office jobs.[83] These have benefited from a respite, thanks to a comparatively greater fog of war than exists in the strict confines of an operator station. But as digital Taylorism explodes, that could change.

In this respect, consider the cultural difference between large and small companies. In the latter, the people make the company. Each employee lends a hand when needed, for instance to answer the phone or unload a container full of merchandise. In large firms, as seen earlier, processes count foremost, relegating staff to automats that follow delineated scripts (with the exception of agile corporations).

Roles reduced to an ever-smaller number of codified tasks, with little space for originality, increase the risks of falling in the automation pit. A grocery store cashier is more prone to automation than the one working in a small hardware dealership, as the latter handles not only cash but also less processed tasks, such as advising customers.

However, smaller companies are more fragile than the behemoths, with scant access to financing, thus meager means to invest in new tech, hire tech-savvy talent and retrain existing staff. Those in small- and medium-sized firms

---

[83] With the notable exception of algorithms or software provided by a third-party, as the vendor will usually account for the customer's size in their quotation, for instance based on its headcount or number of licenses. But as the democratization trend pursues its course, more in-house algorithms could be deployed.

might witness their friends in big corporations sacked by "internal reorgani-zations"—i.e. automation—and sigh in relief for having chosen a different career path. Yet to imagine being spared from the ills of automation would be a grave mistake. As large firms trim on headcount, their cost-savings allow them to drag prices down, threatening small companies. And as their 4^{IR} investments pay off, they gain disproportionate advantages.

Otherwise put, the worker in a big company could see her job threat-ened tomorrow (job disruption), while her peer in a small to medium-sized company stands the risk of the entire organization tanking the following day (corporate disruption). The difference is merely one of timing.

The escape route leads upwards—a rise in the hierarchy. The higher you step up, the less identical positions you'll find. A financial controller is situated on higher grounds than an accountant because the former would represent only, say, 0.2% of the staff (or 1 for 500 employees), versus 5% for the latter (25 accountants for 500 employees). A controller may cost more than a single accountant, but not by a factor of twenty-five. And as the number of identical jobs shrinks, so does the level of structure, thus the inclination for codification.

6.4.7 Demographics

We touched in Chap. 2 on the importance of demographics. Population estimates remain a fiendishly complex business that time and again see demographers err in their predictions. We start this subsection with an overview of the world, followed by a glance at immigration patterns, to conclude with a manifesto of sorts for geographical mobility.

A Mega Middle Class

They say a picture is worth a thousand words. Readers may be familiar with maps that show countries weighted by their population size, a staple of geography schoolbooks, for instance Fig. 6.20 from economist Max Roser.[84]

Quite astonishingly—considering the capitalist world we live in—no such map exists whereby the weight accounts for *only* those people belonging to the middle and upper classes. Perhaps a map that excludes the poor would offend the sensibilities of the politically correct beyond tolerance; yet from a *consumer business* perspective, it would form a prime piece of intel, one that corporate execs could glean on while fomenting their global strategies. And

---

[84] Cf. Max Roser: *Our world in data*, https://ourworldindata.org.

Fig. 6.20 World map with country size based on 2018 population. *Source* Max Roser, https://ourworldindata.org. Reproduced with permission from the publisher

for our humble purpose, juxtaposing such a map circa 1985 with something more recent would illustrate the change that took place in the span of our lifetimes.

By now, readers might be sufficiently acquainted with their author to know that he could not stand by in the presence of so vast a void. Rummaging through the virtual libraries of the web, I unearthed data for people living under $2.15 a day in 1984, and more recently under $5.50 (unfortunately for 1984 I could not find $5.50—a threshold often used to demarcate the middle class).[85] These figures I then deducted from the total population.

Hereafter the resulting maps. Each pixel represents a million of the "qualified" people. As the data can be tricky to come by, the maps should be taken with a pinch of salt (don't bet your hand on North Korea's figures).[86]

Despite the coarseness of these maps, two observations can be derived.

First, the middle class has ballooned: while in the space of these 34 years humanity grew by 57% to reach 7.6 billion souls, in middle and upper classes (this time based on $5.5 from the start, in 2011 PPP) figures rose by a staggering 280%. In 1984, they accounted for approximately a billion humans (and 1.7 billion in Fig. 6.21, based on $2.15 and not $5.50)—roughly one

---

[85] Dollars in 2011 purchasing power parity. The "more recent" data mostly comes for 2016–2019, though for some countries it may be older (cf. next note for sources).

[86] Sources used for Figs. 6.21 and 6.22:

For 1984 population above $2.15: Shaohua Chen and Martin Ravallion, *Absolute poverty measures for the developing world, 1981–2004*, Development Research Group, Proceedings of the National Academy of Sciences (October 23, 2007).

For latest population data above $5.5: data source World Poverty Clock and World Bank data, https://data.worldbank.org/indicator/SI.POV.UMIC; also available on Wikipedia's entry *List of countries by percentage of population living in poverty*, https://en.wikipedia.org/wiki/List_of_countries_by_percentage_of_population_living_in_poverty#cite_note-wdipov_550-6.

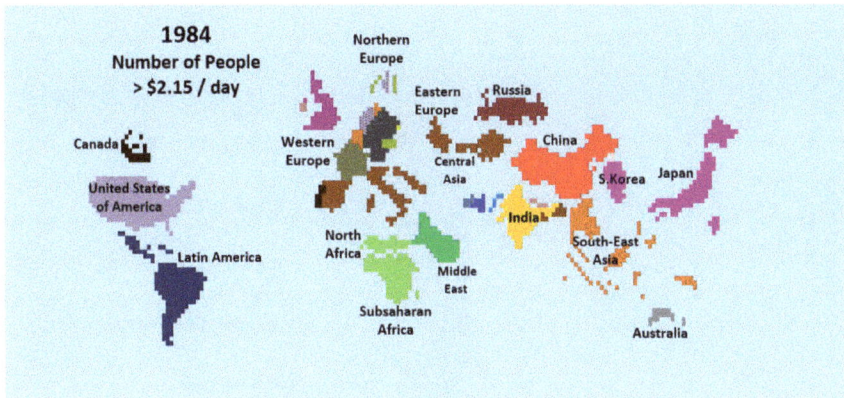

Fig. 6.21 1984 world map, number of people with income above $2.15 per day

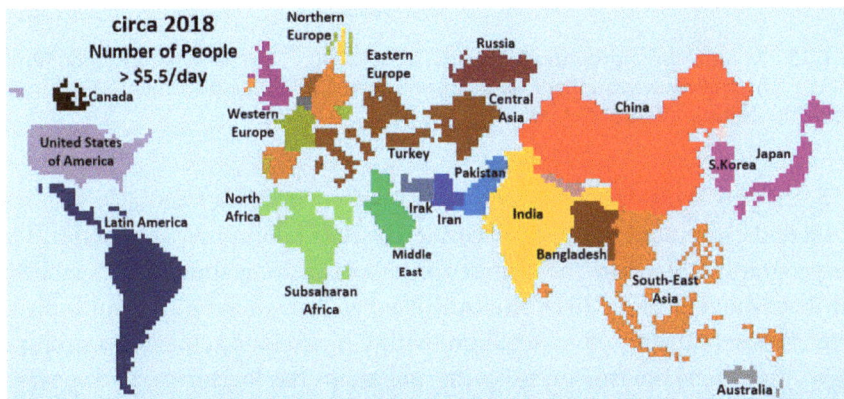

Fig. 6.22 World map circa 2018, number of people with income above $5.50 per day

out of five people.[87] Skip to 2018 and for the first time in history, middle and upper classes tilt the balance to represent over half of the world population.[88]

The second obvious finding shows how 1984 "consumers" occupied the West plus Japan, with a few leftovers sprinkled here and there (again, a split that would have been more pronounced with a $5.5 threshold); whereas by

[87] Homi Kharas: *The Unprecedented Expansion of the Middle Class*, https://www.brookings.edu/wp-con tent/uploads/2017/02/global_20170228_global-middle-class.pdf.

[88] Cf. Brookings Institute 2018 article: *A global tipping point: Half the world is now middle class or wealthier*, https://www.brookings.edu/blog/future-development/2018/09/27/a-global-tipping-point-half-the-world-is-now-middle-class-or-wealthier/; also World Bank 2018: *Nearly Half the World Lives on Less than $5.50 a Day*, https://www.worldbank.org/en/news/press-release/2018/10/17/nearly-half-the-world-lives-on-less-than-550-a-day.

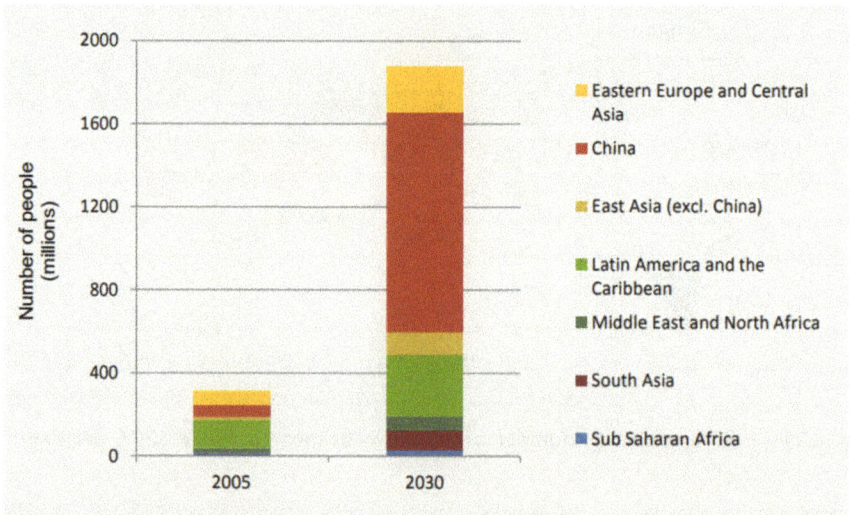

Fig. 6.23 Middle-class growth forecasts, 2005–2030. *Source* Bussolo and Muad (2011) https://www.worldbank.org/content/dam/Worldbank/document/MIC-Forum-Rise-of-the-Middle-Class-SM13.pdf

2018, the fulgurant development of countries previously categorized as Third World had catapulted these to the coveted status of consumerist societies. The first geographic bloc saw the number of people making above $2.15 in 1984 and then above $5.5 in 2018 rise by 20%, versus a swelling by a multiple of three elsewhere, from 1.3 to 4 billion, with China alone achieving a multiple of five.[89] Perhaps the true unease with such maps has little to do with poverty and everything to do with a wakeup call for the West: the momentum is shifting elsewhere.

This shift essentially returns to the East the predominant economic status it had enjoyed for centuries, following an interlude of Western supremacy triggered by the industrial revolutions—a head start coming to an end as the rest of the world catches up. Even Latin America now outnumbers its Northern counterpart in sheer terms of middle-class size.

Figures 6.23 and 6.24 show how researchers are bullish on the continued rise of the East, along with that of Latin America.[90]

---

[89] The percentage of Chinese below $1.25 a day fell from 84% in 1981 to 16% in 2005. Cf. United Nations report on poverty, Chap. 2, p. 25. https://www.un.org/esa/socdev/rwss/docs/2010/chapter2.pdf.

[90] Notice middle class is a porous concept—Fig. 6.23 places the bar higher than the aforementioned 5.5 USD per day.

Table 4: Middle class consumption - top 10 countries, 2015, 2020, and 2030 (PPP, constant 2011 trillion $ and global share)								
Country	2015	Share (%)	Country	2020	Share (%)	Country	2030	Shares (%)
U.S.	4.7	13	China	6.8	16	China	14.3	22
China	4.2	12	U.S.	4.7	11	India	10.7	17
Japan	2.1	6	India	3.7	9	U.S.	4.7	7
India	1.9	5	Japan	2.1	5	Indonesia	2.4	4
Russia	1.5	4	Russia	1.6	4	Japan	2.1	3
Germany	1.5	4	Germany	1.5	4	Russia	1.6	3
Brazil	1.2	3	Indonesia	1.3	3	Germany	1.5	2
U.K.	1.1	3	Brazil	1.2	3	Mexico	1.3	2
France	1.1	3	U.K.	1.2	3	Brazil	1.3	2
Italy	0.9	3	France	1.1	3	U.K.	1.2	2

Fig. 6.24 Middle-class consumption—top 10 countries, 2015–2020, and 2030 (PPP, constant 2011 trillion $ and global share). *Source* Homi Kharas (The Brookings Institution)[91]

McKinsey predicts China's middle class to comprise 550 million souls by 2022[92]—over three times that of the United States; soon India will join. Those who refer to China as the "factory of the world" should reconsider that moniker; it has become as antiquated as tales of a faraway country full of starving children fed to American kids squeamish about finishing their meals. Imagine expanding Henry Ford's "five dollars a day" principle to a billion plus people, and you begin to understand why at times China shows little appetite for coaxing the West: there's plenty of room to fill within its borders.

Alas, note that poverty can always make a forceful comeback at any time. And a clever chap glancing at the above figures could retort that the world counts as many people below the poverty line today as it did in 1984: roughly 4 billion souls.

Southward

It's easy to visualize past changes, but how to augur the future direction?

In a bid to answer this question, our final map projects the current world, only using a different pair of lenses. We now filter out everyone above 25 years old. The scale remains that of one million per pixel, amounting to a globe populated by three billion youngsters (Fig. 6.25).

---

[91] Homi Kharas: *The Unprecedented Expansion of the Middle Class*, https://www.brookings.edu/wp-con tent/uploads/2017/02/global_20170228_global-middle-class.pdf.

[92] *Mapping China's middle class,* https://www.mckinsey.com/industries/retail/our-insights/mapping-chi nas-middle-class. Of course this was prior to Covid and the actual China of 2022.

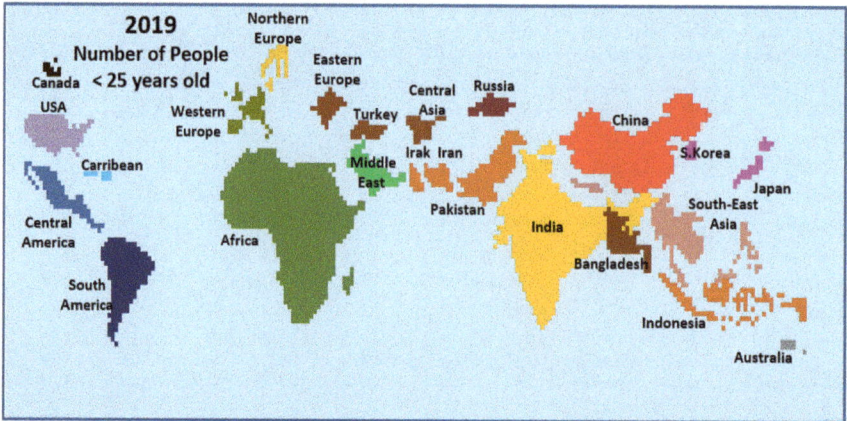

Fig. 6.25 2019 world map, population below 25 years old[93]

Assuming this criterion hints at where the global economic nexus steers next, the direction is clear: Southward. A 2017 MGI report on the future of jobs cites the growing middle class in countries referred to as the "Third World" as the main growth engine for jobs (followed by aging populations creating demand in healthcare). It further claims that increase in income per capita from 2015 to 2030 will be responsible for roughly three-quarters of the global rise in consumption, with the remaining quarter due to (future) population growth.[94]

Home to 1.2 billion souls, the portion of Africa's population under 25 years old stands at 60%, or 730 million youngsters. From the 2010 to 2050 period, half of the births in the world are projected to take place on the continent. By 2050, Nigeria will outnumber the US.[95] In comparison, China has around 420 million people under age 25; the US, 70 million, while the European Union is a bit shy of 100 million. Only India can rival Africa in this respect, with half of its 1.3 billion inhabitants under the age of 25. In other words, setting immigration and early mortality aside, in a twenty-to-thirty-year time span India and Africa will *each* have a middle-aged population larger than that of today's three aforementioned powerhouses, *combined*. No wonder the second half of the twenty-first century is said to belong to them.[96]

---

[93] Source: data compiled by the Author from Population Pyramid.net, https://www.populationpyramid.net/world/2019/.

[94] Cf. *Jobs lost, jobs gained: workforce transitions in a time of* automation, McKinsey Global Institute (December 2017).

[95] Franklin Andrews: *Megachange*, p. 24, The Economist publications (2012).

[96] Strong disparities between African countries warranted a representation of the continent as a whole in Fig. 6.25. Cf. Appendix E for a detail by country.

Big Corp is taking note. From tourism to education and consumer goods, everyone has been vying for the attention of Chinese Millennials. Next batter up: the South. In its Belt Road Initiative, China has poured close to US\$ 50 billion as of 2020, mostly targeting the South.

While traditionally immigrants would flock to the US and Europe, a paradigm shift is taking shape, one that sees this flow reverse course. Take the Cameroonian who sold his house in Orlando, FL, in 2003 to move back to his home country, forsaking a promising career in the US reinsurance business. Now president and CEO of a firm specializing in African infrastructure projects, he is but one of a growing number of African white collars returning to the homeland, invigorated by a desire to participate in its development.[97] In a survey from Irawo, a leading platform for African youth talent with over 50,000 members, 500 youngsters of the African diaspora were asked whether they wished to return to Africa after their studies abroad. A resounding 70% answered positively.[98] And the trend is not limited to the educated elite: disillusioned by limited prospects and overall rough treatment as third-class citizens in the West, the less fortunate are also taunted to return home.

If this reverse migration truly expands from a trickle to a torrent, it may counterbalance the established immigration patterns that economists count on to boost Western labor forces, putting those assumptions at risk.

The detective's advice applies to corporations as much as to individuals: follow the money. Westerners succumb to this false belief that they can walk in the footsteps of their parents. Baby boomers benefited from a golden age of economic growth. Times have changed and the tide has moved. Weighed by unfavorable demographics, Western economies are no longer roaring full steam ahead, they're nearing a standstill.

As a current or future worker, any tie or door to forging ties with (soon-to-be) booming countries is an opportunity to exploit. Don't wait for the dust to settle. There remains scant space for an American dream in a country with a shrinking middle class, whose number of consumers is bound to dwindle by the year. The same goes for Europe and parts of the East. In hindsight, a logical path toward success for those graduating around the turn of the last century was to head Eastwards (guilty as charged). Future graduates may find higher waves lying South.

---

[97] Jean-Philippe von Gastrow: *African White Collars that Return to the Homeland*, Les Echos (August 4th, 2016), https://www.lesechos.fr/2006/08/ces-cadres-africains-qui-retournent-au-pays-577452.

[98] Aldrich Achani: *7 Young Africans out of 10 wish to go home after studying abroad*, https://irawotalents.com/jeunes-africains-retour-afrique-etudes-entrepreneuriat-developpement/.

Aging Populations

The Northern Hemisphere is facing a serious challenge in the upcoming decades as the baby-boomer generation retires. Apart from boosting the elderly care field, some believe it opens opportunities, giving freshly minted graduates a wide range of vacancies to choose from.

If only things could be that simple.

Unfortunately, elderly care is plagued by neglect and inadequate funding, as witnessed by the sector's scandalously low wages: US nursing assistants receive a paltry $15.41 an hour; home healthcare aides, $13.49—less than locker room attendants. No wonder there is a chronic shortage in the sector.[99]

Holder of the oldest population record (with 38% of its inhabitants above 60, and counting), can Japan provide guidance on the effects of an aging and ultimately declining population? If anything, it teaches us that a declining population translates into stalled growth. World Bank figures show annual GDP growth slowing from 4.9% in 1990 to 0.3% in 2019, while data from the country's Ministry of Health, Labor and Welfare show a *decrease* in average annual salary over the period. An aging population affects the banking sector: as less people place their savings in pension funds and more elders take their savings out, it creates an imbalance that leads banks to bleed money. Other nefarious impacts include the skewing of politics toward the concerns of the elderly; this in Japan contributed to the *satori sedai*, a "resignation generation" of youths that purely give up on the pursuit of career and family. A decade after being coined in 2010, it is finding siblings with the "Great Resignation" in the US, and in China with *tangping* (躺平, literally "lie flat"), a nascent trend of renouncing materialist and societal pursuits.

Japan is a harbinger of the storm to come in Western economies that fail to curtail their own aging timebomb. Given their limited power over birth rates (anti-abortion laws in backward stretches notwithstanding), salvation could come from immigration. But as history has proven oft and again, toying too much with this faucet can get one's hands burned.

Immigration Patterns

Uplifting the Third World will level the playing field between nations, flatten the value between passports and facilitate the circulation of peoples. Former head of European Bank for Reconstruction and Development Jacques Attali

---

[99] Dollar figures from 2020. These two jobs comprise roughly four and a half million workers. Cf. Bureau of Labor Statistics, codes 31–1014 (Nursing Assistants) and 31–1120 (Home Health and Personal Care Aides).

surmised that the number of people living out of their country of birth could reach the billion mark by 2035.[100]

Conventionally, manual labor represented the go-to jobs for fresh immigrants. But as robots and algorithms pick up that demand, a new breed of immigrants will rise, one that pursues knowledge jobs. Already governments have adopted selective immigration processes catered to cognitive jobs, in a bid to offset skills mismatch issues at home. Language-fluent and educated online, these newcomers may contribute to plugging the population gap in aging nations, in terms of work, skills, and consumption. The new "social contract": become citizens, enjoy work and life here, in exchange for paying for our retirees and contributing to the economy.

The operation's success will depend on the welcoming countries' aptitude for inclusion. Xenophobic backlashes, lack of integration, and even the local language can deter would-be settlers, who may seek their luck elsewhere. Perceiving them as consumers and taxpayers crucial to growth will rewrite the dynamics of supply and demand, giving immigrants the upper hand (or at least more bargaining power) as countries vie for their (cognitive) labor. And if they choose to stay and work remotely from their home country, the otherwise host country loses out both in terms of consumption and tax revenue.

The model is not short of flaws. Rather than retrain its workforce or improve its education system to foster talent within its constituents, the US forsakes its kin to poach the best talents from abroad. Favorable taxation and policies for the wealthy attract the elites, leading to a brain drain in countries that pour considerable effort into education and better wealth redistribution. Another social timebomb.

Young populations in the likes of India and Indonesia ensure that these countries will face no dearth of workers in the upcoming decades. The same cannot be said of Japan or China. Given how in 2020 Asia surpassed the rest of the world in terms of GDP to become the world's main economic powerhouse,[101] would it not benefit from greater acceptance of multicultural diversity? How the region overcomes this challenge will affect the future landscape.

---

[100] Jacques Attali: *A Short History of the Future: A Brave and Controversial Look at the 21st Century* (2011).

[101] This was expected even before Covid-19 precipitated humanity off its spin. Cf. December 2019 report from World Economic Forum: https://www.weforum.org/agenda/2019/12/asia-economic-growth/.

Making a Move

Figure 6.26 depicts geographical zones based on GDP per capita, in 2019 (horizontal axis) and as a growth percentage since 2000 (vertical axis); the size of the bubble conveys that of population. We grouped the world into six geographical buckets of similar population sizes.

Little growth can be expected from the bottom-right area; the top-left is undergoing an accelerated growth phase, hinting at opportunities for the adventurous, while the bottom-left has yet to take off. China's outlier position is testimony to the "China miracle". Refer to Appendix F for a breakdown by countries of over 30 million inhabitants.

Fulgurant economic growth triggers a gold rush as companies scramble to set up shop. Yet they may face a paucity of talent on the spot, as the education system has yet to adapt and produce a skilled workforce. Locals lack experience in modern management practice and servicing the needs of a buoyant middle class, opening a window for foreigners. Take the case of Western retail firms entering the Middle Kingdom circa 2005, with say a five-year plan to open 100 stores. Hiring quickly proves problematic: local expertise is hard to come by; the market is young, and the company unheard of. The firm would prefer candidates who know its business model, who have a Platonic vision of their store hovering in their minds, something they can aim to replicate. This is a crucial aspect for store construction, merchandizing, marketing, training, and many other areas. In the initial setup phase, multinationals struggle to instill a dose of their DNA.

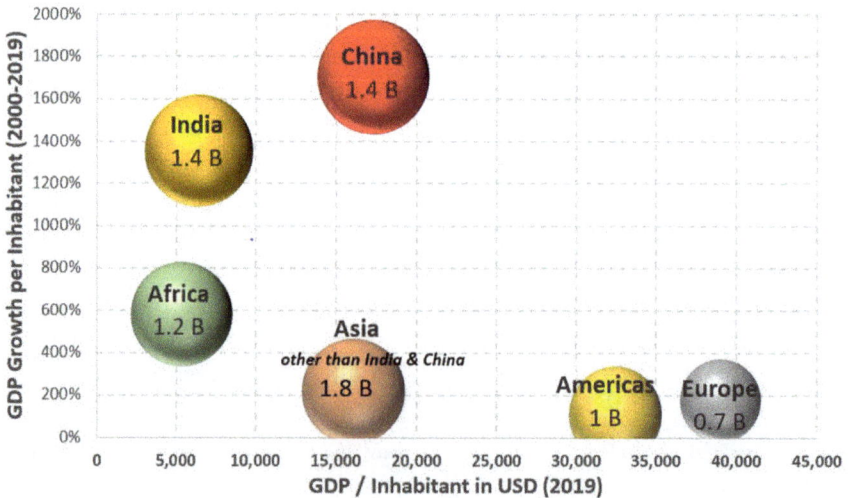

Fig. 6.26 The world in six buckets (with population figures of 2019, in billions)

This cocktail of expertise, knowledge of the company, and of its business model/brand image to convey, translates as an opportunity. I've seen interns promoted to managerial positions in months there where it would take an equal amount of years in a mature market. Of course, local market knowledge and language proficiency also count (I secured my second job in China thanks in part to a first gig in the countryside, hailed by the HR manager as "the real China").

The tide in China has since abated. Its swift rise may have been unique from a historical standpoint; the world nonetheless remains one of vast opportunities, that to be captured require a global mindset. Study the markets to gauge where the next gold rush could be, and what value you could bring to the table.

Do your homework upfront. Whether it's South Koreans in search of meaning who sail off to India, French enamored with K-pop heading to pursue their dreams on the Far-Eastern peninsula, or Americans seeking their *Emily in Paris* moment, the gaping hole between tourism and immigration can quickly turn dreams into a nightmare.

Granted, forsaking one's country of birth may not be everyone's cup of tea. Demographic trends exist within countries too. Atlanta is experiencing a boom, Palo Alto a saturation, and New Mexico lags. A job-seeking American could aim for the Georgian city of Civil War and Civil Rights Movements' fame that has come to epitomize the Southern revival, rather than Silicon Valley. Firms like McKinsey publish studies on regional disparities of future job opportunities in the US[102] that are worthwhile consulting. Take your craft into account. You might want to reconsider that plan about opening a ski shop if you are adamant about remaining in Lubbock, Texas. Identify demand and supply levels.

Organizations such as the World Economic Forum provide annual data and predictions for future jobs per industry and region,[103] while a bevy of countries provide their own employment statistics. The US updates its Occupational Outlook Handbook on a yearly basis; it includes a description of jobs, with insights on average pay, number of workers, stats like the location quotient,[104] and projections for the upcoming decade.

---

[102] McKinsey: *The future of work in America: People and places, today and tomorrow* (July 11, 2019), https://www.mckinsey.com/featured-insights/future-of-work/the-future-of-work-in-america-people-and-places-today-and-tomorrow.

[103] Cf. *The Future of Jobs Report 2020*, World Economic Forum, https://www.weforum.org/reports/the-future-of-jobs-report-2020.

[104] The location quotient compares the ratio of an occupation's share of employment in a given area (e.g. a State or city) to the national ratio. For example, in 2021 the U.S. has 66 dermatologists per million American workers. In the Killeen-Temple-Forth Hood metropolitan area, some 50 miles

It predicts the demand for airline pilots and flight attendants to grow by 13 and 30% respectively from 2020 to 2030; that's 14,700 and 31,100 new jobs. Both hover above the overall 8% jobs growth rate expected over the period.

That's right: the BLS projects an addition of 11.9 million jobs from 2020 to 2030. But please take these forecasts with a grain of salt. Although they strive to account for technological change, forecasts can be wrong—a sum of errors, as the saying goes.[105]

Backtracking to the globalism trend, we must strike a note of caution. It does not result from a heavenly decree. Populist governments toying with ideas of erecting walls on the borders, a new Cold War, Covid-19 that brought international mobility to a halt and is pushing countries to rethink travel are but several counterweights playing against globalism. Rising geopolitical tensions could dissuade people and companies from seeking opportunities abroad. And those who have succeeded oversees can get caught in the crossfires of geopolitical tensions.

6.4.8   Legal and Political

Regulations

Here, we consider laws, norms, and protocols, both local and international.

Areas where regulators are prone to step in respond to certain patterns: a GPT that requires sizeable investments, or a strong ecosystem, or relates to national sovereignty, to maintaining a competitive edge; sectors that organize into influential lobbies, such as farmers and healthcare; areas that involve privacy, safety, and matters of life-and-death, for instance self-driving vehicles, drones, crane operators or again healthcare. Hence why in spite of all the ruckus surrounding AI progress, radiologists and dermatologists should still have bright days ahead. Truck driver jobs are unlikely to disappear until hurdles revolving around responsibility and insurance are lifted. Regulations on drone flight appeared in the US in 2016, and in the EU in 2020,

---

north of Austin, that number rises to 256 per million—a quotient of 3.92, whereas in Dallas Fort Worth it drops to 23 per million workers—a quotient of 0.35. All else considered equal, one would assume better prospects setting up shop in the latter. For State, Metropolitan and Non-Metropolitan data, cf.: https://www.bls.gov/oes/tables.htm.

[105] The self-evaluation of their latest 10-year prediction shows that the BLS was right around 80% of the time as to gauging whether an occupancy grows or declines, and half the time as to whether it grows faster or slower than the overall job market. https://www.bls.gov/emp/evaluations/projections-evaluations.htm.

tampering ambitions with restrictions on maximum load and the obligation for the user to keep their device in sight during flight. Autonomous cars and drones require entire ecosystems to function properly that in turn need regulation. But regulators advance at a notoriously slow pace. This explains why the Boston Consulting Group foresees a mere 10% share of driverless vehicles by 2035.[106]

Complex, structured areas dominated by a handful of corporations that lobby government can slow the march of technology to a crawl, curtailing its otherwise natural development. Finance and healthcare have so far proven resilient to profound disruption. Accounting for 17 and 7% of US GDP respectively, these sectors are notorious for high entry barriers, byzantine bureaucracies, and a myriad of costly inefficiencies. Their lumbering giants exert profound influence over policymakers, basically dictating the pace. Aside from forming a moat against new entrants, this delays tech advancement. Blockchain could bring innovative models in banking and notary work that would greatly benefit consumers, if not for regulations that hamper its otherwise disruptive potential, giving banks and governments the time to ingest it on their own terms. While a booming fintech industry is gnawing at the fringes of their markets, we have yet to witness a major bank collapse due to cryptocurrencies displacing traditional transaction flows. But as tech firms grow, they too can exert influence, as proven by the Uber Papers scandal in Europe.

Government intervention varies by country. China's clampdown on Big Tech has rattled the industry. Its stated crusade on inequality targets private education one day, luxury goods the next, then KOLs—in this last case upsetting marketing strategies just when funds were being funneled *en masse* toward livestreaming. Laudable as the underlying motives may seem, these actions raise the bar of uncertainty for both firms and workers. The threat of a break-up for monopolistic behavior also hangs over behemoth organizations, though anti-monopoly laws may appear somewhat outdated. They were designed to protect the consumer, when today the main victims of firms such as Walmart and Amazon are small companies and mom-and-pop stores.

The most forceful action from governments is to prohibit a product or technology. This can be cause for sectorial disruption, as witnessed with the U.S. Prohibition period (1920-1933). Ditto for lifting restrictions: as it is being legalized, several players in the tobacco and alcohol industries are fearful of marijuana's propensity to substitute for their products.

---

[106] Boston Consulting Group (2015): *Back to the Future: The Road to Autonomous Driving*, http://de.slideshare.net/TheBostonConsultingGroup/the-road-to-autonomous-driving.

Governments exerting their power to outlaw push firms into a strategic inflection point (c.f. Figure 5.3 in the Sectorial Disruption chapter). In the aftermath of the 9/11 attacks, new airlines safety regulations forbade the carrying of knives onboard. This affected Swiss company Victorinox, manufacturer of the iconic Swiss Pocket Knife, as these were sold to a large extent in airports. The company adapted by adding watches, fragrance and other luxury products to its range (a flight measure, aka diversification).

Elsewhere, labor unions and petition groups carry the weight to pressure authorities to shelter their activity, as in the case of taxi drivers. Centuries ago, professionals in Europe formed guilds that defended the interest of their members against outsiders, including the inventors who, with their new equipment and techniques, threatened to disturb their members' economic status.[107]

Lobbies are often found lurking behind new regulations, exerting their clout to shelter their activity from disruption, or to dictate the pace and modalities for an innovation to take hold. For instance, they will participate in the work of the International Organization for Standardization (ISO)—or their country's equivalent—to influence the carving out of protocols. Yet it would be foolish for workers to assume immunity from automation for purely regulatory reasons. Governments come and go, and moods change—especially as other countries march ahead, exhibiting the benefits of a progressive path. If you reside in a sheltered activity or profession, assess how much time this buys you, then use that time to plan a prison break of the types covered in the sectorial and corporate disruption chapter.

In some instances, a lack of regulations can curtail technological progress. The absence of harmonized protocols for the Internet of Things is a case in point. Ecosystems require a healthy regulatory environment that defines the contours of each player's role and rights.

Policies can propel a technology. In 1985, the U.S. Federal Communications Commission released portions of the radio spectrum reserved for industrial, scientific, and medical purposes (ISM bands) for unlicensed use for communication. The tinkering of these bands by IT and telecom groups led to the birth of Wi-Fi in the late 1990s.

In a bid to maintain a competitive edge, governments favor tech via grants and subsidies targeting specific sectors, especially those deemed strategic. ARPANET is famous for organizing tournaments with million-dollar prizes,

---

[107] Hermann Kellenbenz, *The Rise of the European Economy: An Economic History of Continental Europe from the Fifteenth to the Eighteenth Century*, Holmes & Meier (1976).

giving a boost to private businesses in fields from robotics and self-driving vehicles to cybersecurity. Bill Clinton launched the National Nanotech Initiative (NNI) in 2000, pouring $31 billion of funding in the ensuing decade.[108]

Governments can also set targets for the private sector. Several aim for full Electrical Vehicle fleets by 2060. China wants EVs to account for a fourth of total car sales by 2025[109]; the EU targets 30 million EVs by 2030, with Slovenia and France announcing dates to end fossil-fuel cars.[110] Some municipalities push for even more ambitious goals; the Paris mayor plans to banish all but EVs within the city's precincts by 2030.

These efforts follow deeper trends, in this case the urgent need for cleaner technologies. The U.S. achieved a record level of investment in clean energy in 2021, at 105 billion dollars, while China invested 380 billion dollars, or one in every two dollars spent on clean energy in the world.[111]

Alas, one cannot fully account for legislation without considering changes brought to labor laws. Regulatory bodies can alter the economics equation seen previously, by raising minimum wages, and taking more drastic measures to deter firms from having recourse to temps, interns, illegal immigrants, and so on. In doing so, it pushes companies against the wall, leaving them no option but to press the automation button. Interest rates, taxation, and other government policies can also play in favor of or discourage firms from investing in R&D and automation. Earlier we mentioned the impact of generally accepted accounting principles (GAAP). These also dissuade firms from investing in their personnel: staff and training costs are treated as a fixed expense, not as assets that could offset liabilities, even less so as a core competence (as opposed to an asset that deteriorates over time, a core competence appreciates).

Geopolitics

Given its latent potential, superpowers cannot afford to fall behind in the race to develop AI. Big Tech brandish this rhetoric as they whisper in the ears

---

[108] https://www.nano.gov/about-nni/what/funding.

[109] Cf. Bloomberg News, *China Raises 2025 Target of Electric-Car Sales to around 25%*, https://www.bloomberg.com/news/articles/2019-12-03/china-raises-2025-sales-target-for-electrified-cars-to-about-25.

[110] https://www.reuters.com/article/us-climate-change-eu-transport/eu-to-target-30-million-electric-cars-by-2030.

[111] Jacob Dreyer: *China's Revolution Turns Green,* Noema Magazine (October 20, 2022), https://www.noemamag.com/chinasrevolution-turns-green/.

of politicians, advancing their agendas and (so far) preventing their breakup for monopolistic behavior.

China, the US and the EU set forth bold roadmaps to foster dynamism in fields from AI to nanotech and quantum computing. These support the creation of local champions and can be accompanied by a protectionist component. China's blocking of all major US apps circa 2010 (in the backdrop of the Arab Spring) propelled the rise of homegrown players. Geopolitics and protectionism also weigh on regulations. Invocation of national security, with at times farfetched, amplified concerns over hacking and espionage, lead to heavy-handed State interventionism, with cross-border acquisition projects blocked and the banning of Huawei's 5G equipment in several countries.

China is the second biggest spender in terms of R&D and narrowing the gap fast.[112] This puts pressure on the US and may discourage politicians from breaking up its darling behemoths, as it relies ever more on the private sector to support the technologies supposed to help it maintain its edge.

In light of the Cold War 2 brewing between China and the US, workers need to assess the risks of where and who they work for. Multinationals are grudgingly dragged into the spotlight as they are caught in the crosshairs between superpowers. Ease of information access and a hardening of public opinions are making it increasingly challenging to accommodate both sides. Placing Hong Kong separately on a website (Marriott), thanking Xinjiang authorities for their assistance in making a movie (Disney) or making use of produce from that region carries repercussions, and not just in the US or China.[113]

During the First Cold War, countries were pressured to choose between blocs. So far, the brunt of Cold War 2 is on the private sector, catching corporate empires from banks to hotels and luxury groups off-guard. Is a corporate path of non-alignment akin to India's during Cold War 1 feasible, or will brands and apps be forced to pick sides? Note that while the protagonists used carrots to appeal to countries, with companies they seem more inclined to brandish the stick: tariffs and other protectionist measures, bans on materials

---

[112] Cf. *Global Investments in R&D*, http://uis.unesco.org/sites/default/files/documents/fs59-global-inv estments-rd-2020-en.pdf; 2021 data is not available yet at the time of print, but seems to indicate that China may have surpassed the US in R&D spending. If so, the change might be short-lived though, given the impact of China's imposed lockdowns in 2022.

[113] For example, Inditex's Zara saw the extension plan of a store in Bordeaux refused by authorities on the grounds of its use of cotton from Xinjiang. Cf. *Bordeaux: l'extension de Zara refusée sur fond d'exploitation des Ouïghours*, Sud-Ouest (November 11, 2021), https://www.sudouest.fr/gironde/bor deaux/bordeaux-l-extension-de-zara-refusee-sur-fond-d-exploitation-des-ouighours-7030350.php.

or sourcing locations, not to mention the media attention and unpredictable repercussions of viral online posts on image and revenue. Following decades of globalization strategies aimed at achieving global brand dominance, led during an era of relative geopolitical neutrality, corporate empires wake up treading on treacherous grounds, with the need to juggle between capricious nations driven by the whims of hardened citizens.

Such rivalries are a godsend for fields stretching from defense to cybersecurity. Even education may benefit: when Russia launched the first Sputnik satellite into space, ahead of the US, it triggered a wake-up call, with Kennedy's famous speech to put a man on the moon before the end of the decade. In the aftermath, the US took several radical actions to remain competitive, including a revamp of the educational system.[114]

China's attempts to shake off overreliance on United States technologies ranging from microchips to 5G to GPS and the SWIFT payment system[115] have broad repercussions, putting even the future of the Internet as we know it at stake.

In September 2019, a delegation from Huawei stormed the United Nations International Telecommunications Agency in Geneva to present their vision of a future Internet. Dubbed the "New IP", it aims to amend the "failings" of the current Internet Protocol, described as unstable, unfit and suffering from "lots of security and reliability issues".[116] The New IP would help usher us into the 2020s by facilitating applications such as holographic communication and virtual reality. Yet not only does the Chinese version challenge the Internet protocol built by the US army (ARPANET), it also promotes a radically different model, one that gives governments absolute control over content, in a move anathema to the initial mindset behind the Internet—a tool for unhindered global communication between peoples. This top-down vision would mark an end to the democratic dimension heralded by the Internet since its opening to civilian use in the 1990s; it has garnered support from the less democratically inclined usual suspects (Saudi

---

[114] Michael Kanaan: *T-Minus AI: Humanity's Countdown to Artificial Intelligence and the New Pursuit of Global Power.* Chap. 12: *Moments that awaken nations*, Benbella Book (2020).

[115] While based in Belgium and supposedly neutral, the Board of Directors of the Society for Worldwide Interbank Financial Telecommunications (composed of executives from the world's largest banks) have demonstrated a certain obedience to the United States, for instance in 2012 when it cut off ties with Iranian banks. In response, China in 2015 launched its own Cross-Border Interbank Payment System (CIPS) for bank clearing and settlements.

[116] Cf. Financial Times, *Inside China's controversial mission to reinvent the internet*, https://www.ft.com/content/ba94c2bc-6e27-11ea-9bca-bf503995cd6f.

Arabia, Russia, Iran...), feeding fears of an end to the global Internet system, in what has been dubbed the *splinternet*.

The Internet is a paragon of our modern dilemma: maintain the current system designed and presided by the US, or reject the *pax americana* for a fractured constellation of systems based on ideological clusters. China is not always alone in its endeavors—for instance India and Europe also seek to develop their own GPS and satellite systems.

A third alternative could emerge, that of a global system without American roots. A future unfettered from US hegemony, yet that preserves harmony. This would require an overhaul of our rusty international institutions, and a deep level of mutual trust. It could usher us into a new era of *pax mundi*.

6.4.9 Sociocultural

Sociocultural factors pertain to a specific time and place. They can be smattered into aspects such as

- privacy concerns that shield jobs (e.g. guards instead of surveillance cameras);
- AI fears, previous flops, sunk costs or incidents that bury AI's reputation for years;
- confidential information that warrants in-house handling;
- resilient demand for superior quality products of unrivaled human craftsmanship.

Culture permeates society, hinting the direction for successful business ventures while exerting a strong impact on employment.

Eating out has become more of a habit than was the case for previous generations, fueling a boost in F&B jobs. Books on disruption tout the case of Uber supposedly devastating the taxi business. These fail to acknowledge newer generations of urbanites' limited appetite for car ownership, while still "going out" (tougher enforcement on drinking and driving rules no doubt made a dent too). Far from falling, the number of US taxi drivers and chauffeurs has sprung by 60% since 2000, surpassing 200,000 (Uber drivers are not included in that number). Other jobs suffer from a shift in norms: executive secretaries appear more of a luxury nowadays, hence the halving of their numbers over the same timeframe.

Facebook, Snapchat and countless other 2nd wave behemoths monetize on the ubiquity of portable, connected cameras that can access their user platforms with ease—in other words, they capture the *sharing* frenzy.

We've seen several examples of human fear or resentment of new tech. Despite a study by Intel predicting that self-driving cars could save over half a million lives in the 2035–2045 decade,[117] a recent survey from the American Automobile Association (AAA) found that 78% of Americans were afraid to ride in one. 54% of respondents further feared the prospect of sharing the road with self-driving cars.[118] What scale of death could warrant AI? A ratio of 1:1,000? 1:100,000?

Technophobia delays the deployment of new tech, but tech that benefits people adds advocates to its cause. Social norms influence legislation, triggering regulation that favors, restricts or purely bans new tech. Recall the 1980s aerobics trend alluded to earlier. Other than breaking the ceiling for women to partake in sports, Jane Fonda's workout video changed the perception of VHS (up to then conceived primarily as a tool to view pornography). In 1984, two years after the video's release, the US Supreme Court ruled that video cassette recording manufacturers could not be liable for infringement, in effect clearing up a legal gray zone surrounding VCRs. In the aftermath, VCR adoption rate soared from 1% to 50% of US households in the years 1980–1987.[119]

Sociocultural norms vary by location. Japanese embrace the kind of new gadgetry that would make the French grind their teeth. China has little regard for privacy rights, providing fertile grounds for machine learning via the massive troves of data amassed (the world's largest computer vision company hails from China: SenseTime). If this brings it a step ahead of the rest of the horde, might that summon the US to facilitate tech development to the detriment of citizens' privacy concerns?

In the West, people browse via Google, comment on friends' walls, surf YouTube and share photos on Instagram. Data collectors on the other side of the mirror can glean preferences in terms of movies (Netflix), music (Spotify), books and online shopping (Amazon), fish for likes and dislikes, along with some rather creepy info on physical errands via geo-localization, Uber records

[117] *Latest Intel Study Finds People Expect Self-Driving Cars to Be Common in 50 Years* (October 23, 2018), https://newsroom.intel.com/news/latest-intel-study-finds-people-expect-self-driving-cars-common-50-years/#gs.xrkk61.

[118] Cf. *Americans Feel Unsafe Sharing the Road with Fully Self-Driving Cars* (March 7th, 2017), https://newsroom.aaa.com/2017/03/americans-feel-unsafe-sharing-road-fully-self-driving-cars, *Three in Four Americans Remain Afraid of Fully Self-Driving Vehicles* (March 14th, 2019), https://newsroom.aaa.com/2019/03/americans-fear-self-driving-cars-survey.

[119] Cf. Everett M. Rogers in *Media and Values*, Issue #42, http://www.medialit.org/reading-room/video-here-stay.

and so on. These ingredients are then applied to concoct recommendations and targeted ads. In China, the Internet's tentacles sprawl beyond the question of whether you prefer dogs or cats. Online shopping surpasses 20% of total retail sales (a figure likely obsoleted by the time this book hits the shelves), double that of the US, with Alibaba's ecommerce revenue bigger than Amazon's and eBay's combined.

Cultural differences shape other factors, like the human touch. Tourists return from the US dumbfounded by the tipping system, praise Thailand for the warmth of its people and unfailingly return from Paris with horrid stories of the locals that highlight a bad customer experience—a human punch.

Some cultural traits are universal yet purvey a sign of the times. Safety concerns justify having humans fill in jobs like the police force, school bus driver, and air pilot. A pilot in the cockpit keeps everyone reassured, regardless of his price tag and how long he runs the flight in autopilot mode.

Each generation reshapes its elders' culture, and the borders of conventional norms move in parallel. Consider the gap in perception on smoking bans today versus the 1960s, when smoking was allowed even in airplanes. I overhear people of my parent's age reminisce of the "good old days", when they could sneak onto the Orsay museum rooftop and gaze at the stars. In today's highly policed context, this is unthinkable; public areas are sealed off at night, and we expect a prompt arrest for anyone caught attempting to infringe these rules.

This line between private and public space may prove most malleable in the 4^{IR}. In the metaverse, every move you make, every smile you fake, they'll be watching you. As users acclimate to these prying eyes, they may have no qualms about corporate voyeurism spilling over to the physical world, especially as the benefits of algorithm-powered recommendations perfected by these troves of data are unraveled. In a sense, it is but a repetition of the Faustian pact whereby we receive directions and neighborhood recommendations, in exchange for a GPS functionality that tracks our location; or how we forsook cash for smartphone payment methods, never mind the indelible digital trace left behind.

Our stance on digital privacy may appear retrograde to future generations, and fears of State or corporate abuse ease—or on the contrary escalate. China's QR health code, implemented in response to the Covid pandemic, offers a chilling precedent. In 2022, bank depositors protesting for access to their funds, frozen without a plausible explanation, saw their health codes suddenly turn red, in effect banning them from entering venues or taking public transportation (the health code system was ditched later that year).[120] We may witness the advent of less freedom for netizens, perhaps with an end of online anonymity, combined with greater tolerance for corporate eavesdropping on our dwellings both real and virtual.

Time and again, governments seek to instrumentalize cultures. The trick of pointing a finger abroad instead of looking inward is as old as civilizations. With Cold War 2 brewing, the dusty playbooks are once again pulled off the shelves and brought up to the speed of today's technology. Algorithms by design favor shock over moderation, fueling worldwide polarization. The novel forms of nationalism thus bred are pushing multinationals in the ropes, as radicalized citizens denounce their supposed complacency on another's turf, either by selling or sourcing there, compelling tough choices that call into question expansion plans, bottom lines, jobs, and the globalization model itself.

Safety Concerns

Safety concerns are a stout component within the sociocultural trait. From the first locomotives to AI, society's initial reaction toward technology is one of fear, even when proven superior to prior methods. This factor could provide a buffer protecting jobs from pilot to policeman, driver, and flight attendant.

Reversals happen. People may tire at the evidence amassed on car accidents, especially as data sheds light, providing vivid images of driver negligence behind the wheel. We take car deaths as a given. But self-driving car performance will improve over time, while humans remain, well, human (as highlighted by an AAA survey, in which 8 out of 10 males claimed themselves to be "above-average" drivers, in a prime example of cognitive bias[121]).

Big Data and dropping costs could see the addition of controls to ensure driver soberness; minicameras on the lookout for signs of drowsiness. Pressure could mount for regulators to purely outlaw human-steered vehicles. Ditto for police brutality and other "human punch" factors that fragilize the safety concern barricade, making it ripe for tech assaults. The elevator boy precedent illustrates the lurking menace for workers in this category.

---

[120] Engen Tham: *China bank protest stopped by health codes turning red, depositors say*, Reuters (June 16, 2022), https://www.reuters.com/world/china/china-bank-protest-stopped-by-health-codes-turning-red-depositors-say-2022-06-14.

[121] *More Americans Willing to Drive in Fully Self-Driving Cars* (March 7th, 2018), https://newsroom.aaa.com/2018/01/americans-willing-ride-fully-self-driving-cars.

Safety concerns could lead to a prohibition on nanotech to quell public fears of a gray goo scenario[122], or stall gene edition due to a long list of quandaries, from designer babies and enhanced soldiers to irreversibly losing our humanity. Fearing a moratorium on CRISPR/CAS9, Jennifer Doudna, one of the scientists behind its discovery (for which she received the Nobel prize in physics in 2020), urged scientists and policymakers to build an international supervisory entity[123]. When governments outlaw the use of coal, Schumpeter's creative destruction locomotive grinds to a halt.

Workers in existing fields face a similar menace if their sector is abandoned or outlawed for the cause of safety concerns. The nuclear industry employs roughly half a million Americans, or 0.3% of the workforce[124]; France has twice that proportion of its workforce in the sector, with pressure mounting from Europe to exit it entirely. While not a case of job automation but sectorial disruption, and getting the energy from elsewhere will require jobs, those jobs will involve a different skillset.

The safety factor must be accounted for wherever health, security and the environment are involved—an array that spans guns and tobacco, food and beverage, automobiles, mining, plastics, and many more existing fields.

Work Trends

Work trends are too numerous for an exhaustive coverage. We've already discussed the outsourcing paradigm, as well as data analytics pervading office space with the aim of monitoring and improving performance (Digital Taylorism). The following pages zoom in on remote work and the gig economy. Together, these shifts are dislocating the classic office model, for instance by facilitating outsourcing.

Remote Work Several early pioneers of work from home (WFH) reversed course in the 2010s. Yahoo's Marissa Mayer eliminated the WFH perk in 2013. IBM in 2017 asked its home workers, who then comprised 40% of the workforce, to return to the office, or quit, its CFO citing the need to get the teams back physically together to make them "more agile".

---

[122] Whereby self-replicating nanobots go out of control and end up gobbling the planet's entire ecosystem. A recurrent sci-fi theme, from the *Gunnm* manga that saw planet Mercury become inhabitable as a result of uncontrolled autonomous replication of nanobots, to Nick Bostrom's paperclip example, to the 2015 video game *Grey Goo*.

[123] Jennifer A. Doudna, Samuel H. Sternberg: *A Crack in Creation: Gene Editing and the Unthinkable Power to Control our Evolution*, Chap. 8: *What Lies Ahead*, Mariner Books (2017).

[124] Cf. figure from the Nuclear Energy Institute, https://www.nei.org/advantages/jobs.

Then Covid hit. A survey of 50,000 Americans conducted during the second quarter of 2020 shows that 35% of workers had shifted to remote work from home (while another 10% had been laid off).[125] Today talk around work often starts with "Now that companies are OK with home office".

No breakthrough occurred during the 2020–2021 period—not in 5G, nor VR or holograms. The somersault was force-fed by quarantines and safety measures. The response is mixed: some have found a new life-balance by working from home, while others deem the experience isolating, or even challenging with toddlers running around.

The dust has yet to settle on this phenomenon, making it difficult to size up for now. Several companies that gave in to employee demands for the flexibility to WFH found that this did not necessarily lead to greater happiness, as staff would lose the social proximity essential to building a team spirit and corporate culture, while juniors would miss out on training and mentoring opportunities.[126] Climbing in an organization often involves proximity to the central scene, there where games of power and politics take shape. Under the reign of Louis XIV, distance from Versailles would reduce you to inexistence. Granted, the Sun King didn't have Zoom or Teams. But to what extent can ICT effectively supplant physical presence? How can bosses assess their employees' potential for management or leadership if they are never present? The answer will fluctuate based on factors ranging from industry, local practice, corporate culture, and deployment of seamless VR technology. Sticking to our vow to plan for the worse, avoid anything beyond a day per week of home office. Let others bear the risk of fading in obscurity. Bear in mind that when a given job does not require physical presence, management could be tempted to outsource it.

The Gig Economy The outsourcing paradigm favors the big fish. The Apples and Nikes. Their weight grants extra leverage to coerce suppliers for better deals, as size determines supplier-customer dynamics. The other end of the spectrum is populated by an army of little ants called freelancers. These have virtually no bargaining power. Attempts at unionization, for instance between Uber drivers, have so far proven brittle, lacking in unity and leadership. As

125 Erik Brynjolfsson et al.: "COVID-19 and remote work: An early look at U.S. data," NBER working paper 27,344, June 2020.
126 Cf. Mark Mortensen, Amy C. Edmonson: Rethink Your Employee Value Proposition: Offer Your People More Than Just Flexibility, in Harvard Business Review (January-February 2023), p.45-49.

the number of freelancers grows, it gives companies an ever larger and global pool of talent from which to tap—in other words, leverage.

If the task at hand requires such unique skills as to narrow the scope drastically, a freelancer with a good ratings-fueled reputation has a shot at making a decent living. In *Gigged*, programmer Curtis possessed skills in high demand and built a good online reputation over time, thus achieving a comfortable income level. Again, it all comes down to supply and demand. If your "expertise" represents an abundant commodity—as was the case for every other person followed by author Sarah Kessler—you won't have that bargaining power.[127] Time will tell if even Curtis' gold mine one day reaches depletion.

According to one account, the US now has close to 60 million giggers, roughly 40% of all workers.[128] In exchange of forgoing a stable work contract and being chained to a boss, these micro-entrepreneurs are solely responsible for their daily subsistence, with no safety net for the rainy days. This precarious status handicaps freelancers in search of a loan, mortgage or when vying against stable income-earners to rent an apartment. Perhaps one day, giggers will make up a majority of the workforce, forcing a shift in their perception; again, the question is what happens in the meanwhile, especially given the uncertainty about the timing.

Some claim that the gig economy reflects the Millennials' aspiration for independence. But what if that was just a passing fad, a trait of youth? Independence might sound great for those in their 20s and early 30s, full of want and aiming for the stars. Were baby boomers not in a similar mood during the seventies? Millennials might reconsider when looking anew at the pros and cons under the prism of settling down to start a family. This may not list as a goal on their dashboard yet, but unless digitalization has significantly altered their brain wiring, these cravings should manifest at some point. Studies on the liberalization of Japanese women from the seclusion of stereotyped housewives pointed to a shift in the nineties, hailed by feminist advocates as a major victory.[129] Yet a decade later, the dry conclusion was that the fad didn't fare

---

[127] Namely an Uber driver, a Mechanical Turk worker, and the cleaners and janitors of Managed by Q, among a pool of other jobs from proofreaders to call center operators. Reference to the botched attempts at unionization also comes from this book.

[128] Nandita Bose: *U.S. Labor Secretary supports classifying gig workers as employees*, Reuters (April 29, 2021) https://www.reuters.com/world/us/exclusive-us-labor-secretary-says-most-gig-workers-should-be-classified-2021-04-29/; also Forbes: *57 Million U.S. Workers Are Part Of The Gig Economy* (May 13, 2021) https://www.forbes.com/sites/tjmccue/2018/08/31/57-million-u-s-workers-are-part-of-the-gig-economy/.

[129] Cf. Anne Garrigue: *Japonaises, la révolution douce* (Japanese women, the quiet revolution), Editions Picquier (1998).

well in the long term. These women were mostly thriving out of the confines of Japanese society—an unforgiving, misogynist one at that.

If you opt to go freelance, steer your path cautiously. Frame a plan. Gigging has advantages, too, for instance to fill a gap between jobs, or serve as a starting point to gain experience post graduation (especially when every job offer requires a minimum of two to three years of work experience).

Self-entrepreneurship is a risky, high-stress business, not suitable for everyone. Office employees comprise workers with lofty standards for performance and achievement, but also 9-to-5s who seek a balance with family life. The latter group may lack ambition and be content with its pay and position; shy from promotions and the burden of responsibilities. If the gig economy engulfs the labor market, it will hurl these wretched souls onto the battle royale arena. A growing number of occupations are succumbing to this form of disruption. And unlike job automation, this acid attacks the very fundamentals of labor as codified in laws, often the legacy of hallmark achievements during the 2^{IR}.

Conclusion on Macro Trends

Figure 6.27 provides a snapshot of our tour d'horizon of external trends, grouped under headwinds and tailwinds.

Tailwinds	Headwinds
• Convenience	• Regulatory
• Transportation of:	• *Lack of standards, protocols (IoT)*
- People: Uber, Mobike, Hyperloop,	• *Too much regulation (drones)*
UAV for humans	• *Data protection (GDPR)*
- Goods: Alibaba, Amazon, Eleme	• *Self-driving responsibility*
• Added connectivity: IoT	• *Sheltered activities & strategic sectors*
• Payment	• Lack of ecosystem / convergence
• Cold War fuels race to develop best AI	• *VR, IoT…*
• Quantum computing	• Environmental: toll of data centers
• Swarm robots	• Social norms & perceptions
• Automation enabling cost-savings	• *Discomfort (VR), Voyeurism (AR)*
• ERPs, CRM & other Software	• *Privacy concerns (Cambridge Analytica)*
• Optimal Character Recognition	• *Mistrust (vaccination, GMO, Crispr/Cas9)*
• Overcoming Moravec Paradox	• *Safety concerns (autopilot, robot police)*
• More cognitive bots (ChatGPT)	• Risks of hack / cybertheft / virus
• Dearth of labor pushes for emotional robots	• Backlash following overhype
• care for elderly in Japan	• *AI Winters*
• Risky environments (Mars, Fukushima)	• *human genome mapping*
	• *Dolly the sheep*
	• *VR in 2016, metaverse in 2022*

Fig. 6.27 External trends snapshot

6.5   Job Vulnerability to Automation

6.5.1   A Fresh Look at US Jobs

With internal and external factors accounted for, we return to the BLS classification of jobs, using our new lenses to cross-examine these. Figure 6.28 shows US jobs in Minor categories; to make for a digestible visual, we trimmed the number to keep only those with north of a million workers. Among the excluded are some:

– 700,000 ad and marketing managers;
– 800,000 food-processing workers (bakers, butchers, slaughterers…);
– 600,000 production supervisors;
– As many personal appearance workers (hairdressers, manicurists, barbers).

Overall, 18 million workers are missing; still, close to 90% of the workforce is represented (126 million workers). Readers in the excluded categories can assess the traits of their trade in the same manner that we look at those kept in focus.

Workers are once again sorted by increasing levels of wages, arbitrarily split into three groups to reflect low-, middle- and upper-income levels. The year is 2018 (for a clearer, full-page view, refer to Appendix G).

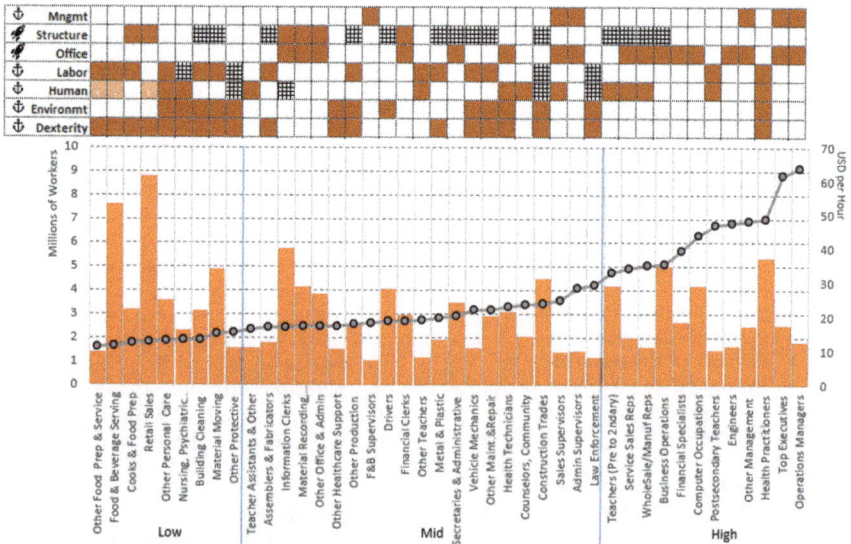

Fig. 6.28   U.S. jobs classification

The top area highlights factors encountered in this chapter. Icons on the left indicate whether a trait is more of a headwind (anchor: ⚓) or tailwind (rocket: 🚀) to automation. The absence of structure underpins cognition, a headwind. Lightly shaded boxes on the Human Touch row represent categories where roughly half of the workers are concerned:

- "Other Foods" includes hosts (with) but also dishwashers (without);
- Food & Beverage is half with (waiters, coffee baristas, and barmen) half without (fast food and cafeterias);
- Retail sales comprises

  - 3.6 million pure cashiers, whose contact with shoppers remains limited (by the time you reach a grocery store's cashier, you've already settled on what to buy);
  - 4.4 million retail salespeople, who use the human touch to guide and assist shoppers, who seal the deal.

Alas, gridded boxes only *partially* possess the given trait. Many jobs are partially structured yet preserve hints of VUCA.

As with any simplification, these classifications are arbitrary. Notwithstanding, they reveal distinct typologies emerging in each of the three wage levels:

- Low-Income Jobs sheltered by

  - An unpredictable Environment (⚓);
  - High manual dexterity (⚓);
  - Mostly manual labor (⚓);
  - The income level, itself a headwind to automation (⚓).

  However,

  - improvements in Machine Learning (object recognition, unsupervised learning, NLP…), robotics (miniaturization, dropping costs…) and other tech (AR, aR…) could fragilize these ramparts.
  - a single headwind taken alone is weak: e.g.:
      a dexterous task within a predictable environment is vulnerable to automation (as in the hamburger-making machine);
      in certain instances, dexterity could be shoved over to the consumer (as with automated scan-and-pay checkouts).
  - displaced workers from middle-class jobs could spill over to the low end, overcrowding these occupations and adding pressure on wages.

- while cheap wages deter companies from automation, thus form a trench against tech replacement, it's not an enviable one.

• in the Mid-Income bracket, we find two types of jobs:

- Highly structured office jobs, or rules-based clerical work, *without* an unpredictable environment, nor dexterity nor manual labor as ramparts (🚀).
  Around 15 million office jobs fit this high-risk profile type.
- Skilled workers in relatively structured jobs yet operating in an unpredictable environment; similar to low-income jobs, these could fall victim to AI progress, and their higher pay level makes for a fatter, juicier target.
  Close to 20 million workers here: repairmen, drivers, construction trades (plumbers, electricians…) that could become the twenty-first century's Luddites.

• High-Income Jobs characterized by

- Little showing in terms of headwinds—yet bear in mind that these are highly unstructured, cognitive jobs to begin with (⚓).

In short, chief areas where automation is encroaching on human tasks relate to

- Rules-based tasks: vulnerable to the top-down approach ("if this then that", or GOFAI).
- Computer vision, dexterity and to a lesser extent, NLP: vulnerable to the bottom-up approach and to a blending with outsourcing of all sorts.

The clerical portion of workers holding mid-level office jobs is at the highest risk of succumbing to automation. While some may achieve the climb to the higher rungs of managers and experts (albeit less plausibly for the latter, given educational requirements), the less fortunate will tumble down to the merciless arena of low-income jobs, deflating wages there. Because that category consists mostly of manual work, that to automate requires robotics translating into higher investments than the replication of cognitive work, jobs there could be sheltered. Again, the data points to the advent of a double-faced society, with first-class citizens on one side, and those who serve them on the other.

Furthermore, we can conjecture that a low-middle-upper class population split moving from, say, 20%-60%-20% to 50%-30%-30% would adversely impact the overall level of consumption, affecting the service sector and beyond, thus the demand for unskilled labor. Because no matter how much richer the rich get, they can only spend so much amount on food, travel, spas, and other niceties (this relates to what economists call the "diminishing marginal utility of income"). Hence, even jobs at the bottom of the pyramid could become rare and difficult to secure.

A Manifesto for Computer Jobs

Using another prism, we split US jobs into three categories, as per Fig. 6.29:

– manual labor, with production, logistics, construction, and maintenance;
– office jobs that to a large extent involve the use of a computer;
– other jobs that mostly relate to service: healthcare, food preparation, sales, and related (including retail).

These clusters are far from perfect: some sales jobs come with a computer, educational ones not, and so on. It's quite irrelevant to the argument exposed hereafter and hinted at earlier as we contemplated job proximity to automation tools; what does matter is to consider your own job and career situation.

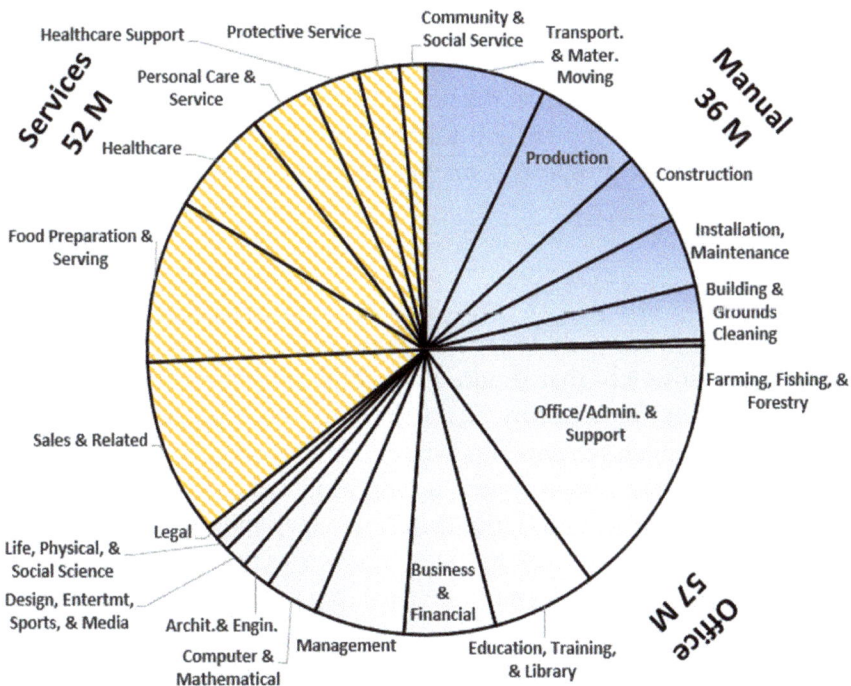

Fig. 6.29 US office jobs, 2018 (with number of workers in millions)

Now, picture each of these three categories as a separate mountain. As a working individual, you naturally seek to climb the mountain you occupy to reach the managerial strata, or at least an altitude with better living conditions, with now the added pressure of establishing grounds safe from automation.

While these mountains share a pyramidal shape, each one has its proper characteristics; for instance, the service mountain is more inclined to reward workers with a strong human touch.

The office mountain's main feature consists in a road that spirals to the top. The other two have no road, making the ascent painstakingly long. Suppose you toil on either of the other two mountains. If your career is well advanced and you are already up in the cognitive clouds, or merely a few years away, then you may conclude that best maintain course.

But if you still face a long, tedious climb that could take a decade before reaching safe heights, consider switching over to the office job mountain. You may need to start back from scratch, at the foothill. But there you will find a parking lot with several cars—the software tools embedded in the computer given to you so that you can do your job. By learning to drive them well, you can speed on the sinusoidal route, pass indolent colleagues lounging on the wayside, ignorant of the shaky grounds they settled on, and exceed altitudes previously reached on the former mountain. The road may not be in great shape; it could be stuffed with VUCA pits and sudden cliffs, but by laying asphalt you can further unleash the power of your car engine.

This pursuit of a computer job followed by that of computer skills as a tactic to bolster your prospects is one of the major themes developed in the next chapter.

Limits

The traits listed in Fig. 6.28 are far from exhaustive.

Highly cognitive jobs that require a dose of creativity are difficult to automate; yet gauging for creativity at this level of coarseness would push the simplification a notch too far. Supervisors, waiters, counselors, law enforcement and others may exert creativity, or not; people of both types can occupy the same job, in the same environment. Some may indeed "blindly" follow a script, but denying creativity to the occupation as a whole would be blasphemy. At best, structured jobs can be perceived as less demanding in terms of critical thinking and creativity.

A monotask job is significantly more vulnerable to automation. It is not feasible to represent it from this vantage point. The Materials Moving category comprises 50,000 crane and tower operators, yet together these monotask jobs represent a drop in that pool's 4 million-strong workforce.

Note that while the cost of automation is not directly shown, it can be worked out from available data: high wage levels times a large number of workers make for an appealing automation case, especially for office jobs as these are cheaper to automate at scale, with algorithms in place of robots (cf. Scalability trait).

Looking at the entire spectrum of US jobs on a single chart has its limits—major occupations are too broad, and we cannot cover each of the 800 more detailed categories. Nor is that the point of this book. Our goal is to empower each reader to look at her own job and assess its strengths and vulnerabilities, to then address these in order to emerge victorious from the battle royale.

6.5.2 Job Vulnerability Canvass

Our tech SWOT culminates with the job vulnerability canvass, a comprehensive tool to zoom in on a job. We illustrate it here with our opening example of airline pilot versus flight attendant.[130]

The grid hereunder picks traits deemed relevant to these jobs. Each is scored on a scale from −5, denoting a strong *headwind* to automation, to +5 for a strong *tailwind* to automation. A positive score favors automation, a negative one slows it.

Several traits reviewed earlier are neglected here for lack of relevance, though that could be debated and warrant extra research. The only form of weighting used is to regroup certain lines under the "Tech" appellation, and others under the "Economics" umbrella (Fig. 6.30).

We used five scores: Tech, Economics, Human Touch, Legal and Sociocultural. The economics was determined by multiplying the number of US airline pilots with their average salary, ditto for flight attendants.[131] We did not provide a precise estimate for the cost for silicon counterparts, but you get the gist.

---

[130] These correspond to the Bureau Labor of Statistics' occupational codes 53–2011 and 53–2031, respectively.

[131] These stats are available for all jobs on the BLS website; here data used from 2019: https://www.bls.gov/oes/special.requests/oesm19st.zip.

	Book Section. Subsection	Topic	Pilot Detail	Score	Flight Attendant Detail	Score
Internal	4.1 Structure	Client VUCA	= back-office job	-	High Client VUCA	-4
	4.3 Dexterity / Recognition	Dexterity	nil	-	cramped space, high dexterity	-4
		Rival Tech	Autopilot & aR, widespread	5	Robots: far from up to the task	-
	4.6 Scalability	Tech	Threat	5	No imminent threat	-4
		Human Cost	High: airline pilots ≈170K$/year	5	Average: ≈57K$/year	2
		Scalable	≈83,000 airline pilots	1	≈120,000 flight attendants	1
		Automation Cost	Low cost, quasi-nil	5	Tangible -> high cost to scale	-5
		Economics	≈$14 Billion/year Vs low cost	4	≈$7 Billion/year Vs high cost	-1
	4.4 Human Touch	Human Touch	Irrelevant - pilot unseen	-	Crucial (health emergency,...)	-4
External	4.7 Demography	Global	Not Applicable	-	Not Applicable	-
	4.8 Regulatory	Political /Legal	Low (insurance claims?)	-1	Low (insurance claims?)	-1
	4.9 SocioCultural	Socio-Cultural	Strong safety concerns	-4	Maintain order on flight	-3
			Total Score	4	Total Score	-13
			Major Tailwinds	2	Major Tailwinds	0
			Major Headwinds	1	Major Headwinds	2

Fig. 6.30 Scoring of pilots versus flight attendants in the United States

Figure 6.31 plots these scores.

Summing the scores produces a total of +4 for the pilots versus −13 for the flight attendants. The pilot's job turns out decidedly more vulnerable to automation

Alternatively, we can neglect low scores to focus on the number of *gales*, or absolute values of 4 and 5. This reveals two strong tailwinds and a sole strong headwind for pilots, with safety concerns at −4 (−5 would equate to replacing the entire police force by LAWS of drones and robots); meanwhile, flight attendants have two substantial headwinds and nothing opposite.

The job vulnerability canvass (Fig. 6.32) depicts the exact same data, in a different format that facilitates comparison between different jobs, should you hesitate between several career paths.

The pilot's sole head-gale remains a fragile one, as demonstrated by the elevator boy precedent from a century ago: exasperation following strikes

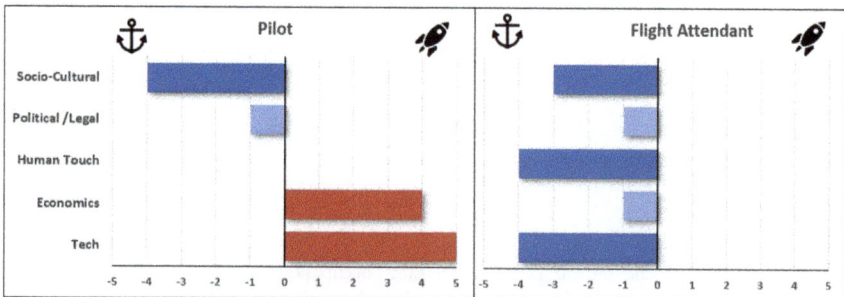

Fig. 6.31 Job trait scoring for pilot and flight attendant

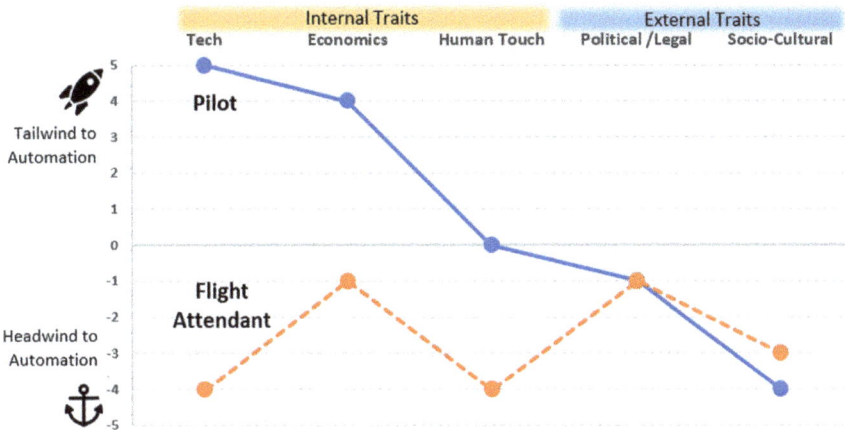

Fig. 6.32 Job vulnerability canvass

led those jobs to vanish. Strikes and scandals of various sorts regarding pay, lousiness, and ripping of managers' clothes to shreds[132] could spell doom for pilots.

Meanwhile, little gain can be squeezed out from automating flight attendants. Certain tasks are automatable: we've seen the little TV screens take over the safety instruction guidelines dispensed to passengers before takeoff; aisle cameras could ensure passengers are seated with belts buckled when needed, sensors identify a seizure, etc. But full automation would prove a costly act to pull, given the cramped environment on a plane, risks of unruly passengers, the need for speed in a crisis situation, and our preference for experienced professionals on board a possibly perilous journey. Flight attendants assist those bearing children or feeling discomfort (human touch) and ensure order during flight, in the microcosm of an airplane 30,000 feet above ground (safety).

Now apply the canvass to your job, or to compare jobs that you hesitate between. Do not reason merely at the occupational level as done hereabove, but descend to your personal situation. This will clear up blurry areas, for instance whether or not you exert creativity or social skills at work, thus revealing areas for improvement. Refer again to Figure 6.18, the star chart that sought to identify gaps between your existing skillset and what it takes to excel in that job.

Not every trait will play a role. Recurrence is rather irrelevant for an actor, to whom factors like cost, human touch and social norms take the front scene

---

[132] Cf. *Air France bosses attacked in jobs protest*, Financial Times, October 6th 2015, https://www.ft.com/content/c0d167e6-6b59-11e5-8171-ba1968cf791a.

amid the growing threat of computer-generated imagery (CGI) actors and deepfakes.[133] Scores fluctuate based on context, such as the country and its relevant labor costs, and by company. AirAsia emphasizes the polished aesthetics of its crews, adding a discerning flavor to their human touch that could help those employees prevail, were automation to take hold elsewhere—the same way posh restaurants will keep waiters when others dismiss them. But social perception could prove a fragile branch to hold on to, as witnessed by the backlash in the West against idealized aesthetics that pushed firms from Abercrombie & Fitch to Hooters to revise their models.

Think out of the box. A pilot playing the devil's advocate could foresee forages in cargo flights, where no passenger safety is at stake (though a malfunctioning plane can still crash in an inhabited area). If proven successful, these precursors could put pressure on passenger flight pilots. The sector counts many low-cost competitors eager to slash prices. Headcount represents around a third of an airline's costs, and pilots roughly a fifth of headcount; automating these jobs could allow from 5 to 10% cost savings, part of which could be passed on to customers.[134]

Account for safety, shelterism, voyeurism, clientele (dis)comfort, and how these may relate to your job. While the focus here is on the threat of job automation, signs of sectorial or corporate fragility should be apprehended if you are chained to either (the air pilot and flight attendant are prime examples of low sectorial mobility). Even without the emergence of a mighty substitute, guns, tobacco and other sectors could suffer from stricter regulations.

In *The Signals Are Talking*, Amy Webb proposes a methodology to uncover emerging, impactful technologies. She starts by digging around for information and developing alertness as to what's happening on the fringes. The information is then funneled and assessed in terms of timing. From this extracted essence, the reader is invited to let her imagination flow free, to allow an unhindered development of future scenarios. Next enters the scientific observer, who drags each scenario into her lab to prod it for flaws in the assumptions and underlying math.

Though the finality is different, assessing a job's fragility drives us near to this methodology. We also need to let our perspective oscillate between the

---

[133] While in the past, actors needed to cope with technological disruption of the enhancement type (recall the movie *Singing in the Rain* for a caricature of the painful move to "talkies"), CGI and deepfakes could amount to a full automation/substitution threat, putting actors in the horses' shoes, so to speak.

[134] Estimates based on publicly available figures from the financials of Delta, United and Southwestern for the year 2019. That is, $32 billion of staff costs for $99 billion of expenses and $113 billion of revenue, and finally the assumption that the 6,000 pilots in these airlines earned at least the BLS's average annual income of 174,870$.

wild dreamer and the pragmatist; explore worst-case scenarios, then poke for holes. Several probable outcomes will surface from this exercise that you can grade from best to worst, then by likelihood to materialize.

Monitor tech and trends, and when this harvesting brings in fresh intel that could alter prior assumptions, review these accordingly, in line with a Bayesian approach.[135] Repeat at least once a year. 2020 saw the addition of the pandemic; the following year, environmentalist pressures, or progress in a new menacing technology, say Hyperloop transportation. Cybersecurity concerns form a strong deterrent against AI—even an unmanned cargo plane can be hacked and weaponized, an argument people are most sensitive to ever since 9/11; ditto self-driving trucks (here the elevator boy comparison hits a ceiling). Add a short comment next to each score to explain it. Let your mind roam free, and alas confront wild ideas with rigorous logic and empirical evidence.

When finished, pull out last year's scoring and observe the changes. Dig deeper where needed.

Actions

If the canvass unveils serious threats, consider what actions can be taken. As stated earlier, these can be of two sorts.

Either the job is hopelessly calcified, a rotten apple. This could result from the occupation itself (e.g. a tollway or parking cashier), the company in which you work or the management style of your boss. Clarifying the source of rigidity determines the action: staff in the latter case could grow wings by changing departments or companies, whereas a tollway cashier had best extricate herself from that occupation altogether.

Workers have less power over external factors, least they move to a region with more favorable laws, or where different demographics translate as a shortage of talent.

Internal traits are comparatively easier for the worker to adjust. Seek valuable tasks to add onto an initially monotask job. Adopt a more customer-centric approach, develop trust and go the extra mile for customers. Strive for a more agile mindset that brings workers closer to humans than automatons.

One limitation with the job vulnerability canvass pertains to the absence of weights. Each factor should be considered from the unique vantage point of

---

[135] Eighteenth-century reverend Thomas Bayes is most revered today for the theorem he developed that describes the probability of an event based on prior knowledge of conditions that might be related to it, and more specifically on how new evidence that pours in effects that likelihood. His formula is widely used in statistics and machine learning.

a job and individual—up to her to apply weights as deemed necessary based on context.

Properly exploiting inner traits, be it the human touch or agility, also demands a certain alignment between you and your organization's motives. A firm that unlike BestBuy dissuades its employees from developing meaningful contact with customers could be a sign of misfit.

In certain contexts (notably in large organizations), efforts can pay off at the team level too. Suppose one day, flight attendant jobs are automatable—perhaps only partially, allowing a 30% workforce reduction. The attendant constantly receiving praise for her friendliness may survive her colleagues; but if the whole team strongly connects with passengers, management may consider it a strength of the airline and maintain all jobs even as rivals slash headcount.

Perhaps the most important part of the exercise is to identify the head-winds: their number, and their resilience in the face of both improving technology and macro trends such as changes in regulation or sociocultural norms. What protective traits come into play? What value do these barricades convey on the job market? Are they a commodity, as in the dexterity involved in low-paid jobs, or the hard-acquired skills of an air pilot?

Conclusion on Job Disruption

This investigation into jobs has led us to reckon with the lurking threats that technology and morphing trends invite into our workspace. We combed through a non-exhaustive list of characteristics that can hamper or speed up the automation push. These traits escape any definite weighing method, given the variety of contexts. Human touch and VUCA may appear sturdier than dexterity or even regulatory barricades. What appears as a critical factor in one environment will be secondary or even irrelevant in another.

Some elements can affect companies and sectors, too (hence the reason for corporate SWOTs). At times, the worker will have little power to alter a given situation. Workers facing strong tailwinds of that blend may consider changing jobs or sectors entirely. This predicament hits most external factors, but at times internal ones, for instance the monotask job of a grocery store cashier. Other traits can be worked on to increase resilience: by taking on more tasks, developing an agile mindset, and delivering value via the human touch or IT proficiency.

The job vulnerability analysis and canvass purport to identify weaknesses. In the process, we hinted at some solutions, yet without a clear exit route. This is the focus of the next chapter.

7

Tasks

After navigating sectorial fields, orbiting global corporations, and exploring jobs, we touch ground on the nitty–gritty: tasks. Here lies the most genuinely actionable part of the smart worker's survival plan.

We start this chapter with a self-assessment exercise (Sect. 7.1), followed by the main steps to up your game—namely automation (Sect. 7.2) and delegation (Sect. 7.3) of existing tasks, and last but not least, aiming for cognitive work (Sect. 7.4).

7.1 Self-assessment

Before we commence, let us bring to light an important remark or two that may have transpired in previous pages. Throughout this investigation, it became resoundingly clear that workers can find inspiration from how companies themselves cope with disruption. What do the prophets advocate for them to become futureproof? Which ones receive praise for their ability to reinvent themselves?

In the sectorial and corporate disruption chapter, we listed corporate actions to remain relevant in the digital age: creating a side project

---

The original version of this chapter was revised: Text correction has been updated. The correction to the chapter is available at https://doi.org/10.1007/978-3-031-19278-4_10

A. M. Recanati, *AI Battle Royale*, Copernicus Books,
https://doi.org/10.1007/978-3-031-19278-4_7

(skunkworks), seeking inspiration from big tech, flipping threat into opportunity…

Firms automate. They outsource. They harness data, develop digital savviness, polish their customer's shoes, finetune their public relations, and create a compelling brand story that resonates with their targeted audience. Many of these actions are replicable at an individual level. Employees can develop a certain entrepreneurial spirit; reason and showcase themselves as a brand; learn to harness new tech. In fact, we have spent much of Part 2 tearing pages from the corporate playbook. Hereafter we pursue, by transposing automation and outsourcing actions to the individual level. On another hand, firms are notoriously slow to digest the implications of new technology on working paradigms. This gap between the new horizons opened and their ability to exploit them gives the company's employees a rare chance to make changes ahead of them.

Task Snapshot

We begin with a little exercise: to score your job in terms of recurrence, and vulnerability to replacement, both by automation and by outsourcing. Doing this properly draws on everything learnt from the previous chapter on Job Disruption. Recall Fig. 6.8 that pictured the correlation between work recurrence and vulnerability to replacement. Here, we drill this relationship down a level.

Start with a white sheet of paper, and jot down the tasks within your job's scope.

Strive for exhaustivity. Reference points may lie within your firm, starting with the original job description, though that may not translate into what you actually do—either that too much time has elapsed and your job has morphed into something quite entirely different, or that it presented an embellished version of the daily hell you go through. Companies that conform to the ISO-9001 management system keep a written track of each department's processes and job definitions.

Surely you know your duties, but the way corporate archives document these can shed a more objective light. Indeed, this exercise demands honesty foremost, not hiding from the truth of what may be a dreary or excruciating job. We tend to flee from the thought of a "job introspection". It's amazing how we go on toiling about without ever pausing to contemplate this major portion of our lives. If one truly desires to engage in any meaningful change, the first step is to look in the mirror; not to daydream what you wish you were, but to assess the "as is" situation, in all its lifeless splendor.

Don't neglect tasks that should fall in your purview, based on your job description or more broadly on what your title assumes, yet that you do not currently handle, for lack of time or whatever reason.

Now observe the result. How many tasks have you listed? Are you in a monotask job, or were you able to exhume a host of chores and undertakings?

Next, add two columns: one to grade each of these tasks in terms of recurrence, the other for how prone it is to replacement. Here replacement refers to automation and/or to a transfer to other people, with either lower or greater skills—*not* organic replacement—whether from within the organization or from the outside (cf. A Protean Threat to Work). Consider each task in light of the traits reviewed in the Job SWOT, only applied to the task. Recurrence links to the first part (cognition, structure, and VUCA); that of replacement, to the other traits (e.g. the human touch). Using these parameters, give each task a score from 0—High recurrence to 10—Low Recurrence, and from 0—Highly Prone to Replacement to 10—Irreplaceable.

Lastly, factor in the time spent on each task. If necessary, split it in two: frequency and average time consumed. Frequency here refers to how often the task is performed and differs from recurrence, meant to highlight the repetitiveness and redundancy of a task. No need to pull out the calculator—stay at a guesstimate level.

At the risk of repeating ourselves, don't sugarcoat it. Keep a neutral tone. Imagine yourself in the shoes of an outside auditor, interrogating from afar. Challenge the ready-made answers sprouting from the ego. Wear the bureaucrat fatigues and take notes coldly, without passing on judgment. You know best what dose of each ingredient makes your job.

If not done from the start, bring the time spent on each task down to a common denominator, for instance average time by week, or as a percentage of your total worktime.

All done! We just pinned each of your tasks with three bits of information:

- a score for recurrence: from 0 (recurrent) to 10 (non-recurrent);
- a score for replaceability: from 0 (easily prone to replacement) to 10 (irreplaceable);
- worktime consumed by each task.

With this, we can now plot tasks using the same recurrence and replaceability axes as in Fig. 6.8—only using a bubble chart to accommodate for time, as exemplified in Figure 7.1 for a financial position.

This snapshot provides a glimpse as to where you stand when automation hits; it also prepares our action plan.

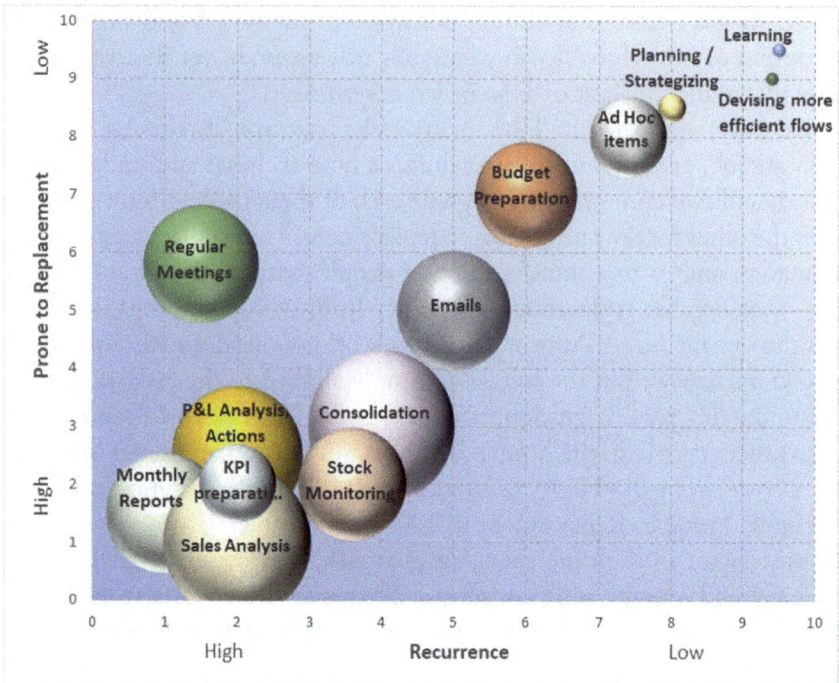

Fig. 7.1 Example of a finance controller's job decomposition into tasks, by recurrence and ease of replacement

If hesitant on a task, say "responding emails", that includes a bit of routine yet also the occasional time-consuming email, consider splitting it into separate bubbles on far sides rather than compromise—for instance a volley of reports to email at regular intervals, and requests from your boss that warrant more digging.

You may uncover outliers, such as the staff meetings shown in the figure. No matter their frequency, teamwork and other forms of human interaction are difficult to supplant, whether by means of automation or outsourcing.

Notice the "ad hoc" bubble on the far right; it comprises emergencies and miscellaneous, unforeseen events that pop up on your dish: In short, VUCA. Beyond it, several dispersed dots represent non-mandatory tasks that you should be doing, yet never seem to find the time for.

Now that we have summarized our position, what's next?

Imagine you've been offered a gig. Your mission, should you choose to accept it, is to venture to a remote desert, excavate precious stones, and bring them back.

After a long walk, you arrive at the site, scoop everything you can lay your bare hands on, seal your bag now filled with stones of all sorts, and prepare for the journey back to town, hoping to fetch a decent price from the dealer who engaged you.

Picture the bubbles in Fig. 7.1 as the stones you've amassed; the bottom-left rocks convey little value—granite and limestone—while the top-right corner features the shinier gems.

On the trek back, you stumble into stormy weather. Flash floods plunge you neck-deep into marshes. You curse and make your way through unscathed, only to halt, seized by an odd sensation of lightness. Opening your bag, you let out a gasp: the low-grade material rocks have eroded, several dissolved entirely. Only the handful of rare gems remain in pristine condition.

Pondering the situation, you wonder whether your dealer will accept so small a bounty, or even consider your services in the future. Worse still, with some ways left before reaching town and clouds forming on the horizon, you could suffer more losses.

Now mentally rewind to the point when you just finished piling up your load. Don't get up and walk the long trudge just yet. Open your bag. With a stick, draw a chart in the ground dirt and place the stones on it. Reflect on your options to avoid the abovementioned, undesirable predicament, knowing that the weather in the area is notoriously unpredictable. Would it not be wise to discard the vulgar rocks? To allocate a little extra time and effort to quarry the finer stones? Not only are these less prone to chafe by automation waters, they also command a higher value on the market. Should the gods of rain and thunder show mercy, you'd still be striking a better deal; why run the risk of filling your bag with lousy rocks that could get washed away, leaving you empty-handed, when little gain can come from them anyway?

Action Plan

With this, we flip over to the action plan. It is devolved at polishing your repertoire, your collection of stones (tasks), and fighting the threat of job loss head-on.

Take your bubble chart of tasks and perform a diagonal incision from top left to bottom right (cf. Fig. 7.2). What percentage of your time is taken by everything on the left side of the line? These constitute the tasks prone to automation, or at best retention by low-paid workers.

Recall the opening advice about taking a cue from companies. These low-to-no valued-added tasks form the burden that lean organizations strive to weed out, the rocks to be discarded. And just how to go about that?

In chess, you don't anticipate your opponent's moves to then do nothing about it. Therefore, take a preemptive strike. *Provoke* the automation. Shift

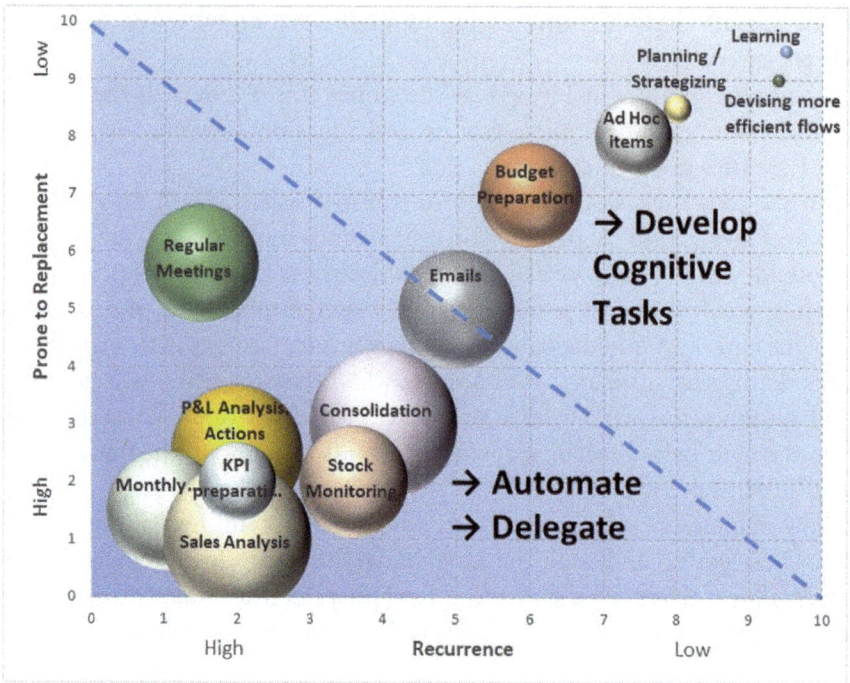

Fig. 7.2 Task actions

redundant tasks of limited value to others. Seek refuge in cognitive, non-recurrent tasks.

The idea of hacking tasks off may feel a bit scary, especially when these comprise an important chunk of your job—what are you left with when it's not just the bark and branches, but a good portion of the trunk sawed off?

Remember Kodak. In 1981, the inventor of the digital camera (yes, a Kodak employee) produced an internal study of the technology's disruptive potential, stating that the company had a decade to prepare for it. Half of Kodak's management proved unable to shake off the idea of digital cameras as a gimmick or a threat rather than an opportunity; the other dangled wishful ideas about embracing a digital future to shareholders, squandering money on acquisitions and stale enterprises, as if to reassure themselves that they were on top of things. Deep down though, they couldn't commit to slaughtering the cash cow. After all, its milk nourished 200,000 employees and earned it a shimmering spot on the Dow Jones. They failed to envisage a radically different form of income stream (and to realize that unlike them, startups like Instagram had nothing to lose). Add a pinch of "too big to fail" hubris, legacy of scores of quasi-monopoly, and the inevitable happened. Polaroid met a similar fate, even as they too appeared to be on the path of digitization. Nokia developed an OS called Symbian to kickstart their smartphone business, only to fail. And Xerox PARC serves as prime example of the chess player who brilliantly foresees several moves ahead, conceiving radical innovations such as the computer mouse and a skeuomorphic user interface, to then do nothing about it (letting Microsoft develop the Windows interface). When I hear my marketing team hesitant to launch a disruptive product or an entry-level range, out of fear that it might cannibalize our star product sales, I roll my eyes. If we don't do it, others will. It's only when you close yourself to opportunities that these morph into threats. It's the difference between Blockbuster and Netflix. The latter's CEO, Reed Hastings, had no qualms when he decided to move into on-demand livestreaming, knowing very well that it would dig the grave for his DVD rental business. Every book on disruption now underscores the need for companies to disrupt from within—not just by identifying future trends, but by fomenting and executing strategies in consequence.[1] The same holds for workers. The point isn't to sabotage your career, but to take a preemptive strike at your own weaknesses in order to emerge stronger.

This may require splitting into an automation devil's advocate, to maliciously review your work, in pure skunkworks fashion.

To unburden your load from worthless rocks, stop viewing your job as set in stone. Every job has a degree of plasticity to it, a potential for redesign and evolution. To what magnitude will depend on.

- your company: not only its organization and culture, but also your superior's openness and managerial abilities.
- you: your performance, the perception you convey to the rest of the team, to bosses and direct reports, and the potential for evolution that they see in you.

Consider it half/half. We talked about the company's role in the corporate disruption chapter, and what to do in the absence of any chemistry. Take responsibility for that second half: this is where you can change the world (and more to the point, *your* world).

Admittedly, certain jobs offer limited career prospects. The truck driver, data labeler, and parking cashier have little chance to shine at work. The

---

[1] Vincent Barabba: *The Decision Loom: A Design for Interactive Decision-making in Organizations*, Triarchy Press Ltd. (2011). Head of Kodak's market intelligence in the early 1980s, Barabba is the inventor who performed the aforementioned study on the digital threat.

employee facing a dead-end had best do everything in her power to switch over to a more malleable position—ideally one that involves a computer.

Which Path

The worker's arsenal contains two weapon shelves: automation and delegation. Which one you turn to depends on the beast of task in sight (the object), which weapon is best suited to take it down (the method), and what ammo you have in storage (your abilities).

As any fresh graduate can attest, one doesn't enter the workforce managing people; it takes years before the concepts taught in fancy lad schools carve a path into daily work. In the early days, the automation shelf is more accessible than the delegation one. Consider your proximity to automation tools, in relation to a given task. Start by splitting physical and cognitive work: the former is harder to automate (you'd need a robot), thus best delegated, whereas computer tasks belong to the realm of automation that a worker can initiate (though that doesn't imply that at times these shouldn't be delegated).

If neither automation nor delegation are an option—say, a manual task with no one to shift it to—then keep it for now. Is the impossibility to delegate due to your rank in the company something likely to improve over time? Or is it intrinsic to the job? A job that can never be automated nor delegated poses a serious quandary. If impregnable to automation, such as tasks in a highly cognitive, managerial position, the worker remains safe. But a job or task susceptible to automation and/or outsourcing, yet that *you* are unable to automate or delegate, spells trouble—like standing on a trap door (cf. Proximity to Automation Tools). Paddle your way out of this sinister spot. Other than pursuing studies on the side, exhibiting IT and people skills can help put distance between you and the danger. For instance in retail, seize any opportunity to navigate the Point of Sales (POS) system, improve stock management and customer experience, learn about and demonstrate leadership, shine with charisma, and strive to take on more.

While physical work provides a buffer against AI, this defense could prove fragile in the face of improving computer vision and dropping robotics costs; lest it involves rare expertise, such a job commands a low wage. Beyond manual labor lies the (generally better paid) cognitive tasks and jobs; these deal with information, a trail that leads straight to computers. The computer wields the power to automate. In the AI Battle Royale, getting your hands on a laptop or desktop represents a major milestone, akin to an initiation or to being knighted (or to grabbing the bow and arrows, if you are a Hunger Games fan). Until you gain seniority, along with the official delegation powers that follow, at best all you have is a computer. Make the most of it.

The following exposé of the respective advantages of automation (Sect. 7.2) and delegation (Sect. 7.3) clarifies which path (or blend of paths) should be favored, based on circumstances.

It's not always evident. Upon closer inspection of the rocks on-site, you may notice composites consisting of various materials, some noble, others alloys, along with the inevitable rubbish. This type of task must be broken first into smaller bits. Recall the billiards allegory: a job composed of tasks. Like when zooming in and out of Brittany's coastline viewed from the sky, only to find the same repeating patterns, zoning in on one of the billiard's task-balls may reveal a billiards-set composition within it, consisting of more or less cognitive balls. Break it into smaller parts, then do the same for those parts, until you reach chunks chewable by automation or delegation. Whether redesigning the task in view of delegating or automating it, you will need to carve up a step-by-step procedure that any chump can execute, no brain-work required. It's the same methodology used by corporations to chop a manufacturing process into clear, repetitive steps, or by a coder to write a program, with a strong emphasis on what the Japanese call *poka-yoke*, literally the fail-safes to "avoid mistakes".[2]

A little practice and computer proficiency will train your ability to cut tasks into smaller pieces and determine which ones to automate, which to delegate, and which to keep.

7.2   Step A as Automate

Task automation forms an essential piece in the smart worker's playbook. Manuals on management tend to neglect its benefits, partly because in the past workers had limited access to tools powerful enough to leapfrog peers by such a magnitude as is possible today.

When a factory rolls out new machinery, workers are trained on it until they achieve the expected output. Office staff receive less formal training, under the naïve assumption that everyone should know how to use Microsoft Office and the rest. Moreover, the metrics to monitor office performance lag the sophistication level present in a workshop. Slow paper-movers survive and thrive thanks to this opacity, sheltered by the difficulty of objectively assessing performance. Since the herd tends to ignore or underestimate its potential, learning efficient use of automation tools gives you an advantage. The results will appear all the more stellar in contrast with the ambient performance

---

[2] The original term was baka-yoke, or "idiot-proofing". No doubt the term "poka", derived from Japanese chess (Shogi) where "poka o yokeru" (ポカを避ける) denotes avoiding an unthinkably bad move, was deemed more palatable for inclusion in the Toyota Production System.

level. As noted earlier, the 4^{IR} will soon shed light on the dark corners of the office, exhibiting each employee's performance (or lack of therein).

The underlying precept is simple: anything that can *will* be automated, with or without you. By whom exactly is irrelevant: as long as you're not in on it, you lose your grip on those tasks, forever.

So where to begin?

At some point, automation may involve coding; but prior to that, the bare bones would be to consider the pros and cons of automation. By now, your sharpened eyes should be able to identify tasks ripe for automation. The ability to project this is a skill that one finetunes by training her teeth to automation.

For a succinct recap, automation marries well with

- quantified data;
- closed environments of perfect information;
- something that can be broken down and written into rules ("if this then that");
- repetitive actions (in coding called loops);
- limited exposure to VUCA;
- a system of stick and carrot (albeit this would be for more advanced, reinforced learning algorithms).

Certain tasks elude this mold, such as dealing with the ill-tempered boss who bursts with sudden requests. But before setting these aside, take a closer look into the problem. Discern patterns in the apparent chaos, and assess whether anything could be done to see the boss coming. Even the BMW engine inside a McLaren is of little use without a flat street to drive it on. The prerequisite here involves rasping sharp VUCA edges. Plant the décor in which requests are likely to spawn. Victory is often secured in battle (at least in the movies) by luring the enemy into familiar terrain that puts them at a disadvantage, via a feigned retreat or some other deceitful plan—in short, by dissipating the fog of war. Devising tactics in your line of work to weed out VUCA lays the asphalt road that will allow you to speed ahead with the full throttle of automation tools.

In the case of the mercurial boss, if you are able to demonstrate superior efficiency when tasks are planned out ahead, find a moment for a conversation to highlight to her how with a better framework, that includes the formalities of your interaction together, overall productivity could soar.

With the contours shaped, turn to your arsenal. Suppose you have a presentation to prepare and regularly update. Over the years, PowerPoint has risen as the undisputed champion in the field. Yet when cast under an automation spectroscope, it's not exactly cutting-edge: akin to a rudimentary spear, in the weapons room it pales in comparison to the glazing Excel gun with its semi-automatic firing options. Realizing that much of the preparatory work can be performed on Excel, reach out for the gun—the needed parts can be copy-pasted into the ppt with such ease as to beg for delegation.

Ditto emails. Responding to a unique query pertaining to a very specific matter may require writing the bloody thing yourself. But for a routine piece of information, such as responding to a client request or providing feedback on sales activity, pull the heavy artillery. Study the structure of the email. Is it not made of consistent blocks, like the following (for a sales report):

1. Dear [x];
2. Please find attached the monthly sales activity for [YYYY-MM];
3. You are [x]% [above/below] Budget, [x]% [above/behind] Last Year;
4. Products [x] and [x] in particular performed well, while sales under [Miss x] and [Mr. y] were behind target;
5. *Optional customized message;*
6. Thanks and Best Regards;
7. [signature].

Each of these bits could be pre-written on a spreadsheet, one per cell, with the parts in brackets referring to other cells containing dynamic data. Only the "*Customized message*" will vary from one email to the next—the "cognitive" part that stays in human hands. Assuming this task is done not only on a monthly basis, but that each time over a dozen emails are fired off to different regional heads, you can save a substantial amount of time (email addresses can be put in other cells, and used by a program like VBA to send the emails automatically).

Let's take another example. Imagine you work in the Front Office department and seek to automate replies to customer requests. This is far trickier than an analysis of numbers. Yet from experience, you have discerned repetitive patterns that underpin recurrent response lines, to conclude that requests fall into the following buckets:

- quotation request;
- after-sales quotation request;
- hotline/troubleshooting issue;

– request that concerns another department;
– other.

Suppose half of the emails turn out as semi-automatable, say the requests for quotations and other departments. For those, elaborate an automatic response. Check for techniques to upload the data into the system automatically. If not possible, at least automate data extraction (Item Number, Quantity, Requested Delivery Date…) onto a spreadsheet, from where it can be copy-pasted onto the system via Excel shortcuts—this beats retyping everything and reduces risks of manual error. Maintaining an FAQ tab for customers up to date can also reduce traffic upfront. You might even devise a program to search for certain keywords that can determine the category.[3]

The first time(s) you automate, it may seem longer than doing it the manual way… and perhaps it is. So was our first time typing on a keyboard with all fingers instead of just indexes. The trial-and-error process of automation can be excruciatingly frustrating for beginners, partly because there is no telling in advance whether the code will work on the first try, nor how many knots reside inside and how long it might take to unravel them. Suppose a full day was consumed to write a program, whereas doing it the old manual way eats up half an hour each Monday. That equates to a four-month payback on invested time.

But that would be missing the point. In the process, you learn the ropes. These knowledge gains will help you automate faster in the future. For starters, you can refer back to the painstakingly built code and copy-paste snippets to new programs, with a few tweaks. Today you learned how to send an email automatically, tomorrow you will find out how to embed a chart in the email body, and so on, like a magician continuously enlarging her repertoire with new tricks.

As far as programming goes, you will also learn quicker ways to achieve feats using less code. Programmers have this obsession for elegancy, not as part of some quirky coder pageantry contest, but to keep the code concise and swift to execute. When dipping back into code you wrote eons ago, whether to reuse bits or debug the occasional error, you will appreciate having laid down each step in an economical manner, with indentation and explicit comments, in dozens instead of thousands of lines.

---

[3] Of course, receiving an email or (worse) phone call represents the most "VUCA" way of dealing with a customer; best if your website has requests already filtered into categories, such as "new product quotation request" or "after-sales quotation request", "technical issue", and so on. Tools such as Oracle's OSC perform these precise actions, and we can expect a major boost in the field following the upheaval of advanced AI demonstrated by ChatGPT. Here again we touch on shaping the environment to tame VUCA.

This calls for a parenthesis. One of the prime downsides of coding is that it can be difficult to transfer the task to someone else. Being indispensable has its advantages, but purposely making your code inscrutable is not a recommended way to get there. Be fair and add explicit comments; leave breadcrumbs so that another coder could use your program in the future, should you leave. It would be a shame to see your hard work go to the bin, and the firm return to the old medieval ways. Besides, certain managers know only too well the inherent risks of processes dependent on a single person, the grand architect who coded the program. They have a (justified) bias against code of any sort. To hush such objections, make your code as clear and self-explanatory as possible. Add comments, procedures, and strive to account for problems down the road, so that even a child can run it. Parenthesis closed.

If 50% of your tasks are prime candidates for semi-automation tricks that enable a 50%-time gain, like our front office clerk handling customer requests, you can save a fourth of your time. Don't brag about it online or drown it on Facebook and video games as legendary Reddit user FiletOfFish1066 did (only to get the sack whence his company found out).[4] Take on more. Alternatively, explain to your boss that you could help others reach a similar performance level so that the whole department benefits. With her blessing, spearhead the change. Spread the net to capture incoming data, unleash a mix of human and machine to analyze, categorize, and treat it efficiently. Leverage the latest tools. Explain to peers the necessary minimum as to how the system functions, and train them for the remaining parts to handle. You may realize that in the process, you are starting to delegate parts of the work you'd been doing up to then. Guess what? You just climbed some steps, scored points with management, and added a new powerful weapon to your arsenal: humans.

7.3   Step B: Delegate

Are you in a position to delegate?

A manager can hand tasks over to her staff or aim to shove them to another department. But if you are solely responsible for making your coffee, you will need to devise subtler methods. Without the leeway and authority to decide who does what, persuasion rules. Not by licking your boss' boots, but by proving over time your ability to take on more demanding, value-added

---

[4] While the story may be fictious, it reverberated around the web, with other users claiming to have performed similar feats. Cf. for example: https://www.techworm.net/2016/06/programmer-automates-job-six-years-forgets-coding-gets-caught-fired.html.

s.

tasks. Demonstrate rare skills; tackle increasingly greater levels of VUCA; sign up for every training course and other opportunity available, for instance by filling in for someone absent. In this last case, dig for any ways that their tasks could be automated, try to set up a more efficient process, and write it into a procedure. In all instances, automate wherever possible to achieve greater efficiency. These actions add fodder to your cannon. Politics aside, a clever boss recognizes valuable elements within the team and seeks to withdraw mundane tasks from them. She has responsibilities that she looks forward to delegating to capable reports one day. When she talks of giving you extra responsibilities or even a promotion, bargain to discard low-value tasks that elude automation to other staff.

You score a double whammy by successfully delegating. This proactively sheds tasks of meager value and prone to vanish soon anyways, disintegrated by automation. And the delegation process involves training and follow-up—a soft power form of management, in case the employee is a colleague over which you have no formal authority. Maintain regular follow-ups until you ensure they get it right. Openly share responsibility in the event of a degradation in quality following the transfer: if she fails to deliver on time, hands in slipshod work, or commits blunders, acknowledge that it tarnishes your credibility. You may be deemed good at doing the task yourself, but ill-equipped to train others. This would limit your potential for vertical ascension and thus should be improved.

Smart bosses categorize the better elements in their teams under two labels: experts and (potential) managers. The first excel at their job, delivering steady triple "A"s. The downside? They lack people and managerial skills. Elevating an expert to management is a common mistake, derived from the Peter Principle—the misconception that a firm has a single ladder, one that ultimately leads to the CEO.[5] The expert proves incapable of managing a team. To be fair, some can be coached and eventually reveal themselves as excellent managers (and thus no longer qualify as mere experts). But the rest, although they may not admit to it (after all, they too are subject to the societal pressure to rise in the ranks), would rather be left alone to focus on what they're good at: dealing with concepts, figures, and *things*, not people.

Poor supervision abilities curb the expert's growth potential. In short, not a desirable label. If you do see yourself as the expert type, acknowledge it and seek a remedy. Either strive to change, for instance via some coaching; or if everything (including yourself) confirms that you are most performant

[5] Rob Ashgar: *Incompetence Rains, Err, Reigns: What The Peter Principle Means Today*, Forbes (August 14, 2014), https://www.forbes.com/sites/robasghar/2014/08/14/incompetence-rains-er-reigns-what-the-peter-principle-means-today.

as an expert, see how your firm might deal with that situation, whether it recognizes the value of experts and has (or can trace) a career path tailored to them.[6]

When promoted to a managerial position and failing to deliver, an expert faces dire consequences as backtracking to his previous role is seldom an option: once the damage is done, the most plausible exit is through the company door. However, if you aptly manage task transfers, and keep colleagues happy in the process, this elevates you in the view of superiors. The line between delegation and management is a blurry one; succeeding in delegation demonstrates managerial skills, paving the path for an ascent.

Even recurrent tasks contain some VUCA. The report needs to accommodate for a leap year, or account for a non-comparable basis following an acquisition; a formula may break down and cause an error; an algorithm's predictions start to fall astray. It's up to you to dose the extent of power you delegate, so that staff can handle certain VUCA situations on their own while relying on you for the thornier issues. If they can't solve chronic issues, it will stifle their work, erode motivation, cause you a nuisance to intervene, and ultimately bring trouble. Knowledge is power, but too obvious a thirst for it could backfire. Staff won't appreciate overly relying on you, especially if they feel you are withholding information or tasks that they qualify for. No one likes the colleague reluctant to share, the boss that lacks recognition for her staff, nor the Machiavellian one constantly scheming in dark corridors.

By feeding them fish instead of teaching them how to fish, you may wind up spending more time troubleshooting their problems than when you handled things on your own, a phenomenon that the mediocre worker might interpret as proof that either she is no good, or she'd be better off doing the task the old way. The capable employee will see through it and sense what you hide deep down under this façade: insecurity, the fear of being surpassed by your own staff. And she may not keep that information to herself.

Beyond spoiling your beach holidays with work emergencies, such behavior blocks your pathway to management. The better approach would be to take the time to deepen their knowledge of tasks. Provide context, the bigger picture, the ins and outs of what comes before, and the impacts and purpose of their work. Employee motivation increases as you share the "why" instead of focusing merely on the "what". It shows you care about their growth. Strike the right balance of handicap, so that like the captain of a ship, your team can navigate on clear days, but needs you to take over

---

[6] Companies from IBM to Microsoft have come to grips with this diversity. They've responded by carving out separate career path for experts and other talents that allow for promotion and recognition without the hassle of managing others.

the wheel during a major storm. The real maestro nurtures her staff and uses their progress as a motivator to continuously push herself to learn more, in order to stay ahead of the pack—all the while cognizant that at some point management takes over expertise, that it's okay then if some of your reports excel better or are more knowledgeable than you in certain feats.

When feasible, outsource. Services from outsourcing platforms don't come free and require monitoring to avoid handing in sloppy work. But in certain contexts, this can be a path worth exploring.

Example Blending Automation, Delegation, and Retention

Imagine you have to get data from several entry points on a weekly basis, analyze it, and report the results to other members of the company. Altogether it takes a good two hours of your time, or 5% of your work, if you're on a 40-h week (that's the equivalent of one billiard ball!).

Your diligent dissection of this job produces the following steps:

(1) extract data from several sources,
(2) format it,
(3) bring parts together,
(4) perform calculations,
(5) synthesize it into a digestible piece of intel (a report that holds on a single A4-size paper),
(6) analyze these results, which may involve,
(7) reaching out to other departments for information (to fill missing parts of the puzzle),
(8) convey your conclusions in an email, and
(9) send the email to the right people

Once dissected, plot each step in terms of automation and delegation. For the latter, do not consider yet whether you have the power to delegate within your firm; rather, reason according to the level of brainwork necessary.

Here we plot the results for our example (Fig. 7.3).

A meticulous engineer might use bubbles to portray time spent and then measure progress in terms of time saved as the plan is rolled out. While we won't insist on that level of detail here, it does convey the underlying idea at stake.

The first step should be delegated as it possesses little value yet in this example resists automation (in other contexts it might be easily automated).

Steps 2–5 can take place in Excel, via formulas; the format can be automated via Power Query or a Macro recorder. The choice to automate or

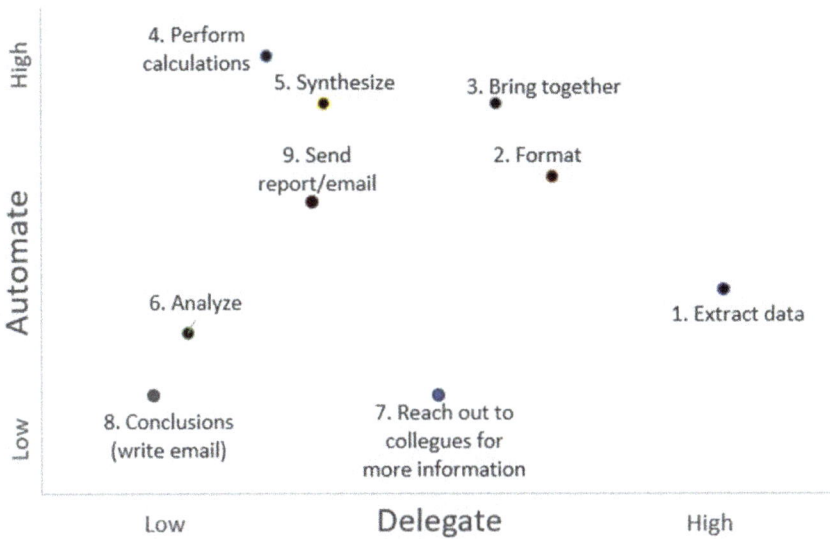

Fig. 7.3 Example of task automation and delegation

delegate as usual depends on your skills in either field and on available tools, both carbon and silicon.

Cognitive skills come into play in steps 6 to 8; keep these on your plate, lest you have capable people in your entourage. If so, that aide could also liaise with other departments for additional intel when needed. Step 8 is earmarked as the most cognitive bit. Best conclude and personalize the message yourself; if the previous part was delegated, this includes a review of that work. Note that the analysis can to a certain extent be automated if rules are clear—e.g. when comparing figures to a given target; so can sending emails, albeit less easily than the formatting step as it requires either coding or a tool such as Microsoft Power BI, with which sharing of reports within the firm can be automated and scheduled).

The task may not emerge on the other end of the tunnel entirely automated/delegated. Yet your time has been slashed, say to a meager 15 min a week, or less than 1% of your worktime. Moreover, by mixing delegation and automation, you blur the trail and alone master the end-to-end process.

A last point to mention when performing this type of exercise: question the tool(s) and framework used. Seek to optimize these for automation. If someone sends you bank data in a PDF, ask them for a comma-separated values (CSV) or Excel format. Perhaps they ignore the automation benefits of the latter two. If they claim that it can't be done, crosscheck just to be sure— perhaps it can only be downloaded when accessing the bank's online portal via Chrome and not Microsoft Edge. They might have limited computer proficiency, period.

7.4 Step C as Cognitive: Strive for Human Value-Added Tasks

Feats like seeing the bigger picture, connecting the dots, weighing in different goals or group brainstorming won't show up on an algorithm's resume anytime soon. Programs work best relative to humans on huge quantities of data or repetitive actions that follow a script: updating information, searching for correlations, a match with certain criteria, pricing analysis, etc.

Our tasks chart contained two areas prone to the discovery of untamed beasts: the ad hoc bubble bustling with VUCA, and new tasks. Your goal should be to wrestle these beasts leftwards, turning art into science by processing and streamlining. Starting with ad hoc tasks already in your purview. This relates to our earlier advice on "laying the asphalt road".

Adverse forces can blow a bubble in the wrong direction, too. Suppose you are responsible for your firm's sourcing and supply chain. The prevailing business as usual was upset in unprecedented ways by the Covid pandemic. What the politically correct have labeled "these uncertain times" translated as skyrocketing raw material prices and shortages of all sorts, from electronics to metals to freight containers and human movers. Your minions actively rummage for deals to secure components, venturing way beyond their habitual supplier base. When they spot one, they must close in fast, lest another firm swoops in and snatches the deal. Yet the normal modus operandi warrants a lengthy vendor approval process that includes supplier audits and several rows of sample testing; moreover, the higher cost of this makeshift source results in a loss of margin that they cannot fathom (it's above their pay grade), to say nothing of the unfavorable payment terms and risks related to unfamiliar players. Only you have the authority to call the shots in such instances; but as the once exceptional situation becomes the new norm, you risk toiling in a mud pool that ultimately forms your grave.

To avoid this, take a step back. Acknowledge that the circumstances have changed, and that yesterday's wisdom no longer prevails. What process design changes can be made to adapt to the new realities? How much should you loosen the leash on your reports? What additional training could accompany these responsibilities, so that they can call the shots without needing to pass everything by you, yet without critically endangering the firm either? What new metrics could provide a better view of performance?

From Art to Science, and Back

Before Ford set up the scientific principles of management, the nascent car manufacturing sector was plain artisanry: a workshop packed with technicians in freestyle mode, and little to no consistency. Taylorism changed all that, turning art into science via processing and streamlining. You need to apply these precepts to your work. Turn the Pollock into a Mondrian.

Scrutinize new tasks, high VUCA work like the one described hereabove and even supposed cognitive tasks. How far out do they lie in unstructured territory? Navigating the VUCA maze sans map requires experience, common sense, and a beacon of the greater objectives enshrined in the company's vision and mission statement; in other words, agility (the kind of thing machines simply don't have). These traits serve as a compass. But as any Zelda fan will recall from the legendary 1986 game, a compass alone still leaves you at the mercy of dead ends. A map improves your odds.

Back in the office, this translates as "map out the process". Then chalk up any risks and events that could materialize at each step of the process. It could range from a bug in a program, a formula that doesn't work, server downtime, to the absence of an employee relied upon to perform a certain task or provide information by a given deadline, a traffic jam delaying your arrival at a meeting or another of the million last-minute surprises that Murphy's Law casts on an event. Assess both the likelihood and impact of each threat with a score from 1 to 5. Then list out preventive actions to contain this type of problem.

Next, suppose every barrier breaks down. What contingency plans could be actioned to confine the damage?

Inscribe these risks and related measures, both preventive and curative, into the process. Challenge the scoring in light of new events; break the rules if they no longer make sense. In our sourcing example, you could consider simplifying the process and sharing information with staff relative to minimum margin targets to increase their autonomy without endangering the business, even if that means getting them to sign an NDA (non-disclosure agreement).

Write the new process out in a clear and concise manner; communicate it to those concerned, organize meetings, train employees, and monitor progress. And acknowledge that which cannot be reduced to deterministic processes but retains a dose of VUCA, in turn requiring higher cognition.

Correctly toying with these levers blows the bubble toward the left, from an impalpable endeavor to a well-oiled process, both workable by less seasoned staff and measurable, with rules and troubleshooting guidelines. This morphs a subtle art into pure science. Some steps may still require a dose of cognitive skills that elude both AI and junior staff, but overall the task should be more structured, less subject to variability in the output, and especially, less time-consuming for you. Handing its execution over to someone or something else shrinks the bubble of *your* time down to its most cognitive essence, plus regular checks that partake in a manager's job. Feel free to keep a bubble chart of your own time, and another for your department, or use separate colors for yourself and others (colors can add a fourth dimension to a chart).

In the above, we discussed under-processed tasks. Yet we've seen how processing improves efficiency at first, to then peak and gradually deteriorate (cf. Structure & Cognition). Staff reduced to mere cogs by over-processing see their motivation erode. Such processes need to be loosened a bit (Fig. 7.4).

Some tasks evade structuring: each occurrence is unique and defies resemblance with anything prior. Not all art can be chained to science. These are the endeavors that AI will have the most trouble dealing with, those where humans keep the upper hand. They often involve either the bigger picture or the future horizon—unsurprisingly both realms are dealt with to a greater extent by the upper rungs of the organization. They require a sound understanding of the ramifications of each possible action in fields ranging from customer satisfaction to the bottom line, the environment, corporate reputation, as well as the company's goals, vision, and mission. What decisions best serve the company's interests in the short and long run?

When confronting a task or process, a capable manager can discern whether it is under- or over-processed. This will partly depend on the external

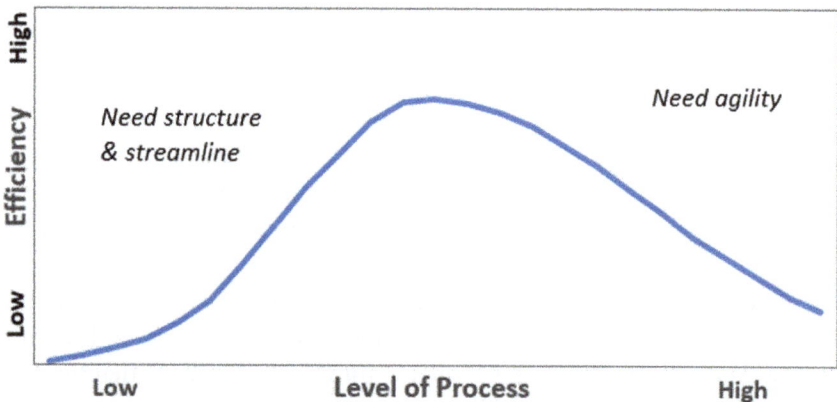

Fig. 7.4   Process versus efficiency

situation. The horizontal axis in Fig. 7.5 depicts the level of structure in the outer context, while the vertical axis shows the internal level of structure, for the organization, department, team, or single individual.

It highlights how striking the right balance of inner structure depends on the outer context. Author Daniel Coyle explains the contrast between a highly structured context where one seeks proficiency foremost, from that of an unstructured context where creativity takes the front seat: the first "needs people to know and feel exactly what to do", while the second needs them "to discover that for themselves".[7]

To bring this idea home in pure Picasso bull-simplification fashion, think of a notebook purchase: should you choose one filled with horizontal lines, or blank pages? The answer depends on context. If it's mainly for writing, pick the one with straight lines; for drawing, or to brainstorm ideas, opt

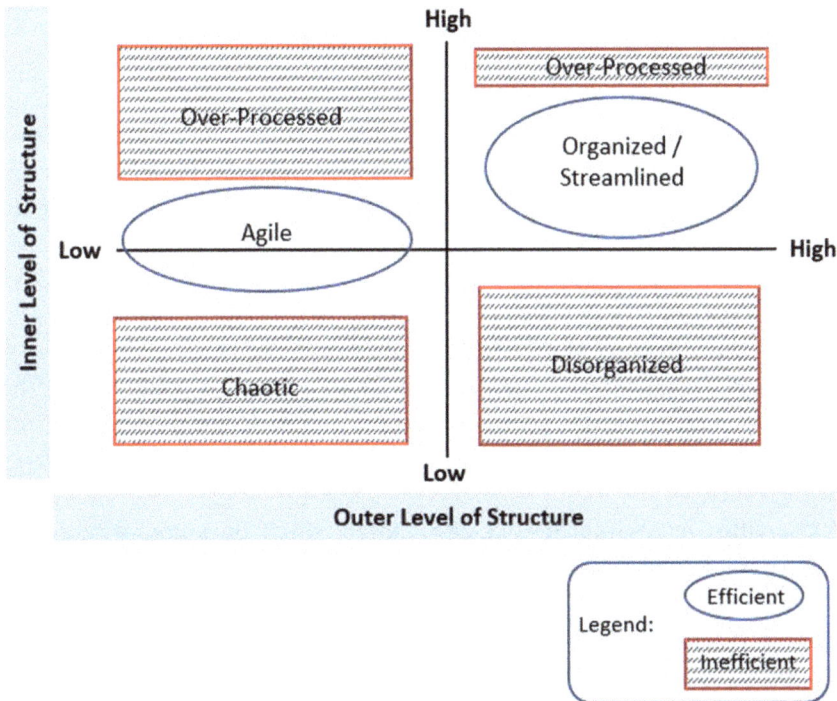

Fig. 7.5 Adapting the inner level of structure to context, i.e. to the outer level of structure

---

[7] Daniel Coyle: *The Culture Code: The Secrets of Highly Successful Groups*, Cornerstone Digital (2018).

for the one with blank pages (or at most faint dots). The lines symbolize processes; a great void, freestyle divagation and creativity.

A last note of caution. As 49ers know only too well, all that glitters is not gold. In the office world, this translates as mistaking a task as highly cognitive when in fact it is not. Mediocre employees may go to great lengths to cover their tracks, deploying cryptic formulas and opaque coding with the sole aim of making their work seem more complicated than it really is, in an antithesis of both lean thinking and teamwork spirit. Or simply they abstain from jotting their processes down in writing.

Beware of the inner voice behind this habit: its motive for maintaining a lowly cognitive task in a darkness that only the employee's magic can dispel stems from a desire to appear irreplaceable, a desire which belies deep inner insecurities. Unfortunately, the absence of rigorous work codification in offices gives workers free rein for recourse to such cloaking devices and subterfuges.

The problem with this fool's gold? It will dupe neither automation tools nor more seasoned experts. Imagine the day this task comes under the spotlight—say, your boss or someone with superior IT skills pulls a chair behind you and asks that you walk them through the process. The stone's glitter will fade, and your black arts crumble as they immediately notice automation opportunities and underpinning time gains. They will perceive the fact that the task isn't rightly addressed as a problem, and the fact that you've been handling it for so long without ever questioning the poor efficiency achieved makes you part of that problem. If they need to do it for you, what does that say about your prospects for growth?

Know to recognize and admit which tasks are truly cognitive. When honing your skills, ensure you are pursuing the philosopher's stone, not some vulgar hunk of pyrite. Others might not be so easily fooled when you dangle it in their face.

Observing the splintered rock bits, judge which ones comprise enough cognitive purities for your handling. Delegate the dull and keep the glossy. If tasks in your scope don't exactly glare with cognitive requirements, search for more promising rocks. We've hinted at the bubbles not yet on your plate. Now that some room has been made, it's time to explore beyond your habitual pasture grounds.

Adding on New Tasks

Venture out to endeavors within your department and beyond. Look upwards, toward your boss, her boss, all the way to top management. As you climb in an organization, the horizon extends ever farther. What questions keep them awake at night as they gaze afar? What do they value that you could intervene on?

Obvious prerequisites to add on tasks include:

- the spare time to take on more work (normally achieved following the previous steps);
- the relevant skills for performing it;
- authorization from above.

The last requirement can come in later, after you've covertly fulfilled the task once or twice, thus proving your valor (desirable especially if others question your skills). Just avoid conveying the impression of going behind people's back.

You might question whether these tasks are within your purview to begin with. Helping others carries the risk that they view this as impinging on their turf, even if in fact they remained too constrained to ever find the time for it. Secure the right support beforehand; avoid casting a threatening shadow. This danger tops Robert Greene's list of 48 laws of power: "Do not go too far in displaying your talents or you might accomplish the opposite—inspire fear and insecurity".[8] Make it appear as if someone else came up with the idea. If the change leads to mundane work for peers, ensure your superior presents the change, not you. Introducing a knowledge matrix in your organization can help advance your agenda, by highlighting areas where too few staff are

> ### The Knowledge Matrix
> A knowledge matrix is a tool to visualize the spread of knowledge of tasks within the organization. Skills and knowledge of how to perform tasks are represented on one end (say, horizontally), and employee names on the other (vertically).
> At each employee/knowledge juncture, tick whether that person has the expertise to handle the task. This helps to identify risks of losing critical knowhow, whether a staff quits for good or goes on leave, ensuring at least one knowledgeable person remains stationed in the office at all times. The firm or department then hedges against this risk by spreading that expertise via training, so that it is shared by at least several people.
> Sophisticated knowledge matrixes go beyond a simple yes/no, applying a scoring or a notation that could for instance indicate whether the staff is novice, autonomous on the task, or capable of training others on it.

---

[8] Robert Greene: *The 48 Laws of Power*, p. 21. Viking Press (1998).

knowledgeable. Use it as a battle plan, strive to gain knowledge in all the tasks of your department. Not only is a knowledge matrix a great tool for the company, it can also help you shed off dull tasks by training others on them, and triggers a quest for more interesting (cognitive) ones on your plate. You can then peel the new process off into bits and seek more efficient ways to perform it.

The ability to achieve work more efficiently and thus liberate time puts you in a position of strength. Request for more or let the idea float around that you could take on increasingly daunting tasks and see what the boss hands over to you.

Don't despair if the new tasks fall on the left-hand side of the bubble chart. Gold seldom surfaces in chunks: most tasks are neither 100% cognitive nor 100% automatable. Taking on automatable tasks allows for easy wins. Slowly but steadily steer toward cognitive work. Managers may praise the employee that speeds up recurrent tasks, but that alone will not guarantee her rise in the company. Aim for the fertile lands of high-reasoning tasks on the right side of the chart; here lies the Holy Grail that workers must strive for to hedge against the threat of AI.

Investigate what's being done in the company at various levels. Tasks performed by your superior(s) represent obvious sniffing grounds. Bosses can appear just as reluctant to take back tasks once delegated as they were to delegate them in the first place. Yet at any point a promotion, transfer, or departure could send them far away, placing you as the sole survivor capable of handling the task, thus a candidate for succession.

We talked earlier about internal quiet hiring. As an employee, you can exploit this trend to take on new tasks. Even if the new role given does not correspond to your dream job (recall the baggage handlers at Qantas), take the opportunity to observe the process. Seek measures that could improve it, be it by streamlining and automating certain aspects, by providing a better human touch, or addressing an unnoticed pain point that could differentiate your firm from its rivals.

Some tasks don't fall in the category of work that *must* be done and have thus been left neglected, perhaps forever, particularly in companies running low on resources or devoid of the right talent. With mandatory work automated-slash-delegated, you can turn your attention to these endeavors. Some may convey greater value than the mandatory stuff—for instance a new indicator that provides valuable insight on a business aspect ignored up to then.

Finding new, cognitive tasks calls for observance and a dose of creativity. While creating tasks for your company both new and valuable may prove a difficult act to pull, the rewards are consistently greater. As conceiver and craftsman, you alone hold the keys to the task, you detain ultimate knowledge of the nuts and bolts. The more value it generates, the more merit you amass.

Figure 7.6 illustrates the decomposition of our financial worker's activity, a year after following the above steps.

We see a distinct shift in overall time consumption from the perilous bottom-left area, as a result of automation and delegation actions, toward more cognitive pastures. Notice how certain bubbles have slid: though still performed with the same frequency (i.e. on a yearly basis), structuring the budget process with templates, a procedure and clear communication has turned it into routine work—a prime example of fool's gold, or a task that once structured was not so cognitive or VUCA-infested, after all. Our employee spends roughly the same amount of time in meetings, but these have changed: they are now high-level ones that engage the fate of the company; less important meetings have been passed onto trained reports. Alas, new tasks have spawned, in particular tasks related to a managerial function—the "work supervision" bubble englobes the supervision of many other tasks.

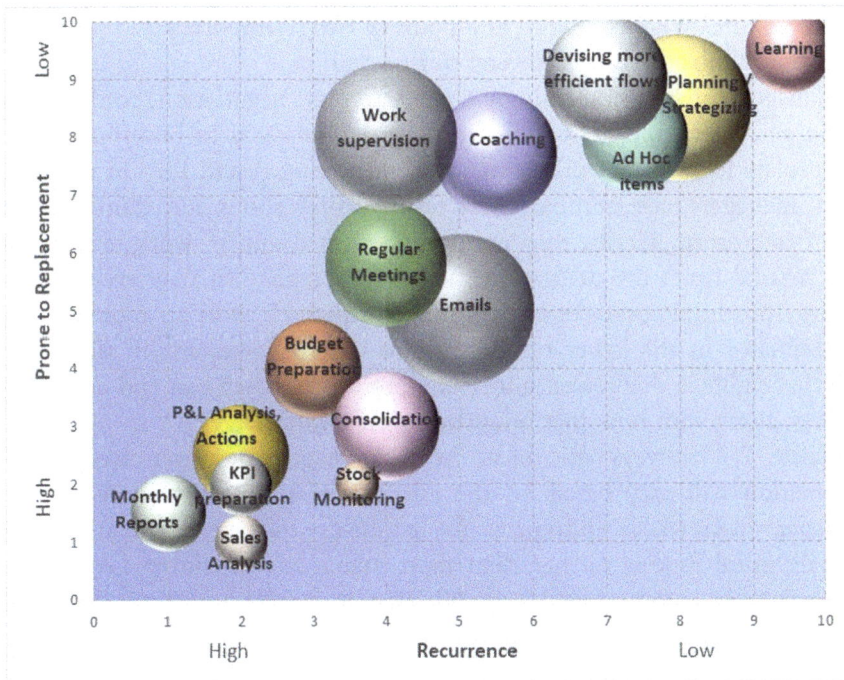

Fig. 7.6 Financial occupation task decomposition after zealous pursuit of automation, delegation, and cognitive tasks

Compared to Fig. 7.1, this employee is now a valued asset within the firm.

Rising in the Ranks

To recapitulate, we can summarize the above steps as follows:

- identify new promising rocks (tasks);
- smatter them into smaller chunks if needed;
- structure them into a step-by-step process to round the edges;
- streamline this process: examine each rock and reroute it toward automation and/or delegation; keep the glittery bits (as in cognitive) to yourself;
- use the time saved to repeat the process.

These steps form a loop. Each iteration frees time, allowing you to take on more, to *manage* more.

This gradual ascension puts you square in the target of books on management and new tech. The latter deal with how to harness technology, digitize the company, morph it into a data-driven business, and triumphantly march it down the 4^{IR} red carpet. We will not cover these aspects in depth, as our focus is less on managers and leaders precisely because that area already bustles with literature. We merely hint at a point or two of importance.

As one climbs the ladder, several shifts occur.

Management skills increasingly come into play: negotiation, conflict resolution and leadership. The knowledge repertoire needs to be broadened to encapsulate legal frameworks, financials, marketing... and IT. On the other hand, managers have comparatively less to worry about automation, for at least two reasons. Firstly, they are immersed in cognitive work. Second, in their arsenal room the delegation shelf is fully replete (it may even include outside subcontractors). All else considered equal, IT skills act more as a key differentiator in the lower rungs of the corporate hierarchy; in the stratospheric heights, a theoretical understanding of what tech can and cannot do suffices, along with how that boundary evolves in time.

Figure 7.7 conveys this idea. At what stage delegation overshadows automation will vary based on the job, sector, and even the style of the manager. Elon Musk epitomizes the hands-on manager who micromanages technical aspects farther than most managers, remaining keenly alert to advances in automation. Meanwhile Warren Buffett and Bernard Arnault may not master the latest IT tools, nor are they expected to—they have armies of capable lieutenants for that.

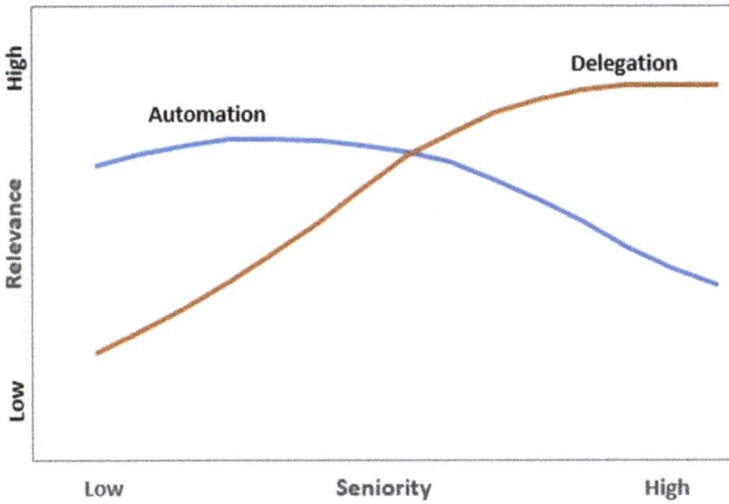

Fig. 7.7 Relevance of automation versus delegation/management skills based on seniority

Take the time to ponder on this chart and gauge where you currently situate yourself. This can help determine if there is an urge to develop proficiency in automation tools, or whether this is less critical. In the latter case, digital tools must not be ignored, but you can rely on others for the heavy lifting. As noted earlier, striving to deepen coding expertise to the detriment of people skills could make for a poor manager.

Forestalling automation and rising in the ranks often coincide. As you climb, reforge alliances and adapt your style to reflect that of the new echelons, so as to appear as "one of them". This may cause envy, but rising seldom happens without shoving elbows, and it takes a thick skin to reach the summit.

Another change in vantage point sees work gradually shift from *tasks* to *responsibilities*. The employee in the former does what she is told to do (till rage against the machine ensues); meanwhile, the latter employee is held *accountable* for achievements broadly defined. The first type of employee has scarce knowledge of the ins and outs of her tasks; the latter conceives her role as part of a grander corporate scheme. She oversees, trains others, and strives to improve execution. When a problem arises, she finds it, fixes it, and does whatever is in her power to prevent future occurrences. She treads the fine line between seemingly contradictory objectives, like short-term goals and long-term objectives, or inventory turnover and on-time delivery targets, while accounting for conjectural factors—best loosen the grip on the just-in-time motto in times of high uncertainty and chronic shortages. She can explain to staff the action's purpose within the corporation, how it links to the strategy, and even to the greater good. As you may have guessed, this has more to do with a mindset than a clear-cut distinction between two strata of workers. To succeed in your ascent, you should have this holistic, responsible mindset from day one on the job, no matter what it is. When Elon Musk wrote an email stating (amongst several guidelines): "Don't follow rules. Follow principles.", he was addressing not only managers but the entirety of his staff. Firms like Pixar go to great lengths to instill this kind of spirit in their recruits, at times leading to wondrous accounts, such as that of the barista-turned-story manager.[9]

Compared to tasks, responsibilities evolve in more abstract settings. We could say tasks are to responsibilities what a Mondrian is to a Rothko. The former is crisp; codified in an SOP, the employee only needs to play it by the book. The latter is more abstract, leaving the nitty–gritty on how to achieve goals to the worker—vague and at times contradictory goals such as "Maximize the bottom-line" and "Customer first". The leeway given to achieve these involves decision-making, and by extension, a broad knowledge of all the ins and outs: In other words, cognition that extends beyond mere task execution. In sum, while a junior is given a narrow, one-dimensional path to tread on, her ascent lifts her to a fully dimensional world of infinite possibilities. Drier grounds safer from automation, but also more treacherous ones, that at times can prove intimidating by their plethora of choices, with VUCA lurking behind every corner, and the added weight of responsibility.

Earlier we talked about the agile organization. As you clamber out of the AI Battle Royale arena and onto managerial grounds, it's on you to foment the agile mindset within your team. The paradigm of transferring only dull tasks to keep the cognitive bits has outlived its purpose. While valid at the lower echelons, a survival technique to emerge from the pit, beyond that it quickly slides toward the caricatural—one can only get so far towering over underlings that act and behave like robots. Where would you place your team on the sumo ring? How would they fare if you took a two-week vacation on a remote island?

A shift is necessary to shape your employees' ability to reason and work solutions out. Instill an entrepreneurial spirit; encourage them, even in the face of apparent failure. Help them see the bigger picture. Favor interdepartmental work, and avoid slipping into a silo. Rehash the corporate goals and vision with concrete illustrations that resonate with staff, and ensure these

---

[9] Cf. Daniel Coyle: *The Culture Code: The Secrets of Highly Successful Groups*, p. 77. Cornerstone Digital (2018).

are understood. Develop your people's faculty to accurately call the shots. Be authentic too: lead by example.

Pull those in a stultifying job out of it, and let them sense its malleable contours, so they can shape it like a clay sculpture. Give them responsibilities and room to experiment. Clarify the contours of the sandbox upfront. The famously decentralized firm Gore & Associates emphasizes this with the "waterline" concept. Picturing the firm as a ship at sea, the staff's understanding of the waterline is most crucial when toying with hazardous materials. If things go awry, damage above the waterline is trivial, whereas blowing a hole below it leads the ship to sink.[10] The company goes to great lengths, using training and mock cases to ensure staff develops the acumen to recognize the waterline. As the authors of *Primed to Perform* observed, too often firms emphasize on giving staff freedom as to *when* or *where* they work, when it's the freedom as to *how* they work that can spark the real magic.[11]

Not everyone succeeds in this transition. Some fear the burden of responsibilities and managing others; they struggle to adapt or simply resist change. Establish an incentivization system that rewards staff in line with the agile culture you strive to instill, to ensure good elements stay while the lesser ones drop out, and not the reverse. Note that the higher spheres grant extra leeway to delegate work to outsiders as well, i.e. to outsource.

At this level, success also entails a tech-savvy person or two under your belt. Reliable members whom you can delegate to for matters of pure IT expertise, for instance, to venture beyond there where your coding skills come to a halt. Ideally, name one of your staff to oversee the review and improvement of processes within the department, the same way an industrial engineer augments productivity on the assembly floor. Without turning the department into a sweatshop of overstressed minions, aim for a culture of excellency. If digital Taylorism performance metrics are necessary, balance these with fair incentives, training, and guidance to help lift the team. Allow your staff a number of hours per week for tutorials, combined with brief reports on what they seek to learn, the tasks addressed, and materialized achievements.

I find the "pulling a chair behind the employee to let her walk me through her work" a fruitful tactic. I provide a few hints at the end of the process on which aspects could be optimized, and some clues for how to improve, all the while making precise the purpose, which includes making her job more interesting (as opposed to making her redundant or burying her with more chores). Typically, the employee comes to grips with reality, acknowledges areas for improvement, and sets out to excel. Some may call on me later to

[10] https://www.gore.com/about/our-beliefs-and-principles.
[11] Neel Doshi and Lindsay McGregor: *Primed to Perform*, p. 179, Harper Business (2015).

review the process and seek guidance, or even with a request for training. As if simply showing interest in their work awakens them from lethargy, making them feel useful to the firm.

One might opine that there are limits to adding on more within the finite brackets of working hours. Indeed, it would be a hard trick to pull if simultaneously keeping all the cognitive stuff to yourself. But brilliant managers know to surround themselves with capable lieutenants. By fostering an agile culture, their vision can play out from top all the way to bottom. As captain of the ship, the CEO is responsible for the entire business; every task "belongs" to her—she has merely delegated or outsourced them to various extents.

8

Other Weapons

What skills are most relevant to success in the 4^{IR}? In line with our A, B, and C steps from the Tasks chapter, we can scoop these into three buckets:

- delegation/management,
- tools leveraging,
- everything (else) that eludes AI and computers—which itself can be split into:

  - higher cognition: creativity, induction, organizational skills, etc.
  - optimizing human actions that are here to stay, like reading, or effective communication.

We covered cognition earlier in our job SWOT (the sumo game and the gang). In this chapter we first investigate human tasks prone to remain with us (Sect. 8.1), before turning to the importance of continuous learning (Sect. 8.2).

Companies have long sought for individuals good at people management, the teachings of which are the focus of business school curriculums and many a book. While comparatively underserved, learning IT tools also deserves a central spot in any worker's battleplan. Therefore, we take the reverse stance, setting management skills aside to tackle tool leveraging (Sect. 8.3).

The original version of this chapter was revised: Text correction has been updated. The correction to the chapter is available at https://doi.org/10.1007/978-3-031-19278-4_10

Alas, other actions can boost our game. We end this chapter by considering the power of social networking (Sect. 8.4), including via online platforms, and the opportunity for developing side-gigs or going full entrepreneur (Sect. 8.5).

8.1 Efficiency in Human Tasks that Are Here to Stay

While fundamental to our survival toolkit in the 4^{IR}, automation and delegation have their limits. Algorithms paired with Big Data can feed us suggestions, yet do not dispense the need for us to digest information. We do not have microchip implants to enhance assimilation and memorization as in *The Matrix*, nor drugs of the type depicted in *Limitless*. No matter how hard we pursue the previous chapter's actions, we still need to attend meetings, read emails, and perform a variety of other tasks. But there is no reason to spare these from our efficiency motto.

Managing Email

The email has risen to embody the twenty-first-century office-sphere. Despite other tools infringing on its turf—instant messaging apps with group chat options and video calls—it remains the cornerstone of communication, the one that makes things *official*. Employees are expected to have read each and every snippet of text hurled in their direction, and dereliction of duty due to an unnoticed email can have dire consequences.

Snippets of vital information drift in a sea of litter, bound to drown to the ocean floor if not caught in time. There is no golden rule to manage this portion of work. Some opt for an edifice of subfolders in their email box, meticulously classifying emails by topic; others are comfortable leaving everything as it comes, use sort and search options to find information, and ignore the rest. Develop the tools and habits that work best for you. Remain alert for more advanced software, for instance the messaging system in Oracle's Service Cloud (OSC). What benefits or efficiencies can they provide compared to your usual communication vehicle?

Speed Reading

An obvious path to efficiency, speed reading is often disregarded, as if it were a prank, in the lines of: "people who speed read do not assimilate or enjoy anything".

Immersion in a novel, poetry recitation—these are activities we indulge in, written to unlock our imagination, create a vicarious vibe with protagonists and share their emotions. A learning child reads aloud, slowly (in fact, *not* reading out loud was likely the exception until a mere 1,000 years ago, at least in Mediterranean civilizations[1]). But reading at work fulfills purposes other than lifting the human soul, purposes that dictate a need for speed. Employers do not pay staff to spend all day reading (with the exception of my publisher). Yet they do expect proper digestion of every scrap of data: emails, procedures, memos, KPIs, reports, and minutes. The ICT revolution elevated the written word to the rank of supreme truth while simultaneously facilitating its propagation at zero marginal cost, overflooding office workers with written documents. Shame on he who misses an email, fails to acknowledge a written process, blindly accepts a website's terms and conditions, or signs a contract without meticulously proofreading the back written in font size 8.

Coupled with the tacit rule that elevates negligence of written information to a quasi-crime, this deluge makes speed reading a no-brainer and a prime candidate for differentiation. Seize this overlooked opportunity to fast-track ahead of the pack. No need to boast about it publicly nor make it too obvious; just apply it at work. Excelling at such an ubiquitous task scores you points.

Several techniques (and more books) develop speedreading; they start by assuring audiences that it is not an innate talent a lucky few are presumably born with. It takes practice. As in learning to drive a car, the first attempts require concentration, until perseverance and training lead to habit, adding an autopilot switch in the cockpit.

Technology (as often) can come to the rescue. Instead of laying out words in the usual pattern (left-to-right, for written English), a digital tool like *Spritz* produces one word at a time in a static space, creating a fast succession of blinks. Users can adjust the number of words per minute. This obviates the need for eye movement, cutting down reading time while reducing strain on eye muscles.[2]

The same goes for audio and video. Firms from Taobao to the Little Red Book (小红书 *XiaoHongShu*) provide livestreaming tutorials at a speed roughly 20% faster. A concentrated viewer can digest the information while saving that much time overall. The fast speed option exists on platforms like YouTube, too; make use of it whenever feasible.

---

[1] Cf. Alberto Manguel: *A History of Reading*, the chapter entitled "The Silent Readers", Penguin Books (2014).

[2] https://spritz.com/.

Break Discipline

In the <u>Workless or Work less?</u> section, we envisioned shorter worktimes. In reality, people *have* been working less, by spending office hours on their smartphone, "possibly the biggest non-drug addiction of the twenty-first century".[3] In a Harris Poll survey commissioned by CareerBuilder in the mid-2010's on 3,000 employees and 1,000 employers, over half of the latter cited the mobile phone as the worst office productivity killer, with 83% estimating at least an hour a day by worker lost to it, and three in four believing it surpasses two hours. 7% of employees in the study confessed using the Internet at work to watch pornography or access dating sites.[4]

When left to their devices, workers have a pesky inclination to waste time. For some, mornings begin by catching up on their social media life. Others deal with urgent tasks first, *then* take a "well-deserved break" online.

Internet breaks have become a pernicious form of slacking. They dig their roots in a deeply ingrained reward mechanism. After achieving a task, we seek a pat on the back, thus feel justified to open the browser or pull out the smartphone. In no time this carrot grows into a sizeable addiction, aggravated by constant feeds from group chats and the latest CNN flash news.

It's OK to take breaks, but these need to be disciplined. One easily loosens control over the number of self-granted breaks, and just as easily loses track of time, to the point where breaks surpass productive worktime. Collateral damage includes procrastinating, by focusing on immediate tasks, or on those imposed by superiors with a nearing deadline. Meanwhile profound, vital work is neglected. And because the latter tends to coincide with higher cognitive requirements, setting it aside leads year-end performance reviewers to conclude that you are unfit for highly cognitive work. Recall the billiards allegory (Fig. 6.13) for a hint at what might happen when the next reorganization surfaces from the corner.

Steering clear from these dangers can place you above less disciplined peers. Even a hare with excellent IT skills loses the race to the tortoise when slacking too much on recreational sites and apps.

Instilling discipline is not rocket science. But as some futurists put it: "A tech detox starts with us, and there are no shortcuts."[5] Tuck the phone in a drawer. Turn off notifications, mute friends. Request a separate phone for

---

[3] Shambare et al. (2012): *The invisible addiction: Cell-phone activities and addiction among male and female college students*, https://www.ncbi.nlm.nih.gov/pmc/articles/PMC4291831.

[4] Susie Poppick: *These are the top workplace productivity killers*, CNBC (June 9, 2016), https://www.cnbc.com/2016/06/09/top-distractions-at-work-and-how-to-increase-productivity.html.

[5] Paul Roehrig, Ben Pring: *Monster: A Tough Love Letter on Taming The Machines That Rule Our Jobs, Lives, and Future*, Wiley (2021), p. 115.

work. If you must take smartphone breaks, use a timer. Give yourself a daily target—for instance 20 min. The simple fact of officializing digital breaks can greatly partake in developing an iron discipline.

Favor *physical* breaks: go to the washroom, grab a coffee, engage with others, for instance by walking over to see that colleague you need intel from instead of skyping her. Make this your new "pat on the back", for both work well done and successful resistance to online temptations. Sitting at the office all day has become the great evil of the twenty-first century; doctors are adamant on the need to get up at least once an hour and exercise, be it just to walk around.[6] You will feel refreshed, will not lose focus, and remain competitive.

The Bigger Picture

Clever organization and time management count among the top actions to improve work. At the most rudimentary level, use a To Do list; taking the game a notch further, an Eisenhower Matrix.

The 2×2 Eisenhower Matrix categorizes work according to urgency and importance. From thereon opinions diverge as to how to address each category for optimal management. Figure 8.1 shows our take on the subject; you might sense a vague resemblance with the task bubble chart (Fig. 7.1). For example, urgent tasks of little value comprise troubleshooting problems—when difficult to automate, these are best delegated.

Improving efficiency implies meticulous self-observation and discipline. 17th century English philosopher Thomas Hobbes remarked that "Man is a wolf to man".[7] Think of this not as directed to another person, but as to oneself. And note that the original saying from two thousand years earlier contained a nuance, stating that this is especially the case "when he does not know what he is like".[8] This echoes the "Know thyself" maxim and relates to our above arguments on self-discipline. Understand that the "not urgent, not important" box includes things unrelated to work, such as chatting with friends on WhatsApp, browsing Facebook or AllRecipies.com.

We hinted at how companies are turning the cameras on their staff, at how they are developing metrics to assess office productivity on par with workshops. Why not set these metrics up yourself? Tidy the room before your

---

[6] Cf. Brigid Schulte: *Health experts have figured out how much time you should sit each day*, The Washington Post (June 2, 2015), https://www.washingtonpost.com/news/wonk/wp/2015/06/02/medical-researchers-have-figured-out-how-much-time-is-okay-to-spend-sitting-each-day/.

[7] Thomas Hobbes: De Cive (On the Citizen), (1642)

[8] « Lupus est homo homini, non homo, quom qualis sit non novit », from Titus Maccius Plautus, Asinaria (circa 195 BC)

		Urgent	Not Urgent
Important	**What is it?**	Crisis Situations Approaching deadlines on crucial projects	Achieving the strategy Brainstorming on new opportunities Developing your network
	How to deal with	**Reduce** Via design & organization, land it in the not urgent. Push back on less-organized stakeholders who make last-minute requests	**Schedule** Or you'll never have time for it The bulk of your work should lie here Apply our motto: automate, delegate, or keep if the task implies cognition
Not Important	**What is it?**	Interruptions, phone calls, weighing in on emails not primarily addressed to you	Trivial matters, slacking activities
	How to deal with	**Delegate** If, for lack of seniority, you cannot delegate it, and the task is recurrent, do it but then automate it for next time	**Delete** Learn to say no to these tasks Discipline yourself against slacking and activities unrelated to achieving the corporate mission

Fig. 8.1 An Eisenhower matrix

company snoops in. Akin to iPhone's Screentime app, tools exist to monitor the amount of time spent on each software. Several apps follow the Eisenhower Matrix approach, such as the freely available Priority Matrix (with a more replete version for $150 a year).

For a deeper dive into time management, check the timeless best-seller *The 7 Habits of Highly Effective People*. Habit number three, or "put first things first", brilliantly exploits the Eisenhower Matrix. Author Stephen Covey outlines the process as one where:

1. priorities are defined based on what matters: the corporate vision, mission and strategy,
2. work is designed and organized around those priorities, and
3. discipline prevails to ensure their achievement

While many people believe that they stagger in step number three, Covey argues that their real issue comes from not properly executing the first two steps.[9]

Stripping it down to its bare bones, in their book *The ONE Thing*, Gary Keller and Jay Papasan frame this line of thought as "What's the one thing

---

[9] Stephen R. Covey: The 7 Habits of Highly Effective People, Free Press (1989).

I can do such that by doing it, everything else will be easier and unnecessary?" They argue that wisely applying this mantra can help you both solve the current issues at hand and remain in synch with the bigger picture.[10]

We merely skimmed through several aspects of efficiency. Much more could be written on the topic.

A last example: we've seen how AI and IT are invading the brain's turf, whether by performing increasingly basic calculations or writing our essays for us. In the Information Age, the brain is your most important muscle. Do not let it sink into numbness. For instance, every once in a while you can take a pen and paper to jot down random series of figures with operators, then perform the calculations without the aid of any device (except later, to review your results). Such little cerebral workouts can also substitute for phone breaks; they contribute to keep your mind sharpened.

Readers are invited to maintain a list of human tasks that are here to stay, then set milestones to improve in each one. Read materials to that purpose, for instance on mental calculation techniques, mnemotechnic tips, and other street-smart tricks to improve thinking and memory.

8.2   Learning Curve

In *The 100 Year Life: Living and Working in an Age of Longevity*, authors Andrew Scott and Lynda Gratton argue that by accounting for progress, we can assume one out of two newborns will live up to 100 years old. They then delve into the ramifications, emphasizing in particular the role of continuous learning to secure a decent life in the later years.[11] Longevity aside, this should come as no surprise given the impacts of acceleration, user-friendliness, and democratization trends.

People tend to rely on the system for their education, leading their learning curve to plateau after school graduation. This type of assumption will not fare well in the twenty-first-century job market. As yesteryear's skills lose relevance, it behooves employees to adapt, via regular training. Make the old saying your mantra: you are solely responsible for your education.

Choose your poison carefully. Time is a luxury. Consider not only on what will aid you in your career, but what is bound to remain relevant in the AI age. This applies especially for the more junior readers, who for instance could

---

[10] Gary Keller, Jay Papasan: *The ONE Thing: The Surprisingly Simple Truth About Extraordinary Results*, Bard Press (2013), p. 122.
[11] Lynda Gratton, Andrew J. Scott: *The 100 Year Life: Living and Working in an Age of Longevity*, Bloomsbury Information (2016).

seek to gain of inkling of statistics, meanwhile eschewing pattern-recognition-based expertise.

Seeking Inspiration

Explore beyond your company perimeter towards other organizations, especially leaders in:

– your sector: e.g. in manufacturing, turn to Toyota (LEAN) or Tesla,
– your function: in finance, look at Big 4 audit firms and top banks,
– tech disruptors attacking your turf (both sector and function), whether Big Tech or startups.

Read up on these companies, especially when their weapon of disruption is a swifter process (rather than a revolutionary product). Magazines like the *Harvard Business Review* provide a well of inspiration, replete with top-notch cases, proven methods, and comprehensive research. Seek for tips actionable in your company in such a way that both you and your firm benefit, whether through better processes, a reorganization, or metrics that address and measure a key issue left ignored until then.

Ideas and best practices can emerge from unexpected fields, there where top performers achieve excellency. The Great Ormond Street Hospital's emergency section improved their handling of patients in critical condition by observing the speed and organization displayed by Ferrari's Formula One team at work in the pit during races, spawning a successful collaboration between teams from industries miles apart.[12]

Look Towards the Top… and Their Schools

One clue to deciphering future jobs in demand comes from observing current top management duties and responsibilities.

Up to the first half of the twentieth century, the accounting profession was quasi-inexistent. Then needs for clarity on taxable income and stakeholder transparency (investors, banks, suppliers, customers, even employees) birthed ever more stringent regulations, spurring demand for financial expertise. So who was assuming the functions of accountant, cost controller, and

---

[12] Shane Snow: *Smartcuts: The Breakthrough Power of Lateral Thinking*, Harper Business (2014), chapter 2. Also Ken R. Catchpole, Marc R. De Leval, Angus McEwan, Nick Pigott, Martin J. Elliott, Annette McQuillan, Carol Macdonald and Allan J. Goldman: *Patient Handover Using Formula 1 Pit-Stop and Aviation Models to Improve Safety and Quality*, Pediatric Anesthesia, 17 (2007): 470–78.

chief financial officer before these terms were coined? The big boss (and often his spouse). The same goes for strategic marketing, public relations, and more.

Business guru Peter Drucker once referred to management as "areas of organized ignorance"[13] (he contributed more than anyone to lift that veil). In small firms the boss still handles these tasks (or neglects them), but the larger they get, the greater the division of labor. With time, these tasks trickle down from the jack-of-all-trades manager towards employees that become specialized, filling the molds for new occupations that land on the Bureau of Labor Statistics' list. Once the apanage of management, they are lifted from art to science and stripped from the boss so that investors' money no longer relies on some alpha's gut instinct.

By eavesdropping on the top brass and getting familiar with their concepts and concerns, one can foresee the type of responsibilities bound to branch out and form the sprouts of tomorrow's jobs. Beyond gleaning over online job descriptions, peruse the curriculums of the world's elite engineering and business schools, the Ivy Leagues and MBAs that top the Economist and Financial Times's rankings. Universities might lag in terms of new areas of value, including skills related to automation[14], but elite business schools lie at the cutting edge of future thinking, thus present excellent sniffing grounds for future skills in demand.

How have their contents evolved today versus a generation ago? New themes may include cross-cultural management, data science, probabilities and statistics, organizational behavior, risk management, crisis management, brand reputation, storytelling, CSR and ESG and other fancy names that mandate a peek at the introduction (or ChatGPT query) to translate into plain English. Meanwhile the more traditional courses morph to integrate new thinking: the ecommerce classes of the 1990s have spawned several offspring, like SEO, harnessing public and private traffic, digital media and branding, or how to succeed as a KOL. And who would have predicted for marketing classes to use R and Python?

Top schools are pricey; money aside, candidates must fulfill certain conditions to qualify. But glimpses of their contents are available online. Alternatively, pose under the guise of a potential applicant and reach out to alumni, if such is your leaning. Alumni are usually a tight community, eager to share their experience and mentor others (in part because the schools rightly

[13] Peter Drucker: *Management: Tasks, Responsibilities, Practices*, New York: Harper & Row (1973), p. 5.
[14] Cf. Teboho Pitso: *Shared Futures: An Exploration of the Collaborative Potential of Intelligent Machines and Human Ingenuity in Cocreating Value*, InTechOpen (2019).

emphasize the benefits of helping others grow). Much of the schools' teachings can be gleaned in books written by eminent scholars. Soak up on the seminal works of Porter, Drucker and others.

Let us take this opportunity for a digression. Polishing your look, vocabulary, and knowledge, how you present and express yourself can greatly help both in work and in life. Human beings self-organize into clusters, each one evolving its feathers to distinguish and spot members of their tribe. Though dressing sharp certainly matters, the point is not to splurge on fancy clothes or unaffordable watches—a right cut and polished shoes usually suffice. Culture and behavior partake in the plumage of higher society at least as much as wealth appurtenances. A great deal can be done by ingesting the ethos, mastering the jargon, learning the memes, mimicking movies, and devouring magazines relating to their concerns in bookstores that tolerate indoor reading.

We are judged by others in the first few seconds of an encounter based on demeanor and parlance. France is no exception, as I got to learn the hard way. Thanks to teenage time spent in the wrong side of the neighborhood, I had developed the accent most despised by the elites. While this boosted survival odds in my living environment, it did not help when seeking for my first long-term internship: the moment I opened my mouth, the interview was over. An invisible barrier made me one of "them". It took no less than thirty failed interviews to land that first... internship. It took an even greater effort to unlearn the accent. Those subject to -isms at work (racism, ageism, sexism…) have no choice but to double-down in order to dispel the tenacious stereotypes that apply to them.

Gather Intel

It is paramount to remain vigilant both to what is happening in your field of activity, and to new technology. These constitute the two vantage points from which to monitor movement.

– On the business end

Watch neighboring companies taking action to veer the ship towards future technologies. How have they evolved in the past five to ten years? How are they leveraging digital tech, both internally (in their processes) and externally (how do they expand their business with data)? What new tech are they incorporating into product launches? What strategy underpins these choices? Or are these mere fist swings in the dark, a display of resource scattering?

- On the technology end

Look out for tech players showing interest in your sector, dipping their toes here and there or leading what amounts to a more serious incursion. Be sure to cover both ends of the spectrum, too: startups sprawling with stated goals aimed at (disrupting) your activities, regardless of how presumptuous they may sound; and Big Tech.

Both types are a potential source of disruption to your company, sector or occupation, thus can also be viewed as a source of inspiration. Hereafter a shortlist of sources to gather intel from, under the two angles:

- Books and professional magazines

When seeking for books, favor those that address both new technologies and your field of activity. The book *Deep Medicine* by Eric Topol deals with the revolution taking place in healthcare; Brett King's books on the future of banking are another prime example. Bear in mind though that books tend to lag behind the latest research in the field: by the time they are published, the information they contain has already aged (and that holds true for this book, too). Hence the importance of consulting reports and articles in magazines to stay up to date with the latest developments. Subscribe to newsletters, consult reviews and articles at the crossroads between new tech and business, or related to your sector in tech magazines like *Wired* or *Inc.*

- Exhibitions

Attend exhibitions in your field to gather what new technologies are being deployed—not just the flashy gimmicks vaunted by competitors, but those from suppliers that could change the game for your processes, or of clients that might reveal a new need. Keep an eye on gadgets with implications in your sector at main tech exhibitions, like the Consumer Electronics Show held annually in Las Vegas. These generate a lot of press, providing insights even without the possibility of physical attendance.

- The Internet

Companies in the industry, magazines, product reviews, research papers, forums—the sky is the limit as everyone now has a digital presence. Find answers on Stack Overflow. Follow tech gurus, futurists and social mavens on websites like LinkedIn and TechCrunch; some specialize in the vulgarization of otherwise arcane concepts, provide insights and book recommendations. Deepen your knowledge while diversifying sources between the sensationalism-chasing tabloids and more serious, albeit abstruse publications from and for academics. As with all news, reaching an objective comprehension requires inputs from diverse horizons.

Check annual or quarterly reports from major businesses in your field and in the tech industry. These are easy to google and download. See how their financials have evolved; squint through letters to shareholders for relevant insights into both their business and how they see the near future.[15]

This exercise takes time; but making it a habit elevates your wisdom level, putting you on par with top managers in terms of knowledge of what is happening in the world. In life I encounter many employees driven by a burning desire to succeed, who display remarkable tenacity to get the job done. However, they seem totally oblivious to an important element in the eyes of top execs. When they talk and share ideas, especially in a casual, out-of-work context, what often rubs off is narrow cultural literacy and intellectual breadth. Take two workers who equally excel at achieving their tasks. One cannot host a quality conversation with the top brass, while the other possesses a breadth of knowledge and cultural awareness that stimulates the minds of listeners, elevating her to a respected fencing partner for debate or to glean ideas from. Developing this cultural luggage can make a substantial difference to a career.

– People

Mingle with those in the business. Devise ways to connect with and make yourself of interest to them. Banter with your R&D, bounce off ideas with customers to see whether these spark any interest. Talk with techies whenever you get a chance. Query them as to how tech might take on your occupation or industry.

As you get immersed in new technologies and gain awareness of the wild things under development, you might notice how easy it is to get the conversation flowing. The field is abuzz with energy, full of enthusiasts both passionate and open to debate on technology's implications (as long as their interlocutor is not a neo-Luddite whose stubbornness is matched only by an ignorance of technology). They may also be on the lookout for the next big game-changer, and appreciate the chance to exchange with someone in the know. Or simply they understand (possibly even fear) technology's ramifications and seek insights. Keep notes on all incoming intel.

---

[15] A compilation of Jeff Bezos' annual letters to shareholders has even been published in a book. Cf. *Invent and Wander: The Collected Writings of Jeff Bezos, with an Introduction by Walter Isaacson*, Harvard Business Review (2020).

Receive each tidbit with a pinch of salt. Place it in context. Who is talking? Under what circumstances? What is their track record? People seeking backers to invest in a project may lack objectivity. When a given technology spurs overhype, you will hear stock recommendations from drivers and hairdressers blabbing as if they were born in it; see tech events swarm with crypto advocates on the verge of an ICO, half of which by the next event will have reconverted into ardent NFT proselytes. AI enthusiasts spread the gospel to reporters only too eager to propagate and amplify anything that can sell. Best do your homework; gather different opinions to forge your own. Crosscheck with players in the field to see what they make of it. Question relentlessly and learn to read between the lines. In the footsteps of Confucius, humbly acknowledge your ignorance.

That goes for this book, too. Take our smart fridge egg replenishment example from the Tech chapter—did it leave you dubious upon lecture? Why eggs in particular? It just so happens that this parable is parroted by every other rag mag marveling about smart homes. As if, apart from being perishable, eggs were the only imaginable food consumed by a broad public *on a regular basis*, something the fridge should never be short of. But this only concerns eggs (if even—vegans would disapprove). No one desires to eat the same dish at every meal. We enjoy variety yet cannot keep stock of everything. Without the ability to read our minds, the smart fridge concept may have limited appeal.

Or consider the rehashed promise of smart homes to be able to detect the presence of occupants in a room, recognize them and adjust the temperature according to their preference. Dazzling. But are there really such wide gaps in our appreciation of room temperature as to justify the cost for this? How should the system respond if people with different preferences occupy the same room? Oh, and who wants to be seen and recognized in their home? Likewise, does it sound plausible for people to install smart mirrors embedded with sensors and cameras in the most intimate part of their home, namely the bathroom?

Pay attention to timing, too. *Science* and *Nature* cover the cutting edge. While only serious breakthroughs make it to these prestigious magazines, their time to hit the market is often measured in years if not decades (or never). Meanwhile tabloids feed on these articles, concocting an astounding story and referencing the original so as to provide a seal of proof, only to amplify the technology as if it were ripe for tomorrow. In another tactic, they carefully pluck an eccentric scientist for an interview, presenting him as the apostle. These sources pursue the sensational to make a quick buck. Take the pains to crosscheck facts: read the original referenced article, and look up quoted scientists.

Staying in the know brings multiple benefits. It sharpens your awareness of new tech and potential encroachments through the four doors of disruption. More generally, it facilitates the exercises in this book: assessing for sectorial disruption risks, the job vulnerability canvass, where and how to automate tasks yourself… It lays communication bridges with those working on technology, creating a virtuous spiral as you then gain insights from those circles. Alas, as already mentioned, such knowledge is increasingly sought by organizations, hence it adds stripes to your blazer.

Learning via Internet

The ICT has revolutionized our access to knowledge. Colleges from Harvard to MIT and Stanford now offer Massive Open Online Courses. Websites that provide a more or less heuristic learning approach include Codecademy, Udacity, fast.ai, Khan Academy, and Coursera. Not all are free, but costs are usually reasonable.

Founded by Andrew Ng and Daphne Koller, Coursera offers courses stretching beyond software and coding to practically any conceivable field. KDnuggets, a discussion forum on data science and analytics, provides all kinds of "how to" tips. Kaggle is a free online community of data scientists, replete with tutorials and datasets to train on, starting with survival stats on the 2,240 passengers onboard the Titanic (a classic ML case for newbies). It includes a Jupyter notebook environment to hone programming skills—and competitions. Organizations can post challenges on Kaggle, with a monetary reward for the winner. One example calls for the use of TensorFlow to

> detect crown-of-thorns starfish in underwater image data: the goal of this competition is to accurately identify starfish in real-time by building an object detection model trained on underwater videos of coral reefs. Your work will help researchers identify species that are threatening Australia's Great Barrier Reef and take well-informed action to protect the reef for future generations.

As if that were not motivation enough, the winner pockets $150,000.[16]

Do not let these challenges deter you; the website is suitable for beginners. 66% of Kaggle users describe themselves as self-taught. Over half claim having learned online.[17]

But perhaps the best way to start is via a mix of Google, Wikipedia, ChatGPT (or some other bot), and YouTube tutorials. Combine these tools

---

[16] https://www.kaggle.com/c/tensorflow-great-barrier-reef.

[17] Richard Waters: *How machine learning creates new professions—and problems*, Financial Times (November 29, 2017), https://www.ft.com/content/49e81ebe-cbc3-11e7-8536-d321d0d897a3.

to grasp the contours of what you *should* learn, based on your current position and situation: to survey available tools, get an inkling of the concepts, such as the difference between an object and a class, or between a package, user interface and library. It will spare you time, as opposed to diving head-first into a potentially fastidious endeavor with little relevance to your work.

8.3   Leveraging Automation Tools

Step by Step

From learning to type on a QWERTY to training artificial neural networks, the range of tools at an individual's disposal has increased phenomenally since the birth of computers. We must not lose our heads as to where to begin.

A sound strategy would be to move upward in the following sequence:

(1) fast-type on a keyboard
(2) the two-to-three tools most called upon in your line of work; usually emailing, perhaps a part of the Microsoft Office or Google Suite package
(3) other software pertaining more to your specialty: Adobe Photoshop or Illustrator for a designer, Dreamweaver for a web designer, Trello, Microsoft or Teamwork Projects for a project manager; SankeyMATIC or Lucid Chart to build diagram visuals, business intelligence tools for analysis; make sure these are:

- Relevant to your job
- Available in your organization, or open source
- For collaborative work: that others possess a minimum knowledge of the tool

(4) Programming (top-down, Good Old-Fashion AI)
(5) Machine Learning

Start with small, simple things. Then advance incrementally. When moving to the next step, ensure it will enhance efficiency beyond the previous one.

Plan Your Tool Learning

Keep a list of the various tools in your arsenal, your level of expertise in each, which ones require more digging into, and a bit of polishing here and there to prevent dust and rust. Where and how do you apply them so far? How beneficial has each one proved in your work, and what more can you expect to achieve by further unlocking the vaults to their secrets?

You basically have two ways to improve your arsenal:

- Horizontally, by adding more weapons to it,
- Vertically, by deepening expertise of the weapons you already have some knowledge of.

Imagine you have inherited a stretch of land reputed to conceal precious resources. Upon arrival, tour the site thoroughly, taking good measure of sections already drilled, to what depths, the deposits uncovered, and the amount of profit streams derived.

Based on this preliminary knowledge of the topography, you can formulate your tool learning plan. Burrow existing tunnels deeper, or explore virgin land parcels in a gamble for new bounty (applications useful to your line of work). Take note of the composition of sediments in different parts of the estate: some may turn out more difficult to drill in than others. You can gain more in a shorter timeframe by digging into limestone than through denser materials (like coding). As easily accessible deposits are depleted, aim for costlier ones. The whole enterprise naturally comprises a dose of luck. As your career evolves, minerals which up to then appeared worthless become of value, prompting you to resume drilling in a previously abandoned quarry.

Not all tools are created equal: Smartsheet, Microsoft Word or LucidChart offer comparatively less depth than Python, Photoshop or even Excel. To stick with Office software, a seasoned Excel user can achieve far greater efficiency than a novice in comparison to what a Word expert could do versus that same novice (assuming both typewrite at similar speeds). Ditto for broadness: Python goes deeper beneath the surface than does Scratch (no pun intended).

Keep your list of IT skills to improve dynamic. View it not as a dull diary of progress, but rather a battle plan. Set goals and subgoals as to where you want to be within a year, a quarter; organize time for research and experimentation. Stick to the plan with the iron discipline of a student learning any other craft, or rather, with more resolve than that (you won't lose your job for giving up on piano lessons). While learning is more accessible, that does not mean it has become easier; it still requires effort and discipline. Of course, goalposts can be adjusted, for instance to make room for a software your company just implemented.

Organize learning time proportionately with that spent (or that should be spent) on each tool. For those tasks on which you spend the bulk of your time, keyboard shortcuts are a no-brainer. Remember that the more structured the task, with little space for VUCA, the easier to automate via GOFAI.

As when walking on the beach into the sea, IT tools can take a sudden, steep veer towards the obscure; refrain from rushing or you might lose your foothold. Do not get lured by book titles that promise to automate everything via Python or other software. If you have never touched code and your statistical knowledge is buried under a thick layer of rust, signing up for MIT's MOOC on machine learning is a certain recipe for failure and frustration.

It makes little sense to learn a coding language like Python or Java with the aim of automating a recurrent task 100% when it could be automated at 80% via benign Excel formulas within grasp. Consider the time to learn coding and the return on time invested, compared to a task that, by setting up a process with a structured spreadsheet, now takes ten minutes per week instead of an hour. Overreaching can cause more harm than good. The effort will be tedious, you will face frequent bugs and fail to comprehend half of what you are doing. Troubleshooting glitches rapidly eclipses any supposed time gains, and blind perseverance is no guarantee of success: at best you may wind up pointing a shiny bazooka to take out a mosquito.

Rather than taking blind swings in the hope of hitting useful skills, focus on the tasks at hand. We saw examples of automation via Excel. Granted, its programming corollary Visual Basic (the thing that makes macros), as a top-down approach will not catapult you into the universe of machine learning; yet it can mark the first baby step towards object-oriented programming (OOP).

Playing with the Sequence

The five learning steps laid above should not be taken unequivocally. Backtrack every once in a while to check out new "basic things" rolled out, courtesy of the user-friendly trait, and include these in your tool bag.

Suppose you frequently automate tasks via code. Suddenly, Microsoft adds the Dictate option in Word.[18] This requires no coding knowledge: simply press the Windows logo key + H and like a scribe, Word takes note of oral speech. It adds a chance to automate more task bits: instant digitization of meetings, interviews, phone calls, and other oral communication. Think of the substantial part of a doctor's time spent with patients, diverted by the computer screen on which she is required to take notes and fill in fields,

---

[18] The exact launch date varies as it was first launched in "soft-opening" in 2018, then expanded in 2020. For now, it is only available in the Office 365 pack.

meanwhile leaving the patient desperately craving for eye contact, just a dose of humanity to hang onto. Would the doctor capable of focusing on her patient, intently leaning forward and maintaining eye contact throughout the consultation, not rake in higher loyalty and repeat visits?

Experiment with these new feats. Tinker for hacks, and perform tests. How could such a feature apply to your work, which tasks might it address, and how much time savings does it enable? Such are the questions that smart workers ponder as they devote time exploring new tools, from Word's Dictate option to the latest Power BI features and ChatGPT plugins. You should do likewise.

The tool may be far from perfect. To stick with the dictation example, you soon realize that humans do much more than dumbly transcribe words: the brain sieves through oral data and synthesizes it in its own words, capturing key points. For the automated version to at least equal the human one implies formatting the discussion upfront to ensure concision and eradicate background noise. This underscores the need to control the ambient environment—the asphalt road that blocks the pesky VUCA weeds from sprouting.

Each step can be further broken in detail. In coding, you could split learning of vocabulary and grammar (including punctuation) from more general concepts like loops or Boolean logic, objects, methods, and properties. Once you grasp the concepts, the bulk of code need not be written from scratch but can come as snippets picked online, or from previous code you wrote, copy/pasted, and adapted to your new program.

Machine Learning: The Final Frontier?

We listed machine learning (ML) in last. Many of us may have no justifiable imperative to learn ML, or a full plate of other tools to catch up on first. Bear in mind that while ML is making strides in fields from prediction to pattern recognition, admittedly receiving all the media attention, much of task automation does not require the bottom-up approach. The recurrent part of work is usually automatable via rules-based coding (top-down approach). Meaning that in many instances GOFAI trumps ML in terms of threat to your work—or opportunity to automate it yourself. Nor would ML prove more apt at solving issues whence the program stumbles onto a VUCA-infested minefield.

Yet just as your tasks should be tested for their resilience to GOFAI, so should they pass an ML test. Prudence warrants vigilance wherever AI shows signs of improvement. In either case, ask yourself the following:

– Is AI starting to encroach on my field? Rephrased using our 2×2 matrix to ensure full coverage: "Is AI encroaching on my sector, my company, my work, or any of the tasks I handle?"
– What is my firm currently deploying in this regard, and how does that reframe the 2×2 matrix assessment? (typically, a company "on top of things" pushes the needle from sectorial or corporate disruption threats towards job automation threats)
– How much time do I have?
– Are the tabs I have in place to track its progress sufficient?
– What new programs, versions, user interfaces (UI), integrated development environments (IDE), no-code AI, and other novelties are surfacing that could contribute to simplify the use of ML, bringing it in reach of my knowledge scope?

Figure 8.2 juxtaposes the decreasing AI complexity trend with your growing expertise; while the figure depicts AI, the concept can be generalized to any IT tool.

The decrease in complexity follows the user-friendly trend (cf. Democratization and User-Friendly). Abrupt inflection points of AI complexity may correspond to a new patch or software update, UI, or the growing number of low-code and no-code AI platforms: Obviously.ai focused on prediction models, Akkio that provides data in tabular format, Lobe.ai for image recognition (acquired by Microsoft in 2018), Baidu's EasyDL… ChatGPT and its successors form the most salient case of recent

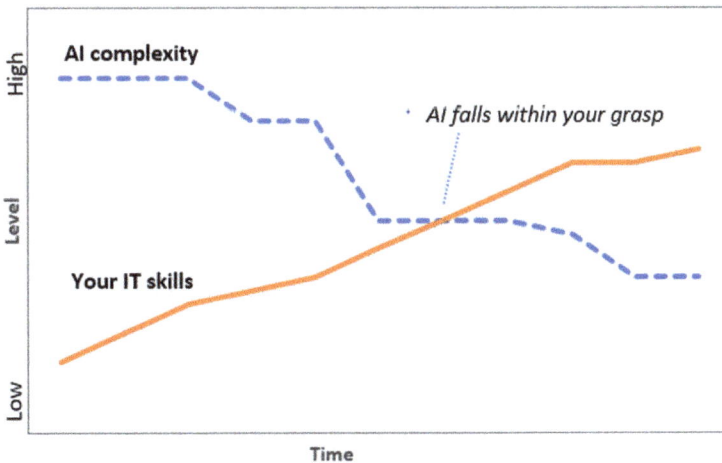

Fig. 8.2 AI complexity versus skills level

times: a chatbot that can obtain information, debate, write essays and code in any language makes for a powerful ally.

As these advances lift the mist of coding complexity, AI's true enemies appear. Due to the black box phenomenon, it is not possible to "peer under the hood". ML provides no explanation on output. Toying with it calls for basic knowledge of the models utilized, from standard vectors to genetic algorithms, Karger–Stein and Monte-Carlo algorithms. How each functions, with comparative advantages and shortcomings. It demands a solid background in statistics and probabilities. Insufficient data, poor prior data cleaning, overfitting, and bias within the training data represent but a handful of the issues that plague the field. The danger with ML lies less in the inability to produce results as to setting the knobs right to prevent rubbish output—as in the tank-detection algorithm that ticks for clouds. That flaw was blatant; the problem will not always lend itself to such easy discovery. The sorcerer's apprentice who blithely ignores these forewarnings while boasting of leveraging ML will run afoul of sharp reefs. Making decisions based on a slanted output can have dire consequences, including, ultimately, for the brazen initiator's job. Correct use of ML takes practice and training, both for the user and the algorithm, both costly and time-consuming. In short, it quickly amounts to a full-time job.

Time permitting, follow two separate paths: a hands-on approach to learn how to deal with the more immediate tasks at hand, accompanied by an itch to broaden your horizon of what is going on in AI. The former is a practical approach, the latter one of theoretical knowledge; one day both ends may meet.

If you believe ML can contribute to efficiency in your line of work, ensure you have the previous bases at least partially covered (the basics, professional software, and rules-based programming). Again, forlorn attempts to shoot for ML while being hamstrung at work by a lack of more basic tool knowledge will put you behind your peers. By focusing instead on fine-tuning and broadening existing skills, all the while observing the ML branch descend evermore within grasp, in time you just might be able to reap its fruit before others beat you to the punch.

Remember that you are in an open competition, as the rarefication of "lovely jobs" pits you against peers. We plot the ideal course by adding this nuance in Fig. 8.3.

While starting from a similar standpoint, here the active pursuit of IT skills catapults you above peers, ensuring you master automation tools first. Colleague A also strives to learn; the most logical step would be for her to in due time fall under your supervision, given her potential—assuming there is a need for a second employee (usually firms favor a backup, for contingency

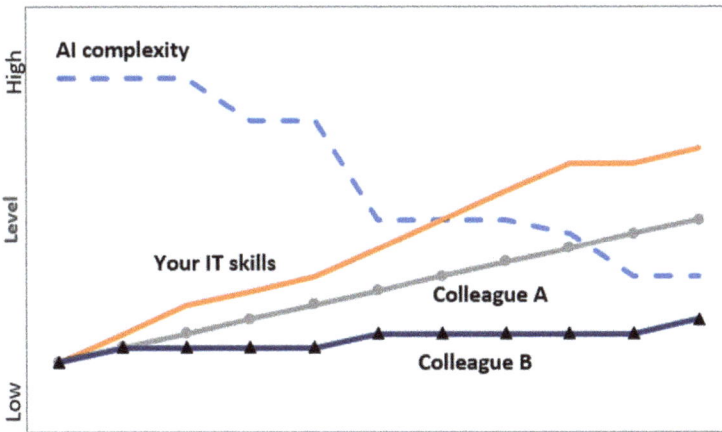

Fig. 8.3 Your skills versus peers

purposes). Colleague B will likely bite the dust, another victim of automation. Do not panic if others in the company have a head-start; set sail in the right direction. Failure to act will put you in colleague A or B's shoes.

Remember that it is the blend of expertise that counts. Fresh graduates may arrive with programming proficiency, but with no knowledge of, well, work. As a data scientist once told me, laymen will learn AI faster than AI experts will learn all other jobs.

Exploiting Tools to Their Advantage

Mastery of IT tools involves more than coding and keyboard shortcuts. It includes leveraging the tools wherever they can exceed our human capabilities. Acknowledge where they surpass us and where they do not (yet). Harness that power, for instance to discern patterns there where we see only a cacophony of data.

Old school managers make decisions based on "gut" instinct, something hard to describe but that rests on a lifetime of experience. While it may suffice for decisions of little relevance, this "I got a hunch" of the type portrayed by Malcolm Gladwell in *Blink* will not convince shareholders when investments turn sour. Christine Lagarde, Janet Yellen, and other smart leaders time and again emphasize this reliance on data to make informed decisions. Books like futurist Mike Walsh's *The Algorithmic Leader: How to Be Smart When Machines Are Smarter Than You* do not purport to teach coding, but rather how to develop the digital mojo in your company and reap the benefits.

Optimizing human–machine collaboration requires more than a software license. Your organization needs the structure in place to collect, store and analyze data, along with a shift in mindset towards Big Data and ML. Think of it as a replay of the must-have internet presence from two decades earlier. Persuading your organization to take steps in this direction grows evermore into duty as you climb the managerial ladder.

Example: Excel and Data Analysis

Suppose you need to polish your repertoire of data analysis skills. Why not begin with Excel?

Microsoft Office, the popularity of which has surpassed even the wildest dreams of its creators, is a plain illustration of the human–machine collaboration. For what is Office but a bundle of collaborative tools, and the worldwide undisputed leader at that? Those who shine in its mastery possess an incredible advantage within practically any organization. This holds especially true for Excel, for several reasons.

First, of the classic Office triad (shared with Word and PowerPoint), Excel has the most depth. Oftentimes, several methods coexist to reach a given goal. While they produce the same result, the most basic could take hours, versus seconds for the more advanced, allowing experts to leap past less skilled peers.

Ubiquity comes next. Excel is the software for data manipulation *per excellence*. Not the most sophisticated or devoid of flaws (far from it), but the only one with north of a billion users worldwide (roughly a third of humanity's workforce!). Few office jobs can forgo Excel skills. Call it a consequence of our increased leaning on data for decision-making. Data circulates in the troves in organizations, on Excel. Despite years of ERPs and business analytics tools assaulting its turf, Excel has held firm—workers often end up transferring data to Excel for analysis. Analytical skills are gaining traction in a wide array of jobs, and that rings true even as one climbs the rungs, adding on tasks like P&L responsibility. One windfall lies in the abundant online forums and tutorials, that make learning on one's own relatively easy.

Some readers may scoff at Excel's limited capabilities. Actuaries and data scientists work with huge troves of data sets, covering many traits (p, equivalent to Excel's columns), with massive sample sizes (n, or Excel's rows). While Excel has increased the size of a sheet from the previous 65,000 odd rows and 256 columns, to above a million rows and sixteen thousand columns, in reality this exceeds the calculating prowess of most computers, considerably slowing down performance.[19] To analyze Big Data, the gold medal goes to Python and R.

---

[19] For an illustration, open an Excel worksheet and press Ctrl + A, 1 and Ctrl + Enter. This simple manipulation (typing "1" in 17 billion cells) is likely to crash your computer.

Excel pyramid: Proficiency

Level	
5	Macros / Statistics / Get & Transform / Add-ons / What if analysis
4	Navigational shortcuts / Text functions / Indirect / Index / Matrix formulas / templates
3	Basic shortcuts / Pivot Table / Vlookup / Sumifs / Boolean functions / Formula auditing / data validation
2	Sort & Filter / Charts / If / Paste Special
1	Basic Math / Navigation / change Font / Print / 1 parameter functions (sum, average) / Cut & Copy / Paste

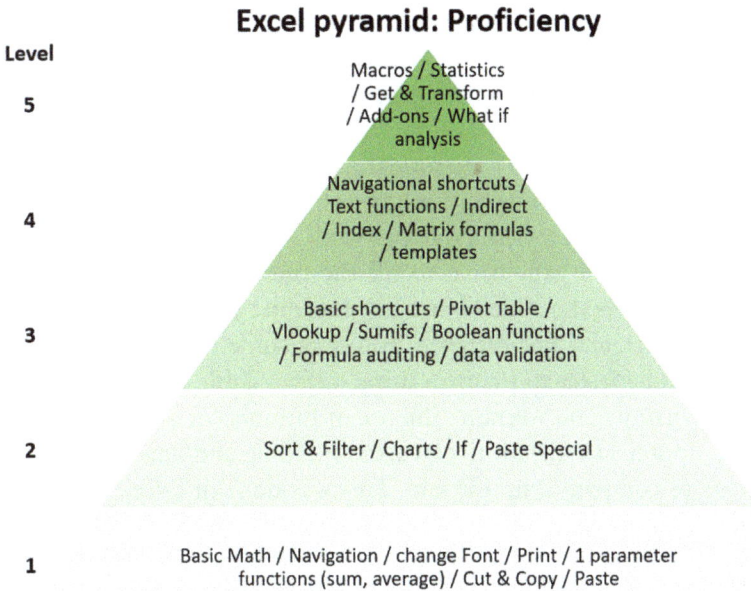

Fig. 8.4 Excel proficiency

Notwithstanding, Excel is a good steppingstone towards programming. Its cell formulas and built-in functions are nothing else but code. Learning them preps the user for concepts such as conditional statements and Boolean logic. The Excel macro recorder creates Visual Basic for Applications code on the fly, allowing non-programmers to tip their toes in the water by creating and visualizing code. While VBA's tentacles do not extend as far as Python, they cover most of the Windows Office ecosystem, including Outlook and Teams. And then comes the user-friendly Windows Task Scheduler, for scheduling macros to run at specific intervals.

Alas, Excel's trademark two-dimensional organization of data in a list constitutes an intuitive database format. As a *Wired* editor noted,

> The user interface—columns and rows—is part of our cognitive canon, and decades of use have trained us in what tech writer Steven Levy neatly dubbed "A Spreadsheet Way of Knowledge" back in 1984.[20]

So how good are your Excel skills? Where would you see yourself in Fig. 8.4?

---

[20] Clive Thompson: *The New Spreadsheet Revolution*, Wired Magazine (June 2022), p. 22–23.

Next, how much time per week do you spend on average on Excel? (Fig. 8.5).

Merging these pyramids can unveil gaps in proficiency (Fig. 8.6).

Suppose you spend 20 h per week on Excel (= Level 4), yet toy with the mouse, master less than a dozen functions and even fewer keyboards shortcuts (= Level 2); with some training you might achieve an efficiency rate in the ballpark of 30%, saving over half a day per week.

Should you identify a gap, strive to fill the breach. This will spare you time in the long run, as the added knowledge enables you to automate work and/or improve efficiency. For instance, you may come to realize that an ad hoc analysis could be faster to perform using a Pivot Table, while a recurrent one based on dynamic data warrants the use of formulas or an Excel Table.

My first computer internship involved the building and analysis of financial statements of companies up for sale. This was done in Excel, of which I then had limited knowledge. The never-ending cycles of repetitive checks and corrections, still invariably leading to incomprehensible errors, were excruciating. The system drove me nuts. Each evening I would return home feeling lobotomized by the grunt ant work, eyes red and sore from what at the time was not the limpid flat screens of today. Within a month I was fired, the boss berating that I must have been on some kind of drug. An astute remark—I

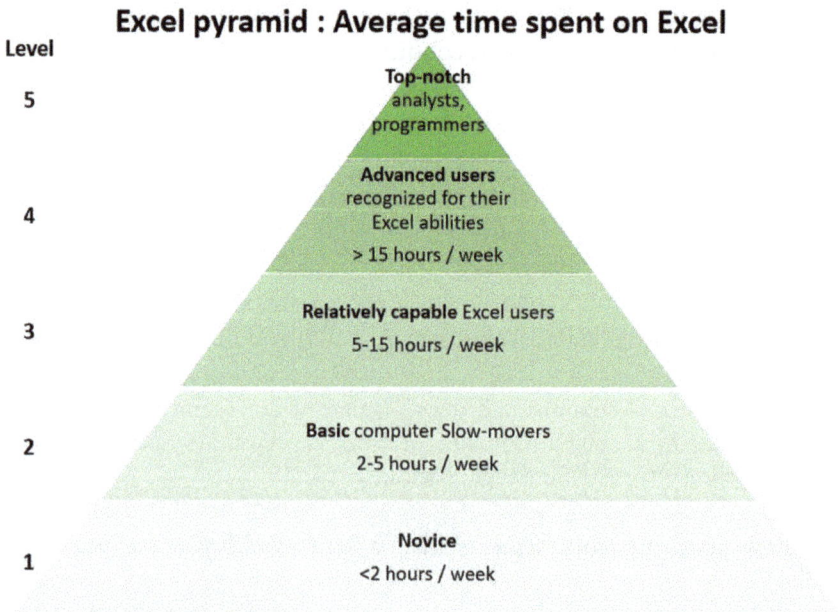

Excel pyramid : Average time spent on Excel

Level

5 — Top-notch analysts, programmers

4 — Advanced users recognized for their Excel abilities
> 15 hours / week

3 — Relatively capable Excel users
5-15 hours / week

2 — Basic computer Slow-movers
2-5 hours / week

1 — Novice
<2 hours / week

Fig. 8.5 Time spent on Excel

Excel pyramid : where do you stand?

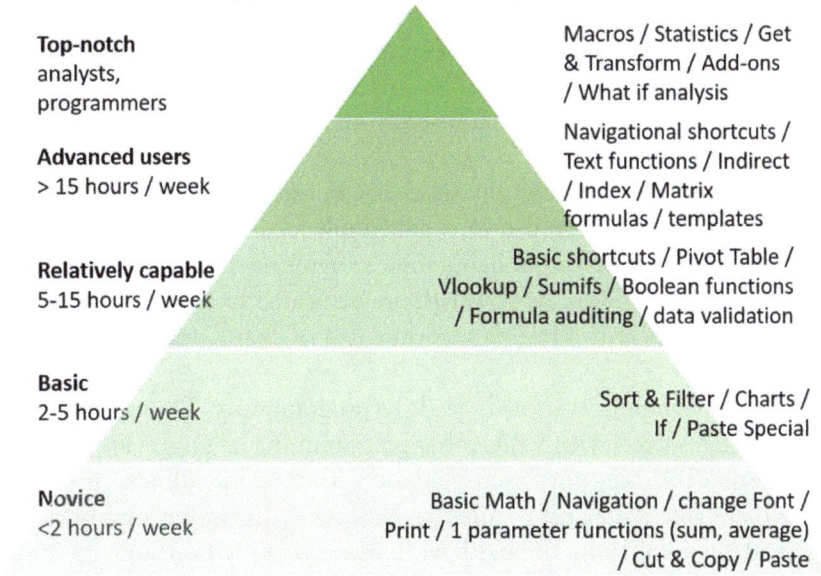

Top-notch analysts, programmers	Macros / Statistics / Get & Transform / Add-ons / What if analysis
Advanced users > 15 hours / week	Navigational shortcuts / Text functions / Indirect / Index / Matrix formulas / templates
Relatively capable 5-15 hours / week	Basic shortcuts / Pivot Table / Vlookup / Sumifs / Boolean functions / Formula auditing / data validation
Basic 2-5 hours / week	Sort & Filter / Charts / If / Paste Special
Novice <2 hours / week	Basic Math / Navigation / change Font / Print / 1 parameter functions (sum, average) / Cut & Copy / Paste

Fig. 8.6 Excel proficiency versus time spent on Excel

had suffered an Excel overdose. Yet with time I learned more, even spending weekends at the nearby library devouring Excel books, taking notes, and gradually upping my level. No one today would believe that I had once been fired for lack of Excel skills.

If data analysis represents a sizable chunk of your work, by no means should you limit your scope to Excel. The market is aflush with tools that connoisseurs will swear outperform it. Several circumvent the need for programming, via ergonomic user interfaces. Microsoft is no stranger to the party: its Power Query feature bridges Excel with Power BI (its business intelligence software).

Seek tools available in your company first. If they have yet to appoint one, test different software, then vouch for a promising one by demonstrating the potential gains at the end of the tunnel. If money is an issue, favor free and open-source software, like RapidMiner (that runs on Java—https://rapidm iner.com) or Orange (using Python—https://orange.biolab.si/). For the sake of collaboration, choose a tool likely to win staff adherence. Unearthing a tool eventually shared by all while deepening your own expertise of it beyond others earns you kudos.

Acutely aware of Excel's shortcomings pertaining to versatility and user-friendliness, a new breed of copycats is rushing to fill in the gaps: Rows,

Smartsheet, Spreadsheet.com… They favor compatibility, collaboration, and ease of use, with drop-lists, drag-and-drop for gifs and pdfs into cells, links between files that actually work (as opposed to Excel's nightmarish referenced links, best avoided at all costs), and less need for coding (i.e. formulaic gibber in cells), following the no-code philosophy. In short, they address Excel's pain points.

These alternative tools typically specialize in one of two fields of the Excel fiefdom: those cited in the previous paragraph focus on lists and databases, often with an emphasis on collaborative use; meanwhile business analytics tools like Orange, Tableau or Power BI are dedicated to analysis and production of neat dashboards, offering a cornucopia of charts, visual graphics and drill downs.

Alas, data wrangling eventually leads to programming. Though the Macro recorder bridges Excel with VBA, other programming languages are worthy of exploration. VBA does not exactly radiate with user-friendliness in comparison to IDEs like PyCharm or Jupyter Notebook. In the upcoming decade, fresh graduates will join onboard with fluency of Python and its Pandas library (the reference for data analysis).[21] Its advantages over Excel include the ingestible amount of data, speed, ergonomics, processing power, and clarity (the code is not hidden in cells), along with the ability to read and categorize data, to support various formats such as SQL, and its multitude of libraries that broaden the spectrum of charts and diagrams. Python cascades to machine learning and other fields, making it the rising general-purpose technology–similar to the English language, only for computers. Given its expansion beyond the realm of data, in a generation's time Python could become more ubiquitous than Excel.

With Big Data emerging as a major trend, in our age more than ever, knowledge is power. Just as the (turn of the) twentieth century witnessed the electrification of our surroundings and products, so the twenty-first is poised to see the cognizance of objects. The IoT will marshal an ever-increasing avalanche of data. Who will process it and how? By printing it out and using a ruler to tick patterns discernable to the human eye? Or setting out to learn how to make the best use of silicon alternatives?

We used Excel here as example, but this type of reasoning, along with the pyramidal figures, can be applied to any software that offers depth, be it for computer-aided design (AutoCAD, SolidWorks…), working with sound (Ableton Live, Sound Forge, Audacity…), etc.

---

[21] For one of the best books for Python and Pandas, in fact written by the developer of Pandas, cf. Wes McKinney: *Python for Data Analysis*, O'Reilly (2012).

8.4   Stay Social

How often do you head out to meet people? Is it always the same tight band of friends? Do you occasionally explore beyond your comfort zone? Or are you constantly on the move, stemming towards new horizons?

Children easily make friends, and the school environment facilitates socializing. Then with age, we turn opiniated, curmudgeonly, and increasingly prone to stick to the bandwagon of pals we have journeyed with forever. For many of us, meeting new people can be exhausting. And as we start families, time becomes scarcer.

With the age of retirement retreating like a desert mirage, forging relationships in and out of work matters more than ever. It is the second key takeaway from Lynda Gratton and Andrew Scott's book, *The 100 Year Life*—and just as for continuous learning, one hard to object against.

How to set about with assessing and developing one's network? Is it reserved to those with the oft-praised "people skills"? Hereafter we provide guidelines while debunking some of the myths.

Guanxi

Modern books emphasize the importance of networking and connections as a means to climb the social ladder, join the ranks of the posh elite and get rich. This narrow mindset hampers chances of success; it saps authenticity. This will transpire as you hop from one group to another—people have a flair for these things.

In contrast, *The Diamond Cutter* recounts the true story of a monk who enters Manhattan's business world, in the diamond trade to be precise. The narrator places authenticity as top core value, a beacon that guides him through perils and misfortunes, all the way to the summit.[22] Authenticity is a powerful weapon in the mingling game, one that easily outshines the more superficial elements. But what is authenticity?

To grasp this notion, along with what should be the core motivation for developing networks, let us introduce the Chinese concept of *guanxi* (关系), a term that loosely translates as web of contacts and relationships.

Understanding the background and ramifications of guanxi can help build sturdy networks. No need to be an orientalist; the Far East may have its unique blend of identities and histories, with traits like filial piety, but the basic outlines of guanxi are quite universal, not limited to the adventurer

---

[22] Geshe Michael Roach and Lama Christie McNally: *The Diamond Cutter: The Buddha on Managing Your Business and Your Life*, Harmony Publishing (2009).

intent on forging business relationships with the Chinese. Guanxi casts light on *why* to cultivate relationships in the first place, feeding a more laudable purpose than social ascent.

An important tenet of guanxi relates to favors. When someone receives a favor or service, they are in debt to the person who provides it. This creates a web of informal bonds, with cycles of favors given and received, that range from paying the bill at restaurants, gift-giving, and other trivialities, to more onerous or consequent "favors", which in high circles can veer towards corruption, what Russians call *blat*.

These drifts into the dark notwithstanding, guanxi's roots stretch back to Confucianism, where it partakes in the emphasis on face, social status, and moral obligations within both family and society—elements alive and vibrant in today's China. Not as a means to suit appearances, but in the echo of old Daoist principles which hold that each person has a given place in society relative to others. Discovering one's role kills two birds with one stone, leading to individual fulfillment while contributing to a harmonious and orderly society, no less. This greater good ideal resonates with the Hindu concept of Dharma, where the quest to find one's place in the cosmos is one of the four life aspirations (*Puruṣārtha*).

The tacit bonds forged between people form a major pillar of human organizations. Ancient societies acknowledged this, hence their accentuation of relationships throughout millennia, reflected in social stratification systems with varying degrees of success. The etymological root of religion points to a "bond" (in Latin *religare*), that of dharma, to a "support" (Sanskrit *dhr-*). While several interpretations of these roots can be advanced (for instance the bond between the profane and sacred by way of *imitatio dei*[23]), one could simply conceive of it as stressing the importance of human bonds, period. Without these, one ceases to exist.

And forging bonds is more than just about meeting people; it involves the impression that you leave them with—the invisible seeds you plant, as the Diamond Cutter would put it.

Illustration

So how to go about it? Hereafter two examples of outsiders landed in a big and frightening metropolis awash with ambitious creatures, where fortunes are built and undone overnight—namely Shanghai, the "Pearl of the Orient".

---

[23] A phenomenon most thoroughly studied by history of religions professor Mircea Eliade. Cf. for instance Mircea Eliade, Willard R. Trask: *The Sacred and The Profane* (1987).

Let us call our first witness to the bar Mr. X. Now Mr. X has a natural gift for sparking conversation in events and garnering attention. His career quite naturally treaded towards marketing and public relations, and over the years he amassed an impressive A-list of contacts, from business leaders to army generals and top Taiwanese celebrities (yes, that is a big deal here). In short, the charismatic type that introverts (myself included) tend to envy.

That is, until one day when a certain Miss Z brought to my attention a disturbing fact: "You know, your friend brags about his contacts, but he never actually *introduces* anyone; on two occasions when I asked him as a favor to be presented to such and such, he just played hard to get". That's when it fell on me: over the years, I had never been acquainted with any of his contacts, invited to activities with them, brought together around a dinner table— *zilch, nada*. Granted, we do not work in the same industry, but regardless, he appears to keep his contacts distant from each other. As if jealously guarding his precious address book to himself.

Back to Miss Z. She arrived on Shanghai's gladiatorial arena a few years after X, started off from a lower rung, generates less attention and on average milks less contacts at events. But what she *does* with her contacts more than catches up for that. She goes out of her way to help people out, and if someone has a need that does not correspond to any of her strengths or is totally foreign to her area of expertise, she will comb through her contacts to find a suitable match. She views these as a catalog of potential supply and demand components of infinite varieties, Lego bricks begging to be nestled in a larger ensemble, with herself in the role of chef *d'orchestre*.

After just one year of such puzzle-assembling, she had built a reputation as someone both trustworthy and resourceful.

This creates virtuous cycles—a positive karma of sorts. Today a week seldom passes by without a headhunter, HR Manager or CEO calling her for a job offer, a business proposition, or simply advice—including whether she might know someone useful to a given purpose. It begins with "I heard of you from such and such", "You come highly recommended", "I was told to reach out to you directly". She seldom turns anyone down straight. For a job offer, she would ponder about the people she worked with in the past. She keeps a tab on those unsatisfied in their current position or open to new opportunities.

Of course, she is not always right; sometimes the chemistry between those she puts together does not work out. They remain grateful to her for the effort. And like a puppeteer, with practice she only gets better.

Miss Z. is no extravert. She does not crave to spend every instant of her spare time outside in society, and at times even complains that it drains her energy.[24] I once asked her what her secret was. "Companies hire people to manage their customer and public relations, she explained. These people work hard to develop the business—but what of themselves? Should we not apply these image branding and customer relationship management precepts to our own lives?" Words that fell spot on taking a cue from what companies do. And apply she did, squelching the inner voice to trek the hard trail, even when that meant forsaking family time to head over to some dull business event serving only orange juice on a Sunday.

What is the difference between Mr. X and Miss Z? The former has a lengthy list of contacts, but without regular maintenance, these rot in an anonymous graveyard. Pull a number out at random, the chances they remember Mr. X are close to nil—at best a hazy memory of an entertaining chap met once, long ago. Like a celebrity's autograph, it is of little practical use. The day he runs into trouble, I doubt the four-star general will pick up his call.

Perhaps Mr. X deems his contact list most valuable closed to prying eyes; he fears that connecting people would erase him from the equation, that they cut him out. He may consider his day job exhausting enough and prefer to relax at home in his own spare time. Or he is content with his rank and pay, thus sees no need to develop guanxi. His job may be relatively sheltered from automation. Alas to his defense, there is nothing wrong with striking the right balance between work and personal life.

But people who are ambitious, who strive to rise above ground bound to fall to automation or prepare for their silver years cannot lie ensconced on the sofa, lest they endure a fundamental contradiction between their aspirations and what they do about them.

Miss. Z understands the value of contacts; like plants in a garden, these need nurturing. Young sprouts in particular require frequent watering to mark an imprint. Granted, not every new contact will lead to something. Attempts hit a wall, some people do not develop the right chemistry, while others indeed bypass her, or play foul game. She stays intact and holds no grudge. Neither should you. Fill in your role as a facilitator, a connector, and leave the rest to serendipity. As a classic book on the sales profession once framed it, by assuming up front that only 10% of leads pursued will materialize into new business, you set the stage to sail off and conquer the world (rather than sulk that nine times out of ten your efforts remain vain).[25]

---

[24] Though by their complexity, introversion and extraversion defy a one-sentence summary, and granted no-one is 100% one or the either, to simplify we can say an extravert draws her energy from the outside, the introvert, from inside. Cf. Carl Gustav Jung, *Psychological Types*.

[25] Tom Hopkins: *How to Master the Art of Selling*, Champion Press (1981).

Do not wait till you need a favor to reach out–no one appreciates this. That might work with your mom, or a handful of closest friends (if even), but not beyond. That is when you realize that you have been procrastinating on your deeds to help others—and by then it's too late. Also, strive to avoid calculated aims from the onset. For instance, the first time a headhunter asks whether you might know anyone that could be suitable for a job opening, your first reaction should not be to ask for a referral fee.

By lending a helping hand first, you forge an invisible bond. Keep in touch with your circles, and schedule lunches with different people as often as your agenda permits. Open yourself up somewhat to put them at ease and let them reciprocate, summarize their words from time to time to reassure them of your intent listening, and mirror their emotions to show empathy. Fulfill the role of a recipient, remain attentive to their needs and when you sense an opening, do not hesitate to offer help. Do not make it *sound* like you are helping them, nor humiliate them by (metaphorically) getting them to beg on their knees. Pretend it is nothing. And do not ostensibly keep track of score.

Limits apply, of course. Your time is precious too and will become more so as the snowball effect catches on, leading to a point where it is no longer possible to handle all incoming traffic. You will need to filter, delegate, and at times even severe ties to achieve a right balance.

That does not imply sneering at people currently beneath you on the totem pole while licking the boots of high society. Today's students, interns, and juniors could in due time rise to important positions. By then, they too will be submerged by incoming requests, with perhaps an assistant serving as filter. Yet rightful people remember those who helped them in the early days, when they were a nobody (as long as you do not brag about it). Those who invest in talent early on reap the highest yields. Can you spot and nurture tomorrow's Amazons and Zao Wou-Kis[26]?

Other criteria apply. Within your circles, recognize the individuals who emit energy, those with potential. This has less to do with their current position or status and more with an attitude towards life, with core beliefs and aspirations. Like you, they acknowledge the importance of *guanxi*, of developing and nurturing relationships. As a fisherman recognizes another

[26] Zao Wou-Ki (赵无极, 1920–2013), a Chinese French abstract painter whose works, much admired by the author, have skyrocketed in price after his death: a 2018 Sotheby's auction saw his largest piece (named *Juin–Octobre 1985*) set the record of the most expensive oil painting by an Asian artist, at 65 million USD.

fisherman at a distance, Miss Z knows which of her contacts share her keenness to help and for instance could produce a recommendation, should she not have one (needless to say, Mr. X is absent from that list).

And what of the bad apples, the type that unravels its miseries, complains nonstop at every encounter, and latches onto you the moment it realizes you put up with their whining act there where everyone else receives an impromptu message that requires their immediate presence elsewhere? You can play patient, strive to understand and guide them as best you can, if you believe there is a glimmer of hope, or present someone who might be of aid. But if several meetings reveal a rotten core whose cure eludes you, incapable of listening, of change, then best part ways. Shun bad vibes that cannot be overturned before they drag you down to the ocean floor.

Another point to underscore: Z initially had no idea what she was good at. She changed jobs frequently, in search of a sector she could feel in synch with and eager to flourish in. She eventually found her calling, and from there on swiftly slalomed upwards. The point is that she began actively developing guanxi only *after* having built this field expertise. While that was pure happenstance, it worked in her favor. Because networking skills are greatly enhanced when one is perceived through the eyes of others as in possession of a core area of expertise, something *other* than simply being good at connecting people. You do not want to be labeled a social butterfly nor social climber, with nothing else to show for. Best when your entourage praises you first and foremost for a core talent or expertise, and only tangentially as a resourceful person.

To make that happen, you must excel in that area so that it outshines your socialite skills. Next, this reputation that precedes you should be a positive one; this leads back to our invisible seeds. Word gets around and the past always catches up. She who remains authentic and holds no grudge even as others wrong her keeps her reputation intact.

Alas, avoid the pitfall of networking with people solely from within your field. Your aura for excelling in a particular endeavor will only radiate stronger to non-expert eyes. Strive to be regarded as a respectable player in a specific domain, *and* a resourceful person in a *borderless* array, rather than the reverse, or than either one taken alone.

Mr. X has talent in his field, makes good coin, and enjoys a comfortable life, but because he fails to leverage his contacts, his guanxi remains weak; meanwhile Miss Z's career has catapulted, she can select the projects she desires to work on, and at any point could attempt a side business with greater chances of success.

Cohesion and Bridge

Take a sheet of paper and draw a dot for each of your contacts. Vary the sketch by playing with colors to express distinct types of relationships, or to highlight expertise fields; use bubbles instead of dots to convey the importance of or the level of contact you have with each person, space to represent geographical areas, or different shapes to distinguish those from within and outside of work.

This exercise is useful in several ways. It helps visualize where you stand, compare it to the past and then to a future rendering, after making the vow to develop your guanxi. Here are a few ways to work on it from there.

First, taking a cue from social media's *active* user metrics, filter out people you have not met with in the past quarter or so. Sieve through distant catchups at large gatherings to preserve only meaningful encounters—one to ones, or at least meetings where you spend an exclusive portion of time together. Build on this to plan your lunches and other activities, in order to ensure you grow the network and keep it alive.

For example, pay attention to those one-time encounters, acquaintances that stroke a chord, with contact information exchanged yet no contact renewed thereafter. You have little to lose in making the first step to try and reconnect with these "strangers", bearing in mind the one-out-of-ten rule.

Sense weaknesses and exploit them. For example, if you message or bump into a faint acquaintance with whom an earlier attempt to connect bore no fruit, but now learn that he is out of a job, that person may be more amenable to catch up for coffee. It puts you in a position of strength, giving you a golden opportunity to help someone in need. Meet and see where it leads.

You can also juxtapose the sketch with a basic list of the types of talent you seek to have in your address book. This can highlight deficiencies in your network: do you know an influential person at the bank? Or who can help with police matters? Someone knowledgeable at the Customs house? Who you can turn to for medical or legal assistance, or whose couch you could crash on for a few days? If you have a specific goal or future project in mind, list out the types of expertise that could be of assistance, then crosscheck your sketch to identify gaps and highlight which distant acquaintances ("friend of a friend") could be worked on.

Third, and very importantly, how do you believe that these people perceive you? Where do they place your value, what might they say of you in your absence? A 360° review typically aims to answer this type of query, and many tools are available to perform one. Do the results conform with your beliefs, or is there a gap? How could you narrow the gap in upcoming meetings and social activities?

The exhaustion from networking stems largely from the masks worn in society. Adjusting demeanor, donning an image, and acting the part demands effort and preparation. Authenticity can reduce the effort, yet should be balanced with audience expectations. This includes the choice of clothes, makeup, and other tribal feathers, but also polishing a knowledge repertoire catered to the audience. Staying up to date on what is going on in the professional sport most coveted in the locality is a no-brainer. Chitchat in elite circles revolves around elite concerns, which usually fall in one of two patterns: the nouveaux-riche discuss luxury brands and recent purchases, tax optimization, business deals, opportunities, and investment yields, or compare the service levels of platinum cards and VIP lounges of first-class flights, the size of their watches and the taste of their chateau's latest vintage wine—whatever vaunts and flaunts their status. Money is more of a taboo for old money: aristocrats indulge in art, culture, poetry, bridge, collectibles, philosophy and philanthropy, horses and Cuban cigars, golf and boat racing, Greek and Latin—all things that share a common denominator: the lack of any utilitarian, moneymaking function, as if to rub in the plebs' face the fact that they are beyond worldly preoccupations.

In any circle, the inability for one to keep pace with the conversation quickly transpires, exposing the outsider and sealing her fate. We touched earlier on the weight that a well-rounded education and broad knowledge can carry. Adhering to the group's etiquette, mastering the lingo and exuding cultural proficiency partake in the first steps to conveying a positive image.

Fourth, what have you done, or could you do to keep these people in your good favor? Though we publicly swore not to keep track of deeds, one must naturally maintain a (top-secret) tab of sorts. Not in the aim of going door-to-door for payback like some lowly loan shark, but to visualize and ensure you are spreading good karma wherever it is in your power to do so. Keep track of favors received, too.

Too many people walk in a social event with targeted aims: What is in it for me? How can I make the most of it? Will I get enough sales leads or business cards to send my resume to? What you should have in mind is how you can be of benefit to others.

Stay on the lookout for little things that could help people out or make them feel better. These need not be lavish gifts. It could be advice, a good tennis coach's number, or help in booking a seat at a coveted restaurant whose owner you happen to know. Sometimes, it can be just lending an ear. Birthdays, giving birth or a hospital operation are occasions to display thoughtfulness and support in ways that trump generic calendar celebrations. Showing that you have paid attention to someone's personal situation will move them; it also facilitates the bid to add a personal touch (as opposed to a Christmas card).

Aim for original, lasting effects, based on a person's affinities or on circumstances. Especially in times of hardship. During Shanghai's harsh 2022 lockdown, I had secured a large quantity of rare fruit that I then dispatched to several contacts; though far from starving (Western media exaggerated the proportions of the food shortages), they appreciated the gesture.

Gifts that contribute to raise the recipient's status in front of others also work marvels. When making introductions between strangers, avoid sticking to stale job titles; take the time to highlight each person's strengths, be it unrivaled knowledge in a given field, or recounting the story of a past achievement. Do not hesitate to use superlatives, of the type: "Perhaps the most intellectual person I have met in a long time." Or: "Her unparalleled knowledge of the city's restaurant scene guarantees for some hidden gems." Just make sure not to diminish the other person to an awkward muteness. Aim for the common ground that can spark mutual interest, be it a sport, past travels to a similar destination, or any shared passion that can serve as harpoon for them to latch onto and get the conversation flowing with no further need of you.

I once worked a stint in La Baule, an area of Western France most prized for its beaches, but also home to some of the world's best salt marshes. This summoned a story I had read, about Sherman's army during the American Civil War. After plundering a farm deep South, the yanks loaded as much meat as each man could carry (by then they had cut all bridges and were living off the land). Except for one soldier, who flummoxed his comrades by instead packing as much salt as he could fit. They soon realized that the meat was best preserved and enjoyed with salt; by bartering his salt against everyone else's meat, the clever soldier enjoyed more meat than any one man could carry.

Inspired by the story, I purchased several bags of local *Fleur de Sel de Guérande*, the *nec plus ultra* of salt, available for a steal. Back in Texas, when invited to a barbecue I would bring a bag of the coveted condiment, regale guests with tremors of gustatory ecstasy, share stories of its origin when prodded, then offer it to the host. For the price of a bottle of wine that would have been inconspicuously drowned on the spot, I provided hosts with a gift that would last them years, allowing them to delight guests during barbecues—a dead-serious business in Texas—each time evoking the memory of yours truly.

But back to networking.

The fifth and last element relates to connecting contacts. People will appreciate you as someone resourceful only if you connect them with others. So how to leap from Mr. X to Miss Z?

Suppose we sketched a vast constellation of contacts. At this stage, there is no telling whether we are looking at a Mr. X or a Miss Z type network. We must dig deeper.

On the sketch, draw lines between the people that know each other, ruling out distant acquaintances. Do not hesitate to vary the thickness of lines to convey degrees of friendship. The difference then emerges like a full moon on a cloudless night: while Mr. X's sketch may contain several nebulae of acquainted shapes, it reveals many more scores of isolated, fading dots devoid of relationships. Meanwhile Miss Z's resembles a vibrant starry night, with a great number of bridges between clusters.

In fact, organizational behaviorists distinguish between these two types of networks. They call the cohesive one the type where your contacts also know each other, whereas in the bridging one you are the sole linkage.[27] Each type has its strengths and weaknesses:

– In a cohesive network:

  • Your value is diminished: it is hard to appear resourceful when everyone you know already knows everyone else, and you fail to produce new contacts,
  • As birds of a feather flock together, cohesive networks tend to share the same beliefs, creating an echo effect that can feel like drinking your own bathwater,
  • In a team: adhesion can be swift for small projects, but a profound overhaul, that involves self-questioning of one's beliefs, can trigger collective resistance; it may prove difficult to win a tight-knit group to a cause deemed too radical,

– In a bridging network:

  • You cast a wide net from which you can reap contrasting ideas and opinions of all sorts, that can broaden your vision and perhaps contain insights that could be turned into opportunities,
  • You appear resourceful by conveying intel from one group to another, and at times connecting people,

---

[27] Cf. Julie Battilana and Tiziana Casciaro: *The Network Secrets of Great Change Agents*, Harvard Business Review (July–August 2013).

- In a team: minor changes may take longer to get through, but radical ones are more likely to find early adopter(s), and you can tailor your message to each audience, fully benefitting from the *divide et impera* maxim.

While a network can be bridged or cohesive, a person's entire network seldom belongs fully to one or the other extreme. Mr. X has a circle of tight-knit friends who hang out together, and not everyone in Miss Z's notebook knows each other. Yet dust off the more superficial relations, based on criteria such as a minimum of three catchups in the past year involving a meaningful exchange, and the view of Mr. X's stars shifts from that of a forest clearing to a bright metropolis, dimming the majority of stars out of sight to preserve only a cluster or two of close friends who all know each other—a cohesive network. Miss Z's sketch proves more resilient to this filter, placing her in a bridging network.

The tricky part with the bridged network lies in the "at times connecting people". For one, it is optional (as Mr. X demonstrated); secondly, the minute you connect two individuals, it sets in motion a new dynamic that could see the three-person network morph, from bridged to cohesive—on condition that they hit it off. Great mixers of disparate, bridged networks typical during weddings or anniversaries do not count as a connection of all participants, unless two invitees are introduced to one another, keep contact and gradually forge a friendship.

The true mastery of social networking lies in maintaining bridging networks while at the same time connecting people that develop some form of chemistry, that find reciprocal value in the relationship. Each time you connect people, your value increases in their eyes, at least in the short term; this value erodes on the long run, especially if they wind up getting along better with each other than with you. To maintain the reputation of a resourceful person (as opposed to a good networker), you need to stay on a streak of connecting your acquaintances; but by doing so, you slowly slide into the trap of a stale cohesive network: given enough time, all of your contacts will end up knowing each other. The escape route: making new acquaintances on a regular basis. Hence the maestro constantly expands her networks and experiments pathways between people, balancing the whole to avoid falling into either extreme.[28]

As super-connector Keith Ferrazzi put it:

---

[28] This is but a glimpse into the topic of networks, the subject of an entire branch of social science. For a deeper dive, backed by a plethora of meta-studies, see Marissa King: *Social Chemistry: Decoding the Patterns of Human Connection*, Penguin Random House (2021).

You can't amass a network of connections without introducing such connections to others with equal fervor. The more people you help, the more help you'll have and the more help you'll have helping others.[29]

One might object to a limit in adding contacts, especially when factoring in the maintenance necessary for these to have an impact. Bear in mind the 10% rule of sales prospection (though of course a 10% conversion rate is something you might wish to seek to improve over time, too). Besides, friends move to faraway cities, start families and fade from the social scene, or simply you grow apart over time. By staying engaged in the social mingling scene and adapting to circumstances (including your own: the networking game differs radically based on whether you are a couple or single, with or without kids), you remain relevant and avoid the pitfall of sticking with pals, for good old times' sake, that deep down you no longer feel in synch with.

Alas, the necessity to actively keep in touch with everyone shrinks as your reputation grows. A (positive) reputation that precedes you wherever you go creates miracles, for instance by halving the time it would normally take for strangers to get to trust you (contrast that with the impacts of a bad reputation).

Effective networking and continuous learning both imply a broadening of one's horizon, a positive outlook on the world and a thirst for knowledge, not unlike the attitude displayed in the movie *Yes Man* starring Jim Carrey and Terence Stamp. While the movie was purposely caricatural, readers are invited to experiment with a shift of this type, recognizing and challenging their assumptions, and to observe the results after a few months.

Networks represent an insurance for later years: when the time comes to develop a side business, you will most regret not having nurtured past acquaintances. And for many people, the notion of developing a venture is shaping as a prerequisite for happy post-retirement years.

8.5 Spreading Your Eggs—Entrepreneurial Aspirations

You may have passions related or totally foreign to your job. Might these one day translate into additional revenue, or grow into a full-time endeavor?

A side-business related to work lets you harness your expertise and reputation while leveraging contacts forged over the years. The right dose of both expertise and network permitting (along with an itch for entrepreneurship),

[29] Keith Ferrazzi, Tahl Raz: *Never Eat Alone, and Other Secrets to Success,* One Relationship at a Time, Crown Business (2005)

one can quite naturally hop from employee to consultant. The expertise underpins a rare skill that conveys value, while the network ensures a trusting clientele hungry for your services. But read the details of your non-compete before setting sail.

The pursuit of side hobbies can in time turn us into seasoned connoisseurs. Who might appreciate and value this knowledge? Is it sufficiently rare to differentiate you? Check whether it is something for which there is demand, looking through the angles of ongoing trends met earlier—demographics, human needs, and so on.

When I was a teen, computer nerds were belittled, graffiti and video games scorned. Today top gamers earn good coin, Banksy is showcased in the world's most prestigious galleries, and 80's nostalgia has made a forceful comeback, for instance in the bestselling novels of Ernest Cline, the super-geek who roams California in a DMC DeLorean, replete with a (non-functional) flux capacitor. An inveterate fan of 8-bit games who spends late nights creating music could include those pixelized sound effects as a signature mark, present her creations to other tinkerers, collaborate, perform in the vicinity, and slowly develop a following.

Whether painting or coding, cooking, gardening or disc-jockeying, it's all the more important to hone the craft when it differs from your daytime work. Replace Hulu binge-watching with the pursuit of a side gig.

The endeavor need not be a creative one. It can be a high sense of aesthetics, or rare-to-come-by expertise. Suppose you regularly indulge in a great cup of coffee, slowly elevating your taste buds, until the quality of coffee takes precedence over that of food whence facing the ageless question of where to brunch at. Why not push beyond the stage of dilettante? Read books, follow online tutorials, chat with baristas whence sipping that *Yirgacheffe*. Slowly lift your level to that of cognoscente, while developing auxiliary networks that can support the passion. There is no telling where this road may take you: the opening of your own coffee shop, an invitation to visit coffee plantations in the Southern Hemisphere, or more broadly to live your passion after passing a certain age, by rebranding yourself.

Look for training opportunities in your neighborhood—ideally with a degree at the end to officialize your newly acquired expertise. Finetuning the craft in this manner during your spare time, for example on weekends, also serves as a trial to validate whether you have the belly for it. In the process you will meet like-minded enthusiasts, people you can bounce ideas with, perhaps uncovering future partners for a promising venture.

As you indulge in these recesses from work, toy with monetization ideas. Remain vigilant for flaws and shortcomings. What recurrent complaints circulate in your social circles? As hinted above, coffee freaks might lament the lack of a place that serves *both* good coffee and decent food. Restaurant owners may retort that they need not bother with the hassle of fine coffee to fill their venue. There lies your value proposition. Or perhaps the developed palette of coffee flavors favors a model that associates fine coffees paired with high-end chocolates? Are you better off opening a coffee shop that addresses the issue? Is your objective to grow it into an imposing chain? Or would you rather set up a user-friendly distribution channel that targets existing restaurants? Or sell direct to consumers online? Find a value proposition that addresses a pain point no one noticed or cared about, then explore ways to address it.

The following illustrates the discovery of a pain point and its prompt exploitation. While pregnant, former ballerina and by then gym-owner Brynn Putnam could no longer work out at her gym. Unnerved with home tryouts at having to follow instructions on a smartphone screen, she started to tinker with the idea of a screen embedded in a wall mirror. After one of her studios underwent a renovation that included the adding of mirrors, she sent out a survey to query members on the changes. The feedback was unequivocal: people liked mirrors. In 2016, she secured her first investment, and after shipping free smart mirrors to celebrities, in 2018 a post by Alicia Keys highlighting one went viral. Then the pandemic hit. As the Gold Gym chain of Schwarzenegger fame filed for bankruptcy,[30] Brynn's mirror business exploded.[31] In 2020, Lululemon purchased Mirror for 500 million dollars; soon after, its CFO stated: "Mirror sales exceeded our initial expectations in 2020".[32]

Suppose smart mirrors go mainstream. Would these not be to Jane Fonda's video what fintech was to ATMs, in other words, the coach and gym instructor gravedigger (as opposed to a propeller of more jobs)? Could smart mirrors not concurrently unleash a fertile ecosystem for other apps surfing on the narcissist wave (wardrobe, makeup, health…)?

The human touch is another obvious chord to exploit—a business where proximity matters. People often invoke skills like programming, web design,

---

[30] Forbes: *Bodybuilding Favorite Gold's Gym Files For Chapter 11 Bankruptcy Protection* (May 5, 2020), https://www.forbes.com/sites/isabeltogoh/2020/05/05/bodybuilding-favourite-golds-gym-files-for-chapter-11-bankruptcy-protection.

[31] Forbes: *How a Former Ballerina turned Mirror into a Buzzy $300 Million Exercise Phenomenon* https://www.forbes.com/sites/amyfeldman/2020/05/28/how-a-former-ballerina-turned-mirror-into-a-buzzy-300-million-exercise-phenomenon.

[32] John Ballard: *The Mirror Acquisition Is Already Exceeding Lululemon's Expectations*, The Motley Fool (April 12, 2021) https://www.fool.com/investing/2021/04/12/mirror-already-exceeding-lululemons-expectations/.

or innate strengths like that of a polyglot sufficient in today's world, especially to succeed remotely. Working on a laptop from a Starbucks in Bali might sound alluring; the only hiccup is that this type of work pitches you against a world swarming with talented people content with $3 an hour gigs. As the saying goes: "if you can do your job from anywhere, someone anywhere can do your job".[33]

American Lexie Comstock arrived in Shanghai in 2010. After her day job in marketing and PR, she enjoyed baking cookies. Hearing the grumble in expat circles on the lack of Western-style desserts, she started selling her produce to cafes and individuals. Then took the leap. Her business has spawned into a full-time endeavor named *Strictly Cookies*, now an iconic presence in over 60 locations.[34]

Reflect on where the ideal location might be, how to pique interest, preserve traffic, the right price point, and what pent-up frustration you bring a solution to. Do the whiskey lovers also adore cigars, and deplore the dearth of bars offering both, or the absence of a heated terrace on which they could be consumed together, if local regulations forbid inside smoking? Is the market growing? Make a (business) SWOT, on which for instance deteriorating climatic conditions, or geopolitical risks surrounding Cuba, including that of tariffs, would appear. What margins can you expect? Is it becoming a collector's item? Or is the market saturated, like Shanghai's dense coffee scene (over 7,000 cafes and counting, with one every several yards in some parts of town). This begs the question of entry barriers to stave off future competition. Smart mirrors and beauty sponges are easily copied, making differentiation key to survival on the long run.

While fulfilling a passion should be your goal, take into account the scarcity factor. The Internet is emblematic of plethoric offer. On the other side of the spectrum, an interest so narrow as to border the unique could conceal a goldmine (though oftentimes there is a reason why it does not exist). It may only turn popular in a decade, or the underlying tech has yet to mature; but by nurturing it early on, when ripe you could emerge an uncontested expert and reap the fruit. In her book *Reinventing You*, Dorie Clark offers countless examples of workers who successfully turned their life around by allying work with passion, such as the cycling fanatic turned real

[33] Simon Kuper: *Are Superstar Employees about to be Offshored?* Financial Times (March 25, 2021) https://www.ft.com/content/9414f45c-6f03-4b8f-85c5-537d7e4f4932.

[34] https://strictlycookies.com/.

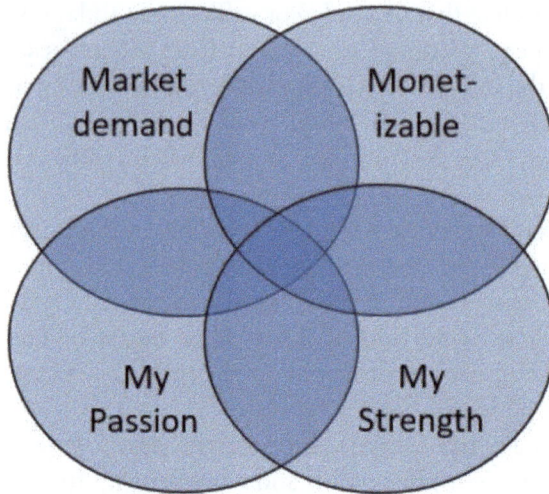

Fig. 8.7 Success lies at the confluence of four elements

estate agent, who inspects the biking tracks and environment around properties, takes his clients on biking tours and shows whether it's safe for the kids to bike to school.[35]

One of my aunts is a musicologist who moved to Israel in the 1970s to teach. A rather lugubrious fascination with the Holocaust branched into an investigation into the music sung by Jews in Nazi camps. She spent a good portion of her free time consulting archives, interviewing survivors, and documenting lyrics. As time passed by (and with it the remaining witnesses of World War 2 horrors), this combination of talent (musicology) and passion (Shoah) has turned her into one of the world's leading experts on Holocaust music.

Before taking the leap, account for potential demand, as alluded to earlier with our Texas panhandle ski shop. One CEO expressed the potential for success as the intersection of four circles, depicted in Figure 8.7.[36]

Note the balanced proportion of inner and outer aspects at the confluence of:

– what the world needs
– something that can be turned into nickels and pennies

---

[35] Page 80, Dorie Clark: *Reinventing You: Define Your Brand, Imagine Your Future*, Harvard Business Press (2013).

[36] Hubert Joly, former CEO of Best Buy. Cited in *CEO Excellence: The Six Mindsets that Distinguish the Best Leaders from the Rest*, p.22. Carolyn Dewar, Scott Keller, Vikram Malhotra. Scribner (2022).

– what you are good at
– what you are passionate about

A passion lifts your spirits. It should last beyond the daydreaming joys of an evanescent fling, extending to the following morning, and the next one, and again when projecting life a decade down the road of that path–as opposed to a drudgery that triggers a headlong rush to bury your head in phone notifications, friend posts and other ostrich holes.

Some start pursuing their passion on the side while employed, developing apps, freelancing designs, or baking cookies. When the income derived by the "side-job" overshadows that provided by the employer, it triggers a moment of reckoning, a time to sit down and ponder on what you have created: a new alternative path for your future. You have reached a crossroads: stay employed or pursue the entrepreneurial route?

The passion can be kept on the side, something for post-retirement years. When tough times strike, easy-to-activate skills offer a buffer. In a poignant moment of the movie *Central do Brazil*, the heroine is left penniless in deep rural Brazil. She then sits in the street to perform a most basic task, yet one that calls on rare skills in that particular location: namely to write letters for the illiterate, in exchange of a small fee.[37]

If you wish to open your options in terms of geographic mobility for later years, pencil that desire in when fathoming on the ideal side gig. Expertise can lead to greater mobility: design, sports, and language (as a coach or teacher), IT and crafts of all sorts, be it photography, antique clock repairman or *kintsugi* master (an ancient Japanese art of mending broken pottery with a technique of lacquer mixed with powdered gold). If you have no entrepreneurial aspirations, perhaps the side skill you have developed could interest a company willing to hire you as a consultant. A deep expertise in a field with strong demand lays the ground for authoring a book, giving lectures, and speaking at conferences.

Alas, upon retirement, the passion could help ends meet. Especially as the prospects of living off retirement funds and 401(k)s dwindle, in the context of prolonged life. And as Voltaire noted, with work comes solace—a sense of purpose.

Build a Platform

When starting a business, expertise alone is no failsafe against catastrophe.

---

[37] Directed by Walter Sales, *Central do Brasil* (1998), in English: *Central Station*.

As stressed earlier, setting sail for the entrepreneurial horizon quickly unveils the importance of networks, for better or worse. Someone with passable expertise but well-nurtured platforms counting many devotees stands a better chance of succeeding than a hard-skills expert with no believers. If you have only one of these strengths, finding a suitable partner versed in the other can help, as in the tale of Steve and Steve (Jobs and Wozniak).

Figure 8.8 highlights the importance of combining these two strengths (most certainly tailed by a hands-on attitude to get the job done, boldness, creativity and other aspects). Those who develop deep expertise yet forgo networking efforts are likely to remain in the position of employee for life, with the added risk of AI encroaching on that expertise. Starting a business involves finding and convincing various stakeholders—customers, bankers, investors, partners, and even employees. These people are unlikely to line up on your porch to hear your brilliant ideas. However, as Miss Z has shown, fostering a healthy network recognizant of your talent upfront maximizes the odds for the cards to fall in the right spot when the moment comes.

Building trust, maintaining good relationships with (potential) clients, keeping that flicker of human touch alive can make or break a business plan. And thanks to the Internet revolution, now anyone can reach out to the world.

In the twenty-first century, the use of digital media is a powerful tool to reckon with. From livestreaming to Instagram, LinkedIn and YouTube, a growing number of people derive income from building communities of followers. It starts with something as trivial as posting creations online, sharing photos, or giving regular advice on a topic you are passionate about, be it vegan cooking, how to handle a cross-cultural relationship, or repair vintage guitars. Then comes that spark, when you grab a leading influencer's

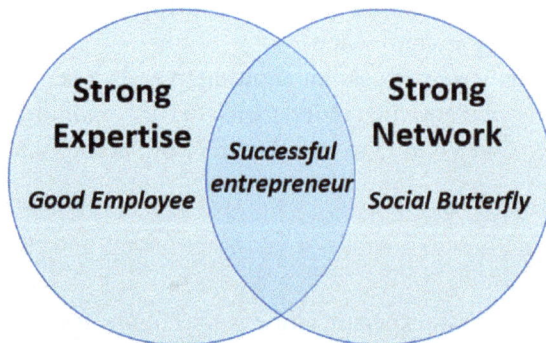

Fig. 8.8 The combination of strong skills and strong network contribute to a business' success

attention; a single like or repost can trigger a chain reaction that catapults you to stardom, by harnessing other peoples' networks.

On YouTube alone, content creators have several ways of making money: by selling products, crowdfunding, licensing, or receiving brand sponsorship as a recognized influencer. They can rely on fan donations to support their work ("fan funding") or join the YouTube Partner Program (YPP) for greater access to YouTube resources and monetization features. With YPP, creators receive a share of the income from ads served on their content (YPP creators must also abide by YouTube's rules, reflective of American values[38]).

Following O2O logic, a fanbase can propel a brick-and-mortar business. To stick with our cigar lounge example, clients could scan a QR code in the facility for access to a WhatsApp or WeChat group—a community of cigar afficionados administered by the owner, who uses the platform to announce events, new stock arrivals, late night screenings, and flash sale discounts. Of course, members can also freely discuss and share theme-related photos. A business that creates a community capable of giving users a sense of belonging scores points, with monetizable opportunities a step away.

A fanbase community also embodies a sampling of customers, that can be prodded for information on relevant features for a product launch, the title bound to maximize a video's views, or the importance of mirrors in a gym. Experiments conducted on these guinea pigs prior to full-scale launch can provide insights that prove tantamount to success. Gauge reactions, take note of evidence garnered, and steer in the direction that seems most promising.

In a nod to the power of platforms, corporate interest in influencers is growing. And not just for freelancing or livestream ads. Influencers are landing jobs in communications departments of large organizations, as brand ambassadors, or recognized and hired for their talent in a specific craft. For example, when securing Big Data expertise, talent-seeking firms can turn to LinkedIn to get a measure of applicants via their number of posted articles, views, and followers. Fanbase sizes now figure prominently on certain resumes.

Nor are platforms constrained to the online world. Forging relationships in the workplace builds trust over the years, with peers, vendors, customers, and other stakeholders—acquaintances that may reach out to you later.

---

[38] Repulsed by what they view as an imposition of American puritanism to the rest of the world, a growing fringe of creators is forsaking YPP for the fan funding model, in a new bucket of thorns for YouTube (who loses advertising dollars). For an example, google the controversy on user *Joueur du Grenier* (literally the "attic player").

9

Conclusion

As we approach the shores, let us contemplate the ground covered along the journey. Looking at past, present, and possible futures; fathoming the development of 4^{IR} technologies, and potential collisions with the workplace; devising tools to assess threats and remedies to traverse the storm intact or even stronger.

(Too) much of the 4^{IR} talk revolves around whether this time is different; whether smart bots and swarm bots could generate unbearable levels of unemployment, or perhaps worse, a society of haves and have-nots that cunningly preserves the right dose of low-paid jobs to assuage rebellious aspirations. Another equally impressive throng of books focuses on corporate leadership in the digital age, with advice on how to make the best of 4^{IR} tech, to avoid falling face down in the dirt while FAANG speed ahead, reaping the benefits. Fascinating as they may be, these topics primarily address academics, political elites, and top execs. While acknowledging trialing times ahead for workers, subject to a middle-class squeeze that obturates upward mobility routes, these books make no focal point of the issue; as if it were a hopeless case not worth tackling, the outcome preordained.

In contrast, we sought the worker's stance, despite how vague or even presumptuous that may sound given the diversity of occupations and backgrounds defined by age, education, gender, geography, and more.

The original version of this chapter was revised: Text correction has been updated. The correction to the chapter is available at https://doi.org/10.1007/978-3-031-19278-4_10

Alternating between a macro and a more personal level, we conceived of work under four angles: sector, company, occupation, and tasks—each one a door susceptible to a specific breed of disruption in upcoming years. After considering the risks of sectorial and corporate disruption, and noting the modest powers of employees over these, we turned our full weight to job and task disruption. Here the threat can take the form of automation, a lowering of skill requirements, or enhancement. The third case points to the most desirable escape route, the threat-turned-opportunity. It also highlights the importance of tool proficiency.

Our SWOT framework led to the job vulnerability canvass, whereby like a chemist testing various acids, we scanned for human strengths and weaknesses in the face of emerging technologies. External factors ranging from demographics, human needs, and legislation partook in this tableau. And by forging insidious alliances with technology, outsourcing in all its forms—not merely offshoring—raises the risks. Among inner traits, we pinned down a job's level of structure, recurrence, and narrowness, to what extent it relies on cognition, dexterity and pattern recognition, and finally the importance of the human touch and IT versatility.

A person seldom identifies 100% with a job description. Educational background, past achievements, seniority, charisma, reputation, networks, side hobbies, and more combine to produce unique snowflakes. Toss in the salt and pepper of being at the right place and time for the full recipe. It is up to the reader to put together the pieces of the puzzle known only to her.

Granted, that's a lot to factor in. Yet here lie the crumbs to a true reckoning. The outcome will vary by individual, producing a more or less urgent need for change, itself more or less radical.

Several trails lead to high grounds safe from the mounting waters of automation. What we propose is but one of these paths, albeit with variations—for instance reliance on the human touch takes precedence in a customer-facing job. To fight automation, aim for the center of the sumo ring: high-level reasoning, creativity, working with others, an unpredictable environment (VUCA). Exploit the human touch to build up a reputation, then go beyond. As reputation turns into personal branding, the loyal customer base spills over to become a loyal *stakeholder* base that includes vendors, devoted employees, potential investors, fans, influencers, and so on.

If the path to cognition is obstructed, as so often happens early in a career (and sadly further down the road for many), we advise starting with ruthless automation of one's own tasks. This begs the question of feasibility: cashiers, truck drivers, and coffee baristas cannot automate their work for lack of access to the right tools. Automating physical labor involves costly robots and machinery. Our advice to anyone in that predicament—an automatable job yet without the means to automate it yourself (and far from both management and retirement)—is to strive for a position that puts the tools in your bare hands. In other words, a desktop job, regardless of where you land on the corporate rungs.

Before taking the leap, reflect on your rank in the corporate ladder, on your strengths and weaknesses. If you have no knack for computer tools, but excel at socializing, or sense a promotion nearing, perhaps best stay in the service or physical labor arena, in a bid for middle management. Otherwise, the tunnel may be a long and arduous one, that involves years of sedulous moiling. When you perceive light at the end, it could be that of a speeding train named automation.

Unlike physical labor, computer work is automatable and scalable via easily accessible software, courtesy of the zero marginal cost paradigm and the democratization trend. This rings most true for low-cognitive work, the type that follows a standard process and thus sits square in the path of automation. Due to the exponential gap, many firms simply have not made it there yet. This gives you a window of opportunity. Once wired to a computer, wield it to take the lead and automate tasks in your scope. Leverage the cornucopia of learning methods and tutorials brought by the Information Age to investigate and experiment with faster ways to get the job done. Bit by bit, demonstrate the ability to achieve higher efficiency, to take on and manage more. Doing so lifts you above the crowd. From thereon, waddle toward cognitive work and gradually capture the management of other humans.

This does not happen overnight. It calls for dedication, iron self-discipline, continuous learning, and a little networking.

Avoid overshooting for full task automation from the start; rather, strive for efficiency with widespread tools like Excel, business analytics, whatever ERP or design software your firm utilizes. Experiment with new features such as ChatGPT, that bring previously arcane tools into the hands of commoners. Spend a disproportionate amount of time to master these, be it off-hours. Sharpening your knowledge repertoire in this way gives you the ammo to question the status quo and see through existing procedures, possibly written by less tech-savvy people. And to seek improvements. Oftentimes, expertise is a prerequisite to successful creativity.

Aim for programming only if it appears sensical (as in, it could unlock greater efficiencies) and you have a flair for it. If your work involves a lot of Excel, try the natural route paved by VBA. Start with the Macro recorder and read the code created on the go; parse your nearby library for a good book on

Visual Basic (avoid using only digital learning formats); seek and share information on forums like Stack Overflow. Keep a notebook titled "My VBA" or "My Python", and make it your bedside companion. Remember that routine work is automatable via GOFAI—rules-based procedures, that in terms of programming and other areas of knowledge (notably statistics) remain more accessible than machine learning and unsupervised algorithms.

Recall the shifting importance of automating versus delegating tasks as one rises in seniority. This change may occur before the urge for programming surfaces. From there on, people and management skills take the front seat. By then, you are nearing grounds safe from automation, immersed in cognitive work.

Even so, keep on the lookout for tech enhancement opportunities, whether for yourself or your team. This mountain lion lurks in the higher rungs, ready to spring on white collars lacking IT sensitivity, making them irrelevant, bested by more tech-savvy peers. Hone new tools to outmaneuver rivals. AI foremost, but also AR, 3D printing and other technologies where applicable—for instance quantum computing in cybersecurity, or the impact of NFTs for customer relationship management and loyalty programs. Approach AI as a pathway to automate redundant work, to mine data and harness the powers conferred by it, rather than to gain raw coding expertise as an end in itself. Best to have one or two elements within your team capable of coding, that remain up to date and who can advise you on these matters.

One thing is certain: until recently, middle-class workers could either aim to shoot higher or be content with their position, cash in the monthly checks and focus more on family life. As tech both propels automation and facilitates outsourcing, it shepherds employees toward a battle royale arena of colossal proportions, making staying put and rehearsing the script the relic of a bygone era. There will not be enough room to accommodate everyone at the top—after all, it is not a ladder, but a pyramid. Start the climb now, or risk tumbling down to an overcrowded base.

Acknowledging this tense future lays the groundwork, providing a strong impetus to act. It's not as simple as: "Become a data scientist" or "Learn Mandarin". There is no future-proof, one-size-fits-all silver bullet. Besides, one must account for the scaffolding that makes up the equation of personal goals:

- where you stand today, that includes where you come from,
- where you need to be,
- where you want to be.

The rest then consists in how to reach that destination—a journey already well begun whence these three elements are sorted out. The first cannot be overlooked, it is the starting point from which to foment a pragmatic plan. Hence the focus of our job introspection and listing of salient traits. Market needs and disruptive tides fuel the second. The third accounts for personal preferences and aspirations, to the extent there is space left for these. The above are listed in order of importance; at certain stages of life, your desired destination may be a luxury to set aside. Know to bid your time.

At regular intervals, take a step back to look at the bigger picture. Some people do this on a yearly basis, typically with their New Year's Eve resolutions. See over your shoulder how far you've come and what you achieved in the past year. Then look ahead. One should keep a notebook for this sole purpose and update it at least once a year. Pinning down the resolutions in writing greatly emphasizes discipline. Remember that you are sole responsible for your own education.

Our lives are but imperfect stones that need refining. As French poet Nicolas Boileau once wrote: "Polish it constantly, then repolish it".

The diagram hereunder provides a snapshot of this book, from identifying threats posed by technology to defining the type of disruption they may cause, to actionable prevention measures and countermoves (Fig. 9.1).

The top half shows the macro environment, the bottom half the more personal level of work, in its four dimensions, each one a door prone to a form of disruption that warrants a different cocktail of actions. Task actions will vary based on the type of job and on which of the three types of job disruption one faces. The power to self-automate, or lack of therein, makes a compelling case for manual and service workers far from the cognition center of the sumo ring to move over to a computer job.

As with any snapshot, it remains far from exhaustive. Measures and advice omitted include the benefits of integrating Big Data and other new tech in your leadership, self-discipline, looking toward corporations for inspiration as to how to deal with the threat of new tech, etc.

Critics may object that these actions are self-centered. As announced from the start, we provide no holistic plan to save the world from the claws of disruption, leaving that topic to policymakers. Instead we focused on what measures working individuals can set in motion, knowing very well going in that there will be winners and losers—hence this book's title.

We are only at the dawn of the 4th Industrial Revolution; it will arguably create lasting ripple effects, for better or worse. The nature, volume, and quality of work are but several of the aspects bound for seismic transformation. The ramifications extend beyond the scope of any single book. While

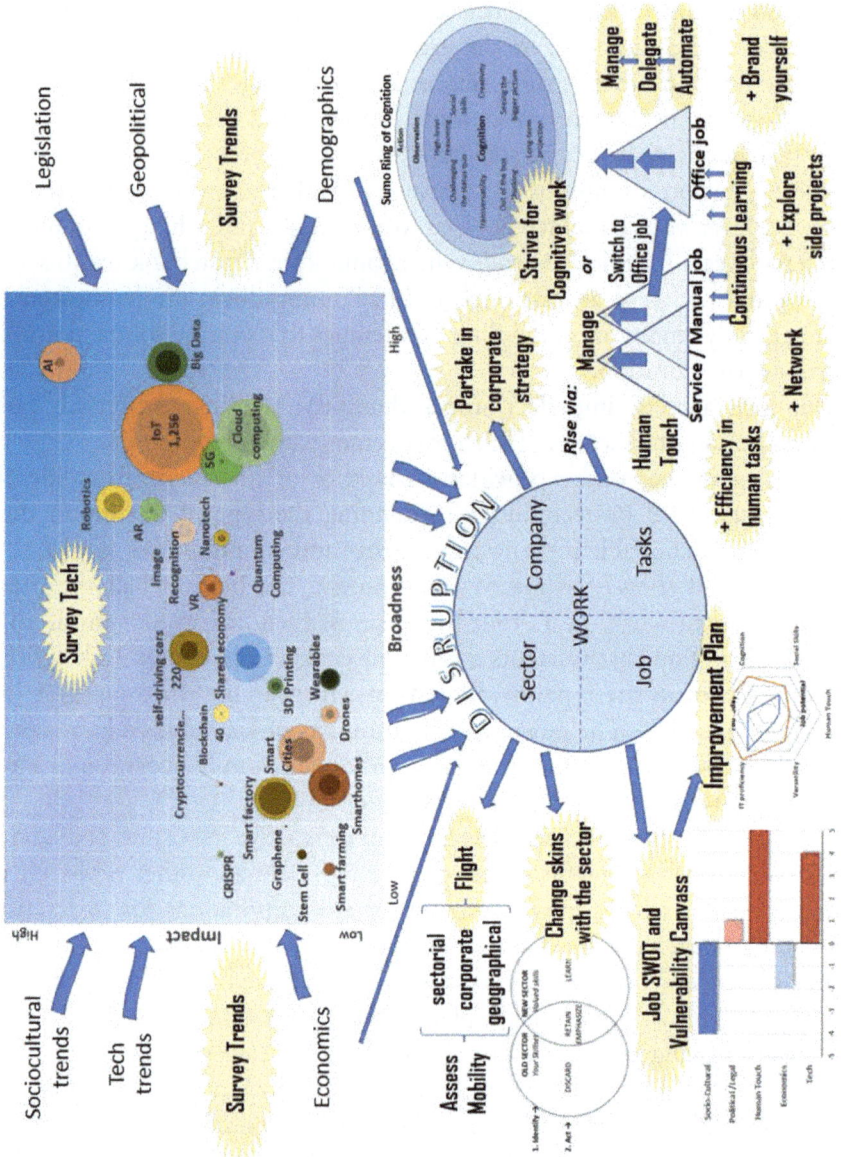

Fig. 9.1 Conclusion

we strived to condense major trends here, no doubt crucial elements have sieved through without the proper attention they deserve—for instance the growing and multifarious issues surrounding global warming.

Regardless of the severity and urgency of threats you face, keep a tab on evolving trends, both within technology and in society at large. Each of us has a duty to fulfill, if not as a worker to remain relevant and competitive, then as a citizen, to ensure the upholding of ethical standards in our deployment of AI and to nurture the building of a fairer digital world for future generations.

Correction to: AI Battle Royale

Correction to:
A. M. Recanati, *AI Battle Royale*, Copernicus Books,
https://doi.org/10.1007/978-3-031-19278-4

In the original version of the book, author provided belated corrections has been incorporated in the following chapters 1, 2, 4, 5, 6, 7, 8, 9.

The correction chapters and the book have been updated with the changes.

The updated versions of these chapters can be found at
https://doi.org/10.1007/978-3-031-19278-4_1
https://doi.org/10.1007/978-3-031-19278-4_2
https://doi.org/10.1007/978-3-031-19278-4_4
https://doi.org/10.1007/978-3-031-19278-4_5
https://doi.org/10.1007/978-3-031-19278-4_6
https://doi.org/10.1007/978-3-031-19278-4_7
https://doi.org/10.1007/978-3-031-19278-4_8
https://doi.org/10.1007/978-3-031-19278-4_9

Appendix A: U.S. Job Openings in 2021

The Covid pandemic strongly impacted the job market. The charts in Appendix A highlight this by using 2021 as reference point, as opposed to Fig. 2.5 which used 2018. The axes remain similar to those used in Fig. 2.5, i.e.:

– Vertical axis: number of job openings as a rate of total jobs in that field
– Horizontal axis: evolution of this rate from 2001 to 2021
– Bubble size: the number of job openings.

The rates shown correspond to the monthly average during the year. Notice the scale of the axes that can differ from one chart to another.

The first chart shows a dramatic shortage in manual labor jobs, to the extent that the rest of the job categories are shoehorned in the bottom-left corner. This warrants a second chart to focus more specifically on that zone.

© The Editor(s) (if applicable) and The Author(s), under exclusive
license to Springer Nature Switzerland AG 2023, corrected publication 2023
A. M. Recanati, *AI Battle Royale*, Copernicus Books,
https://doi.org/10.1007/978-3-031-19278-4

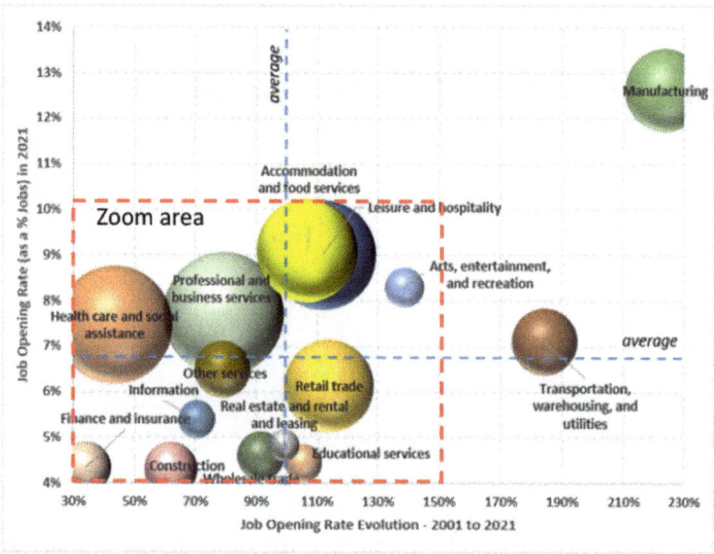

Overall the rate of job openings has increased dramatically as the U.S. tilts toward full employment.

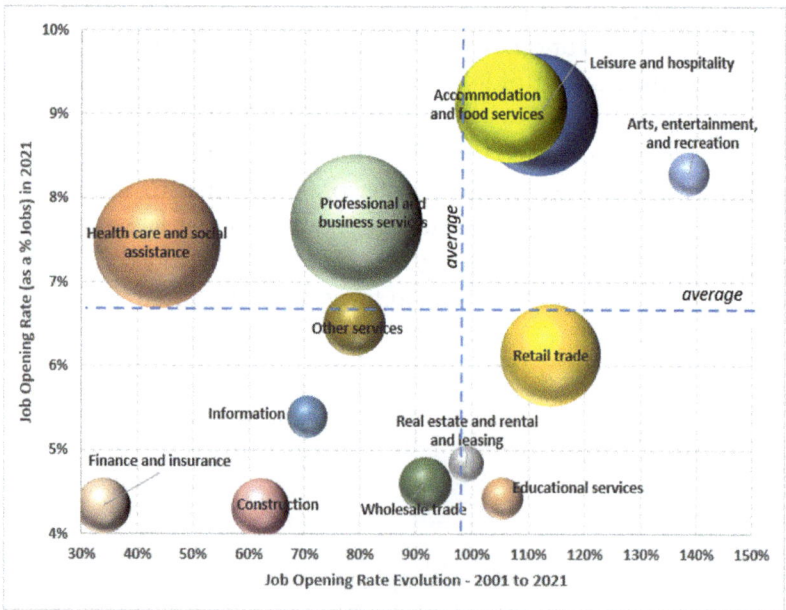

Zoom Area

The third chart shows the same data, only using 2018 instead of 2001 as starting point, in order to focus on the impact of the Covid pandemic.

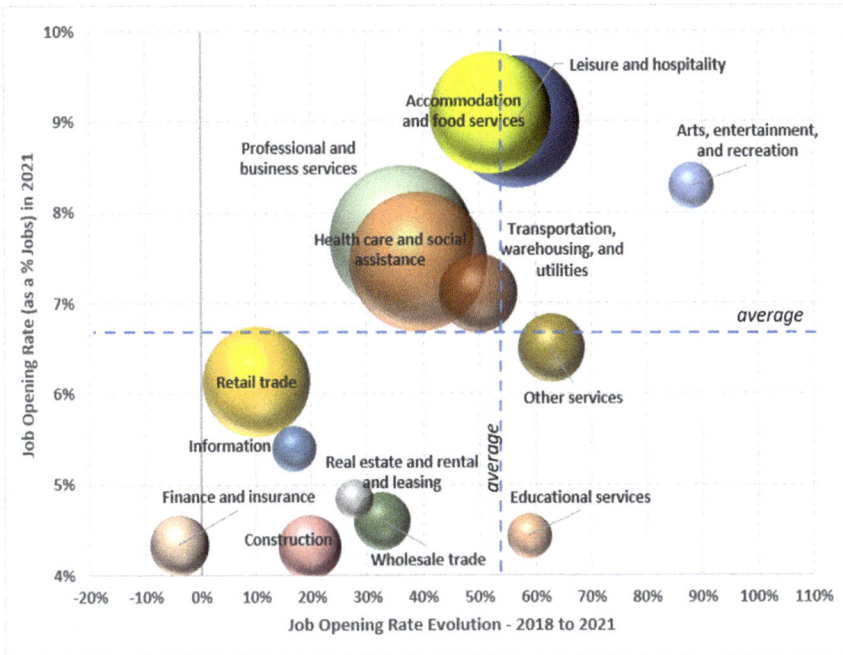

Job Opening Rate evolution, since 2018

Absent from this chart and still hovering high at 12.6%, the Rate of Manu-facturing Job Openings relative to Manufacturing Jobs increased by 78% in the space of three years (from 7.1% to 12.6%).

The Rate of Job Openings in Finance and Insurance improved over the period, while the hit taken by Retail is also apparent.

For the reminder, all the above data comes from the U.S. Bureau of Labor Statistics Jobs Opening and Labor Turnover Survey. Using not seasonally adjusted figures from the private sector (government jobs are excluded).

Appendix B: Vertical Waterfall Chart by Minor Job Categories

Showing changes in the Number of Jobs from 2000 to 2018.
 Sorted top-down by increasing the level of wages.
 (Split into two detailed charts on the next pages for better visibility).

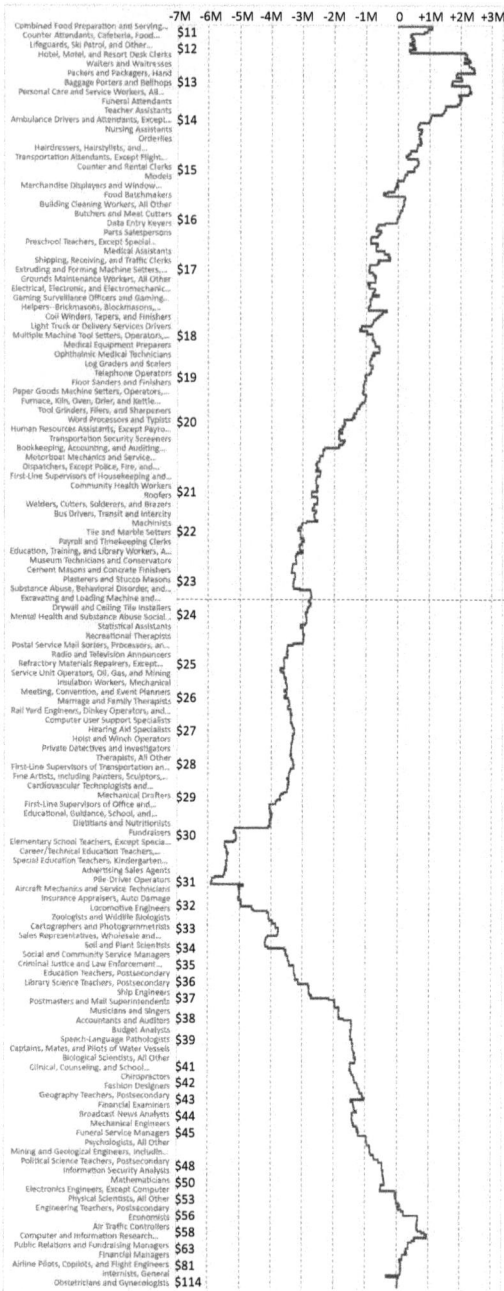

-7M -6M -5M -4M -3M -2M -1M 0 +1M +2M +3M

Job Category	
Combined Food Preparation and Serving...	
Counter Attendants, Cafeteria, Food...	$11
Lifeguards, Ski Patrol, and Other...	
Hotel, Motel, and Resort Desk Clerks	$12
Waiters and Waitresses	
Packers and Packagers, Hand	
Baggage Porters and Bellhops	$13
Personal Care and Service Workers, All...	
Funeral Attendants	
Teacher Assistants	
Ambulance Drivers and Attendants, Except...	$14
Nursing Assistants	
Orderlies	
Hairdressers, Hairstylists, and...	
Transportation Attendants, Except Flight...	
Counter and Rental Clerks	$15
Models	
Merchandise Displayers and Window...	
Food Batchmakers	
Building Cleaning Workers, All Other	
Butchers and Meat Cutters	$16
Data Entry Keyers	
Parts Salespersons	
Preschool Teachers, Except Special...	
Medical Assistants	
Shipping, Receiving, and Traffic Clerks	
Extruding and Forming Machine Setters,...	$17
Grounds Maintenance Workers, All Other	
Electrical, Electronic, and Electromechanic...	
Gaming Surveillance Officers and Gaming...	
Helpers--Brickmasons, Blockmasons,...	
Coil Winders, Tapers, and Finishers	
Light Truck or Delivery Services Drivers	
Multiple Machine Tool Setters, Operators,...	$18
Medical Equipment Preparers	
Ophthalmic Medical Technicians	
Log Graders and Scalers	
Telephone Operators	
Floor Sanders and Finishers	$19
Paper Goods Machine Setters, Operators,...	
Furnace, Kiln, Oven, Drier, and Kettle...	
Tool Grinders, Filers, and Sharpeners	
Word Processors and Typists	$20
Human Resources Assistants, Except Payro...	
Transportation Security Screeners	
Bookkeeping, Accounting, and Auditing...	
Motorboat Mechanics and Service...	
Dispatchers, Except Police, Fire, and...	
First-Line Supervisors of Housekeeping and...	
Community Health Workers	$21
Roofers	
Welders, Cutters, Solderers, and Brazers	
Bus Drivers, Transit and Intercity	
Machinists	
Tile and Marble Setters	$22
Payroll and Timekeeping Clerks	
Education, Training, and Library Workers, A...	
Museum Technicians and Conservators	
Cement Masons and Concrete Finishers	
Plasterers and Stucco Masons	$23
Substance Abuse, Behavioral Disorder, and...	
Excavating and Loading Machine and...	
Drywall and Ceiling Tile Installers	
Mental Health and Substance Abuse Social...	$24
Statistical Assistants	
Recreational Therapists	
Postal Service Mail Sorters, Processors, an...	
Radio and Television Announcers	
Refractory Materials Repairers, Except...	$25
Service Unit Operators, Oil, Gas, and Mining	
Insulation Workers, Mechanical	
Meeting, Convention, and Event Planners	
Marriage and Family Therapists	$26
Rail Yard Engineers, Dinkey Operators, and...	
Computer User Support Specialists	
Hearing Aid Specialists	$27
Hoist and Winch Operators	
Private Detectives and Investigators	
Therapists, All Other	
First-Line Supervisors of Transportation an...	$28
Fine Artists, including Painters, Sculptors,...	
Cardiovascular Technologists and...	
Mechanical Drafters	$29
First-Line Supervisors of Office and...	
Educational, Guidance, School, and...	
Dietitians and Nutritionists	
Fundraisers	
Elementary School Teachers, Except Specia...	$30
Career/Technical Education Teachers,...	
Special Education Teachers, Kindergarten-...	
Advertising Sales Agents	
Pile-Driver Operators	$31
Aircraft Mechanics and Service Technicians	
Insurance Appraisers, Auto Damage	
Locomotive Engineers	$32
Zoologists and Wildlife Biologists	
Cartographers and Photogrammetrists	$33
Sales Representatives, Wholesale and...	
Soil and Plant Scientists	$34
Social and Community Service Managers	
Criminal Justice and Law Enforcement...	$35
Education Teachers, Postsecondary	
Library Science Teachers, Postsecondary	$36
Ship Engineers	
Postmasters and Mail Superintendents	$37
Musicians and Singers	
Accountants and Auditors	$38
Budget Analysts	
Speech-Language Pathologists	$39
Captains, Mates, and Pilots of Water Vessels	
Biological Scientists, All Other	$41
Clinical, Counseling, and School...	
Chiropractors	$42
Fashion Designers	
Geography Teachers, Postsecondary	$43
Financial Examiners	
Broadcast News Analysts	$44
Mechanical Engineers	
Funeral Service Managers	$45
Psychologists, All Other	
Mining and Geological Engineers, includin...	
Political Science Teachers, Postsecondary	$48
Information Security Analysts	
Mathematicians	$50
Electronics Engineers, Except Computer	
Physical Scientists, All Other	$53
Engineering Teachers, Postsecondary	
Economists	$56
Air Traffic Controllers	
Computer and Information Research...	$58
Public Relations and Fundraising Managers	$63
Financial Managers	
Airline Pilots, Copilots, and Flight Engineers	$81
Internists, General	
Obstetricians and Gynecologists	$114

Detail 1

Detail 2

Detail 1

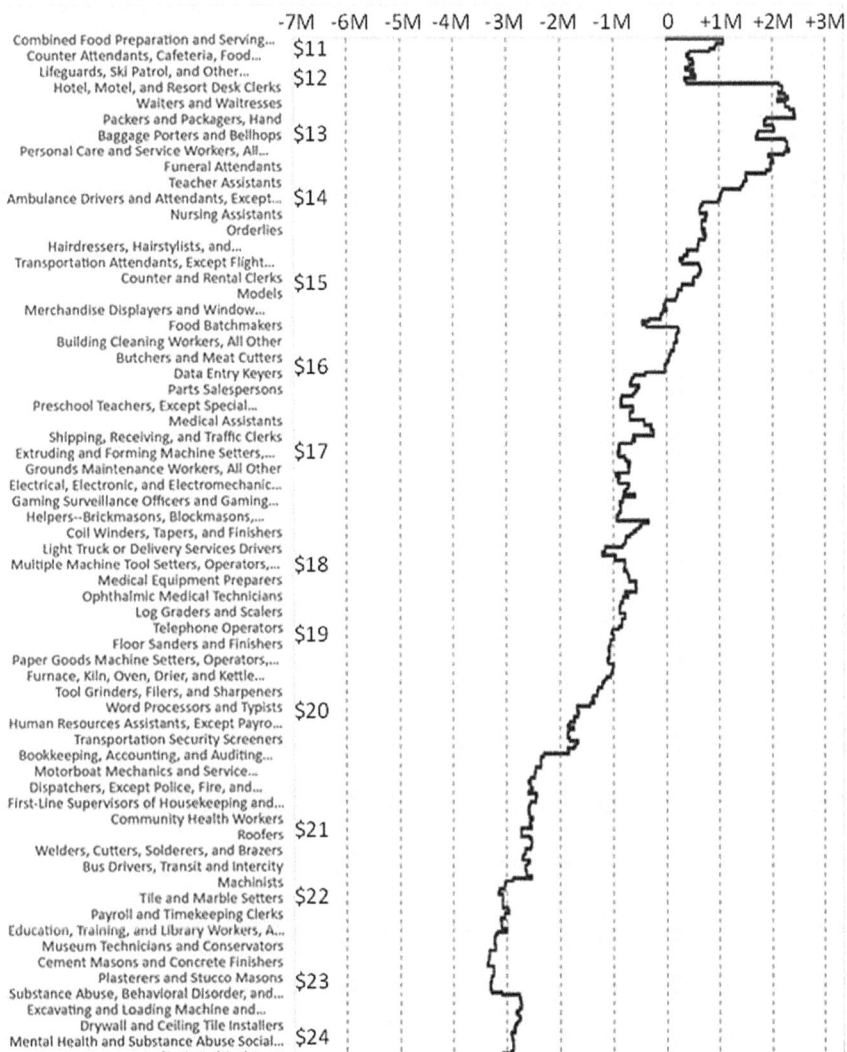

	-7M	-6M	-5M	-4M	-3M	-2M	-1M	0	+1M	+2M	+3M

Combined Food Preparation and Serving... $11
Counter Attendants, Cafeteria, Food...
Lifeguards, Ski Patrol, and Other... $12
Hotel, Motel, and Resort Desk Clerks
Waiters and Waitresses
Packers and Packagers, Hand
Baggage Porters and Bellhops $13
Personal Care and Service Workers, All...
Funeral Attendants
Teacher Assistants
Ambulance Drivers and Attendants, Except... $14
Nursing Assistants
Orderlies
Hairdressers, Hairstylists, and...
Transportation Attendants, Except Flight...
Counter and Rental Clerks $15
Models
Merchandise Displayers and Window...
Food Batchmakers
Building Cleaning Workers, All Other
Butchers and Meat Cutters $16
Data Entry Keyers
Parts Salespersons
Preschool Teachers, Except Special...
Medical Assistants
Shipping, Receiving, and Traffic Clerks
Extruding and Forming Machine Setters,... $17
Grounds Maintenance Workers, All Other
Electrical, Electronic, and Electromechanic...
Gaming Surveillance Officers and Gaming...
Helpers--Brickmasons, Blockmasons,...
Coil Winders, Tapers, and Finishers
Light Truck or Delivery Services Drivers
Multiple Machine Tool Setters, Operators,... $18
Medical Equipment Preparers
Ophthalmic Medical Technicians
Log Graders and Scalers
Telephone Operators $19
Floor Sanders and Finishers
Paper Goods Machine Setters, Operators,...
Furnace, Kiln, Oven, Drier, and Kettle...
Tool Grinders, Filers, and Sharpeners
Word Processors and Typists $20
Human Resources Assistants, Except Payro...
Transportation Security Screeners
Bookkeeping, Accounting, and Auditing...
Motorboat Mechanics and Service...
Dispatchers, Except Police, Fire, and...
First-Line Supervisors of Housekeeping and...
Community Health Workers
Roofers $21
Welders, Cutters, Solderers, and Brazers
Bus Drivers, Transit and Intercity
Machinists
Tile and Marble Setters $22
Payroll and Timekeeping Clerks
Education, Training, and Library Workers, A...
Museum Technicians and Conservators
Cement Masons and Concrete Finishers
Plasterers and Stucco Masons $23
Substance Abuse, Behavioral Disorder, and...
Excavating and Loading Machine and...
Drywall and Ceiling Tile Installers
Mental Health and Substance Abuse Social... $24

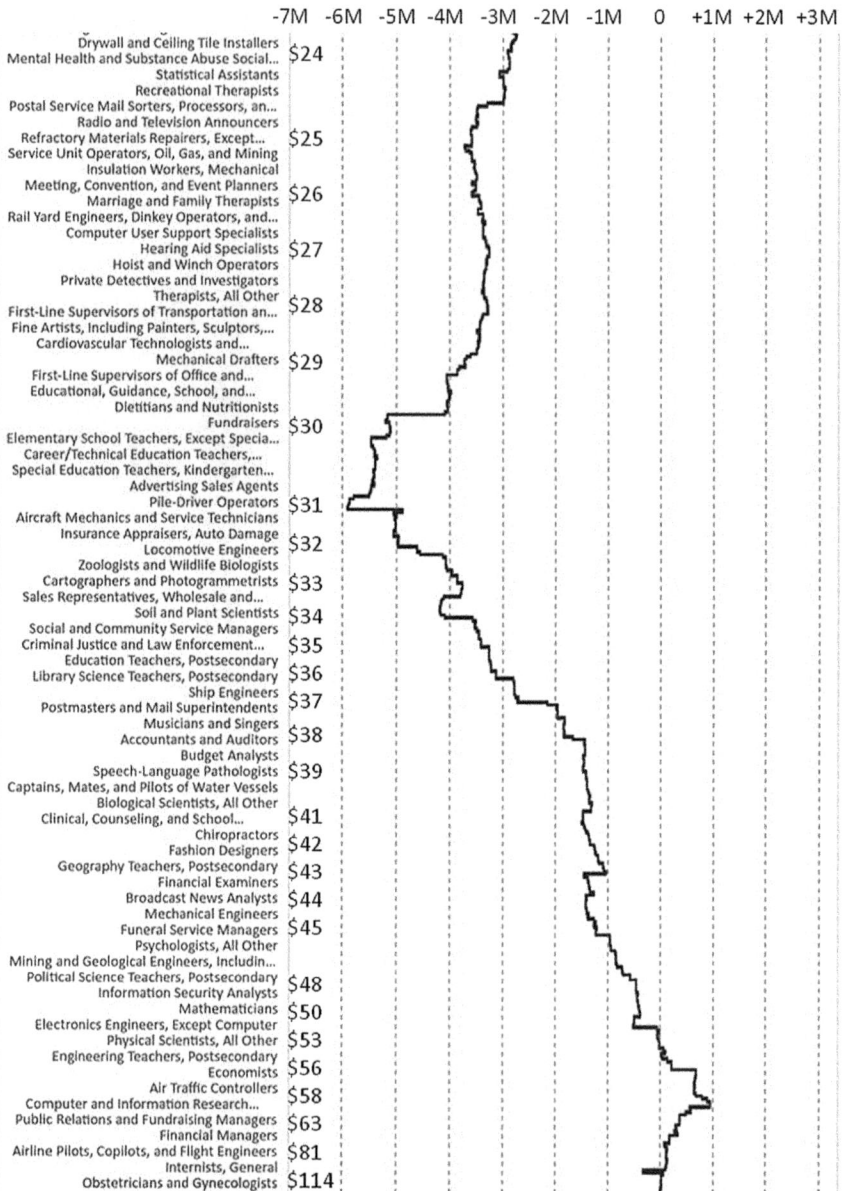

Detail 2

	-7M	-6M	-5M	-4M	-3M	-2M	-1M	0	+1M	+2M	+3M

Drywall and Ceiling Tile Installers $24
Mental Health and Substance Abuse Social...
Statistical Assistants
Recreational Therapists
Postal Service Mail Sorters, Processors, an...
Radio and Television Announcers
Refractory Materials Repairers, Except... $25
Service Unit Operators, Oil, Gas, and Mining
Insulation Workers, Mechanical
Meeting, Convention, and Event Planners
Marriage and Family Therapists $26
Rail Yard Engineers, Dinkey Operators, and...
Computer User Support Specialists
Hearing Aid Specialists $27
Hoist and Winch Operators
Private Detectives and Investigators
Therapists, All Other $28
First-Line Supervisors of Transportation an...
Fine Artists, Including Painters, Sculptors,...
Cardiovascular Technologists and...
Mechanical Drafters $29
First-Line Supervisors of Office and...
Educational, Guidance, School, and...
Dietitians and Nutritionists
Fundraisers $30
Elementary School Teachers, Except Specia...
Career/Technical Education Teachers,...
Special Education Teachers, Kindergarten...
Advertising Sales Agents
Pile-Driver Operators $31
Aircraft Mechanics and Service Technicians
Insurance Appraisers, Auto Damage
Locomotive Engineers $32
Zoologists and Wildlife Biologists
Cartographers and Photogrammetrists $33
Sales Representatives, Wholesale and...
Soil and Plant Scientists $34
Social and Community Service Managers
Criminal Justice and Law Enforcement... $35
Education Teachers, Postsecondary
Library Science Teachers, Postsecondary $36
Ship Engineers
Postmasters and Mail Superintendents $37
Musicians and Singers
Accountants and Auditors $38
Budget Analysts
Speech-Language Pathologists $39
Captains, Mates, and Pilots of Water Vessels
Biological Scientists, All Other
Clinical, Counseling, and School... $41
Chiropractors
Fashion Designers $42
Geography Teachers, Postsecondary $43
Financial Examiners
Broadcast News Analysts $44
Mechanical Engineers
Funeral Service Managers $45
Psychologists, All Other
Mining and Geological Engineers, Includin...
Political Science Teachers, Postsecondary $48
Information Security Analysts
Mathematicians $50
Electronics Engineers, Except Computer
Physical Scientists, All Other $53
Engineering Teachers, Postsecondary
Economists $56
Air Traffic Controllers $58
Computer and Information Research...
Public Relations and Fundraising Managers $63
Financial Managers
Airline Pilots, Copilots, and Flight Engineers $81
Internists, General
Obstetricians and Gynecologists $114

Appendix C: U.S. Sales Jobs by Detailed Category, 2000 and 2018

Sorted in increasing order of wages, as per the gray background.

While Fig. 2.9 shows Sales jobs as a whole belonging to the middle-class, behind the average wage of $20 an hour lie huge disparities. The majority of

2018 sales jobs (8 out of 14.5 million) consists of cashiers and retail sales, whose hourly wages averaged $11.17 and $13.61, respectively.

A waterfall chart of the type presented in Fig. 2.11 shows middle-class squeeze dynamics at play here too:

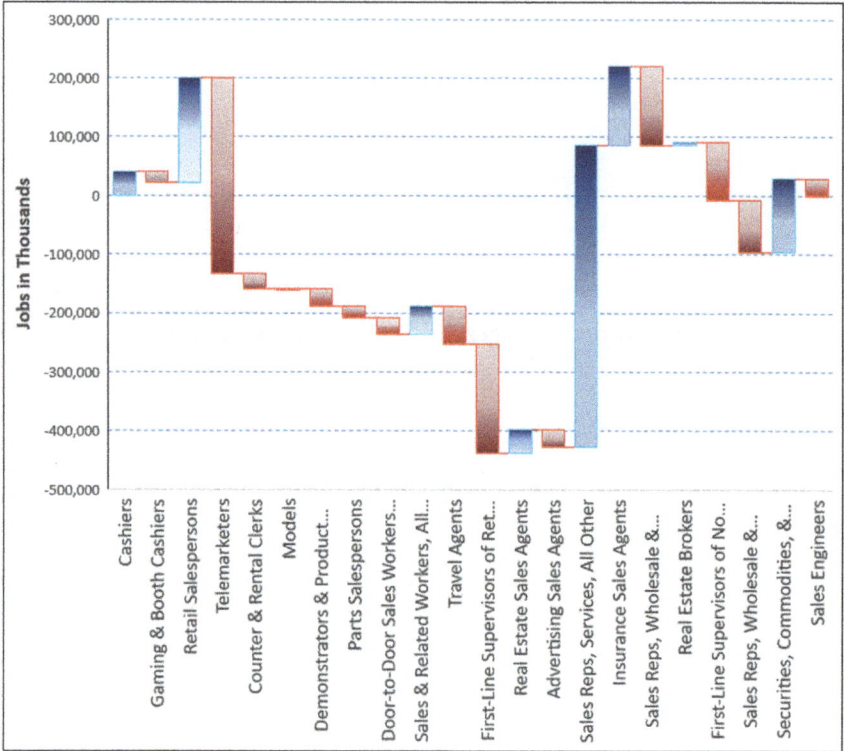

2000 to 2018 U.S. Sales Jobs Evolution by Major Category.Sorted by increasing wage level & adjusted for overall workforce increase (11.6%)

Appendix D: Big Tech (GAFAM) Versus Rest of the U.S.—Sales, Headcount and R&D Spending

Namely Alphabet (Google), Apple, Facebook, Amazon and Microsoft.

GAFAM % of total USA	2016	2021
Sales	3.0%	6.0%
Headcount	0.4%	1.4%
R&D	11.7%	24.0%

2021 Sales (in M$)

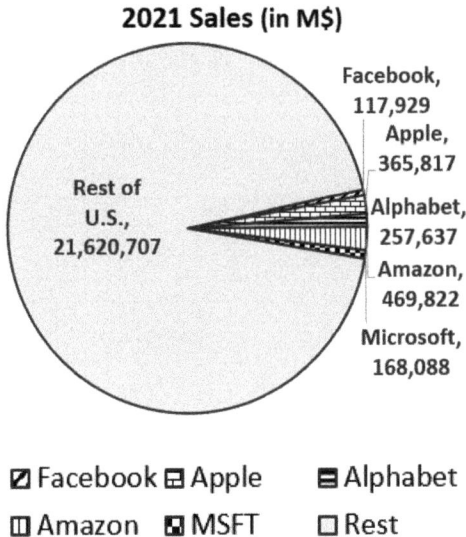

Facebook, 117,929
Apple, 365,817
Alphabet, 257,637
Amazon, 469,822
Microsoft, 168,088
Rest of U.S., 21,620,707

☑ Facebook ⊞ Apple ☰ Alphabet
⬚ Amazon ⊠ MSFT ☐ Rest

© The Editor(s) (if applicable) and The Author(s), under exclusive license to Springer Nature Switzerland AG 2023, corrected publication 2023
A. M. Recanati, *AI Battle Royale*, Copernicus Books,
https://doi.org/10.1007/978-3-031-19278-4

**2021 Headcount
(in number of workers)**

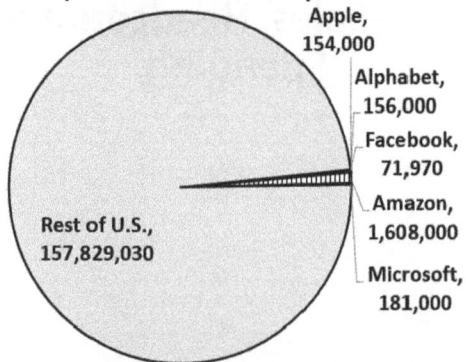

Apple,
154,000

Alphabet,
156,000

Facebook,
71,970

Amazon,
1,608,000

Rest of U.S.,
157,829,030

Microsoft,
181,000

2021 R&D Spending (in M$)

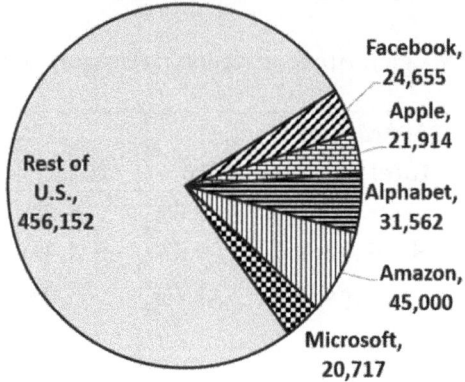

Facebook,
24,655

Apple,
21,914

Rest of
U.S.,
456,152

Alphabet,
31,562

Amazon,
45,000

Microsoft,
20,717

Appendix E: African Countries, Weighted by Population Size Under 25 Years Old, as of 2019

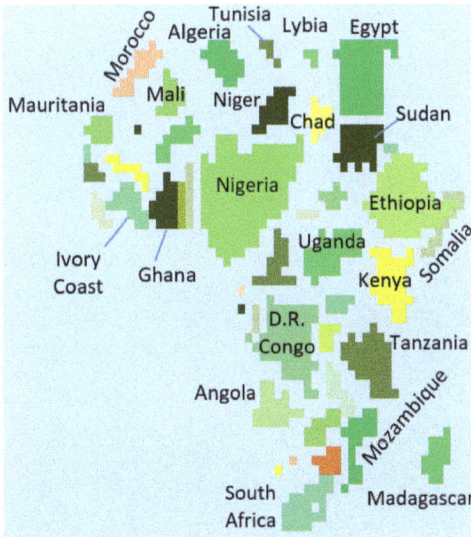

With countries in their normal position

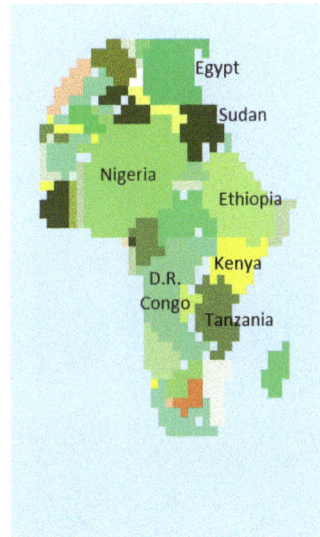

Without gaps between countries

The challenge with building such maps: either respect the overall shape of the continent (left-side map), with as a result large swaths of empty space in between countries, that betray actual landmass size (making it appear exaggeratingly big, especially when represented on a world map), or "stitch" the countries together in what produces a lopsided continent (right-side map).

© The Editor(s) (if applicable) and The Author(s), under exclusive
license to Springer Nature Switzerland AG 2023, corrected publication 2023
A. M. Recanati, *AI Battle Royale*, Copernicus Books,
https://doi.org/10.1007/978-3-031-19278-4

Appendix F: 2019 GDP per Capita in USD, 2000–2019 GDP per Capita Growth, for Countries with a population size above 30 Million as of 2019

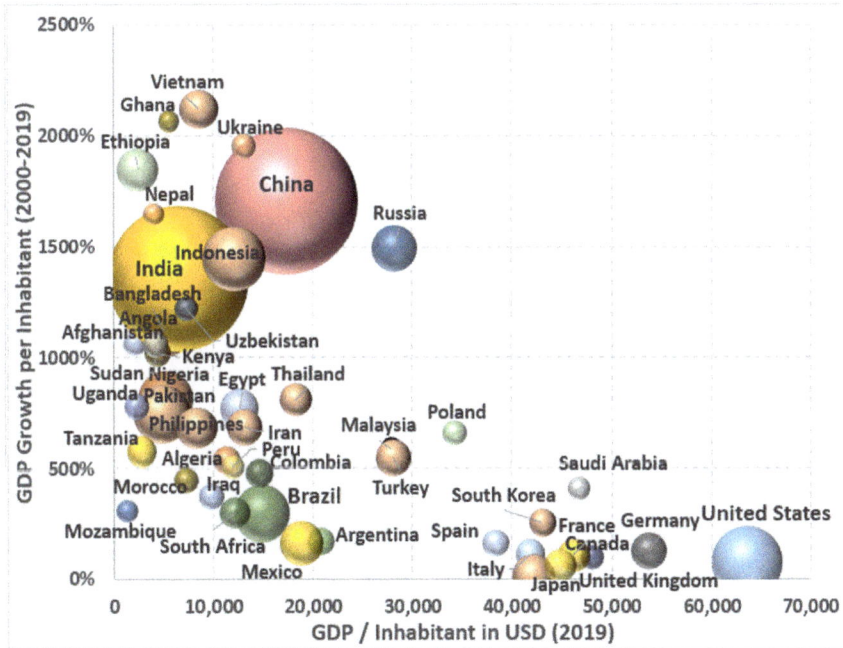

Bubble size based on size of population. These countries totalize 88% of the world population in 2019, or 6.6 out of 7.5 billion people.

© The Editor(s) (if applicable) and The Author(s), under exclusive license to Springer Nature Switzerland AG 2023, corrected publication 2023
A. M. Recanati, *AI Battle Royale*, Copernicus Books,
https://doi.org/10.1007/978-3-031-19278-4

Appendix G: Full Page View of Job Classification with Traits

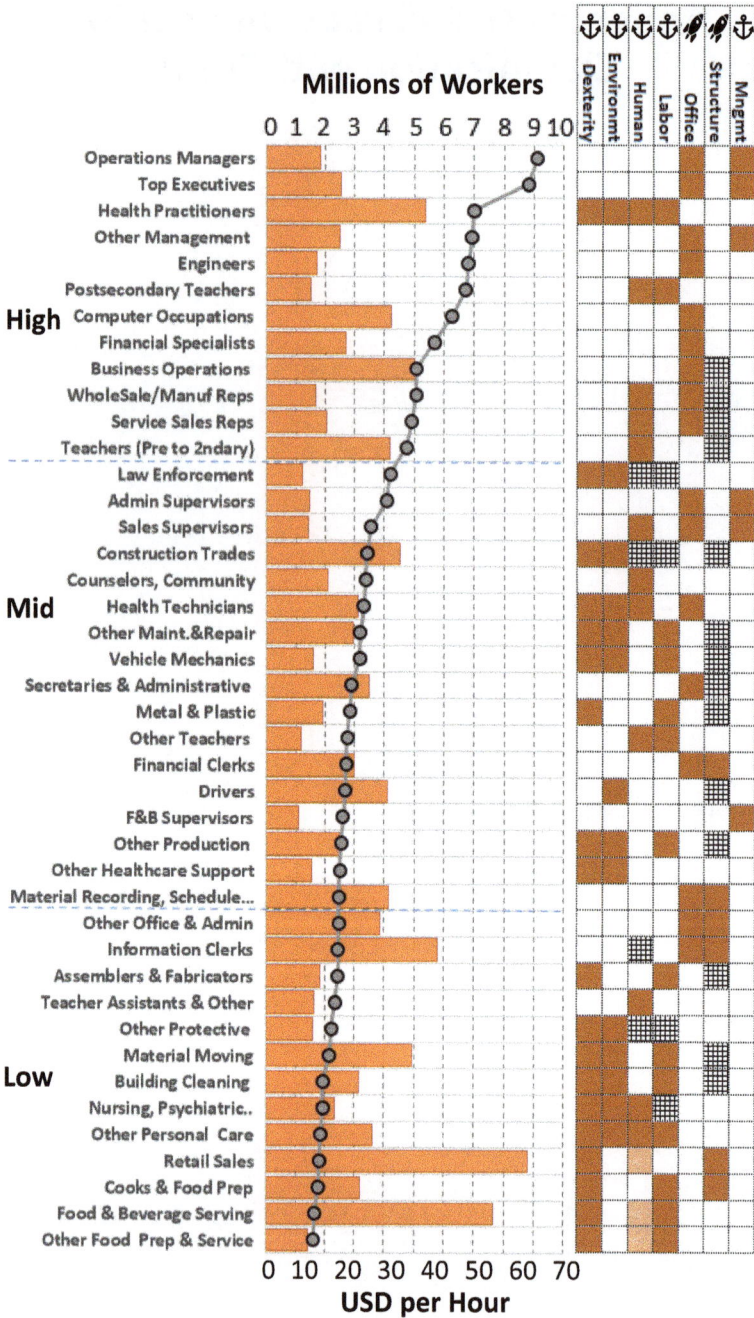

Millions of Workers

0 1 2 3 4 5 6 7 8 9 10

| | Dexterity | Environm. | Human | Labor | Office | Structure | Mngmt |

High
- Operations Managers
- Top Executives
- Health Practitioners
- Other Management
- Engineers
- Postsecondary Teachers
- Computer Occupations
- Financial Specialists
- Business Operations
- WholeSale/Manuf Reps
- Service Sales Reps
- Teachers (Pre to 2ndary)

Mid
- Law Enforcement
- Admin Supervisors
- Sales Supervisors
- Construction Trades
- Counselors, Community
- Health Technicians
- Other Maint.&Repair
- Vehicle Mechanics
- Secretaries & Administrative
- Metal & Plastic
- Other Teachers
- Financial Clerks
- Drivers
- F&B Supervisors
- Other Production
- Other Healthcare Support
- Material Recording, Schedule...

Low
- Other Office & Admin
- Information Clerks
- Assemblers & Fabricators
- Teacher Assistants & Other
- Other Protective
- Material Moving
- Building Cleaning
- Nursing, Psychiatric..
- Other Personal Care
- Retail Sales
- Cooks & Food Prep
- Food & Beverage Serving
- Other Food Prep & Service

0 10 20 30 40 50 60 70

USD per Hour

Glossary

3D Printing a manufacturing process by which an object is produced by adding single grains of material, layer upon layer.

5G the fifth generation of technology standard for broadband cellular networks. Provides better connection speeds (up to 10 GB by second) and forms a building block for the Internet of Things.

Additive Manufacturing cf. 3D printing.

Amara's Law the tendency for people to overestimate technology's effects in the short term, and underestimate its effects in the long run.

ARPANET the Advanced Research Projects Agency Network. Set up by the Defense Advanced Research Projects Agency (DARPA), a sub-division of the U.S. Department of Defense, ARPANET was the precursor of the Internet.

Artificial General Intelligence (AGI) Artificial Intelligence that achieves an intelligence level equivalent to that of a human brain. Characterized by strong cognitive abilities, it can connect the dots between different types of information, and induce general rules from observation. AGI is not restrained to a closed system of perfect information, the way narrow AI is.

Artificial Narrow Intelligence (ANI) AI that excels at a narrow task but is incapable of performing several different tasks (for instance processing language while simultaneously decrypting the speaker's facial expressions, body language and tone of voice). All AI as of today is narrow; also called "weak AI".

Artificial Neural Networks computing systems inspired by the biological neural networks present in animals, ANN use a collection of connected nodes (called neurons) organized in layers, that act like brain synapses. Each connection and neuron have a weight that changes as the learning improves.

Artificial Super Intelligence (ASI) an Artificial Intelligence level that exceeds human intelligence.

Asimov's Laws introduced in Isaac Asimov's short story *Runaround*, the three laws are: "A robot may not injure a human being or, through inaction, allow a human being to come to harm. A robot must obey orders given to it by human beings except where such orders would conflict with the First Law. A robot must protect its own existence as long as such protection does not conflict with the First or Second Law." These laws serve as the backbone for a number of his novels, providing early insights into the challenges and limitations of a top-down approach to AI for real-world applications.

Assisted Reality (aR) allows one to remotely view a screen within her immediate field of vision, with the possibility of superimposing information without blocking the user's vision. Usually the device used is hands-free (for instance smart glasses). It can greatly enhance collaborative work at a distance but also enable new forms of outsourcing that erode the value of skills.

Augmented Reality (AR) an interactive experience of a real-world environment with computer-generated information or objects overlaid, using head-mounted gear.

Backpropagation short for "backward propagation of errors". A type of algorithm used for supervised machine learning of artificial neural networks.

Bayes' Theorem named after Thomas Bayes, the theorem describes the probability of an event, based on prior knowledge of conditions that might be related to it. Bayes' formula is as follows: the conditional probability of an event based on the occurrence of another event equals the likelihood of the second event given the occurrence of the first, multiplied by the probability of the first event, divided by the probability of the second event. It is of great use in statistics and machine learning, especially as with time new events are added.

Beaudry Effect a term we coin, based on economist Paul Beaudry's remark that once an innovative technology is up and running, less labor is necessary than was the case to set it up, therefore resulting in a decline in number of jobs.

Big Data refers to the copious amounts of data that pour in via a variety of inputs. The size of the data makes it challenging to analyze by humans alone, yet with the aid of machines, it can be mined for information, analyzed and used by data-hungry algorithms for machine learning, classification, predictive modeling, and other applications.

Billiards Allegory an illustration of the limited rigidity and sturdiness of a job. A reorganization can rip a job description to bits, in a shakeup that sends tasks flying apart, similar to the break shot of a stack of billiards, dismembering and reshaping jobs into different settings which entail new job requirements. Technology is often the true cue stick that shatters the job. The metaphor serves as a counterargument to the oft-rehashed objection that as long as certain of the tasks that compose it resist automation, a job cannot be harmed by automation.

Black Box highlights our inability to "look under the hood", into the inner cogs of an algorithm. As we cannot scrutinize its reasoning, we cannot understand by what means it produces an output based on inputs, in other words how it reaches a given conclusion.

Cambrian Explosion a period around 540 million years ago that saw the gradual introduction of a great diversity of new life species, as per fossil records. It is hypothesized that this explosion in life forms was consequent to a biological novelty: eyes. Some AI experts conjecture that advances in computer vision will soon lead to a "Cambrian Explosion" in robotics.

ChatGPT an artificial intelligence chatbot developed by OpenAI and launched in November 2022. Using both supervised and reinforcement learning techniques, ChatGPT represents a major leap in terms of abilities "commonly associated with intelligent beings". It quickly garnered attention for its detailed responses and articulate answers across many domains of knowledge, breaching the million-user threshold in a record time, and raising anew concerns over the future of the job market.

Chinese Room a thought experiment used to argue that a digital computer executing a program does not have a "mind", "understanding", nor a "consciousness", regardless of how intelligent or human-like it may appear to human observers.

Cloud Computing the availability of data and computational resources on a third-party server, as opposed to storage on one's own physical hard drives; it marks the case of buying a service instead of hardware. Main providers include Microsoft, Amazon and Alibaba. Advantages include flexibility, bypassing upfront investments in IT infrastructure, computational power and security.

Combinatorial Explosion the rapid growth of complexity arising from added inputs that have an exponential effect.

Computer Vision a subfield of AI that deals with image recognition, enabling computers to derive meaningful information from images and videos.

Corporate Dystopia a dystopia refers to a nightmarish society where the strong dominate the weak, in opposition to the ideal society, or utopia. A popular theme in cyberpunk, the *corporate* dystopia sees power centralized in the hands of large corporations.

Counterfactual Explanations Method describes a causal situation in the form of "if I had not sipped that coffee, I would not have burned my lips". Can be used in machine learning to test the output by tweaking the inputs.

Codecademy a free-access website to learn how to code.

Creative Destruction the destruction of the old brought forth by the introduction of the new. Though in a broad sense it encapsulates disruptive processes and products, we use the term in the narrow sense of an emerging market or sector of activity, that disrupts an existing market or sector by substitution.

CRISPR/CAS9 a revolutionary form of gene-editing discovered in 2012, using a natural process that calls on sequences of clustered regularly interspaced short palindromic repeats (CRISPR) along with the Cas9 enzyme (CRISPR-associated protein 9) to identify, cut and paste specific parts of DNA.

Crowdfunding an alternative financing method to bank loans and traditional capital raising, that consists in presenting a project or venture online to seek and receive funds from the internet community. Several types exist; a common one sees a minimum threshold of funds to collect specified upfront for the project to move forward; if not reached, the money is returned to investors (called seeders). If the threshold is met, the project moves forward and seeders can receive a prototype or other reward for their support.

Deep Learning a subset of Machine Learning that uses three or more layers of artificial neural networks.

Deepfake a portmanteau of deep learning and fake, deepfakes are synthetic media that appear to be real, usually involving the image or video of a person. The fabrication can show that person doing or saying things convincingly, thus duping viewers, and posing grave ethical issues.

"Digidend" a hypothetical monetary retribution given by an organization to people in exchange for their digital data.

Digital Taylorism a modern take on Taylorism, applied to the service and office working areas, with the aim of routinizing tasks and streamlining processes; it involves the use of new technologies to devise metrics for monitoring worker performance.

Digital Twin a virtual representation that serves as a digital counterpart of a physical object or process. The term was first used by NASA to create a simulation of space conditions. Interest in digital twins is growing, for their ability to generate data, thus train algorithms.

Disruptive Innovation an innovative process, usually introduced on the low-end market, but that gradually gains traction, displacing market-leaders.

eDiscovery in a lawsuit or investigation, the electronic aspect of identifying, collecting and producing electronically stored information.

Engel's Pause a term coined by economic historian Robert C. Allen to describe the period from 1790 to 1840 that saw British working-class wages stagnate in spite of rapid per-capita gross domestic product expansion.

Fan Funding a form of crowd funding, more commonly used for music and video content creation.

General-Purpose Technology (GPT) a technology with broad, deep and long-lasting impacts on the economy. Often found at the epicenter of industrial revolutions.

Generative Adversarial Network (GAN) consists in two neural networks. The first one generates candidates from data, the second one evaluates them.

Genetic Algorithm an algorithm that relies on biologically inspired operators such as mutation, gene crossover and selection. Used to solve optimization and search problems.

Gini Index a measure of income or wealth dispersion developed Corrado Gini, with 0 representing perfect equality and 1 maximum inequality (everything is held by a single person).

GitHub a provider of internet hosting for software development and version control using Git software. Acquired by Microsoft in 2018.

Grey Goo Scenario also called ecophagy; a hypothetical global catastrophe caused by nanotechnology in which out-of-control self-replicating machines consume all biomass while building more of themselves.

Holacracy a decentralized method of management and organizational governance, where authority and decision-making are distributed through self-organizing teams rather than vertically in a management hierarchy.

Internet of Things (IoT) refers to physical objects embedded with sensors, processing ability and a connection device (such as a Bluetooth module), enabling them to send and receive data, or even perform actions.

Internet Waves a concept we use to demarcate the periods where PCs dominated, to that of smartphones, soon to be followed by headsets and smartglasses (3rd wave), and eventually brain implants (4th wave).

Job Polarization the tendency for middle-class jobs to disappear, leading to a pileup at the top and bottom extremes. Observed in Western economies since the 1970s, with names such as middle-class squeeze, hollowing out of the middle-class, or ALM hypothesis.

Kaggle a free machine learning platform and community, with open competitions that often involve a monetary reward. Acquired by Google in 2017.

Key Opinion Consumer an active Internet user with a community of followers, who approaches brands to test and post about their products.

Key Opinion Leader influencers with a large fanbase, that brands contact and offer incentives to, in exchange for posting about them.

Labor Force Participation Rate the population working or actively seeking for a job, divided by the overall population that qualifies for work. In the United States, this includes everyone above 16 years old that is not in the army or imprisoned; e.g. retirees and students are included.

Live-Streaming a live online broadcast, used to promote products (similarly to TV-shopping), but also to offer advice, do a performance, etc.

Location Quotient a statistic used by the U.S. Bureau of Labor to measure the ratio of an occupation's share of employment in a given area, compared to that occupation's share of employment in the U.S. as a whole. For example, an occupation that makes up 10% of employment in a specific metropolitan area compared with 2% of U.S. employment would have a location quotient of 5 for the area in question.

Luddites name given at the start of the 19th Century to bands of English textile workers who revolted against the introduction of novel machinery that made their skills irrelevant, reducing their value in the supply chain as it allowed low-skilled workers to take over their work. It has since become a derogatory term to designate people refractory to new technology (though the more proper term would be neo-Luddite, or technophobe).

Machine Learning the subfield of AI that leverages data to learn and improve a given task, for instance prediction or classification.

Macro a set of instructions that uses Microsoft's Visual Basic for Applications (VBA) program to execute tasks within Microsoft software. While mostly used for Excel, Macros also work on Word, Outlook, and within Windows (for instance to count the number of files of a certain extension in a given folder).

Metaverse virtual worlds of online 3D animated objects that aim to convey a semblance of realism indistinguishable from the physical world, where people can connect and interact.

Mixed Reality a medium of immersive computer-generated environments in which elements of a physical (AR) and virtual environment (VR) are combined.

MOOC massive open online courses are online courses available to the public, either for free or for a modest fee (in comparison with the cost of the curriculum of the schools offering the course).

Moore's Law a prognostic formulated by Gordon Moore in 1965 and based on past observation, that states that continuous transistor miniaturization would allow for the number of transistors placed on an integrated circuit chip to double roughly every 18 months. This exponential shrinkage of transistors is at the heart of the 3rd Industrial Revolution.

Moravec Paradox an observation made in the 1980s by roboticist Hans Moravec that for computers, reasoning requires little computational power in comparison to perception and dexterity. For humans it is the opposite: toddlers can easily perceive and manipulate objects.

Nanotechnology the use of matter on nanoscales—atomic, molecular or supramolecular—for industrial purposes.

Overfitting is said of a model that follows too closely a set of training data. It risks failing to achieve reliable efficiency when exposed to test data (i.e. new data).

Pattern Recognition machine learning methods geared to identify patterns and regularities in data. The data can be anything from the evolution of a price to commonalities in the genetic code of people with a proclivity for a particular disease, to images of people's faces or weapons, sounds and other definable qualities.

Polanyi Paradox the notion that human knowledge of how the world functions lies to a large extent beyond our explicit understanding. Named in honor of the British-Hungarian philosopher Michael Polanyi. For a job, refers to difficulties in writing down the contents of a job in minutiae, in reducing it to a list of instructions.

Quantified Self a cultural trend, whose adherents use technology to self-track aspects of their health and daily life or ("lifelogging"), often with the goal of improving health or mental performance.

Quantum Computing a type of computation that harnesses the properties of quantum states, such as superposition, interference and entanglement, to perform calculations. The devices that perform quantum computing are called quantum computers; the bits used are called qubits. These have the particular property of being equal to 0 and 1 simultaneously, in the same way that an electron spins both up and down.

Quiet Hiring A term used to describe the trend of companies to add on labor without actually hiring full-time employees. This is done typically by hiring short-term contractors, or by encouraging existing employees to temporarily take on a new role, usually when there is a sudden need to be filled somewhere.

Reinforcement Learning a type of algorithm that uses a performance score; the score serves as a feedback loop that guides it to improve. Through what begins as random actions, the algorithm gradually learns which actions can maximize its score.

Sectorial Mobility a term we use to describe the level of ease with which someone in an occupation can hop from one sector to another. An accountant has a high sectorial mobility, while a cardiologist is pinned down to the healthcare sector.

Servitization the "product as a service" model, whereby customers pay a recurrent service fee instead of a one-type product purchase. Also called "sales as a service", or SaaS. Note that SaaS initially referred to *software* as a service, only to spread beyond software to tangible goods, and partly as a result of the IoT trend turning tangible goods digital.

Shadow Data digital traces of data created by individuals unintentionally during their activities, for instance when surfing online.

Singularity in AI parlance, refers to an artificial intelligence that grows exponentially to achieve a super-intelligence level that by far surpasses human intelligence, leading to unforeseeable consequences.

Standard Operating Procedure (SOP) A set of step-by-step instructions to help workers carry out routine operations.

Sumo Challenge a term we use to assess, in a job that relies on so-called human–computer collaboration, which of these two agents retains the largest portion of cognition necessary to perform the job, for instance when it comes to decision-making.

Supervised Learning a type of algorithm that learns based on training data which has been tagged by humans. The algorithm is then exposed to untagged, test data, and attempts to achieve an optimal performance (or accuracy), using the training data similarly to how humans rely on experience.

Taylorism the scientific management of work, named after Frederick Taylor (1856–1915), that most notably involves division of labor and specialization, a meticulous inventory of tasks along with the timing of each action against a standard.

Turing Test initially called the Imitation Game, Alan Turing devised the test in 1950 as a method to determine whether a computer could exhibit intelligent behavior. The test consists in an evaluator asking questions to and receiving responses from two hidden subjects, one human, the other a machine. The machine passes the test if by the end of the exchange, the evaluator is unable to distinguish which is which.

Unsupervised Learning a type of algorithm that does not require human intervention to tag data. The algorithm learns patterns by drawing from large, untagged datasets.

Virtual Reality cf. *Metaverse*.

VUCA acronym for volatility, uncertainty, complexity and ambiguity. It aims to describe the realities of the outer world. When it comes to designing and performing a job, VUCA limits the propensity for a standard operating procedure to work smoothly, especially when followed blindly, without any brainwork required, the way good-old fashioned AI executes a program.

Zero Marginal Cost marginal cost designates the cost required to produce one extra unit—for instance the cost of raw material or labor involved—as opposed to a fixed cost like office rent. Zero marginal cost is a situation where units can be added with no extra cost incurred. It serves primarily to describe digital goods, such as online music or videos.

Bibliography

Abnett, Kate. 2020. "EU to target 30 million electric cars by 2030." *Reuters*, December 5. https://www.reuters.com/article/us-climate-change-eu-transport/eu-to-target-30-million-electric-cars-by-2030.

Acemoglu, Daron, and James A. Robinson. 2012. *Why nations fail: the origins of power, prosperity, and poverty.* Profile Books.

Acemoğlu, Daron, and Pascual Restrepo. 2018. *Artificial Intelligence, Automation and Work.* National Bueau of Economic Research, The University of Chicago Press. https://doi.org/10.3386/w24196.

Acemoglu, Daron, David Daron, and Pascual Restrepo. 2018. "The Race between Man and Machine: Implications of Technology for Growth, Factor Shares, and Employment." *American Economic Review (American Economic Review)* 108 (6): 1488–1542. https://doi.org/10.1257/aer.20160696.

Achani, Aldrich. n.d. "7 Young Africans out of 10 wish to go home after studying abroad." https://irawotalents.com/jeunes-africains-retour-afrique-etudes-entrepreneuriat-developpement/.

Adner, Ron, and Rahul Kapoor. 2016. "It's not the Tech, it's the Timing." *Harvard Business Review*, November.

Agrawal, Ajay, Joshua Gans, and Avi Goldfarb. 2018. *Prediction Machines: The Simple Economics of Artificial Intelligence.* Harvard Business Review Press.

2015. "Air France bosses attacked in jobs protest, Financial Times." *Financial Times.* https://www.ft.com/content/c0d167e6-6b59-11e5-8171-ba1968cf791a.

Allen, Robert C. 2009. "Engels' pause: Technical change, capital accumulation, and inequality in the British industrial revolution." *Explorations in economic history* (Elsevier) 46 (4): 418–435. https://doi.org/10.1016/j.eeh.2009.04.004.

© The Editor(s) (if applicable) and The Author(s), under exclusive license to Springer Nature Switzerland AG 2023, corrected publication 2023
A. M. Recanati, *AI Battle Royale*, Copernicus Books,
https://doi.org/10.1007/978-3-031-19278-4

Allen, Robert. 2009. *The British Industrial Revolution in Global Perspective*. Cambridge University Press.

Amazon staff. n.d. *What robots do (and don't do) at Amazon fulfilment centres.* https://www.aboutamazon.co.uk/amazon-fulfilment/what-robots-do-and-dont-do-at-amazon-fulfilment-centres.

Andrews, Franklin. 2012. *Megachange: The world in 2050.* Economist Books.

Arntz, Melanie, Terry Gregory, and Ulrich Zierahn. 2016. "The Risk of Automation for Jobs in OECD Countries: A Comparative Analysis." OECD Social, Employment and Migration Working Paper, OECD. https://doi.org/10.1787/5jlz9h56d vq7-en.

Arntz, Melanie, Terry Gregory, and Ulrich Zierahn. n.d. *The Risk of Automation for Jobs in OECD Countries: A Comparative Analysis.* Working Papers, OECD Social, Employment and Migration, OECD, Paris: OECD Publishing. https://doi.org/10.1787/5jlz9h56dvq7-en.

Ashgar, Rob. 2014. "Incompetence Rains, Err, Reigns: What The Peter Principle Means Today." *Forbes.* https://www.forbes.com/sites/robasghar/2014/08/14/incompetence-rains-er-reigns-what-the-peter-principle-means-today.

Asimov, Isaac. 1942. *Runaround.* Street & Smith.

Attali, Jacques. 2006. *Une Brève Histoire de l'Avenir (English: A Short History of the Future: A Brave and Controversial Look at the 21st Century).* Fayard (English: Arcade).

2017. *Augmented reality on AGCO's factor floor.* May 10. http://blog.agcocorp.com/2017/05/google-glass-placeholder/.

Autor, David H. 2015. "Why are there still so many jobs? The history and future workplace of automation." *Journal of Economic Perspectives* 29 (3): 3–30.

Autor, David. 2003. "Outsourcing at Will: The Contribution of Unjust Dismissal Doctrine to the Growth of Employment Outsourcing." *Journal of Labor Economics* 21 (1): 1–42. https://doi.org/10.1086/344122.

Autor, David. 2014. "Polanyi's Paradox and the Shape of Employment Growth." *Federal Reserve Bank of Kansas City: Economic Policy Proceedings.* 129–177.

Autor, David. 2010. *The Polarization of Job Opportunities in the U.S. Labor Market: Implications for Employment and Earnings, (April 2010).* Department of Economics and National Bureau of Economic Research, The Center for American Progress and The Hamilton Project. www.americanprogress.org.

Autor, David. 2017. *Will Automation Take Away All our Jobs?* https://www.youtube.com/watch?v=th3nnEpITz0.

Autor, David, and David Dorn. 2013. "The Growth of Low-Skill Service Jobs and the Polarization of the U.S. Labor Market." *American Economic Review* 5.

Autor, David, Frank Levy, and Richard Murnane. 2003. "The Skill Content of Recent Technological Change: an Empirical Exploration." *Quarterly Journal of Economics* (Harvard College and the Massachusetts Institute of Technology) (118).

Autor, David, Frank Levy, and Richard Murnane. 2003. "The Skill Content of Recent Technological Change: an Empirical Exploration." *Quarterly Journal of Economics* (118).

Azhar, Azeem. 2021. *The Exponential Age: How Accelerating Technology is Transforming Business, Politics and Society.* Diversion Books.

Baer, Drake. 2014. "Why Apple employees learn design from Pablo Picasso." *Business Insider*, August 15. https://www.businessinsider.com/why-apple-employees-learn-design-from-pablo-picasso-2014-8.

Baldwin, Richard. 2020. *The Globotics Upheaval: Globalization, Robotics and the Future of Work.* W&N.

Ballard, John. 2021. "The Mirror Acquisition Is Already Exceeding Lululemon's Expectations." *The Motley Fool*, April 12. https://www.fool.com/investing/2021/04/12/mirror-already-exceeding-lululemons-expectations/.

Barabba, P Vincent. 2011. *The Decision Loom: A Design for Interactive Decision-making in Organizations.* Triarchy Press Ltd.

Barjavel, René. 1968. *La Nuit des Temps (Engish: The Ice People).* Pocket.

Bartlett, Albert A. 1969. "Arithmetic, Population and Energy—a talk by Al Bartlett."

Battilana, Julie, and Tiziana Casciaro. 2013. "The Network Secrets of Great Change Agents." *Harvard Business Review*, July–August.

Beaudry, Paul, David A. Green, and Benjamin M. Sand. 2016. "The Great Reversal in the Demand for Skill and Cognitive Tasks." *Journal of Labor Economics* 34 (1).

Benavav, Aaron. 2020. *Automation and the Future of Work.* Verso publications.

Bezos, Jeff. 2020. *Invent and Wander: the Collected Writings of Jeff Bezos, with an Introduction by Walter Isaacson.* Harvard Business Review.

Biggs, John. 2009. "Senseg: amazing haptic technology that could be coming to a device near you." *Techcrunch*, April 29. https://techcrunch.com/2009/04/28/senseg-amazing-haptic-technology-that-could-come-to-a-device-near-you/.

Blinder, Alan S. 2007. "How Many U.S. Jobs Might Be Offshorable?" *The CEPS working paper series* (Princeton, NJ: Center for Economic Policy Studies) 142.

Bloomberg News. 2020. "China Raises 2025 Target of Electric-Car Sales to about 25%." December 3. https://www.bloomberg.com/news/articles/2019-12-03/china-raises-2025-sales-target-for-electrified-cars-to-about-25.

2018. *Boeing Tests Augmented Reality in the Factory.* January 19. https://www.boeing.com/features/2018/01/augmented-reality-01-18.page.

Bose, Nandita. 2021. "U.S. Labor Secretary supports classifying gig workers as employees." *Reuters.* https://www.reuters.com/world/us/exclusive-us-labor-secretary-says-most-gig-workers-should-be-classified-2021-04-29/.

Boston Consulting Group. 2015. "Back to the Future: The Road to Autonomous Driving." January 8. http://de.slideshare.net/TheBostonConsultingGroup/the-road-to-autonomous-driving.

Bostrom, Nick. 2003. *Ethical Issues in Advanced Artificial Intelligence.* Vol. 2, in *Cognitive, Emotive and Ethical Aspects of Decision Making in Humans and in Artificial Intelligence*, 12–17. Intrenational Institute of Advanced Studies in Systems Research and Cybernetics.

Bostrom, Nick. 2014. *Superintelligence: Paths, Dangers, Strategies.* OUP Oxford.

Bresnahan, Timothy F, and Manuel Trajtenberg. 1992. "General-Purpose Technologies: Engines of Growth." *National Bureau of Economic Research.* https://doi.org/10.3386/w4148.

Brown, John S., and Paul Duguid. 2017 updated edition. *The Social Life of Information.* Harvard Business Review Press.

Brynjolfsson, Erik, and Andrew McAfee. 2011. *Race Against the Machine: How the Digital Revolution is Accelerating Innovation, Driving Productivity, and Irreversibly Transforming Employment and the Economy.* Digital Frontier Press.

Brynjolfsson, Erik, and Andrew McAfee. 2014. *The Second Machine Age: Work, Progress, and Prosperity in a Time of Brilliant Technologies.* Norton & Company.

Brynjolfsson, Erik, et al. 2020. "COVID-19 and remote work: An early look at U.S. data." *National Burau of Economic Research.* http://www.nber.org/papers/w27344.

Bughin, Jacques, Jeongmin Seong, James Manyika, Michael Chui, and Raoul Joshi. 2018. *Notes from the AI frontier: Modeling the impact of AI on the world economy.* McKinsey Global Institute. https://www.mckinsey.com/featured-insights/artificial-intelligence/notes-from-the-ai-frontier-modeling-the-impact-of-ai-on-the-world-economy#part1.

Cappelli, Peter. 2023. "How Financial Accounting Screw Up HR." *Harvard Business Review*, January–February: 39–44.

Carr, Nicholas. 2010. *The Shallows: What the Internet is Doing to Our Brains.* W. W. Norton & Company.

Casadesus-Masanell, Ramon, Oliver Gassmann, and Roman Sauer. 2017. "Hilti Fleet Management: Turning a Successful Business Model on Its Head, (May 2017)." *Harvard Business School*, May. https://www.hbs.edu/faculty/Pages/item.aspx?num=52550.

Catchpole, Ken R., Marc R. De Leval, Angus McEwan, Nick Pigott, Martin J. Elliott, Annette McQuillan, Carol Macdonald, and Allan J. Goldman. 2007. "Patient Handover Using Formula 1 Pit-Stop and Aviation Models to Improve Safety and Quality." *Pediatric Anesthesia* (17): 470–478.

Chakravorti, Bhaskar, Ajay Bhalla, and Ravi Shankar Chaturvedi. 2019. "Which Countries are Leading the Data Economy." *The Harvard Business Review*, January 24.

Chen, Chi, and Leo Zhou. 2022. *How China's data privacy and security rules could impact your business.* July 18. Accessed October 01, 2022. https://www.ey.com/en_ae/forensic-integrity-services/how-chinas-data-privacy-and-security-rules-could-impact-your-business.

Chen, Shaohua, and Martin Ravaillon. 2007. "Absolute poverty measures for the developing world, 1981–2004." *The Proceedings of the National Academy of Sciences* 104: 16757–16762. https://doi.org/10.1073/pnas.0702930104.

Chetty, Raj, John N. Friedman, Emmanuel Saez, Nicholas Turner, and Danny Yagan. 2017. "Mobility Report Cards: The Role of Colleges in Intergenerational Mobility." *National Bureau of Economic Research* (National Bureau of Economic Research). https://doi.org/10.3386/w23618.

Christensen, Clayton. 1997. *The innovator's dilemma: when new technologies cause great firms to fail.* Harvard Business School Press.

Chui, Michael, James Manyika, and Mehdi Miremadi. 2015. "Four Fundamentals of Workplace Automation." *McKinsey Quarterly*, November 1. https://www.mck insey.com/business-functions/mckinsey-digital/our-insights/four-fundamentals-of-workplace-automation.

Clark, Dorie. 2013. *Reinventing You: Define Your Brand, Imagine Your Future.* Harvard Business Press.

Clark, Gregory. 2008. *A Farewell to Arms.* Princeton University Press.

Clery, Daniel. 2013. *A Piece of the Sun, the Quest for Fusion Energy.* Gildan Media, LLC.

Cline, Ernest. 2015. *Armada.* Ballantine Books.

Cline, Ernest. 2011. *Ready Player One.* Ballantine Books.

Cline, Ernest. 2020. *Ready Player Two.* Ballantine Books.

Codella, Noel, Quoc-Bao Nguyen, and et al. 2017. "Deep Learning Ensembles for Melanoma Recognition in Dermoscopy Images." *IBM Journal of Research and Development* 61.

Cohany, Sharon R. 1998. "Workers in Alternative Employment Arrangements: a Second Look." *Monthly Labor Review* 121 (11): 3–21. https://www.bls.gov/opub/mlr/1998/11/art1full.pdf.

Cole, David. 2004. "The Chinese Room Argument." *Stanford Encyclopedia of Philosophy.* March 19. https://plato.stanford.edu/entries/chinese-room/.

Comin, Diego, and Bart Hobjin. 2010. "An Exploration of Technology Diffusion." *American Economic Review* 100 (5).

Covey, Stephen R. 1989. *The 7 Habits of Highly Effective People.* Free Press.

Coyle, Daniel. 2018. *The Culture Code: The Secrets of Highly Successful Groups.* Bantam.

Crevier, Daniel. 1993. *AI: The Tumultuous History of the Search for Artificial Intelligence.* Basic Books.

2019. *Data Economy: Radical Transformation or Dystopia?* Department of Economic and Social Affairs, United Nations, Economic Analysis and Policy Division, Frontier Technology Quarterly. https://www.un.org/development/desa/dpad/wp-content/uploads/sites/45/publication/FTQ_1_Jan_2019.pdf.

David, Paul A. 1990. "The Dynamo and the Computer: An Historical Perspective on the Modern Productivity Paradox." *The American Economic Review* (American Economic Association) 80: 355–361. http://www.jstor.org/stable/2006600.

Davie, Anna, Devin Fidler, and Marina Gorbis. 2011. "Future Work Skills 2020." Institute for the Future, University of Phoenix Research Institute.

Dawkins, Richard. 1976. *The Selfish Gene.* Oxford University Press.

De Sautoy, Marcus. 2019. *The Creativity Code, How AI is Learning to Write, Paint and Think*. 4th Estate.

Dennett, Daniel C. 2017. *From Bacteria to Bach and Back: The Evolution of Minds*. W. W. Norton & Company.

Desai, Sujay, et al. 2017. "MoS2 transistors with 1-nanometer gate lengths." *Science Magazine* 354. https://science.sciencemag.org/content/354/6308/99.

Dewar, Carolyn, Scott Keller, and Vikram Malhotra. 2022. *CEO Excellence: The Six Mindsets That Distinguish the Best Leaders from the Rest*. Scribner.

Diamandis, Peter H. 2020. *The Future Is Faster Than You Think: How Converging Technologies Are Transforming Business, Industries, and Our Lives*. Simon & Schuster.

Diamandis, Peter H., and Steven Kotler. 2015. *Bold, How to Grow Big, Create Wealth and Impact the World*. Simon & Schuster.

Diamond, Jared. 2019. *Upheaval: Turning Points for Nations in Crisis*. Little, Brown and Company.

Dickson, Ben. 2021. "Google's new deep learning system can give a boost to radiologists." *Venture Beat*, September 16. https://venturebeat.com/2021/09/16/goo gles-new-deep-learning-system-can-give-a-boost-to-radiologists/.

Domingos, Pedro. 2015. *The Master Algorithm: How the Quest for the Ultimate Learning Machine Will Remake Our World*. Basic Books.

Doshi, Neel, and Lindsay McGregor. 2015. *Primed to Perform*. Harper Business.

Doudna, Jennifer A., and Samuel H. Sternberg. 2017. *A Crack in Creation: Gene Editing and the Unthinkable Power to Control our Evolution*. Mariner Books.

Dreyer, Jacob. 2022. "China's Revolution Turns Green." *Noema Magazine*, October 20. https://www.noemamag.com/chinas-revolution-turns-green.

Dreyfus, Herbert L., and Stuart E. Dreyfus. 1992. "What artificial experts can and cannot do." *AI and Society* 6: p.21. https://doi.org/10.1007/BF02472766.

Drucker, Peter. 1973. *Management: Tasks, Responsibilities, Practices*. Harper & Row.

Dwoskin, Elizabeth. 2021. "Misinformation on Facebook got six times more clicks than factual news during the 2020 election, study says." *The Washington Post*, September 4. https://www.washingtonpost.com/technology/2021/09/03/fac ebook-misinformation-nyu-study/.

Edmonds, Ellen. 2017. "Americans Feel Unsafe Sharing the Road with Fully Self-Driving Cars." American Automobile Association. https://newsroom.aaa.com/2017/03/americans-feel-unsafe-sharing-road-fully-self-driving-cars/.

Edmonds, Ellen. 2019. "Three in Four Americans Remain Afraid of Fully Self-Driving Vehicles." Amrican Automobile Association. https://newsroom.aaa.com/2019/03/americans-fear-self-driving-cars-survey/.

Eliade, Mircea, and Willard R. Trask. 1987. *The Sacred and The Profane: The Nature of Religion*. Harcourt Brace Jovanovich.

Esteva, A., B. Kuprel, R. Novoa, et al. 2017. "Dermatologist-level classification of skin cancer with deep neural networks." Nature, 115–118. https://doi.org/10.1038/nature21056.

Fan, Shelley, and Matthew Taylor. 2019. *Will AI Replace US?* Thames & Hudson Ltd.

Feinstein, Charles. 1998. "Pessimism Perpetuated: Real Wages and the Standard of Living in Britain during and after the Industrial Revolution." *Journal of Economic History* (Cambridge University Press) 58 (3): 625–658.

Feinstein, Charles. 1998. *Pessimism Perpetuated: Real Wages and the Standard of Living in Britain during and after the Industrial Revolution.* Cambridge University Press.

Feldman, Amy. 2020. "How a Former Ballerina turned Mirror into a Buzzy $300 Million Exercise Phenomenon." *Forbes*, May 28. https://www.forbes.com/sites/amyfeldman/2020/05/28/how-a-former-ballerina-turned-mirror-into-a-buzzy-300-million-exercise-phenomenon/.

Feloni, Richard. 2016. "A Zappos employee had the company's longest customer-service call at 10 hours, 43 minutes." *Business Insider*, July 27. https://www.businessinsider.com/zappos-employee-sets-record-for-longest-customer-service-call-2016-7.

Ferrazzi, Keith, and Tahl Raz. 2005. *Never Eat Alone, and Other Secrets to Success, One Relationship at a Time.* Crown Business.

Financial Times. 2020. "Inside China's controversial mission to reinvent the internet." March 27. https://www.ft.com/content/ba94c2bc-6e27-11ea-9bca-bf503995cd6f.

Fitzgerald, McKenna, Aaron Boddy, and Seth D. Baum. 2020. "2020 Survey of Artificial General Intelligence Projects for Ethics, Risk, and Policy." Global Catastrophic Risk Institute. https://gcrinstitute.org/papers/055_agi-2020.pdf.

Ford, Martin. 2015. *Rise of the Robots: Technology and the Threat of a Jobless Future.* Basic Books.

Fox, Douglas. 2016. "What sparked the Cambrian explosion?" *Nature* 530 (7590). https://www.nature.com/news/what-sparked-the-cambrian-explosion-1.19379.

Franklin, Daniel. 2018. *Megatech: Technology in 2050.* Economist Books.

Frey, Carl Benedikt. 2019. *The Technology Trap: Capital, Labor, and Power in the Age of Automation.* Princeton University Press.

Frey, Carl Benedikt, and Michael O. Osborne. 2013. "The future of employment: how susceptible are jobs to computerization?" *Technological Forecasting and Social Change.* https://doi.org/10.1016/j.techfore.2016.08.019.

Friedman, Milton, and Binyamin Appelbaum. 1962. *Capitalism and Freedom.* University of Chicago Press.

Friedman, Milton, and Rose D. Friedman. 1980. *Free to Choose.* Harcourt.

Friend, Tad. 2018. "How Frightened Should We Be of A.I.?" *The New Yorker*, May 7. https://www.newyorker.com/magazine/2018/05/14/how-frightened-should-we-be-of-ai.

Fukuyama, Francis. 2015. *Political Order and Political Decay: From the Industrial Revolution to the Globalisation of Democracy.* Profile Books.

Garcia, Tristan. 2016. *La Vie Intense. Une Obsession Moderne.* Autrement.

Garfinkel, Harold. 1967. *Studies in ethnomethodology.* Englewood Cliffs.

Garfinkle, Madeline. 2023. *Quiet Hiring' Is on the Horizon – Here's What Employers and Employees Need to Know.* January 4. Accessed January 5, 2023. https://www.entrepreneur.com/business-news/what-is-quiet-hiring-and-how-you-can-use-it-to-your.

Garrigue, Anne. 1998. "Japonaises, la révolution douce." Picquier.

Gibbons, Ann. 2019. "Spotting Evolution Among Us." *Science magazine* 363: 21–23.

Giffard, Pierre. 1899. *La fin du cheval (The end of the horse).* PU Valenciennes (2015 publication).

Gladwell, Malcolm. 2009. *Blink: The Power of Thinking Without Thinking.* Back Bay Books.

2020. "Global Investments in R&D." Fact Sheet, Institute for Statistics estimates, UNESCO. http://uis.unesco.org/sites/default/files/documents/fs59-global-invest ments-rd-2020-en.pdf.

Golden, Hallie. 2020. "'Just walk out': Amazon debuts its first supermarket with no checkout lines." *The Guardian,* February 27. https://www.theguardian.com/us-news/2020/feb/25/amazon-go-grocery-supermarket-seattle-technology.

Goldin, Claudia. 2006. "The Quiet Revolution That Transformed Women's Employment, Education, and Family." *American Economic Review* 96: 1–21. https://doi.org/10.1257/000282806777212350.

Goldin, Claudia, and Lawrence Katz. 2009. *The Race between Education and Technology.* Harvard University Press.

Golson, Jordon. 2015. "Well, That Didn't Work: The Segway Is a Technological Marvel. Too Bad It Doesn't Make Any Sense." *Wired magazine,* January 16. https://www.wired.com/2015/01/well-didnt-work-segway-technological-mar vel-bad-doesnt-make-sense.

Goos, Maarten, and Alan Manning. 2007. "Lousy and Lovely Jobs: The Rising Polarization of Work in Britain." *The Review of Economics and Statistics.*

Gordon, Edward. 2013. *Future Jobs: Solving the Employment and Skills Crisis.* Praeger.

Gratton, Lynda, and Andrew J. Scott. 2016. *The 100-Year Life: Living and Working in an Age of Longevity.* Bloomsbury Information.

Greene, Robert. 1998. *The 48 Laws Of Power.* Viking Press.

Greenemeier, Larry. 2015. "Fukushima Disaster Inspires Better Emergency-Response Robots." *Scientific American,* May 18. https://www.scientificamerican.com/article/fukushima-disaster-inspires-better-emergency-response-robots/.

Guan, Mingyu, Paul Gao, Arthur Wang, Daniel Zipser, and Pei Shen. 2019. *2019 China Auto Consumer Insights.* McKinsey. https://www.mckinsey.com/industries/automotive-and-assembly/our-insights/china-auto-consumer-insights-2019.

Guido, Cortes Matias, Nir Jaimovich, and Henry E. Siu. 2017. "Disappearing routine jobs: Who, how, and why?" *Journal of Monetary Economics* (Elsevier) 91 (C): 69–87. https://doi.org/10.1016/j.jmoneco.2017.09.006.

Gupta, Sidhant, Dan Morris, Shwetak N. Patel, and Desney Tan. 2013. "AirWave: Non-Contact Haptic Feedback Using Air Vortex Rings." *UbiComp '13: Proceedings of the 2013 ACM international joint conference on Pervasive and ubiquitous computing.* ACM. 419–428. https://doi.org/10.1145/2493432.2493463.

Harari, Yuval Noah. 2018. *21 Lessons for the 21st Century.* Random House.

Harari, Yuval Noah. 2016. *Homo Deus: A Brief History of Tomorrow.* Harvill Secker.

Haraway, Donna J. 1990. *Simians, Cyborgs and Women: The Reinvention of Nature.* Routledge.

Harris, Michael. 2014. *The End of Absence: Reclaiming What We've Lost in a World of Constant Connection.* Current.

Heater, Brian. 2022. https://techcrunch.com/. June 23. https://techcrunch.com/2022/06/22/amazon-debuts-a-fully-autonomous-warehouse-robot/.

Heater, Brian, and Lucas Matney. 2020. "Magic Leap reportedly slashes 1,000 jobs and steps away from consumer plans." *Techcrunch,* April 22. https://techcrunch.com/2020/04/22/magic-leap-announces-layoffs-amid-covid-19-slowdown/.

High, Peter. 2017. "Under Armour Is Now The Largest Digital Health And Fitness Company On Earth." *Forbes,* September 18. https://www.forbes.com/sites/peterhigh/2017/09/18/under-armour-is-now-the-largest-digital-health-and-fitness-company-on-earth/?sh=1c1f77c85dfc.

Hill, David J. 2013. ""Keep Calm and Rape a Lot" T-Shirts show Growing Automation Pains." *Singularity Hub,* March 20. https://singularityhub.com/2013/03/20/keep-calm-and-rape-a-lot-t-shirts-show-automation-growing-pains/.

Hoadley, Daniel S., and Kelly M. Sayler. 2020. "Artificial Intelligence and National Security." Congressional Research Service. https://crsreports.congress.gov/.

Hobbes, Thomas. 1642. *De Cive (On the Citizen).*

Hopkins, Tom. 1981. *s, How to Master the Art of Selling, Champion Press (1981).* Champion Press.

Hou, Felicia. 2021. "This A.I. entrepreneur is working to bring machine learning to more industries." *Fortune,* November 9. https://fortune.com/2021/11/08/andrew-ng-data-centric-artificial-intelligence-machine-learning-braianstorm-ai-landing-ai/.

n.d. https://jkrishnamurti.org. https://jkrishnamurti.org/content/ojai-10th-public-talk-1945.

n.d. https://spritz.com. https://spritz.com.

n.d. https://strictlycookies.com. https://strictlycookies.com.

Iansiti, Marco, and Karim R. Lakhani. 2021. "How AI is Changing Work." *Harvard Business Review Special Issue.*

Ikenaga, Toshie, and Ryo Kambayashi. 2016. "Task Polarization in the Japanese Labor Market: Evidence of a Long-Term Trend." *Industrial Relations A Journal of Economy and Society* 55 (2): 267–293. https://doi.org/10.1111/irel.12138.

Intel News. 2018. "Latest Intel Study Finds People Expect Self-Driving Cars to Be Common in 50 Years." October 23. https://newsroom.intel.com/news/latest-intel-study-finds-people-expect-self-driving-cars-common-50-years/#gs.xrkk61.

Isaacson, Walter. 2014. *The Innovators: How a Group of Hackers, Geniuses, and Geeks Created the Digital Revolution.* Simon & Schuster.

Jung, Carl G. 1921. *Psychological Types.* Rascher Verlag.

Kahn, Jeremy. 2021. "Data-labeling company Scale AI valued at $7.3 billion with new funding." *Fortune Magazine*, April 14. https://fortune.com/2021/04/13/scale-ai-valuation-new-funding-fundraising-data-labeling-company-startups-vc/.

Kahneman, Daniel. 2011. *Thinking Fast and Slow.* Penguin.

Kaiser, Jocelyn, and Ann Gibbons. 2019. "Biology in the Bank." *Science* 363: 18–20.

Kanaan, Michael. 2020. *T-Minus AI: Humanity's Countdown to Artificial Intelligence and the New Pursuit of Global Power.* BenBella Books.

Kanterman, Matthew, and Nathan Naidu. 2021. "Metaverse may be $800 billion market, next tech platform." *Bloomberg*, December 1. https://www.bloomberg.com/professional/blog/metaverse-may-be-800-billion-market-next-tech-platform/.

Kelleher, Suzanne Rowan. 2022. *Qantas Asks Executives To Be Baggage Handlers Amid Labor Shortage, Forbes (August 8th, 2022).* August 8. Accessed November 01, 2022. https://www.forbes.com/sites/suzannerowankelleher/2022/08/08/qantas-asks-executives-to-be-baggage-handlers-amid-labor-shortage.

Kellenbenz, Hermann. 1976. *The Rise of the European Economy: An Economic History of Continental Europe from the Fifteenth to the Eighteenth Century.* Holmes & Meier.

Keller, Gary W., and Jay Papasan. 2013. *The ONE Thing: The Surprisingly Simple Truth About Extraordinary Results.* John Murray.

Kellogg, Katherine C, and Valentine A Melissa. 2022. "Five Mistakes Bosses Make When Introducing AI—and How to Fix Them." *The Wall Street Journal*, November 9.

Kelly, Kevin. 2016. *The Inevitable: Understanding The 12 Technological Forces That Will Shape Our Future.* Penguin Books.

Kenny, Charles, and George Yang. 2021. "Can Africa Help Europe Avoid Its Looming Aging Crisis?" Center for Global Development.

Kessler, Sarah. 2018. *Gigged: The End of the Job and the Future of Work.* St Martin's Press.

Keynes, John Maynard. 1930. *Essays in Persuasion.* Palgrave Macmillan. https://doi.org/10.1007/978-1-349-59072-8_25.

Kharas, Homi. 2017. "The Unprecedented Expansion of the Middle Class." The Brookings Institution. https://www.brookings.edu/wp-content/uploads/2017/02/global_20170228_global-middle-class.pdf.

Kharas, Homi, and Kristofer Hamel. 2018. "A global tipping point: Half the world is now middle class or wealthier." September 27. https://www.brookings.edu/blog/future-development/2018/09/27/a-global-tipping-point-half-the-world-is-now-middle-class-or-wealthier.

Kim, Chan W., and Renée A. Mauborgne. 2014. *Blue Ocean Strategy, Expanded Edition: How to Create Uncontested Market Space and Make the Competition Irrelevant.* Harvard Business Review Press.

King, Brett. 2018. *Bank 4.0: Banking Everywhere, Never at a Bank.* Wiley.

King, Marissa. 2021. *Social Chemistry: Decoding the Patterns of Human Connection.* Penguin Random House.

2011–2019. *Suits.* Directed by Aaron Korsh.

Kremen, Gladys Roth. n.d. "MDTA: The Origins of the Manpower Development and Training Act of 1962." https://www.dol.gov/. https://www.dol.gov/general/aboutdol/history/mono-mdtatext.

Krugman, Paul. 2013. "Lumps of Labor." *The New York Times.*

Kuper, Simon. 2021. "Financial Times: Are Superstar Employees about to be Offshored?" *Financial Times*, March 25. https://www.ft.com/content/9414f45c-6f03-4b8f-85c5-537d7e4f4932.

Kurzweil, Ray. 2000. *The Age of Spiritual Machines: When Computers Exceed Human Intelligence.* Penguin Books.

Kurzweil, Ray. 2006. *The Singularity is Near: When Humans Transcend Biology.* Duckworth.

Laws, David. 2018. "13 Sextillion & Counting: The Long & Winding Road to the Most Frequently Manufactured Human Artifact in History." *Computer History Museum*, April 2. https://computerhistory.org/blog/13-sextillion-counting-the-long-winding-road-to-the-most-frequently-manufactured-human-artifact-in-history/.

Lee, Kai-Fu. 2018. *Ai Superpowers: China, Silicon Valley, and the New World Order.* Mariner Books.

Lee, Kai-Fu, and Chen Qiufan. 2021. *AI 2041: Ten Visions for Our Future.* WH Allen.

Leontief, Wassily. 1983. "Technological Advance, Economic Growth, and the Distribution of Income." *Population and Development Review* (Population Council) 9 (3): 403–410. https://doi.org/10.2307/1973315.

Lesnes, Corinc. 2021. "Le Monde, Inégalités, pollution, vieillissement… le déclin du rêve californien." *Le Monde*, January 29.

Levesque, Hector J. 2018. *Common Sense, the Turing Test, and the Quest for Real AI.* The MIT press.

Lévi-Strauss, Claude. 1955. *Tristes Tropiques.* Librairie Plon.

Levit, Alexandra. 2018. *Humanity Works: Merging Technologies and People for the Workforce of the Future.* Kogan Page.

Levy, Frank, and Richard Murnane. 2005. *The New Division of Labor: How Computers are Creating the Next Job Market.* Princeton University Press.

Liao, Rita. 2021. "Pinduoduo steals Alibaba's crown with 788M annual active users." *Tech Crunch*, March 17. https://techcrunch.com/2021/03/17/pinduoduo-surpasses-alibaba/.

Lund, Susan, James Manyika, Liz H. Segel, André Dua, Bryan Hancock, Scott Rutherford, and Brent Macon. 2019. "The future of work in

America: People and places, today and tomorrow." McKinsey Global Institute. https://www.mckinsey.com/featured-insights/future-of-work/the-future-of-work-in-america-people-and-places-today-and-tomorrow.

Manguel, Alberto. 2014. *A History of Reading*. Penguin Books.

Manyika, James, Susan Lund, Michael Chui, Jacques Bughin, Jonathan Woetzel, Parul Batra, Ryan Ko, and Saurabh Sanghvi. 2017. "Jobs lost, jobs gained: workforce transitions in a time of automation." McKinsey Global Institute. https://www.mckinsey.com/~/media/BAB489A30B724BECB5 DEDC41E9BB9FAC.ashx.

Markoff, John. 2012. "How Many Computers to Identify a Cat? 16,000." June 25.

Matney, Lucas. 2019. "An AR Pioneer Collapses." *TechCrunch*, January 11. https://techcrunch.com/2019/01/10/an-ar-glasses-pioneer-collapses.

May, Matthew E. 2012. "The Rules of Successful Skunkworks Projects." *Fast Company*, October 9. http://www.fastcompany.com/3001702/rules-successful-skunk-works-projects.

McAfee, Andrew, and Erik Brynjolfsson. 2017. *Machine, Platform, Crowd: Harnessing Our Digital Future*. W.W.Norton & Company.

McCue, TJ. 2021. "57 Million U.S. Workers Are Part Of The Gig Economy." *Forbes*. https://www.forbes.com/sites/tjmccue/2018/08/31/57-million-u-s-workers-are-part-of-the-gig-economy.

McKeand, Kirk. 2020. "Half-Life: Alyx review—VR's killer app is a key component in the Half-Life story." *VG247*, March 23. https://www.vg247.com/half-life-alyx-review.

McKenzie, Theodore. 2022. "ZooBuilder: Ubisoft's AI-Based Tool for Animating Animals." *80 Level*, March 24. https://80.lv/articles/zoobuilder-ubisoft-s-ai-based-tool-for-animating-animals.

McKie, Robin. 2004. "Japanese boffins spawn almost invisible man." *The Guardian*, June 13. https://www.theguardian.com/science/2004/jun/13/japan.research.

McKinney, Wes. 2012. *Python for Data Analysis*. O'Reilly.

Miller, Steven, and Debbie Hughes. 2017. "The Quant Crunch: how the demand for data science skills is disrupting the job market." https://www.ibm.com. https://www.ibm.com/downloads/cas/3RL3VXGA.

Millward, Alan S. 1980. *War Economy and Society 1939–1945*. University of California Press.

Minsky, Marvin. 1986. *The Society of Mind*. Simon and Schuster.

Molinier, Jean. 1977. "L'évolution de la population agricole du XVIIIe siècle à nos jours." *Economie et Statistique*, 79–84.

Moravec, Hans. 1988. *Mind Children*. Harvard University Press.

Morris, Desmond. 1994. *The Human Zoo*. Vintage.

Myers, Joe. July 25th, 2016. *China's working-age population will fall 23% by 2050*. World Economic Forum.

Mortensen, Mark, and Amy C. Edmonson. 2023. "Rethink Your Employee Value Proposition: Offer Your People More Than Just Flexibility." *Harvard Business Review*, January–February: 45–49.

Nature. 2021. "Concrete needs to lose its colossal carbon footprint, Nature." September 28: 593–594. https://doi.org/10.1038/d41586-021-02612-5.

Nguyen, Tuong H. 2021. "5 Impactful Technologies From the Gartner Emerging Technologies and Trends Impact Radar for 2022." *Gartner*, December 8. https://www.gartner.com/en/articles/5-impactful-technologies-from-the-gartner-emerging-technologies-and-trends-impact-radar-for-2022.

n.d. *Nuclear Energy Institute.* https://www.nei.org/advantages/jobs.

Olazaran, Mikel. 1996. "A sociological study of the official history of the perceptrons controversy." *Social Studies of Science* 26 (3): 611–659. https://doi.org/10.1177/030631296026003005.

Olga, Kharif. 2013. "Shoppers' "Mobile Blinders" Force Checkout-Aisle Changes." *Bloomberg*, March 21. https://www.bloomberg.com/news/articles/2013-03-21/shoppers-mobile-blinders-force-checkout-aisle-changes.

Oloman, Jordan. 2020. "Half-Life: Alyx is a watershed moment for virtual reality." *Techradar*, March 24. https://www.techradar.com/uk/news/half-life-alyx-is-a-watershed-moment-for-virtual-reality.

O'Neil, Cathy. 2016. *Weapons of Math Destruction: How Big Data Increases Inequality and Threatens Democracy.* Crown.

Onnela, Jukka-Pekka, Benjamin N. Waber, and et al. 2014. "Using sociometers to quantify social interaction patterns." (Nature).

Oppenheimer, Andres. 2019. *The Robots are Coming! The Future of Jobs in the Age of Automation.* Vintage.

Orr, Julian. 1996. *Talking About Machines: An Ethnography of a Modern Job.* ILR PRess.

Perrigo, Billy. 2021. "Time Magazine." *Inside Facebook's African Sweatshop*, February 17. https://time.com/6147458/facebook-africa-content-moderation-employee-treatment/.

Phelan, David. 2017. "Apple CEO Tim Cook: As Brexit hands over UK, times are not really awful, there's some great things happening." *The Independent*, February 10.

Piketty, Thomas. 2014. *Capital in the 21st Century.* Harvard University Press.

Pinker, Steven. 2018. *Enlightment, Now: The Case for Reason, Science, Humanism, and Progress.* Penguin.

Pitso, Teboho. 2019. "Shared Futures: An Exploration of the Collaborative Potential of Intelligent Machines and Human Ingenuity in Cocreating Value." *InTechOpen.*

Pitso, Teboho. 2020. *Privileged.* Teboho Pitso.

Plautus, Titus Maccius. 195 BC. *Asinaria.*

Polanyi, Michael. 1967. *The Tacit Dimension.* Anchor Books.

Poppick, Susie. 2016. "These are the top workplace productivity killers." *CNBC*, June 9. https://www.cnbc.com/2016/06/09/top-distractions-at-work-and-how-to-increase-productivity.html.

n.d. *Population Pyramid.* https://www.populationpyramid.net/world/2019.

Porter, Michael E. 1980. *Competitive Strategy: Techniques for Analyzing Industries and Competitors.* Free Press.

Porter, Michael, and Mark Kramer. 2011. "Creating Shared Value." *Harvard Business Review*.

Prahalad, C.K., and Gary Hamel. 1990. "The Core Competence of the Corporation." *Harvard Business review*, May–June. https://hbr.org/1990/05/the-core-competence-of-the-corporation.

Pratt, Gill A. 2015. "Is a Cambrian Explosion Coming for Robotics?." *Journal of Economic Perspectives* 29 (3): 51–60.

Pugliano, John. 2017. *The Robots are Coming: A Human's Survivl Guide to Profiting in the Age of Automation*. Ulysses Press.

Rao, Lina, and Leena Rao. 2011. "Flurry: Time Spent on Mobile Apps has Surpassed Web Browsing." *Techcrunch*, June 20. https://techcrunch.com/2011/06/20/flurry-time-spent-on-mobile-apps-has-surpassed-web-browsing/.

Reece, Byron. 2018. *The Fourth Age: Smart Robots, Conscious Computers, and the Future of Humanity*. Atria Books.

Reese, Hope. 2016. "Is 'data labeling' the new blue-collar job of the AI era?" *Tech Republic*, March 10. https://www.techrepublic.com/article/is-data-labeling-the-new-blue-collar-job-of-the-ai-era/.

Richards, Douglas E. 2017. *Infinity Born*. Paragon Press.

Rifkin, Jeremy. 1996. *The End of Work: The Decline of the Global Labor Force and the Dawn of the Post-Market Era*. G.P. Putnam's Sons.

Ritchie, Hannah, and Max Roser. n.d. *Our World in Data*. https://ourworldindata.org/technology-adoption.

Roach, Geshe Michael, and Christie Lama McNally. 2009. *The Diamond Cutter: The Buddha on Managing Your Business and Your Life*. Harmony Publishing.

Roberts, James A., Luc Honore Petnji Yaya, and Chris Manolis. 2014. "The invisible addiction: Cell-phone activities and addiction among male and female college students." *National Library of Medecine* 245–265. https://doi.org/10.1556/JBA.3.2014.015.

Robinson, Andy. 2020. "Review: Half-Life Alyx is VR's stunning killer app." *Videogame chronicle.com*, March 23. https://www.videogameschronicle.com/review/half-life-alyx/.

2021. "Robots replace humans as labour shortages bite." *The Financial Times*.

Roehrig, Paul, and Ben Pring. 2021. *Monster: A Tough Love Letter On Taming The Machines That Rule Our Jobs, Lives, and Future*. Wiley.

Rogers, Everett. n.d. "Media is Here to Stay." *Media and Values*. http://www.medialit.org/reading-room/video-here-stay.

Roose, Kevin. 2021. *Futureproof: 9 Rules for Humans in the Age of Automation*. Random House.

Ross, Alec. 2016. *The Industries of the Future*. Simon & Schuster.

Rothman, Denis. 2020. *Hands-On Explainable AI (XAI) with Python: Interpret, visualize, explain, and integrate reliable AI for fair, secure, and trustworthy AI apps*. Packt Publishing.

Schulte, Brigid. 2015. "Health experts have figured out how much time you should sit each day." *The Washington Post*, June 2. https://www.washingtonpost.com/news/wonk/wp/2015/06/02/medical-researchers-have-figured-out-how-much-time-is-okay-to-spend-sitting-each-day/.

Schuman, Lucy. 1987. "Plans and Situated Actions, The Problem of Human Machine Collaboration." *International Conference on Computational Linguistics.*

Schumpeter, Joseph A. 1942. *Capitalism, Socialism and Democracy.* Harper & Brothers.

Schwab, Karl. 2017. *The Fourth Industrial Revolution.* Penguin.

Scoble, Robert, and Shel Israel. 2016. *The Fourth Transformation: How Augmented Reality and Artificial Intelligence will Change Everything.* Patrick Brewster Press.

Scott, James, and Nick Polson. 2018. *AIQ: How People and Machines are Smarter Together.* St. Martin's Press.

Searle, John. 1980. "Chinese Room Argument, in Minds, brains, and programs." *Behavioral and Brain Sciences*, September: 417–424. https://doi.org/10.1017/S0140525X00005756.

Shambare, Richard, Robert Rugimbana, and Takesure Zhowa. 2012. "Are mobile phones the 21St century addiction?" *African Journal of Business Management* 6 (2): 573–577. https://doi.org/10.5897/AJBM11.1940.

Sharkey, Linda, and Morag Barrett. 2017. *The Future-Proof Workplace: Six Strategies to Accelerate Talent Development, Reshape Your Culture, and Succeed with Purpose.* Wiley.

Shontell, Alyson. 2011. "Flashback: This is What the First-Ever Website Looked Like." *Business Insider*, June 29. www.businessinsider.com/flashback-this-is-what-the-first-website-ever-looked-like-2011-6.

Simonite, Tom. 2016. "Mark Zuckerberg Says It Will Take 10 Years for Virtual Reality to Reach Mass Market." *MIT Technology Review*, February 29. https://www.technologyreview.com/2016/02/29/161822/mark-zuckerberg-says-it-will-take-10-years-for-virtual-reality-to-reach-mass.

Simonite, Tom. 2017. "For Superpowers, Artificial Intelligence Fuels New Global Arms Race." *Wired magazine*, September. https://www.wired.com/story/for-superpowers-artificial-intelligence-fuels-new-global-arms-race/.

n.d. *Skunkworks Origin Story.* http://www.lockheedmartin.com/us/aeronautics/skunkworks/origin.html.

Snow, Shane. 2014. *Smartcuts: The Breakthrough Power of Lateral Thinking.* Harper Business.

Solow, Robert M. 1956. "A Contribution to the Theory of Economic Growth." *The Quarterly Journal of Economics* (Oxford University Press) 70 (1).

Solow, Robert M. 1987. "We'd Better Watch Out." *The New York Timees Book Review*, July 12: 36. http://www.standupeconomist.com/pdf/misc/solow-computer-productivity.pdf.

Staune, Jean. 2015. *Les Clés du Futur.* Place des éditeurs.

Stephenson, Neal. 1992. *Snow Crash.* Bantam Books.

Stokel-Walker, Chris. 2016. "Sound waves that mimic the touch of a button? That's the future." *Wired magazine*, November 9. https://www.wired.co.uk/art icle/touch-the-future.

Stone, Peter, Rodney Brooks, Erik Brynjolfsson, Ryan Calo, Oren Etzioni, Greg Hager, Julia Hirschberg, et al. 2016. *Report of the 2015–2016 Study Panel on Artificial Intelligence and Life in 2030.* The 100 Year Study on Artificial Intelligence (September 2016), Stanford University. http://ai100.stanford.edu/2016-report.

Sud-Ouest. 2021. "Bordeaux: l'extension de Zara refusée sur fond d'exploitation des Ouïghours." November 11. https://www.sudouest.fr/gironde/bordeaux/bor deaux-l-extension-de-zara-refusee-sur-fond-d-exploitation-des-ouighours-703035 0.php.

Taleb, Nassim Nicholas. 2010. *The Black Swan: The Impact of the Highly Improbable.* Penguin.

Tegmark, Max. 2017. *Life 3.0: Being Human in the Age of Artificial Intelligence.* Vintage Publishing.

The Economist. 2016. "Automation and anxiety—Will smarter machines cause mass unemployment?" June 25.

The Economist. 2017. "The world's most valuable resource is no longer oil, but data." May 6.

2020. "The Future of Jobs Report 2020." World Economic Forum. https://www. weforum.org/reports/the-future-of-jobs-report-2020.

The Guardian. 2016. "Our Problem isn't Robots, it's the low-wage car-wash economy." December 12. https://www.theguardian.com/commentisfree/2016/ dec/12/mark-carney-britains-car-wash-economy-low-wage-jobs.

The Guardian. 2016. "The Snowbot: how Edward Snowden gets around his exile." June 27. https://www.theguardian.com/us-news/shortcuts/2016/jun/27/ snowbot-edward-snowden-telepresence-robot.

The New York Times. n.d. "Economic Diversity and Student Outcomes at Stanford University." https://www.nytimes.com/interactive/projects/college-mobility/ stanford-university.

The New York Times. 1958. "New Navy device learns by doing; Psychologist Shows Embryo of Computer Designed to Read and Grow Wiser." July 8.

n.d. *The Skin Cancer Foundation.* https://www.skincancer.org/skin-cancer-inform ation/skin-cancer-facts/.

n.d. *The Winograd challenge.* https://commonsensereasoning.org/winograd.html.

Thompson, Clive. 2022. "The New Spreadsheet Revolution." *Wired Magazine*, June: 22–23.

Tirole, Jean. 2017. *Economics for the Common Good.* Princeton University Press.

Togoh, Isabel. 2020. "Bodybuilding Favorite Gold's Gym Files For Chapter 11 Bankruptcy Protection." *Forbes*, May 5. https://www.forbes.com/sites/isabel togoh/2020/05/05/bodybuilding-favourite-golds-gym-files-for-chapter-11-ban kruptcy-protection.

Topol, Eric. 2019. *Deep Medicine: How Artificial Intelligence Can Make Healthcare Human Again.* Basic Books.

Townsend, Anthony M. 2013. "Smart Cities: Big Data, Civic Hackers, and the Quest for a New Utopia." W. W. Norton & Company.

Turing, Alan. 1950. "Computing Machinery and Intelligence." https://www.csee.umbc.edu/courses/471/papers/turing.pdf.

n.d. *Tuvalu Department of Foreign Affairs.* https://dfa.gov.tv/index.php/future-now-project.

Twain, Mark. 1867. "Letter to San Francisco Alta California, June 5, 1867." June 5. http://www.twainquotes.com/18670811.html.

n.d. *UNESCO Institute for Statistics.* http://uis.unesco.org.

n.d. *United States Bureau of Labor Statistics.* https://www.bls.gov.

n.d. *U.S. Census.* https://www.census.gov/programs-surveys/decennial-census/decade/decennial-publications.1790.html.

Vespa, Jonathan. 2018. *The Graying of America, More Adults than Kids by 2035.* United States Census Bureau. https://www.census.gov/library/stories/2018/03/graying-america.html.

Viramontes, Helena Maria. 2021. "Pay Inequity is persistent, shameful—and still widely tolerated." *National Geographic*, October. https://www.nationalgeographic.com/magazine/article/pay-inequity-is-persistent-shameful-and-still-widely-tolerated.

Von Gastrow, Jean-Philippe. 2016. "African White Collars that Return to the Homeland." *Les Echos*, August 4. https://www.lesechos.fr/2006/08/ces-cadres-africains-qui-retournent-au-pays-577452.

Voytko, Lisette. 2021. "How Beautyblender Founder Rea Ann Silva Reinvented A Sponge And Created A New Category." *Forbes*, June 2. https://www.forbes.com/sites/lisettevoytko/2021/06/02/how-beautyblender-founder-rea-ann-silva-reinvented-a-sponge-and-created-a-new-category/?sh=4603da1033f0.

Walsh, Mike. 2019. *The Algorithmic Leader: How to Be Smart When Machines Are Smarter Than You.* Page Two Books, Inc.

Wang, Zixu. 2021. https://supchina.com. April 20. https://supchina.com/2021/04/20/in-china-delivery-workers-struggle-against-a-rigged-system/.

Waters, Richard. 2017. "How machine learning creates new professions—and problems." *Financial Times*, November 29. https://www.ft.com/content/49e81ebe-cbc3-11e7-8536-d321d0d897a3.

Waters, Richard. 2017. "How machine-learning creates new professions—and problems." *The Financial Times*, November 29. https://www.ft.com/content/49e81ebe-cbc3-11e7-8536-d321d0d897a3.

Watkins, Michael D. 2013. *The First 90 Days.* Harvard Business Press Review.

Watts, Humphrey S. 1989. *Managing the Software Process.* Addison-Wesley Professional.

Webb, Amy. 2016. *The Signals Are Talking: Why Today's Fringe Is Tomorrow's Mainstream.* PublicAffairs.

Wenzhuo, Wu. 2020. "Can Harmay Take Out Sephora in China?" *Jing Daily*, February 6. https://jingdaily.com/can-harmay-take-out-sephora-in-china/.

2009. *White Paper on the US Security Guard Market*. Robert H. Perry & Associates. https://www.roberthperry.com/publications.

Wilkinson, Endymion. 1980. *Studies in Chinese Price History*. Garland.

Wilson, James, and Paul R. Daugherty. 2018. "Collaborative Intelligence: Humans and AI Are Joining Forces." *The Harvard Business Review*, July-August.

n.d. *Word Bank Gini index estimates*. https://data.worldbank.org/indicator/SI.POV.GINI.

World Bank. 2018. "Nearly Half the World Lives on Less than $5.50 a Day." October 17. https://www.worldbank.org/en/news/press-release/2018/10/17/nearly-half-the-world-lives-on-less-than-550-a-day.

Wurmser, Yoram. 2019. "US Time Spent with Mobile 2019." *eMarketer*, May 30. https://www.emarketer.com/content/us-time-spent-with-mobile-2019.

n.d. www.akila3d.com. https://www.akila3d.com.

2014. www.gartner.com. February 13. Accessed January 16, 2020. https://www.gartner.com/en/newsroom/press-releases/2014-02-13-gartner-says-annual-smartphone-sales-surpassed-sales-of-feature-phones-for-the-first-time-in-2013.

n.d. www.gore.com. https://www.gore.com/about/our-beliefs-and-principles.

n.d. www.kaggle.com. https://www.kaggle.com/c/tensorflow-great-barrier-reef.

n.d. www.nano.gov. https://www.nano.gov/about-nni/what/funding.

Yang, Andrew. 2018. *The War on Normal People: The Truth About America's Disappearing Jobs and Why Universal Basic Income Is Our Future*. Hachette Books.

Yendamiru, Praneeth, and Zara Ingilizian. 2019. "In 2020 Asia will have the world's largest GDP. Here's what that means." *World Economic Forum*, December 20. https://www.weforum.org/agenda/2019/12/asia-economic-growth.

Yonck, Richard. 2017. *Heart of the Machine: Our Future in a World of Artificial Emotional Intelligence*. Arcade Publishing.

n.d. *Youtube*. The Backwards Brain Bicycle—Smarter Every Day 133.

Zeeberg, Amos. 2017. "D.I.Y. Artificial Intelligence Comes to a Japanese Family Farm." *The New Yorker*, August 10. https://www.newyorker.com/tech/annals-of-technology/diy-artificial-intelligence-comes-to-a-japanese-family-farm.

Zhou, Naaman. 2017. "Volvo admits its self-driving cars are confused by kangaroos." *The Guardian*, July 1. https://www.theguardian.com/technology/2017/jul/01/volvo-admits-its-self-driving-cars-are-confused-by-kangaroos.

Zhuangzi. n.d. "The Basic Writings."

Index

Milton Keynes UK
Ingram Content Group UK Ltd.
UKHW021831081123
432225UK00002B/11

9 783031 192777